New Perspectives on

# MICROSOFT®
# OFFICE XP

## Brief

JUNE JAMRICH PARSONS
DAN OJA

PATRICK CAREY
Carey Associates, Inc.

ROY AGELOFF
University of Rhode Island

JOSEPH J. ADAMSKI
Grand Valley State University

ROBIN M. ROMER
ANN SHAFFER
KATHLEEN T. FINNEGAN

S. SCOTT ZIMMERMAN
Brigham Young University

BEVERLY B. ZIMMERMAN
Brigham Young University

**COURSE TECHNOLOGY**
**THOMSON LEARNING** ™

Australia • Canada • Mexico • Singapore • Spain • United Kingdom • United States

**COURSE TECHNOLOGY**

**THOMSON LEARNING**

**New Perspectives on Microsoft® Office XP—Brief**

is published by Course Technology.

**Managing Editor:**
Greg Donald

**Senior Editor:**
Donna Gridley

**Series Technology Editor:**
Rachel Crapser

**Senior Product Manager:**
Kathy Finnegan

**Product Manager:**
Melissa Hathaway

**Web Associate Project Manager:**
Amanda Young

**Editorial Assistant:**
Jessica Engstrom

**Marketing Manager:**
Sean Teare

**Developmental Editors:**
Jessica Evans, Mary Kemper, Rose Marie Kuebbing, Jane Pedicini, Lisa Ruffolo

**Production Editors:**
Daphne Barbas, Jennifer Goguen, Kristen Guevara, Elena Montillo, Aimee Poirier

**Composition:**
GEX Publishing Services

**Text Designer:**
Meral Dabcovich

**Cover Designer:**
Efrat Reis

Disclaimer
Course Technology reserves the right to revise this publication and make changes from time to time in its content without notice.

Some of the product names and company names used in this book have been used for identification purposes only and may be trademarks or registered trademarks of their respective manufacturers and sellers.

Microsoft and the Office logo are either registered trademarks or trademarks of Microsoft Corporation in the United States and/or other countries. Course Technology is an independent entity from the Microsoft Corporation, and not affiliated with Microsoft in any manner.

ISBN 0-619-02096-2

# Preface

Course Technology is the world leader in information technology education. The New Perspectives Series is an integral part of Course Technology's success. Visit our Web site to see a whole new perspective on teaching and learning solutions.

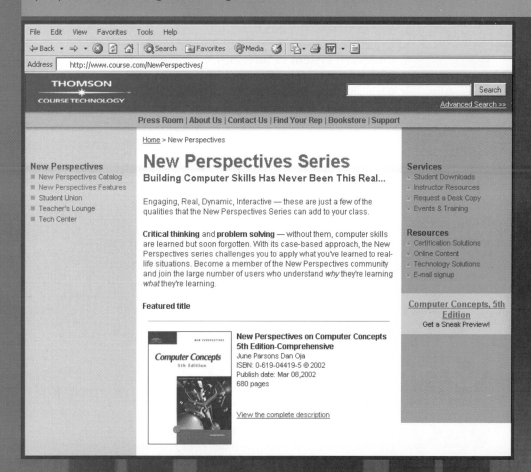

**New Perspectives—Building Computer Skills Has Never Been This Real**

# Why New Perspectives will work for you.

**Critical thinking** and **problem solving**—without them, computer skills are learned but soon forgotten. With its **case-based** approach, the New Perspectives Series challenges students to apply what they've learned to real-life situations. Become a member of the New Perspectives community and watch your students not only **master** computer skills, but also **retain** and carry this **knowledge** into the world.

### New Perspectives catalog
Our online catalog is never out of date! Go to the Catalog link on our Web site to check out our available titles, request a desk copy, download a book preview, or locate online files.

### Complete system of offerings
Whether you're looking for a Brief book, an Advanced book, or something in between, we've got you covered. Go to the Catalog link on our Web site to find the level of coverage that's right for you.

### Instructor materials
We have all the tools you need—data files, solution files, figure files, a sample syllabus, and ExamView, our powerful testing software package.

### How well do your students know Microsoft Office?
Experience the power, ease, and flexibility of SAM XP and TOM. These innovative software tools provide the first truly integrated technology-based training and assessment solution for your applications course. Click the Tech Center link to learn more.

### Get certified
If you want to get certified, we have the titles for you. Find out more by clicking the Teacher's Lounge link.

### Interested in online learning?
Enhance your course with rich online content for use through MyCourse 2.0, WebCT, and Blackboard. Go to the Teacher's Lounge to find the platform that's right for you.

## Your link to the future is at
## www.course.com/NewPerspectives

# What *you need to know about this book.*

- Student Online Companion takes students to the Web for additional work.

- ExamView testing software gives you the option of generating a printed test, LAN-based test, or test over the Internet.

- New Perspectives Labs provide students with self-paced practice on computer-related topics.

- This edition includes NEW tutorial cases and case problem scenarios throughout!

- Each Word tutorial emphasizes the importance of planning the work to be done in the document.

- Our coverage of Excel functions is more extensive and complete than that of other texts. Students work with financial functions to calculate the cost of mortgages and loans; calculate a payments schedule using financial and logical functions; and work with text and date functions.

- Students will appreciate our clear and concise coverage of database concepts, which gives them the solid foundation they need as they progress to creating and working with Access database objects.

- Our coverage takes full advantage of the new PowerPoint Task Pane, Slides Tab, and Outline Tab.

| CASE | TROUBLE? | SESSION 1.1 | QUICK CHECK | RW |
|---|---|---|---|---|
| **Tutorial Case** Each tutorial begins with a problem presented in a case that is meaningful to students. The case sets the scene to help students understand what they will do in the tutorial. | **TROUBLE? Paragraphs** These paragraphs anticipate the mistakes or problems that students may have and help them continue with the tutorial. | **Sessions** Each tutorial is divided into sessions designed to be completed in about 45 minutes each. Students should take as much time as they need and take a break between sessions. | **Quick Check Questions** Each session concludes with conceptual Quick Check questions that test students' understanding of what they learned in the session. | **Reference Windows** Reference Windows are succinct summaries of the most important tasks covered in a tutorial. They preview actions students will perform in the steps to follow. |

**www.course.com/NewPerspectives**

# BRIEF CONTENTS

# TABLE OF CONTENTS

## Microsoft Office XP                    OFF 1

## Microsoft Word 2002
### Level I Tutorials                     WD 1.01

## Tutorial 1                             3

### Introducing Microsoft Office XP

**Preparing Promotional Materials for Delmar Office Supplies**

## Tutorial 1                             WD 1.03

### Creating a Document

**Writing a Business Letter for Art4U Inc.**

# Tutorial 3 — EX 3.01

*Developing a Professional-Looking Worksheet*

**Formatting a Sales Report**

## Tutorial 3                                      AC 3.01

*Querying a Database*

**Retrieving Information About Employers and Their Positions**

## Microsoft PowerPoint 2002

# Tutorial 1      PPT 1.03

*Creating a PowerPoint Presentation*

**Presentation on Information about Global Humanitarian**

# Tutorial 1                              OUT 1.03

*Communicating with Outlook 2002*

**Sending and Receiving E-mail Messages for The Express Lane**

*New Perspectives on*

# MICROSOFT®

# WINDOWS® 2000

# PROFESSIONAL

# Read This Before You Begin

## To the Student

### Make Data Disk Program

To complete the Level I tutorials, Review Assignments, and Projects, you need three Data Disks. Your instructor will either provide you with Data Disks or ask you to make your own.

If you are making your own Data Disks you will need three blank, formatted high-density disks and access to the Make Data Disk program. If you want to install the Make Data Disk program to your home computer, you can obtain it from your instructor or from the Web. To download the Make Data Disk program from the Web, go to **www.course.com**, click Data Disks, and follow the instructions on the screen.

To install the Make Data Disk program, select and click the file you just downloaded from **www.course.com**, 6548-9.exe. Follow the onscreen instructions to complete the installation. If you have any trouble obtaining or installing the Make Data Disk program, ask your instructor or technical support person for assistance.

Once you have obtained and installed the Make Data Disk program, you can use it to create your Data Disks according to the steps in the tutorials.

### Course Labs

The Level I tutorials in this book feature three interactive Course Labs to help you understand Using a Keyboard, Using a Mouse, and Using Files concepts. There are Lab Assignments at the end of Tutorials 1 and 2 that relate to these Labs. To start a Lab, click the **Start** button on the Windows 2000 taskbar, point to **Programs**, point to **Course Labs**, point to **New Perspectives Course Labs**, and click the name of the Lab you want to use.

### Using Your Own Computer

If you are going to work through this book using your own computer, you need:

- **Computer System** Microsoft Windows 2000 Professional must be installed on a local hard drive or on a network drive. This book is about Windows 2000 Professional—for those who have Windows 2000 Millennium, you might notice some differences.

- **Data Disks** You will not be able to complete the tutorials or exercises in this book using your own computer until you have your Data Disks. See "Make Data Disk Program" above for details on obtaining your Data Disks.

- **Course Labs** See your instructor or technical support person to obtain the Course Lab software for use on your own computer.

### Visit Our World Wide Web Site

Additional materials designed especially for you are available on the World Wide Web. Go to **http://www.course.com**.

## To the Instructor

The Make Data Disk Program and Course Labs for this title are available in the Instructor's Resource Kit for this title. Follow the instructions in the Help file on the CD-ROM to install the programs to your network or standalone computer. For information on using the Make Data Disk Program or the Course Labs, see the "To the Student" section above. Students will be switching the default installation settings to Web style in Tutorial 2. You are granted a license to copy the Data Files and Course Labs to any computer or computer network used by students who have purchased this book.

## OBJECTIVES

In this tutorial you will:

- Start and shut down Windows 2000

- Identify the objects on the Windows 2000 desktop

- Practice mouse functions

- Run software programs, switch between them, and close them

- Identify and use the controls in a window

- Use Windows 2000 controls such as menus, toolbars, list boxes, scroll bars, option buttons, tabs, and check boxes

- Explore the Windows 2000 Help system

## LABS

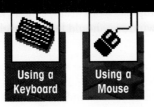

Using a Keyboard    Using a Mouse

# EXPLORING THE BASICS

*Investigating the Windows 2000 Operating System*

## CASE

## Your First Day on the Computer

You walk into the computer lab and sit down at a desk. There's a computer in front of you, and you find yourself staring dubiously at the screen. Where to start? As if in answer to your question, your friend Steve Laslow appears.

"You start with the operating system," says Steve. Noticing your puzzled look, Steve explains that the **operating system** is software that helps the computer carry out operating tasks such as displaying information on the computer screen and saving data on your disks. (Software refers to the **programs**, or **applications**, that a computer uses to perform tasks.) Your computer uses the **Microsoft Windows 2000 Professional** operating system—Windows 2000, for short.

Steve explains that much of the software available for Windows 2000 has a standard graphical user interface. This means that once you have learned how to use one Windows program, such as Microsoft Word word-processing software, you are well on your way to under-standing how to use other Windows software. Windows 2000 lets you use more than one program at a time, so you can easily switch between them—between your word-processing software and your appointment book software, for example. Finally, Windows 2000 makes it very easy to access the **Internet**, the worldwide collection of com-puters connected to one another to enable communication. All in all, Windows 2000 makes your computer effective and easy to use.

Steve recommends that you get started right away by starting Microsoft Windows 2000 and practicing some basic skills.

# SESSION 1.1

In this session, in addition to learning basic Windows terminology, you will learn how to use a pointing device, how to start and close a program, and how to use more than one program at a time.

## Starting Windows 2000

**Using a Keyboard**

Windows 2000 automatically starts when you turn on the computer. Depending on the way your computer is set up, you might be asked to enter your username and password.

### To start Windows 2000:

**1.** Turn on your computer.

TROUBLE? If you are asked to select an operating system, do not take action. Windows 2000 will start automatically after a designated number of seconds. If it does not, ask your technical support person for help.

TROUBLE? If prompted to do so, type your assigned username and press the Tab key. Then type your password and press the Enter key to continue.

TROUBLE? If this is the first time you have started your computer with Windows 2000, messages might appear on your screen informing you that Windows is setting up components of your computer. If the Getting Started with Windows 2000 box appears, press and hold down the Alt key on your keyboard and then, while you hold down the Alt key, press the F4 key. The box closes.

After a moment, Windows 2000 starts. Windows 2000 has a **graphical user interface** (**GUI,** pronounced "gooey"), which uses **icons,** or pictures of familiar objects, such as file folders and documents, to represent items in your computer such as programs or files. Microsoft Windows 2000 gets its name from the rectangular work areas, called "windows," that appear on your screen as you work (although no windows should be open right now).

### The Windows 2000 Desktop

In Windows terminology, the area displayed on your screen when Windows 2000 starts represents a **desktop**—a workspace for projects and the tools needed to manipulate those projects. When you first start a computer, it uses **default** settings, those preset by the operating system. The default desktop, for example, has a plain blue background. However, Microsoft designed Windows 2000 so that you can easily change the appearance of the desktop. You can, for example, add color, patterns, images, and text to the desktop background.

Many institutions design customized desktops for their computers. Figure 1-1 shows the default Windows 2000 desktop and two other examples of desktops, one designed for a business, North Pole Novelties, and one designed for a school, the University of Colorado. Although your desktop might not look exactly like any of the examples in Figure 1-1, you should be able to locate objects on your screen similar to those in Figure 1-1. Look at your screen and locate the objects labeled in Figure 1-1. The objects on your screen might appear larger or smaller than those in Figure 1-1, depending on your monitor's settings.

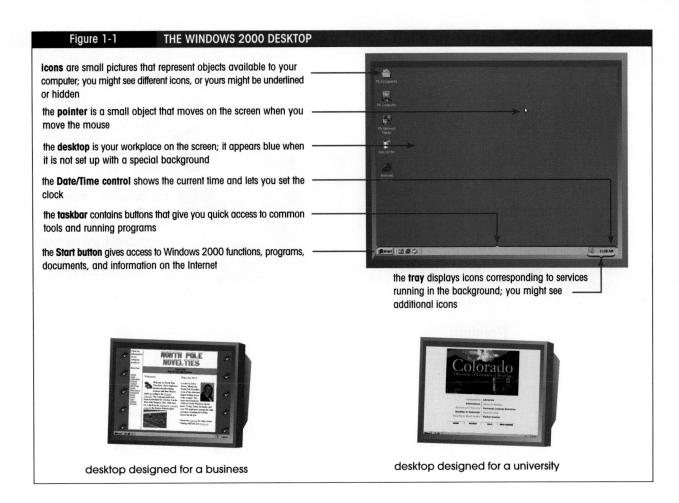

| Figure 1-1 | THE WINDOWS 2000 DESKTOP |

**icons** are small pictures that represent objects available to your computer; you might see different icons, or yours might be underlined or hidden

the **pointer** is a small object that moves on the screen when you move the mouse

the **desktop** is your workplace on the screen; it appears blue when it is not set up with a special background

the **Date/Time control** shows the current time and lets you set the clock

the **taskbar** contains buttons that give you quick access to common tools and running programs

the **Start button** gives access to Windows 2000 functions, programs, documents, and information on the Internet

the **tray** displays icons corresponding to services running in the background; you might see additional icons

desktop designed for a business

desktop designed for a university

If the screen goes blank or starts to display a moving design, press any key to restore the Windows 2000 desktop.

# Using a Pointing Device

**Using a Mouse**

A **pointing device** helps you interact with objects on the screen. Pointing devices come in many shapes and sizes; some are designed to ensure that your hand won't suffer fatigue while using them. Some are directly attached to your computer via a cable, whereas others function like a TV remote control and allow you to access your computer without being right next to it. Figure 1-2 shows examples of common pointing devices.

The most common pointing device is called a **mouse**, so this book uses that term. If you are using a different pointing device, such as a trackball, substitute that device whenever you see the term "mouse." Because Windows 2000 uses a graphical user interface, you need to know how to use the mouse to manipulate the objects on the screen. In this session you will learn about pointing and clicking. In Session 1.2 you will learn how to use the mouse to drag objects.

You can also interact with objects by using the keyboard; however, the mouse is more convenient for most tasks, so the tutorials in this book assume you are using one.

**Figure 1-2** | **POINTING DEVICES**

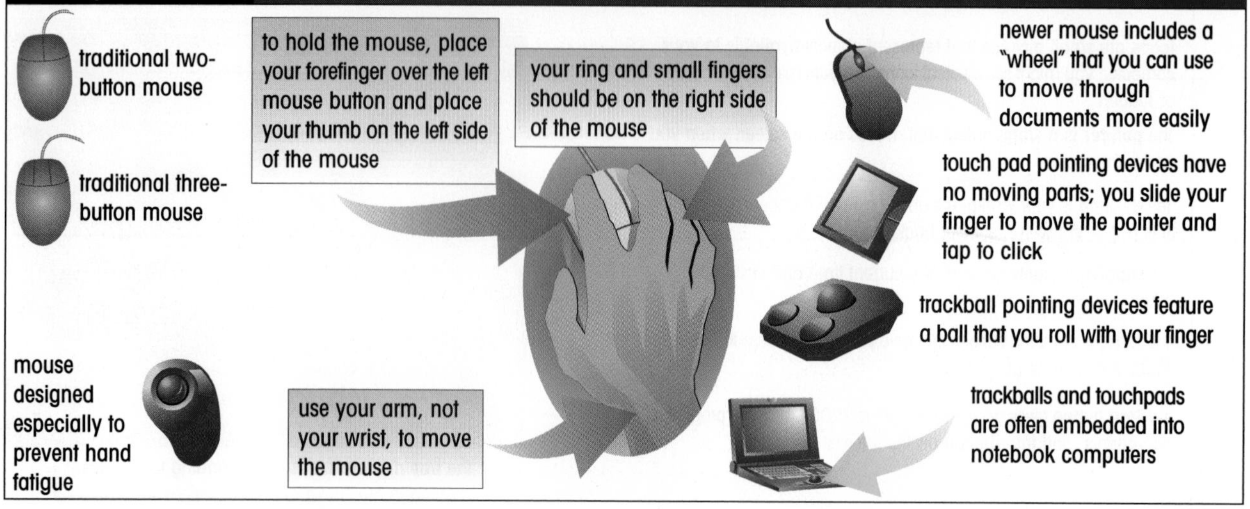

traditional two-button mouse

traditional three-button mouse

to hold the mouse, place your forefinger over the left mouse button and place your thumb on the left side of the mouse

your ring and small fingers should be on the right side of the mouse

newer mouse includes a "wheel" that you can use to move through documents more easily

touch pad pointing devices have no moving parts; you slide your finger to move the pointer and tap to click

trackball pointing devices feature a ball that you roll with your finger

mouse designed especially to prevent hand fatigue

use your arm, not your wrist, to move the mouse

trackballs and touchpads are often embedded into notebook computers

## Pointing

You use a pointing device to move the pointer over objects on the desktop. The pointer is usually shaped like an arrow ℞ , although it can change shape depending on where it is on the screen and on what tasks you are performing. Most computer users place the mouse on a **mouse pad**, a flat piece of rubber that helps the mouse move smoothly. As you move the mouse on the mouse pad, the pointer on the screen moves in a corresponding direction.

You begin most Windows operations by positioning the pointer over a specific part of the screen. This is called **pointing**.

### To move the pointer:

**1.** Position your right index finger over the left mouse button, as shown in Figure 1-2, but don't click yet. Lightly grasp the sides of the mouse with your thumb and little fingers.

TROUBLE? If you want to use the mouse with your left hand, ask your instructor or technical support person to help you use the Control Panel to swap the functions of the left and right mouse buttons. Be sure to find out how to change back to the right-handed mouse setting, so that you can reset the mouse each time you are finished in the lab.

**2.** Place the mouse on the mouse pad and then move the mouse. Watch the movement of the pointer.

TROUBLE? If you run out of room to move your mouse, lift the mouse and place it in the middle of the mouse pad. Notice that the pointer does not move when the mouse is not in contact with the mouse pad.

When you position the mouse pointer over certain objects, such as the objects on the taskbar, a "tip" appears. These "tips" are called **ScreenTips**, and they tell you the purpose or function of an object.

## To view ScreenTips:

1. Use the mouse to point to the **Start** button Start, but don't click it. After a few seconds, you see the tip "Click here to begin," as shown in Figure 1-3.

   TROUBLE? If the Start button and taskbar don't appear, point to the bottom of the screen. They will then appear.

| Figure 1-3 | VIEWING SCREENTIPS |
| --- | --- |

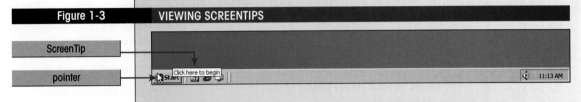

ScreenTip

pointer

2. Point to the time on the right end of the taskbar. Notice that today's date (or the date to which your computer's time clock is set) appears.

## Clicking

**Clicking** is when you press a mouse button and immediately release it. Clicking sends a signal to your computer that you want to perform an action on the object you click. In Windows 2000 most actions are performed using the left mouse button. If you are told to click an object, click it with the left mouse button, unless instructed otherwise.

When you click the Start button, the Start menu appears. A **menu** is a list of options that you use to complete tasks. The **Start menu** provides you with access to programs, documents, and much more. Try clicking the Start button to open the Start menu.

## To open the Start menu:

1. Point to the **Start** button Start.

2. Click the left mouse button. An arrow ▶ following an option on the Start menu indicates that you can view additional choices by navigating a **submenu**, a menu extending from the main menu. See Figure 1-4.

| Figure 1-4 | START MENU |
| --- | --- |

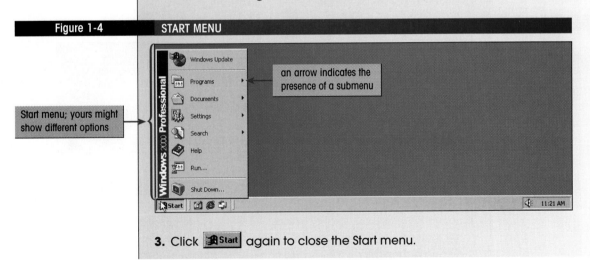

Start menu; yours might show different options

an arrow indicates the presence of a submenu

3. Click Start again to close the Start menu.

Next you'll learn how to select items on a submenu.

## Selecting

In Windows 2000, pointing and clicking are often used to **select** an object, in other words, to choose it as the object you want to work with. Windows 2000 shows you which object is selected by highlighting it, usually by changing the object's color, putting a box around it, or making the object appear to be pushed in, as shown in Figure 1-5.

| Figure 1-5 | SELECTED OBJECTS |
|---|---|

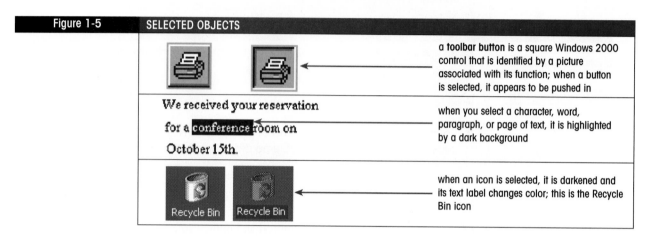

In Windows 2000, depending on your computer's settings, some objects are selected when you simply point to them, others when you click them. Practice selecting the Programs option on the Start menu to open the Programs submenu.

### To select an option on a menu:

1. Click the **Start** button 🏁 Start and notice how it appears to be pushed in, indicating it is selected.

2. Point to (but don't click) the **Programs** option. After a short pause, the Programs submenu opens, and the Programs option is highlighted to indicate it is selected. See Figure 1-6.

| Figure 1-6 | PROGRAMS SUBMENU |
|---|---|

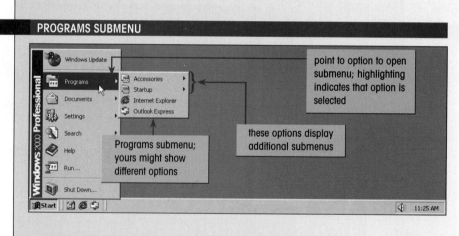

TROUBLE? If a submenu other than the Programs menu opens, you selected the wrong option. Move the mouse so that the pointer points to Programs.

TROUBLE? If the Programs option doesn't appear, your Start menu might have too many options to fit on the screen. If that is the case, a double arrow ☒ appears at the top or bottom of the Start menu. Click first the top and then the bottom arrow to view additional Start menu options until you locate the Programs menu option, and then point to it.

**3.** Now close the Start menu by clicking 🞄Start again.

You return to the desktop.

## Right-Clicking

Pointing devices were originally designed with a single button, so the term "clicking" had only one meaning: you pressed that button. Innovations in technology, however, led to the addition of a second and even a third button (and more recently, options such as a wheel) that expanded the pointing device's capability. More recent software—especially that designed for Windows 2000—takes advantage of the additional buttons, especially the right button. However, the term "clicking" continues to refer to the left button; clicking an object with the *right* button is called **right-clicking**.

In Windows 2000, right-clicking both selects an object and opens its **shortcut menu**, a list of options directly related to the object you right-clicked. You can right-click practically any object—the Start button, a desktop icon, the taskbar, and even the desktop itself—to view options associated with that object. For example, the first desktop shown in Figure 1-7 illustrates what happens when you click the Start button with the left mouse button to open the Start menu. Clicking the Start button with the right button, however, opens the Start button's shortcut menu, as shown in the second desktop.

| Figure 1-7 | CLICKING WITH THE LEFT AND RIGHT MOUSE BUTTONS |
| --- | --- |

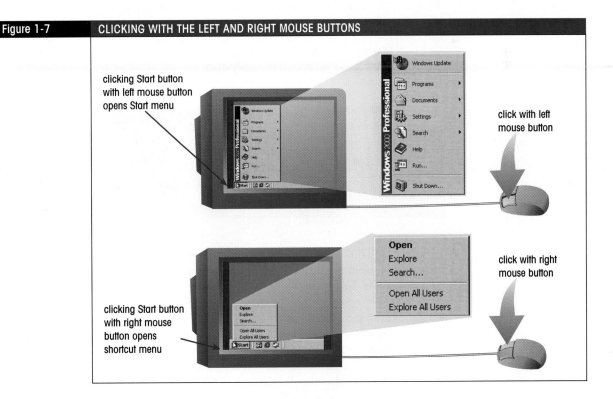

Try using right-clicking to open the shortcut menu for the Start button.

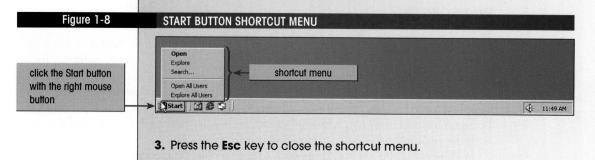

*To right-click an object:*

1. Position the pointer over the Start button.

2. Right-click the **Start** button [Start]. The shortcut menu that opens offers a list of options available to the Start button.

   TROUBLE? If you are using a trackball or a mouse with three buttons or a wheel, make sure you click the button on the far right, not the one in the middle.

   TROUBLE? If your menu looks slightly different from the one in Figure 1-8, don't worry. Different systems will have different options.

| Figure 1-8 | START BUTTON SHORTCUT MENU |
| --- | --- |

click the Start button with the right mouse button

Open
Explore
Search...
Open All Users
Explore All Users

shortcut menu

Start                                11:49 AM

3. Press the **Esc** key to close the shortcut menu.

You again return to the desktop.

# Starting and Closing a Program

To use a program, such as a word-processing program, you must first start it. With Windows 2000 you usually start a program by clicking the Start button and then you locate and click the program's name in the submenus.

The Reference Window below explains how to start a program. Don't do the steps in the Reference Windows as you go through the tutorials; they are for your later reference.

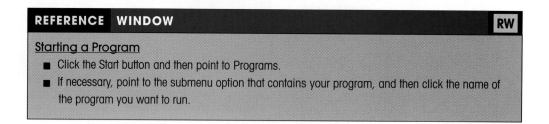

**REFERENCE WINDOW**    **RW**

Starting a Program
- Click the Start button and then point to Programs.
- If necessary, point to the submenu option that contains your program, and then click the name of the program you want to run.

Windows 2000 includes an easy-to-use word-processing program called WordPad. Suppose you want to start the WordPad program and use it to write a letter or report. You open Windows 2000 programs from the Start menu. Programs are usually located on the Programs submenu or on one of its submenus. To start WordPad, for example, you select the Programs and Accessories submenus.

If you can't locate an item that is supposed to be on a menu, it is most likely temporarily hidden. Windows 2000 menus use a feature called **Personalized Menus** that hides menu options you use infrequently. You can access hidden menu options by pointing to the menu name and then clicking the double arrow ⌄ (sometimes called a "chevron") at the bottom of the menu. You can also access the hidden options by holding the pointer over the menu name.

## *To start the WordPad program from the Start menu:*

1. Click the **Start** button 🏁Start to open the Start menu.

2. Point to **Programs**. The Programs submenu appears.

3. Point to **Accessories**. The Accessories submenu appears. Figure 1-9 shows the open menus.

   TROUBLE? If a different menu opens, you might have moved the mouse diagonally so that a different submenu opened. Move the pointer to the right across the Programs option, and then move it up or down to point to Accessories. Once you're more comfortable moving the mouse, you'll find that you can eliminate this problem by moving the mouse quickly.

   TROUBLE? If WordPad doesn't appear on the Accessories submenu, continue to point to Accessories until WordPad appears.

| Figure 1-9 | START MENU |
| --- | --- |

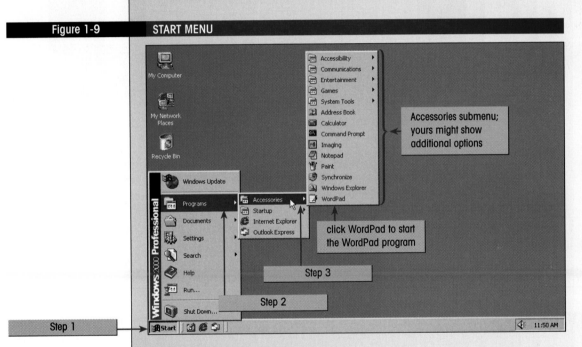

4. Click **WordPad**. The WordPad program opens, as shown in Figure 1-10. If the WordPad window fills the entire screen, don't worry. You will learn how to manipulate windows in Session 1.2.

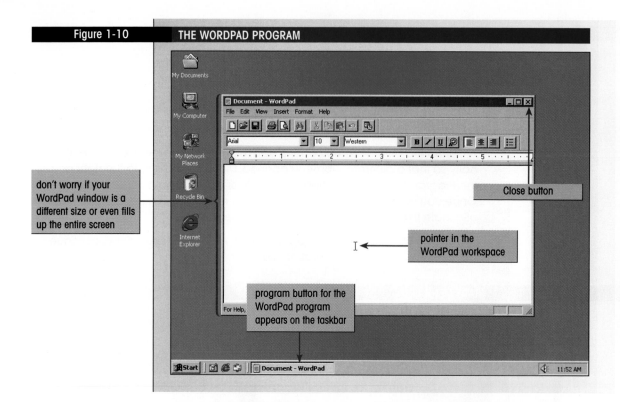

Figure 1-10    THE WORDPAD PROGRAM

When a program is started, it is said to be **open** or **running**. A **program button** appears on the taskbar for each open program. You click program buttons to switch between open programs. When you are finished using a program, click the Close button ☒.

### To exit the WordPad program:

**1.** Click the **Close** button ☒. See Figure 1-10. You return to the Windows 2000 desktop.

## Running **Multiple Programs**

One of the most useful features of Windows 2000 is its ability to run multiple programs at the same time. This feature, known as **multitasking**, allows you to work on more than one project at a time and to switch quickly between projects. For example, you can start WordPad and leave it running while you then start the Paint program.

### To run WordPad and Paint at the same time:

**1.** Start WordPad again and then click the **Start** button 🔲Start again.

**2.** Point to **Programs** and then point to **Accessories**.

**3.** Click **Paint**. The Paint program opens, as shown in Figure 1-11. Now two programs are running at the same time.

   TROUBLE? If the Paint program fills the entire screen, don't worry. You will learn how to manipulate windows in Session 1.2.

| Figure 1-11 | THE PAINT PROGRAM |
| --- | --- |

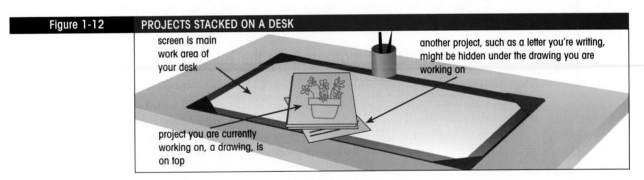

What happened to WordPad? The WordPad program button is still on the taskbar, so even if you can't see it, WordPad is still running. You can imagine that it is stacked behind the Paint program, as shown in Figure 1-12. Paint is the active program because it is the one with which you are currently working.

| Figure 1-12 | PROJECTS STACKED ON A DESK |
| --- | --- |

screen is main work area of your desk

another project, such as a letter you're writing, might be hidden under the drawing you are working on

project you are currently working on, a drawing, is on top

## Switching Between Programs

The easiest way to switch between programs is to use the buttons on the taskbar.

### To switch between WordPad and Paint:

1. Click the button labeled **Document - WordPad** on the taskbar. The Document - WordPad button now looks as if it has been pushed in, to indicate that it is the active program, and WordPad moves to the front.
2. Next, click the button labeled **untitled - Paint** on the taskbar to switch to the Paint program.

The Paint program is again the active program.

## Accessing the Desktop from the Quick Launch Toolbar

The Windows 2000 taskbar, as you've seen, displays buttons for programs currently running. It also can contain **toolbars**, sets of buttons that give single-click access to programs or documents that aren't running or open. In its default state, the Windows 2000 taskbar displays the **Quick Launch toolbar**, which gives quick access to Web programs and to the desktop. Your taskbar might contain additional toolbars, or none at all.

When you are running more than one program but you want to return to the desktop, perhaps to use one of the desktop icons such as My Computer, you can do so by using one of the Quick Launch toolbar buttons. Clicking the Show Desktop button [ ] returns you to the desktop. The open programs are not closed; they are simply made inactive and reduced to buttons on the taskbar.

### To return to the desktop:

1. Click the **Show Desktop** button [ ] on the Quick Launch toolbar. The desktop appears, and both the Paint and WordPad programs are temporarily inactive. See Figure 1-13.

   TROUBLE? If the Quick Launch toolbar doesn't appear on your taskbar, right-click the taskbar, point to Toolbars, and then click Quick Launch and try Step 1 again.

| Figure 1-13 | ACCESSING THE DESKTOP |

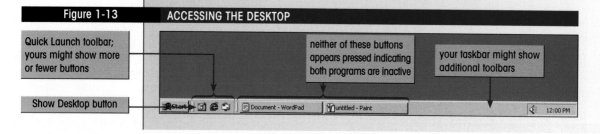

Quick Launch toolbar; yours might show more or fewer buttons

neither of these buttons appears pressed indicating both programs are inactive

your taskbar might show additional toolbars

Show Desktop button

## Closing Inactive Programs from the Taskbar

It is good practice to close each program when you are finished using it. Each program uses computer resources, such as memory, so Windows 2000 works more efficiently when only the programs you need are open. You've already seen how to close an open program using the Close button [X]. You can also close a program, whether active or inactive, by using the shortcut menu associated with the program button on the taskbar.

### To close WordPad and Paint using the program button shortcut menus:

1. Right-click the **untitled – Paint** button on the taskbar. To right-click something, remember that you click it with the right mouse button. The shortcut menu for that program button opens. See Figure 1-14.

2. Click **Close**. The button labeled "untitled – Paint" disappears from the taskbar, indicating that the Paint program is closed.

3. Right-click the **Document – WordPad** button on the taskbar, and then click **Close**. The WordPad button disappears from the taskbar.

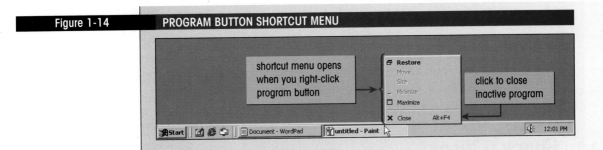

Figure 1-14 | PROGRAM BUTTON SHORTCUT MENU

shortcut menu opens when you right-click program button

click to close inactive program

## Shutting Down Windows 2000

It is very important to shut down Windows 2000 before you turn off the computer. If you turn off your computer without correctly shutting down, you might lose data and damage your files.

You should typically use the "Shut Down" option when you want to turn off your computer. However, your school might prefer that you select the Log Off option in the Shut Down Windows dialog box. This option logs you out of Windows 2000, leaves the computer turned on, and allows another user to log on without restarting the computer. Check with your instructor or technical support person for the preferred method at your lab.

*To shut down Windows 2000:*

**1.** Click the **Start** button ![Start] on the taskbar to display the Start menu.

**2.** Click the **Shut Down** menu option. A box titled "Shut Down Windows" opens.

TROUBLE? If you can't see the Shut Down menu option, your Start menu has more options than your screen can display. A double arrow ☆ appears at the bottom of the Start menu. Click this button until the Shut Down menu option appears, and then click Shut Down.

TROUBLE? If you are supposed to log off rather than shut down, click the Log Off option instead and follow your school's logoff procedure.

**3.** Make sure the **Shut Down** option appears in the box shown in Figure 1-15.

TROUBLE? If "Shut down" does not appear, click the arrow to the right of the box. A list of options appears. Click Shut Down.

Figure 1-15 | SHUTTING DOWN

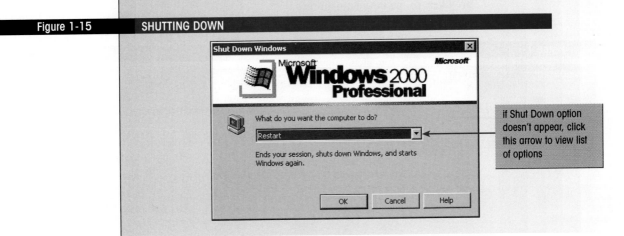

if Shut Down option doesn't appear, click this arrow to view list of options

4. Click the **OK** button.

5. Wait until you see a message indicating it is safe to turn off your computer. If your lab staff has requested you to switch off your computer after shutting down, do so now. Otherwise leave the computer running. Some computers turn themselves off automatically.

## Session 1.1 QUICK CHECK

1. What is the purpose of the taskbar?

2. The _____ feature of Windows 2000 allows you to run more than one program at a time.

3. The _____ is a list of options that provides you with access to programs, documents, submenus, and more.

4. What should you do if you are trying to move the pointer to the left edge of your screen, but your mouse bumps into the keyboard?

5. Even if you can't see an open program on your desktop, the program might be running. How can you tell if a program is running?

6. Why is it good practice to close each program when you are finished using it?

7. Why should you shut down Windows 2000 before you turn off your computer?

## SESSION 1.2

In this session you will learn how to use many of the Windows 2000 controls to manipulate windows and programs. You will also learn how to change the size and shape of a window; how to move a window; and how to use menus, dialog boxes, tabs, buttons, and lists to specify how you want a program to carry out a task.

## Anatomy of a Window

When you run a program in Windows 2000, it appears in a window. A **window** is a rectangular area of the screen that contains a program or data. Windows, spelled with an uppercase "W," is the name of the Microsoft operating system. The word "window" with a lowercase "w" refers to one of the rectangular areas on the screen. A window also contains controls for manipulating the window and for using the program. Figure 1-16 describes the controls you are likely to see in most windows.

| Figure 1-16 | WINDOW CONTROLS |
|---|---|
| **CONTROL** | **DESCRIPTION** |
| Menu bar | Contains the titles of menus, such as File, Edit, and Help |
| Sizing buttons | Let you enlarge, shrink, or close a window |
| Status bar | Provides you with messages relevant to the task you are performing |
| Title bar | Contains the window title and basic window control buttons |
| Toolbar | Contains buttons that provide you with shortcuts to common menu commands |
| Window title | Identifies the program and document contained in the window |
| Workspace | Part of the window you use to enter your work—to enter text, draw pictures, set up calculations, and so on |

WordPad is a good example of a typical window, so try starting WordPad and identifying these controls in the WordPad window.

## To look at window controls:

**1.** Make sure Windows 2000 is running and you are at the Windows 2000 desktop.

**2.** Start WordPad.

TROUBLE? To start WordPad, click the Start button, point to Programs, point to Accessories, and then click WordPad.

**3.** On your screen, identify the controls labeled in Figure 1-17. Don't worry if your window fills the entire screen or is a different size. You'll learn to change window size shortly.

| Figure 1-17 | WORDPAD WINDOW CONTROLS |
| --- | --- |

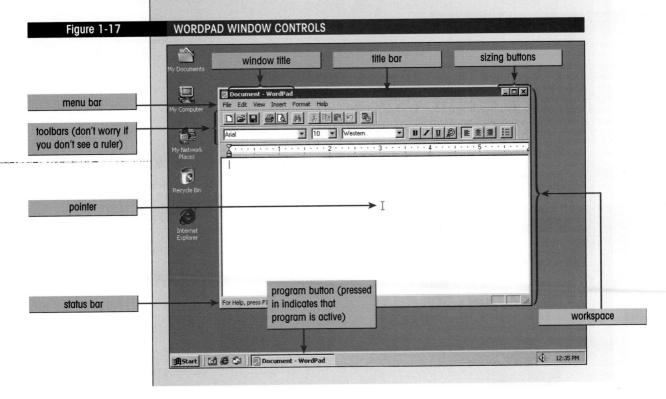

## Manipulating a Window

There are three buttons located on the right side of the title bar. You are already familiar with the Close button. The Minimize button ▬ hides the window so that only its program button is visible on the taskbar. The other button changes name and function depending on the status of the window (it either maximizes the window or restores it to a predefined size). Figure 1-18 shows how these buttons work.

### Minimizing a Window

The Minimize button hides a window so that only the button on the taskbar remains visible. You can use the Minimize button when you want to temporarily hide a window but keep the program running.

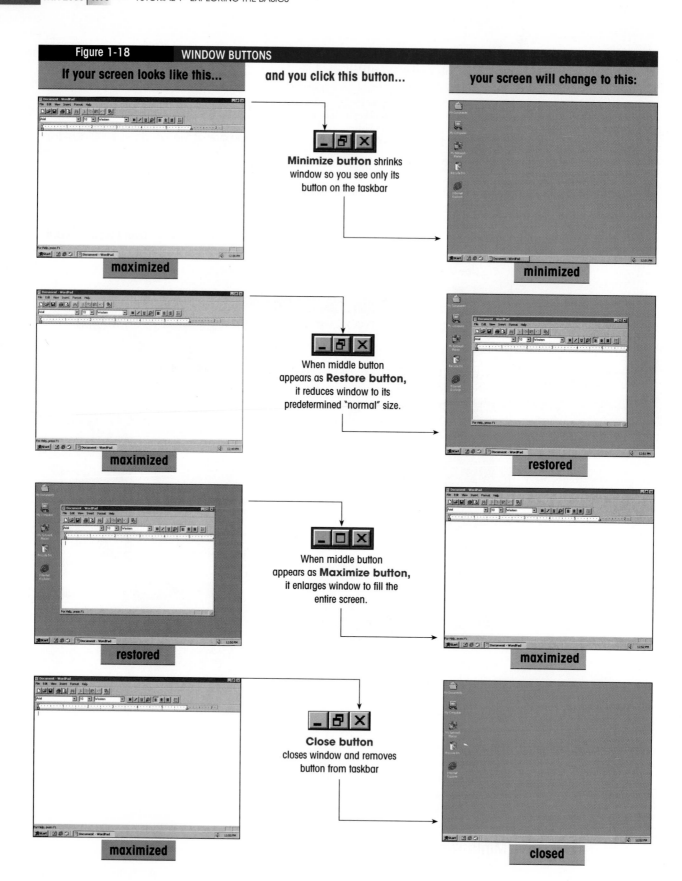

**Figure 1-18**    WINDOW BUTTONS

**If your screen looks like this...**    **and you click this button...**    **your screen will change to this:**

maximized

**Minimize button** shrinks window so you see only its button on the taskbar

minimized

maximized

When middle button appears as **Restore button**, it reduces window to its predetermined "normal" size.

restored

restored

When middle button appears as **Maximize button**, it enlarges window to fill the entire screen.

maximized

maximized

**Close button** closes window and removes button from taskbar

closed

> **To minimize the WordPad window:**
>
> 1. Click the **Minimize** button ▬. The WordPad window shrinks so that only the Document - WordPad button on the taskbar is visible.
>
> TROUBLE? If you accidentally clicked the Close button and closed the window, use the Start button to start WordPad again.

## Redisplaying a Window

You can redisplay a minimized window by clicking the program's button on the taskbar. When you redisplay a window, it becomes the active window.

> **To redisplay the WordPad window:**
>
> 1. Click the **Document - WordPad** button on the taskbar. The WordPad window is restored to its previous size. The Document - WordPad button looks pushed in as a visual clue that WordPad is now the active window.
>
> 2. The taskbar button provides another means of switching a window between its minimized and active state: Click the **Document - WordPad** button on the taskbar again to minimize the window.
>
> 3. Click the **Document - WordPad** button once more to redisplay the window.

## Maximizing a Window

The Maximize button enlarges a window so that it fills the entire screen. You will probably do most of your work using maximized windows because they allow you to see more of your program and data.

> **To maximize the WordPad window:**
>
> 1. Click the **Maximize** button ▢ on the WordPad title bar.
>
> TROUBLE? If the window is already maximized, it will fill the entire screen, and the Maximize button won't appear. Instead, you'll see the Restore button ▣. Skip Step 1.

## Restoring a Window

The Restore button ▣ reduces the window so it is smaller than the entire screen. This is useful if you want to see more than one window at a time. Also, because of its smaller size, you can drag the window to another location on the screen or change its dimensions.

> **To restore a window:**
>
> 1. Click the **Restore** button ▣ on the WordPad title bar. Notice that once a window is restored, ▣ changes to the Maximize button ▢.

## Moving a Window

You can use the mouse to move a window to a new position on the screen. When you click an object and hold down the mouse button while moving the mouse, you are said to be **dragging** the object. You can move objects on the screen by dragging them to a new location. If you want to move a window, you drag its title bar. You cannot move a maximized window.

> *To drag the WordPad window to a new location:*
>
> 1. Position the mouse pointer on the WordPad window title bar.
> 2. While you hold down the left mouse button, move the mouse to drag the window. A rectangle representing the window moves as you move the mouse.
> 3. Position the rectangle anywhere on the screen, then release the left mouse button. The WordPad window appears in the new location.
> 4. Now drag the WordPad window to the upper-left corner of the screen.

## Changing the Size of a Window

You can also use the mouse to change the size of a window. Notice the sizing handle at the lower-right corner of the window. The **sizing handle** provides a visible control for changing the size of a window.

> *To change the size of the WordPad window:*
>
> 1. Position the pointer over the sizing handle . The pointer changes to a diagonal arrow .
> 2. While holding down the mouse button, drag the sizing handle down and to the right.
> 3. Release the mouse button. Now the window is larger.
> 4. Practice using the sizing handle to make the WordPad window larger or smaller, and then maximize the WordPad window.

You can also drag the window borders left, right, up, or down to change a window's size.

# Using **Program Menus**

Most Windows programs use menus to organize the program's menu options. The menu bar is typically located at the top of the program window and shows the titles of menus such as File, Edit, and Help.

Windows menus are relatively standardized—most Windows programs include similar menu options. It's easy to learn new programs, because you can make a pretty good guess about which menu contains the option you want.

## Selecting Options from a Menu

When you click any menu title, choices for that menu appear below the menu bar. These choices are referred to as **menu options** or **commands**. To select a menu option, you click it. For example, the File menu is a standard feature in most Windows programs and contains the options typically related to working with a file: creating, opening, saving, and printing a file or document.

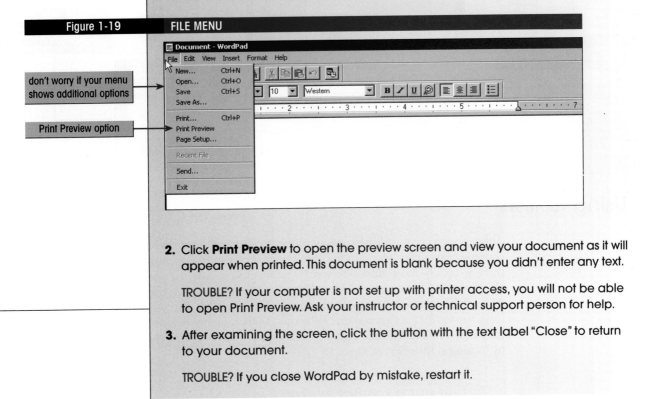

## *To select the Print Preview menu option on the File menu:*

**1.** Click **File** on the WordPad menu bar to display the File menu. See Figure 1-19.

TROUBLE? If you open a menu but decide not to select any of the menu options, you can close the menu by clicking its title again.

**Figure 1-19          FILE MENU**

don't worry if your menu shows additional options

Print Preview option

**2.** Click **Print Preview** to open the preview screen and view your document as it will appear when printed. This document is blank because you didn't enter any text.

TROUBLE? If your computer is not set up with printer access, you will not be able to open Print Preview. Ask your instructor or technical support person for help.

**3.** After examining the screen, click the button with the text label "Close" to return to your document.

TROUBLE? If you close WordPad by mistake, restart it.

Not all menu options immediately carry out an action—some show submenus or ask you for more information about what you want to do. The menu gives you hints about what to expect when you select an option. These hints are sometimes referred to as **menu conventions**. Figure 1-20 describes the Windows 2000 menu conventions.

**Figure 1-20          MENU CONVENTIONS**

| CONVENTION | DESCRIPTION |
|---|---|
| **Check mark** | Indicates a toggle, or "on-off" switch (like a light switch) that is either checked (turned on) or not checked (turned off) |
| **Ellipsis** | Three dots that indicate you must make additional selections after you select that option. Options without dots do not require additional choices—they take effect as soon as you click them. If an option is followed by an ellipsis, a dialog box opens that allows you to enter specifications for how you want a task carried out. |
| **Triangular arrow** | Indicates the presence of a submenu. When you point at a menu option that has a triangular arrow, a submenu automatically appears. |
| **Grayed-out option** | Option that is not available. For example, a graphics program might display the Text Toolbar option in gray if there is no text in the graphic to work with. |
| **Keyboard shortcut** | A key or combination of keys that you can press to activate the menu option without actually opening the menu |
| **Double arrow** | Indicates that additional menu options are available; click the double arrow to access them |

Figure 1-21 shows examples of these menu conventions.

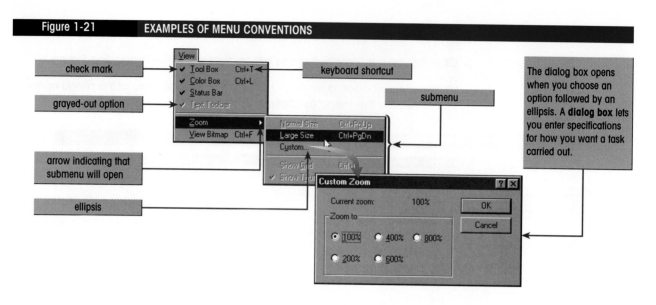

Figure 1-21 EXAMPLES OF MENU CONVENTIONS

# Using Toolbars

Although you can usually perform all program commands using menus, toolbar buttons provide convenient one-click access to frequently used commands. For most Windows 2000 functions, there is usually more than one way to accomplish a task. To simplify your introduction to Windows 2000 in this tutorial, we will usually show you only one method for performing a task. As you become more accomplished at using Windows 2000, you can explore alternate methods.

In Session 1.1 you learned that Windows 2000 programs include ScreenTips, which indicate the purpose and function of a tool. Now is a good time to explore the WordPad toolbar buttons by looking at their ScreenTips.

## To find out a toolbar button's function:

1. Position the pointer over any button on the toolbar, such as the Print Preview button ⬚. After a short pause, the name of the button appears in a box near the button, and a description of the button appears in the status bar just above the Start button. See Figure 1-22.

Figure 1-22 TOOLBAR BUTTON AIDS

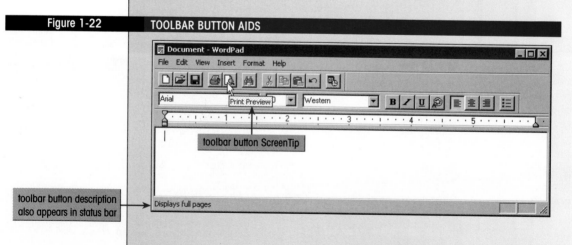

2. Move the pointer over each button on the toolbar to see its name and purpose.

You select a toolbar button by clicking it.

*To select the Print Preview toolbar button:*

**1.** Click the **Print Preview** button ⬚. The Print Preview screen appears. This is the same screen that appeared when you selected Print Preview from the File menu.

**2.** After examining the screen, click the button with the text label "Close" to return to your document.

## Using **List Boxes and Scroll Bars**

As you might guess from the name, a **list box** displays a list of choices. In WordPad, date and time formats are shown in the Date/Time list box. List box controls usually include arrow buttons, a scroll bar, and a scroll box, as shown in Figure 1-23.

*To use the Date/Time list box:*

**1.** Click the **Date/Time** button ⬚ to display the Date and Time dialog box. See Figure 1-23.

| Figure 1-23 | LIST BOX |

click up arrow button to move toward top of list

scroll bar appears when list is too long to fit in list box

list box shows available date formats

drag scroll box up or down to view different parts of list

click down arrow button to move toward bottom of list

**2.** To scroll down the list, click the **down arrow** button ⬚. See Figure 1-23.

**3.** Find the scroll box on your screen. See Figure 1-23.

**4.** Drag the **scroll box** to the top of the scroll bar. Notice how the list scrolls back to the beginning.

TROUBLE? You learned how to drag when you learned to move a window. To drag the scroll box up, point to the scroll box, press and hold down the mouse button, and then move the mouse up.

**5.** Find a date in the format "July 07, 2002." Click that date format to select it.

**6.** Click the **OK** button to close the Date and Time dialog box. This inserts the current date in your document.

You can access some list boxes directly from the toolbar. When a list box is on the toolbar, only the current option appears in the list box. A **list arrow** appears on the right of the box and you can click it to view additional options.

## To use the Font Size list box:

**1.** Click the **Font Size** list arrow, as shown in Figure 1-24.

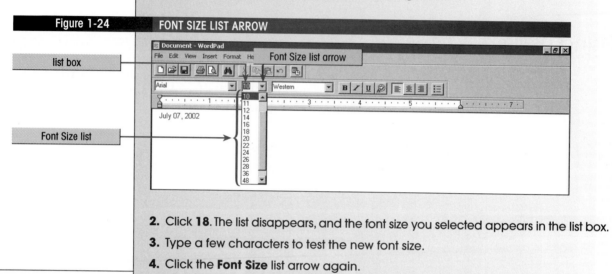

**Figure 1-24**    FONT SIZE LIST ARROW

list box

Font Size list

**2.** Click **18**. The list disappears, and the font size you selected appears in the list box.

**3.** Type a few characters to test the new font size.

**4.** Click the **Font Size** list arrow again.

**5.** Click **12**.

**6.** Type a few characters to test this type size.

**7.** Click the **Close** button ☒ to close WordPad.

**8.** When you see the message "Save changes to Document?" click the **No** button.

# Using **Dialog Box Controls**

Recall that when you select a menu option or button followed by an ellipsis, a dialog box opens that allows you to provide more information about how a program should carry out a task. Some dialog boxes group different kinds of information into bordered rectangular areas called **panes**. Within these panes, you will usually find tabs, option buttons, check boxes, and other controls that the program uses to collect information about how you want it to perform a task. Figure 1-25 describes common dialog box controls.

**Figure 1-25**    DIALOG BOX CONTROLS

| CONTROL | DESCRIPTION |
| --- | --- |
| **Tabs** | Modeled after the tabs on file folders, tab controls are often used as containers for other Windows 2000 controls such as list boxes, radio buttons, and check boxes. Click the appropriate tabs to view different pages of information or choices. |
| **Option buttons** | Also called **radio buttons**, option buttons allow you to select a single option from among one or more options. |
| **Check boxes** | Click a check box to select or deselect it; when it is selected, a check mark appears, indicating that the option is turned on; when deselected, the check box is blank and the option is off. When check boxes appear in groups, you can select or deselect as many as you want; they are not mutually exclusive, as option buttons are. |
| **Spin boxes** | Allow you to scroll easily through a set of numbers to choose the setting you want |
| **Text boxes** | Boxes into which you type additional information |

Figure 1-26 displays examples of these controls.

Figure 1-26          EXAMPLES OF DIALOG BOX CONTROLS

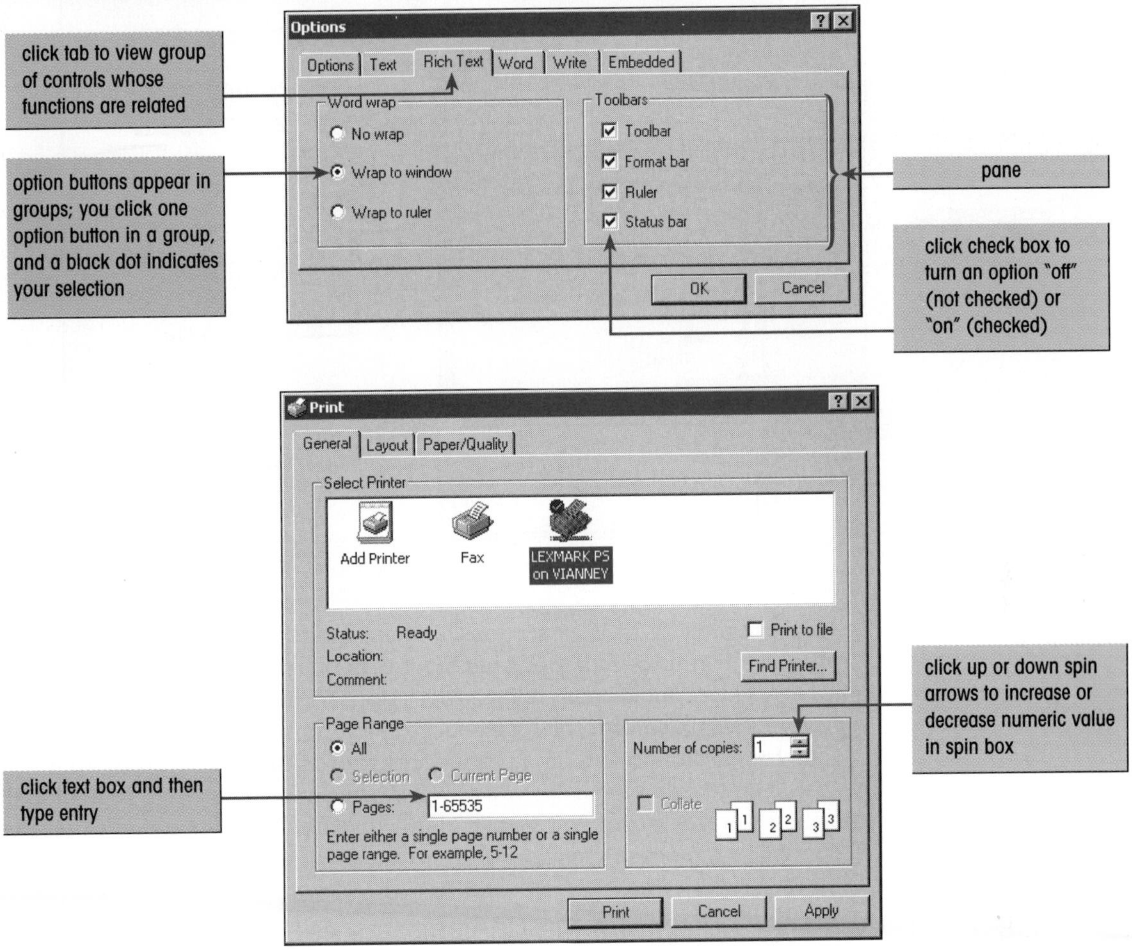

click tab to view group of controls whose functions are related

option buttons appear in groups; you click one option button in a group, and a black dot indicates your selection

pane

click check box to turn an option "off" (not checked) or "on" (checked)

click up or down spin arrows to increase or decrease numeric value in spin box

click text box and then type entry

## Using Help

Windows 2000 **Help** provides on-screen information about the program you are using. Help for the Windows 2000 operating system is available by clicking the Start button on the taskbar, then selecting Help from the Start menu. If you want Help for a program, such as WordPad, you must first start the program, then click Help on the menu bar.

When you start Help, a Windows Help window opens, which gives you access to help files stored on your computer as well as help information stored on Microsoft's Web site. If you are not connected to the Web, you have access only to the help files stored on your computer.

### To start Windows 2000 Help:

1. Click the **Start** button.

2. Click **Help**. The Windows 2000 window opens to the Contents tab. See Figure 1-27.

   TROUBLE? If the Contents tab is not in front, click the Contents tab to view the table of contents.

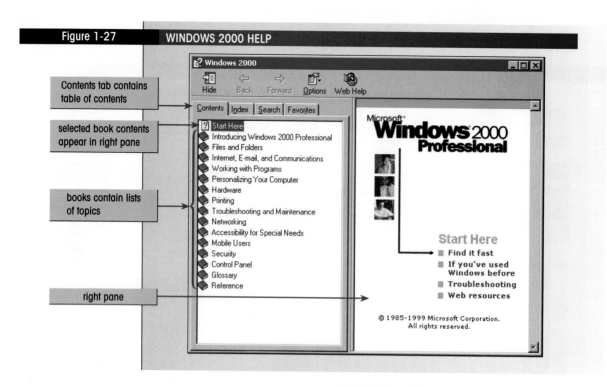

**Figure 1-27** WINDOWS 2000 HELP

Contents tab contains table of contents

selected book contents appear in right pane

books contain lists of topics

right pane

Help uses tabs for the four sections of Help: Contents, Index, Search, and Favorites. The **Contents tab** groups Help topics into a series of books. You select a book 📚 by clicking it. The book opens, and a list of related topics appears from which you can choose. Individual topics are designated with the ? icon. Overview topics are designated with the 📖 icon.

The **Index tab** displays an alphabetical list of all the Help topics from which you can choose. The **Search tab** allows you to search the entire set of Help topics for all topics that contain a word or words you specify. The **Favorites tab** allows you to save your favorite Help topics for quick reference.

## Viewing Topics from the Contents Tab

You know that Windows 2000 gives you easy access to the Internet. Suppose you're wondering how to connect to the Internet from your computer. You can use the Contents tab to find more information on a specific topic.

### To use the Contents tab:

1. Click the **Internet, E-mail, and Communications** book icon 📚. A list of topics and an overview appear below the book title.

2. Click the **Connect to the Internet** topic icon ?. Information about connecting to the Internet appears in the right pane. See Figure 1-28.

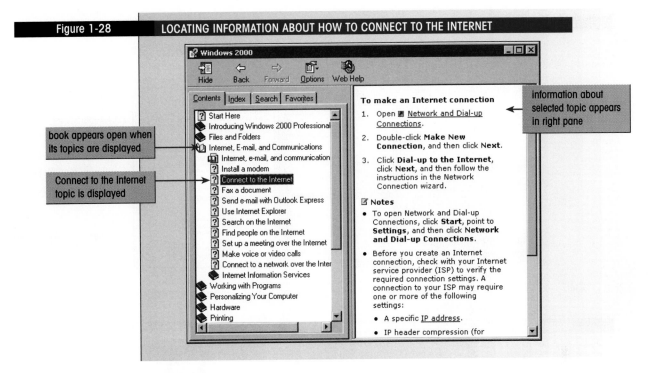

Figure 1-28  **LOCATING INFORMATION ABOUT HOW TO CONNECT TO THE INTERNET**

## Selecting a Topic from the Index

The Index tab allows you to jump to a Help topic by selecting a topic from an indexed list. For example, you can use the Index tab to learn more about the Internet.

### To find a Help topic using the Index tab:

1. Click the **Index** tab. A long list of indexed Help topics appears.

   TROUBLE? If this is the first time you've used Help on your computer, Windows 2000 needs to set up the Index. This takes just a few moments. Wait until you see the list of index entries in the left pane, and then proceed to Step 2.

2. Drag the scroll box down to view additional topics.

3. You can quickly jump to any part of the list by typing the first few characters of a word or phrase in the box above the Index list. Click the box and then type **Internet**.

4. Click the topic **searching the Internet** (you might have to scroll to see it) and then click the **Display** button. When there is just one topic, it appears immediately in the right pane; otherwise, the Topics Found window opens, listing all topics indexed under the entry you're interested in. In this case, there are four choices.

5. Click **Using Internet Explorer** and then click the **Display** button. The information you requested appears in the right pane. See Figure 1-29. Notice in this topic that there are a few underlined words. You can click underlined words to view definitions or additional information.

| Figure 1-29 | USING THE INDEX TO LOCATE INFORMATION |

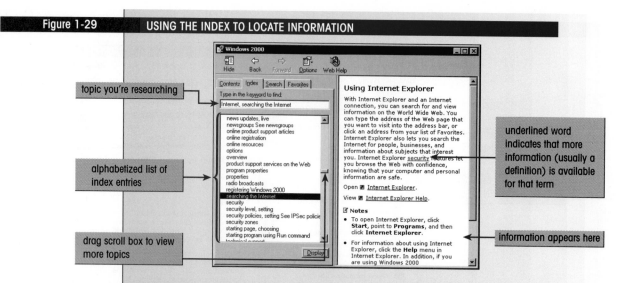

**6.** Click **security**. A small box appears that defines the term "security." See Figure 1-30.

| Figure 1-30 | VIEWING ADDITIONAL INFORMATION |

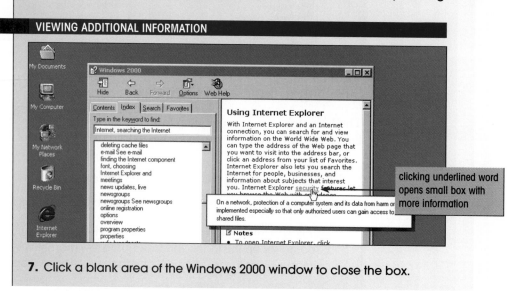

**7.** Click a blank area of the Windows 2000 window to close the box.

The third tab, the Search tab, works similarly to the Index tab, except that you type a word, and then the Help system searches for topics containing that word. You'll get a chance to experiment with the Search and Favorites tabs in the Review Assignments.

## Returning to a Previous Help Topic

You've looked at a few topics now. Suppose you want to return to the one you just saw. The Help window includes a toolbar of buttons that help you navigate the Help system. One of these buttons is the **Back** button, which returns you to topics you've already viewed. Try returning to the help topic on connecting to the Internet.

*To return to a Help topic:*

**1.** Click the **Back** button. The Internet topic appears.

**2.** Click the **Close** button ⊠ to close the Windows 2000 window.

**3.** Log off or shut down Windows 2000, depending on your lab's requirements.

Now that you know how Windows 2000 Help works, don't forget to use it! Use Help when you need to perform a new task or when you forget how to complete a procedure.

You've finished the tutorial, and as you shut down Windows 2000, Steve Laslow returns from class. You take a moment to tell him all you've learned: you know how to start and close programs and how to use multiple programs at the same time. You have learned how to work with windows and the controls they employ. Finally, you've learned how to get help when you need it. Steve is pleased that you are well on your way to mastering the fundamentals of using the Windows 2000 operating system.

## Session 1.2 QUICK CHECK

1. What is the difference between the title bar and a toolbar?

2. Provide the name and purpose of each button:
   a. ☐     b. ☐     c. ☐     d. ☒

3. Describe what is indicated by each of the following menu conventions:
   a. Ellipsis...     b. Grayed-out     c. ▶     d. ✔

4. A(n) _____ consists of a group of buttons, each of which provides one-click access to important program functions.

5. What is the purpose of the scroll bar? What is the purpose of the scroll box?

6. Option buttons allow you to select _____ option(s) at a time.

7. It is a good idea to use _____ when you need to learn how to perform new tasks.

## REVIEW ASSIGNMENTS

1. **Running Two Programs and Switching Between Them** In this tutorial you learned how to run more than one program at a time, using WordPad and Paint. You can run other programs at the same time, too. Complete the following steps and write out your answers to questions b through f:
   a. Start the computer. Enter your username and password if prompted to do so.
   b. Click the Start button. How many menu options are on the Start menu?
   c. Run the Calculator program located on the Accessories menu. How many program buttons are now on the taskbar (don't count toolbar buttons or items in the tray)?
   d. Run the Paint program and maximize the Paint window. How many programs are running now?
   e. Switch to Calculator. What are two visual clues that tell you that Calculator is the active program?
   f. Multiply 576 by 1457 using the Calculator accessory. What is the result?
   g. Close Calculator, then close Paint.

*Explore*

2. **WordPad Help** In Tutorial 1 you learned how to use Windows 2000 Help. Almost every Windows 2000 program has a Help feature. Many users can learn to use a program just by using Help. To use Help, start the program, then click the Help menu at the top of the screen. Try using WordPad Help:
   a. Start WordPad.
   b. Click Help on the WordPad menu bar, and then click Help Topics.
   c. Using WordPad Help, write out your answers to questions 1 through 4.
      1. How do you create a bulleted list?
      2. How do you set the margins in a document?
      3. How do you undo a mistake?
      4. How do you change the font style of a block of text?
   d. Close WordPad.

**Explore**

3. **The Search Tab** In addition to the Contents and Index tabs you worked with in this tutorial, Windows 2000 Help also includes a Search tab. Windows 2000 makes it possible to use a microphone to record sound on your computer. You could browse through the Contents tab, although you might not know where to find information about microphones. You could also use the Index tab to search through the indexed entry. Or you could use the Search tab to find all Help topics that mention microphones.

   a. Start Windows 2000 Help and use the Index tab to find information about microphones. How many topics are listed?
   b. Now use the Search tab to find information about microphones. Type "microphone" in the box on the Search tab, and then click the List Topics button.
   c. Write a paragraph comparing the two lists of topics. You don't have to view them all, but indicate which tab seems to yield more information, and why. Close Help.

4. **Getting Started** Windows 2000 includes Getting Started, an online "book" that helps you discover more about your computer and the Windows 2000 operating system. You can use this book to review what you learned in this tutorial and pick up some tips for using Windows 2000. Complete the following steps and write out your answers to questions d–j.

   a. Start Help, click the Contents tab, click Introducing Windows 2000 Professional, and then click Getting Started online book. Read the information and then click Windows 2000 Professional Getting Started.
   b. In the right pane, click New to Windows? Notice the book icons in the upper-right and upper-left corners of the right pane.
   c. Read each screen, and then click the right book icon to proceed through the Help topics. Alternately, you can view specific Getting Started Help topics by clicking them on the Contents tab. To answer the following questions, locate the information on the relevant Help topic. All the information for these questions is located in Chapter 4—"Windows Basics." When you are done, close Help.
   d. If your computer's desktop style uses the single-click option, how do you select a file? How do you open a file?
   e. What features are almost always available on your desktop, regardless of how many windows you have open?
   f. How can you get information about a dialog box or an area of the dialog box?
   g. How does the Getting Started online book define the word "disk"?
   h. If your computer is connected to a network, what Windows 2000 feature can you use to browse network resources?
   i. Why shouldn't you turn off your computer without shutting it down properly?

5. **Favorite Help Topics** You learned in this tutorial that you can save a list of your favorite Help topics on the Favorites tab. Try adding a topic to your list of favorites.

   a. Open a Help topic in the Help system. For this assignment, click the Contents tab, click Personalizing Your Computer, and then click Personalizing your workspace overview.
   b. Click the Favorites tab. The topic you selected appears on the right, and the topic name appears in the lower-left corner.
   c. Click the Add button. The topic appears in the box on the Favorites tab. This provides you an easy way to return to this topic.
   d. Click the Remove button to remove the topic from the Favorites list.

## PROJECTS

1. There are many types of pointing devices on the market today. Go to the library and research the types of devices available. Consider what devices are appropriate for these situations: desktop or laptop computers, connected or remote devices, and ergonomic or standard designs (look up the word "ergonomic").

Use up-to-date computer books, trade computer magazines such as *PC Computing* and *PC Magazine*, or the Internet (if you know how) to locate information. Your instructor might suggest specific resources you can use. Write a one-page report describing the types of devices available, the differing needs of users, special features that make pointing devices more useful, price comparisons, and what you would choose if you needed to buy a pointing device.

2. Using the resources available to you, either through your library or the Internet (if you know how), locate information about the release of Windows 2000. Computing trade magazines are an excellent source of information about software. Read several articles about Windows 2000 and then write a one-page essay that discusses the features that are most important to the people who evaluated the software. If you find reviews of the software, mention the features that reviewers had the strongest reaction to, pro or con.

3. Upgrading is the process of placing a more recent version of a product onto your computer. When Windows 2000 first came out, people had to decide whether or not they wanted to upgrade to Windows 2000. Interview several people you know who are well-informed Windows computer users. Ask them whether they are using Windows 2000 or an older version of Windows. If they are using an older version, ask why they have chosen not to upgrade. If they are using Windows 2000, ask them why they chose to upgrade. Ask such questions as:

   a. What features convinced you to upgrade or made you decide to wait?
   b. What role did the price of the upgrade play?
   c. Would you have had (or did you have) to purchase new hardware to make the upgrade? How did this affect your decision?
   d. If you did upgrade, are you happy with that decision? If you didn't, do you intend to upgrade in the near future? Why, or why not?

   Write a single-page essay summarizing what you learned from these interviews.

4. Choose a topic to research using the Windows 2000 online Help system. Look for information on your topic using three tabs: the Contents tab, the Index tab, and the Search tab. Once you've found all the information you can, compare the three methods (Contents, Index, Search) of looking for information. Write a paragraph that discusses which tab proved the most useful. Did you reach the same information topics using all three methods? In a second paragraph, summarize what you learned about your topic. Finally, in a third paragraph, indicate under what circumstances you'd use which tab.

## LAB ASSIGNMENTS

**Using a Keyboard** Keyboard To become an effective computer user, you must be familiar with your primary input device—the keyboard. See the Read This Before You Begin page for information on installing and starting the lab.

1. The Steps for the Using a Keyboard Lab provide you with a structured introduction to the keyboard layout and the function of special computer keys. Click the Steps button and begin the Steps. As you work through the Steps, answer all of the Quick Check questions that appear. When you complete the Steps, you will see a Summary Report that summarizes your performance on the Quick Checks. Follow the directions on the screen to print the Summary Report.

2. In Explore, start the typing tutor. You can develop your typing skills using the typing tutor in Explore. Take the typing test and print out your results.

3. In Explore, try to improve your typing speed by 10 words per minute. For example, if you currently type 20 words per minute, your goal will be 30 words per minute. Practice each typing lesson until you see a message that indicates that you can proceed to the next lesson.

Create a Practice Record, as shown here, to keep track of how much you practice. When you have reached your goal, print out the results of a typing test to verify your results.

Practice Record
Name:
Section:
Start Date:   Start Typing Speed:        wpm
End Date:    End Typing Speed:         wpm
Lesson #:    Date Practiced/Time Practiced

**Using a Mouse**

*Using a Mouse*  A mouse is a standard input device on most of today's computers. You need to know how to use a mouse to manipulate graphical user interfaces and to use the rest of the Labs. See the Read This Before You Begin page for information on installing and starting the lab.

1. The Steps for the Using a Mouse Lab show you how to click, double-click, and drag objects using the mouse. Click the Steps button and begin the Steps. As you work through the Steps, answer all of the Quick Check questions that appear. When you complete the Steps, you will see a Summary Report that summarizes your performance on the Quick Checks. Follow the directions on the screen to print the Summary Report.

2. In Explore, create a poster to demonstrate your ability to use a mouse and to control a Windows program. To create a poster for an upcoming sports event, select a graphic, type the caption for the poster, then select a font, font styles, and a border. Print your completed poster.

# QUICK CHECK ANSWERS

*Session 1.1*

1. The taskbar contains buttons that give you access to tools and programs.
2. multitasking
3. Start menu
4. Lift the mouse up and move it to the right.
5. Its button appears on the taskbar.
6. To conserve computer resources such as memory.
7. To ensure you don't lose data and damage your files.

*Session 1.2*

1. The title bar identifies the window and contains window controls; toolbars contain buttons that provide you with shortcuts to common menu commands.
2. a. Minimize button shrinks window so you see button on taskbar
   b. Maximize button enlarges window to fill entire screen
   c. Restore button reduces window to predetermined size
   d. Close button closes window and removes button from taskbar
3. a. ellipsis indicates a dialog box will open
   b. grayed-out indicates option is not currently available
   c. arrow indicates a submenu will open
   d. check mark indicates a toggle option
4. toolbar
5. Scroll bars appear when the contents of a box or window are too long to fit; you drag the scroll box to view different parts of the contents.
6. one
7. online Help

# WORKING WITH FILES

*Creating, Saving, and Managing Files*

## Distance Education

You recently purchased a computer in order to gain new skills so you can stay competitive in the job market. You hope to use the computer to enroll in a few distance education courses. **Distance education** is formalized learning that typically takes place using a computer and the Internet, replacing normal classroom interaction with modern communications technology. Distance education teachers often make their course material available on the **World Wide Web**, a popular service on the Internet that makes information readily accessible.

Your computer came loaded with Windows 2000. Your friend Shannon suggests that before you enroll in any online courses, you should get more comfortable with your computer and with Windows 2000. Knowing how to save, locate, and organize your files will make your time spent at the computer much more productive. A **file**, often referred to as a **document**, is a collection of data that has a name and is stored in a computer. Once you create a file, you can open it, edit its contents, print it, and save it again—usually using the same program you used to create it.

Shannon suggests that you become familiar with how to perform these tasks in Windows 2000 programs. Then she'll show you how to choose different ways of viewing information on your computer. Finally, you'll spend time learning how to organize your files.

## SESSION 2.1

In Session 2.1, you will learn how to format a disk so it can store files. You will create, save, open, and print a file. You will find out how the insertion point differs from the mouse pointer, and you will learn the basic skills for Windows 2000 text entry, such as entering, selecting, inserting, and deleting. For the steps of this tutorial you will need two blank 3½-inch disks.

## Formatting a Disk

Before you can save files on a floppy disk, the disk must be formatted. When the computer **formats** a disk, the magnetic particles on the disk surface are arranged so that data can be stored on the disk. Today, many disks are sold preformatted and can be used right out of the box. However, if you purchase an unformatted disk, or if you have an old disk you want to completely erase and reuse, you can format the disk using the Windows 2000 Format command. This command is available through the **My Computer window**, a feature of Windows 2000 that you use to view, organize, and access the programs, files, drives and folders on your computer. You open My Computer by using its icon on the desktop. You'll learn more about the My Computer window later in this tutorial.

The following steps tell you how to format a 3½-inch high-density disk, using drive A. Your instructor will tell you how to revise the instructions given in these steps if the procedure is different for your lab.

*Make sure you are using a blank disk (or one that contains data you no longer need) before you perform these steps.*

### To format a disk:

1. Start Windows 2000, if necessary.

2. Write your name on the label of a 3½-inch disk and insert your disk in drive A. See Figure 2-1.

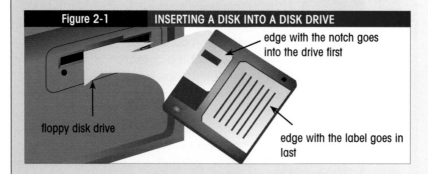

Figure 2-1    INSERTING A DISK INTO A DISK DRIVE

edge with the notch goes into the drive first

floppy disk drive

edge with the label goes in last

TROUBLE? If your disk does not fit in drive A, put it in drive B and substitute drive B for drive A in all of the steps for the rest of the tutorial.

3. Click the **My Computer** icon on the desktop. The icon is selected. Figure 2-2 shows this icon on your desktop.

TROUBLE? If the My Computer window opens, skip Step 4. Your computer is using different settings, which you'll learn to change in Session 2.2.

4. Press the **Enter** key to open the My Computer window. See Figure 2-2 (don't worry if your window opens maximized).

TROUBLE? If you see a list of items instead of icons like those in Figure 2-2, click View, and then click Large Icons. Don't worry if your toolbars don't exactly match those in Figure 2-2.

TROUBLE? If you see additional information or a graphic image on the left side of the My Computer window, Web view is enabled on your computer. Don't worry. You will learn how to return to the default Windows 2000 settings in Session 2.2.

| Figure 2-2 | MY COMPUTER WINDOW |
| --- | --- |

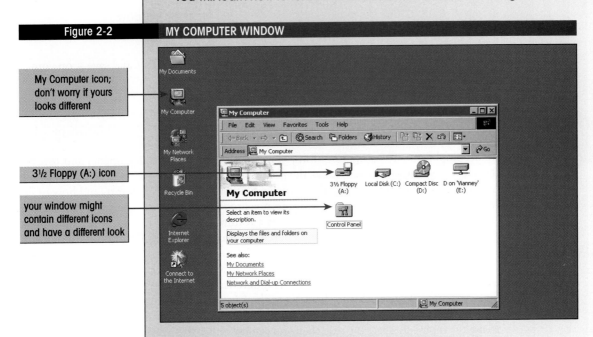

My Computer icon; don't worry if yours looks different

3½ Floppy (A:) icon

your window might contain different icons and have a different look

5. Right-click the **3½ Floppy (A:)** icon to open its shortcut menu, and then click **Format**. The Format dialog box opens.

6. Make sure the dialog box settings on your screen match those in Figure 2-3.

| Figure 2-3 | FORMATTING A FLOPPY DISK |
| --- | --- |

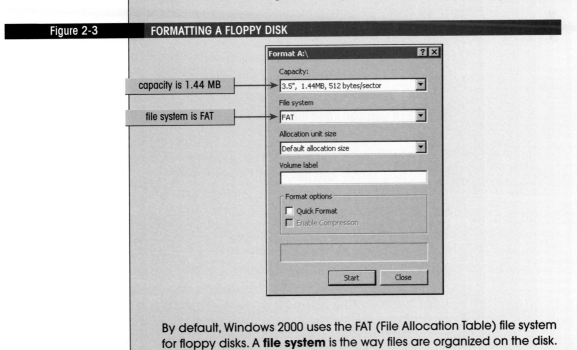

capacity is 1.44 MB

file system is FAT

By default, Windows 2000 uses the FAT (File Allocation Table) file system for floppy disks. A **file system** is the way files are organized on the disk. Windows 2000 supports other file systems such as FAT32 and NTFS, but this is a more advanced topic.

7. Click the **Start** button to start formatting the disk.

8. Click the **OK** button to confirm that you want to format the disk (the actual formatting will take a minute to perform). Click the **OK** button again when the formatting is complete.

9. Click the **Close** button.

10. Click the **Close** button [X] to close the My Computer window.

Now that you have a formatted disk, you can create a document and save it on your disk. First you need to learn how to enter text into a document.

# Working with Text

To accomplish many computing tasks, you need to enter text in documents and text boxes. This involves learning how to move the pointer so the text will appear where you want it, how to insert new text between existing words or sentences, how to select text, and how to delete text. When you type sentences of text, do not press the Enter key when you reach the right margin of the page. Most software contains a feature called **word wrap**, which automatically continues your text on the next line. Therefore, you should press Enter only when you have completed a paragraph.

If you type the wrong character, press the Backspace key to back up and delete the character. You can also use the Delete key. What's the difference between the Backspace and Delete keys? The **Backspace** key deletes the character to the left, while the **Delete** key deletes the character to the right. If you want to delete text that is not next to where you are currently typing, you need to use the mouse to select the text; then you can use either the Delete key or the Backspace key.

Now you will type some text, using WordPad, to practice text entry. When you first start WordPad, notice the flashing vertical bar, called the **insertion point**, in the upper-left corner of the document window. The insertion point indicates where the characters you type will appear.

*To type text in WordPad:*

1. Start WordPad and locate the insertion point.

   TROUBLE? If the WordPad window does not fill the screen, click the Maximize button [□].

   TROUBLE? If you can't find the insertion point, click in the WordPad **document window**, the white area below the toolbars and ruler.

2. Type your name, pressing the Shift key at the same time as the appropriate letter to type uppercase letters and using the Spacebar to type spaces, just as on a typewriter.

3. Press the **Enter** key to move the insertion point down to the next line.

4. As you type the following sentences, watch what happens when the insertion point reaches the right edge of the page:

   **This is a sample typed in WordPad. See what happens when the insertion point reaches the right edge of the page. Note how the text wraps automatically to the next line.**

   TROUBLE? If you make a mistake, delete the incorrect character(s) by pressing the Backspace key on your keyboard. Then type the correct character(s).

TROUBLE? If your text doesn't wrap, your screen might be set up to display more information than the screen used for the figures in this tutorial, or your WordPad program might not be set to use Word Wrap. Click View, click Options, make sure the Rich Text tab is selected, click the Wrap to window option button, and then click the OK button.

## The Insertion Point Versus the Pointer

The insertion point is not the same as the mouse pointer. When the mouse pointer is in the text-entry area, it is called the **I-beam pointer** and looks like ⌶. Figure 2-4 explains the difference between the insertion point and the I-beam pointer.

| Figure 2-4 | THE INSERTION POINT VS. THE POINTER |

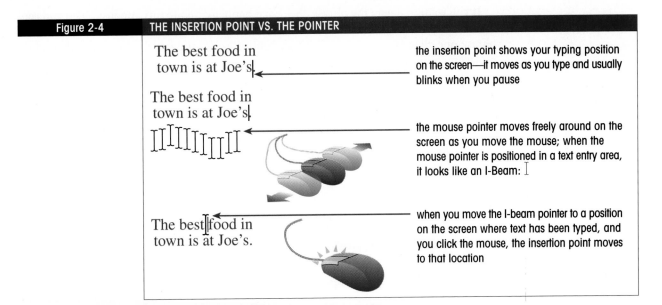

The best food in town is at Joe's.  — the insertion point shows your typing position on the screen—it moves as you type and usually blinks when you pause

The best food in town is at Joe's. — the mouse pointer moves freely around on the screen as you move the mouse; when the mouse pointer is positioned in a text entry area, it looks like an I-Beam: ⌶

The best food in town is at Joe's. — when you move the I-beam pointer to a position on the screen where text has been typed, and you click the mouse, the insertion point moves to that location

When you enter text, the insertion point moves as you type. If you want to enter text in a location other than where the mouse pointer is currently positioned, you move the I-beam pointer to the location where you want to type, and then click. The insertion point jumps to the location you clicked. In most programs, the insertion point blinks, making it easier for you to locate it on a screen filled with text.

*To move the insertion point:*

1. Check the locations of the insertion point and the I-beam pointer. The insertion point should be at the end of the sentence you typed in the last set of steps. The easiest way to locate the I-beam pointer is to move your mouse gently until you see the pointer. Remember that it will look like ⌖ until you move the pointer into the document window.

2. Use the mouse to move the I-beam pointer just to the left of the word "sample" and then click the mouse button. The insertion point should be just to the left of the "s."

   TROUBLE? If you have trouble clicking just to the left of the "s," try clicking in the word and then using the arrow keys to move the insertion point one character at a time.

**3.** Move the I-beam pointer to a blank area near the bottom of the workspace and then click. Notice the insertion point does not jump to the location of the I-beam pointer. Instead the insertion point jumps to the end of the last sentence or to the point in the bottom line directly above where you clicked. The insertion point can move only within existing text. It cannot be moved out of the existing text area.

## Selecting Text

Many text operations are performed on a **block** of text, which is one or more consecutive characters, words, sentences, or paragraphs. Once you select a block of text, you can delete it, move it, replace it, underline it, and so on. To deselect a block of text, click anywhere outside the selected block.

If you want to delete the phrase "See what happens" in the text you just typed and replace it with the phrase "You can watch word wrap in action," you do not have to delete the first phrase one character at a time. Instead, you can select the entire phrase and then type the replacement phrase.

### To select and replace a block of text:

**1.** Move the I-beam pointer just to the left of the word "See."

**2.** While holding down the mouse button, drag the I-beam pointer over the text to the end of the word "happens." The phrase "See what happens" should now be highlighted. See Figure 2-5.

TROUBLE? If the space to the right of the word "happens" is also selected, don't worry. Your computer is set up to select spaces in addition to words. After completing Step 4, simply press the Spacebar to type an extra space if required.

| Figure 2-5 | SELECTING TEXT |
| --- | --- |

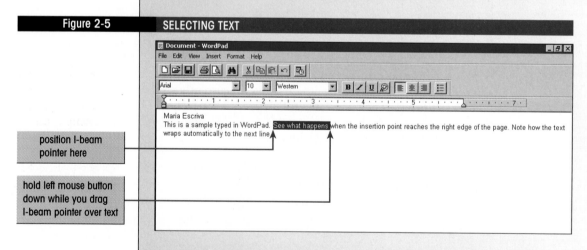

position I-beam pointer here

hold left mouse button down while you drag I-beam pointer over text

**3.** Release the mouse button.

TROUBLE? If the phrase is not highlighted correctly, repeat Steps 1 through 3.

**4.** Type **You can watch word wrap in action**

The text you typed replaces the highlighted text. Notice that you did not need to delete the selected text before you typed the replacement text.

## Inserting a Character

Windows 2000 programs usually operate in **insert mode**—when you type a new character, all characters to the right of the insertion point are pushed over to make room.

Suppose you want to insert the word "page" before the word "typed" in your practice sentences.

---

*To insert text:*

1. Move the I-beam pointer just before the word "typed" and then click to position the insertion point.

2. Type **page**

3. Press the **Spacebar**.

---

Notice how the letters in the first line are pushed to the right to make room for the new characters. When a word gets pushed past the right margin, the word-wrap feature moves it down to the beginning of the next line.

# Saving a File

As you type text, it is held temporarily in the computer's memory, which is erased when you turn off the computer. For permanent storage, you need to save your work on a disk. In the computer lab, you will probably save your work on a floppy disk in drive A.

When you save a file, you must give it a name, called a **filename**. Windows 2000 allows you to use up to 255 characters in a filename—this gives you plenty of room to name your file accurately enough so that you'll know the contents of the file by just looking at the filename. You may use spaces and certain punctuation symbols in your filenames. You cannot use the symbols \ / ? : * " < > | in a filename, because Windows uses those for designating the location and type of the file, but other symbols such as & ; - and $ are allowed.

Another thing to consider is whether you might use your files on a computer running older programs. Programs designed for the Windows 3.1 and DOS operating systems (which were created before 1995) require that files be eight characters or less with no spaces. Thus when you save a file with a long filename in Windows 2000, Windows 2000 also creates an eight-character filename that can be used by older programs. The eight-character filename is created from the first six nonspace characters in the long filename, with the addition of a tilde (~) and a number. For example, the filename Car Sales for 1999 would be converted to Carsal~1.

Most filenames have an extension. An **extension** (a set of no more than three characters at the end of a filename, separated from the filename by a period) is used by the operating system to identify and categorize the file. In the filename Car Sales for 1999.doc, for example, the file extension "doc" identifies the file as one created with Microsoft Word. You might also have a file called Car Sales for 1999.xls—"xls" identifies the file as one created with Microsoft Excel, a spreadsheet program. When pronouncing filenames with extensions, say "dot" for the period, so that the file Resume.doc is pronounced "Resume dot doc."

You usually do not need to add extensions to your filenames because the program you use to create the file does this automatically. Also, Windows 2000 keeps track of file extensions, but not all computers are set to display them. The steps in these tutorials refer to files by using the filename without its extension. So if you see the filename Practice Text in the steps, but "Practice Text.doc" appears on your screen, don't worry—these refer to the same file. Also don't worry if you don't use consistent lowercase and uppercase letters when saving files. Usually the operating system doesn't distinguish between them. Be aware, however, that some programs are "case-sensitive"—they check for case in filenames.

Now you can save the WordPad document you typed.

*To start saving a document:*

**1. Click the Save button** 🖫 **on the toolbar. The Save As dialog box opens, as shown in Figure 2-6.**

| Figure 2-6 | SAVING A FILE |
| --- | --- |

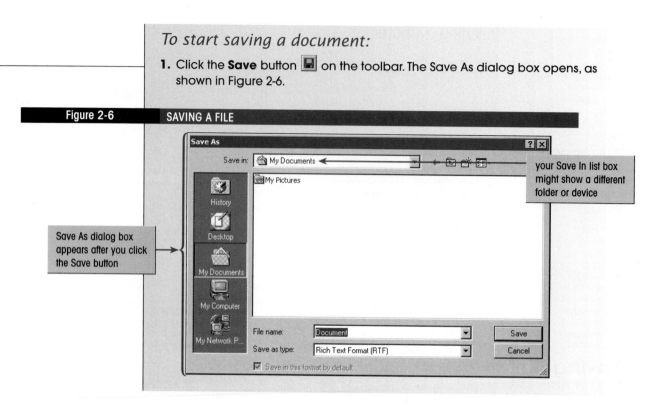

Save As dialog box appears after you click the Save button

your Save In list box might show a different folder or device

You use the Save As dialog box to specify where you want to save your file (on the hard drive or on a floppy disk, in a folder or not, and so on). Before going further with the process of saving a file, let's examine some of the features of the Save As dialog box so that you learn to save your files exactly where you want them.

## Specifying the File Location

In the Save As dialog box, Windows 2000 provides the **Places Bar**, a list of important locations on your computer. When you click the different icons in the Places Bar, the contents of those locations will be displayed in the white area of the Save As dialog box. You can then save your document directly to those locations. Figure 2-7 displays the icons in the Places Bar and gives their function.

| Figure 2-7 | ICONS IN THE PLACES BAR |
| --- | --- |

| ICON | DESCRIPTION |
| --- | --- |
| History | Displays a list of recently opened files, folders, and objects |
| Desktop | Displays a list of files, folders, and objects on the Windows 2000 desktop |
| My Documents | Displays a list of files, folders, and objects in the My Documents folder |
| My Computer | Displays a list of files, folders, and objects in the My Computer window |
| My Network P... | Displays a list of computers and folders available on the network |

To see this in action, try displaying different locations in the dialog box.

## *To use the Places Bar:*

1. Click the **Desktop** icon in the Places Bar.

2. The Save As dialog box now displays the contents of the Windows 2000 desktop. See Figure 2-8.

| Figure 2-8 | USING THE PLACES BAR |

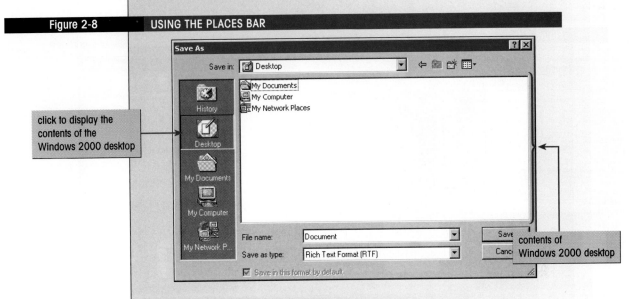

click to display the contents of the Windows 2000 desktop

contents of Windows 2000 desktop

3. Click the **My Documents** icon to display the contents of the My Documents folder.

Once you've clicked an icon in the Places Bar, you can open any file displayed in that location, and you can save a file into that location. The Places Bar doesn't have an icon for every location on your computer, however. The **Save in** list box (located at the top of the dialog box) does. Use the Save in list box now to save your document to your floppy disk.

## *To use the Save in list box:*

1. Click the **Save in** list arrow to display a list of drives.

2. Click **3½ Floppy (A:)**.

   Now that you've specified where you want to save your file, you can specify a name and type for the file.

## Specifying the File Name and Type

After choosing the location for your document, you have to specify the name of the file. You should also specify (or at least check) the file's format. A file's **format** determines what type of information you can place in the document, the document's appearance, and what kind of programs can work with the document. There are five file formats available in WordPad: Word for Windows 6.0, Rich Text Format (RTF), Text, Text for MS-DOS, and Unicode Text. The Word and RTF formats allow you to create documents with text that can use bold-faced or italicized fonts as well as documents containing graphic images and scanned photos. However, only word-processing programs like WordPad or Microsoft Word can work with those files. The three text formats allow only simple text with no graphics or special formatting, but such documents are readable by a wider range of programs. The default format for WordPad documents is RTF, but you can change that, as you'll see shortly.

Continue saving the document, using the name "Practice Text" and the file type Word 6.0.

## To finish saving your document:

1. Select the text **Document** in the File name text box and then type **Practice Text** in the File name text box. The new text replaces "Document."

2. Click the **Save as type** list arrow and then click **Word for Windows 6.0** in the list. See Figure 2-9.

| Figure 2-9 | COMPLETED SAVE AS DIALOG BOX |
| --- | --- |

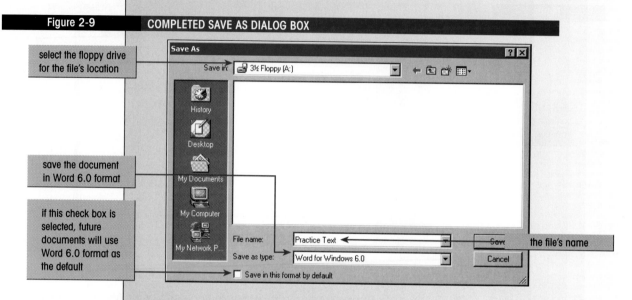

select the floppy drive for the file's location

save the document in Word 6.0 format

if this check box is selected, future documents will use Word 6.0 format as the default

the file's name

Note that if you want all future documents saved by WordPad to use the Word 6.0 format as the default format rather than RTF, you can select the Save in this format by default check box. If you select it, the next time you save a document in WordPad, this format will be the initial choice, so you won't have to specify it.

3. Click the **Save** button in the lower-right corner of the dialog box.

4. If you are asked whether you are sure that you want to save the document in this format, click the **Yes** button.

Your file is saved on your Data Disk, and the document title, "Practice Text," appears on the WordPad title bar.

Note that after you save the file the document appears a little different. What has changed? By saving the document in Word 6.0 format rather than RTF, you've changed the format of the document slightly. One change is that the text is wrapped differently in Word 6.0 format. A Word 6.0 file will use the right margin and, in this case, limit the length of a single line of text to 6 inches.

What if you try to close WordPad before you save your file? Windows 2000 will display a message—"Save changes to Document?" If you answer "Yes," Windows will display the Save As dialog box so you can give the document a name. If you answer "No," Windows 2000 will close WordPad without saving the document. Any changes you made to the document will be lost, so when you are asked if you want to save a file, answer "Yes," unless you are absolutely sure you don't need to keep the work you just did.

After you save a file, you can work on another document or close WordPad. Since you have already saved your Practice Text document, you'll continue this tutorial by closing WordPad.

## To close WordPad:

1. Click the **Close** button ⊠ to close the WordPad window.

# Opening a File

Suppose you save and close the Practice Text file, then later you want to revise it. To revise a file you must first open it. When you open a file, its contents are copied into the computer's memory. If you revise the file, you need to save the changes before you close the program. If you close a revised file without saving your changes, you will lose them.

There are several methods to open a file. You can select the file from the Documents list (available through the Start menu) if you have opened the file recently, since the Documents list contains the 15 most recently opened documents. This list is very handy to use on your own computer, but in a lab, other student's files quickly replace your own. You can also locate the file in the My Computer window (or in **Windows Explorer**, another file management tool) and then open it. And finally, you can start a program and then use the Open button within that program to locate and open the file. Each method has advantages and disadvantages.

The first two methods for opening the Practice Text file simply require you to select the file from the Documents list or locate and select it from My Computer or Windows Explorer. With these methods the document, not the program, is central to the task; hence, this method is sometimes referred to as **document-centric**. You need only to remember the name of your file—you do not need to remember which program you used to create it.

## Opening a File from the My Computer Window

If your file is not in the Documents list, you can open the file by selecting it from the My Computer window. Either way, Windows 2000 uses the file extension (whether it is displayed or not) to determine which program to start so you can manipulate the file. It starts the program, and then automatically opens the file. The advantage of both methods is simplicity. The disadvantage is that Windows 2000 might not start the program you expect. For example, when you select Practice Text, you might expect Windows 2000 to start WordPad because you used WordPad to create it. Depending on the programs installed on your computer system, however, Windows 2000 might start Microsoft Word instead. Usually this is not a problem. Although the program might not be the one you expect, you can still use it to revise your file.

---

*To open the Practice Text file by selecting it from My Computer:*

**1.** Open the **My Computer** window, located on the desktop.

**2.** Click the **3½ Floppy (A:)** icon in the My Computer window.

TROUBLE? If the 3½ Floppy (A:) window opens, skip Step 3.

**3.** Press the **Enter** key. The 3½ Floppy (A:) window opens.

**4.** Click the **Practice Text** file icon.

TROUBLE? If the Practice Text document opens, skip Step 5.

**5.** Press the **Enter** key. Windows 2000 starts a program, and then automatically opens the Practice Text file. You could make revisions to the document at this point, but instead, you'll close all the windows on your desktop so you can try the other method for opening files.

TROUBLE? If Windows 2000 starts Microsoft Word or another word-processing program instead of WordPad, don't worry. You can use Microsoft Word to revise the Practice Text document.

**6.** Close all open windows on the desktop.

## Opening a File from Within a Program

The third method for opening the Practice Text file requires you to open WordPad, and then use the Open button to select the Practice Text file. The advantage of this method is that you can specify the program you want to use—WordPad, in this case. This method, however, involves more steps than the method you tried previously.

You can take advantage of the Places Bar to reduce the number of steps it takes to open a file from within a program. Recall that one of the icons in the Places Bar is the History icon, which displays a list of recently opened files or objects. One of the most recently opened files was the Practice Text file, so it should appear in the list.

*To start WordPad and open the Practice Text file:*

1. Start **WordPad** and, if necessary, maximize the WordPad window.

2. Click the **Open** button 📂 on the toolbar.

3. Click **History** in the Places Bar.

The Practice Text file doesn't appear in the list. Why not? Look at the Files of Type list box. The selected entry is "Rich Text Format (*.rtf)". What this means is that the Open dialog box will display only RTF files (as well as drives). This frees you from having to deal with the clutter of unwanted or irrelevant files. The downside is that unless you're aware of how the Open dialog box will filter the list of files, you may mistakenly think that the file you're looking for doesn't exist. You can change how the Open dialog box filters this file list. Try this now by changing the filter to show only Word documents.

*To change the types of files displayed:*

1. Click the **Files of type** list arrow and then click **Word for Windows (*.doc)**

   The Practice Text file now appears in the list.

2. Click **Practice Text** in the list of files. See Figure 2-10.

| Figure 2-10 | THE OPEN DIALOG BOX |
| --- | --- |

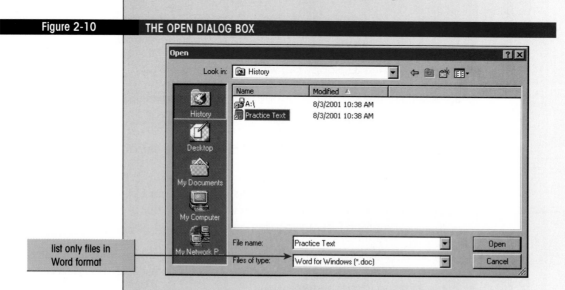

list only files in
Word format

3. Click the **Open** button. The document should once again appear in the WordPad window.

Now that the Practice Text file is open, you can print it.

# Printing a File

Windows 2000 provides easy access to your printer or printers. You can choose which printer to use, you can control how the document is printed, and you can control the order in which documents will be printed.

## Previewing your Document Before Printing

It is a good idea to use Print Preview before you send your document to the printer. **Print Preview** shows on the screen exactly how your document will appear on paper. You can check your page layout so that you don't waste time and paper printing a document that is not quite the way you want it. Your instructor might supply you with additional instructions for printing in your school's computer lab.

*To preview, then print, the Practice Text file:*

1. Click the **Print Preview** button 🔍 on the toolbar.

   TROUBLE? If an error message appears, printing capabilities might not be set up on your computer. Ask your instructor or technical support person for help, or skip this set of steps.

2. Look at your document in the Print Preview window. Before you print the document, you should make sure the font, margins, and other document features look the way you want them to.

   TROUBLE? If you can't read the document text on screen, click the Zoom In button as many times as needed to view the text.

3. Click the **Close** button to close Print Preview and return to the document.

Now that you've verified that the document looks the way you want, you can print it.

## Sending the Document to the Printer

There are three ways to send your document to the printer. The first approach is to print the document directly from the Print Preview window by clicking the Print button. Thus once you are satisfied with the document's appearance, you can quickly move to printing it.

Another way is to click the Print button 🖨 on your program's toolbar. This method will send the document directly to your printer without any further action on your part. It's the quickest and easiest way to print a document, but it does not allow you to change settings such as margins and layout. What if you have access to more than one printer? In that case, Windows 2000 sends the document to the default printer, the printer that has been set up to handle most print jobs.

If you want to select a different printer, or if you want to control how the printer prints your document, you can opt for a third method—selecting the Print command from the File menu. Using this approach, your program will open the Print dialog box, allowing you to choose which printer to use and how that printer will operate. Note that clicking the Print button from within the Print Preview window will also open the Print dialog box so you can verify or change settings.

*To open the Print dialog box:*

**1.** Click **File** on the WordPad menu bar and then click **Print**.

**2.** The Print dialog box opens, as displayed in Figure 2-11. Familiarize yourself with the controls in the Print dialog box.

Figure 2-11    THE PRINT DIALOG BOX

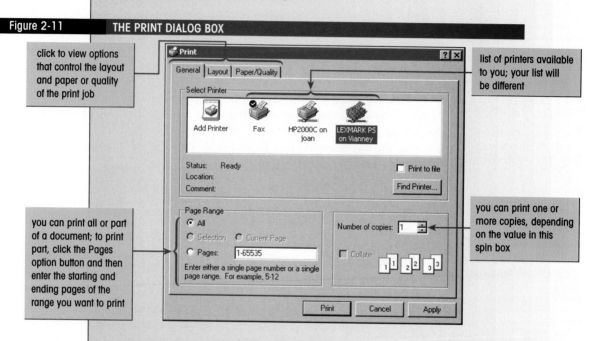

click to view options that control the layout and paper or quality of the print job

list of printers available to you; your list will be different

you can print all or part of a document; to print part, click the Pages option button and then enter the starting and ending pages of the range you want to print

you can print one or more copies, depending on the value in this spin box

**3.** Make sure your Print dialog box shows the Print range set to "All" and the Number of copies set to "1."

**4.** Select one of the printers in the list (your instructor may indicate which one you should select) and then click the **Print** button. The document is printed.

**5.** Close WordPad.

TROUBLE? If you see the message "Save changes to Document?" click the No button.

You've now learned how to create, save, open, and print word-processed files—essential skills for students in distance education courses that rely on word-processed reports transmitted across the Internet. Shannon assures you that the techniques you've just learned apply to most Windows 2000 programs.

# Session 2.1 QUICK CHECK

**1.** A(n) _____ is a collection of data that has a name and is stored on a disk or other storage medium.

**2.** _____ erases all the data on a disk and arranges the magnetic particles on the disk surface so that the disk can store data.

**3.** True or False: When you move the mouse pointer over a text entry area, the pointer shape changes to an I-beam.

4. What indicates where each character you type will appear?

5. What does the History icon in the Places Bar display?

6. A file that you saved does not appear in the Open dialog box. Assuming that the file is still in the same location, what could be the reason that the Open dialog box doesn't display it?

7. What are the three ways to print from within a Windows 2000 application? If you want to print multiple copies of your document, which method(s) should you use and why?

## SESSION 2.2

In this session, you will learn how to change settings in the My Computer window to control its appearance and the appearance of desktop objects. You will then learn how to use My Computer to manage the files on your disk; view information about the files on your disk; organize the files into folders; and move, delete, copy, and rename files. For this session you will use a second blank 3½-inch disk.

## Creating Your Data Disk

Starting with this session, you must create a Data Disk that contains some practice files. You can use the disk you formatted in the previous session.

If you are using your own computer, the NP on Microsoft Windows 2000 menu option will not be available. Before you proceed, you must go to your school's computer lab and find a computer that has the NP on Microsoft Windows 2000 program installed. If you cannot get the files from the lab, ask your instructor or technical support person for help. Once you have made your own Data Disk, you can use it to complete this tutorial on any computer running Windows 2000.

### To add the practice files to your Data Disk:

1. Write "Disk 1 - Windows 2000 Tutorial 2 Data Disk" on the label of your formatted disk (the same disk you used to save your Practice Text file).

2. Place the disk in drive A.

3. Click the **Start** button  .

4. Point to **Programs**.

5. Point to **NP on Microsoft Windows 2000 – Level I**.

   TROUBLE? If NP on Microsoft Windows 2000 - Level I is not listed, ask your instructor or technical support person for help.

6. Click **Disk 1 (Tutorial 2)**. A message box opens, asking you to place your disk in drive A (which you already did, in Step 2).

7. Click the **OK** button. Wait while the program copies the practice files to your formatted disk. When all the files have been copied, the program closes.

Your Data Disk now contains practice files you'll use throughout the rest of this tutorial.

## My Computer

The My Computer icon, as you have seen, represents your computer, with its storage devices, printers, and other objects. The My Computer icon opens into the My Computer window, which contains an icon for each of the storage devices on your computer. My Computer also gives you access to the **Control Panel**, a feature of Windows 2000 that controls the behavior of other devices and programs installed on your computer. Figure 2-12 shows how the My Computer window relates to your computer's hardware.

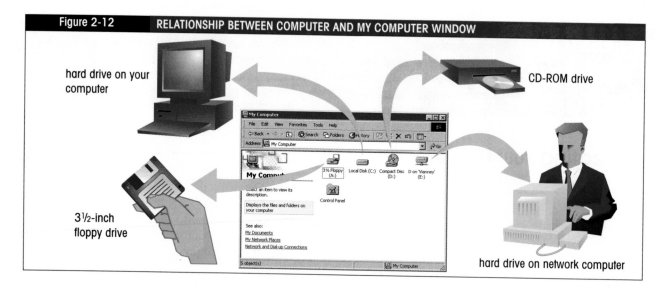

**Figure 2-12** RELATIONSHIP BETWEEN COMPUTER AND MY COMPUTER WINDOW

Each storage device that you have access to has a letter associated with it. The first floppy drive on a computer is usually designated as drive A (if you add a second floppy drive, it is usually designated as drive B), and the first hard drive is usually designated drive C. Additional hard drives will have letters D, E, F and so forth. If you have a CD-ROM drive, it will usually have the next letter in the alphabetic sequence. If you have access to hard drives located on other computers on a network, those drives will sometimes (though not always) have letters associated with them. In the example shown in Figure 2-12, the network drive has the drive letter E.

You can use the My Computer window to organize your files. In this section of the tutorial, you'll use the My Computer window to move and delete files on your Data Disk, which is assumed to be in drive A. If you use your own computer at home or work, you will probably store your files on drive C instead of drive A. In a school lab environment, you can't always save your files to drive C, so you need to carry your files with you on a floppy disk. Most of what you learn about working on the floppy drive will also work on your home or work computer when you use drive C (or other hard drives).

Now you'll open the My Computer window.

*To open the My Computer window and explore the contents of your Data Disk:*

1. Open the My Computer window.

2. Click the **3½ Floppy (A:)** icon and then press the **Enter** key. A window appears showing the contents of drive A; maximize this window if necessary. See Figure 2-13.

Figure 2-13    CONTENTS OF DATA DISK

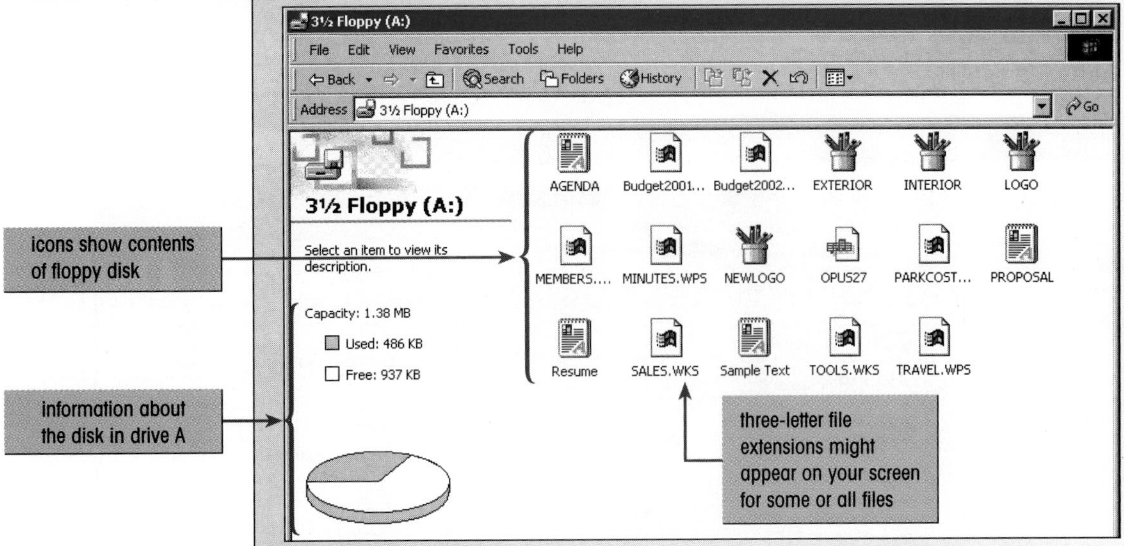

icons show contents of floppy disk

information about the disk in drive A

three-letter file extensions might appear on your screen for some or all files

TROUBLE? If the window appears before you press the Enter key, don't worry. Windows 2000 can be configured to use different keyboard and mouse combinations to open windows. You'll learn about these configuration issues shortly.

TROUBLE? If you see a list of filenames instead of icons, click View on the menu bar and then click Large Icons on the menu.

# Changing the Appearance of the My Computer Window

Windows 2000 offers several different options that control how toolbars, icons, and buttons appear in the My Computer window. To make the My Computer window look the same as it does in the figures in this book, you need to ensure three things: that only the Address and Standard toolbars are visible, that files and other objects are displayed using large icons, and that the configuration of Windows 2000 uses the default setting. Setting your computer to match the figures will make it easier for you to follow the steps.

## Controlling the Toolbar Display

The My Computer window, in addition to displaying a Standard toolbar, allows you to display the same toolbars that can appear on the Windows 2000 taskbar, such as the Address toolbar or the Links toolbar. These toolbars make it easy to access the Web from the My Computer window. In this tutorial, however, you need to see only the Address and Standard toolbars.

*To display only the Address and Standard toolbars:*

1. Click **View**, point to **Toolbars**, and then examine the Toolbars submenu. The Standard Buttons and Address Bar options should be preceded by a check mark. The Links and Radio options should not be checked. Follow the steps below to ensure that you have check marks next to the correct options.

2. If the Standard Buttons and Address Bar options *are not checked*, then click them to select them (you will have to repeat Step 1 to view the Toolbars submenu to do this for each option).

**3.** If the Links or Radio options *are checked*, then click them to deselect them (you will have to repeat Step 1 to view the Toolbars submenu to do this for each option).

**4.** Click **View** and then point to **Toolbars** one last time and verify that your Toolbars submenu and the toolbar display look like Figure 2-14.

| Figure 2-14 | CHECKING VIEW OPTIONS |
| --- | --- |

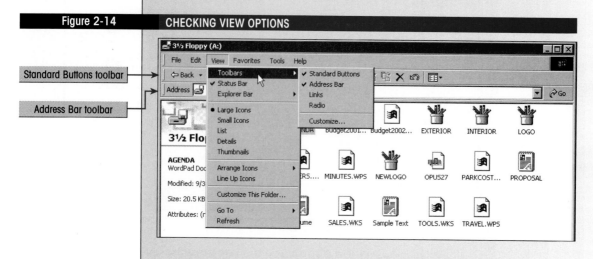

TROUBLE? If the check marks are distributed differently than in Figure 2-14, repeat Steps 1–4 until the correct options are checked.

TROUBLE? If your toolbars are not displayed as shown in Figure 2-14 (for example, both the Standard and Address toolbars might be on the same line, or the Standard toolbar might be above the Address toolbar), you can easily rearrange them. To move a toolbar, drag the vertical bar at the far left of the toolbar. By dragging that vertical bar, you can drag the toolbar left, right, up, or down.

## Changing the Icon Display

Windows 2000 provides five ways to view the contents of a disk—Large Icons, Small Icons, List, Details, and Thumbnails. Figure 2-15 shows examples of these five styles.

| Figure 2-15 | VIEWING STYLES |
| --- | --- |

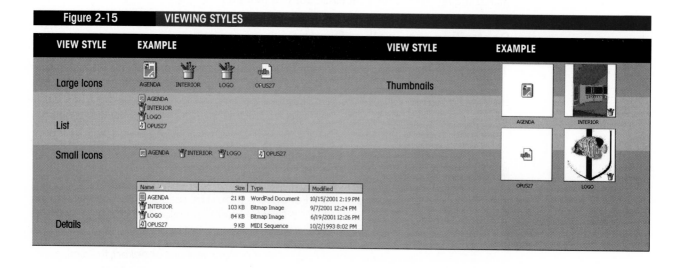

The default view, **Large Icons view**, displays a large icon and title for each file. The icon provides a visual cue to the type of the file, as Figure 2-16 illustrates. You can also get this same information with the smaller icons displayed in the **Small Icons** and **List** views, but in less screen space. In Small Icons and List views, you can see more files and folders at one time, which is helpful when you have many files in one location.

| Figure 2-16 | TYPICAL ICONS IN WINDOWS 2000 |
| --- | --- |

| **FILE AND FOLDER ICONS** | |
| --- | --- |
| 🗒 | Text documents that you can open using the Notepad accessory are represented by notepad icons. |
| ✏ | Graphic image documents that you can open using the Paint accessory are represented by drawing instruments. |
| 🗒 | Word-processed documents that you can open using the WordPad accessory are represented by a formatted notepad icon, unless your computer designates a different word-processing program to open files created with WordPad. |
| 🗎 | Word-processed documents that you can open using a program such as Microsoft Word are represented by formatted document icons. |
| 🗎 | Files created by programs that Windows does not recognize are represented by the Windows logo. |
| 📁 | A folder icon represents folders. |
| 📁 📁 | Certain folders created by Windows 2000 have a special icon design related to the folder's purpose. |

| **PROGRAM ICONS** | |
| --- | --- |
| 🖩 | Icons for programs usually depict an object related to the function of the program. For example, an icon that looks like a calculator represents the Calculator accessory. |
| ⬜ | Non-Windows programs are represented by the icon of a blank window. |

All of the three icon views (Large Icons, Small Icons, and List) help you quickly identify a file and its type, but what if you want more information about a set of files? **Details view** shows more information than the Large Icon, Small Icon, and List views. Details view shows the file icon, the filename, the file size, the program you used to create the file, and the date and time the file was created or last modified.

Finally, if you have graphic files, you may want to use **Thumbnails view**, which displays a small "preview" image of the graphic, so that you can quickly see not only the filename, but also which picture or drawing the file contains. Thumbnails view is great for browsing a large collection of graphic files, but switching to this view can be time-consuming, since Windows 2000 has to create all of the preview images.

To see how easy it is to switch from one view to another, try displaying the contents of drive A in Details view.

### To view a detailed list of files:

**1.** Click **View** and then click **Details** to display details for the files on your disk, as shown in Figure 2-17. Your files might be listed in a different order.

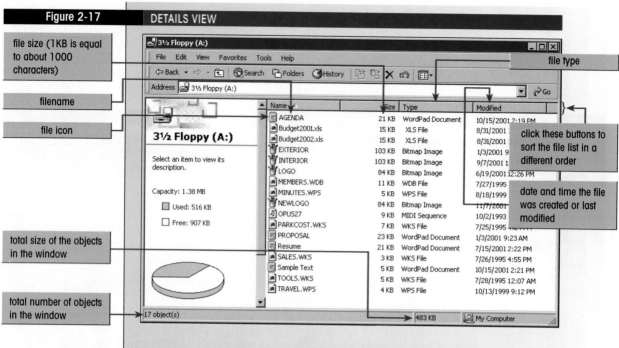

**Figure 2-17**  **DETAILS VIEW**

file size (1KB is equal to about 1000 characters)

filename

file icon

total size of the objects in the window

total number of objects in the window

file type

click these buttons to sort the file list in a different order

date and time the file was created or last modified

**2.** Look at the file sizes. Do you see that Exterior and Interior are the largest files?

**3.** Look at the dates and times the files were modified. Which is the oldest file?

One of the advantages that Details view has over other views is that you can sort the file list by filename, size, type, or the date the file was last modified. This helps if you're working with a large file list and you're trying to locate a specific file.

## To sort the file list by type:

**1.** Click the **Type** button at the top of the list of files.

The files are now sorted in alphabetical order by type, starting with the "Bitmap Image" files and ending with the "XLS File" files. This would be useful if, for example, you were looking for all the .doc files (those created with Microsoft Word), because they would all be grouped together under "M" for "Microsoft Word."

**2.** Click the **Type** button again.

The sort order is reversed with the "XLS File" files now at the top of the list.

**3.** Click the **Name** button at the top of the file list.

The files are now sorted in alphabetical order by filename.

Now that you have looked at the file details, switch back to Large Icon view.

## To switch to Large Icon view:

**1.** Click **View** and then click **Large Icons** to return to the large icon display.

## Restoring the My Computer Default Settings

Windows 2000 provides other options in working with your files and windows. These options fall into two general categories: Classic style and Web style. **Classic style** is a mode of working with windows and files that resembles earlier versions of the Windows operating system. **Web style** allows you to work with your windows and files in the same way you work with Web pages on the World Wide Web. For example, to open a file in Classic style, you can double-click the file icon (a **double-click** is clicking the left mouse button twice quickly) or click the file icon once and press the Enter key. To open a file in Web style, you would simply click the file icon once, and the file would open. You could also create your own style, choosing elements of both the Classic and Web styles, and add in a few customized features of your own.

In order to simplify matters, this book will assume that you're working in the Default style, that is the configuration that Windows 2000 uses when it is initially installed. No matter what changes you make to the configuration of Windows 2000, you can always revert back to the Default style. Try switching back to Default style now.

---

*To switch to the Default style:*

1. Click **Tools** and then click **Folder Options** on the menu.

2. If it is not already selected, click the **General** tab.

   The General sheet displays general options for working with files and windows. Take some time to look over the list of options available.

3. Click the **Restore Defaults** button.

4. Click the **View** tab.

   The View sheet displays options that control the appearance of files and other objects. You should set these options to their default values as well.

5. Click the **Restore Defaults** button.

6. Click the **OK** button to close the Folder Options dialog box.

---

# Working **with Folders and Directories**

Up to now, you've done a little work with files and windows, but before going further you should look at some of the terminology used to describe these tasks. Any location where you can store files on a computer is referred to as a **directory**. The main directory of a disk is sometimes called the **root directory**, or the **top-level directory**. All of the files on your Data Disk are currently in the root directory of your floppy disk.

If too many files are stored in a directory, the list of files becomes very long and difficult to manage. You can divide a directory into **subdirectories**, also called **folders**. The number of files for each folder then becomes much fewer and easier to manage. A folder within a folder is called a **subfolder**. The folder that contains another folder is called the **parent folder**.

All of these objects exist in a **hierarchy**, which begins with your desktop and extends down to each subfolder. Figure 2-18 shows part of a typical hierarchy of Windows 2000 objects.

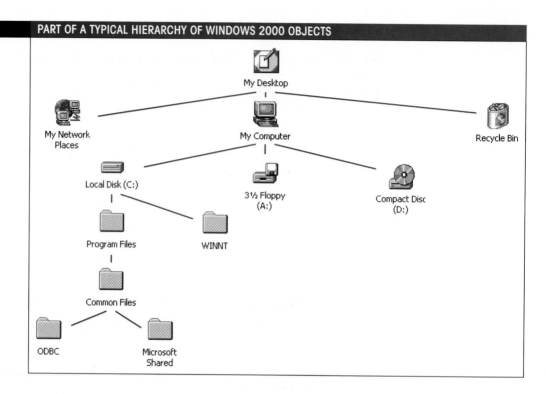

**Figure 2-18** | **PART OF A TYPICAL HIERARCHY OF WINDOWS 2000 OBJECTS**

## Creating a Folder

You've already seen folder icons in the various windows you've previously opened. Now, you'll create your own folder called Practice to hold your documents.

### To create a Practice folder:

1. Click **File** and then point to **New** to display the submenu.

2. Click **Folder**. A folder icon with the label "New Folder" appears.

3. Type **Practice** as the name of the folder.

   TROUBLE? If nothing happens when you type the folder name, it's possible that the folder name is no longer selected. Right-click the Practice folder, click Rename, and then repeat Step 3.

4. Press the **Enter** key.

   The folder is now named "Practice" and is the selected item on your Data Disk.

5. Click a blank area next to the Practice folder to deselect it.

## Navigating Through the Windows 2000 Hierarchy

Now that you've created a subfolder, how do you move into it? You've seen that to view the contents of a file, you open it. To move into a subfolder, you open it in the same way.

## To view the contents of the Practice folder:

1. Click the **Practice** folder and press the **Enter** key.

2. The Practice folder opens. Because there are no files in the folder, there are no items to display. You'll change that shortly.

You've seen that to navigate through the devices and folders on your computer, you open My Computer and then click the icons representing the objects you want to explore. But what if you want to move back to the root directory? The Standard toolbar, which stays the same regardless of which folder or object is open, includes buttons that help you navigate through the hierarchy of drives, directories, folders, subfolders and other objects in your computer. Figure 2-19 summarizes the navigation buttons on the Standard toolbar.

| Figure 2-19 | | NAVIGATION BUTTONS |
|---|---|---|
| **BUTTON** | **ICON** | **DESCRIPTION** |
| Back | ⬅ | Returns you to the folder, drive, directory, or object you were most recently viewing. The button is active only when you have viewed more than one window in the current session. |
| Forward | ➡ | Reverses the effect of the Back button. |
| Up | ⬆ | Moves you up one level in the hierarchy of directories, drives, folders, and other objects on your computer. |

You can return to your floppy's root directory by using the Back or the Up button. Try both of these techniques now.

## To move up to the root directory:

1. Click the **Back** button ⬅.

   Windows 2000 moves you back to the previous window, in this case the root directory of your Data Disk.

2. Click the **Forward** button ➡.

   The Forward button reverses the effect of the Back button and takes you to the Practice folder.

3. Click the **Up** button ⬆.

   You move up one level in hierarchy of Windows 2000 objects, going to the root directory of the Data Disk.

Another way of moving around in the Windows 2000 hierarchy is through the Address toolbar. By clicking the Address list arrow, you can view a list of the objects in the top part of the Windows 2000 hierarchy (see Figure 2-20). This gives you a quick way of moving to the top without having to navigate through the intermediate levels.

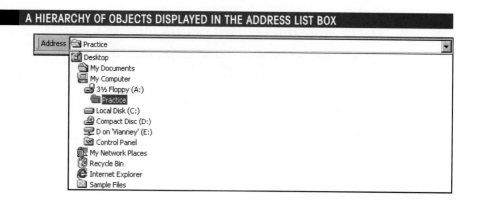

Figure 2-20 | A HIERARCHY OF OBJECTS DISPLAYED IN THE ADDRESS LIST BOX

Now that you know how to move among the folders and devices on your computer, you can practice manipulating files. The better you are at working with the hierarchy of files and folders on your computer, the more organized the hierarchy will be, and the easier it will be to find the files you need.

# Working with Files

As you've seen, the Practice folder doesn't contain any files. In the next set of steps, you will place a file from the root directory into it.

## Moving and Copying a File

If you want to place a file into a folder from another location, you can either move the file or copy it. **Moving** a file takes it out of its current location and places it in the new location. **Copying** places the file in both locations. Windows 2000 provides several different techniques for moving and copying files. One way is to make sure that both the current and the new location are visible on your screen and then hold down the right mouse button and drag the file from the old location to the new location. A menu will then appear, and you can then select whether you want to move the file to the new location or make a copy in the new location. The advantage of this technique is that you are never confused as to whether you copied the file or merely moved it. Try this technique now by placing a copy of the Agenda file in the Practice folder.

*To copy the Agenda file:*

1. Point to the **Agenda** file in the root directory of your Data Disk and press the *right* mouse button.

2. With the right mouse button still pressed down, drag the **Agenda** file icon to the **Practice** folder icon; when the Practice folder icon turns blue, release the button.

3. A menu appears, as shown in Figure 2-21. Click **Copy Here**.

Figure 2-21 | COPYING A FILE

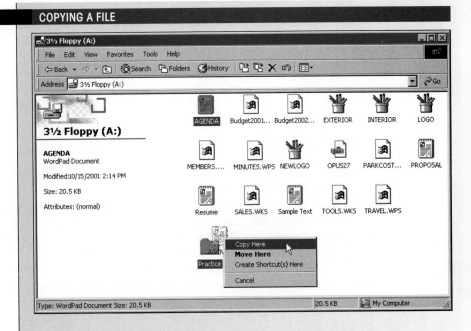

TROUBLE? If you release the mouse button by mistake before dragging the Agenda icon to the Practice folder, the Agenda shortcut menu opens. Press the Esc key and then repeat Steps 1 and 2.

**4.** Double-click the **Practice** folder.

The Agenda file should now appear in the Practice folder.

Note that the "Move Here" command was also part of the menu. In fact, the command was in boldface, indicating that it is the default command whenever you drag a document from one location to another on the same drive. This means that if you were to drag a file from one location to another on the same drive using the left mouse button (instead of the right), the file would be moved and not copied.

## Renaming a File

You will often find that you want to change the name of files as you change their content or as you create other files. You can easily rename a file by using the Rename option on the file's shortcut menu or by using the file's label.

Practice using this feature by renaming the Agenda file "Practice Agenda," since it is now in the Practice folder.

### To rename the Agenda file:

**1.** Right-click the **Agenda** icon.

**2.** Click **Rename**. After a moment the filename is highlighted and a box appears around it.

**3.** Type **Practice Agenda** and press the **Enter** key.

TROUBLE? If you make a mistake while typing and you haven't pressed the Enter key yet, you can press the Backspace key until you delete the mistake, then complete Step 3. If you've already pressed the Enter key, repeat Steps 1-3 to rename the file a second time.

The file appears with a new name.

## Deleting a File

You should periodically delete files you no longer need so that your folders and disks don't get cluttered. You delete a file or folder by deleting its icon. Be careful when you delete a folder, because you also delete all the files it contains! When you delete a file from a hard drive on your computer, the filename is deleted from the directory but the file contents are held in the Recycle Bin. The Recycle Bin is an area on your hard drive that holds deleted files until you remove them permanently; an icon on the desktop allows you easy access to the Recycle Bin. If you change your mind and want to retrieve a file deleted from your hard drive, you can recover it by using the Recycle Bin. However, once you've emptied the Recycle Bin, you can no longer recover the files that were in it.

When you delete a file from a floppy disk or a disk that exists on another computer on your network, it does not go into the Recycle Bin. Instead, it is deleted as soon as its icon disappears—and you can't recover it.

Try deleting the Practice Agenda file from your Data Disk. Because this file is on a floppy disk and not on the hard disk, it will not go into the Recycle Bin, and if you change your mind you won't be able to get it back.

### To delete the Practice Agenda file:

1. Right-click the icon for the Practice Agenda file.

2. Click **Delete** on the menu that appears.

3. Windows 2000 asks if you're sure that you want to delete this file. Click the **Yes** button.

4. Click the **Close** button ☒ to close the My Computer window.

If you like using your mouse, another way of deleting a file is to drag its icon to the Recycle Bin on the desktop. Be aware that if you're dragging a file from your floppy disk or a network disk, the file will *not* be placed in the Recycle Bin—it will still be permanently deleted.

## Other Copying and Moving Techniques

As was noted earlier, there are several ways of moving and copying. As you become more familiar with Windows 2000, you will no doubt settle on the technique you like best. Figure 2-22 describes some of the other ways of moving and copying files.

| Figure 2-22 | METHODS FOR MOVING AND COPYING FILES | |
|---|---|---|
| **METHOD** | **TO MOVE** | **TO COPY** |
| Cut, copy, and paste | Select the file icon. Click **Edit** on the menu bar and **Cut** on the menu bar. Move to the new location. Click **Edit** and **Paste**. | Select the file icon. Click **Edit** on the menu bar and **Copy** on the menu bar. Move to the new location. Click **Edit** and **Paste**. |
| Drag and drop | Click the file icon. Drag and drop the icon in the new location. | Click the file icon. Hold down the Ctrl key and drag and drop the icon in the new location. |
| Right-click, drag and drop | With the right mouse button pressed down, drag the file icon to the new location. Release the mouse button and click **Move Here** on the menu. | With the right mouse button pressed down, drag the file icon to the new location. Release the mouse button and click **Copy Here** on the menu. |
| Move to folder and copy to folder | Click the file icon. Click **Edit** on the menu bar and **Move to Folder** on the menu bar. Select the new location in the Browse for Folder dialog box. | Click the file icon. Click **Edit** on the menu bar and **Copy to Folder** on the menu bar. Select the new location in the Browse for Folder dialog box. |

The techniques shown in Figure 2-22 are primarily for document files. Because a program might not work correctly if moved into a new location, the techniques for moving program files are slightly different. See the Windows 2000 online Help for more information on moving or copying a program file.

## Copying an Entire Floppy Disk

You can have trouble accessing the data on your floppy disk if the disk is damaged, is exposed to magnetic fields, or picks up a computer virus. To avoid losing all your data, it is a good idea to make a copy of your floppy disk.

If you wanted to make a copy of an audiocassette, your cassette player would need two cassette drives. You might wonder, therefore, how your computer can make a copy of your disk if you have only one floppy disk drive. Figure 2-23 illustrates how the computer uses only one disk drive to make a copy of a disk.

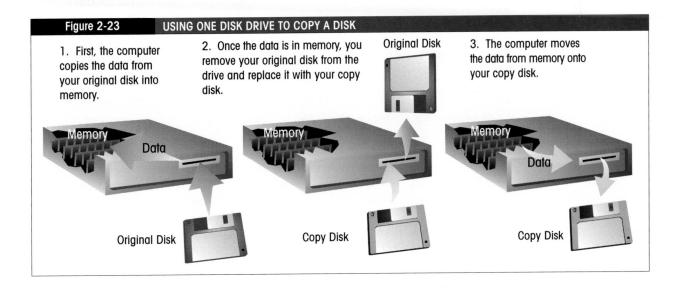

| Figure 2-23 | USING ONE DISK DRIVE TO COPY A DISK |
|---|---|

1. First, the computer copies the data from your original disk into memory.

2. Once the data is in memory, you remove your original disk from the drive and replace it with your copy disk.

Original Disk

3. The computer moves the data from memory onto your copy disk.

Memory
Data
Original Disk

Memory
Copy Disk

Memory
Data
Copy Disk

**Copying a Disk**
- Insert the disk you want to copy in drive A.
- In My Computer, right-click the 3½ Floppy (A:) icon, and then click Copy Disk.
- Click Start to begin the copy process.
- When prompted, remove the disk you want to copy, place your second disk in drive A, and then click OK.

If you have an extra floppy disk, you can make a copy of your Data Disk now. Make sure you copy the disk regularly so that as you work through the tutorials in this book it will stay updated.

## To copy your Data Disk:

1. Write your name and "Windows 2000 Disk 1 Data Disk Copy" on the label of your second disk. Make sure the disk is blank and formatted.

   TROUBLE? If you aren't sure if the disk is blank, place it in the disk drive and open the 3½ Floppy (A:) window to view its contents. If the disk contains files you need, get a different disk. If it contains files you don't need, you could format the disk now, using the steps you learned at the beginning of this tutorial.

2. Make sure your original Data Disk is in drive A and the My Computer window is open.

3. Right-click the **3½ Floppy (A:)** icon, and then click **Copy Disk**. The Copy Disk dialog box opens.

4. Click the **Start** button and then the **OK** button to begin the copy process.

5. When the message "Insert the disk you want to copy to (destination disk)..." appears, remove your Data Disk and insert your Windows 2000 Disk 1 Data Disk Copy in drive A.

6. Click the **OK** button. When the copy is complete, you will see the message "Copy completed successfully." Click the **Close** button.

7. Close the My Computer window.

8. Remove your disk from the drive.

As you finish copying your disk, Shannon emphasizes the importance of making copies of your files frequently, so you won't risk losing important documents for your distance learning course. If your original Data Disk were damaged, you could use the copy you just made to access the files.

Keeping copies of your files is so important that Windows 2000 includes a program called Backup that automates the process of duplicating and storing data. In the Projects at the end of the tutorial you'll have an opportunity to explore the difference between what you just did in copying a disk and the way in which a program such as the Windows 2000 Backup program helps you safeguard data.

## Session 2.2  QUICK CHECK

1. If you want to find out about the storage devices and printers connected to your computer, what window could you open?

2. If you have only one floppy disk drive on your computer, it is usually identified by the letter _____.

3. The letter C is typically used for the _____ drive of a computer.

4. What information does Details view supply about a list of folders and files?

5. The main directory of a disk is referred to as the _____ directory.

6. What is the topmost object in the hierarchy of Windows 2000 objects?

7. If you have one floppy disk drive, but you have two disks, can you copy the files on one floppy disk to the other?

## REVIEW ASSIGNMENTS

1. **Opening, Editing, and Printing a Document**  In this tutorial you learned how to create a document using WordPad. You also learned how to save, open, and print a document. Practice these skills by copying the document called **Resume** into the Practice folder on your Data Disk. Rename the file **Woods Resume**. This document is a resume for Jamie Woods. Make the changes shown in Figure 2-24. Save your revisions in Word for Windows 6.0 format, preview, and then print the document. Close WordPad.

**Figure 2-24**

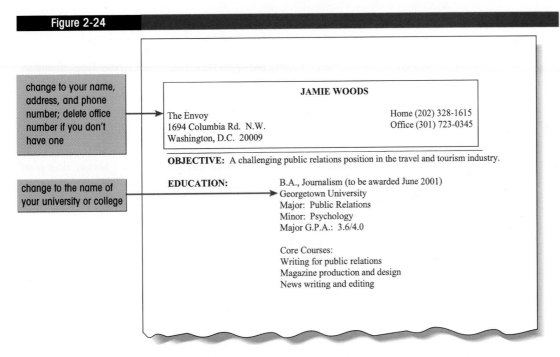

change to your name, address, and phone number; delete office number if you don't have one

change to the name of your university or college

**JAMIE WOODS**

The Envoy
1694 Columbia Rd. N.W.
Washington, D.C. 20009

Home (202) 328-1615
Office (301) 723-0345

**OBJECTIVE:**  A challenging public relations position in the travel and tourism industry.

**EDUCATION:**

B.A., Journalism (to be awarded June 2001)
Georgetown University
Major: Public Relations
Minor: Psychology
Major G.P.A.: 3.6/4.0

Core Courses:
Writing for public relations
Magazine production and design
News writing and editing

2. **Creating, Saving, and Printing a Letter**  Use WordPad to write a one-page letter to a relative or a friend. Save the document in the Practice folder on your Data Disk with the name **Letter**. Use the Print Preview feature to look at the format of your finished letter, then print it, and be sure to sign it. Close WordPad.

3. **Managing Files and Folders**  Using the copy of the disk you made at the end of the tutorial, complete steps a through f below to practice your file-management skills, and then answer the questions below.

   a. Create a folder called Spreadsheets on your Data Disk.
   b. Move the files **Parkcost**, **Budget2001**, **Budget2002**, and **Sales** into the Spreadsheets folder.
   c. Create a folder called Park Project.
   d. Move the files **Proposal**, **Members**, **Tools**, **Logo**, and **Newlogo** into the Park Project folder.
   e. Delete the file called **Travel**.
   f. Switch to the Details view and write out your answers to Questions 1 through 5:
      1. What is the largest file or files in the Park Project folder?
      2. What is the newest file or files in the Spreadsheets folder?
      3. How many files (don't include folders) are in the root directory of your Data Disk?
      4. How are the Opus and Exterior icons different? Judging from the appearance of the icons, what would you guess these two files contain?
      5. Which file in the root directory has the most recent date?

4. **More Practice with Files and Folders**  For this assignment, you need a third blank disk. Complete steps a through g below to practice your file-management skills.

   a. Write "Windows 2000 Tutorial 2 Assignment 4" on the label of the blank disk, and then format the disk if necessary.
   b. Create another copy of your original Data Disk, using the Assignment 4 disk. Refer to the section "Creating Your Data Disk" in Session 2.2.
   c. Create three folders on the Assignment 4 Data Disk you just created: Documents, Budgets, and Graphics.
   d. Move the files **Interior**, **Exterior**, **Logo**, and **Newlogo** to the Graphics folder.
   e. Move the files **Travel**, **Members**, and **Minutes** to the Documents folder.
   f. Move **Budget2001** and **Budget2002** to the Budgets folder.
   g. Switch to Details view and write out your answers to Questions 1 through 6:
      1. What is the largest file or files in the Graphics folder?
      2. How many word-processed documents are in the root directory? *Hint*: These documents will appear with the WordPad, Microsoft Word, or some other word-processing icon, depending on what software you have installed.
      3. What is the newest file or files in the root directory (don't include folders)?
      4. How many files in all folders are 5 KB in size?
      5. How many files in the root directory are WKS files? *Hint*: Look in the Type column to identify WKS files.
      6. Do all the files in the Graphics folder have the same icon? What type are they?

5. **Searching for a File**  Windows 2000 Help includes a topic that discusses how to search for files on a disk without looking through all the folders. Start Windows Help, then locate this topic, and answer Questions a through c:

   a. To display the Search dialog box, you must click the _____ button, then point to _____ on the menu, and finally click _____ on the submenu.
   b. Do you need to type in the entire filename to find the file?
   c. How do you perform a case-sensitive search?

6. **Help with Files and Folders**  In Tutorial 2 you learned how to work with Windows 2000 files and folders. What additional information on this topic does Windows 2000 Help provide? Use the Start button to access Help. Use the Index tab to locate topics related to files and folders. Find at least two tips or procedures for working with files and folders that were not covered in the tutorial. Write out the tip in your own words and include the title of the Help screen that contains the information.

7. **Formatting Text**  You can use a word processor such as WordPad to format text, that is, to give it a specific look and feel by using bold, italics, and different fonts, and by applying other features. Using WordPad, type the title and words to one of your favorite songs and

then save the document on your Data Disk (make sure you use your original Data Disk) with the filename Song.

a. Select the title, and then click the Center ![icon], Bold **B**, and Italic *I* buttons on the toolbar.

b. Click the Font list arrow and select a different font. Repeat this step several times with different fonts until you locate a font that is appropriate for the song.

c. Experiment with other formatting options until you find a look you like for your document. Save and print the final version.

## PROJECTS

1. Formatting a floppy disk removes all the data on a disk. Answer the following questions using full sentences:

   a. What other method did you learn in this tutorial for removing data from a disk?

   b. If you wanted to remove all data from a disk, which method would you use? Why?

   c. What method would you use if you wanted to remove only one file? Why?

2. A friend who is new to computers is trying to learn how to enter text into WordPad. She has just finished typing her first paragraph when she notices a mistake in the first sentence. She can't remember how to fix a mistake, so she asks you for help. Write the set of steps she should try.

3. Computer users usually develop habits about how they access their files and programs. Follow the steps below to practice methods of opening a file, and then evaluate which method you would be likely to use and why.

   a. Using WordPad, create a document containing the words to a favorite poem, and save it on your Data Disk with the name Poem.

   b. Close WordPad and return to the desktop.

   c. Open the document using a document-centric approach.

   d. After a successful completion of step c, close the program and reopen the same document using another approach.

   e. Write the steps you used to complete steps c and d of this assignment. Then write a paragraph discussing which approach is most convenient when you are starting from the desktop, and indicate what habits you would develop if you owned your own computer and used it regularly.

*Explore* 4. The My Computer window gives you access to the objects on your computer. In this tutorial you used My Computer to access your floppy drive so you could view the contents of your Data Disk. The My Computer window gives you access to other objects too. Open My Computer and write a list of the objects you see, including folders. Then open each icon and write a two-sentence description of the contents of each window that opens.

*Explore* 5. In this tutorial you learned how to copy a disk to protect yourself in the event of data loss. If you had your own computer with an 80 MB hard drive that was being used to capacity, it would take many 1.44 MB floppy disks to copy the contents of the entire hard drive. Is copying to floppy disks a reasonable method to use for protecting the data on your hard disk? Why, or why not?

   a. As mentioned at the end of the tutorial, Windows 2000 also includes an accessory called Backup that helps you safeguard your data. Backup doesn't just copy the data—it organizes it so that it takes up much less space than if you simply copied it. This program might not be installed on your computer, but if it is, try starting it (click the Start button, point to Programs, point to Accessories, point to System Tools, and then click Backup) and opening the Help files to learn what you can about how it functions. If it is not installed, skip Part a.

   b. Look up the topic of backups in a computer concepts textbook or in computer trade magazines. You could also interview experienced computer owners to find out which method they use to protect their data. When you have finished researching the concept of the backup, write a single-page essay that explains the difference between copying and backing up files, and evaluates which method is preferable for backing up large amounts of data, and why.

**Using Files**

## LAB ASSIGNMENTS

*Using Files* In this Lab you manipulate a simulated computer to view what happens in memory and on disk when you create, save, open, revise, and delete files. Understanding what goes on "inside the box" will help you quickly grasp how to perform basic file operations with most application software. See the Read This Before You Begin page for instructions on starting the Using Files Course Lab.

1. Click the Steps button to learn how to use the simulated computer to view the contents of memory and disk when you perform basic file operations. As you proceed through the Steps, answer all of the Quick Check questions that appear. After you complete the Steps, you will see a Quick Check Summary Report. Follow the instructions on the screen to print this report.

2. Click the Explore button and use the simulated computer to perform the following tasks:
   a. Create a document containing your name and the city in which you were born. Save this document as NAME.
   b. Create another document containing two of your favorite foods. Save this document as FOODS.
   c. Create another file containing your two favorite classes. Call this file CLASSES.
   d. Open the FOOD file and add another one of your favorite foods. Save this file without changing its name.
   e. Open the NAME file. Change this document so that it contains your name and the name of your school. Save this as a new document called SCHOOL.
   f. Write down how many files are on the simulated disk and the exact contents of each file.
   g. Delete all the files.

3. In Explore, use the simulated computer to perform the following tasks.
   a. Create a file called MUSIC that contains the name of your favorite CD.
   b. Create another document that contains eight numbers and call this file LOTTERY.
   c. You didn't win the lottery this week. Revise the contents of the LOTTERY file, but save the revision as LOTTERY2.
   d. Revise the MUSIC file so that it also contains the name of your favorite musician or composer, and save this file as MUSIC2.
   e. Delete the MUSIC file.
   f. Write down how many files are on the simulated disk and the exact contents of each file.

## QUICK CHECK ANSWERS

*Session 2.1*
   1. file
   2. Formatting
   3. True
   4. insertion point
   5. a list of recently opened files and objects
   6. The Files of Type list box could be set to display files of a different type than the one you're looking for.
   7. From the Print Preview window, using the Print button on the toolbar, and using the Print command from the File menu. If you want to print multiple copies of a file, use either the Print button from the Print Preview window or the Print command from the File menu—both of these techniques will display the Print dialog box containing the options you need to set.

*Session 2.2*
   1. My Computer
   2. A
   3. hard
   4. filename, size, type, and date modified
   5. root or top-level
   6. the Desktop
   7. yes

*New Perspectives on*

# MICROSOFT®
# OFFICE XP

**TUTORIAL 1   OFF 3**

*Introducing Microsoft Office XP*

# Read This Before You Begin

## To the Student

### Data Disks

To complete this tutorial and the Review Assignments, you need one Data Disk. Your instructor will either provide you with the Data Disk or ask you to make your own.

If you are making your own Data Disk, you will need **one** blank, formatted high-density disk. You will need to copy a set of files and/or folders from a file server, standalone computer, or the Web onto your disk. Your instructor will tell you which computer, drive letter, and folder contain the files you need. You could also download the files by going to www.course.com and following the instructions on the screen.

The information below shows you which folder goes on your disk, so that you will have enough disk space to complete the tutorial and Review Assignments:

### Data Disk 1

Write this on the disk label:
Data Disk 1: Introducing Office XP

Put this folder on the disk:
Tutorial.01

When you begin the tutorial, be sure you are using the correct Data Disk. Refer to the "File Finder" chart at the back of this text for more detailed information on which files are used in the tutorial. See the inside front or inside back cover of this book for more information on Data Disk files, or ask your instructor or technical support person for assistance.

### Using Your Own Computer

If you are going to work through this tutorial using your own computer, you need:

- **Computer System** Microsoft Windows 98, NT, 2000 Professional, or higher must be installed on your computer. This book assumes a typical installation of Microsoft Office XP.

- **Data Disk** You will not be able to complete this tutorial or Review Assignments using your own computer until you have your Data Disk.

### Visit Our World Wide Web Site

Additional materials designed especially for you are available on the World Wide Web.
Go to www.course.com/NewPerspectives.

## To the Instructor

The Data Disk Files are available on the Instructor's Resource Kit for this title. Follow the instructions in the Help file on the CD-ROM to install the programs to your network or standalone computer. For information on creating the Data Disk, see the "To the Student" section above.

You are granted a license to copy the Data Disk Files to any computer or computer network used by students who have purchased this book.

In this tutorial you will:

- Explore the programs that comprise Microsoft Office

- Explore the benefits of integrating data between programs

- Start programs and switch between them

- Use personalized menus and toolbars

- Save and close a file

- Open an existing file

- Print a file

- Get Help

- Close files and exit programs

# INTRODUCING MICROSOFT OFFICE XP

*Preparing Promotional Materials for Delmar Office Supplies*

CASE

## Delmar Office Supplies

Delmar Office Supplies, a company in Wisconsin founded by Nicole Delmar in 1996, sells recycled office supplies to businesses and home-based offices around the world. The demand for quality recycled papers, reconditioned toner cartridges, and renovated office furniture has been growing each year. Nicole and all her employees use Microsoft Office XP, which provides everyone in the company the power and flexibility to store a variety of information, create consistent documents, and share data. In this tutorial, you'll review some of the latest documents the company's employees have created using Microsoft Office XP.

# Exploring Microsoft Office XP

**Microsoft Office XP**, or simply **Office**, is a collection of the most popular Microsoft programs: Word, Excel, PowerPoint, Access, and Outlook. Each Office program contains valuable tools to help you accomplish many tasks, such as composing reports, analyzing data, preparing presentations, and compiling information.

**Microsoft Word 2002**, or simply **Word**, is a **word processing program** you use to create text documents. The files you create in Word are called **documents**. Word offers many special features that help you compose and update all types of documents, ranging from letters and newsletters to reports, fliers, faxes, and even books—all in attractive and readable formats. You also can use Word to create, insert, and position figures, tables, and other graphics to enhance the look of your documents. Figure 1 shows a business letter that a sales representative composed with Word.

| Figure 1 | LETTER COMPOSED IN A WORD DOCUMENT |
| --- | --- |

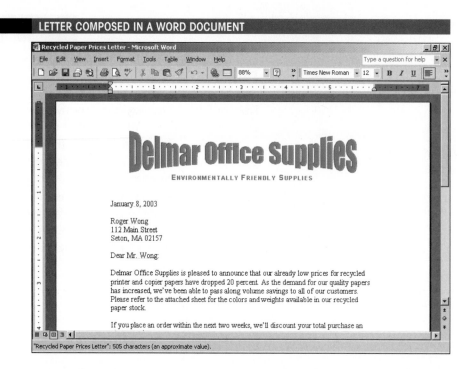

**Microsoft Excel 2002**, or simply **Excel**, is a **spreadsheet program** you use to display, organize, and analyze numerical information. You can do some of this in Word with tables, but Excel provides many more tools for performing calculations than Word does. Its graphics capabilities also enable you to display data visually. You might, for example, generate a pie chart or bar chart to help readers quickly see the significance of and the connections between information. The files you create in Excel are called **workbooks**. Figure 2 shows an Excel workbook with a line chart that the Operations Department uses to track the company's financial performance.

**Figure 2**      **FINANCIAL DATA IN AN EXCEL WORKBOOK**

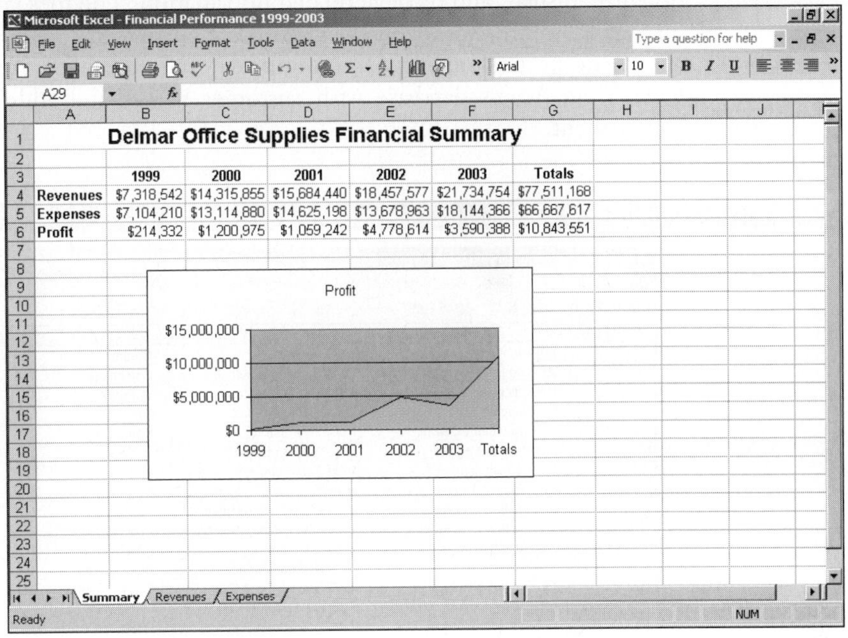

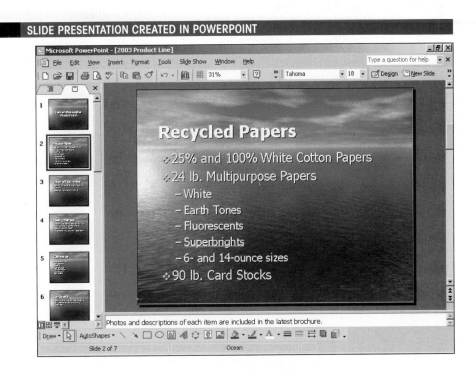

Microsoft **PowerPoint 2002**, or simply **PowerPoint**, is a **presentation graphics program** you use to create a collection of "slides" that can contain text, charts, pictures, and so on. The files you create in PowerPoint are called **presentations**. You can show these presentations on your computer monitor, project them onto a screen as a slide show, print them, share them over the Internet, or display them on the World Wide Web. You also can use PowerPoint to generate presentation-related documents such as audience handouts, outlines, and speakers' notes. Figure 3 shows an effective slide presentation the Sales Department created with PowerPoint to promote the latest product line.

**Figure 3**      **SLIDE PRESENTATION CREATED IN POWERPOINT**

**Microsoft Access 2002**, or simply **Access**, is a **database program** you use to enter, organize, display, and retrieve related information. The files you create in Access are called **databases.** With Access you can create data entry forms to make data entry easier, and you can create professional reports to improve the readability of your data. Figure 4 shows a table in an Access database with customer names and addresses compiled by the Sales Department.

Figure 4 CUSTOMER ADDRESSES COMPILED IN AN ACCESS DATABASE

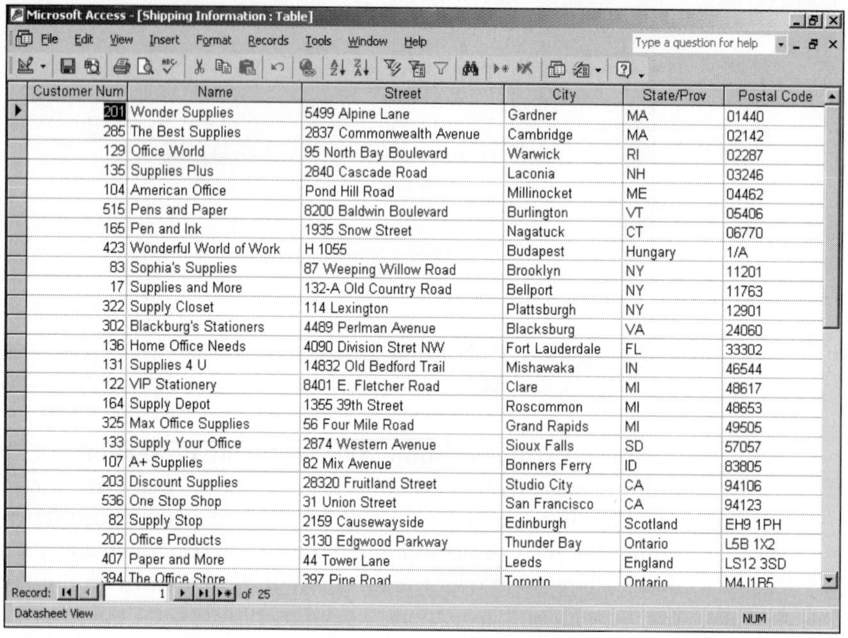


| Customer Num | Name | Street | City | State/Prov | Postal Code |
|---|---|---|---|---|---|
| 201 | Wonder Supplies | 5499 Alpine Lane | Gardner | MA | 01440 |
| 285 | The Best Supplies | 2837 Commonwealth Avenue | Cambridge | MA | 02142 |
| 129 | Office World | 95 North Bay Boulevard | Warwick | RI | 02287 |
| 135 | Supplies Plus | 2840 Cascade Road | Laconia | NH | 03246 |
| 104 | American Office | Pond Hill Road | Millinocket | ME | 04462 |
| 515 | Pens and Paper | 8200 Baldwin Boulevard | Burlington | VT | 05406 |
| 165 | Pen and Ink | 1935 Snow Street | Nagatuck | CT | 06770 |
| 423 | Wonderful World of Work | H 1055 | Budapest | Hungary | 1/A |
| 83 | Sophia's Supplies | 87 Weeping Willow Road | Brooklyn | NY | 11201 |
| 17 | Supplies and More | 132-A Old Country Road | Bellport | NY | 11763 |
| 322 | Supply Closet | 114 Lexington | Plattsburgh | NY | 12901 |
| 302 | Blackburg's Stationers | 4489 Perlman Avenue | Blacksburg | VA | 24060 |
| 136 | Home Office Needs | 4090 Division Stret NW | Fort Lauderdale | FL | 33302 |
| 131 | Supplies 4 U | 14832 Old Bedford Trail | Mishawaka | IN | 46544 |
| 122 | VIP Stationery | 8401 E. Fletcher Road | Clare | MI | 48617 |
| 164 | Supply Depot | 1355 39th Street | Roscommon | MI | 48653 |
| 325 | Max Office Supplies | 56 Four Mile Road | Grand Rapids | MI | 49505 |
| 133 | Supply Your Office | 2874 Western Avenue | Sioux Falls | SD | 57057 |
| 107 | A+ Supplies | 82 Mix Avenue | Bonners Ferry | ID | 83805 |
| 203 | Discount Supplies | 28320 Fruitland Street | Studio City | CA | 94106 |
| 536 | One Stop Shop | 31 Union Street | San Francisco | CA | 94123 |
| 82 | Supply Stop | 2159 Causewayside | Edinburgh | Scotland | EH9 1PH |
| 202 | Office Products | 3130 Edgwood Parkway | Thunder Bay | Ontario | L5B 1X2 |
| 407 | Paper and More | 44 Tower Lane | Leeds | England | LS12 3SD |
| 394 | The Office Store | 397 Pine Road | Toronto | Ontario | M4J1B5 |

**Microsoft Outlook 2002**, or simply **Outlook**, is an **information management program** you use to send, receive, and organize e-mail; plan your schedule; arrange meetings; organize contacts; create a to-do list; and jot down notes. You also can use Outlook to print schedules, task lists, or phone directories and other documents. Figure 5 shows how Nicole Delmar uses Outlook to plan her schedule and create a to-do list.

| Figure 5 | CALENDAR AND TASKS IN OUTLOOK |
| --- | --- |

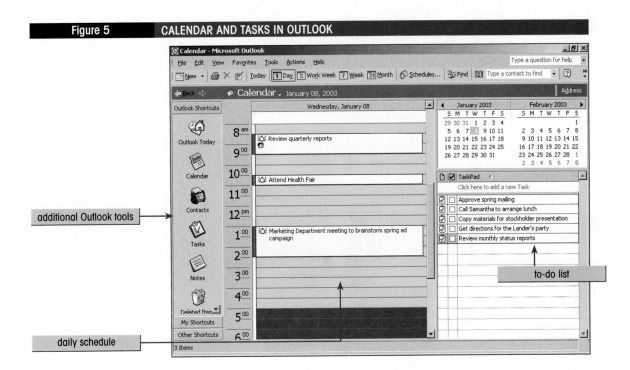

additional Outlook tools

to-do list

daily schedule

Although each Office program individually is a strong tool, their potential is even greater when used together.

## Integrating Programs

One of the main advantages of Office is **integration**, the ability to share information between programs. Integration ensures consistency and accuracy, and it saves time because you don't have to re-enter the same information in several Office programs. The staff at Delmar Office Supplies uses the integration features of Office daily, including the following examples:

■ The Accounting Department created an Excel bar chart on the last two years' fourth-quarter results, which they inserted into the quarterly financial report, created in Word. They added a hyperlink to the Word report that employees can click to open the Excel workbook and view the original data. See Figure 6.

**Figure 6    WORD DOCUMENT WITH AN EXCEL CHART**

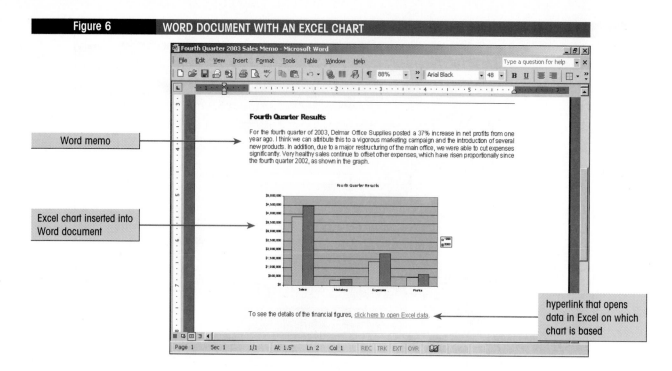

Word memo

Excel chart inserted into Word document

hyperlink that opens data in Excel on which chart is based

■ An Excel pie chart of sales percentages by divisions of Delmar Office Supplies can be duplicated on a PowerPoint slide. The slide is part of the Operations Department's presentation to stockholders. See Figure 7.

**Figure 7    POWERPOINT PRESENTATION WITH AN EXCEL CHART**

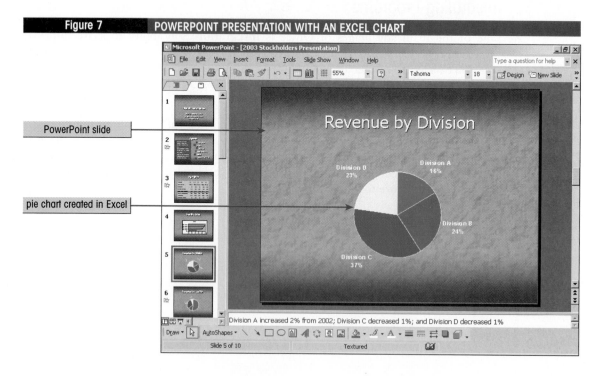

PowerPoint slide

pie chart created in Excel

■ An Access database or an Outlook contact list that stores the names and addresses of customers can be combined with a form letter that the Marketing Department created in Word, to produce a mailing promoting the company's newest products. See Figure 8.

| Figure 8 | WORD LETTER WITH ACCESS OR OUTLOOK DATA |

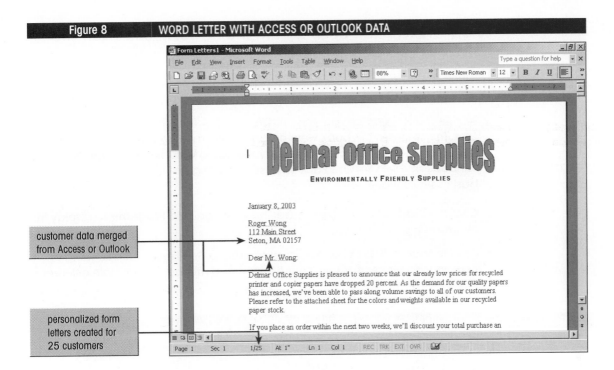

customer data merged from Access or Outlook

personalized form letters created for 25 customers

These are just a few examples of how you can take information from one Office program and integrate it into another.

# Starting Office Programs

All Office programs start the same way—from the Programs menu on the Start button. You select the program you want, and then the program starts so you can immediately begin to create new files or work with existing ones.

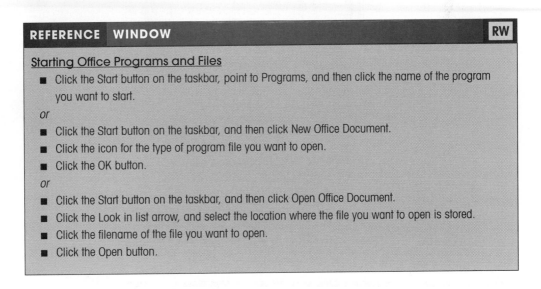

**REFERENCE    WINDOW**    RW

### Starting Office Programs and Files

- Click the Start button on the taskbar, point to Programs, and then click the name of the program you want to start.

*or*

- Click the Start button on the taskbar, and then click New Office Document.
- Click the icon for the type of program file you want to open.
- Click the OK button.

*or*

- Click the Start button on the taskbar, and then click Open Office Document.
- Click the Look in list arrow, and select the location where the file you want to open is stored.
- Click the filename of the file you want to open.
- Click the Open button.

You'll start Excel using the Start button.

## To start Excel and open a new, blank workbook from the Start menu:

1. Make sure your computer is on and the Windows desktop appears on your screen.

   TROUBLE? Don't worry if your screen differs slightly from those shown in the figures. The figures in this book were created while running Windows 2000 in its default settings, but Office runs equally well using Windows 98 or later or Windows NT 4 with Service Pack 5. These operating systems share the same basic user interface.

2. Click the **Start** button on the taskbar, and then point to **Programs** to display the Programs menu.

3. Point to **Microsoft Excel** on the Programs menu. See Figure 9. Depending on how your computer is set up, your desktop and menu might contain different icons and commands.

**Figure 9**     START MENU WITH PROGRAMS MENU DISPLAYED

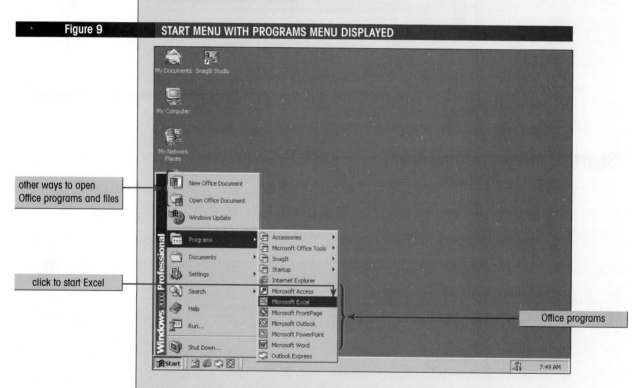

other ways to open Office programs and files

click to start Excel

Office programs

TROUBLE? If you don't see Microsoft Excel on the Programs menu, point to Microsoft Office, and then point to Microsoft Excel. If you still don't see Microsoft Excel, ask your instructor or technical support person for help.

4. Click **Microsoft Excel** to start Excel and open a new, blank workbook. See Figure 10.

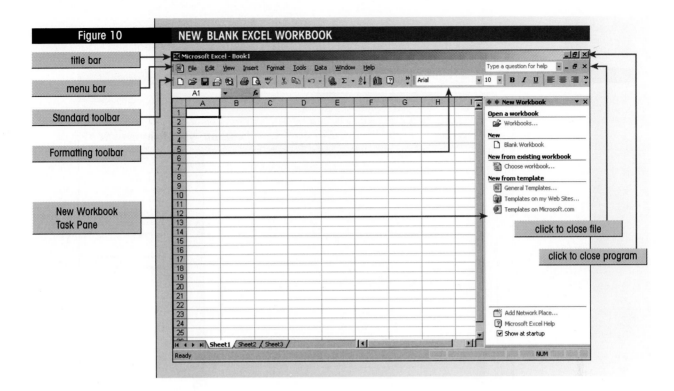

**Figure 10** NEW, BLANK EXCEL WORKBOOK

title bar

menu bar

Standard toolbar

Formatting toolbar

New Workbook
Task Pane

click to close file

click to close program

An alternate method for starting programs with a blank file is to click the New Office Document command on the Start menu; the kind of file you choose determines which program opens. You'll use this method to start Word and open a new, blank document.

## To start Word and open a new, blank document with the New Office Document command:

**1.** Leaving Excel open, click the **Start** button on the taskbar, and then click **New Office Document**. The New Office Document dialog box opens, providing another way to start Office programs. See Figure 11.

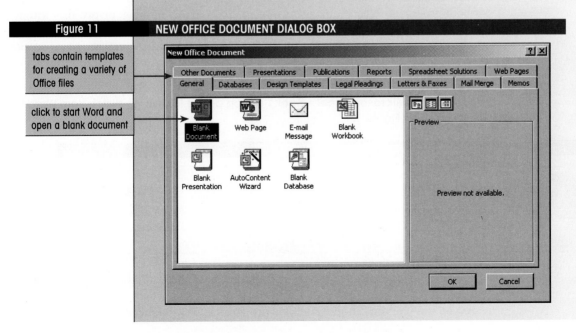

**Figure 11** NEW OFFICE DOCUMENT DIALOG BOX

tabs contain templates
for creating a variety of
Office files

click to start Word and
open a blank document

**2.** If necessary, click the **General** tab, click the **Blank Document** icon, and then click the **OK** button. Word opens with a new, blank document. See Figure 12.

| Figure 12 | NEW, BLANK DOCUMENT IN WORD |
| --- | --- |

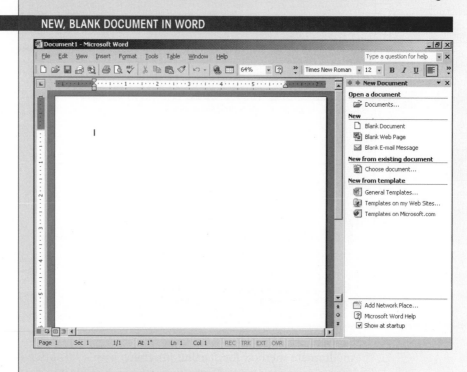

TROUBLE? If you don't see the New Document Task Pane, click File on the Word menu bar, and then click New.

You've tried two ways to start a program. There are several methods for performing most tasks in Office. This flexibility enables you to use Office in the way that fits how you like to work.

## Switching Between Open Programs and Files

Two programs are running at the same time—Excel and Word. The taskbar contains buttons for both programs. When you have two or more programs running, or two files within the same program open, you can use the taskbar buttons to switch from one program or file to another. The employees at Delmar Office Supplies often work in several programs at once.

### To switch between Word and Excel:

**1.** Click the **Microsoft Excel – Book1** button on the taskbar to switch from Word to Excel. See Figure 13.

| Figure 13 | EXCEL AND WORD PROGRAMS OPENED |
| --- | --- |

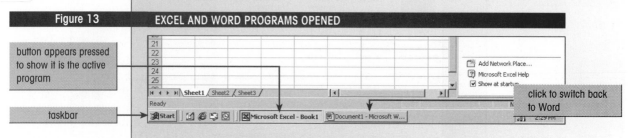

**2.** Click the **Document1 – Microsoft Word** button on the taskbar to return to Word.

As you can see, you can start multiple programs and switch between them in seconds.

The Office programs also share many features, so once you've learned one program, it's easy to learn the others. One of the most visible similarities among all the programs is the "personalized" menus and toolbars.

# Using Personalized Menus and Toolbars

In each Office program, you perform tasks using a menu command, a toolbar button, or a keyboard shortcut. A **menu command** is a word on a menu that you click to execute a task; a **menu** is a group of related commands. For example, the File menu contains commands for managing files, such as the Open command and the Save command. A **toolbar** is a collection of **buttons** that correspond to commonly used menu commands. For example, the Standard toolbar contains an Open button and a Save button. **Keyboard shortcuts** are combinations of keys you press to perform a command. For example, Ctrl+S is the keyboard shortcut for the Save command (you hold down the Ctrl key while you press the S key). Keyboard shortcuts are displayed to the right of many menu commands.

When you first use a newly installed Office program, the menus and toolbars display only the basic and most commonly used commands and buttons, streamlining the program window. The other commands and buttons are available, but you have to click an extra button to see them (the double-arrow button on a menu and the Toolbar Options button on a toolbar). As you select commands and click buttons, the ones you use often are put on the short, personalized menu and on the visible part of the toolbars. The ones you don't use remain available on the full menus and toolbars. This means that the Office menus and toolbars might display different commands and buttons on each person's computer.

## To view a personalized and full menu:

1. Click **Insert** on the Word menu bar to display the short, personalized menu. See Figure 14. The Bookmark command, for example, does not appear on the short menu.

| Figure 14 | SHORT, PERSONALIZED MENU |

double-arrow button

TROUBLE? If the Insert menu displays different commands than shown in Figure 14, you need to reset the menus. Click Tools on the menu bar, click Customize (you might need to pause until the full menu appears to see that command), and then click the Options tab in the Customize dialog box. Click the Always show full menus check box to remove the check mark if necessary, and then click the Show full menus after a short delay check box to insert a check mark if necessary. Click the Reset my usage data button, and then click the Yes button to confirm that you want to reset the commands. Click the Close button. Repeat Step 1.

You can display the full menu in one of three ways: (1) pause until the full menu appears, which might happen as you read this; (2) click the double-arrow button at the bottom of the menu; or (3) double-click the menu name on the menu bar.

**2.** Pause until the full Insert menu appears, as shown in Figure 15. The Bookmark command and other commands are now visible.

| Figure 15 | EXPANDED, FULL MENU |
| --- | --- |

commands with light border appear on short menu

commands with dark border appear only on full menu

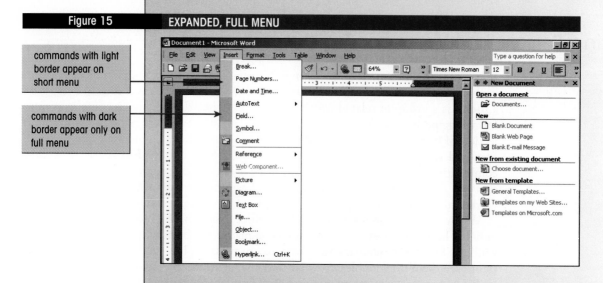

**3.** Click the **Bookmark** command. A dialog box opens when you click a command whose name is followed by an ellipsis (...). In this case, the Bookmark dialog box opens.

**4.** Click the **Cancel** button to close the Bookmark dialog box.

**5.** Click **Insert** on the menu bar again to display the short, personalized menu. The Bookmark command appears on the short, personalized menu because you used it.

**6.** Press the **Esc** key to close the menu.

As you can see, the menu changed based on your actions. Over time, only the commands you use frequently will appear on the personalized menu. The toolbars work similarly.

## To use the personalized toolbars:

**1.** Observe that the Standard and Formatting toolbars appear side by side below the menu bar.

TROUBLE? If the toolbars appear on two rows, you need to reset them. Click Tools on the menu bar, click Customize, and then click the Options tab in the Customize dialog box. Click the Show Standard and Formatting toolbars on two rows check box to remove the check mark. Click the Reset my data usage button, and then click the Yes button to confirm you want to reset the commands. Click the Close button. Repeat Step 1.

The Formatting toolbar sits to the right of the Standard toolbar. You can see most of the Standard toolbar buttons, but only a few Formatting toolbar buttons.

**2.** Click the **Toolbar Options** button ⯆ at the right side of the Standard toolbar. See Figure 16.

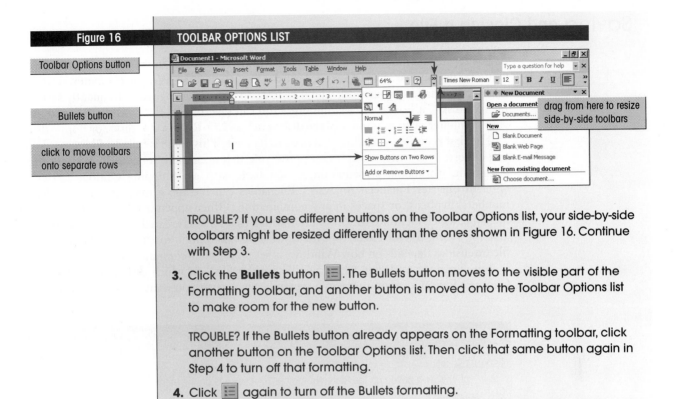

Figure 16     TOOLBAR OPTIONS LIST

TROUBLE? If you see different buttons on the Toolbar Options list, your side-by-side toolbars might be resized differently than the ones shown in Figure 16. Continue with Step 3.

3. Click the **Bullets** button . The Bullets button moves to the visible part of the Formatting toolbar, and another button is moved onto the Toolbar Options list to make room for the new button.

TROUBLE? If the Bullets button already appears on the Formatting toolbar, click another button on the Toolbar Options list. Then click that same button again in Step 4 to turn off that formatting.

4. Click again to turn off the Bullets formatting.

Some people like that the menus and toolbars change to meet their work habits. Others prefer to see all the menu commands or to display the toolbars on different rows so that all the buttons are always visible. You'll change the toolbar setting now.

### *To turn off the personalized toolbars:*

1. Click the **Toolbar Options** button at the right side of the Standard toolbar.

2. Click the **Show Buttons on Two Rows command**. The toolbars move to separate rows (the Standard toolbar on top) and you can see all the buttons on each toolbar.

You can easily access any button on the toolbars with one mouse click. The drawback is that the toolbars take up more space in the program window.

## Using Speech Recognition

Another way to perform tasks in Office is with your voice. Office's **speech recognition technology** enables you to say the names of the toolbar buttons, menus, menu commands, dialog box items, and so forth, rather than clicking the mouse or pressing keys to select them. The Language toolbar includes the Speech Balloon, which displays the voice command equivalents of a selected button or command. If you switch from Voice mode to Dictation mode, you can dictate the contents of your files rather than typing the text or numbers. For better accuracy, complete the Training Wizard, which helps Office learn your vocal quality, rate of talking, and speech patterns. To start using speech recognition, click Tools on the menu bar in any Office program, and then click Speech. The first time you start this feature, the Training Wizard guides you through the setup process.

# Saving and Closing a File

As you create and modify Office files, your work is stored only in the computer's temporary memory, not on disk. If you were to exit the programs, turn off your computer, or experience a power failure, your work would be lost. To prevent losing work, frequently save your file to a disk—at least every ten minutes. You can save files to the hard disk located inside your computer or to portable storage disks, such as CD-ROMs, Zip disks, or floppy disks.

The first time you save a file, you need to name it. This name is called a **filename**. When you choose a filename, select a descriptive one that accurately reflects the content of the document, workbook, presentation, or database, such as "Shipping Options Letter" or "Fourth Quarter Financial Analysis." Filenames can include a maximum of 255 letters, numbers, hyphens, or spaces in any combination. Office appends a **file extension** to the filename, which identifies the program in which that file was created. The file extensions are .doc for Word, .xls for Excel, .ppt for PowerPoint, and .mdb for Access. Whether you see file extensions depends on how Windows is set up for your computer.

You also need to decide where you'll save the file—on which disk and in what folder. Choose a logical location that you'll remember whenever you want to use the file again.

---

**REFERENCE WINDOW**    **RW**

### Saving a File

- Click the Save button on the Standard toolbar (*or* click File on the menu bar, and then click Save or Save As).
- Click the Save in list arrow, and then select the location where you want to save the file.
- Type a filename in the File name text box.
- Click the Save button.
- To resave the named file to the same location, click the Save button on the Standard toolbar (*or* click File on the menu bar, and then click Save).

---

Nicole has asked you to start working on the agenda for the stockholder meeting. You enter text in a Word document by typing. After you type some text, you'll save the file.

### To enter text in a document:

1. Type **Delmar Office Supplies**, and then press the **Enter** key. The text you typed appears on one line in the Word document.

   TROUBLE? If you make a typing error, press the Backspace key to delete the incorrect letters, and then retype the text.

2. Type **Stockholder Meeting Agenda**, and then press the **Enter** key. The text you typed appears on the second line.

The two lines of text you typed are not yet saved on disk. You'll do that now.

## To save a file for the first time:

**1.** Insert your Data Disk in the appropriate drive.

**TROUBLE?** If you don't have a Data Disk, you need to get one before you can proceed. Your instructor or technical support person will either give you one or ask you to make your own by following the instructions on the "Read This Before You Begin" page at the beginning of this tutorial. See your instructor or technical support person for more information.

**2.** Click the **Save** button 🖫 on the Standard toolbar. The Save As dialog box opens. See Figure 17. The first few words of the first line appear in the File name text box, as a suggested filename. You'll replace this with a more descriptive filename.

| Figure 17 | SAVE AS DIALOG BOX |
| --- | --- |

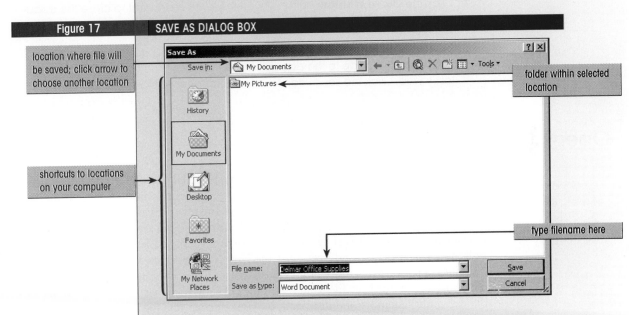

location where file will be saved; click arrow to choose another location

folder within selected location

shortcuts to locations on your computer

type filename here

**TROUBLE?** If the .doc file extension appears after the filename, then your computer is configured to show file extensions. Just continue with Step 3.

**3.** Type **Stockholder Meeting Agenda** in the File name text box.

**4.** Click the **Save in** list arrow, and then click the drive that contains your Data Disk.

**5.** Double-click the **Tutorial.01** folder in the list box, and then double-click the **Tutorial** folder. This is the location where you want to save the document.

**6.** Click the **Save** button. The Save As dialog box closes, and the name of your file appears in the program window title bar.

The saved file includes everything in the document at the time you saved. Any edits or additions you then make to the document exist only in the computer's memory and are not saved in the file on the disk. As you work, remember to save frequently so that the file is updated to reflect the latest content of the document.

Because you already named the document and selected a storage location, the second and subsequent times you save, the Save As dialog box doesn't open. If you wanted to save a copy of the file with a different filename or to a different location, you would reopen the Save As dialog box by clicking File on the menu bar, and then clicking Save As. The previous version of the file remains on your disk as well.

You need to add your name to the agenda. Then you'll save your changes and close the file. You can close a file by clicking the Close command on the File menu or by clicking the Close Window button in the upper-right corner of the menu bar.

---

### To modify, save, and close a file:

1. Type your name, and then press the **Enter** key. The text you typed appears on the next line.

2. Click the **Save** button 🖫 on the Standard toolbar.

   The updated document is saved to the file. When you're done with a file, you can close it. Although you can keep multiple files open at one time, you should close any file you are no longer working on to conserve system resources.

3. Click the **Close Window** button ☒ on the Word menu bar to close the document. Word is still running, but no documents are open.

   TROUBLE? If a dialog box opens and asks whether you want to save the changes you made to the document, you modified the document since you last saved. Click the Yes button to save the current version and close it.

---

## Opening a File

Once you have a program open, you can create additional new files for the open programs or you can open previously created and saved files. You can do both of these from the New Task Pane. The New Task Pane enables you to create new files and open existing ones. The name of the Task Pane varies, depending on the program you are using: Word has the New Document Task Pane, Excel has the New Workbook Task Pane, PowerPoint has the New Presentation Task Pane, and Access has the New File Task Pane.

When you want to work on a previously created file, you must open it first. Opening a file transfers a copy of the file from the storage disk (either a hard disk or a portable disk) to the computer's memory and displays it on your screen. The file is then in your computer's memory and on the disk.

---

**REFERENCE WINDOW**　　　　　　　　　　　　　　　　　　　**RW**

Opening an Existing or New File

- Click File on the menu bar, click New, and then (depending on the program) click the More documents, More workbooks, More presentations, or More files link in the New Task Pane (*or* click the Open button on the Standard toolbar *or* click File on the menu bar, and then click Open).
- Click the Look in list arrow, and then select the storage location of the file you want to open.
- Click the filename of the file you want to open.
- Click the Open button.

*or*

- Click File on the menu bar, click New, and then (depending on the program) click the Blank Document, Blank Workbook, Blank Presentation, or Blank Database link in the New Task Pane (*or* click the New button on the Standard toolbar).

Nicole asks you to print the agenda. To do that, you'll reopen the file. Because Word is still open, you'll use the New Document Task Pane.

## To open an existing file:

1. If necessary, click **File** on the menu bar, and then click **New** to display the New Document Task Pane. See Figure 18.

| Figure 18 | NEW DOCUMENT TASK PANE |
|---|---|

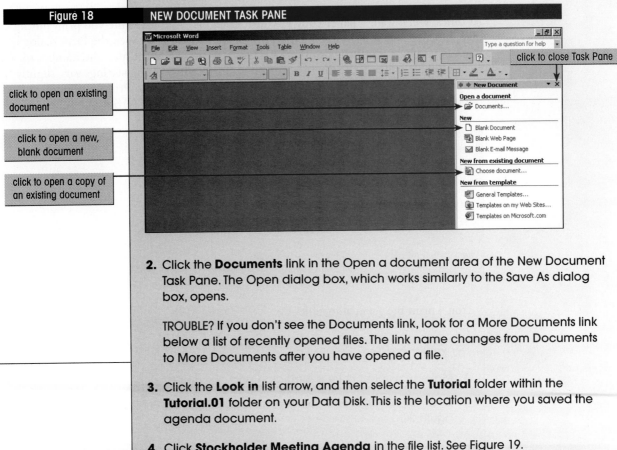

click to open an existing document

click to open a new, blank document

click to open a copy of an existing document

click to close Task Pane

2. Click the **Documents** link in the Open a document area of the New Document Task Pane. The Open dialog box, which works similarly to the Save As dialog box, opens.

   TROUBLE? If you don't see the Documents link, look for a More Documents link below a list of recently opened files. The link name changes from Documents to More Documents after you have opened a file.

3. Click the **Look in** list arrow, and then select the **Tutorial** folder within the **Tutorial.01** folder on your Data Disk. This is the location where you saved the agenda document.

4. Click **Stockholder Meeting Agenda** in the file list. See Figure 19.

| Figure 19 | OPEN DIALOG BOX |
|---|---|

files in this folder are displayed below

agenda file to open and print

**5.** Click the **Open** button. The file you saved earlier reopens in the Word program window, and the New Document Task Pane closes.

After the file is open, you can view, edit, print, or resave it.

# Printing a File

At times, you'll want a paper copy of your Office file. The first time you print during each computer session, you should use the Print menu command to open the Print dialog box so you can verify or adjust the printing settings. You can select a printer, the number of copies to print, the portion of the file to print, and so forth; the printing settings vary slightly from program to program. For subsequent print jobs you can use the Print button to print without opening the dialog box, if you want to use the same default settings.

---

**REFERENCE  WINDOW**                                                   **RW**

**Printing a File**
- Click File on the menu bar, and then click Print.
- Verify the print settings in the Print dialog box.
- Click the OK button.

*or*

- Click the Print button on the Standard toolbar.

---

You'll print the agenda document.

### To print a file:

**1.** Make sure your printer is turned on and contains paper.

**2.** Click **File** on the menu bar, and then click **Print**. The Print dialog box opens. See Figure 20.

---

**Figure 20**                    **PRINT DIALOG BOX**

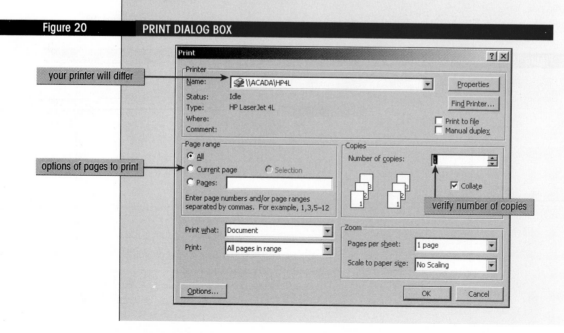

your printer will differ

options of pages to print

verify number of copies

3. Verify that the correct printer appears in the Name list box. If the wrong printer appears, click the **Name** list arrow, and then click the correct printer from the list of available printers.

4. Verify that **1** appears in the Number of copies text box.

5. Click the **OK** button to print the document. See Figure 21.

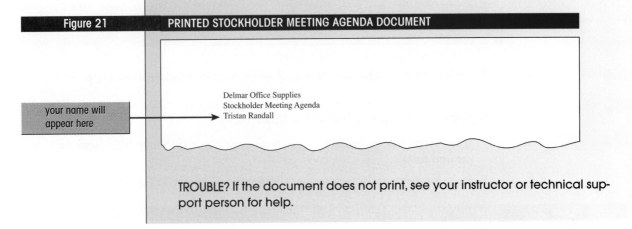

| Figure 21 | PRINTED STOCKHOLDER MEETING AGENDA DOCUMENT |
|---|---|

Delmar Office Supplies
Stockholder Meeting Agenda
Tristan Randall

your name will appear here

TROUBLE? If the document does not print, see your instructor or technical support person for help.

Another important aspect of Office is the ability to get help right from your computer.

# Getting Help

If you don't know how to perform a task or want more information about a feature, you can turn to Office itself for information on how to use it. This information, referred to simply as **Help**, is like a huge encyclopedia stored on your computer. You can access it in a variety of ways.

There are two fast and simple methods you can use to get Help about objects you see on the screen. First, you can position the mouse pointer over a toolbar button to view its **ScreenTip**, a yellow box with the button's name. Second, you can click the **What's This?** command on the Help menu to change the pointer to ▷?, which you can click on any toolbar button, menu command, dialog box option, worksheet cell, or anything else you can see on your screen to view a brief description of that item.

For more in-depth help, you can use the **Ask a Question** box, located on the menu bar of every Office program, to find information in the Help system. You simply type a question using everyday language about a task you want to perform or a topic you need help with, and then press the Enter key to search the Help system. The Ask a Question box expands to show Help topics related to your query. You click a topic to open a Help window with step-by-step instructions that guide you through a specific procedure and explanations of difficult concepts in clear, easy-to-understand language. For example, you might ask how to format a cell in an Excel worksheet; a list of Help topics related to the words you typed will appear. The Help window also has Contents, Answer Wizard, and Index tabs, which you can use to look up information directly from the Help window.

If you prefer, you can ask questions of the **Office Assistant**, an interactive guide to finding information from the Help system. In addition, the Office Assistant can provide Help topics and tips on tasks as you work. For example, it might offer a tip when you select a menu command instead of clicking the corresponding toolbar button. You can turn on or off the tips, depending on your personal preference.

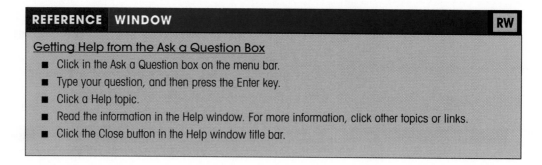

**REFERENCE  WINDOW**                                                                    RW

Getting Help from the Ask a Question Box
- Click in the Ask a Question box on the menu bar.
- Type your question, and then press the Enter key.
- Click a Help topic.
- Read the information in the Help window. For more information, click other topics or links.
- Click the Close button in the Help window title bar.

You'll use the Ask a Question box to obtain more information about Help.

## To use the Ask a Question box:

1. Click in the **Ask a Question** box on the menu bar, and then type **How do I search help?**.

2. Press the **Enter** key to retrieve a list of topics, as shown in Figure 22.

Figure 22            ASK A QUESTION BOX WITH HELP TOPICS

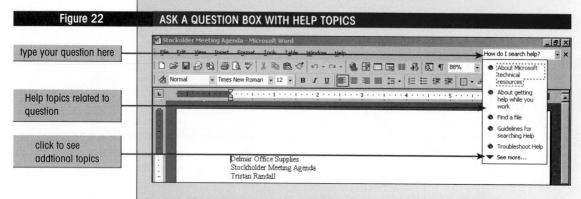

type your question here

Help topics related to question

click to see addtional topics

3. Click the **See more** link, review the additional Help topics, and then click the **See previous** link.

4. Click **About getting help while you work** to open the Help window and learn more about the various ways to obtain assistance in Office. See Figure 23.

Figure 23            HELP WINDOW

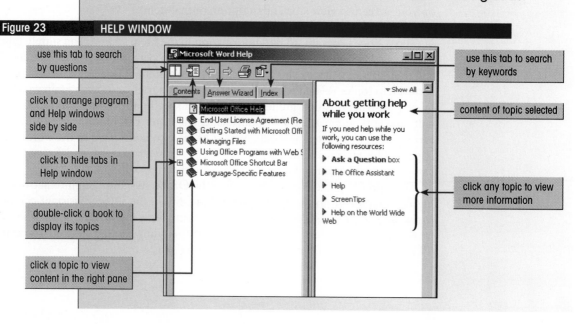

use this tab to search by questions

click to arrange program and Help windows side by side

click to hide tabs in Help window

double-click a book to display its topics

click a topic to view content in the right pane

use this tab to search by keywords

content of topic selected

click any topic to view more information

5. Click **Help** in the right pane to display information about that topic.

6. Click the other links about Help features and read the information.

7. When you're done, click the **Close** button ☒ in the Help window title bar to return to the Word window.

The Help features enable the staff at Delmar Office Supplies to get answers to questions they have about any task or procedure when they need it. The more you practice getting information from the Help system, the more effective you will be at using Office to its full potential.

# Exiting Programs

Whenever you finish working with a program, you should exit it. As with many other aspects of Office, you can exit programs with a button or from a menu. You'll use both methods to close Word and Excel.

*To exit a program:*

1. Click the **Close** button ☒ in the upper-right corner of the screen to exit Word. Word exits, and the Excel window is visible again on your screen.

   TROUBLE? If a dialog box opens, asking whether you want to save the document, you may have inadvertently made a change to the document. Click the No button.

2. Click **File** on the menu bar, and then click **Exit**. The Excel program exits.

Exiting programs after you are done using them keeps your Windows desktop uncluttered for the next person using the computer, frees up your system's resources, and prevents data from being lost accidentally.

## QUICK CHECK

1. Which Office program would you use to write a letter?
2. Which Office programs could you use to store customer names and addresses?
3. What is integration?
4. Explain the difference between Save As and Save.
5. What is the purpose of the New Task Pane?
6. When would you use the Ask a Question box?

## REVIEW ASSIGNMENTS

Before the stockholders meeting at Delmar Office Supplies, you'll open and print documents for the upcoming presentation.

1. Start PowerPoint using the Start button and the Programs menu.

2. Use the Ask a Question box to learn how to change the toolbar buttons from small to large, and then do it. Use the same procedure to change the buttons back to regular size. Close the Help window when you're done.

3. Open a blank Excel workbook using the New Office Document command on the Start menu.

*Explore*  4. Switch to the PowerPoint window using the taskbar, and then close the presentation but leave open the PowerPoint program. (*Hint:* Click the Close Window button in the menu bar.)

*Explore*  5. Open a new, blank PowerPoint presentation from the New Presentation Task Pane. (*Hint:* Click Blank Presentation in the New area of the New Presentation Task Pane.)

6. Close the PowerPoint presentation and program using the Close button in the PowerPoint title bar; do not save changes if asked.

*Explore*  7. Open a copy of the Excel **Finances** workbook located in the **Review** folder within the **Tutorial.01** folder on your Data Disk using the New Workbook Task Pane. (*Hint:* Click File on the Excel menu bar and then click New to open the Task Pane. Click Choose Workbook in the New from existing workbook area of the New Workbook Task Pane; the dialog box functions similarly to the Open dialog box.)

8. Type your name, and then press the Enter key to insert your name at the top of the worksheet.

9. Save the worksheet as **Delmar Finances** in the **Review** folder within the **Tutorial.01** folder on your Data Disk.

10. Print one copy of the worksheet using the Print command on the File menu.

11. Exit Excel using the File menu.

*Explore*  12. Open the **Letter** document located in the **Review** folder within the **Tutorial.01** folder on your Data Disk using the Open Office Document command on the Start menu.

13. Use the Save As command to save the document with the filename **Delmar Letter** in the **Review** folder within the **Tutorial.01** folder on your Data Disk.

*Explore*  14. Press and hold the Ctrl key, press the End key, and then release both keys to move the insertion point to the end of the letter, and then type your name.

15. Use the Save button on the Standard toolbar to save the change to the Delmar Letter document.

16. Print one copy of the document, and then close the document.

17. Exit the Word program using the Close button on the title bar.

# QUICK | CHECK ANSWERS

1. Word
2. Access or Outlook
3. the ability to share information between programs
4. Save As enables you to change the filename and save location of a file. Save updates a file to reflect its latest contents using its current filename and location.
5. enables you to create new files and open existing files
6. when you don't know how to perform a task or want more information about a feature

*New Perspectives on*

# MICROSOFT®
# WORD 2002

# Read This Before You Begin

## To the Student

### Data Disks

To complete these tutorials, Review Assignments, and Case Problems, you need one Data Disk. Your instructor will either provide you with the Data Disk or ask you to make your own.

If you are making your own Data Disk, you will need **one** blank, formatted high-density disk. You will need to copy a set of files and/or folders from a file server, standalone computer, or the Web onto your disk. Your instructor will tell you which computer, drive letter, and folders contain the files you need. You could also download the files by going to **www.course.com** and following the instructions on the screen.

The information below shows you which folders go on your disk, so that you will have enough disk space to complete all the tutorials, Review Assignments, and Case Problems:

### Data Disk 1

Write this on the disk label:
Data Disk 1: Word 2002 Tutorials 1-2
Put these folders on the disk:
Tutorial.01 and Tutorial.02

When you begin each tutorial, be sure you are using the correct Data Disk. Refer to the "File Finder" chart at the back of this text for more detailed information on which files are used in which tutorials. See the inside front or inside back cover of this book for more information on Data Disk files, or ask your instructor or technical support person for assistance.

### Course Labs

The Word tutorials feature an interactive Course Lab to help you understand word processing concepts. There are Lab Assignments at the end of Tutorial 1 that relate to this Lab.

To start a Lab, click the **Start** button on the Windows taskbar, point to **Programs**, point to **Course Labs**, point to **New Perspectives Course Labs**, and then click the name of the Lab you want to use.

### Using Your Own Computer

If you are going to work through this book using your own computer, you need:

- **Computer System** Microsoft Windows 98, NT, 2000 Professional, or higher must be installed on your computer. This book assumes a typical installation of Microsoft Word.

- **Data Disk** You will not be able to complete the tutorials or exercises in this book using your own computer until you have your Data Disk.

- **Course Labs** See your instructor or technical support person to obtain the Course Lab software for use on your own computer.

### Visit Our World Wide Web Site

Additional materials designed especially for you are available on the World Wide Web.
Go to **www.course.com/NewPerspectives**.

## To the Instructor

The Data Disk Files and Course Labs are available on the Instructor's Resource Kit for this title. Follow the instructions in the Help file on the CD-ROM to install the programs to your network or standalone computer. For information on creating Data Disks or the Course Labs, see the "To the Student" section above.

You are granted a license to copy the Data Files and Course Labs to any computer or computer network used by students who have purchased this book.

## OBJECTIVES

In this tutorial you will:

- Plan a document

- Identify the components of the Word window

- Choose commands using toolbars and menus

- Create a new document

- Scroll a document

- Correct errors

- Save, preview, and print a document

- Enter the date with AutoComplete

- Remove Smart Tags

- Create an envelope

## LAB

Word Processing

# CREATING A DOCUMENT

*Writing a Business Letter for Art4U Inc.*

### CASE

### Creating a Contract Letter for Art4U Inc.

Megan Grahs is the owner and manager of Art4U Inc., a graphics design firm in Tucson, Arizona. When Megan founded Art4U in the early 1980s, the company drew most of its revenue from design projects for local magazines, newspapers, advertising circulars, and other print publications. The artists at Art4U laboriously created logos, diagrams, and other illustrations by hand, using watercolors, ink, pastels, and a variety of other media. Since the advent of the Internet, however, Art4U has become one of the Southwest's leading creators of electronic artwork. The firm's artists now work exclusively on computers, saving each piece of art as an electronic file that they can e-mail to a client in a matter of minutes.

Thanks to e-mail, Art4U is no longer limited to the local Tucson market. As a result, Art4U has nearly doubled in size over the past few years. Most of the increase in business has come from Web page designers, who continually need fresh and innovative graphics to use in their Web pages. In fact, Megan has just signed a contract with Web Time Productions agreeing to create a series of logos for a high-profile Web site. She needs to return the signed contract to Web Time's office in Chicago.

In this tutorial, you will create the cover letter that will accompany the contract. You will create the letter using Microsoft Word 2002, a popular word-processing program. Before you begin typing the letter, you will learn to start the Word program, identify and use the elements of the Word screen, and adjust some Word settings. Next you will create a new Word document, type the text of the cover letter, save the letter, and then print the letter for Megan. In the process of entering the text, you'll learn several ways to correct typing errors.

## SESSION 1.1

In this session you will learn how to start Word, identify and use the parts of the Word window, and adjust some Word settings. With the skills you learn in this session, you'll be prepared to use Word to create a variety of documents, such as letters, reports, and memos.

## Four Steps to a Professional Document

Word helps you produce quality work in minimal time. Not only can you type a document in Word, but you can also quickly make revisions and corrections, adjust margins and spacing, create columns and tables, and add graphics to your documents. The most efficient way to produce a document is to follow these four steps: (1) planning and creating, (2) editing, (3) formatting, and (4) printing.

In the long run, *planning* saves time and effort. First, you should determine what you want to say. State your purpose clearly and include enough information to achieve that purpose without overwhelming or boring your reader. Be sure to *organize* your ideas logically. Decide how you want your document to look as well. In this case, your letter to Web Time Productions will take the form of a standard business letter. It should be addressed to Web Time's president, Nicholas Brower. Megan has given you a handwritten note indicating what she would like you to say in the letter. This note is shown in Figure 1-1.

| Figure 1-1 | MEGAN'S NOTES FOR CONTRACT LETTER |
|---|---|

Please write a cover letter for the Web Time Productions contract. In the letter please include the following questions:

- When will we receive a complete schedule for the project?
- How many preliminary designs do you require?
- Will you be available to discuss the project with our artists via a conference call next week?

Send the letter to Web Time's president, Nicholas Brower. The address is: 2210 West Sycamore Avenue, Chicago, IL 60025.

After you plan your document, you can go ahead and *create* it using Word. This generally means typing the text of your document. The next step, *editing*, consists of reading the document you've created, correcting your errors, and, finally, adding or deleting text to make the document easy to read.

Once your document is error-free, you can *format* it to make it visually appealing. Formatting features, such as adjusting margins to create white space (blank areas of a page), setting line spacing, and using boldface and italics, can help make your document easier to read. *Printing* is the final phase in creating an effective document. In this tutorial, you will preview your document before you spend time and resources to print it.

## Exploring the Word Window

Before you can apply these four steps to produce a letter in Word, you need to start Word and learn about the general organization of the Word window. You'll do that now.

## To start Microsoft Word:

1. Make sure Windows is running on your computer and that you can see the Windows desktop on your screen.

2. Click the **Start** button on the taskbar to display the Start menu, and then point to **Programs** to display the Programs menu.

3. Point to **Microsoft Word** on the Programs menu. Depending on how your computer is set up, you might see a small yellow box (called a ScreenTip) containing an explanation of some common uses for Microsoft Word. See Figure 1-2.

| Figure 1-2 | STARTING MICROSOFT WORD |
| --- | --- |

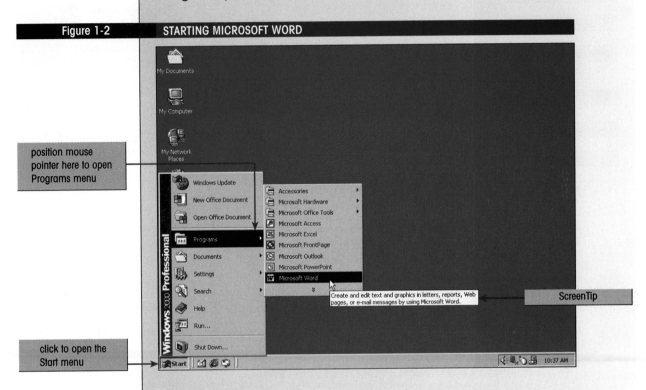

position mouse pointer here to open Programs menu

ScreenTip

click to open the Start menu

TROUBLE? Don't worry if your screen differs slightly from Figure 1-2. Although the figures in this book were created while running Windows 2000 in its default settings, Microsoft Word should run equally well using Windows 98, Windows 2000, Windows Millennium Edition, or Windows NT 4 (with Service Pack 6 installed).

TROUBLE? If you don't see the Microsoft Word option on the Programs menu, ask your instructor or technical support person for help.

TROUBLE? If the Office Shortcut Bar appears on your screen, your system is set up to display it. Because the Office Shortcut Bar is not required to complete these tutorials, it has been omitted from the figures in this text. You can close it or simply ignore it.

4. Click **Microsoft Word**. After a short pause, the Microsoft Word copyright information appears in a message box and remains on the screen until the Word program window opens. See Figure 1-3.

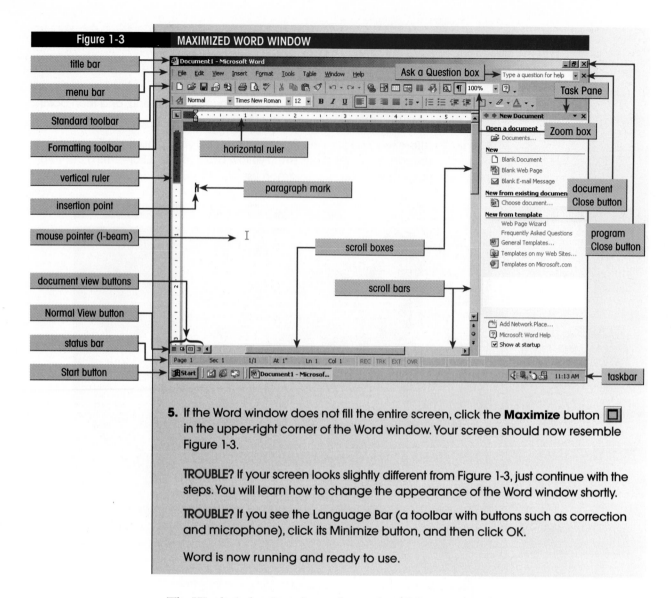

Figure 1-3    MAXIMIZED WORD WINDOW

5. If the Word window does not fill the entire screen, click the **Maximize** button ▢ in the upper-right corner of the Word window. Your screen should now resemble Figure 1-3.

   **TROUBLE?** If your screen looks slightly different from Figure 1-3, just continue with the steps. You will learn how to change the appearance of the Word window shortly.

   **TROUBLE?** If you see the Language Bar (a toolbar with buttons such as correction and microphone), click its Minimize button, and then click OK.

   Word is now running and ready to use.

The Word window is made up of a number of elements which are described in Figure 1-4. You are already familiar with some of these elements, such as the menu bar, title bar, and status bar, because they are common to all Windows programs. Don't be concerned if you don't see everything shown in Figure 1-3. You'll learn how to adjust the appearance of the Word window soon.

Figure 1-4    PARTS OF THE WORD WINDOW

| SCREEN ELEMENT | DESCRIPTION |
| --- | --- |
| Ask a Question box | Allows you to type a question for Word Help |
| Document Close button | Closes the current document |
| Document view buttons | Switches the document between four different views: Normal view, Web Layout view, Print Layout view, and Outline view |
| Document window | Area where you enter text and graphics |
| Formatting toolbar | Contains buttons to activate common font and paragraph formatting commands |

| Figure 1-4 | PARTS OF THE WORD WINDOW (CONTINUED) |
|---|---|
| **SCREEN ELEMENT** | **DESCRIPTION** |
| Horizontal ruler | Adjusts margins, tabs, and column widths; vertical ruler appears in Print Layout view |
| Insertion point | Indicates location where characters will be inserted or deleted |
| Menu bar | Contains lists or menus of all the Word commands. When you first display a menu, you see a short list of the most frequently used commands. To see the full list of commands in the menu, you can either click the menu and then wait a few seconds for the remaining commands to appear, or click the menu and then click or point to the downward-facing double-arrow at the bottom of the menu. |
| Mouse pointer | Changes shape depending on its location on the screen (i.e., I-beam pointer in text area; arrow in nontext areas) |
| Paragraph mark | Marks the end of a paragraph |
| Program Close button | Closes the current document if more than one document is open; closes Word if one or no document is open |
| Scroll bars | Shift text vertically and horizontally on the screen so you can see different parts of the document |
| Scroll box | Helps you move quickly to other pages of your document |
| Standard toolbar | Contains buttons to activate frequently used commands |
| Start button | Starts a program, opens a document, provides quick access to Windows Help |
| Status bar | Provides information regarding the location of the insertion point |
| Taskbar | Shows programs that are running and allows you to switch quickly from one program to another |
| Task Pane | Contains buttons and options for common tasks |
| Title bar | Identifies the current application (i.e., Microsoft Word); shows the filename of the current document |
| Zoom box | Changes the document window magnification |

If at any time you would like to check the name of a Word toolbar button, position the mouse pointer over the button without clicking. A **ScreenTip**, a small yellow box with the name of the button, will appear. (If you don't see ScreenTips on your computer, click Tools on the Word menu bar, click Options, click the View tab, click the ScreenTips check box to insert a check, and then click OK.)

Keep in mind that the commands on the menu bars initially display the commands that are used most frequently on your particular computer. When you leave the menu open for a few seconds or point to the double-arrow, a complete list of commands appears. Throughout these tutorials, you should point to the double-arrow on a menu if you do not see the command you need.

## Setting Up the Window Before You Begin Each Tutorial

Word provides a set of standard settings, called **default settings**, that control how the screen is set up, and how a document looks when you first start typing. These settings are appropriate for most situations. However, these settings are easily changed, and most people begin a work session by adjusting Word to make sure it is set up the way they want it.

When you become more comfortable using Word, you will learn how to customize Word to suit your needs. But to make it easier to follow the steps in these tutorials, you should take care to arrange your window to match the tutorial figures. The rest of this section explains what your window should look like and how to make it match those in the tutorials. Depending on how many people use your computer (and how much they adjust Word's appearance), you might have to set up the window to match the figures each time you start Word.

## Closing the Task Pane

The **Task Pane** is part of the Word window that you can use to perform common chores, such as sending e-mail. By default, the Task Pane appears on the right side of the Word window (as in Figure 1-5) when you start Word.

| Figure 1-5 | TASK PANE IN THE WORD WINDOW |
|---|---|

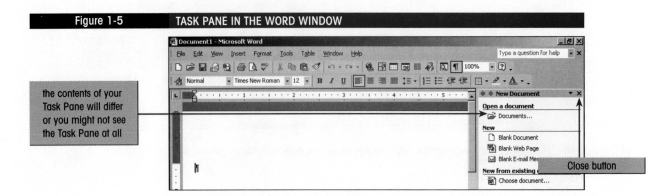

the contents of your Task Pane will differ or you might not see the Task Pane at all

Close button

Depending on how your computer is currently set up, your Task Pane might look different from the one in Figure 1-5, or you might not see the Task Pane at all. When you become a more experienced Word user, you will learn how to take advantage of the Task Pane to work more efficiently. But for now you will close it, using the Close button shown in Figure 1-5.

### To close the Task Pane:

1. If the Task Pane is open on your computer, click its **Close** button ☒. The Document window expands to fill the space left by the Task Pane.

## Setting the Document View to Normal

You can view your document in one of four ways—Normal, Web Layout, Print Layout, or Outline. **Web Layout view** and **Outline view** are designed for special situations that you don't need to worry about now. You will learn more about **Print Layout view**—which allows you to see a page's overall design and format—in later tutorials. In Print Layout view, Word displays both a horizontal ruler (below the toolbars) and a vertical ruler (along the left side of the Document window). For this tutorial you will use **Normal view**, which allows you to see more of the document than Print Layout view. By default, Word often displays the document in Print Layout view, just as it is in Figure 1-5. For this tutorial, you need to display the document in Normal view.

### To make sure the Document window is in Normal view:

1. Click the **Normal View** button ☰ to the left of the horizontal scroll bar. See Figure 1-6. If your Document window was not in Normal view, it changes to Normal view now. The Normal View button is outlined, indicating that it is selected.

| Figure 1-6 | CHANGING TO NORMAL VIEW |
|---|---|

Outline View button
Print Layout button
Web Layout button
Normal View button

Page 1   Sec 1      1/1    At 1"   Ln 1   Col 1    REC TRK EXT OVR    ← status bar

Start   Document1 - Microsof...    11:15 AM

## Displaying the Toolbars and Ruler

The Word toolbars allow you to perform common tasks quickly by clicking a button. In the Word tutorials, you will most often use the Standard toolbar and the Formatting toolbar. While working through these tutorials, you should check to make sure that only the Formatting and Standard toolbars appear on your screen. The Standard toolbar should be positioned on top of the Formatting toolbar, just as they are in Figure 1-7.

| Figure 1-7 | STANDARD TOOLBAR ON TOP OF FORMATTING TOOLBAR |
|---|---|

Standard toolbar

Formatting toolbar

Depending on the settings specified by the last person to use your computer, you may not see both toolbars or your toolbars may all appear on one row. You also may see additional toolbars, such as the Drawing toolbar. In the following steps, you will make sure that your Word window shows only the Standard and Formatting toolbars. Later you will make sure that they are stacked on top of each other.

### To verify that your Word window shows the correct toolbars:

1. Position the pointer over any toolbar and click the right mouse button. A shortcut menu appears. The menu lists all available toolbars with a check mark next to those currently displayed. If the Standard and Formatting toolbars are currently displayed on your computer, you should see check marks next to their names.

   TROUBLE? If you don't see any toolbars on your screen, click Tools on the menu bar, click Customize, and then click the Toolbars tab. Click the Standard and Formatting check boxes to insert a check in each, and then click Close. To gain practice using a shortcut menu, begin again with Step 1, above.

2. Verify that you see a check mark next to the word "Standard" in the shortcut menu. If you do not see a check mark, click **Standard** now. (Clicking any item on the shortcut menu closes the menu, so you will need to re-open it in the next step.)

3. Redisplay the shortcut menu, if necessary, and look for a check mark next to the word "Formatting."

**4.** Redisplay the shortcut menu, if necessary. If any toolbars besides the Formatting and Standard toolbars have check marks, click each one to remove the check mark and hide the toolbar. When you are finished, only the Standard and Formatting toolbars should have check marks.

If the toolbars appear on one row, perform the next steps to arrange the toolbars on two rows.

*To arrange the Standard toolbar and the Formatting toolbar on two rows:*

**1.** Click **Tools** on the menu bar, and then click **Customize**. The Customize dialog box opens.

TROUBLE? If you don't see the Customize command on the Tools menu, point to the double arrow, as explained earlier in this tutorial, to show the full list of commands.

**2.** Click the **Options** tab, and then click the **Show Standard and Formatting toolbars on two rows** check box to select it (that is, to insert a check).

**3.** Click **Close**. The Customize dialog box closes. The toolbars on your screen should now match those shown earlier in Figure 1-7.

## Displaying the Horizontal Ruler

In Normal view, you can use the **Horizontal ruler** to position text on the page. As you complete these tutorials, the ruler should be visible to help you place items precisely. If the ruler is not displayed on your screen as it is in Figure 1-8, you need to perform the following steps.

| Figure 1-8 | HORIZONTAL RULER DISPLAYED IN NORMAL VIEW |
| --- | --- |

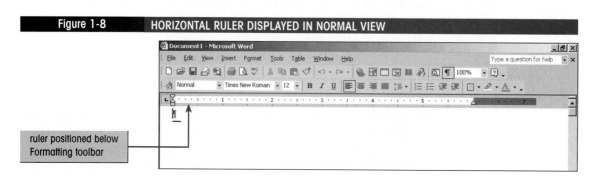

ruler positioned below Formatting toolbar

*To display the ruler:*

**1.** Click **View** on the menu bar, and then point to the **double-arrow** at the bottom of the menu to display the hidden menu commands.

**2.** If "Ruler" does not have a check mark next to it, click **Ruler**. The horizontal ruler should now be displayed, as shown earlier in Figure 1-8.

## Selecting a Zoom Setting

You can use the **Zoom box** on the Standard toolbar to change the magnification of the Document window. (The Zoom box is shown in Figure 1-9.) This is useful when you need a close-up view of a document—especially if you have difficulty reading small print on a computer screen. You will learn how to use the Zoom box later. For now you just need to know how to make the Zoom setting match the figures in these tutorials. By default, the Zoom setting is 100% when you first start Word (as it is in Figure 1-9). But the Zoom setting you see now depends on the setting used by the last person to work with Word on your computer. If your Zoom setting is not 100%, you need to perform the following steps.

| Figure 1-9 | ZOOM BOX IN STANDARD TOOLBAR |

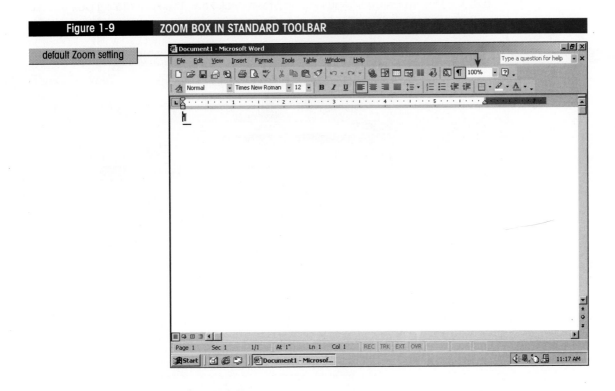

default Zoom setting

## To adjust the Zoom setting:

1. Click the **list arrow** in the Zoom box. A list of settings appears.

2. Click **100%**. The list box closes, and 100% appears in the Zoom box, as shown in Figure 1-9.

## Setting the Font and Font Size

A **font** is a set of characters that has a certain design, shape, and appearance. Each font has a name, such as Courier, Times New Roman, or Arial. The **font size** is the actual height of a character, measured in points, where one point equals 1/72 of an inch in height. You'll learn more about fonts and font sizes later, but for now keep in mind that most documents you create will use the Times New Roman font in a font size of 12 points. Word usually uses a default setting of Times New Roman 12 point, but someone else might have changed the setting after Word was installed on your computer. You can see your computer's current settings in the Font list box and the Font Size list box in the Formatting toolbar, as shown in Figure 1-10.

| Figure 1-10 | DEFAULT FONT AND FONT SIZE SETTINGS |

default font                                                      default font size

If your font setting is not Times New Roman 12 point, you should change the default setting now. You'll use the menu bar to choose the commands.

## To change the default font and font size:

1. Click **Format** on the menu bar, and then click **Font**. The Font dialog box opens. If necessary, click the **Font** tab. See Figure 1-11.

**Figure 1-11**        FONT DIALOG BOX

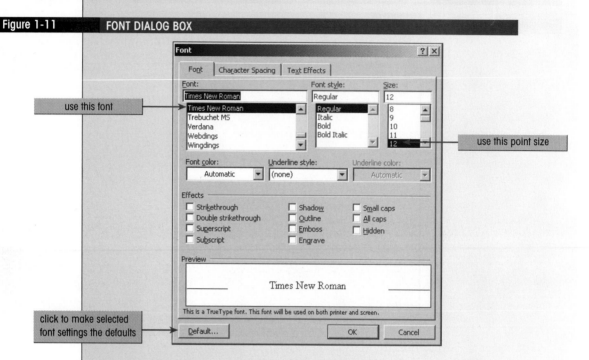

2. In the Font text box, click **Times New Roman**.

3. In the Size list box, click **12**.

4. Click the **Default** button to make Times New Roman and 12 point the default settings. Word displays a message asking you to verify that you want to make 12 point Times New Roman the default font.

5. Click **Yes**.

## Displaying Nonprinting Characters

**Nonprinting characters** are symbols that can appear on the screen but do not show up when you print a document. You can display nonprinting characters when you are working on the appearance, or **format**, of your document. For example, one nonprinting character marks the end of a paragraph (¶), and another marks the space between words (•). It's helpful to display nonprinting characters so you can see whether you've typed an extra space, ended a paragraph, and so on.

Depending on how your computer is set up, nonprinting characters might have been displayed automatically when you started Word. In Figure 1-12, you can see the paragraph symbol (¶) in the blank Document window. Also, the Show/Hide ¶ button is outlined in the Standard toolbar. Both of these indicate that nonprinting characters are displayed. If they are not displayed on your screen, you need to perform the following steps.

| Figure 1-12 | NONPRINTING CHARACTERS DISPLAYED |
|---|---|

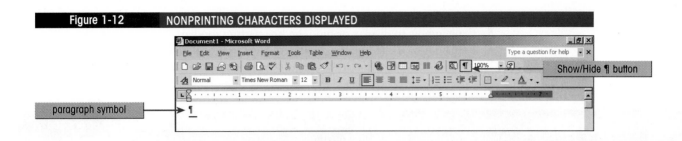

*paragraph symbol*

*Show/Hide ¶ button*

## To display nonprinting characters:

1. Click the **Show/Hide ¶** button ¶ on the Standard toolbar. A paragraph mark (¶) appears at the top of the Document window. Your screen should now match Figure 1-12. To make sure your window always matches the figures in these tutorials, remember to complete the checklist in Figure 1-13 each time you sit down at the computer.

   **TROUBLE?** If the Show/Hide ¶ button was already highlighted before you clicked it, you have now deactivated it. Click the Show/Hide ¶ button a second time to select it.

| Figure 1-13 | WORD WINDOW CHECKLIST |
|---|---|

| SCREEN ELEMENT | SETTING | CHECK |
|---|---|---|
| Document view | Normal view | ☐ |
| Word window | Maximized | ☐ |
| Standard toolbar | Displayed, below the menu bar | ☐ |
| Formatting toolbar | Displayed, below the Standard toolbar | ☐ |
| Other toolbars | Hidden | ☐ |
| Nonprinting characters | Displayed | ☐ |
| Font | Times New Roman | ☐ |
| Point size | 12 point | ☐ |
| Ruler | Displayed | ☐ |
| Task Pane | Closed | ☐ |
| Zoom box | 100% | ☐ |

Now that you have planned your letter, opened Word, identified screen elements, and adjusted settings, you are ready to begin typing a letter. In the next session, you will create Megan's letter to Web Time Productions.

## Session 1.1 QUICK CHECK

1. In your own words, list the steps in creating a document.
2. How do you start Word from the Windows desktop?
3. Define each of the following in your own words:
   **a.** nonprinting characters      **c.** font size
   **b.** document view buttons      **d.** default settings

4. Explain how to change the default font size.
5. Explain how to display or hide the Formatting toolbar.
6. Explain how to change the document view to Normal view.
7. To close the Task Pane, you need to use a command on the menu bar. True or False?

## SESSION 1.2

In this session you will create a one-page document using Word. You'll correct errors and scroll through your document. You'll also name, save, preview, and print the document. Finally, you will create an envelope for the letter.

# Beginning a Letter

Word Processing

You're ready to begin typing Megan's letter to Nicholas Brower at Web Time Productions. Figure 1-14 shows the completed letter printed on company letterhead. You'll begin by opening a new blank page (in case you accidentally typed something in the current page). Then you'll move the insertion point to about 2.5 inches from the top margin of the paper to allow space for the Art4U letterhead.

| Figure 1-14 | COMPLETED LETTER |

Art4U, Inc.
1921 Sedona Avenue
Tucson, AZ 85701
Art4U@WorldNet.com

February 21, 2003

Nicholas Brower, President
Web Time Productions
2210 West Sycamore Avenue
Chicago, IL 60025

Dear Nicholas:

Enclosed you will find the signed contract. As you can see, I am returning all three pages, with my signature on each.

Now that we have finalized the contract, I have a few questions: When will we receive a complete schedule for the project? Also, how many preliminary designs do you require? Finally, will you be available to discuss the project with our artists via a conference call some afternoon next week?

Thanks again for choosing Art4U. We look forward to working with you.

Sincerely yours,

Megan Grahs

## To open a new document:

1. If you took a break after the previous session, make sure the Word program is running, that nonprinting characters are displayed, and that the font settings in the Formatting toolbar are set to 12 point Times New Roman. Also verify that the toolbars and the ruler are displayed. Currently, you have one document open in Word. This document is named Document1. If you have the taskbar displayed at the bottom of your screen, it should contain a button named Document1. If for some reason you need to switch between Word and another Windows program, you could click this taskbar button to redisplay the Word window. In the next steps, you'll try using this button, just for practice.

2. Click the **Minimize** button ___ in the Word title bar. The Word window minimizes, revealing the Windows desktop. (If you couldn't see the taskbar earlier, you should see it now.)

3. Click the **Document1** button in the taskbar. The Word window maximizes again. Now you can open a new document where you can type Megan's letter.

4. Click the **New Blank Document** button 🗋 on the Standard toolbar. A new document, named Document2, opens, as shown in Figure 1-15.

| Figure 1-15 | NEWLY OPENED DOCUMENT |
| --- | --- |

name of new document

new taskbar button for Document 2

button for Document 1

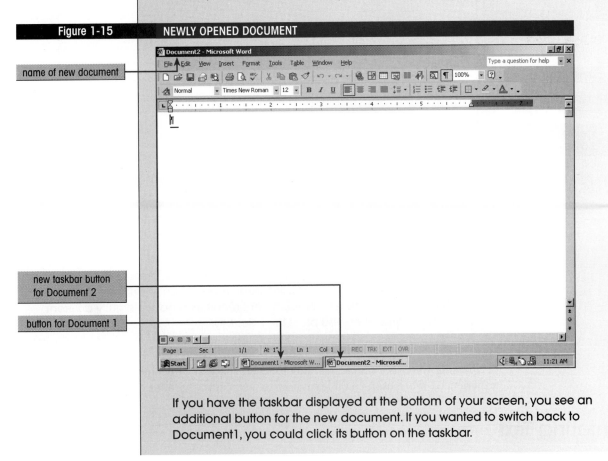

If you have the taskbar displayed at the bottom of your screen, you see an additional button for the new document. If you wanted to switch back to Document1, you could click its button on the taskbar.

Now that you have opened a new document, you need to insert some blank lines in the document so you leave enough room for the company letterhead.

## To insert blank lines in the document:

1. Press the **Enter** key eight times. Each time you press the Enter key, a nonprinting paragraph mark appears. In the status bar (at the bottom of the Document window), you should see the setting "At 2.5"," indicating that the insertion point is approximately 2.5 inches from the top of the page. Another setting in the status bar should read "Ln 9," indicating the insertion point is in line 9 of the document. See Figure 1-16. (Your settings may be slightly different.)

| Figure 1-16 | DOCUMENT WINDOW AFTER INSERTING BLANK LINES |
|---|---|

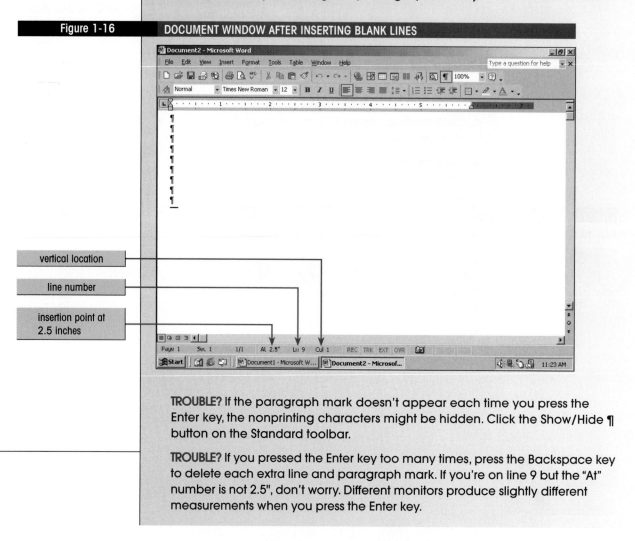

vertical location

line number

insertion point at 2.5 inches

**TROUBLE?** If the paragraph mark doesn't appear each time you press the Enter key, the nonprinting characters might be hidden. Click the Show/Hide ¶ button on the Standard toolbar.

**TROUBLE?** If you pressed the Enter key too many times, press the Backspace key to delete each extra line and paragraph mark. If you're on line 9 but the "At" number is not 2.5", don't worry. Different monitors produce slightly different measurements when you press the Enter key.

Pressing Enter is a simple, fast way to insert space in a document. When you are a more experienced Word user, you'll learn how to insert space without using the Enter key.

## Entering Text

Normally, you begin typing a letter by entering the date. However, Megan tells you that she's not sure whether the contract will be ready to send today or tomorrow. So she asks you to skip the date for now and begin with the inside address. Making changes to documents is easy in Word, so you can easily add the date later.

In the following steps, you'll type the inside address (shown on Megan's note, in Figure 1-1). If you type a wrong character, press the Backspace key to delete the mistake and then retype the correct character.

## To type the inside address:

1. Type **Nicholas Brower, President** and then press the **Enter** key. As you type, the nonprinting character (•) appears between words to indicate a space. Depending on how your computer is set up, you may also see a dotted underline beneath the name, Nicholas Brower, as shown in Figure 1-17. You'll learn the meaning of this underline later in this tutorial, when you type the date. For now you can just ignore it and concentrate on typing the letter.

| Figure 1-17 | FIRST LINE OF INSIDE ADDRESS |
| --- | --- |

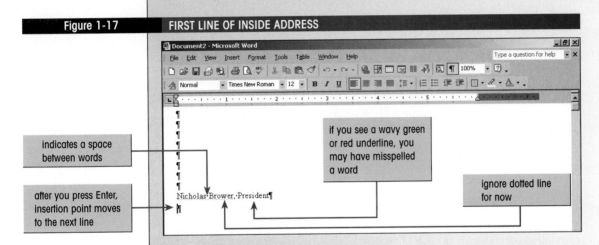

indicates a space between words

after you press Enter, insertion point moves to the next line

if you see a wavy green or red underline, you may have misspelled a word

ignore dotted line for now

Nicholas·Brower,·President¶

TROUBLE? If a wavy line (as opposed to a dotted line) appears beneath a word, check to make sure you typed the text correctly. If you did not, use the Backspace key to remove the error, and then retype the text correctly.

2. Type the following text, pressing the **Enter** key after each line to complete the inside address:
**Web Time Productions**
**2210 West Sycamore Avenue**
**Chicago, IL 60025**

Ignore the dotted underline below the street address. As mentioned earlier, you'll learn the meaning of this type of underline later in this tutorial.

3. Press the **Enter** key again to add a blank line after the inside address. (You should see a total of two paragraph marks below the inside address.) Now you can type the salutation.

4. Type **Dear Nicholas:** and press the **Enter** key twice to double space between the salutation and the body of the letter. When you press the Enter key the first time, the Office Assistant might appear, asking if you would like help writing your letter, as in Figure 1-18. (Depending on the settings on your computer, you might see a different Office Assistant.)

Figure 1-18 | OFFICE ASSISTANT

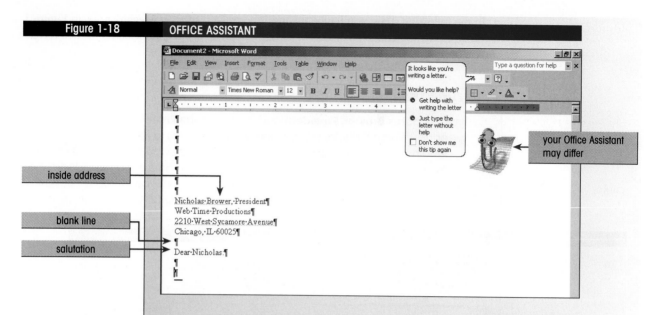

inside address

blank line

salutation

As you know, the Office Assistant is an interactive feature that sometimes appears to offer help on routine tasks. In this case, you could click "Get help with writing the letter" and have the Office Assistant lead you through a series of dialog boxes designed to set up the basic elements of a letter. For now, though, you'll close the Office Assistant and continue writing your letter.

5. Click **Just type the letter without help**. The Office Assistant closes.

   **TROUBLE?** If the Office Assistant remains open, right-click the Office Assistant, and then click Hide.

Before you continue with the rest of the letter, you should save what you have typed so far.

### To save the document:

1. Place your Data Disk in the appropriate disk drive.

   **TROUBLE?** If you don't have a Data Disk, see the "Read This Before You Begin" page at the beginning of this tutorial.

2. Click the **Save** button 🖫 on the Standard toolbar. The Save As dialog box opens, similar to Figure 1-19. (Your Save As dialog box might be larger than the one shown in Figure 1-19.) Note that Word suggests using the first few words of the letter ("Nicholas Brower") as the filename. You will first replace the suggested filename with something more descriptive.

| Figure 1-19 | SAVE AS DIALOG BOX |
| --- | --- |

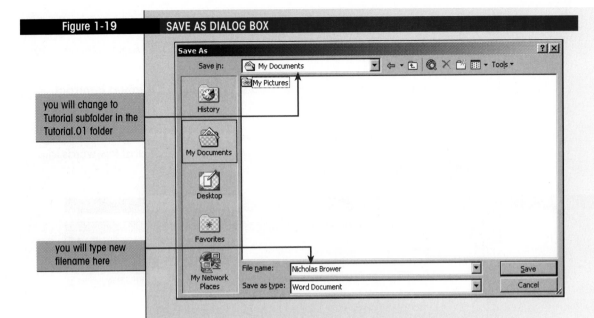

you will change to
Tutorial subfolder in the
Tutorial.01 folder

you will type new
filename here

3. Type **Web Time Contract Letter** in the File name text box. Next, you need to tell Word where you want to save the document. In this case, you want to use the Tutorial subfolder in the Tutorial.01 folder on your Data Disk.

4. Click the **Save in** list arrow, click the drive containing your Data Disk, double-click the **Tutorial.01** folder, and then double-click the **Tutorial** folder. The word "Tutorial" is now displayed in the Save in box, indicating that the Tutorial folder is open and ready for you to save the document.

   **TROUBLE?** If Word automatically adds the .doc extension to your filename, your computer is configured to show filename extensions. Just continue with the tutorial.

5. Click the **Save** button in the Save As dialog box. The dialog box closes, and you return to the Document window. The new document name (Web Time Contract Letter) appears in the title bar.

Note that Word automatically appends the .doc extension to the filename to identify the file as a Microsoft Word document. However, unless your computer is set up to display file extensions, you won't see the .doc extension in any of the Word dialog boxes or in the title bar. These tutorials assume that filename extensions are hidden.

## Taking **Advantage of Word Wrap**

Now that you have saved your document, you're ready to continue working on Megan's letter. As you type the body of the letter, you do not have to press the Enter key at the end of each line. Instead, when you type a word that extends into the right margin, both the insertion point and the word moves automatically to the next line. This automatic line breaking is called **word wrap**. You'll see how word wrap works as you type the body of the letter.

### *To observe word wrap while typing a paragraph:*

1. Make sure the insertion point is at Ln 16 (according to the settings in the status bar). If it's not, move it to line 16 by pressing the arrow keys.

2. Type the following sentence: **Enclosed you will find the signed contract.**

3. Press the **spacebar**.

4. Type the following sentence: **As you can see, I am returning all three pages, with my signature on each.** Notice how Word moves the last few words to a new line when the preceding line is full. See Figure 1-20.

| Figure 1-20 | WORD WRAPPING TEXT |
| --- | --- |

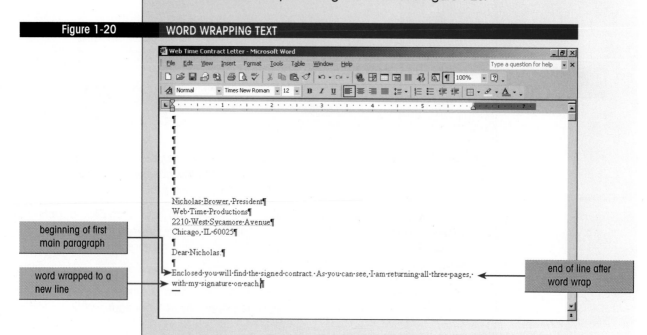

beginning of first main paragraph

word wrapped to a new line

end of line after word wrap

**TROUBLE?** If your screen does not match Figure 1-20 exactly, don't be concerned. The Times New Roman font can have varying letter widths and produce slightly different measurements on different monitors. As a result, the word or letter where the line wraps in your document might be different from the one shown in Figure 1-20. Continue with Step 5.

5. Press the **Enter** key to end the first paragraph, and then press the **Enter** key again to double space between the first and second paragraphs.

6. Type the following text:

   **Now that we have finalized the contract, I have a few questions: When will we receive a complete schedule for the project? Also, how many preliminary designs do you require?**

   When you are finished, your screen should look similar to Figure 1-21, although the line breaks on your screen might be slightly different.

| Figure 1-21 | BEGINNING OF SECOND MAIN PARAGRAPH |

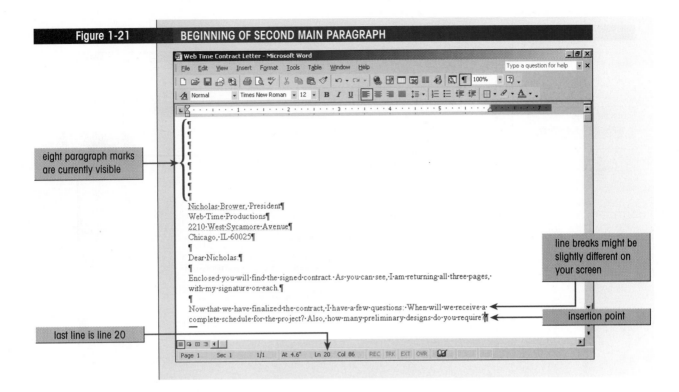

**eight paragraph marks are currently visible**

**line breaks might be slightly different on your screen**

**insertion point**

**last line is line 20**

## Scrolling a Document

After you finish the last set of steps, the insertion point should be near the bottom of the Document window. It looks like there's not enough room to type the rest of Megan's letter. However, as you continue to add text at the end of your document, the text that you typed earlier will **scroll** (or shift up) and disappear from the top of the Document window. You'll see how scrolling works as you enter the rest of the second paragraph.

### To observe scrolling while you're entering text:

1. Make sure the insertion point is positioned to the right of the question mark after the word "require" in the second main paragraph. In other words, the insertion point should be positioned at the end of line 20. (See Figure 1-21 above.)

   **TROUBLE?** If you are using a very large monitor, your insertion point may still be some distance from the bottom of the screen. In that case, you may not be able to perform the scrolling steps that follow. Read the steps to familiarize yourself with the process of scrolling. You'll have a chance to scroll longer documents later.

2. Press the **spacebar**, and then type the following text:

   **Finally, will you be available to discuss the project with our artists via a conference call some afternoon next week?**

   Notice that as you begin to type the text, Word moves the insertion point to a new line. Also, the first paragraph mark at the top of the letter scrolls off the top of the Document window to make room for the end of the question. When you are finished typing, your screen should look like Figure 1-22. (Don't worry if you make a mistake in your typing. You'll learn a number of ways to correct errors in the next section.)

**Figure 1-22** PARAGRAPH MARK SCROLLED OFF THE SCREEN

first paragraph mark scrolled off the screen

now only seven paragraph marks are visible

Nicholas·Brower,·President¶
Web·Time·Productions¶
2210·West·Sycamore·Avenue¶
Chicago,·IL·60025¶
¶
Dear·Nicholas:¶
¶
Enclosed·you·will·find·the·signed·contract.·As·you·can·see,·I·am·returning·all·three·pages,·
with·my·signature·on·each.¶
¶
Now·that·we·have·finalized·the·contract,·I·have·a·few·questions.·When·will·we·receive·a·
complete·schedule·for·the·project?·Also,·how·many·preliminary·designs·do·you·require?·
Finally,·will·you·be·available·to·discuss·the·project·with·our·artists·via·a·conference·call·
some·afternoon·next·week?¶

Page 1    Sec 1    1/1    At 5"    Ln 22    Col 26    REC TRK EXT OVR

3. Press the **Enter** key twice. The document scrolls up to make room for the new lines at the bottom.

4. Type the following text:

   **Thanks again for choosing Art4U. We look forward to working with you.**

5. Press the **Enter** key twice.

6. Type **Sincerely yours,** (including the comma) to enter the complimentary closing.

7. Press the **Enter** key five times to allow space for a signature. Unless you have a very large monitor, part of the inside address scrolls off the top of the Document window.

8. Type **Megan Grahs**. If you see a wavy underline below Megan's name, ignore it for now. You'll learn the meaning of this underline in the next section. You've completed the letter, so you should save your work.

9. Click the **Save** button 🖫 on the Standard toolbar. Word saves your letter with the same name and to the same location you specified earlier. Your letter should look like Figure 1-23. Don't be concerned about any typing errors. You'll learn how to correct them in the next section.

**Figure 1-23** SIGNATURE PORTION OF LETTER

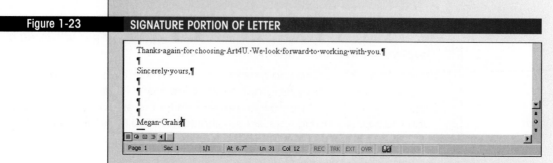

Thanks·again·for·choosing·Art4U.·We·look·forward·to·working·with·you.¶
¶
Sincerely·yours,¶
¶
¶
¶
¶
Megan·Grahs¶

Page 1    Sec 1    1/1    At 6.7"    Ln 31    Col 12    REC TRK EXT OVR

In the last set of steps, you watched the text at the top of your document move off your screen. You can scroll this hidden text back into view so you can read the beginning of the letter. When you do, the text at the bottom of the screen will scroll out of view. To scroll the Document window, you can click the up or down arrows in the vertical scroll bar, click anywhere in the vertical scroll bar, or drag the scroll box. Figure 1-24 summarizes these options.

**Figure 1-24**    SCROLLING THE DOCUMENT WINDOW

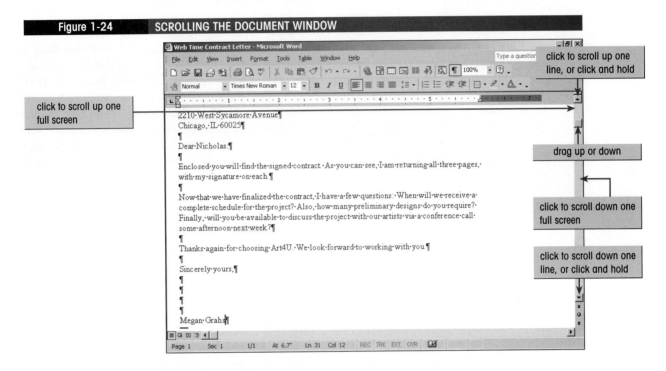

In the next set of steps, you will practice using the vertical scroll bar.

### To scroll the document using the vertical scroll bar:

1. Position the mouse pointer on the up arrow at the top of the vertical scroll bar. Press and hold the mouse button to scroll the text. When the text stops scrolling, you have reached the top of the document and can see the beginning of the letter. Note that scrolling does not change the location of the insertion point in the document.

2. Click the down arrow on the vertical scroll bar. The document scrolls down one line.

3. Click anywhere in the vertical scroll bar, below the scroll box. The document scrolls down one full screen.

4. Drag the scroll box up until the first line of the inside address ("Nicholas Brower, President") is positioned at the top of the Document window.

## Correcting **Errors**

If you discover a typing error as soon as you make it, you can press the Backspace key to erase the characters and spaces to the left of the insertion point one at a time. Backspacing erases both printing and nonprinting characters. After you erase the error, you can type the correct characters. (You can also press the Delete key to delete characters to the right of the insertion point.)

In many cases, however, Word's **AutoCorrect** feature will do the work for you. This helpful feature automatically corrects common typing errors, such as entering "adn" for "and." You might have noticed AutoCorrect at work if you forgot to capitalize the first letter in a sentence as you typed the letter. AutoCorrect automatically corrects this error as you type the rest of the sentence. For example, if you happened to type "enclosed" at the beginning of the first sentence, Word would capitalize the initial "e" automatically.

In the case of more complicated errors, you can take advantage of Word's **Spelling and Grammar** checker. This feature continually checks your document against Word's built-in dictionary and a set of grammar rules. If a word is spelled differently from how it is in Word's dictionary, or if a word isn't in the dictionary at all (for example, a person's name), a wavy *red* line appears beneath the word. A wavy red line also appears if you type duplicate words (such as "the the"). If you accidentally type an extra space between words or make a grammatical error (such as typing "He walk to the store." instead of "He walks to the store."), a wavy *green* line appears beneath the error. The easiest way to see how these features work is to make some intentional typing errors.

## To correct intentional typing errors:

1. Click the **Document1** button in the taskbar.

   **TROUBLE?** If you closed Document1 earlier, click the New Blank Document button in the Standard toolbar to open a blank document.

2. Carefully and slowly type the following sentence exactly as it is shown, including the spelling errors and the extra space between the last two words: **microsoft Word corects teh commen typing misTakes you  make.** Press the **Enter** key when you are finished typing. Notice that as you press the spacebar after the word "commen," a wavy red line appears beneath it, indicating that the word might be misspelled. Notice also that when you pressed the spacebar after the words "corects," "teh," and "misTakes," Word automatically corrected the spelling. After you pressed the Enter key, a wavy green line appeared under the last two words, alerting you to the extra space. See Figure 1-25.

| Figure 1-25 | DOCUMENT WITH INTENTIONAL TYPING ERRORS |
| --- | --- |

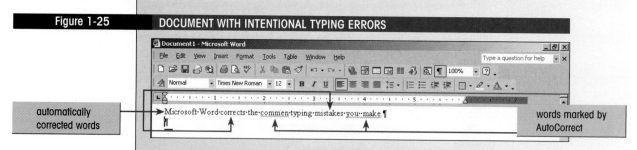

automatically corrected words

words marked by AutoCorrect

**TROUBLE?** If red and green wavy lines do not appear beneath mistakes, Word is probably not set to check spelling and grammar automatically as you type. Click Tools on the menu bar, and then click Options to open the Options dialog box. Click the Spelling & Grammar tab. If necessary, insert check marks in the "Check spelling as you type" and the "Check grammar as you type" check boxes, and click OK. If Word does not automatically correct the incorrect spelling of "the," click Tools on the menu bar, click AutoCorrect Options, and make sure that all seven boxes at the top of the AutoCorrect tab have check marks. Then scroll down the AutoCorrect list to make sure that there is an entry that changes "teh" to "the," and click OK.

## Working with AutoCorrect

Whenever AutoCorrect makes a change, Word inserts an **AutoCorrect Options button** in the document. You can use this button to undo a change, or to prevent AutoCorrect from making the same change in the future. To see an AutoCorrect Options button, you position the mouse pointer over a word that has been changed by AutoCorrect.

### To display the AutoCorrect Options buttons:

1. Position the mouse pointer over the word "corrects." A small blue rectangle appears below the first few letters of the word, as in Figure 1-26.

   **TROUBLE?** If you see a blue button with a lightning bolt, you pointed to the blue rectangle after it appeared. Move the pointer so that only the rectangle is visible, and continue with the next step.

| Figure 1-26 | WORD CHANGED BY AUTOCORRECT |
| --- | --- |

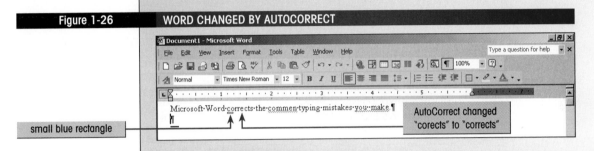

small blue rectangle

Microsoft·Word·corrects·the·commen·typing·mistakes·you··make.¶

AutoCorrect changed
"corects" to "corrects"

2. Point to the **blue rectangle** below "corrects". The blue rectangle is replaced by the AutoCorrect Options button.

3. Click the **AutoCorrect Options** button. A menu with commands related to AutoCorrect appears. You could choose to change "corrects" back to "corects". You could also tell AutoCorrect to stop automatically correcting "corects".

4. Click anywhere in the document. The AutoCorrect menu closes.

## Correcting Spelling and Grammar Errors

After you verify that AutoCorrect made changes you want, you should scan your document for wavy underlines. Again, the red underlines indicate potential spelling errors, while the green underlines indicate potential grammar or punctuation problems. In the following steps, you will learn a quick way to correct such errors.

### To correct spelling and grammar errors:

1. Position the I-Beam pointer ⌶ over the word "commen" and click the right mouse button. A shortcut menu appears with suggested spellings. See Figure 1-27.

**Figure 1-27**    SHORTCUT MENU WITH SUGGESTED SPELLINGS

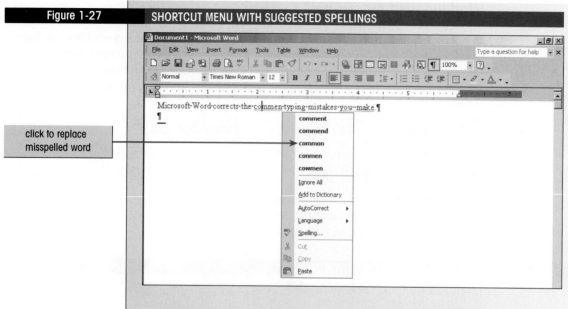

click to replace misspelled word

**TROUBLE?** If the shortcut menu doesn't appear, repeat Step 1, making sure you click the right mouse button, not the left one. If you see a different menu from the one shown in Figure 1-27, you didn't right-click exactly on the underlined word. Press the Esc key to close the menu, and then repeat Step 1.

2. Click **common** in the shortcut menu. The menu disappears, and the correct spelling appears in your document. Notice that the wavy red line disappears after you correct the error.

3. Click to the right of the letter "u" in the word "you". Press the **Delete** key to delete the extra space.

You can see how quick and easy it is to correct common typing errors with AutoCorrect and the Spelling and Grammar checker. Remember, however, to thoroughly proofread each document you create. AutoCorrect will not catch words that are spelled correctly, but used improperly (such as "your" for "you're").

## Proofreading the Letter

Before you can proofread your letter, you need to close the document with the practice sentence. You don't need to save this document, because you only created it to practice correcting errors.

### To close the practice document:

1. Click the **Document Close** button ☒ (on the right end of the menu bar). You see a dialog box asking if you want to save your changes to the document.

2. Click **No**. You return to the document named Web Time Contract Letter.

Now you can proofread the letter for any typos. You can also get rid of the wavy red underline below Megan's last name.

## To respond to possible spelling errors:

1. Scroll down until the signature line is visible. Because Word doesn't recognize "Grahs" as a word, it marked it as a potential error. You need to tell Word to ignore this name wherever it occurs in the letter.

2. Right-click **Grahs**. A shortcut menu opens.

3. Click **Ignore All**. The wavy red underline disappears from below "Grahs".

4. Scroll up to the beginning of the letter, and proofread it for typos. If a word has a wavy red or green underline, right-click it and choose an option in the shortcut menu. To correct other errors, click to the right or left of the error, use the Backspace or Delete key to remove it, and then type a correction.

# Inserting a Date with AutoComplete

The beauty of using a word processing program such as Microsoft Word is that you can easily make changes to text you have already typed. In this case, you need to insert the current date at the beginning of the letter. Megan tells you that she wants to send the contract to Web Time Productions on February 21, so you need to insert that date into the letter now.

Before you can enter the date, you need to move the insertion point to the right location. In a standard business letter, the date belongs approximately 2.5 inches from the top. (As you recall, this is where you started the inside address earlier.) You also need to insert some blank lines to allow enough space between the date and the inside address.

## To move the insertion point and add some blank lines:

1. Scroll up to display the top of the document.

2. Click to the left of the "N" in "Nicholas Brower," in the inside address. The status bar indicates that the insertion point is on line 9, 2.5 inches from the top. (Your status bar might show slightly different measurements.) You might see a square with a lowercase "i" displayed just above the name. Ignore this for now. You'll learn about this special button (called a Smart Tag Actions button) later in this tutorial.

3. Press **Enter** four times, and then press the ↑ key four times. Now the insertion point is positioned at line 9, with three blank lines between the inside address and the line where you will insert the date. See Figure 1-28.

| Figure 1-28 | POSITION OF INSERTION POINT |
|---|---|

insert date here

three blank lines
between date and
inside address

Nicholas·Brower,·President¶
Web·Time·Productions¶
2210·West·Sycamore·Avenue¶
Chicago,·IL·60025¶

You're ready to insert the date. To do this you can take advantage of Word's **AutoComplete** feature, which automatically inserts dates and other regularly used items for you. In this case, you can type the first few characters of the month, and let Word insert the rest. (This only works for long month names like February.)

## To insert the date:

1. Type **Febr** (the first four letters of February). A small yellow box, called an AutoComplete suggestion, appears above the line, as shown in Figure 1-29. If you wanted to type something other than February, you could continue typing to complete the word. In this case, though, you want to accept the AutoComplete tip, so you will press the Enter key in the next step.

| Figure 1-29 | AUTOCOMPLETE SUGGESTION |
|---|---|

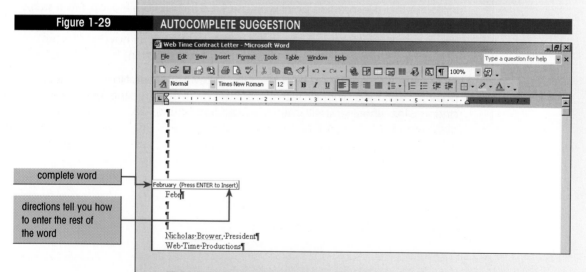

complete word

directions tell you how
to enter the rest of
the word

February  (Press ENTER to Insert)
Febr¶

Nicholas·Brower,·President¶
Web·Time·Productions¶

**TROUBLE?** If the AutoComplete tip doesn't appear, this feature may not be active. Click Tools on the menu bar, click AutoCorrect Options, click the AutoText tab, click the "Show AutoComplete suggestions" check box to insert a check, and then click OK.

2. Press **Enter**. The rest of the word "February" is inserted in the document.

**3.** Press the **spacebar** and then type **21, 2003**.

> **TROUBLE?** If February happens to be the current month, you will see an AutoComplete suggestion displaying the current date after you press the spacebar. To accept that AutoComplete tip, press Enter. Otherwise type the rest of the date as instructed in Step 3.

**4.** Click one of the blank lines below the date. Depending on how your computer is set up, you may see a dotted underline below the date. (You will learn the meaning of this underline in the next section.) You have finished entering the date. See Figure 1-30.

| Figure 1-30 | DATE ENTERED IN THE DOCUMENT |
| --- | --- |

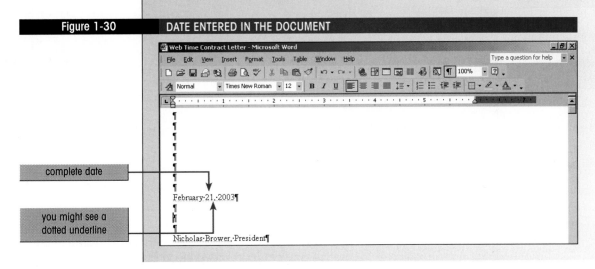

complete date

you might see a dotted underline

February·21,·2003¶

Nicholas·Brower,·President¶

## Removing **Smart Tags**

A dotted underline below a date, name, or address indicates that Word has inserted a Smart Tag in the document. A **Smart Tag** is a feature that that allows you to perform actions (such as sending e-mail or scheduling a meeting) that would normally require a completely different program. Word attaches Smart Tag Action buttons to certain kinds of text, including dates and names. You can click this button to open a menu (similar to a shortcut menu) where you can select commands related to that item. (For example, you might click a Smart Tag on a name to add that name to your e-mail address book.) You don't really need Smart Tags in this document, though, so you will delete them. (Your computer may not be set up to show Smart Tags at all, or it might show them on dates and addresses, but not names. If you do not see any Smart Tags in your document, simply read the following steps.)

### To remove the Smart Tags from the document:

**1.** If you see a dotted underline below the date, position the mouse pointer over the date. A Smart Tag icon ⊙ appears over the date.

**2.** Move the mouse pointer over the Smart Tag icon. The Smart Tag Actions button ⊙▾ appears, as shown in Figure 1-31.

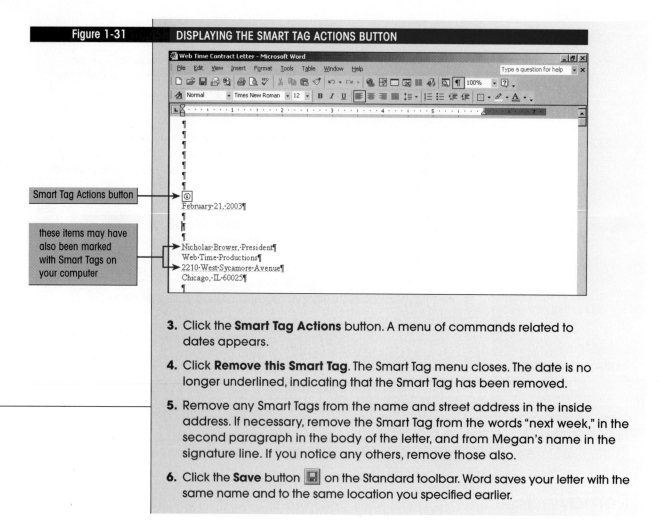

**Figure 1-31**   DISPLAYING THE SMART TAG ACTIONS BUTTON

Smart Tag Actions button

these items may have also been marked with Smart Tags on your computer

3. Click the **Smart Tag Actions** button. A menu of commands related to dates appears.

4. Click **Remove this Smart Tag**. The Smart Tag menu closes. The date is no longer underlined, indicating that the Smart Tag has been removed.

5. Remove any Smart Tags from the name and street address in the inside address. If necessary, remove the Smart Tag from the words "next week," in the second paragraph in the body of the letter, and from Megan's name in the signature line. If you notice any others, remove those also.

6. Click the **Save** button 🖫 on the Standard toolbar. Word saves your letter with the same name and to the same location you specified earlier.

# Previewing and Printing a Document

Do you think the letter is ready to print? You could find out by clicking the Print button on the Standard toolbar and then reviewing the printed page. In doing so, however, you risk wasting paper and printer time. For example, if you failed to insert enough space for the company letterhead, you would have to add more space, and then print the letter all over again. To avoid wasting paper and time, you should first display the document in the Print Preview window. By default, the Print Preview window shows you the full page; there's no need to scroll through the document.

## To preview the document:

1. Click the **Print Preview** button 🔍 on the Standard toolbar. The Print Preview window opens and displays a full-page version of your letter, as shown in Figure 1-32. This shows how the letter will fit on the printed page. The Print Preview toolbar includes a number of buttons that are useful for making changes that affect the way the printed page will look.

| Figure 1-32 | FULL PAGE DISPLAYED IN PRINT PREVIEW WINDOW |
| --- | --- |

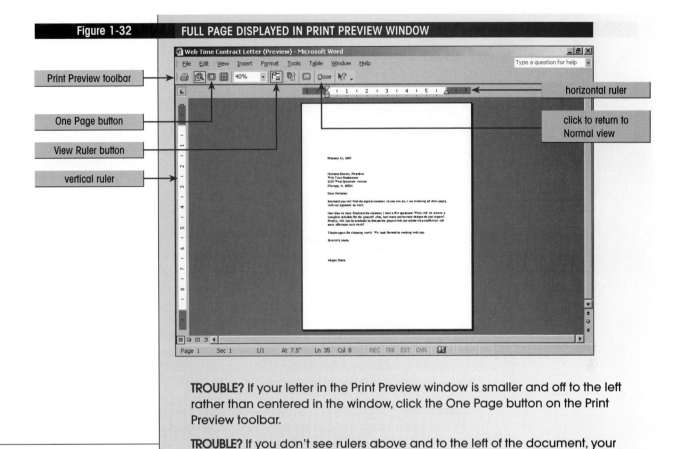

Print Preview toolbar

One Page button

View Ruler button

vertical ruler

horizontal ruler

click to return to Normal view

**TROUBLE?** If your letter in the Print Preview window is smaller and off to the left rather than centered in the window, click the One Page button on the Print Preview toolbar.

**TROUBLE?** If you don't see rulers above and to the left of the document, your rulers are not displayed. To show the rulers in the Print Preview window, click the View Rulers button on the Print Preview toolbar.

**2.** Click **Close** on the Print Preview toolbar to return to Normal view.

Note that it is especially important to preview documents if your computer is connected to a network so that you don't keep a shared printer tied up with unnecessary printing. In this case, the text looks well spaced and the letterhead will fit at the top of the page. You're ready to print the letter.

When printing a document, you have two choices. You can use the Print command on the File menu, which opens the Print dialog box in which you can adjust some printer settings. Or, if you prefer, you can use the Print button on the Standard toolbar, which prints the document using default settings, without opening a dialog box. In these tutorials, the first time you print from a shared computer, you should check the settings in the Print dialog box and make sure the number of copies is set to one. After that, you can use the Print button.

### To print a document:

**1.** Make sure your printer is turned on and contains paper.

**2.** Click **File** on the menu bar, and then click **Print**. The Print dialog box opens. See Figure 1-33.

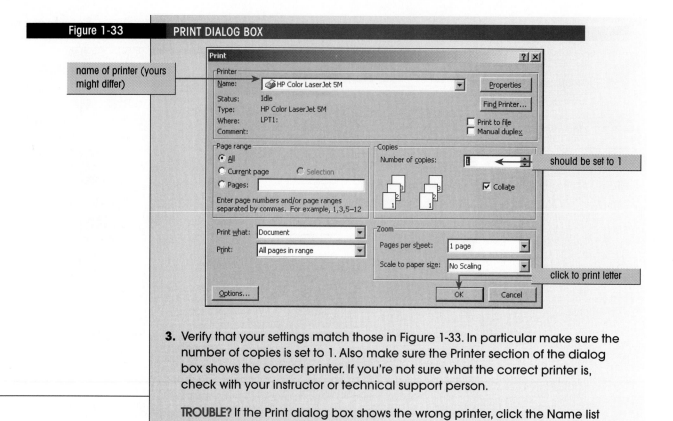

Figure 1-33    PRINT DIALOG BOX

name of printer (yours might differ)

should be set to 1

click to print letter

3. Verify that your settings match those in Figure 1-33. In particular make sure the number of copies is set to 1. Also make sure the Printer section of the dialog box shows the correct printer. If you're not sure what the correct printer is, check with your instructor or technical support person.

   **TROUBLE?** If the Print dialog box shows the wrong printer, click the Name list arrow, and then select the correct printer from the list of available printers.

4. Click **OK**. Assuming your computer is attached to a printer, the letter prints.

Your printed letter should look similar to Figure 1-14, but without the Art4U letterhead. The word wraps, or line breaks, might not appear in the same places on your letter because the size and spacing of characters vary slightly from one printer to the next.

## Creating an Envelope

After you print the letter, Megan stops by your desk and asks you to print an envelope in which to mail the contracts. Creating an envelope is a simple process because Word automatically uses the inside address from the letter as the address on the envelope.

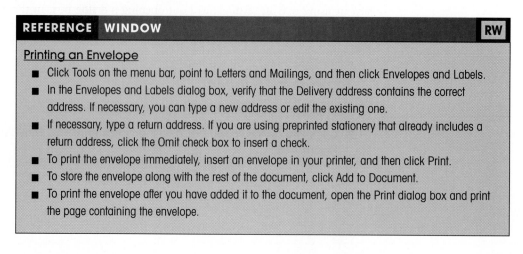

**REFERENCE WINDOW**    **RW**

Printing an Envelope
- Click Tools on the menu bar, point to Letters and Mailings, and then click Envelopes and Labels.
- In the Envelopes and Labels dialog box, verify that the Delivery address contains the correct address. If necessary, you can type a new address or edit the existing one.
- If necessary, type a return address. If you are using preprinted stationery that already includes a return address, click the Omit check box to insert a check.
- To print the envelope immediately, insert an envelope in your printer, and then click Print.
- To store the envelope along with the rest of the document, click Add to Document.
- To print the envelope after you have added it to the document, open the Print dialog box and print the page containing the envelope.

Megan tells you that your printer is not currently stocked with envelopes. She asks you to create the envelope and add it to the document. Then she will print the envelope later, when she is ready to mail the contracts to Web Time Productions.

## To create an envelope:

1. Click **Tools** on the menu bar, point to **Letters and Mailings**, and then click **Envelopes and Labels**. The Envelopes and Labels dialog box opens, as shown in Figure 1-34. By default, Word uses the inside address from the letter as the delivery address. Depending on how your computer is set up, you might see an address in the Return address box. Since you will be using Art4U's printed envelopes, you don't need to include a return address on this envelope.

| Figure 1-34 | ENVELOPES AND LABELS DIALOG BOX |

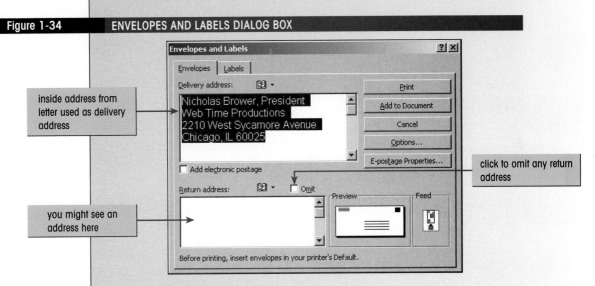

inside address from letter used as delivery address

click to omit any return address

you might see an address here

2. Click the **Omit** check box to insert a check, if necessary.

3. Click **Add to Document**. The dialog box closes, and you return to the Document window. The envelope is inserted at the top of the document, above a double line with the words "Section Break (Next Page)". The double line indicates that the envelope and the letter are two separate parts of the document. The envelope will print in the standard business envelope format. The letter will still print on standard 8.5 × 11-inch paper. (You'll have a chance to actually print an envelope in the exercises at the end of this tutorial.)

4. Click the **Save** button 🖫 on the Standard toolbar.

Congratulations on creating your first letter in Microsoft Word. Since you are finished with the letter and the envelope, you can close the document and exit Word.

## To close the document and exit Word:

1. Click the **Close** button ☒ in the menu bar. The Web Time Contract Letter closes.

   **TROUBLE?** If you see a dialog box with the message "Do you want to save the changes to 'Web Time Contract Letter?'", you didn't save your most recent changes. Click Yes.

**2.** If necessary, close other open documents without saving them.

**3.** Click the **Close** button ☒ in the upper-right corner of the Word window. Word closes, and you return to the Windows desktop.

## Session 1.2 QUICK CHECK

1. Explain how to save a document for the first time.
2. Explain how to enter the name of a month using AutoCorrect.
3. Explain how word wrap works in a Word document.
4. List the steps required to print an envelope.
5. In your own words, define each of the following:
   a. Scrolling
   b. AutoComplete
   c. AutoCorrect
   d. Print Preview
   e. Smart Tag

## REVIEW ASSIGNMENTS

Megan received an e-mail from Nicholas Brower at Web Time Productions, confirming their plans for a conference call. Megan has e-mailed the graphic artists at Art4U, informing them about the call. To make sure everyone remembers, she would like you to post a memo on the bulletin board in the break room. Create the memo shown in Figure 1-35 by completing the following steps.

**Figure 1-35**

Art4U, Inc.
1921 Sedona Avenue
Tucson, AZ 85701
Art4U@WorldNet.com

TO:            Art4U Staff Artists

FROM:       Megan Grahs

DATE:        February 27, 2003

SUBJECT:   Conference Call

Please plan to join us for a conference call at 3 P.M. on Friday, March 1. Nicholas Brower, president of Web Time Productions, will be taking part, as will five of the company's most experienced Web page designers. This will be your chance to ask the designers some important questions.

You will be able to join the call from your desk by dialing an 800 number and a special access code. You'll receive both of these numbers via e-mail the day of the call.

1. If necessary, start Word and make sure your Data Disk is in the appropriate disk drive, and then check your screen to make sure your settings match those in the tutorials. In particular, make sure that nonprinting characters are displayed.

2. If the Office Assistant is open, hide it.

3. Click the New Blank Document button on the Standard toolbar to open a new document.

4. Press the Enter key eight times to insert enough space for the company letterhead.

5. Press the Caps Lock key, and then type "TO:" in capital letters.

*Explore* ▶ 6. You can use the Tab key to align text as a column. In this case, you want to align the To, From, Date, and Subject information. To begin, press the Tab key three times. Word inserts three nonprinting characters (right-pointing arrows), one for each time you pressed the Tab key.

7. Press the Caps Lock key to turn off capitalization, and then type "Art4U Staff Artists".

8. Press the Enter key twice, type "FROM:", press the Tab key twice, and then type your name in lowercase. Throughout the rest of this exercise, use the Caps Lock key as necessary to turn capitalization on and off.

9. Press the Enter key twice, type "DATE:", and then press the Tab key three times.

*Explore* ▶ 10. You can take advantage of AutoCorrect to type the current date. To try it now, type the name of the current month. If an AutoCorrect suggestion appears, press Enter to complete the name of the month; otherwise, continue typing. Press the spacebar. After you press the spacebar, an AutoCorrect suggestion appears with the current date. Press Enter to accept the suggestion.

11. Press the Enter key twice, type "SUBJECT:" and then press the Tab key two times. Type "Conference Call" and then press the Enter key twice.

12. Continue typing the rest of the memo as shown in Figure 1-35. (You will have a chance to correct any typing errors later.) Ignore any AutoCorrect suggestions that are not relevant to the text you are typing.

13. Save your work as **Conference Call Memo** in the Review folder for Tutorial 1.

14. Scroll to the beginning of the document and proofread your work.

15. Correct any misspelled words marked by wavy red lines. If the correct spelling of a word does not appear in the list box, press the Escape key to close the list, and then make the correction yourself. Remove any red wavy lines below words that are actually spelled correctly. Then correct any grammatical or other errors indicated by wavy green lines. Use the Backspace or Delete key to delete any extra words or spaces.

16. Remove any Smart Tags.

17. Save your most recent changes.

18. Preview and print the memo.

19. Close the document. Save any changes if necessary.

*Explore* ▶ 20. If you will be sending mail to someone regularly, it's helpful to add an envelope to a blank document, and then save the document, so that you can print the envelope in the future, whenever you need it. Open a new, blank document. Create an envelope for Nicholas Brower at Web Time Productions. Use the address you used as the inside address in the tutorial. For the return address, type your own address. Add the envelope to the document. If you are asked if you want to save the return address as the new default return address, click No. If your computer is connected to a printer that is stocked with envelopes, click File on the menu bar, click Print, click the Pages option button, type 1 in the Pages text box, and then click OK.

21. Save the document as **Web Time Envelope** in the Review folder for Tutorial 1.

22. Close any open documents and then exit Word.

## CASE PROBLEMS

### Case 1. Letter to Request Information about a Field Trip to Roaring Rapids Water Park

You are a teacher at Luis Sotelo Elementary School. Your students have been raising money all year for a trip to Roaring Rapids Water Park. Before you can plan the outing, you need to write for some information. Create the letter by doing the following:

1. If necessary, start Word, make sure your Data Disk is in the appropriate disk drive, and check your screen to make sure your settings match those in the tutorials.

2. Open a new blank document.

3. Type your name, press Enter, and then type the following address:

   Luis Sotelo Elementary School

   1521 First Avenue

   Durham, North Carolina 27701

*Explore*

4. Press the Enter key four times, and then type the name of the current month. (If an AutoCorrect suggestion appears, press Enter to complete the name of the month.) Press the spacebar. After you press the spacebar, an AutoCorrect suggestion appears with the current date. Press Enter to accept the suggestion.

5. Press the Enter key four times after the date, and, using the proper business letter format, type the inside address: "Scott Rowland, Roaring Rapids Water Park, 2344 West Prairie Street, Durham, North Carolina 27704".

6. Double space after the inside address (that is, press the Enter Key twice), type the salutation "Dear Mr. Rowland:" and then insert another blank line. Close the Office Assistant if it opens.

7. Type the first paragraph as follows: "I'd like some information about a class field trip to Roaring Rapids Water Park. Please answer the following questions:"

8. Save your work as **Water Park Information Letter** in the Cases folder for Tutorial 1.

9. Insert one blank line, and then type these questions on separate lines with one blank line between each:
   How much is a day pass for a 10-year-old child?
   How much is a day pass for an adult?
   Can you offer a discount for a group of 25 children and 5 adults?
   Are lockers available for storing clothes and other belongings?

10. Correct any typing errors indicated by wavy lines. (*Hint*: Because "Sotelo" is spelled correctly, click Ignore All on the shortcut menu to remove the wavy red line under the word "Sotelo" and prevent Word from marking the word as a misspelling.)

11. Insert another blank line at the end of the letter, and type the complimentary closing "Sincerely," (include the comma).

12. Press the Enter key four times to leave room for the signature, and type your full name. Then press the Enter key and type "Luis Sotelo Elementary School". Notice that "Sotelo" is not marked as a spelling error this time.

13. Scroll up to the beginning of the document, and then remove any Smart Tags in the letter.

14. Save your changes to the letter, and then preview it using the Print Preview button.

15. Print the letter, close the document, and exit Word.

### Case 2. Letter to Confirm Food Service During the National Purchasing Management Association Conference

As catering director for the Madison Convention and Visitors Bureau, you are responsible for managing food service at the city's convention center. The National Physical Therapy Association has scheduled a daily breakfast buffet during its annual convention (which runs July 6–10, 2003). You need to write a letter confirming plans for the daily buffet.

Create the letter using the skills you learned in the tutorial. Remember to include today's date, the inside address, the salutation, the date of the reservation, the complimentary closing, and your name and title. If the instructions show quotation marks around text you type, do not include the quotation marks in your letter. To complete the letter, do the following:

1. If necessary, start Word, make sure your Data Disk is in the appropriate disk drive, and check your screen to make sure your settings match those in the tutorials.

2. Open a new, blank document and press the Enter key until the insertion point is positioned about 2 inches from the top of the page. (Remember that you can see the exact position of the insertion point, in inches, in the status bar.)

3. Enter "June 6, 2003" as the date.

4. Press the Enter key four times after the date, and, using the proper business letter format, type the inside address: "Charles Quade, National Physical Therapy Association, 222 Sydney Street, Whitewater, WI 57332".

5. Double space after the inside address (that is, press the Enter key twice), type the salutation "Dear Mr. Quade:", and then double space again. If the Office Assistant opens, close it.

6. Write one paragraph confirming the daily breakfast buffets for July 6–10, 2003.

7. Insert a blank line and type the complimentary closing "Sincerely,".

8. Press the Enter key four times to leave room for the signature, and then type your name and title.

9. Save the letter as **Confirmation Letter** in the Cases folder for Tutorial 1.

10. Remove any Smart Tags. Reread your letter carefully, and correct any errors.

11. Save any new changes, and then preview and print the letter.

*Explore* 12. Create an envelope for the letter, and add it to the document. For the return address, type your own address. Add the envelope to the document. If you are asked if you want to save the return address as the new default return address, click No. If your computer is connected to a printer that is stocked with envelopes, click File on the menu bar, click Print, click the Pages option button, type 1 in the Pages text box, and then click OK.

13. Save your work and close the document, then exit Word.

*Case 3. Letter Congratulating a Professor* Liza Morgan, a professor of e-commerce at Kentucky State University, was recently honored by the Southern Business Council for her series of free public seminars on developing Web sites for nonprofit agencies. She also was recently named Teacher of the Year by a national organization called Woman in Technology. As one of her former students, you need to write a letter congratulating her on these honors. To write this letter, do the following:

1. If necessary, start Word, make sure your Data Disk is in the appropriate disk drive, and check your screen to make sure your settings match those in the tutorials.

2. Write a brief letter congratulating Professor Morgan on her awards. Remember to use the four-part planning process. You should plan the content, organization, and style of the letter, and use a standard letter format. For the inside address, use the following: Professor Liza Morgan, Department of Business Administration, Kentucky State University, 1010 College Drive, Frankfort, Kentucky 40601.

3. Save the document as **Liza Morgan Letter** in the Cases folder for Tutorial 1.

4. Correct any typing errors, remove any Smart Tags, and then preview and print the memo.

*Explore* 5. Create an envelope for the letter, and add it to the document. For the return address, type your own address. Add the envelope to the document. If you are asked if you want to save the return address as the new default return address, click No. If your computer is connected to a printer that is stocked with envelopes, click File on the menu bar, click Print, click the Pages option button, type 1 in the Pages text box, and then click OK.

6. Save the document and close it, and then exit Word.

*Case 4. Memo Created With a Template*  You are the office manager for Head for the Hills, a small company that sells hiking equipment over the Internet. The company has just moved to a new building which requires a special security key card after hours. Some employees have had trouble getting the key cards to work properly. You decide to hold a meeting to explain the security policies for the new building and to demonstrate the key cards. But first you need to post a memo announcing the meeting. The recently ordered letterhead (with the company's new address) has not yet arrived, so you will use a Word template to create the memo. Word provides templates—that is, models with predefined formatting—to help you create complete documents (including a professional-looking letterhead) quickly. To create the memo, do the following:

1. If necessary, start Word, make sure your Data Disk is in the appropriate disk drive, and check your screen to make sure your settings match those in the tutorials.

*Explore*  2. If the Task Pane is not displayed, click View on the menu bar, and then click Task Pane. The Task Pane is displayed on the right side of the Word window. You see a number of options related to creating new documents.

*Explore*  3. Under "New from template," click General Templates. The Templates dialog box opens.

*Explore*  4. Click the Memos tab, click Professional Memo, and then click the OK button. A memo template opens containing generic, placeholder text that you can replace with your own information.

5. Make sure the template is displayed in Normal View. Click at the end of the line "Company Name Here" (at the top of the document), press Backspace to delete the text, and type "Head for the Hills".

6. Click the text "Click here and type name," and in the To: line, type "All Employees". After "From," replace the current text with your name.

7. Click after "CC:" and then press Delete to delete the placeholder text. Use the Backspace key to delete the entire "CC" line. Note that Word inserts the current date automatically after the heading "Date."

8. After "Re:" type "Meeting to discuss building security".

9. Delete the placeholder text in the body of the letter, and replace it with a paragraph announcing the meeting, which is scheduled for tomorrow at 2 P.M. in the Central Conference Room.

10. Save the letter as **Meeting Memo** (in the Cases folder for Tutorial 1).

*Explore*  11. The memo text is in a small font, which is hard to read. To make it easier to review your work, you can change the Zoom setting in Normal view. Click the Zoom list arrow in the Standard toolbar, and then click 150%.

12. Review the memo. Correct any typos and delete any Smart Tags. Save the memo again, preview it, and then print it.

13. Close the document and exit Word.

## LAB ASSIGNMENTS

Word Processing

The New Perspectives Labs are designed to help you master some of the key computer concepts and skills presented in each chapter of the text. If you are using your school's lab computers, your instructor or technical support person should have installed the Labs software for you. If you want to use the Labs on your home computer, ask your instructor for the appropriate software. See the Read This Before You Begin page for more information on installing and starting the Lab.

Each Lab has two parts: Steps and Explore. Use Steps first to learn and review concepts. Read the information on each page and do the numbered steps. As you work through the Lab, you will be asked to answer Quick Check questions about what you have learned. At the end of the Lab, you will see a Summary Report of your answers to the Quick Checks. If your instructor wants you to turn in this Summary Report, click the Print button on the Summary Report screen.

When you have completed the Steps, you can click the Explore button to complete the Lab Assignments. You also can use Explore to practice the skills you learned and to explore concepts on your own.

*Word Processing* Word-processing software is the most popular computerized productivity tool. In this Lab you will learn how word-processing software works. When you have completed this Lab, you should be able to apply the general concepts you learned to any word-processing package you use at home, at work, or in your school lab.

1. Click the Steps button to learn how word-processing software works. As you proceed through the Steps, answer all of the Quick Check questions that appear. After you complete the Steps, you will see a Quick Check Summary Report. Follow the instructions on the screen to print this report.

2. Click the Explore button to begin. Click File, and then click Open to display the Open dialog box. Click the file **Timber.tex**, and then press the Enter key to open the letter to Northern Timber Company. Make the following modifications to the letter, and then print it. You do not need to save the letter.
   a. In the first and last lines of the letter, change "Jason Kidder" to your name.
   b. Change the date to today's date.
   c. The second paragraph begins "Your proposal did not include…". Move this paragraph so it is the last paragraph in the text of the letter.
   d. Change the cost of a permanent bridge to $20,000.
   e. Spell check the letter.

3. In Explore, open the file **Stars.tex**. Make the following modifications to the document and then print it. You do not need to save the document.
   a. Center and boldface the title.
   b. Change the title font to size —16-point Arial.
   c. Boldface the DATE, SHOWER, and LOCATION.
   d. Move the January 2–3 line to the top of the list.
   e. Double-space the entire document.

4. In Explore, compose a one-page double-spaced letter to your parents or to a friend. Make sure you date the letter and check your spelling. Print the letter and sign it. You do not need to save your letter.

## INTERNET ASSIGNMENTS

**Student Union**

The purpose of the Internet Assignments is to challenge you to find information on the Internet that you can use to create effective documents. The actual assignments are updated and maintained on the Course Technology Web site. Log on to the Internet and use your Web browser to go to the Student Union on the New Perspectives Series site at **www.course.com/NewPerspectives/studentunion**. Click the Online Companions link, and then click the link for this text.

# QUICK CHECK ANSWERS

*Session 1.1*

**1.** (1) Plan the content, purpose, organization, and look of your document. (2) Create and then edit the document. (3) Format the document to make it visually appealing. (4) Preview and then print the document.

**2.** Click the Start button, point to Programs, and then click Microsoft Word.

**3. a.** symbols you can display on-screen but that don't print
  **b.** buttons to the left of the horizontal status bar that switch the document to Normal view, Web Layout view, Print Layout view, or Outline view
  **c.** actual height of a character measured in points
  **d.** standard settings

**4.** Click Format on the menu bar, click Font, select the font size in the Size list box, click the Default button, and then click Yes.

**5.** Right-click a toolbar, and then click Formatting on the shortcut menu.

**6.** Click the Normal View button.

**7.** False

*Session 1.2*

**1.** Click the Save button on the Standard toolbar, switch to the drive and folder where you want to save the document, enter a filename in the File name text box, and then click the Save button.

**2.** Type the first few characters of the month. When an AutoCorrect suggestion appears, press the Enter key.

**3.** When you type a word that extends into the right margin, Word moves that word and the insertion point to the next line.

**4.** Click Tools on the menu bar, point to Letters and Mailings, and then click Envelopes and Labels. In the Envelopes and Labels dialog box, verify that the Delivery address contains the correct address. If necessary, you can type a new address or edit the existing one. If necessary, type a return address. If you are using preprinted stationery that already includes a return address, click the Omit check box to insert a check. To print the envelope immediately, insert an envelope in your printer, and click Print. To store the envelope along with the rest of the document, click Add to Document. To print the envelope after you have added it to the document, open the Print dialog box and print the page containing the envelope.

**5. a.** The means by which text at the bottom of the document shifts out of view when you display the top of the document, and text at the top shifts out of view when you display the bottom of the document.
  **b.** A feature that automatically enters dates and other regularly used items.
  **c.** A feature that fixes common typing errors automatically.
  **d.** A window in which you can see how the document will look when printed.
  **e.** A feature that that allows you to perform actions (such as sending e-mail or scheduling a meeting) that would normally require a completely different program. Word attaches Smart Tag Action buttons to certain kinds of text, including dates and names.

OBJECTIVES

In this tutorial you will:

- Check spelling and grammar

- Move the insertion point around the document

- Select and delete text

- Reverse edits using the Undo and Redo buttons

- Move text within the document

- Find and replace text

- Change margins, line spacing, alignment, and paragraph indents

- Copy formatting with the Format Painter

- Change fonts and adjust font sizes

- Emphasize points with bullets, numbering, boldface, underlining, and italics

- Add a comment to a document

# EDITING AND FORMATTING A DOCUMENT

*Preparing a FAQ Document for Long Meadow Gardens*

CASE

## Long Meadow Gardens

Marilee Brigham is the owner of Long Meadow Gardens, a landscape and gardening supply company. The firm's large nursery provides shrubs and trees to professional landscape contractors throughout the Minneapolis/St. Paul area. At the same time, Long Meadow's retail store caters to home gardeners, who often call the store with questions about planting and caring for their purchases.

Marilee has noticed that retail customers tend to ask the same set of questions. To save time in answering these questions, she would like a series of handouts designed to answer these common questions. (Such a document is sometimes known as a FAQ—which is short for "frequently asked questions.") The company's chief horticulturist, Peter Chi, has just finished creating a FAQ containing information on planting trees. Now that Marilee has commented on and corrected the draft, Peter asks you to make the necessary changes and print the document.

In this tutorial, you will edit the FAQ according to Marilee's comments. You will open a draft of the document, resave it, and edit it. You will check the document's grammar and spelling, and then move text using two different methods. You will also find and replace one version of the company name with another.

Next, you will change the overall look of the document by changing margins and line spacing, indenting and justifying paragraphs, and copying formatting from one paragraph to another. You'll create a bulleted list to emphasize the species of water-tolerant trees and a numbered list for the steps involved in removing the burlap from around the base of a tree. Then you'll make the title more prominent by centering it, changing its font, and enlarging it. You'll add boldface to the questions to set them off from the rest of the text and underline an added note about how to get further information. Finally, you will add a comment, and then print the FAQ document.

## SESSION 2.1

In this session you will learn how to use the Spelling and Grammar checker to correct any errors in your document. You will also learn how to undo and redo changes in a document. Then you will edit the draft of the FAQ document by deleting words and moving text. Finally, you'll find and replace text throughout the document.

## Reviewing the Document

Marilee's editing marks and notes on the first draft are shown in Figure 2-1. You'll begin by opening the first draft of the document, which has the filename FAQ.

Figure 2-1    DRAFT OF FAQ WITH MARILEE'S EDITS (PAGE 1)

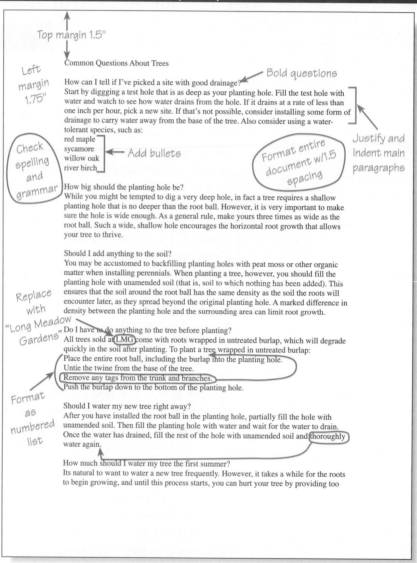

| Figure 2-1 | DRAFT OF FAQ WITH MARILEE'S EDITS (PAGE 2) |
| --- | --- |

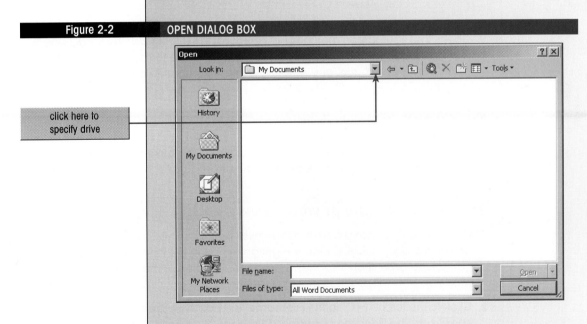

## To open the document:

**1.** Place your Data Disk into the appropriate disk drive.

**2.** Start Word as usual.

**3.** Click the **Open** button 🖻 on the Standard toolbar to display the Open dialog box, shown in Figure 2-2.

| Figure 2-2 | OPEN DIALOG BOX |
| --- | --- |

click here to specify drive

**4.** Click the **Look in** list arrow. The list of drives and files appears.

**5.** Click the drive that contains your Data Disk.

**6.** Double-click the **Tutorial.02** folder, and then double-click the **Tutorial** folder.

**7.** Click **FAQ** to select the file, if necessary.

**TROUBLE?** If you see "FAQ.doc" in the folder, Windows might be configured to display filename extensions. Click FAQ.doc and continue with Step 8. If you can't find the file with or without the filename extension, make sure you're looking in the Tutorial subfolder within the Tutorial.02 folder on the drive that contains your Data Disk, and check to make sure the Files of type text box displays All Word Documents or All Files. If you still can't locate the file, ask your instructor or technical support person for help.

8. Click the **Open** button. The document opens with the insertion point at the beginning of the document. See Figure 2-3.

---

**Figure 2-3**    **OPEN DOCUMENT**

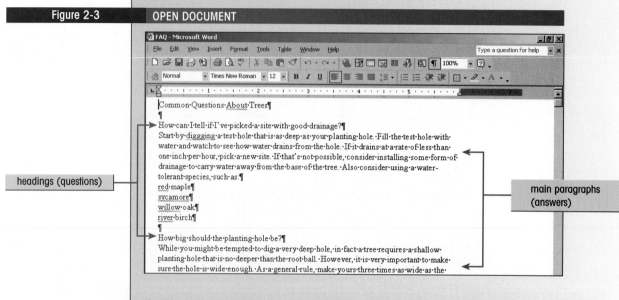

headings (questions)

main paragraphs (answers)

---

9. Check that your screen matches Figure 2-3. For this tutorial, use the Show/Hide ¶ button to display nonprinting characters. This will make formatting elements (tabs, paragraph marks, and so forth) visible and easier to change.

Now that you've opened the document, you can save it with a new name. To avoid altering the original file, FAQ, you will save the document using the filename Tree FAQ. Saving the document with another filename creates a copy of the file and leaves the original file unchanged in case you want to work through the tutorial again.

---

### To save the document with a new name:

1. Click **File** on the menu bar, and then click **Save As**. The Save As dialog box opens with the current filename highlighted in the File name text box. You could type an entirely new filename, or you could edit the current one. In the next step, you will practice editing a filename.

2. Click to the left of "FAQ" in the File name text box, type **Tree**, and then press the **spacebar**. The filename changes to "Tree FAQ."

3. Verify that the Tutorial folder for Tutorial 2 is selected in the Save in box.

4. Click the **Save** button. The document is saved with the new filename.

---

Now you're ready to begin working with the document. First, you will check it for spelling and grammatical errors.

# Using the Spelling and Grammar Checker

When typing a document, you can check for spelling and grammatical errors by looking for words underlined in red (for spelling errors) or green (for grammatical errors). But when you're working on a document that someone else typed, it's a good idea to start by using the Spelling and Grammar checker. This feature automatically checks a document word by word for a variety of errors. Among other things, the Spelling and Grammar checker can sometimes find words that, though spelled correctly, are not used properly. For example, it highlights the word "their" when it is mistakenly used instead of the word "there."

---

**REFERENCE WINDOW**    **RW**

## Checking a Document for Spelling and Grammatical Errors

- Click at the beginning of the document, and then click the Spelling and Grammar button on the Standard toolbar.
- In the Spelling and Grammar dialog box, review any errors highlighted in color. Grammatical errors appear in green; spelling errors appear in red. Review the possible corrections in the Suggestions list box.
- To accept a suggested correction, click on it in the Suggestions list box. Then click Change to make the correction and continue searching the document for errors.
- Click Ignore Once to skip the current instance of the highlighted text and continue searching the document for errors.
- Click Ignore All to skip all instances of the highlighted text and continue searching the document for spelling errors. Click Ignore Rule to skip all instances of a particular grammatical error.
- To type your correction directly in the document, click outside the Spelling and Grammar dialog box, make the correction, and then click Resume in the Spelling and Grammar dialog box.

---

You'll see how the Spelling and Grammar checker works as you check the FAQ document for mistakes.

---

### To check the FAQ document for spelling and grammatical errors:

1. Verify that the insertion point is located at the beginning of the document, to the left of the "C" in "Common Questions."

2. Click the **Spelling and Grammar** button ABC on the Standard toolbar. The Spelling and Grammar dialog box opens with the word "About" highlighted in green, indicating a possible grammatical error. The word "about" (with a lowercase "a") is suggested as a possible replacement. The line immediately under the title bar indicates the type of possible problem, in this case, Capitalization. See Figure 2-4. Normally, prepositions of fewer than six letters are not capitalized in titles. But Marilee prefers to keep this word capitalized because she thinks it makes the title look better.

   TROUBLE? If you see the word "diggging" selected instead of "About", your computer is not set up to check grammar. Click the Check grammar check box to insert a check, and then click Cancel to close the Spelling and Grammar dialog box. Next, click at the beginning of the document, and then repeat Step 2.

**Figure 2-4** | SPELLING AND GRAMMAR DIALOG BOX

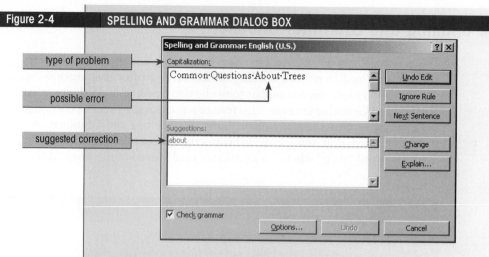

3. Click the **Ignore Rule** button. The word "diggging" is highlighted in red, with "digging" and "diggings" listed as possible corrections.

4. Verify that "digging" is highlighted in the Suggestions list box, and then click the **Change** button. "Digging" is inserted into the document. The word "horizontall" is highlighted in red.

5. Verify that "horizontal" is highlighted in the Suggestions box, and then click the **Change** button.

At this point the word "composts" is highlighted in green, with "and composts" listed as a possible correction. It's not clear why Word suggests this change, so you need to request an explanation.

### To ask the Spelling and Grammar Checker for an explanation:

1. Click the **Explain** button. The Office Assistant opens, showing an explanation of the rule in question.

2. Read the explanation, and then click the **Ignore Rule** button. The last sentence of the document is highlighted in green. The Office Assistant indicates that the highlighted text is a sentence fragment. In this case, Word is correct. The word "call" lacks a direct object—that is, you need to indicate whom the reader should call. You'll fix this problem later, when you insert your name in this sentence.

3. Click **Ignore Once**. The Office Assistant closes, and you see a message indicating that the spelling and grammar check is complete.

4. Click the **OK** button. The Spelling and Grammar dialog box and the Office Assistant close. You return to the FAQ document.

Although the Spelling and Grammar checker is a useful tool, remember that there is no substitute for careful proofreading. Always take the time to read through your document to check for errors the Spelling and Grammar checker might have missed. Keep in mind that the Spelling and Grammar checker probably won't catch *all* instances of words that are spelled correctly but used improperly. And of course, the Spelling and Grammar checker cannot pinpoint phrases that are confusing or inaccurate. To produce a professional document, you must read it carefully several times, and, if necessary, ask a co-worker to read it, too.

## To proofread the FAQ document:

**1.** Scroll to the beginning of the document and begin proofreading. When you get near the bottom of the document, notice that the word "Too" is used instead of the word "Two" in the paragraph on mulch. See Figure 2-5. You will correct this error later in this tutorial, after you learn how to move the insertion point in a document.

| Figure 2-5 | WORD "TOO" USED INCORRECTLY |

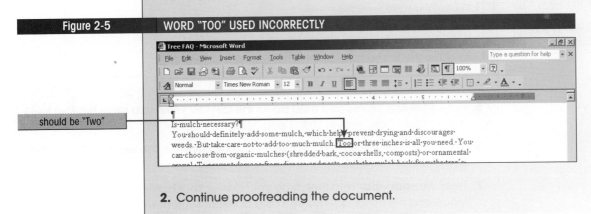

should be "Two"

**2.** Continue proofreading the document.

To make the proofreading corrections, and to make all of Marilee's changes, you need to learn how to move the insertion point quickly to any location in the document.

## Moving the Insertion Point Around a Document

The arrow keys on your keyboard, ↑, ↓, ←, and →, allow you to move the insertion point one character at a time to the left or right, or one line at a time up or down. If you want to move more than one character or one line at a time, you can point and click in other parts of a line or the document. You also can press a combination of keys to move the insertion point. As you become more experienced with Word, you'll decide which method you prefer.

To see how quickly you can move through the document, you'll use keystrokes to move the insertion point to the beginning of the second page and to the end of the document.

## To move the insertion point with keystrokes:

**1.** Press the **Ctrl** key and hold it down while you press the **Home** key. The insertion point moves to the beginning of the document.

**2.** Press the **Page Down** key to move the insertion point down to the next screen.

**3.** Press the **Page Down** key again to move the insertion point down to the next screen. Notice that the status bar indicates the location of the insertion point.

**4.** Press the ↑ or ↓ key to move the insertion point to just below the dotted line that spans the width of the page. The insertion point is now at the beginning of page 2, as shown in Figure 2-6. The dotted line is an **automatic page break** that Word inserts to mark the beginning of the new page. As you insert and delete text or change formatting in a document, the location of the automatic page breaks in your document continually adjust.

**Figure 2-6** | AUTOMATIC PAGE BREAK

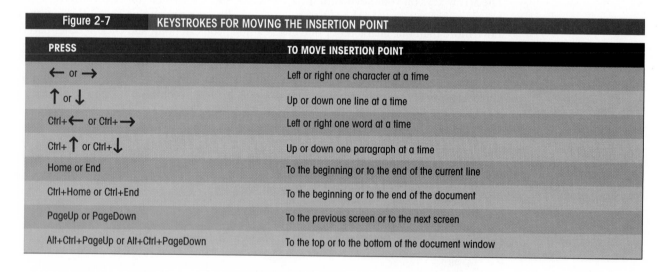

automatic page break

insertion point at the beginning of page 2

5. Press **Ctrl+End**. (Press and hold down the Ctrl key while you press the End key.) The insertion point moves to the end of the document.

6. Use the ← key to position the insertion point between the word "call" and the comma that follows it.

7. Press the **spacebar** and then type your name. Your name completes the sentence and it is no longer marked as a possible sentence fragment.

8. Move the insertion point back to the beginning of the document.

Figure 2-7 summarizes the keystrokes you can use to move the insertion point around the document. When you simply need to display a part of a document, you'll probably want to use the vertical scroll bar. But when you actually need to move the insertion point to a specific spot, it's helpful to use these special keystrokes.

**Figure 2-7** | KEYSTROKES FOR MOVING THE INSERTION POINT

| PRESS | TO MOVE INSERTION POINT |
|---|---|
| ← or → | Left or right one character at a time |
| ↑ or ↓ | Up or down one line at a time |
| Ctrl+← or Ctrl+→ | Left or right one word at a time |
| Ctrl+↑ or Ctrl+↓ | Up or down one paragraph at a time |
| Home or End | To the beginning or to the end of the current line |
| Ctrl+Home or Ctrl+End | To the beginning or to the end of the document |
| PageUp or PageDown | To the previous screen or to the next screen |
| Alt+Ctrl+PageUp or Alt+Ctrl+PageDown | To the top or to the bottom of the document window |

# Selecting **Parts of a Document**

Before you can do anything to text (such as deleting, moving, or formatting it), you often need to highlight, or **select** it. You can select text by using the mouse or the keyboard, although the mouse is usually easier and more efficient. With the mouse you can quickly select a line or paragraph by clicking the **selection bar** (the blank space in the left margin area of the Document window). You can also select text using various combinations of keys.

Figure 2-8 summarizes methods for selecting text with the mouse and the keyboard. The notation "Ctrl+Shift" means you press and hold the two keys at the same time. Note that you will use the methods described in Figure 2-8 as you work on the FAQ document.

| Figure 2-8 | METHODS FOR SELECTING TEXT | | |
| --- | --- | --- | --- |
| **TO SELECT** | **MOUSE** | **KEYBOARD** | **MOUSE AND KEYBOARD** |
| A word | Double-click the word. | Move the insertion point to the beginning of the word, hold down Ctrl+Shift, and then press ⟶. | |
| A line | Click in the selection bar next to the line. | Move the insertion point to the beginning of the line, hold down Ctrl+Shift, and then press ⟶ until the line is selected. | |
| A sentence | | | Press and hold down the Ctrl key, and click within the sentence. |
| Multiple lines | Click and drag in the selection bar next to the lines. | Move the insertion point to the beginning of the first line, hold down Ctrl+Shift, and then press ⟶ until all the lines are selected. | |
| A paragraph | Double-click in the selection bar next to the paragraph, or triple-click within the paragraph. | Move the insertion point to the beginning of the paragraph, hold down Ctrl+Shift, and then press ↓. | |
| Multiple paragraphs | Click and drag in the selection bar next to the paragraphs, or triple-click within the first paragraph and drag. | Move the insertion point to the beginning of the first paragraph, hold down Ctrl+Shift, and then press ↓ until all the paragraphs are selected. | |
| Entire document | Triple-click in the selection bar. | Press Ctrl+A. | Press and hold down the Ctrl key and click in the selection bar. |
| A block of text | Click at the beginning of the block, then drag the pointer until the entire block is selected. | | Click at the beginning of the block, press and hold down the Shift key, and then click at the end of the block. |
| Multiple blocks of text | Press and hold the Ctrl key, then drag the mouse pointer to select multiple blocks of nonadjacent text. | | |

## Deleting Text

When editing a document, you frequently need to delete text. You already have experience using the Backspace and Delete keys to delete a few characters. When you need to delete an entire word or multiple words, it's faster to select the text. After you select the text, you can either replace it with something else by typing over it, or by pressing the Delete key. You need to delete the word "Too" and replace it with "Two," so you'll use the first method now.

*To replace "Too" with "Two":*

1. Press **Ctrl+End**. The insertion point moves to the end of the document.

2. Press and hold the **Ctrl** key while you press ↑ three times. The insertion point is now positioned at the beginning of the paragraph that begins "You should definitely add some mulch." (The status bar indicates that this is line 5 of page 2.)

3. In the second line of the paragraph, double-click the word **Too**. The entire word is highlighted.

4. Type **Two**. The selected word is replaced with the correction. The sentence now correctly reads: "Two or three inches are all you need."

Next, Marilee wants you to delete the phrase "or problems" and the word "any" in the paragraph before the one you've just corrected. Peter explains that you can do this quickly by selecting multiple items and then pressing Delete. As you'll see in the following steps, selecting parts of a document by clicking and dragging takes a little practice, so don't be concerned if you don't get it right the first time. You can always try again.

## To select and delete multiple items:

1. Press ↑ five times. As shown in Figure 2-9, the insertion point is now located in the sentence that begins "To avoid any root damage or problems." The status bar indicates that this is line 1 of page 2.

| Figure 2-9 | TEXT TO BE DELETED |
| --- | --- |

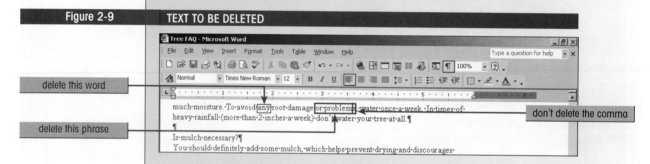

2. Double-click the word **any**. The word and the space following it are selected.

3. Press and hold the **Ctrl** key, and then click and drag to select the phrase "or problems." Do not select the comma after the word "problems". At this point the word "any" and the phrase "or problems" should be selected.

   **TROUBLE?** If you don't get Step 3 right the first time (for instance, if you accidentally selected the word "damage"), click anywhere in the document and then repeat Steps 2 and 3.

4. Press the **Delete** key. The selected items disappear and the words around them move in to fill the space. As you can see in Figure 2-10, you need to delete the extra space before the comma.

   **TROUBLE?** If you deleted the wrong text, click the Undo button (not the Redo button) on the Standard toolbar to reverse your mistake.

| Figure 2-10 | PARAGRAPH AFTER DELETING PHRASE |
| --- | --- |

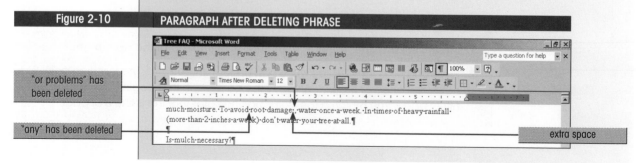

> **TROUBLE?** If your screen looks slightly different than Figure 2-10, don't be concerned. The text may wrap differently on your monitor. Just make sure the text has been deleted.
>
> **5.** Click to the right of the word "damage", and then press the **Delete** key. The extra space is removed.

After rereading the paragraph, Peter wonders if perhaps the text shouldn't have been deleted after all. You can retype the text, but there's an easier way to restore the phrase.

## Using the Undo and Redo Commands

To undo (or reverse) the very last thing you did, click the **Undo button** on the Standard toolbar. If you want to restore your original change, the **Redo button** reverses the action of the Undo button (or redoes the undo). To undo more than your last action, you can click the Undo list arrow on the Standard toolbar. This list shows your most recent actions. Undo reverses the action only at its original location. You can't delete a word or phrase, move the surrounding text, and then undo the deletion at a different location.

You decide to undo the deletion to see how the sentence reads. Rather than retype the phrase, you will reverse the edit using the Undo button.

### To undo the deletion:

**1.** Place the mouse pointer over the Undo button 🔙 on the Standard toolbar. The label "Undo Clear" appears in a ScreenTip, indicating that your most recent action involved deleting (or clearing) something from the document (in this case, a space).

**2.** Click the **Undo** button 🔙 . The space after the word "damage" reappears.

**TROUBLE?** If the space doesn't reappear and something else changes in your document, you probably made another edit or change to the document between the deletion and the undo. Click the Undo button on the Standard toolbar until the space reappears in your document. If a list of possible changes appears under the Undo button, you clicked the list arrow next to the Undo button rather than the Undo button itself. Click the Undo button to restore the deleted phrase and close the list box.

**3.** Click 🔙 again. The deleted text reappears highlighted within the sentence.

**4.** Click in the paragraph to deselect the phrase.

As you read the sentence, you decide that it reads better without the word "any" and the phrase "or problems". Instead of deleting these items again, you'll redo the undo. As you place the pointer over the Redo button, notice that its ScreenTip indicates the action you want to redo.

**5.** Place the mouse pointer over the Redo button 🔜 on the Standard toolbar and observe the "Redo Clear" label.

**6.** Click the **Redo** button 🔜 . The text disappears from the document again.

**7.** Click 🔜 again. The extra space after "damage" disappears again.

**8.** Click the **Save** button 💾 on the Standard toolbar to save your changes to the document.

You have edited the document by replacing "Too" with "Two", and by removing the text that Marilee marked for deletion. Now you are ready to make the rest of the edits she suggested.

# Moving Text Within a Document

One of the most useful features of a word-processing program is the ability to move text. For example, Marilee wants to reorder the four points Peter made in the section "Do I have to do anything to the tree before planting?" on page 1 of his draft. You could reorder the list by deleting the item and then retyping it at a new location, but it's easier to select and then move the text. Word provides several ways to move text: drag and drop, cut and paste, and copy and paste.

## Dragging and Dropping Text

One way to move text within a document is called drag and drop. With **drag and drop**, you select the text you want to move, press and hold down the mouse button while you drag the selected text to a new location, and then release the mouse button.

---

**REFERENCE WINDOW**                                                                      **RW**

**Dragging and Dropping Text**
- Select the text you want to move.
- Press and hold down the mouse button until the drag-and-drop pointer appears, and then drag the selected text to its new location.
- Use the dotted insertion point as a guide to determine exactly where the text will be inserted.
- Release the mouse button to drop the text at the insertion point.

---

Marilee wants you to change the order of the items in the list on page 1 of the document. You'll use the drag-and-drop method to reorder these items. At the same time, you'll practice using the selection bar to highlight a line of text.

---

### To move text using drag and drop:

1. Scroll up until you see "Do I have to do anything to the tree before planting?" (line 29 of page 1). In the list of steps involved in planting a tree, Marilee wants you to move the third step ("Remove any tags from the trunk and branches.") to the top of the list.

2. Move the pointer to the selection bar to the left of the line "Remove any tags from the trunk and branches." The pointer changes from an I-beam ⌶ to a right-facing arrow ⇗.

3. Click to the left of the line "Remove any tags from the trunk and branches." The line is selected. Notice that the paragraph mark at the end of the line is also selected. See Figure 2-11.

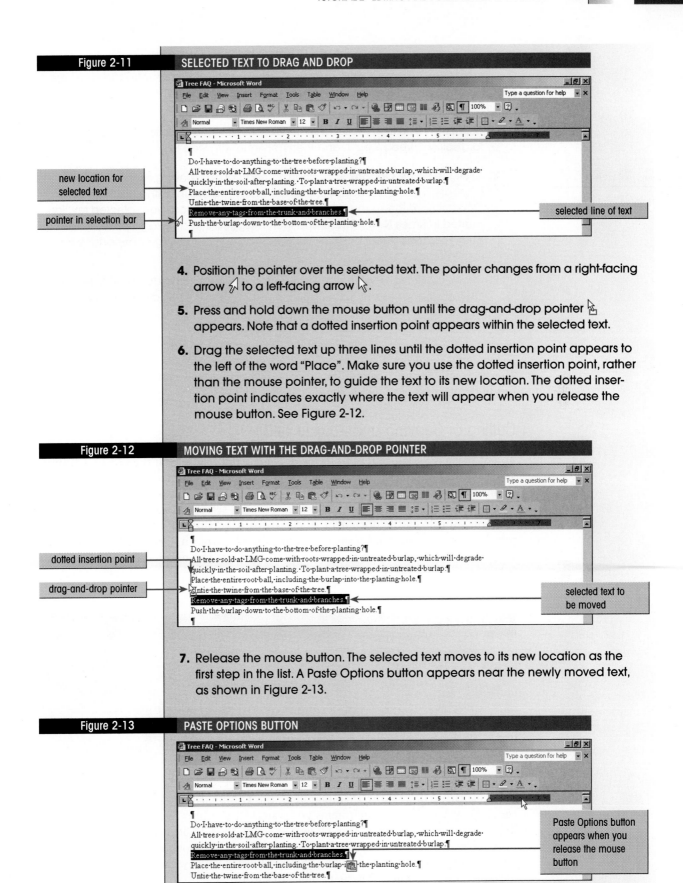

**Figure 2-11**  SELECTED TEXT TO DRAG AND DROP

new location for selected text

pointer in selection bar

selected line of text

**4.** Position the pointer over the selected text. The pointer changes from a right-facing arrow 🔼 to a left-facing arrow 🔼.

**5.** Press and hold down the mouse button until the drag-and-drop pointer 🔼 appears. Note that a dotted insertion point appears within the selected text.

**6.** Drag the selected text up three lines until the dotted insertion point appears to the left of the word "Place". Make sure you use the dotted insertion point, rather than the mouse pointer, to guide the text to its new location. The dotted insertion point indicates exactly where the text will appear when you release the mouse button. See Figure 2-12.

**Figure 2-12**  MOVING TEXT WITH THE DRAG-AND-DROP POINTER

dotted insertion point

drag-and-drop pointer

selected text to be moved

**7.** Release the mouse button. The selected text moves to its new location as the first step in the list. A Paste Options button appears near the newly moved text, as shown in Figure 2-13.

**Figure 2-13**  PASTE OPTIONS BUTTON

Paste Options button appears when you release the mouse button

**TROUBLE?** If the selected text moves to the wrong location, click the Undo button on the Standard toolbar, and then repeat Steps 2 through 7. Be sure you hold the mouse button until the dotted insertion point appears to the left of the word "Place".

**TROUBLE?** If you don't see the Paste Options button, your computer is not set up to display it. Read Step 7, and then continue with Step 8.

8. Click the **Paste Options** 📋 button. A menu of text-moving commands appears. These commands are useful when you are inserting text that looks different from the surrounding text. For instance, suppose you selected text formatted in Times New Roman and then dragged it to a paragraph formatted in Arial. You could then use the Match Destination Formatting command to format the moved text in Arial.

9. Deselect the highlighted text by clicking anywhere in the document. The Paste Options menu closes, but the button remains visible. It will disappear as soon as you perform another task.

Dragging and dropping works well if you're moving text a short distance in a document. However, Word provides another method, called cut and paste, that works well for moving text both long and short distances.

## Cutting or Copying and Pasting Text

To **cut** means to remove text from the document and place it on the **Office Clipboard**, a feature that temporarily stores text or graphics until you need them later. To **paste** means to transfer a copy of the text from the Clipboard into the document at the insertion point. To perform a **cut-and-paste** action, you select the text you want to move, cut (or remove) it from the document, and then paste (or insert) it into the document in a new location. If you don't want to remove the text from its original location, you can copy it (rather than cutting it) and then paste the copy in a new location. This procedure is known as **copy and paste**.

| REFERENCE WINDOW | RW |
|---|---|

**Cutting or Copying and Pasting Text**
- Select the text you want to cut or copy.
- To remove the text, click the Cut button on the Standard toolbar.
- To make a copy of the text, click the Copy button.
- Move the insertion point to the target location in the document.
- Click the Paste button on the Standard toolbar.

If you cut or copy more than one item, the **Clipboard Task Pane** opens, making it easier for you to select which items you want to paste into the document. This special Task Pane contains a list of all the items copied to the Clipboard.

As indicated earlier in Figure 2-1, Marilee suggested moving the word "thoroughly" (in the paragraph under the heading "Should I water my new tree right away?") to a new location. You'll use cut and paste to move this word.

## To move text using cut and paste:

1. If necessary, scroll down until you can see the paragraph below the heading "Should I water my new tree right away?" near the bottom of page 1.

2. Double-click the word **thoroughly**. As you can see in Figure 2-14, you need to move this word to the end of the sentence.

| Figure 2-14 | TEXT TO MOVE USING CUT AND PASTE |
| --- | --- |

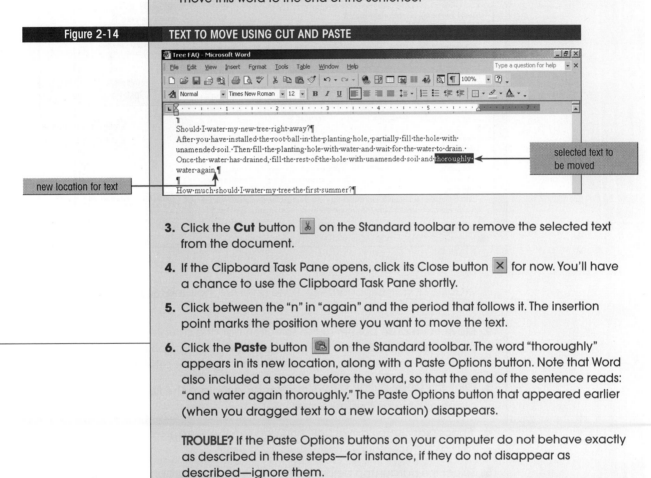

3. Click the **Cut** button ✂ on the Standard toolbar to remove the selected text from the document.

4. If the Clipboard Task Pane opens, click its Close button ✕ for now. You'll have a chance to use the Clipboard Task Pane shortly.

5. Click between the "n" in "again" and the period that follows it. The insertion point marks the position where you want to move the text.

6. Click the **Paste** button 📋 on the Standard toolbar. The word "thoroughly" appears in its new location, along with a Paste Options button. Note that Word also included a space before the word, so that the end of the sentence reads: "and water again thoroughly." The Paste Options button that appeared earlier (when you dragged text to a new location) disappears.

**TROUBLE?** If the Paste Options buttons on your computer do not behave exactly as described in these steps—for instance, if they do not disappear as described—ignore them.

Peter stops by your desk and mentions that he'll be using the paragraph on mulch and the paragraph on watering for the FAQ he plans to write on flowering shrubs. He asks you to copy that information and paste it in a new document that he can use as the basis for the new FAQ. You can do this using copy and paste. This technique is similar to cut and paste. In the process you'll have a chance to use the Clipboard Task Pane.

## To copy and paste text:

1. Click **Edit** on the menu bar, and then click **Office Clipboard**. The Office Clipboard Task Pane opens on the right side of the Document window. It contains the message "Clipboard empty. Copy or cut to collect items." See Figure 2-15.

**Figure 2-15**    CLIPBOARD TASK PANE

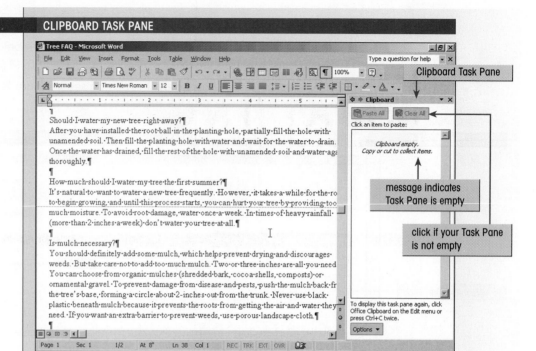

**TROUBLE?** If your Clipboard Task Pane does not show this message, click the Clear All button.

2. Move the mouse pointer to the selection bar and double-click next to the paragraph you edited in the last section (the paragraph that begins "After you have installed the root ball"). The entire paragraph is selected.

3. Click the **Copy** button [icon] on the Standard toolbar. The first part of the paragraph appears in the Task Pane.

4. If necessary, scroll down until you can see the paragraph below the heading "Is mulch necessary?"

5. Select the paragraph below the heading (the paragraph that begins "You should definitely add . . . ").

6. Click [icon]. The first part of the paragraph appears in the Task Pane, as shown in Figure 2-16. An icon appears in the Windows taskbar indicating that the Clipboard Task Pane is currently active.

| Figure 2-16 | ITEMS IN THE CLIPBOARD TASK PANE |
| --- | --- |

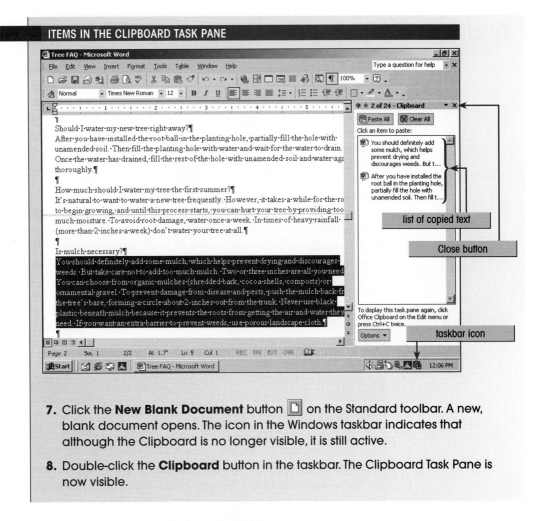

**7.** Click the **New Blank Document** button 🗋 on the Standard toolbar. A new, blank document opens. The icon in the Windows taskbar indicates that although the Clipboard is no longer visible, it is still active.

**8.** Double-click the **Clipboard** button in the taskbar. The Clipboard Task Pane is now visible.

Now you can use the Clipboard Task Pane to insert the copied text into the new document.

## To insert the copied text into the new document:

**1.** In the Clipboard Task Pane, click the item that begins "You should definitely add . . ." The text is inserted in the document.

**2.** Press **Enter** to insert a blank line, and then click the item that begins "After you have installed the root ball . . ." in the Task Pane. The text is inserted in the document.

**3.** Save the document as **Flowering Shrub FAQ** in the Tutorial folder for Tutorial 2, and then close the document. You return to the Tree FAQ document, where the Clipboard Task Pane is still open. You are finished using the Clipboard Task Pane, so you will delete its contents.

**4.** Click the **Clear All** button 🗑 Clear All on the Clipboard Task Pane. The copied items are removed from the Clipboard Task Pane.

**5.** Click the **Close** button ⊠ on the Clipboard Task Pane. The Clipboard Task Pane disappears.

**6.** Click anywhere in the document to deselect the highlighted paragraph.

**7.** Save the document.

# Finding **and Replacing Text**

When you're working with a longer document, the quickest and easiest way to locate a particular word or phrase is to use the **Find command**. If you want to replace characters or a phrase with something else, you can use the **Replace command**, which combines the Find command with a substitution feature. The Replace command searches through a document and substitutes the text you're searching for with the replacement text you specify. As you perform the search, Word stops and highlights each occurrence of the search text. You must determine whether or not to substitute the replacement text, and do so by clicking the Replace button.

If you want to substitute every occurrence of the search text with the replacement text, you can click the Replace All button. When using the Replace All button with single words, keep in mind that the search text might be found within other words. To prevent Word from making incorrect substitutions in such cases, it's a good idea to select the Find whole words only check box along with the Replace All button. For example, suppose you want to replace the word "figure" with "illustration". Unless you select the Find whole words only check box, Word would replace "configure" with "conillustration."

As you search through a document, you can search from the current location of the insertion point down to the end of the document, from the insertion point up to the beginning of the document, or throughout the document.

---

**REFERENCE WINDOW** **RW**

<u>Finding and Replacing Text</u>

- Click Edit on the menu bar, and then click either Find or Replace.
- To find text, click the Find tab. To find and replace text, click the Replace tab.
- Click the More button to expand the dialog box to display additional options (including the Find whole words only option). If you see the Less button, the additional options are already displayed.
- In the Search list box, select Down if you want to search from the insertion point to the end of the document, select Up if you want to search from the insertion point to the beginning of the document, or select All to search the entire document.
- Type the characters you want to find in the Find what text box.
- If you are replacing text, type the replacement text in the Replace with text box.
- Click the Find whole words only check box to search for complete words.
- Click the Match case check box to insert the replacement text just as you specified in the Replace with text box.
- Click the Find Next button.
- Click the Replace button to substitute the found text with the replacement text and find the next occurrence.
- Click the Replace All button to substitute all occurrences of the found text with the replacement text.

---

Marilee wants the company initials, LMG, to be spelled out as "Long Meadow Gardens" each time they appear in the text.

### To replace "LMG" with "Long Meadow Gardens":

1. Press **Ctrl+Home** to move the insertion point to the beginning of the document.

2. Click **Edit** on the menu bar, and then click **Replace**. The Find and Replace dialog box opens.

3. If you see a **More** button, click it to display the additional search options. (If you see a Less button, the additional options are already displayed.) Also, if necessary, click the **Search** list arrow, and then click **All**.

4. Click the **Find what** text box, type **LMG**, press the **Tab** key, and then type **Long Meadow Gardens** in the Replace with text box.

   **TROUBLE?** If you already see the text "LMG" and "Long Meadow Gardens" in your Find and Replace dialog box, someone has already performed these steps on your computer. Continue with Step 7.

5. Click the **Find whole words only** check box to insert a check.

6. Click the **Match case** check box to insert a check. This ensures that Word will insert the replacement text using initial capital letters, as you specified in the Replace with text box. Your Find and Replace dialog box should now look like Figure 2-17.

| Figure 2-17 | FIND AND REPLACE DIALOG BOX |
| --- | --- |

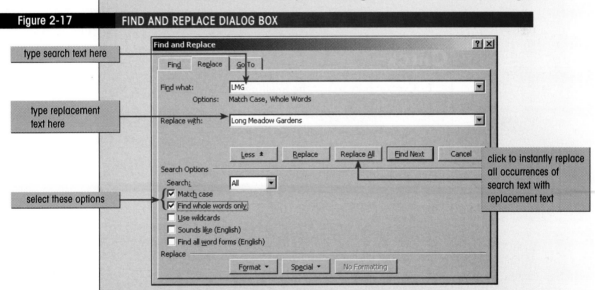

type search text here

type replacement text here

select these options

click to instantly replace all occurrences of search text with replacement text

7. Click the **Replace All** button to replace all occurrences of the search text with the replacement text. When Word finishes making the replacements, you see a dialog box telling you that two replacements were made.

8. Click the **OK** button to close the dialog box, and then click the **Close** button in the Find and Replace dialog box to return to the document. The full company name has been inserted into the document, as shown in Figure 2-18. (You may have to scroll down to see this section.)

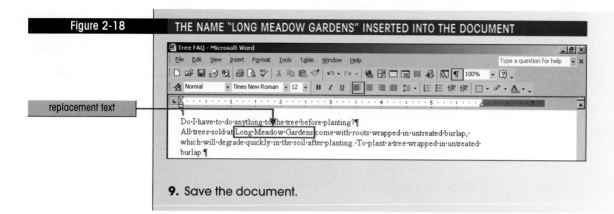

**Figure 2-18**    THE NAME "LONG MEADOW GARDENS" INSERTED INTO THE DOCUMENT

replacement text

**9.** Save the document.

Note that you can also search for and replace formatting, such as bold, and special characters in the Find and Replace dialog box. Click in the Find what text box or the Replace with text box, enter any text if necessary, click the Format button, click Font to open the Font dialog box, and then select the formatting you want to find or replace. Complete the search or replace as usual.

You have completed the content changes Marilee requested. In the next session, you will make some changes that will affect the document's appearance.

## Session 2.1 QUICK CHECK

1. Explain how to use the Spelling and Grammar Checker.

2. Which key(s) do you press to move the insertion point to the following places:
   **a.** down one line
   **b.** to the end of the document
   **c.** to the next screen

3. Explain how to select the following items using the mouse:
   **a.** one word
   **b.** a block of text
   **c.** one paragraph

4. Define the following terms in your own words:
   **a.** selection bar
   **b.** Redo button
   **c.** drag and drop

5. Describe a situation in which you would use the Undo button and then the Redo button.

6. True or False: You can use the Redo command to restore deleted text at a new location in your document.

7. What is the difference between cut and paste, and copy and paste?

8. List the steps involved in finding and replacing text in a document.

## SESSION 2.2

In this session you will make the formatting changes Marilee suggested. You'll use a variety of formatting commands to change the margins, line spacing, text alignment, and paragraph indents. You'll also learn how to use the Format Painter, how to create bulleted and numbered lists, and how to change fonts, font sizes, and emphasis. Finally, you will add a comment to the document.

# Changing the Margins

In general, it's best to begin formatting by making the changes that affect the document's overall appearance. Then you can make changes that affect only selected text. In this case, you need to adjust the document's margin settings.

Word uses default margins of 1.25 inches for the left and right margins and 1 inch for the top and bottom margins. The numbers on the ruler (displayed below the Formatting toolbar) indicate the distance in inches from the left margin, not from the left edge of the paper. Unless you specify otherwise, changes you make to the margins affect the entire document, not just the current paragraph or page.

---

**REFERENCE WINDOW** **RW**

### Changing Margins for the Entire Document

- With the insertion point anywhere in your document and no text selected, click File on the menu bar, and then click Page Setup.
- If necessary, click the Margins tab to display the margin settings.
- Use the arrows to change the settings in the Top, Bottom, Left, or Right text boxes, or type a new margin value in each text box.
- Make sure the Apply to list box displays Whole document.
- Click the OK button.

---

You need to change the top margin to 1.5 inches and the left margin to 1.75 inches, per Marilee's request. The left margin needs to be wider than usual to allow space for making holes so that the document can be inserted in a three-ring binder. In the next set of steps, you'll change the margins with the Page Setup command. You also can change margins in Print Layout view by dragging an icon on the horizontal ruler. You'll have a chance to practice this technique in the Review Assignments at the end of this tutorial.

### To change the margins in the Tree FAQ document:

1. If you took a break after the previous session, make sure Word is running, the Tree FAQ document is open, and nonprinting characters are displayed.

2. Press **Ctrl+Home** to move the insertion point to the top of the document. This should also ensure that no text is selected in the document.

3. Click **File** on the menu bar, and then click **Page Setup** to open the Page Setup dialog box.

4. If necessary, click the **Margins** tab to display the margin settings. The Top margin setting is selected. See Figure 2-19. As you complete the following steps, keep an eye on the document preview, which will change to reflect any changes you make to the margins.

Figure 2-19 | PAGE SETUP DIALOG BOX

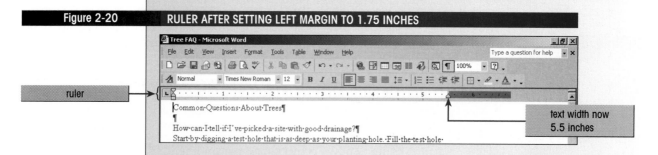

**Margins tab selected** → **Top margin setting**

**new margin settings will apply to whole document** →

**preview illustrates changes to margins**

5. Type **1.5** to change the Top margin setting. (You do not have to type the inches symbol.)

6. Press the **Tab** key twice to select the Left text box and highlight the current margin setting. Notice how the text area in the Preview box moves down to reflect the larger top margin.

7. Type **1.75** and then press the **Tab** key. Watch the Preview box to see how the margin increases.

8. Make sure the **Whole document** option is selected in the Apply to list box, and then click the **OK** button to return to your document. Notice that the right margin on the ruler has changed to reflect the larger margins and the resulting reduced page area. The document text is now 5.5 inches wide. See Figure 2-20.

Figure 2-20 | RULER AFTER SETTING LEFT MARGIN TO 1.75 INCHES

**ruler** →

**text width now 5.5 inches**

**TROUBLE?** If a double dotted line and the words "Section Break" appear in your document, Whole document wasn't specified in the Apply to list box. If this occurs, click the Undo button on the Standard toolbar and then repeat Steps 1 through 8, making sure you select the Whole document option in the Apply to list box.

Next, you will change the amount of space between lines of text.

# Changing **Line Spacing**

The line spacing in a document determines the amount of vertical space between lines of text. In most situations, you will want to choose from three basic types of line spacing: **single spacing** (which allows for the largest character in a particular line as well as a small amount of extra space); **1.5 line spacing** (which allows for one and one-half times the space of single spacing); and **double spacing** (which allows for twice the space of single spacing). The FAQ document is currently single-spaced because Word uses single spacing by default. Before changing the line-spacing setting, you should select the text you want to change. The easiest way to change line spacing is to use the Line Spacing button on the Formatting toolbar. You can also use the keyboard to apply single, double, and 1.5 line spacing.

---

**REFERENCE   WINDOW**                                                                            **RW**

Changing Line Spacing in a Document

- Select the text you want to change.
- Click the list arrow next to the Line Spacing button on the Formatting toolbar, and then click the line spacing you want.
- Now that you have selected a line spacing, apply it by selecting a block of text, and then clicking the Line Spacing button.

*or*

- Select the text you want to change.
- Press Ctrl+1 for single spacing, Ctrl+5 for 1.5 line spacing, or Ctrl+2 for double spacing.

---

Marilee has asked you to change the line spacing for the entire FAQ document to 1.5 line spacing. You will begin by selecting the entire document.

## *To change the document's line spacing:*

**1.** Triple-click in the selection bar to select the entire document.

**2.** Move the mouse pointer over the Line Spacing button 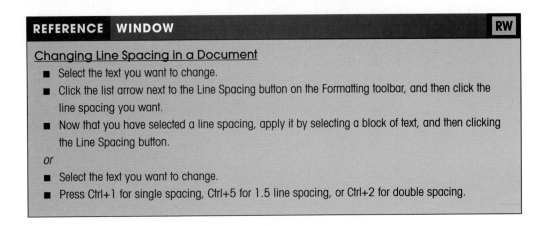 to display its ScreenTip. You see the text "Line Spacing (1)", indicating that single spacing is currently selected.

**3.** Click the **Line Spacing** list arrow. A list of line spacing options appears, as shown in Figure 2-21. To double-space the document, you click 2, while to triple-space it, you click 3. In this case, you need to apply 1.5 line spacing.

| Figure 2-21 | LINE SPACING LIST BOX |
| --- | --- |

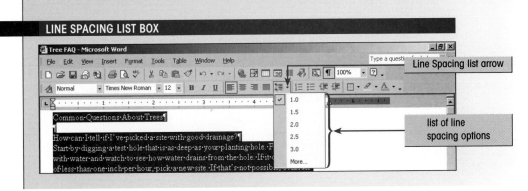

> **4.** Click **1.5**. Notice the additional space between every line of text in the document.
>
> **5.** Move the mouse pointer over 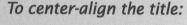 to display its ScreenTip. You see the text "Line Spacing (1.5)", indicating that 1.5 spacing is currently selected.

Now you are ready to make formatting changes that affect individual paragraphs.

# Aligning Text

As you begin formatting individual paragraphs in the FAQ document, keep in mind that in Word, a **paragraph** is defined as any text that ends with a paragraph mark symbol (¶). A paragraph can also be blank, in which case you see a paragraph mark alone on a single line. (The FAQ document includes one blank paragraph before each question heading.)

The term **alignment** refers to how the text of a paragraph lines up horizontally between the margins. By default, text is aligned along the left margin but is **ragged**, or uneven, along the right margin. This is called **left alignment**. With **right alignment**, the text is aligned along the right margin and is ragged along the left margin. With **center alignment**, text is centered between the left and right margins. With **justified alignment**, full lines of text are spaced between or aligned along both the left and the right margins. The paragraph you are reading now is justified. The easiest way to apply alignment settings is by clicking buttons on the Formatting toolbar.

Marilee indicates that the title of the FAQ should be centered and that the main paragraphs should be justified. First, you'll center the title.

### To center-align the title:

**1.** Click anywhere in the title "Common Questions About Trees" at the beginning of the document.

**2.** Click the **Center** button ![center icon] on the Formatting toolbar. The text centers between the left and right margins. See Figure 2-22.

| Figure 2-22 | CENTERED TITLE |
| --- | --- |

Center button

formatted with Center alignment

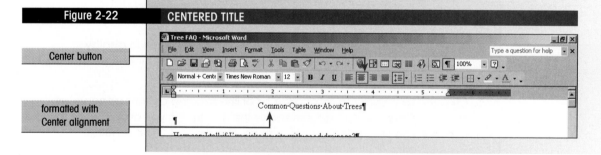

Next, you'll justify the text in the first two main paragraphs.

### To justify the first two paragraphs using the Formatting toolbar:

1. Click anywhere in the first main paragraph, which begins "Start by digging a test hole . . . "

2. Click the **Justify** button 🔳 on the Formatting toolbar. The paragraph text spreads out, so that it lines up evenly along the left and right margins.

3. Move the insertion point to anywhere in the second main paragraph, which begins "While you might be tempted . . . "

4. Click 🔳 again. The text is evenly spaced between the left and right margins. See Figure 2-23.

| Figure 2-23 | JUSTIFIED PARAGRAPHS |
|---|---|

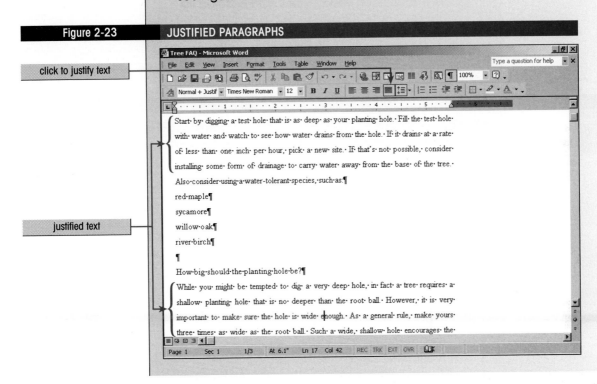

You'll justify the other paragraphs later. Now that you've learned how to change the paragraph alignment, you can turn your attention to indenting a paragraph.

## Indenting a Paragraph

When you become a more experienced Word user, you might want to do some paragraph formatting, such as a **hanging indent** (where all lines except the first line of the paragraph are indented from the left margin) or a **right indent** (where all lines of the paragraph are indented from the right margin). You can select these types of indents on the Indents and Spacing tab of the Paragraph dialog box. (To open this dialog box, you click Format on the menu bar and then click Paragraph.)

In this document, though, you need to indent only the main paragraphs 0.5 inches from the left margin. This left indent is a simple paragraph indent, which requires only a quick click on the Formatting toolbar's Increase Indent button. According to Marilee's notes, you need to indent all of the main paragraphs.

### To indent a paragraph using the Increase Indent button:

1. Click anywhere in the first main paragraph, which begins "Start by digging a test hole . . ."

2. Click the **Increase Indent** button ⯐ on the Formatting toolbar twice. (Don't click the Decrease Indent button by mistake.) The entire paragraph moves right 0.5 inches each time you click the Increase Indent button. The paragraph is indented 1 inch, 0.5 inches more than Marilee wants.

3. Click the **Decrease Indent** button ⯐ on the Formatting toolbar to move the paragraph left 0.5 inches. The paragraph is now indented 0.5 inches from the left margin. Don't be concerned about the list of tree species. You will indent it later, when you format it as a bulleted list.

4. Move the insertion point to anywhere in the second main paragraph, which begins "While you might be tempted . . ."

5. Click ⯐. The paragraph is indented 0.5 inches. See Figure 2-24.

| Figure 2-24 | INDENTED PARAGRAPH |

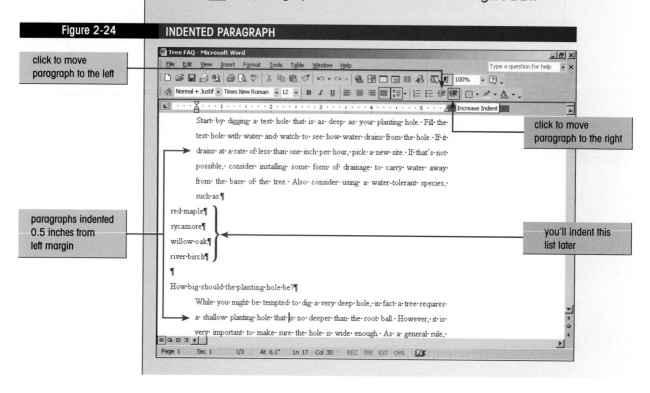

You can continue to indent and then justify each paragraph, or simply use the Format Painter command. The Format Painter allows you to copy both the indentation and alignment changes to all paragraphs in the document.

## Using **Format Painter**

The **Format Painter** makes it easy to copy all the formatting features of one paragraph to other paragraphs. You can use this button to copy formatting to one or multiple items.

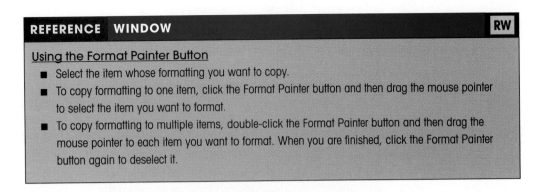

<u>Using the Format Painter Button</u>
- Select the item whose formatting you want to copy.
- To copy formatting to one item, click the Format Painter button and then drag the mouse pointer to select the item you want to format.
- To copy formatting to multiple items, double-click the Format Painter button and then drag the mouse pointer to each item you want to format. When you are finished, click the Format Painter button again to deselect it.

Use the Format Painter now to copy the formatting of the second paragraph to other main paragraphs. Begin by moving the insertion point to the paragraph whose format you want to copy.

## To copy paragraph formatting with the Format Painter:

1. Verify that the insertion point is located in the second main paragraph, which begins "While you might be tempted . . ."

2. Double-click the **Format Painter** button on the Standard toolbar. The Format Painter button will stay highlighted until you click the button again. When you move the pointer over text, the pointer changes to indicate that the format of the selected paragraph can be painted (or copied) onto another paragraph.

3. Scroll down, and then click anywhere in the third main paragraph, which begins "You may be accustomed . . ." The format of the third paragraph shifts to match the format of the first two main paragraphs. See Figure 2-25. Both paragraphs are now indented and justified. The Format Painter pointer is still visible.

**Figure 2-25** **FORMATS COPIED WITH FORMAT PAINTER**

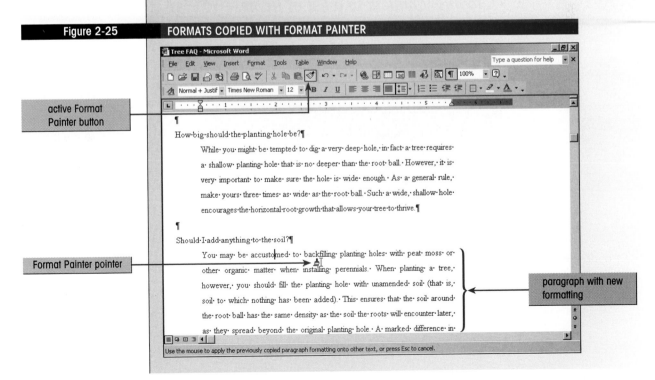

**4.** Click the remaining paragraphs that are preceded by a question heading. Take care to click only the paragraphs below the question headings. Do not click the document title, the one-line questions, the lists, or the last paragraph in the document.

**TROUBLE?** If you click a paragraph and the formatting doesn't change to match the second paragraph, you single-clicked the Format Painter button rather than double-clicked it. Select a paragraph that has the desired format, double-click the Format Painter button, and then repeat Step 4.

**TROUBLE?** If you accidentally click a title or one line of a list, click the Undo button on the Standard toolbar to return the line to its original formatting. Then select a paragraph that has the desired format, double-click the Format Painter button, and finish copying the format to the desired paragraphs.

**5.** After you are finished formatting paragraphs with the Format Painter pointer, click to turn off the feature.

**6.** Save the document.

All the main paragraphs in the document are formatted with the correct indentation and alignment. Your next job is to make the lists easier to read by adding bullets and numbers.

## Adding Bullets and Numbers

You can emphasize a list of items by adding a heavy dot, or **bullet**, before each item in the list. For consecutive items, you can use numbers instead of bullets. Marilee requests that you add bullets to the list of tree species on page 1 to make them stand out.

### To apply bullets to a list of items:

**1.** Scroll to the top of the document until you see the list of tree species below the text "Also consider using a water-tolerant species such as:".

**2.** Select the four items in the list (from "red maple" to "river birch").

**3.** Click the **Bullets** button on the Formatting toolbar. A bullet, a dark circle, appears in front of each item. Each line indents to make room for the bullet.

**4.** In order to make the bullets align with the first paragraph, make sure the list is still selected, and then click the **Increase Indent** button on the Formatting toolbar. The bulleted list moves to the right.

**5.** Click anywhere within the document window to deselect the text. Figure 2-26 shows the indented bulleted list.

**Figure 2-26** INDENTED BULLETED LIST

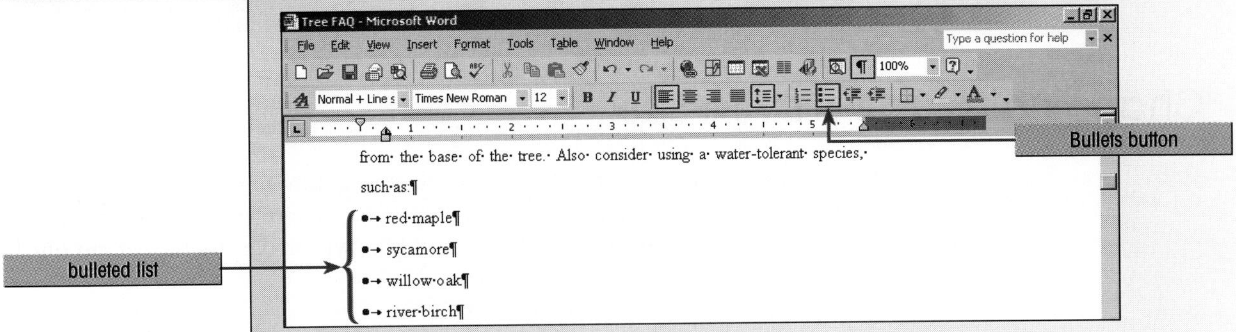

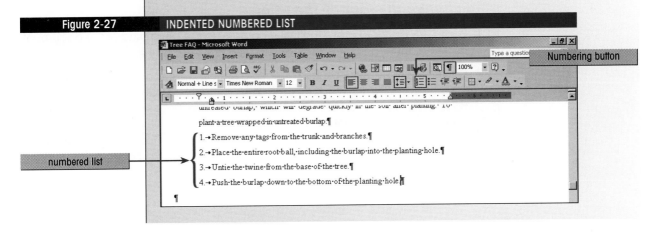

Next, you need to format the list of steps involved in planting a tree. Marilee asks you to format this information as a numbered list, an easy task thanks to the Numbering button, which automatically numbers selected paragraphs with consecutive numbers. If you insert a new paragraph, delete a paragraph, or reorder the paragraphs, Word automatically adjusts the numbers to make sure they remain consecutive.

## To apply numbers to the list of items:

1. Scroll down until you see the list that begins "Remove any tags . . . " and ends with "of the planting hole."

2. Select the entire list.

3. Click the **Numbering** button on the Formatting toolbar. Consecutive numbers appear in front of each item in the indented list. The list is indented, similar to the bulleted list. The list would look better if it was indented to align with the paragraph.

4. Click the **Increase Indent** button on the Formatting toolbar. The list moves to the right, so that the numbers align with the preceding paragraph.

5. Click anywhere in the document to deselect the text. Figure 2-27 shows the indented and numbered list.

**Figure 2-27** INDENTED NUMBERED LIST

The text of the document is now properly aligned and indented. The bullets and numbers make the lists easy to read and give readers visual clues about the type of information they contain. Next, you need to adjust the formatting of individual words.

# Changing the Font and Font Size

All of Marilee's remaining changes concern changing fonts, adjusting font sizes, and emphasizing text with font styles. The first step is to change the font of the title from 12-point Times New Roman to 14-point Arial. This will make the title stand out from the rest of the text.

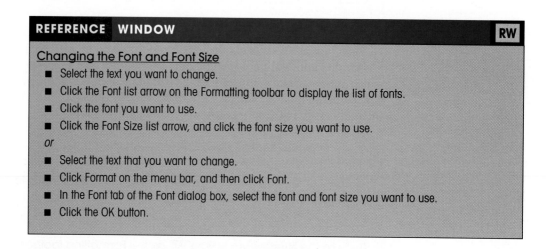

**REFERENCE WINDOW** **RW**

Changing the Font and Font Size
- Select the text you want to change.
- Click the Font list arrow on the Formatting toolbar to display the list of fonts.
- Click the font you want to use.
- Click the Font Size list arrow, and click the font size you want to use.

*or*

- Select the text that you want to change.
- Click Format on the menu bar, and then click Font.
- In the Font tab of the Font dialog box, select the font and font size you want to use.
- Click the OK button.

Marilee wants you to change the font of the title as well as its size and style. To do this, you'll use the Formatting toolbar. Marilee wants you to use a **sans serif** font, which is a font that does not have the small horizontal lines (called serifs) at the tops and bottoms of the letters. Sans serif fonts are often used in titles so they contrast with the body text. Times New Roman is a serif font, and Arial is a sans serif font. The text you are reading now is a serif font, and the text in the following steps is a sans serif font.

### To change the font of the title:

1. Press **Ctrl+Home** to move the insertion point to the beginning of the document, and then select the title **Common Questions About Trees**.

2. Click the **Font** list arrow on the Formatting toolbar. A list of available fonts appears in alphabetical order, with the name of the current font in the Font text box. See Figure 2-28. (Your list of fonts might be different from those shown.) Fonts that have been used recently might appear above a double line. Note that each name in the list is formatted with the relevant font. For example, "Arial" appears in the Arial font, and "Times New Roman" appears in the Times New Roman font.

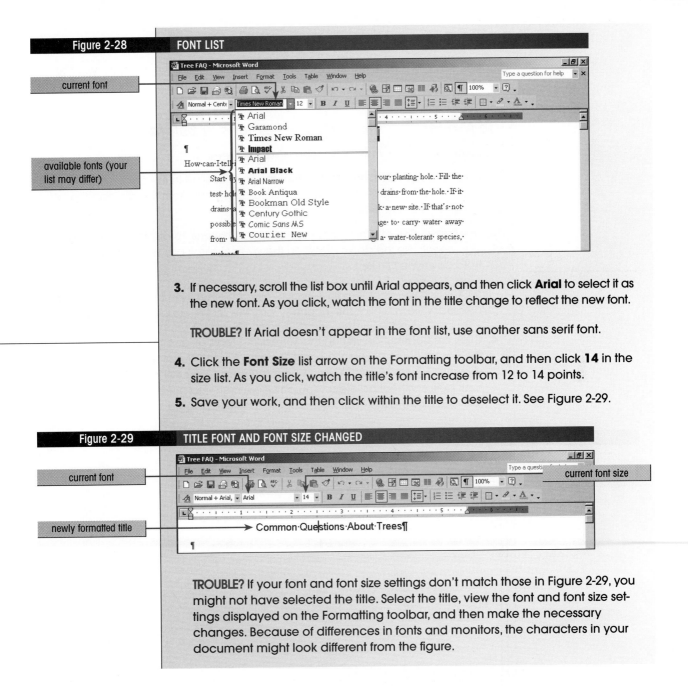

**Figure 2-28**   **FONT LIST**

current font

available fonts (your list may differ)

3. If necessary, scroll the list box until Arial appears, and then click **Arial** to select it as the new font. As you click, watch the font in the title change to reflect the new font.

   TROUBLE? If Arial doesn't appear in the font list, use another sans serif font.

4. Click the **Font Size** list arrow on the Formatting toolbar, and then click **14** in the size list. As you click, watch the title's font increase from 12 to 14 points.

5. Save your work, and then click within the title to deselect it. See Figure 2-29.

**Figure 2-29**   **TITLE FONT AND FONT SIZE CHANGED**

current font

current font size

newly formatted title

Common·Questions·About·Trees¶

TROUBLE? If your font and font size settings don't match those in Figure 2-29, you might not have selected the title. Select the title, view the font and font size settings displayed on the Formatting toolbar, and then make the necessary changes. Because of differences in fonts and monitors, the characters in your document might look different from the figure.

# Emphasizing **Text with Boldface, Underlining, and Italics**

You can emphasize words in your document with boldface, underlining, or italics. These styles help make specific thoughts, ideas, words, or phrases stand out. (You can also add special effects such as shadows to characters.) Marilee marked a few words on the document draft (shown in Figure 2-1) that need this kind of special emphasis. You add boldface, underlining, or italics by using the relevant buttons on the Formatting toolbar. These buttons are **toggle buttons**, which means you can click them once to format the selected text, and then click again to remove the formatting from the selected text.

## Bolding Text

Marilee wants to draw attention to the title and all of the question headings. You will do this by bolding them.

### To format the title and the questions in boldface:

1. Select the title **Common Questions About Trees**.

2. Press and hold **Ctrl**, and then select the first question in the document ("How can I tell if I've picked a site with good drainage?"). Both the title and the first question are now selected.

3. Hold down **Ctrl** and select the remaining questions. To display more of the document, use the down arrow on the vertical scroll bar while you continue to hold down the Ctrl key.

   **TROUBLE?** If you accidentally select something other than a question, keep Ctrl pressed while you click the incorrect item. This should deselect the incorrect item.

4. Click the **Bold** button **B** on the Formatting toolbar, and then click anywhere in the document to deselect the text. The title and the questions appear in bold, as shown in Figure 2-30. After reviewing this change, you wonder if the title would look better without boldface. You can easily remove boldface by selecting the text and clicking the Bold button again to turn, or toggle, off boldfacing.

| Figure 2-30 | TEXT IN BOLDFACE |

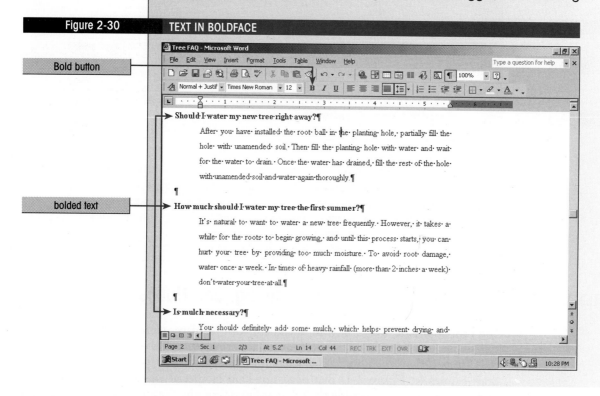

**5.** To remove the boldface, select the title, and then click **B**. The title now appears without boldface. You decide you prefer to emphasize the title with boldface after all.

**6.** Verify that the title is still selected, and then click **B**. The title appears in boldface again.

## Underlining Text

The Underline button works in the same way as the Bold button. Marilee's edits indicate that the word "Note" should be inserted and underlined at the beginning of the final paragraph. Using the Underline button, you'll make both of these changes at the same time.

*To underline text:*

**1.** Press **Ctrl+End** to move the insertion point to the end of the document. Then move the insertion point to the left of the word "Any" in the first line of the final paragraph.

**2.** Click the **Underline** button **U** on the Formatting toolbar to turn on underlining. The Underline button remains highlighted. Whatever text you type now will be underlined on your screen and in your printed document.

**3.** Type **Note:** and then click **U** to turn off underlining. See how the Underline button is no longer pressed, and "Note:" is now underlined.

**4.** Press the **spacebar**. See Figure 2-31.

| Figure 2-31 | WORD TYPED WITH UNDERLINE |
| --- | --- |

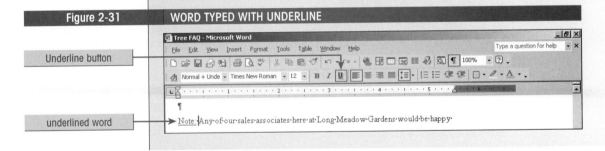

Underline button

underlined word

## Italicizing Text

Next, you'll format each instance of "Long Meadow Gardens" in italics. This helps draw attention to the company name.

*To italicize the company name:*

**1.** Scroll up to the question, "Do I have to do anything to the tree before planting?"

**2.** In the first line below the question, select **Long Meadow Gardens**.

**3.** Click the **Italic** button **I** on the Formatting toolbar. The company name changes from regular to italic text. In the next step, you'll learn a useful method for repeating the task you just performed.

**4.** Scroll down to the last paragraph of the document, select the company name, and then press the **F4** key. Keep in mind that you can use the F4 key to repeat your most recent action. It is especially helpful when formatting parts of a document.

**5.** Save the document.

# Adding **Comments**

Peter stops by your desk to review your work. He's happy with the document's appearance, but wonders if he should add some information about fertilizing new trees. He asks you to insert a note to Marilee about this using Word's Comment feature. A **comment** is an electronic version of an adhesive note that you might attach to a piece of paper. To attach a comment to a Word document, select a block of text, click Comment on the Insert menu, and then type your comment in the Reviewing Pane. To display the comment, place the mouse pointer over text to which a comment has been attached. Comments are very useful when you are exchanging Word documents with co-workers electronically, either via e-mail or on floppies, because they allow you to make notes or queries without affecting the document itself.

You'll attach Peter's comment to the document title so that Marilee will be sure to see it as soon as she opens the document.

*To attach a comment:*

**1.** Scroll up to the top of the document, and then select the title **Common Questions About Trees**.

**2.** Click **Insert** on the menu bar, and then click **Comment**. The Reviewing Pane opens at the bottom of the document window. Depending on how your computer is set up, you might see your name, as well as the current date and time in the Reviewing Pane. The insertion point is positioned in the Reviewing Pane, ready for you to type the comment. Also, the Reviewing toolbar is displayed below the Formatting toolbar. Finally, notice that the title is enclosed in brackets. See Figure 2-32.

| Figure 2-32 | INSERTING A COMMENT |
|---|---|

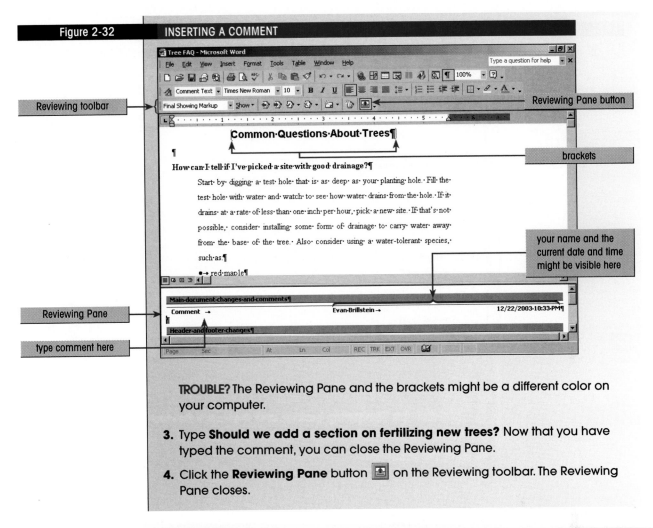

**TROUBLE?** The Reviewing Pane and the brackets might be a different color on your computer.

3. Type **Should we add a section on fertilizing new trees?** Now that you have typed the comment, you can close the Reviewing Pane.

4. Click the **Reviewing Pane** button 📧 on the Reviewing toolbar. The Reviewing Pane closes.

After you insert a comment, you should display it once to make sure you included all the necessary information.

### To display a comment:

1. Move the mouse pointer over the title. The comment is displayed in a box over the title. Depending on how your computer is set up, you might see your name in the comment, as well as the date and time the comment was attached. See Figure 2-33.

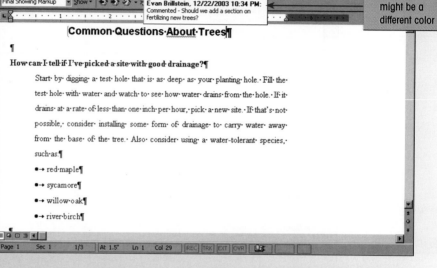

**Figure 2-33    VIEWING A COMMENT**

You won't be using the Reviewing toolbar anymore, so you can close it.

**2.** Right-click the **Reviewing** toolbar, and then click **Reviewing** in the shortcut menu. The Reviewing toolbar disappears.

**3.** Save the document.

# Previewing **Formatted Text**

You have made all the editing and formatting changes that Marilee requested for the FAQ. It's helpful to preview a document after formatting it, because the Print Preview window makes it easy to spot text that is not aligned correctly.

> ## To preview and print the document:
>
> **1.** Click the **Print Preview** button 🔍 on the Standard toolbar and examine the first page of the document. Notice the box in the right margin of the document, indicating that a comment has been attached to the document title. Use the vertical scroll bar to display the second page. (If you notice any formatting errors, click the Close button on the Print Preview toolbar, correct the errors in Normal view, save your changes, and then return to the Print Preview window.)
>
> **2.** Click the **Print** button 🖨 on the Print Preview toolbar. After a pause, the document prints. Note that the comment you inserted into the document earlier is not printed.
>
> **3.** Click the **Close** button on the Print Preview toolbar.
>
> **4.** Close the document and then close Word.

You now have a hard copy of the final FAQ, as shown in Figure 2-34.

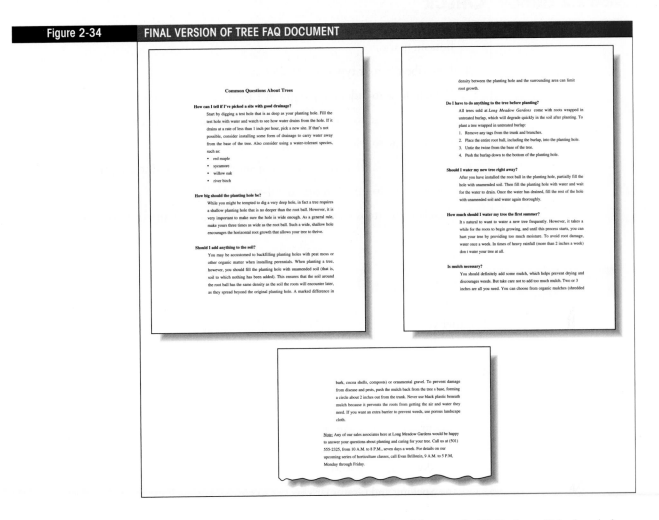

In this tutorial, you have helped Peter edit and format the FAQ that will be handed out to all customers purchasing a tree at Long Meadow Gardens. Peter will e-mail the file to Marilee later so that she can review your work and read the comment you attached.

# Session 2.2 QUICK CHECK

1. What are Word's default margins for the left and right margins? For the top and bottom margins?

2. Describe the four types of text alignment.

3. Explain how to indent a paragraph 1 inch or more from the left margin.

4. Describe a situation in which you would use the Format Painter.

5. Explain how to add underlining to a word as you type it.

6. Explain how to transform a series of short paragraphs into a numbered list.

7. Explain how to format a title in 14-point Arial.

8. Describe the steps involved in changing the line spacing in a document.

## REVIEW ASSIGNMENTS

Now that you have completed the FAQ, Marilee asks you to help her create a statement summarizing customer accounts for the Long Meadow Garden's wholesale nursery. She would also like you to create a document that contains contact information for Long Meadow Gardens. Remember to use the Undo and Redo buttons as you work to correct any errors.

1. If necessary, start Word, make sure your Data Disk is in the appropriate disk drive, and check your screen to make sure your settings match those in the tutorial.

2. Open the file **Statmnt** from the Review folder for Tutorial 2 on your Data Disk, and save the document as **Monthly Statement** in the same folder.

3. Use the Spelling and Grammar checker to correct any spelling or grammatical errors. If the Suggestions list box does not include the correct replacement, click outside the Spelling and Grammar dialog box, type the correction yourself, click Resume in the Spelling and Grammar dialog box, and continue checking the document.

4. Proofread the document carefully to check for any additional errors. Look for two words that are spelled correctly but used improperly.

5. Change the right margin to 2 inches using the Page Setup dialog box.

*Explore*

6. Change the left margin using the ruler in Print Layout view, as follows:
   a. Select the entire document.
   b. Position the pointer on the small gray square on the ruler at the left margin. A ScreenTip with the words "Left Indent" appears.
   c. Press and hold down the mouse button. A vertical dotted line appears in the document window, indicating the current left margin. Drag the margin left to the 0.5-inch mark on the ruler, and then release the mouse button.

7. Make all edits and formatting changes shown in Figure 2-35, and save your work.

**Figure 2-35**

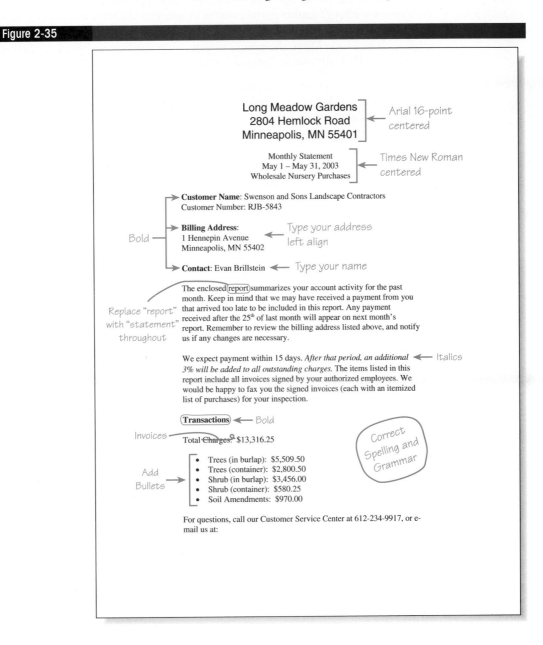

8. Remove any Smart Tags in the document.

*Explore*   9. When you type Web addresses or e-mail addresses in a document, Word automatically formats them as links. When you click a Web address formatted as a link, Windows automatically opens a Web browser (such as Microsoft Internet Explorer) and, if your computer is connected to the Internet, displays that Web page. If you click an e-mail address formatted as a link, Windows opens a program where you can type an e-mail message. The address you clicked is automatically included as the recipient of the e-mail. You'll see how this works as you add a Web address and e-mail address to the statement. In the address centered at the top of the document, click at the end of the ZIP code, add a new line, and then type the address for the company's Web site: www.longmeadowgardens.com. When you are finished, press Enter. Notice that as soon as you press Enter, Word formats the address in blue with an underline, marking it as a link. Move the mouse pointer over the link and read the ScreenTip. Because this Web address is fictitious, clicking it will not actually display a Web page.

*Explore*   10. Move the insertion point to the end of the document, press the spacebar, type long_meadow_gardens@worldlink.com and then press Enter. Word formats the e-mail address as a link. Press and hold the Ctrl button and then click the link. (If you see a message asking if you want to make Outlook Express your default mail client, click No.) You see a window where you could type an e-mail message to Long Meadow Gardens. (If your computer is not set up for e-mail, close any error messages that open.) Close the e-mail window without saving any changes. The link is now formatted in purple, indicating that the link has been clicked.

11  Move the last sentence of the document (which begins "For questions, call . . . ") to a new paragraph, just above the heading "Transactions".

12. Select the last Transactions portion of the document, from the heading "Transactions" down to the end of the document. Indent the selected text 1 inch by clicking the Increase Indent button twice.

13. Open the Clipboard Task Pane. Select the company name, address, and Web address at the top of the document and copy it to the Clipboard, and then copy the company e-mail address to the Clipboard.

*Explore*   14. Open a new, blank document and display the Clipboard Task Pane. In the Clipboard Task Pane, click the company address to insert this information at the top of the document. Insert two blank lines, type "Send all e-mail correspondence to YOUR NAME:" (replace YOUR NAME with your first and last name). Type a space and then, in the Clipboard Task Pane, click the company e-mail address. Type a period at the end of the e-mail address.

15. Clear the contents of the Clipboard Task Pane and then close the Task Pane.

*Explore* ▶ 16. If necessary, switch to Print Layout view. Then attach the following comment to the company name: "Marilee, please let me know how you want this document formatted." Notice that in Print Layout view you type the comment in a small comment window directly in the margin. Switch to Normal view, and display the comment by positioning the pointer over the company name.

17. Save the document as **LMG Contact Information** in the Review folder for Tutorial 2. Print and close the document.

18. Save the Monthly Statement document, preview and print it, and then close it. Also close the Clipboard Task Pane, if necessary. Then exit Word.

## CASE PROBLEMS

*Case 1. Authorization Form for Gygs and Bytes*  Melissa Martinez is the purchasing manager for Gygs and Bytes, a wholesale distributor of computer parts based in Portland, Oregon. Most of the company's business is conducted via catalog or through the company's Web site, but local customers sometimes drop by to pick up small orders. In the past Melissa has had problems determining which of her customers' employees were authorized to sign credit invoices. To avoid confusion, she has asked all local customers to complete a form listing employees who are authorized to sign invoices. She plans to place the completed forms in a binder at the main desk, so the receptionist at Gygs and Bytes can find the information quickly.

1. Open the file **Form** from the Cases folder for Tutorial 2 on your Data Disk, and save the file as **Authorization Form** in the same folder.

*Explore* ▶ 2. Correct any spelling or grammar errors. Ignore any words that are spelled correctly, but that are not included in Word's dictionary. When the Spelling and Grammar Checker highlights the word "sining", click the appropriate word in the Suggestions box, and then click Change.

*Explore* ▶ 3. If necessary, read Steps 9 and 10 in the Review Assignments to learn about adding Web addresses and e-mail addresses to a document. Below the company's mailing address, add the company Web address in all uppercase: WWW.G&B.NET.

4. Change the top and left margins to 1.5 inches.

5. Center the first five lines of the document (containing the form title and the company address).

6. Format the first line of the document (the form title) in 16-point Arial, with italics.

7. Format lines 2 through 5 (the address, including the Web address) in 12-point Arial.

*Explore*     8. Replace all instances of G&B, except the first one (in the Web address), with the complete company name, Gygs and Bytes. Use the Find Next button to skip an instance of the search text.

9. Format the blank ruled lines as a numbered list. Customers will use these blank lines to write in the names of authorized employees.

*Explore*     10. Format the entire document using 1.5 spacing. Then triple-space the numbered list (with the blank lines) and the Signature and Title lines as follows:
    a. Select the numbered list with the blank lines.
    b. Triple-space the selected text using the line spacing button on the Formatting toolbar.
    c. Select the "Signed:" and the "Title:" lines, and then press F4.

11. Save the document.

12. Drag "Customer Number:" up to position it above "Customer Name".

*Explore*     13. Select "Customer Name:", "Customer Number:", and "Address:". Press Ctrl+B to format the selected text in bold. Note that it is sometimes easier to use this keyboard shortcut instead of the Bold button on the Formatting toolbar.

14. Delete the phrase "all employees" and replace it with "all authorized personnel".

*Explore*     15. Select the phrase "all authorized personnel will be required to show a photo I.D." Press Ctrl+I to format the selected text in italics. It is sometimes easier to use this keyboard shortcut instead of the Italic button on the Formatting toolbar.

16. Insert your name in the form, in the "Customer Name:" line. Format your name without boldface, if necessary.

17. Insert your address, left aligned, without bold, below the heading "Address:".

18. Click the Print Preview button on the Standard toolbar to check your work.

*Explore*     19. Click the Shrink to Fit button on the Print Preview toolbar to reduce the entire document to one page. Word reduces the font sizes slightly in order to fit the entire form on one page. Close the Print Preview window and save your work.

*Explore*     20. Use the Print command on the File menu to open the Print dialog box. Print two copies of the document by changing the Number of copies setting in the Print dialog box.

*Explore*     21. You can find out the number of words in your documents by using the Word Count command on the Tools menu. Use this command to determine the number of words in the document, and then write that number in the upper-right corner of the printout.

22. Save and close the document, and then exit Word.

*Case 2. Advertising Brochure for the CCW Web Site*  The *Carson College Weekly* is a student-run newspaper published through the Carson College Student Services Association. The newspaper is distributed around campus each Friday. The online version of the newspaper is posted on the CCW Web site on Thursdays. Local businesses have a long-established tradition of advertising in the print version of the newspaper, and the paper's advertising manager, Noah McCormick, would like to ensure that this same tradition carries over to the online newspaper. When he sends out the monthly statements to his print advertisers, he would like to include a one-page brochure encouraging them to purchase an online ad. He has copied the text of the brochure from the CCW Web site and saved it as unformatted text in a Word document.

1. Open the file **CCW** from the Cases folder for Tutorial 2 on your Data Disk, and save the file as **CCW Brochure** in the same folder.

2. Correct any spelling or grammar errors. Take time to make sure the right correction is selected in the Suggestions list box before you click Change. Proofread for any words that are spelled correctly but used incorrectly.

***Explore***
3. If necessary, read Steps 9 and 10 in the Review Assignments to learn about adding Web addresses and e-mail addresses to a document. Below *Carson College Weekly*, add the newspaper's Web address in all uppercase: WWW.CARSON.CCW.EDU, and then press Enter. At the end of the document, insert a space, type "advertising@carson.ccw.edu", (without the quotation marks), type a period, and then press Enter.

4. In the second to last sentence, replace "the CCW Advertising Office" with your name.

5. Change the right margin to 1.5 inches and the left margin to 2 inches.

6. Format the entire document in 12-point Times New Roman.

7. Format the four paragraphs below "Did you know?" as a bulleted list.

8. Drag the third bullet (which begins "You can include . . . ") up to the top of the bulleted list.

9. Format the first two lines of the document using a font, font size, and alignment of your choice. Use bold or italics for emphasis.

10. Format the entire document using 1.5 line spacing.

11. Add a comment to the first line (*Carson College Weekly*) asking Noah if he would like you to leave a printed copy of the brochure in his mailbox. Close the Reviewing Pane and the Reviewing toolbar when you are finished.

12. Save your work, preview the document, and then switch back to Normal view to make any changes you think necessary.

13. Print the document.

14. Save and close the document, and then exit Word.

*Case 3. Productivity Training Summary for UpTime* Matt Patterson is UpTime's marketing director for the Northeast region. The company provides productivity training for large companies across the country. Matt wants to provide interested clients with a one-page summary of UpTime's productivity training sessions.

1. If necessary, start Word, make sure your Data Disk is in the appropriate disk drive, and check your screen to make sure your settings match those in the tutorials.

2. Open the file **UpTime** from the Tutorial 2 Cases folder on your Data Disk, and save it as **UpTime Training Summary** in the same folder.

3. Change the title at the beginning of the document to a 16-point sans serif font. Be sure to pick a font that looks professional and is easy to read. (Remember to use the Undo and Redo buttons as you work to correct any editing mistakes.)

4. Center and bold the title and Web address.

5. Delete the word "general" from the second sentence of the first paragraph after the document title.

6. Convert the list of training components following the first paragraph to an indented, numbered list.

7. Under the heading "Personal Productivity Training Seminar," delete the last sentence from the first paragraph, the one beginning with "This seminar improves".

8. Under the heading "Personal Productivity Training Seminar," delete the phrase "at the seminar" from the first sentence in the second paragraph.

9. In the first paragraph under the heading "Management Productivity Training," move the first sentence (beginning with "UpTime provides management training") to the end of the paragraph.

10. Switch the order of the first and second paragraphs under the "Field Services Technology and Training" heading.

11. Search for the text "your name", and replace it with your first and last name. Use the Bold button and the Underline button on the Formatting toolbar to format your name in boldface, with an underline.

12. Change the top margin to 1.5 inches.

13. Change the left margin to 1.75 inches.

14. Bold and italicize the heading "Personal Productivity Training Seminar" and then use the Format Painter to copy this heading's format to the headings "Management Productivity Training" and "Field Services Technology and Training". Turn off the Format Painter when you're finished.

*Explore* ▶

15. Select both occurrences of the word "free" in the second paragraph under the "Field Services Technology and Training" heading. Press Ctrl+I to format the selected text in italics.

16. Save and preview the document.

17. Print the document, and then close the file, and exit Word.

**Case 4. *Product Description for Ridge Top*** Thomas McGee is vice president of sales and marketing at Ridge Top, an outdoor and sporting-gear store in Conshohocken, Pennsylvania. Each year Thomas and his staff mail a description of new products to Ridge Top's regular customers. Thomas has asked you to edit and format the first few pages of this year's new products' description.

1. If necessary, start Word, make sure your Data Disk is in the appropriate disk drive, and check your screen to make sure your settings match those in the tutorials.

2. Open the file **Ridge** from the Tutorial 2 Cases folder on your Data Disk, and save it as **Ridge Top Guide** in the same folder.

3. Use the Spelling and Grammar checker to correct any errors in the document. Because of the nature of this document, it contains some words that the Word dictionary on your computer may not recognize. It also contains headings that the Spelling and Grammar checker may consider sentence fragments. As you use the Spelling and Grammar checker, use the Ignore All button, if necessary, to skip over brand names.

4. Delete the phrase "a great deal" from the first sentence of the paragraph below the heading "Snuggle Up to These Prices." (Remember to use the Undo and Redo buttons to correct any editing mistakes as you work.)

5. Reverse the order of the first two paragraphs under the heading, "You'll Eat Up the Prices of This Camp Cooking Gear!"

6. Cut the last sentence of the first full paragraph ("Prices are good through . . . ") from the document. Then move the insertion point to the end of the document, press the Enter key twice, and insert the cut sentence as a new paragraph. Format it in 12-point Arial, and italicize it.

7. Format the Ridge Top tip items as a numbered list.

**Explore** ▷ 8. Reorder the items under the "Ridge Top Tips" heading by moving the fourth product idea and the following blank paragraph to the top of the list.

9. Search for the text "your name", and replace with your first and last name.

**Explore** ▷ 10. Experiment with two special paragraph alignment options: first line and hanging. First, select everything from the heading "Ridge Top Guarantees Warmth at Cool Prices" through the paragraph just before the heading "Ridge Top Tips". Next, click Format on the menu bar, click Paragraph, click the Indents and Spacing tab if necessary, click the Help button in the upper-right corner of the dialog box, click the Special list arrow, and review the information on the special alignment options. Experiment with both the First line and the Hanging options. When you are finished, return the document to its original format by choosing the none option.

11. Justify all the paragraphs in the document. (*Hint*: To select all paragraphs in the document at one time, click Edit on the menu bar, and then click Select All.)

12. Replace all occurrences of "RidgeTop" with "Ridge Top". (You may have already made this correction when you checked spelling in the document.)

13. Apply a 12-point, bold, sans serif font to each of the headings. Be sure to pick a font that looks professional and is easy to read. Use the Format Painter to copy the formatting after you apply it once using the Font list box.

14. Change the title's and subtitle's font to the same font you used for the headings, except set the size to 16 point.

15. Bold the title and subtitle.

16. Underline the names and prices for all of the brand name products.

17. Save and preview the document.

18. Print the document, and then close the file, and exit Word.

## INTERNET ASSIGNMENTS

**Student Union**

The purpose of the Internet Assignments is to challenge you to find information on the Internet that you can use to create effective documents. The actual assignments are updated and maintained on the Course Technology Web site. Log on to the Internet and use your Web browser to go to the Student Union on the New Perspectives Series site at **www.course.com/NewPerspectives/studentunion**. Click the Online Companions link, and then click the link for this text.

## QUICK | CHECK ANSWERS

*Session 2.1*

1. Click at the beginning of the document, and then click the Spelling and Grammar button on the Standard toolbar. In the Spelling and Grammar dialog box, review any errors highlighted in color. Grammatical errors appear in green; spelling errors appear in red. Review the possible corrections in the Suggestions list box. To accept a suggested correction, click it in the Suggestions list box. Then click Change to make the correction and continue searching the document for errors.

2. (a)↓; (b) Ctrl+End; (c) Page Down

3. (a) Double-click the word; (b) click at the beginning of the block, and then drag until the entire block is selected; (c) double-click in the selection bar next to the paragraph, or triple-click in the paragraph.

4. (a) the blank space in the left margin area of the Document window that allows you to easily select entire lines or large blocks of text; (b) the button on the Standard toolbar that redoes an action you previously reversed using the Undo button; (c) the process of moving text by first selecting the text, and then pressing and holding the mouse button while moving the text to its new location in the document, and finally releasing the mouse button

5. You might use the Undo button to remove the bold formatting you had just applied to a word. You could then use the Redo button to restore the bold formatting to the word.

6. False

7. Cut and paste removes the selected material from its original location and inserts it in a new location. Copy and paste makes a copy of the selected material and inserts the copy in a new location; the original material remains in its original location.

8. Click Edit on the menu bar, click Replace, type the search text in the Find what text box, type the replacement text in the Replace with text box, click Find Next or click Replace all.

*Session 2.2*

1. The default top and bottom margins are 1 inch. The default left and right margins are 1.25 inches.

2. Align-left: each line flush left, ragged right; Align-right: each line flush right, ragged left; Center: each line centered, ragged right and left.; Justify: each line flush left and flush right

4. You might use the Format Painter to copy the formatting of a heading to the other headings in the document.

5. Click the Underline button on the Formatting toolbar, type the word, and then click the Underline button again to turn off underlining.

6. Select the paragraphs, and then click the Numbering button on the Formatting toolbar.

7. Select the title, click the Font list arrow, and click Arial in the list of fonts. Then click the Font Size list arrow, and click 14.

8. Select the text you want to change, click the Line Spacing list arrow on the Formatting toolbar, and then click the line spacing option you want. Or select the text, and then press Ctrl+1 for single spacing, Ctrl+5 for 1.5 line spacing, or Ctrl+2 for double spacing.

*New Perspectives on*

# MICROSOFT®
# EXCEL

# Read **This Before You Begin**

## To the Student

### Data Disks

To complete these tutorials, Review Assignments, and Case Problems, you need two Data Disks. Your instructor will either provide you with these Data Disks or ask you to make your own.

If you are making your own Data Disks, you will need **two** blank, formatted high-density disks. You will need to copy a set of files and/or folders from a file server, standalone computer, or the Web onto your disks. Your instructor will tell you which computer, drive letter, and folders contain the files you need. You could also download the files by going to **www.course.com** and following the instructions on the screen.

The information below shows you which folders go on each of your disks, so that you will have enough disk space to complete all the tutorials, Review Assignments, and Case Problems:

### Data Disk 1

Write this on the disk label:
Data Disk 1: Excel 2002 Tutorials 1-2
Put these folders on the disk:
Tutorial.01
Tutorial.02

### Data Disk 2

Write this on the disk label:
Data Disk 2: Excel 2002 Tutorial 3
Put these folders on the disk:
Tutorial.03

When you begin each tutorial, be sure you are using the correct Data Disk. Refer to the "File Finder" chart at the back of this text for more detailed information on which files are used in which tutorials. See the inside front or inside back cover of this book for more information on Data Disk files, or ask your instructor or technical support person for assistance.

### Course Labs

The Excel tutorials feature an interactive Course Lab to help you understand spreadsheet concepts. There are Lab Assignments at the end of Tutorial 1 that relate to this Lab.

To start a Lab, click the **Start** button on the Windows taskbar, point to **Programs**, point to **Course Labs**, point to **New Perspectives Course Labs**, and then click the name of the Lab you want to use.

### Using Your Own Computer

If you are going to work through this book using your own computer, you need:

- **Computer System** Microsoft Windows 98, NT, 2000 Professional, or higher must be installed on your computer. This book assumes a typical installation of Microsoft Excel.

- **Data Disks** You will not be able to complete the tutorials or exercises in this book using your own computer until you have your Data Disks.

- **Course Labs** See your instructor or technical support person to obtain the Course Lab software for use on your own computer.

### Visit Our World Wide Web Site

Additional materials designed especially for you are available on the World Wide Web.
Go to **www.course.com/NewPerspectives**.

## To the Instructor

The Data Disk Files and Course Labs are available on the Instructor's Resource Kit for this title. Follow the instructions in the Help file on the CD-ROM to install the programs to your network or standalone computer. For information on creating Data Disks or the Course Labs, see the "To the Student" section above.

You are granted a license to copy the Data Files and Course Labs to any computer or computer network used by students who have purchased this book.

## OBJECTIVES

In this tutorial you will:

- Identify major components of the Excel window

- Navigate within and between worksheets

- Select and move worksheet cells

- Insert text, values, and formulas into a worksheet

- Insert and delete worksheet rows and columns

- Resize worksheet rows and columns

- Insert, move, and rename worksheets

- Print a workbook

## LAB

Spreadsheets

# USING EXCEL TO MANAGE FINANCIAL DATA

*Creating an Income Statement*

CASE

## Lawn Wizards

Lawn Wizards is a small company that specializes in lawn, bush, and tree care. The company started out as a two-person operation, but in recent years the service has gained in popularity. In the last few months, Lawn Wizards has added three employees—two of them full-time workers. The sudden growth in his small business has caught the owner of the company, Mike Bennett, by surprise. Up to now, he has been entering his financial records using a paper financial ledger. However, he realizes that with the growth of his business he needs to store his documents in electronic form.

Mike has just purchased Microsoft Excel 2002 for the business. He has come to you for help. He has many projects for you to work on, but first he needs help with electronic spreadsheets so he can prepare his income figures. Mike needs to know what electronic spreadsheets can do, and he needs to become familiar with the basics of Excel.

In this tutorial you will use Excel to help Mike understand electronic spreadsheets. You will explain the different parts of the Excel document window and show him how to move around an Excel worksheet. You will show him how Excel works by modifying an Excel workbook that contains some of the monthly income figures for Mike's lawn service business.

# SESSION 1.1

In this session, you will learn about electronic spreadsheets and how they can be used in business. You will explore the components of the Excel window and learn how to move around within an Excel worksheet. Finally, you will select cells and cell ranges and move the selections to a new location within the worksheet.

## Introducing Excel

Spreadsheets

Mike has just purchased Excel and has loaded it on one of his computers. Before working with his financial records, you and Mike sit down to learn about the fundamental parts of Excel. Understanding why electronic spreadsheets such as Excel have become an essential tool for businesses will help Mike to use Excel more fully and help him run his business efficiently.

### Understanding Spreadsheets

Excel is a computerized spreadsheet. A **spreadsheet** is an important business tool that helps you report and analyze information. Spreadsheets are often used for cash flow analysis, budgeting, inventory management, market forecasts, and decision making. For example, an accountant might use a spreadsheet like the one shown in Figure 1-1 to record budget information.

| Figure 1-1 | BUDGET SPREADSHEET |
|---|---|

### Cash Budget Forecast

|  | January Estimated | January Actual |
|---|---|---|
| Cash in Bank (Start of Month) | $1,400.00 | $1,400.00 |
| Cash in Register (Start of Month) | 100.00 | 100.00 |
| *Total Cash* | $1,500.00 | $1,500.00 |
|  |  |  |
| Expected Cash Sales | $1,200.00 | $1,420.00 |
| Expected Collections | 400.00 | 380.00 |
| Other Money Expected | 100.00 | 52.00 |
| *Total Income* | $1,700.00 | $1,852.00 |
| **Total Cash and Income** | $3,200.00 | $3,352.00 |
|  |  |  |
| **All Expenses (for Month)** | $1,200.00 | $1,192.00 |
|  |  |  |
| **Cash Balance at End of Month** | $2,000.00 | $2,160.00 |

In this spreadsheet, the accountant has recorded predicted and observed income and expenses for the month of January. Each line, or row, in this spreadsheet displays a different income or expense. Each column contains the predicted or observed values or text that describes those values. The accountant has also entered the income and expense totals, perhaps having used a calculator to do the calculations.

Figure 1-2 shows the same spreadsheet in Excel. The spreadsheet is now laid out in a grid in which the rows and columns are easily apparent. As you will see later, calculations are also part of this electronic spreadsheet, so that the expense and income totals are calculated automatically rather than entered manually. If an entry in the spreadsheet is changed, the spreadsheet will automatically update any calculated values based on that entry. Thus an electronic spreadsheet provides more flexibility in entering and analyzing your data than the paper version.

| Figure 1-2 | BUDGET SPREADSHEET IN EXCEL |
| --- | --- |

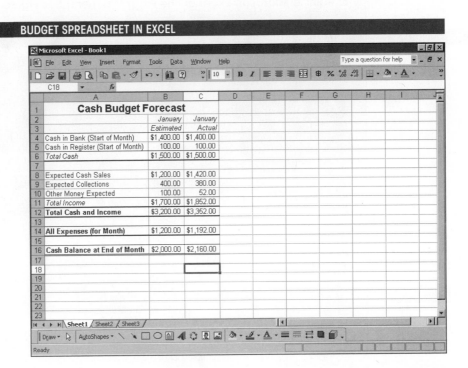

Excel stores electronic spreadsheets in documents called **workbooks**. Each workbook is made up of individual **worksheets**, or **sheets**, just as Mike's spiral-bound ledger is made up of sheets of paper. You will learn more about multiple worksheets later in this tutorial. For now, just keep in mind that the terms *worksheet* and *sheet* are used interchangeably.

## Parts of the Excel Window

Excel displays workbooks within a window that contains many tools for entering, editing, and viewing the data. You will view some of these tools after starting Excel. By default, Excel will open with a blank workbook.

## To start Excel:

**1.** Make sure Windows is running on your computer and the Windows desktop appears on your screen.

**2.** Click the **Start** button on the taskbar to display the Start menu, and then point to **Programs** to display the Programs menu.

**3.** Point to **Microsoft Excel** on the Programs menu. See Figure 1-3.

| Figure 1-3 | STARTING EXCEL |
| --- | --- |

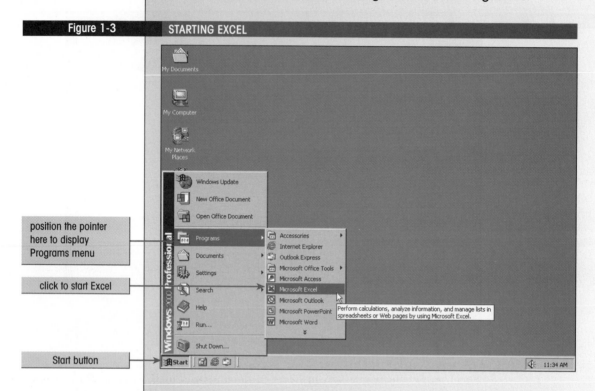

position the pointer here to display Programs menu

click to start Excel

Start button

**TROUBLE?** Do not worry if your screen differs slightly. Although the figures in this book were created while running Windows 2000 in its default settings, the Windows 98 and Windows NT operating systems share the same basic user interface as Windows 2000, and Excel runs equally well using any of these.

**TROUBLE?** Depending on how your system was set up, the menu entry for Excel may appear in a different location on the Programs menu. If you cannot locate Excel, ask your instructor for assistance.

**4.** Click **Microsoft Excel**. After a short pause, the Excel program window and a blank workbook appear. See Figure 1-4.

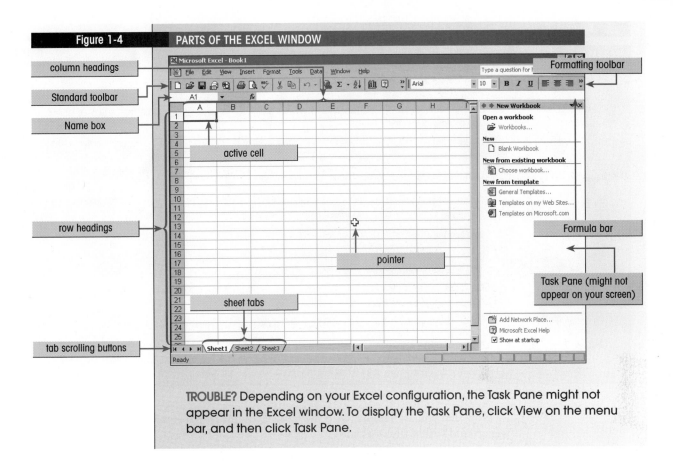

| Figure 1-4 | PARTS OF THE EXCEL WINDOW |

The Excel window has features similar to other Windows programs. It contains a title bar, menu bar, scroll bars, and a status bar. The Excel window also contains features that are unique to the program itself. Within the Excel program window is the document window, which is also referred to as the **workbook window** or **worksheet window**. The worksheet window provides a grid of columns and rows in which the intersection of a column and row is called a **cell**. Figure 1-4 identifies many of the other components of the Excel window. Take a look at each of these components so you are familiar with their location and purpose. Figure 1-5 summarizes the properties of each of these components.

| Figure 1-5 | EXCEL WINDOW COMPONENTS |
| --- | --- |
| **FEATURE** | **DESCRIPTION** |
| Active cell | The **active cell** is the cell in which you are currently working. A dark border outlining the cell identifies the active cell. |
| Column headings | **Column headings** list the columns in the worksheet. Columns are listed alphabetically from A to IV (a total of 256 possible columns). |
| Formula bar | The **Formula bar**, which is located immediately below the toolbars, displays the contents of the active cell. As you type or edit data, the changes appear in the Formula bar. |
| Name box | The **Name box** displays the location of the currently active cell in the workbook window. |
| Pointer | The **pointer** indicates the current location of your mouse pointer. The pointer changes shape to reflect the type of task you can perform at a particular location in the Excel window. |
| Row headings | **Row headings** list the rows in the worksheet. Rows are numbered consecutively from 1 up to 65,536. |
| Sheet tabs | Each worksheet in the workbook has a **sheet tab** that identifies the sheet's name. To move between worksheets, click the appropriate sheet tab. |
| Task Pane | The **Task Pane** appears when you initially start Excel, and it displays a list of commonly used tasks. The Task Pane will disappear once you open a workbook. |
| Tab scrolling buttons | The **tab scrolling buttons** are used to move between worksheets in the workbook. |
| Toolbars | **Toolbars** provide quick access to the most commonly used Excel menu commands. The **Standard toolbar** contains buttons for Excel commands such as Save and Open. The **Formatting toolbar** contains buttons used to format the appearance of the workbook. Additional toolbars are available. |

Now that you are familiar with the basic layout of an Excel workbook, you can try moving around within the workbook.

# Navigating in a Workbook

You can navigate in a workbook by moving from worksheet to worksheet or in a worksheet by moving from cell to cell. Each cell is identified by a **cell reference**, which indicates its row and column location. For example, the cell reference B6 indicates that the cell is located where column B and row 6 intersect. The column letter is always first in the cell reference. B6 is a correct cell reference; 6B is not. One cell in the worksheet, called the **active cell**, is always selected and ready for receiving data. Excel identifies the active cell with a dark border outlining it. In Figure 1-4, cell A1 is the active cell. Notice that the cell reference for the active cell appears in the Name box next to the Formula bar. You can change the active cell by selecting another cell in the worksheet.

## Navigating Within a Worksheet

Excel provides several ways of moving around in the worksheet. The most direct way is to use your mouse. To change the active cell, move the mouse pointer over a different cell and click anywhere within the cell with your left mouse button. If you need to move to a cell that is not currently displayed in the workbook window, use the vertical and horizontal scroll bars to display the area of the worksheet containing the cell.

The second way of moving around the worksheet is through your keyboard. Excel provides you with many keyboard shortcuts for moving to different cells within the worksheet. Figure 1-6 describes some of these keyboard shortcuts.

| Figure 1-6 | KEYS FOR NAVIGATING WITHIN A WORKSHEET |
|---|---|
| **KEYSTROKE** | **ACTION** |
| ↑ , ↓ , ← , → | Moves the active cell up, down, left, or right one cell |
| Enter | Moves the active cell down one cell |
| Tab | Moves the active cell to the right one cell |
| Page Up | Moves the active cell up one full screen |
| Page Down | Moves the active cell down one full screen |
| Home | Moves the active cell to column A of the current row |
| Ctrl + Home | Moves the active cell to cell A1 |
| F5 (function key) | Opens the Go To dialog box in which you can enter the cell address of the cell that you want to make active |

Finally, you can enter a cell reference in the Name box to move directly to that cell in the worksheet.

Explore these techniques by moving around the worksheet using your keyboard and mouse.

## To move around the worksheet:

1. Position the mouse pointer over cell E8, and then click the left mouse button to make cell E8 the active cell.

   Notice that cell E8 is surrounded by a black border, indicating it is the active cell, and that the Name box displays the cell reference "E8." Note also that the row and column headings for row 8 and column E are highlighted, giving another visual indication about the location of the active cell.

2. Click cell **B4** to make it the active cell.

3. Press the → key on your keyboard to make cell C4 the active cell.

4. Press the ↓ key to make cell C5 the active cell. See Figure 1-7.

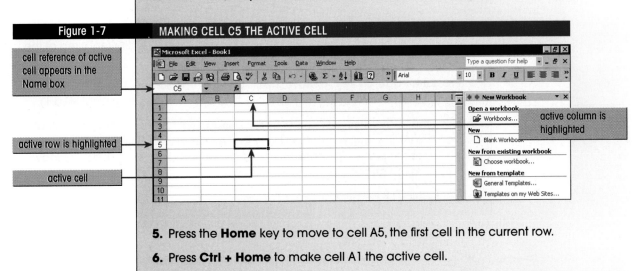

| Figure 1-7 | MAKING CELL C5 THE ACTIVE CELL |
|---|---|

cell reference of active cell appears in the Name box

active column is highlighted

active row is highlighted

active cell

5. Press the **Home** key to move to cell A5, the first cell in the current row.

6. Press **Ctrl + Home** to make cell A1 the active cell.

So far you have moved around the portion of the worksheet displayed in the workbook window. The content of many worksheets will not fit into the workbook window, so you may have to move to cells that are not currently displayed by Excel. You can do this using your keyboard or the scroll bars.

## To bring other parts of the worksheet into view:

1. Press the **Page Down** key on your keyboard to move the display down one screen. The active cell is now A26 (the active cell on your screen may be different). Notice that the row numbers on the left side of the worksheet indicate you have moved to a different area of the worksheet. See Figure 1-8.

| Figure 1-8 | MOVING TO A DIFFERENT AREA OF THE WORKSHEET |

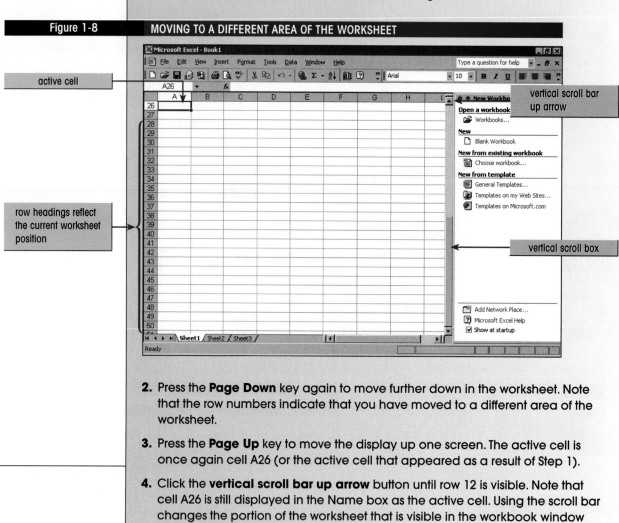

2. Press the **Page Down** key again to move further down in the worksheet. Note that the row numbers indicate that you have moved to a different area of the worksheet.

3. Press the **Page Up** key to move the display up one screen. The active cell is once again cell A26 (or the active cell that appeared as a result of Step 1).

4. Click the **vertical scroll bar up arrow** button until row 12 is visible. Note that cell A26 is still displayed in the Name box as the active cell. Using the scroll bar changes the portion of the worksheet that is visible in the workbook window but does not change the active cell.

5. Click cell **C12** to make it the active cell.

6. Click the blank area above the vertical scroll box to move up one full screen, and then click the blank area below the vertical scroll box to move down a full screen.

7. Click the **vertical scroll box** and drag it to the top of the scroll bar to again change the area of the worksheet being displayed in the window.

You can also use the Go To dialog box and the Name box to jump directly to a specific cell in the worksheet, whether the cell is currently visible in the workbook window or not. Try this now.

### To use the Go To dialog box and Name box:

1. Press the **F5** key to open the Go To dialog box.

2. Type **K55** in the Reference text box, and then click the **OK** button. Cell K55 is now the active cell.

3. Click the **Name** box, type **E6**, and then press the **Enter** key. Cell E6 becomes the active cell.

4. Press **Ctrl + Home** to make cell A1 the active cell.

## Navigating Between Worksheets

A workbook is usually composed of several worksheets. The workbook shown in Figure 1-8 contains three worksheets (this is the default for new blank workbooks) labeled Sheet1, Sheet2, and Sheet3. To move between the worksheets, you click the sheet tab of the worksheet you want to display.

### To move between worksheets:

1. Click the **Sheet2** tab. Sheet2, which is blank, appears in the workbook window. Notice that the Sheet2 tab is now white with the name "Sheet2" in a bold font. This is a visual indicator that Sheet2 is the active worksheet.

2. Click the **Sheet1** tab to return to the first sheet in the workbook.

Some workbooks will contain so many worksheets that some sheet tabs will be hidden from view. If that is the case, you can use the tab scrolling buttons located in the lower-left corner of the workbook window to scroll through the list of sheet tabs. Figure 1-9 describes the actions of the four tab scrolling buttons. Note that clicking the tab scrolling buttons does not change the active sheet; clicking the tab scrolling buttons allows you to view the other sheet tabs in the workbook. To change the active sheet, you must click the sheet tab itself.

| Figure 1-9 | TAB SCROLLING BUTTONS |
| --- | --- |

first sheet → |◄  ◄  ►  ►| ← last sheet

previous sheet → next sheet

Now that you have some basic skills navigating through a worksheet and a workbook, you can begin working with Mike's financial records. Some of the figures from the Lawn Wizards' April income statement have already been entered in an Excel workbook.

## Opening and Saving a Workbook

There are several ways of accessing a saved workbook. To open a workbook, you can click the Open command on Excel's File menu or you can click the Open button found on the Standard toolbar. You can also click the Workbooks link found in the Task Pane (if the Task Pane is visible to you). Any of these methods will display the Open dialog box. Once the Open dialog box is displayed, you have to navigate through the hierarchy of folders and drives on your computer or network to locate the workbook file.

Mike has saved the income statement with the filename "Lawn1." Locate and open this file now.

### To open the Lawn1 workbook:

1. Place your Excel Data Disk in the appropriate drive.

   TROUBLE? If you don't have a Data Disk, you need to contact your instructor or technical support person who will either give you one or give you instructions for creating your own. You can also review the instructions on the Read This Before You Begin page located at the front of this book.

2. Click the **Open** button 🗁 on the Standard toolbar. The Open dialog box is displayed. See Figure 1-10.

| Figure 1-10 | OPEN DIALOG BOX |
| --- | --- |

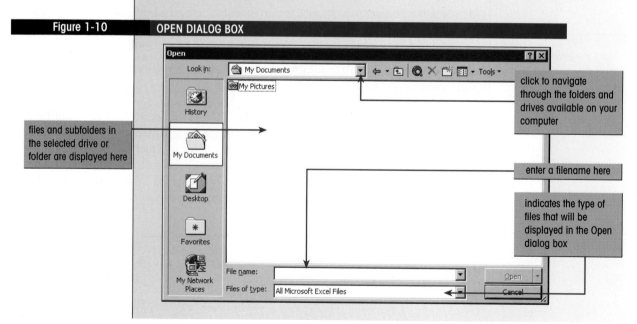

3. Click the **Look in** list arrow to display the list of available drives. Locate the drive that contains your Data Disk. This text assumes your Data Disk is a 3½-inch disk in drive A.

4. Click the drive that contains your Data Disk. A list of documents and folders on your Data Disk appears in the list box.

5. In the list of file and folder names, double-click **Tutorial.01**, double-click **Tutorial** to display the contents of the folder, and then click **Lawn1**.

6. Click the **Open** button (you could also have double-clicked Lawn1 to open the file). The workbook opens, displaying the income figures in the Sheet1 worksheet. Note that if the Task Pane was previously visible, it has now disappeared. See Figure 1-11.

| Figure 1-11 | LAWN1 WORKBOOK |
| --- | --- |

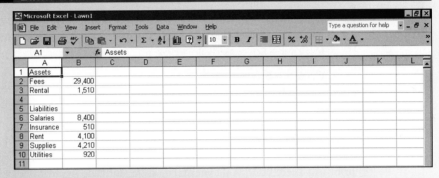

**TROUBLE?** In true accounting terminology, the word "Revenues" should be used in this income statement instead of the word "Assets," and the word "Expenses" should be used instead of the word "Liabilities." If requested by your instructor, you can change these terms to reflect accounting practices. Making this change will cause discrepancies between your screen and the figures and text references throughout the rest of this tutorial; however, such discrepancies will not interfere with your ability to complete the tasks in the tutorial.

Sometimes you will want to open a new blank workbook. Excel allows you to have several workbooks open at the same time. To create a new blank workbook, you can click the New button on the Standard toolbar.

Before going further in the Lawn1 workbook, you should make a copy of the file with a new name. This will allow you to go back to the original version of the file if necessary.

Mike suggests that you save the file with the name "Lawn2."

## To save the workbook with a different name:

1. Click **File** on the menu bar, and then click **Save As**. The Save As dialog box opens with the current workbook name in the File name text box. Note that the Tutorial folder on your Data Disk is automatically opened, so you do not have to navigate through your computer's hierarchy of folders and drives.

2. Click immediately to the right of "Lawn1" in the File name text box, press the **Backspace** key, and then type **2**.

3. Make sure that "Microsoft Excel Workbook" is displayed in the Save as type list box. See Figure 1-12.

Figure 1-12   SAVE AS DIALOG BOX

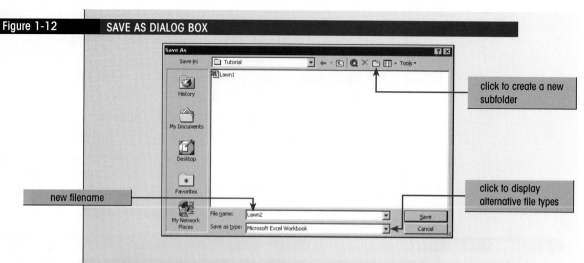

new filename

click to create a new
subfolder

click to display
alternative file types

Note that if you want to save the file to a new folder, you can create a new
folder "on the fly" by clicking the Create New Folder button located at the
top of the Save As dialog box.

4. Click the **Save** button. Excel saves the workbook under the new name and
closes the Save As dialog box.

By default, Excel saves the workbooks in Microsoft Excel Workbook format. If you are
creating a report that will be read by applications other than Excel (or versions of Excel
prior to Excel 2002), you can select a different type from the Save as type list box in the Save
(or Save As) dialog box.

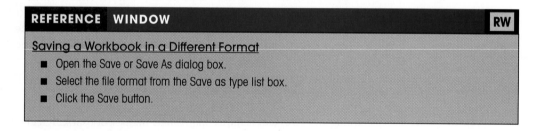

**REFERENCE  WINDOW**                                                      **RW**

Saving a Workbook in a Different Format
- Open the Save or Save As dialog box.
- Select the file format from the Save as type list box.
- Click the Save button.

Figure 1-13 displays a partial list of the other formats you can save your workbook as.
You can add other formats by running the Excel 2002 or Office XP installation program.
Note that some of the formats described in Figure 1-13 save only the active worksheet, not
the entire workbook.

| Figure 1-13 | SOME OF THE FILE FORMATS SUPPORTED BY EXCEL |
|---|---|

| FORMAT | DESCRIPTION |
|---|---|
| CSV (Comma delimited) | Saves the active worksheet as a text file with columns separated by commas |
| DBF2, DBF3, DBF4 | Saves the active worksheet as a dBASE table in the different versions of dBASE |
| Formatted Text (Space delimited) | Saves the active worksheet as a text file with columns separated by spaces |
| Microsoft Excel 2.1, 3.0, 4.0 Worksheet | Saves the workbook in the earliest versions of Excel |
| Microsoft Excel 5.0, 95, 97, 2000 Workbook | Saves the workbook in an earlier version of Excel |
| Text (Tab delimited) | Saves the active worksheet as a text file with columns separated by tabs |
| Web Archive | Saves the workbook as a Web site, enclosed within a single file |
| Web Page | Saves the workbook in HTML format, suitable for use as a Web page |
| WK1, WK2, WK3 | Saves the active worksheet as a Lotus 1-2-3 spreadsheet |
| WK4 (1-2-3) | Saves the workbook as a Lotus 1-2-3 document |
| WQ1 | Saves the active worksheet as a Quattro Pro spreadsheet |
| XML Spreadsheet | Saves the workbook in XML format, suitable for use in Web queries |

In this text you will use only the Microsoft Excel Workbook format.

# Working with Ranges

The data in the Lawn2 workbook contains the assets and liabilities for Lawn Wizards during the month of April, 2003. Mike would like to include this information in a title at the top of the worksheet. To make room for the title, you have to move the current content down a few rows. To move a group of cells in a worksheet, you have to first understand how Excel handles cells.

A group of worksheet cells is called a **cell range**, or **range**. Ranges can be either adjacent or nonadjacent. An **adjacent range** is a single rectangular block such as all of the data entered in cells A1 through B10 of the Lawn2 workbook. A **nonadjacent range** is comprised of two or more separate adjacent ranges. You could view the Lawn2 workbook as containing two non-adjacent ranges: the first range, cell A1 through cell B3, contains the company's assets, and the second range, cell A5 through cell B10, displays the company's liabilities.

Just as a cell reference indicates the location of the cell on the worksheet, a range reference indicates the location and size of the range. For adjacent ranges, the range reference identifies the cells in the upper-left and lower-right corners of the rectangle, with the individual cell references separated by a colon. For example, the range reference for Mike's income statement is A1:B10. If the range is nonadjacent, a semicolon separates the rectangular blocks, such as A1:B3;A5:B10, which refers to data in Mike's income statement, but does not include the blank row (row 4), which separates the assets from the liabilities.

## Selecting Ranges

Working with ranges of cells makes working with the data in a worksheet easier. Once you know how to select ranges of cells, you can move and copy the data anywhere in the worksheet or workbook.

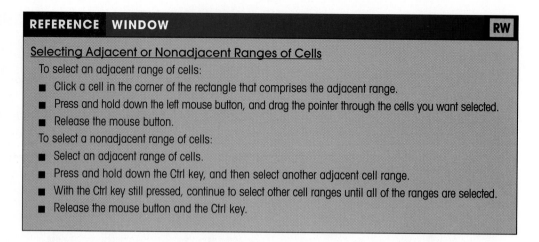

Next you'll select the adjacent range A1 through B10.

## To select the range A1:B10:

1. Click cell **A1** (if necessary) to make it the active cell, and then press and hold down the left mouse button.

2. With the mouse button still pressed, drag the pointer to cell **B10**.

3. Release the mouse button. All of the cells in the range A1:B10 are now highlighted, indicating that they are selected. See Figure 1-14.

| Figure 1-14 | SELECTING RANGE A1:B10 |

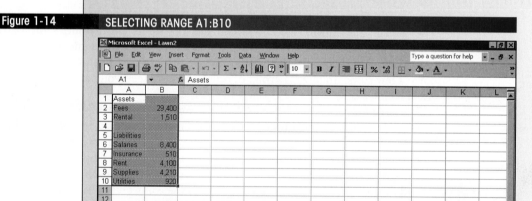

To deselect the range, you can click any cell in the worksheet.

4. Click cell **C1** to deselect the range.

To select a nonadjacent range, you begin by selecting an adjacent range, and then you press and hold down the Ctrl key and select other adjacent ranges. Release the Ctrl key and the mouse button when you are finished. Next you'll select the assets and then select the liabilities in the income statement.

## To select the nonadjacent range A1:B3;A5:B10:

**1.** Select the range **A1:B3**.

**2.** Press and hold down the **Ctrl** key.

**3.** Select the range **A5:B10**. See Figure 1-15.

| Figure 1-15 | SELECTING THE NONADJACENT RANGE A1:B3;A5:B10 |
|---|---|

**4.** Click any cell in the worksheet to deselect the range.

## Other Selection Techniques

To select a large range of data, Excel will automatically scroll horizontally or vertically to display additional cells in the worksheet. Selecting a large range of cells using the mouse drag technique can be slow and frustrating. For this reason, Excel provides keyboard shortcuts to quickly select large blocks of data without having to drag through the worksheet to select the necessary cells. Figure 1-16 describes some of these selection techniques.

| Figure 1-16 | OTHER RANGE SELECTION TECHNIQUES |
|---|---|

| TO SELECT... | ACTION |
|---|---|
| A large range of cells | Click the first cell in the range, press and hold down the Shift key, and then click the last cell in the range. All of the cells between the first and last cell are selected. |
| All cells on the worksheet | Click the Select All button, the gray rectangle in the upper-left corner of the worksheet where the row and column headings meet. |
| All cells in an entire row or column | Click the row or column heading. |
| A range of cells containing data | Click the first cell in the range, press and hold down the Shift key, and then double-click the side of the active cell in which you want to extend the selection. Excel extends the selection up to the first empty cell. |

Try some of the techniques described in Figure 1-16 using the income statement.

## To select large ranges of cells:

**1.** Click cell **A1** to make it the active cell.

**2.** Press and hold down the **Shift** key, and then click cell **B10**. Note that all of the cells between A1 and B10 are selected.

**TROUBLE?** If the range A1:B10 is not selected, try again, but make sure you hold down the Shift key while you click cell B10.

3. Release the Shift key.

4. Click cell **A1** to remove the selection.

5. Press and hold down the **Shift** key, and move the pointer to the bottom edge of cell A1 until the mouse pointer changes to ⇕.

6. Double-click the bottom edge of cell **A1**. The selection extends to cell A3, the last cell before the blank cell A4.

7. With the Shift key still pressed, move the pointer to the right edge of the selection until, once again, the pointer changes to ⇕.

8. Double-click the right edge of the selection. The selection extends to the last non-blank column in the worksheet.

9. Click the **A** column heading. All of the cells in column A are selected.

10. Click the **1** row heading. All of the cells in the first row are selected.

# Moving a Selection of Cells

Now that you know various ways to select a range of cells, you can move the income statement data to another location in the worksheet. To move a cell range, you first select it and then position the pointer over the selection border and drag the selection to a new location. Copying a range of cells is similar to moving a range. The only difference is that you must press the Ctrl key while you drag the selection to its new location. A copy of the original data appears at the location of the pointer when you release the mouse button.

You can also move a selection to a new worksheet in the current workbook. To do this, you press and hold down the Alt key and then drag the selection over the sheet tab of the new worksheet. Excel will automatically make that worksheet the active sheet, so you can drag the selection into its new location on the worksheet.

Next you'll move the cells in the range A1:B10 to a new location, beginning at cell A5.

*To move the range A1:B10 down four rows:*

1. Select the range **A1:B10**.

2. Move the pointer over the bottom border of the selection until the pointer changes to ⇕.

3. Press and hold down the left mouse button, and then drag the selection down four rows. A ScreenTip appears indicating the new range reference of the selection. See Figure 1-17.

| Figure 1-17 | MOVING A SELECTION TO THE RANGE A5:B14 |
|---|---|

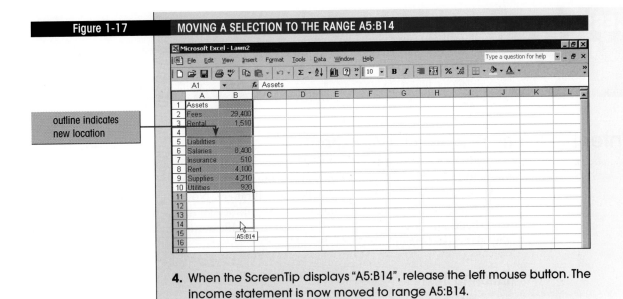

outline indicates new location

**4.** When the ScreenTip displays "A5:B14", release the left mouse button. The income statement is now moved to range A5:B14.

**5.** Click cell **A1** to remove the selection.

At this point, you have made space for a title and other information to be placed above the income statement. In the next session you will learn how to enter the new text into the worksheet, as well as how to edit the contents already there.

## To exit Excel:

**1.** Click **File** on the menu bar, and then click **Exit**.

**2.** When Excel prompts you to save your changes, click the **Yes** button. Excel saves the changes to the workbook and closes.

# Session 1.1 QUICK CHECK

**1.** A(n) _____ is the place on the worksheet where a column and row intersect.

**2.** Cell _____ refers to the intersection of the fourth column and second row.

**3.** What combination of keys can you press to make A1 the active cell in the worksheet?

**4.** To make Sheet2 the active worksheet, you _____.

**5.** Describe the two types of cell ranges in Excel.

**6.** What is the cell reference for the rectangular group of cells that extends from cell A5 down to cell F8?

**7.** Describe how you move a cell range from the Sheet1 worksheet to the Sheet2 worksheet.

**SESSION 1.2**

In this session, you will enter text and values into a worksheet. You will also enter formulas using basic arithmetic operators. You will use Excel's edit mode to change the value in a cell. You will insert rows and columns into a worksheet and modify the width of a column. You will insert, delete, and move worksheets, and you will rename sheet tabs. Finally, you will create a hard copy of your workbook by sending its contents to a printer.

## Entering Information into a Worksheet

In the previous session, you learned about the different parts of Excel's workbook window, and you learned how to work with cells and cell ranges. Now you will enter some new information in Mike's April income statement. The information that you enter in the cells of a worksheet can consist of text, values, or formulas. Mike wants you to enter text that describes the income statement located on Sheet1.

### Entering Text

Text entries include any combination of letters, symbols, numbers, and spaces. Although text is sometimes used as data, text is more often used to describe the data contained in the workbook. For example, the range A5:A14 of the income statement indicates the various asset and liability categories.

To enter text in a worksheet, you click the cell in which you want the text placed and then type the text you want entered. Excel automatically aligns text with the left edge of the cell. Mike wants you to enter the text labels "Lawn Wizards" in cell A1 and "Income Statement" in cell A2.

### To enter labels in cell A1 and A2:

1. If you took a break after the previous session, make sure Excel is running and the Lawn2 workbook is open.

2. Verify that Sheet1 is the active worksheet in the Lawn2 workbook.

3. Click cell **A1** if necessary to make it the active cell.

4. Type **Lawn Wizards** and then press the **Enter** key.

5. In cell A2, type **Income Statement** and then press the **Enter** key. See Figure 1-18.

   TROUBLE? If you make a mistake as you type, you can correct the error with the Backspace key. If you realize you made an error after pressing the Enter key, reenter the text by repeating Steps 3 through 5.

Figure 1-18    **ADDING NEW TEXT TO THE INCOME STATEMENT**

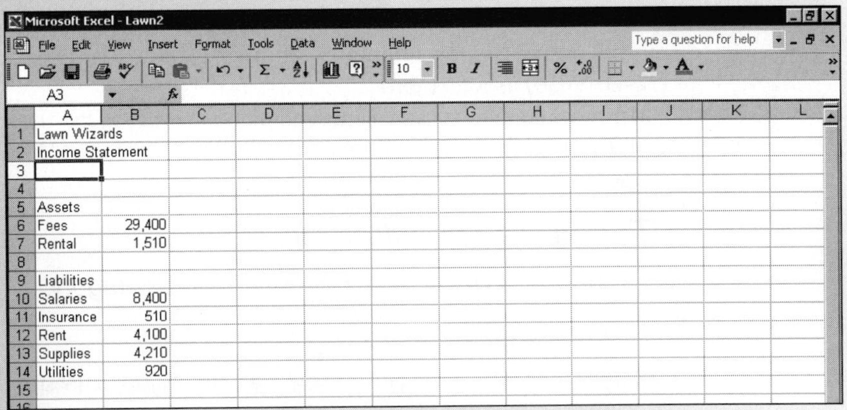

Note that even though you entered text in cells A1 and A2, the text appears to flow into cells B1 and B2. When you enter a text string longer than the width of the active cell, Excel will display the additional text if the cells to the right of the active cell are blank. If those cells are not blank, then Excel will truncate the display (though the entire text is still present in the cell). As you will see later, you can increase the width of the column if the text is cut off.

## Entering Dates

Dates are treated as separate from text in Excel. As you will learn later, Excel includes several special functions and commands to work with dates. For example, you can insert a function that will calculate the number of days between two dates (you will learn more about this in the next tutorial). To enter a date, separate the parts of the date with a slash or hyphen. For example, the date April 1, 2003 can be entered as either "4/1/2003" or "1-Apr-2003".

You can also enter the date as the text string "April 1, 2003", in which case Excel might automatically convert the text to "1-Apr-2003". You can change the format used by Excel to display dates by changing the cell's format. You will learn about date formats in Tutorial 3.

Mike wants the date "4/1/2003" to appear in cell A3.

### To insert the date in cell A3:

1. Verify that cell A3 is the active cell.

2. Type **4/1/2003** and then press the **Enter** key.

   TROUBLE? Your system may be set up to display dates using the mm/dd/yy format; therefore, you may see the date displayed as 4/1/03 rather than 4/1/2003.

## Entering Values

**Values** are numbers that represent a quantity of some type: the number of units in an inventory, stock prices, an exam score, and so on. Values can be numbers such as 378 and 25.275, or negative numbers such as –55.208. Values can also be expressed as currency ($4,571.25) or percentages (7.5%). Dates and times are also values, though that fact is hidden from you by the way Excel displays date information.

As you type information into a cell, Excel determines whether the information you have entered can be treated as a value. If so, Excel will automatically recognize the value type and right-align the value within the cell. Not all numbers are treated as values. For example, Excel treats a telephone number (1-800-555-8010) or a Social Security number (372-70-9654) as a text entry.

Mike would like to add a miscellaneous category to the list of monthly liabilities. In April, the total miscellaneous expenses incurred by Lawn Wizards totaled $351.

### To add the miscellaneous expenses:

1. Click cell **A15** and then type **Misc** as the category.

2. Press the **Tab** key to move to the next column.

3. Type **351** and then press the **Enter** key. Figure 1-19 shows the new entry in the income statement.

**Figure 1-19** ADDING A NEW CATEGORY AND VALUE TO THE INCOME STATEMENT

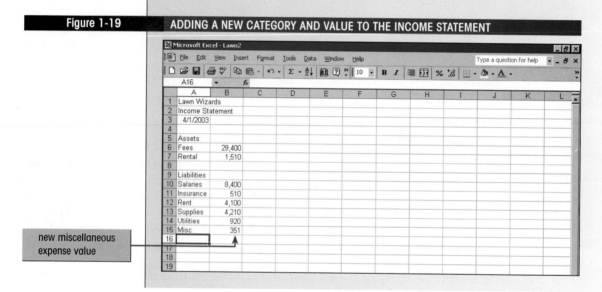

new miscellaneous expense value

## Entering Formulas

A **formula** is an expression that is used to calculate a value. You can enter a formula by typing the expression into the active cell, or in special cases Excel will automatically insert the formula for you. Excel formulas always begin with an equal sign (=) followed by an expression that calculates a value. If you do not start with an equal sign, Excel will treat the expression you enter as text. The expression can contain one or more **arithmetic operators**, such as +, −, *, or /, that are applied to either values or cells in the workbook. Figure 1-20 gives some examples of Excel formulas.

| Figure 1-20 | ARITHMETIC OPERATORS USED IN FORMULAS | | |
|---|---|---|---|
| **ARITHMETIC OPERATION** | **ARITHMETIC OPERATOR** | **EXAMPLE** | **DESCRIPTION** |
| Addition | + | =10+A5 | Adds 10 to the value in cell A5 |
| | | =B1+B2+B3 | Adds the values of cells B1, B2, and B3 |
| Subtraction | − | =C9−B2 | Subtracts the value in B2 from the value in cell C9 |
| | | =1−D2 | Subtracts the value in cell D2 from 1 |
| Multiplication | * | =C9*B9 | Multiplies the value in cell C9 by the value in cell B9 |
| | | =E5*0.06 | Multiplies the value in cell E5 by 0.06 |
| Division | / | =C9/B9 | Divides the value in cell C9 by the value in cell B9 |
| | | =D15/12 | Divides the value in cell D15 by 12 |
| Exponentiation | ^ | =B5^3 | Raises the value in cell B5 to the third power |
| | | =3^B5 | Raises 3 to the power specified in cell B5 |

---

**REFERENCE  WINDOW**                                                     **RW**

### Entering a Formula

- Click the cell where you want the formula value to appear.
- Type = and then type the expression that calculates the value you want.
- For formulas that include cell references, such as B2 or D78, you can type the cell reference or you can use the mouse or arrow keys to select each cell.
- When the formula is complete, press the Enter key.

---

If an expression contains more than one arithmetic operator, Excel performs the calculation in the order of precedence. The **order of precedence** is a set of predefined rules that Excel follows to unambiguously calculate a formula by determining which operator is applied first, which operator is applied second, and so forth. First, Excel performs exponentiation (^). Second, Excel performs multiplication (*) or division (/). Third, Excel performs addition (+) or subtraction (-).

For example, because multiplication has precedence over addition, the formula =3+4*5 has the value 23. If the expression contains two or more operators with the same level of precedence, Excel applies them going from left to right in the expression. In the formula =4*10/8, Excel first multiplies 4 by 10 and then divides the product by 8 to return the value 5.

You can add parentheses to a formula to make it easier to interpret or to change the order of operations. Excel will calculate any expression contained within the parentheses before any other part of the formula. The formula =(3+4)*5 first calculates the value of 3+4 and then multiplies the total by 5 to return the value 35 (note that without the parentheses, Excel would return a value of 23 as noted in the previous paragraph). Figure 1-21 shows other examples of Excel formulas in which the precedence order is applied to return a value.

**Figure 1-21**  **EXAMPLES ILLUSTRATING ORDER OF PRECEDENCE RULES**

| FORMULA VALUE A1=10, B1=20, C1=3 | ORDER OF PRECEDENCE RULE | RESULT |
|---|---|---|
| =A1+B1*C1 | Multiplication before addition | 70 |
| =(A1+B1)*C1 | Expression inside parentheses executed before expression outside | 90 |
| =A1/B1+C1 | Division before addition | 3.5 |
| =A1/(B1+C1) | Expression inside parentheses executed before expression outside | .435 |
| =A1/B1*C1 | Two operators at same precedence level, leftmost operator evaluated first | 1.5 |
| =A1/(B1*C1) | Expression inside parentheses executed before expression outside | .166667 |

The Lawn2 workbook contains the asset and liability values for various categories, but it doesn't include the total assets and liabilities, nor does it display Lawn Wizards' net income (assets minus liabilities) for the month of April. Mike suggests that you add formulas to calculate these values now.

## To calculate the total assets for the month of April:

1. Click cell **A8** to make it the active cell.

2. Type **Total** and then press the **Tab** key twice.

3. In cell C8, type **=B6+B7** (the income from fees and rental for the month).

   Note that as you type in the cell reference, Excel surrounds each cell with a different colored border that matches the color of the cell reference in the formula. As shown in Figure 1-22, Excel surrounds cell B6 with a blue border matching the blue used for the cell reference. Green is used for the B7 cell border and cell reference.

**Figure 1-22**  **TYPING A FORMULA INTO A CELL**

cell B6 is displayed with a blue border ...

... matching the color of its cell reference in the formula

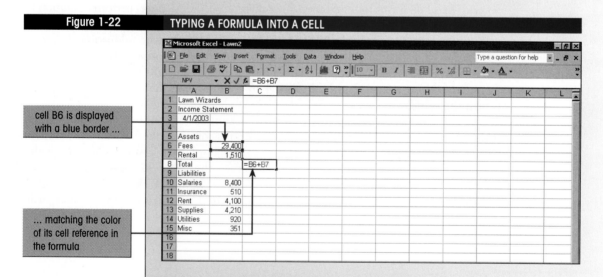

4. Press the **Enter** key.

   The total assets value displayed in cell C8 is 30,910.

You can also enter formulas interactively by clicking each cell in the formula rather than typing in the cell reference. Using this approach reduces the possibility of error caused by typing in an incorrect cell reference.

## To enter a formula by pointing and clicking:

1. Click cell **A16** to make it the active cell.

2. Type **Total** and then press the **Tab** key twice.

   **TROUBLE?** Note that when you started to type the word "Total" in cell A16, Excel automatically completed it for you. Since some worksheets will repeat the same word or phrase several times within a row or column, this AutoComplete feature can save you time.

3. In cell C16, type **=** and then click cell **B10**. Excel automatically inserts the reference to cell B10 into your formula.

4. Type **+** and then click cell **B11**.

5. Type **+** and then click cell **B12**.

6. Continue to select the rest of the liabilities in the range B13:B15, so that the formula in cell C16 reads **=B10+B11+B12+B13+B14+B15**. Do not type an equal sign after you click cell B15.

7. Press the **Enter** key. The total liabilities value "18,491" appears in cell C16.

   Now you can calculate the net income for the month of April.

8. In cell A18, enter **Net Income** and then press the **Tab** key twice.

9. In cell C18, enter the formula **=C8–C16** by clicking to select the cell references, and then press the **Enter** key. Figure 1-23 shows the completed formulas in the income statement.

| Figure 1-23 | TOTAL ASSETS, LIABILITIES, AND NET INCOME |

# Working **with Rows and Columns**

Mike examines the worksheet and points out that it is difficult to separate the assets from the liabilities. He would like you to insert a blank row between row 8 and row 9. You could do this by moving the cell range A9:C18 down one row, but there is another way. Excel allows you to insert rows or columns into your worksheet.

## Inserting a Row or Column

To insert a new row, you select a cell in the row where you want the new row placed. You then select Rows from the Insert menu. Excel will shift that row down, inserting a new blank row in its place. Inserting a new column follows the same process. Select a cell in the column where you want the new column inserted, and click Columns on the Insert menu. Excel will shift that column to the right, inserting a new blank column in its place.

To insert multiple rows or columns, select multiple cells before applying the Insert command. For example, to insert two new blank rows, select two adjacent cells in the same column, and click Rows on the Insert menu. To insert three new blank columns, select three adjacent cells in the same row, and click Columns on the Insert menu.

You can also insert individual cells within a row or column (rather than an entire row or column). To do this, select the range where you want the new cells placed, and click Cells on the Insert menu. Excel provides four options:

| | |
|---|---|
| ■ **Shift cells right** | Inserts new blank cells into the selected region, and moves the selected cells to the right. The new cells will have the same number of rows and columns as the selected cells. |
| ■ **Shift cells down** | Inserts new blank cells into the selected region, and moves the selected cells down. The new cells will have the same number of rows and columns as the selected cells. |
| ■ **Entire row** | Inserts an entire blank row. |
| ■ **Entire column** | Inserts an entire blank column. |

You can also insert rows and columns by right-clicking the selected cells and choosing Insert on the shortcut menu. This is equivalent to clicking the Cells command on the Insert menu.

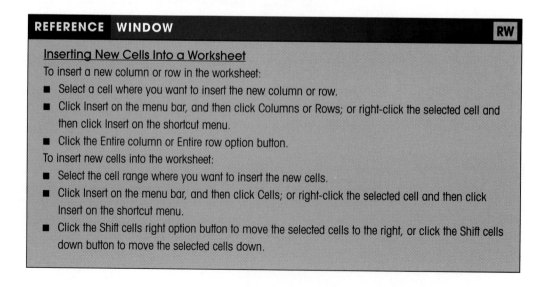

**REFERENCE   WINDOW**                                                                   **RW**

Inserting New Cells Into a Worksheet

To insert a new column or row in the worksheet:
■ Select a cell where you want to insert the new column or row.
■ Click Insert on the menu bar, and then click Columns or Rows; or right-click the selected cell and then click Insert on the shortcut menu.
■ Click the Entire column or Entire row option button.

To insert new cells into the worksheet:
■ Select the cell range where you want to insert the new cells.
■ Click Insert on the menu bar, and then click Cells; or right-click the selected cell and then click Insert on the shortcut menu.
■ Click the Shift cells right option button to move the selected cells to the right, or click the Shift cells down button to move the selected cells down.

Now that you have seen how to insert new cells into your worksheet, you'll insert three new blank cells into the range A9:C9.

## To insert three new cells into the worksheet:

**1.** Select the range **A9:C9**.

**2.** Click **Insert** on the menu bar, and then click **Cells**.

**3.** Click the **Shift cells down** option button, if necessary. See Figure 1-24.

| Figure 1-24 | INSERT DIALOG BOX |
| --- | --- |

**4.** Click the **OK** button.

Excel inserts new blank cells in the range A9:C9 and shifts the rest of the income statement down one row.

**TROUBLE?** Excel displays an Insert Options button ⬦ on the lower-right corner of cell C9. You can use this button to define how the new cells should be formatted. You will learn about formatting in Tutorial 3.

When you insert a new row, the formulas in the worksheet are automatically updated to reflect the changing position. For example, the formula for Net Income has changed from *=C8–C16* to *=C8–C17* to reflect the new location of the total liabilities cell. You will learn more about how formulas are adjusted in Tutorial 2.

## Clearing or Deleting a Row or Column

Mike wants to make one further change to the income statement. He wants to consolidate the supplies and miscellaneous categories into one entry. Your first task will be to remove the current contents of the range A14:B14 (the supplies category). Excel provides two ways of removing data. One way, called **clearing**, simply deletes the contents of the cells. To clear the contents of a cell, you use either the Delete key or the Clear command on the Edit menu. Clearing the contents of a cell does not change the structure of the workbook; that is, the row is not removed from the worksheet. Do not press the spacebar to enter a blank character in an attempt to clear a cell's content. Excel treats a blank character as text, so even though the cell appears to be empty, it is not.

## To remove the supplies category data:

1. Select the range **A14:B14**.

2. Press the **Delete** key. The text and values in the range A14:B14 are cleared.

   Now you can enter the text for the supplies and miscellaneous category.

3. In cell A14, type **Supplies & Misc.** and then press the **Tab** key.

   Now enter the total for the new category.

4. In cell B14, type **4,561** and then press the **Enter** key.

   **TROUBLE?** Do not worry that the Supplies & Misc category label in cell A14 appears to be cut off. The adjacent cell is no longer empty, and cell A14 is not wide enough to display the entire text entry. You will correct this problem shortly.

Now you need to delete the miscellaneous category from the income statement. Excel provides similar options for deleting rows, columns, and cells as it does for inserting them. To delete a row, column, or cell from the worksheet, you first select the cell or range and then click Delete on the Edit menu (you can also right-click the selected range and choose Delete on the shortcut menu). Excel provides you with the following delete options:

- **Shift cells left**   Deletes the selected cells and shifts cells from the right into the selected region
- **Shift cells up**   Deletes the selected cells and shifts cells from the bottom up into the selected region
- **Entire row**   Deletes the entire row
- **Entire column**   Deletes the entire column

Because you no longer need the miscellaneous category, you will delete the cell range A16:C16.

## To delete the cell range A16:C16:

1. Select the range **A16:C16**.

2. Click **Edit** on the menu bar, and then click **Delete**.

3. Select the **Shift cells up** option button if necessary, and then click the **OK** button. Excel deletes the contents of the cell range and moves the cells below up one row. See Figure 1-25.

| Figure 1-25 | DELETING THE MISCELLANEOUS CATEGORY FROM THE INCOME STATEMENT |
| --- | --- |

width of column A
needs to be increased

#REF! indicates that
there is an invalid cell
reference in the formula

Mike immediately sees two problems. One problem is that the text entry in cell A14 is cut off. The second is that the liabilities total in cell C16 and the net income in cell C18 have been replaced with *#REF!* The *#REF*! entry is Excel's way of indicating that there is an invalid cell reference in a formula. Because Excel cannot calculate the formula's value, Excel displays this text as a warning. The invalid cell reference occurred when the miscellaneous total was deleted. Since that cell no longer exists, any formula that is based on that cell, such as the formula that calculates the liability, will return an error message, and since the total liability now returns an error message, the formula for the net income on which the total liability value is based also returns an error.

So you need to do two things: 1) increase the width of column A so that no text is truncated, and 2) revise the formula in cell C16 to remove the error message. First you will change the width of column A.

## Increasing the Width of a Column or the Height of a Row

Excel provides several methods for changing the width of a column or the height of a row. You can click the dividing line of the column or row, or you can drag the dividing line to change the width of the column or the height of the row. You can also double-click the border of a column heading, and the column will increase in width to match the length of the longest entry in the column. Widths are expressed either in terms of the number of characters or the number of screen pixels.

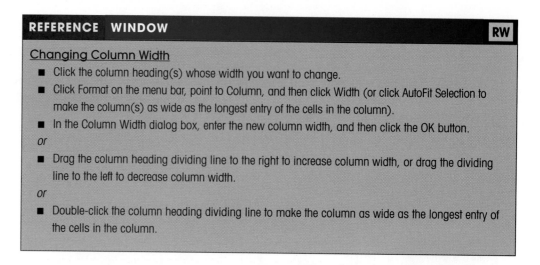

You'll drag the dividing line between columns A and B to increase the width of column A enough to display the complete text in cell A14.

## To increase the width of column A:

1. Move the mouse pointer to the dividing line between the column A and column B headings until the pointer changes to ✛.

2. Click and drag the pointer to the right to a length of about **15** characters (or 110 pixels).

3. Release the mouse button. The entire text in cell A14 should now be visible. See Figure 1-26.

**Figure 1-26**    INCREASING THE WIDTH OF COLUMN A

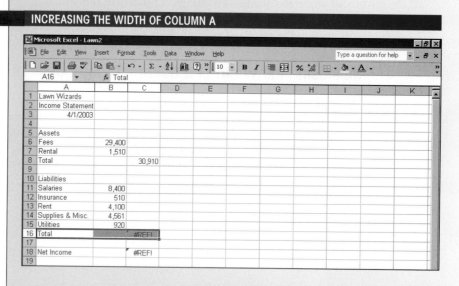

**TROUBLE?** If the text in cell A14 is still truncated, drag the dividing line further to the right.

# Editing **Your Worksheet**

When you work in Excel you might make mistakes that you want to correct or undo. You have an error in the Lawn2 workbook of an invalid cell reference in cell C16. You could simply delete the formula in cell C16 and reenter the formula from scratch. However, there may be times when you will not want to change the entire contents of a cell, but merely edit a portion of the entry. For example, if a cell contains a large block of text or a complicated formula, you might not want to retype the text or formula completely. Instead, you can edit a cell by either selecting the cell and then clicking in the Formula bar to make the changes or by double-clicking the cell to open the cell in **edit mode**.

## Working in Edit Mode

When you are working in edit mode or editing the cell using the Formula bar, some of the keys on your keyboard act differently than they do when you are not editing the content of a cell. For example, the Home, Delete, Backspace, and End keys do not move the insertion point to different cells in the worksheet; rather they move the insertion point to different locations within the cell. The Home key, for example, moves the insertion point to the beginning of whatever text has been entered into the cell. The End key moves the insertion point to the end of the cell's text. The left and right arrow keys move the insertion point backward and forward through the text in the cell. The Backspace key deletes the character immediately to the left of the insertion point, and the Delete key deletes the character at the location of the insertion point. Once you are finished editing the cell, press the Enter key to leave editing mode or to remove the insertion point from the Formula bar.

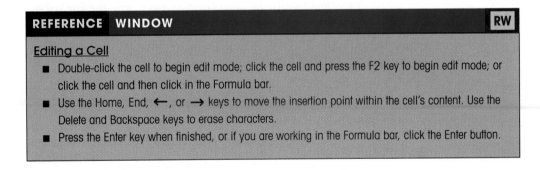

**REFERENCE WINDOW**                                                                 **RW**

**Editing a Cell**

■ Double-click the cell to begin edit mode; click the cell and press the F2 key to begin edit mode; or click the cell and then click in the Formula bar.

■ Use the Home, End, ←, or → keys to move the insertion point within the cell's content. Use the Delete and Backspace keys to erase characters.

■ Press the Enter key when finished, or if you are working in the Formula bar, click the Enter button.

Now you'll use edit mode to change the formula in cell C16.

*To edit the formula in cell C16:*

**1.** Double-click cell **C16**.

An insertion point appears in the cell, indicating where new text will be inserted into the current cell expression. Note that the formula appears fine except for the *+#REF!* at the end of the expression. See Figure 1-27. This notation indicates that the cell reference used in the formula no longer points to a valid cell reference. In this case, the cell referenced was deleted. You can fix the error by deleting the *+#REF!* from the formula.

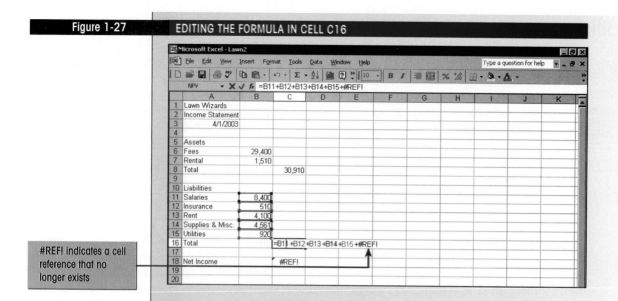

**Figure 1-27**   EDITING THE FORMULA IN CELL C16

#REF! indicates a cell reference that no longer exists

2. Press the **End** key to move the blinking insertion point to the end of the cell.

3. Press the **Backspace** key six times to delete *+#REF!* from the formula.

4. Press the **Enter** key. The value 18,491 appears in cell C16, and the net income for the company is 12,419.

If you make a mistake as you type, you can press the Esc key or click the Cancel button on the Formula bar to cancel all changes you made while in edit mode.

## Undoing an Action

Another way of fixing a mistake is to undo the action. Undoing an action cancels it, returning the workbook to its previous state. To undo an action, click the Undo button located on the Standard toolbar. As you work, Excel maintains a list of your actions, so you can undo most of the actions you perform on your workbook during your current session. To reverse more than one action, click the list arrow next to the Undo button and click the action you want to undo from the list. To see how this works, use the Undo button to remove the edit you just made to cell C16.

### To undo your last action:

1. Click the **Undo** button 🔄 on the Standard toolbar. The value *#REF!* appears again in cells C16 and C18 indicating that your last action, editing the formula in cell C16, has been undone.

If you find that you have gone too far in undoing your previous actions, you can go forward in the action list and redo those actions. To redo an action, you click the Redo button on the Standard toolbar. Use the Redo button now to return the formula in cell C16 to its edited state.

### To redo your last action:

**1.** Click the **Redo** button [ ] on the Standard toolbar. The edited formula has been reinserted into cell C16 and the value 18,491 again appears in the cell.

**TROUBLE?** If you don't see the Redo button, click the Toolbar Options button [ ] located on the right edge of the Standard toolbar, and then click [ ] to repeat the delete (the Redo button will now appear on the toolbar). You can also click the Repeat Delete command on the Edit menu (you might have to wait a few seconds for Excel to display the full Edit menu). After you undo an action, the Repeat command changes to reflect the action that has been undone so you can choose to repeat the action if undoing the action does not give you the result you want.

Through the use of edit mode and the Undo and Redo buttons, you should be able to correct almost any mistake you make in your Excel session.

# Working with Worksheets

By default, Excel workbooks contain three worksheets labeled Sheet1, Sheet2, and Sheet3. You can add new worksheets or remove old ones. You can also give your worksheets more descriptive names. In the Lawn2 workbook, there is no data entered in the Sheet2 or Sheet3 worksheets. Mike suggests that you remove these sheets from the workbook.

## Adding and Removing Worksheets

To delete a worksheet, you first select its sheet tab to make the worksheet the active sheet; then right-click the sheet tab and choose Delete from the shortcut menu. Try this now by deleting the Sheet2 and Sheet3 worksheets.

### To delete the Sheet2 and Sheet3 worksheets:

**1.** Click the **Sheet2** tab to make Sheet2 the active sheet.

**2.** Right-click the sheet tab, and then click **Delete** on the shortcut menu. Sheet2 is deleted and Sheet3 becomes the active sheet.

**3.** Right-click the **Sheet3** tab, and then click **Delete**.

There is now only one worksheet in the workbook.

After you have deleted the two unused sheets, Mike informs you that he wants to include a description of the workbook content and purpose. In other words, Mike wants to include a **documentation sheet**, a worksheet that provides information about the content and purpose of the workbook. A documentation sheet can be any information that you feel is important, for example, the name of the person who created the workbook or instructions on how to use the workbook. A documentation sheet is a valuable element if you intend to share the workbook with others. The documentation sheet is often the first worksheet in the workbook, though in this case Mike wants to place it at the end of the workbook.

To insert a new worksheet, you can either use the Insert Worksheet command or the right-click method. Using either method will insert a new worksheet before the active sheet.

### To insert a new worksheet in the workbook:

1. Click **Insert** on the menu bar.

2. Click **Worksheet**. A new worksheet with the name "Sheet2" is placed at the beginning of your workbook.

Mike wants the documentation sheet to include the following information:

- The company name
- The date the workbook was originally created
- The person who created it
- The purpose of the workbook

You'll add this information to the new sheet in the Lawn2 workbook.

### To insert the documentation information in the new worksheet:

1. Click cell **A1** if necessary, and then type **Lawn Wizards**.

2. Click cell **A3**, type **Date:** and then press the **Tab** key.

3. Enter the current date using the date format, mm/dd/yyyy. For example, if the date is April 5, 2003, enter the text string "4/5/2003." Press the **Enter** key.

4. In cell A4, type **Created By:** and then press the **Tab** key.

5. Enter your name in cell B4, and then press the **Enter** key.

6. Type **Purpose:** in cell A5, and then press the **Tab** key.

7. In cell B5, type **To record monthly income statements for the Lawn Wizards,** and then press the **Enter** key.

8. Increase the width of column A to **15** characters. Figure 1-28 shows the completed documentation sheet (your sheet will display a different name and date).

| Figure 1-28 | CREATING A DOCUMENTATION SHEET |
|---|---|

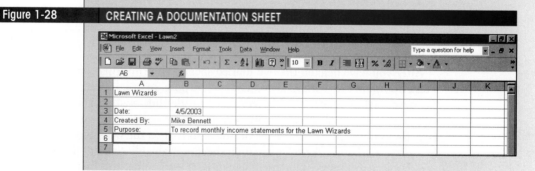

## Renaming a Worksheet

The current sheet names "Sheet2" and "Sheet1" are not very descriptive. Mike suggests that you rename Sheet2 "Documentation" and Sheet1 "April Income". To rename a worksheet, you double-click the sheet tab to select the sheet name, and then you type a new name for the sheet.

Rename the sheet tabs using more meaningful names.

### To rename the worksheets:

1. Double-click the **Sheet2** tab. Note that the name of the sheet is selected.

2. Type **Documentation** and then press the **Enter** key. The width of the sheet tab adjusts to the length of the name you type.

3. Double-click the **Sheet1** tab.

4. Type **April Income** and then press the **Enter** key.

## Moving a Worksheet

Finally, Mike wants the Documentation sheet to appear last in the workbook. He feels that the actual data should be displayed first. To move the position of a worksheet in the workbook, you click the worksheet's sheet tab, and drag and drop it to a new location relative to the other worksheets.

You can create a copy of the entire worksheet by holding down the Ctrl key as you drag and drop the sheet tab. When you release the mouse button, a copy of the original worksheet will be placed at the new location, while the original sheet will stay at its initial position in the workbook.

| REFERENCE WINDOW | RW |
| --- | --- |

**Moving or Copying a Worksheet**
- Click the sheet tab of the worksheet you want to move (or copy).
- Drag the sheet tab along the row of sheet tabs until the small arrow appears in the desired location. To create a copy of the worksheet, press and hold down the Ctrl key as you drag the sheet tab to the desired location.
- Release the mouse button. Release the Ctrl key if necessary.

You'll move the Documentation sheet now.

### To move the Documentation worksheet:

1. Click the **Documentation** tab to make it the active worksheet.

2. Click the **Documentation** tab again, and then press and hold down the left mouse button so the pointer changes to ⏳. A small arrow appears in the upper-left corner of the sheet tab.

3. Drag the pointer to the right of the April Income tab, and then release the mouse button. The Documentation sheet is now the second sheet in the workbook.

# Printing a Worksheet

Now that you are finished editing the Lawn2 workbook, you can create a hard copy of its contents for your records. You can print the contents of your workbook using either the Print command on the File menu or by clicking the Print button on the Standard toolbar. If you use the Print command, Excel displays a dialog box in which you can specify which worksheets you want to print, the number of copies, and the print quality (or resolution). If you click the Print button, you will not have a chance to set these options, but if you do not need to do so, clicking the Print button is a faster way of generating your output. Finally, you can also choose the Print Preview command on the File menu or click the Print Preview button on the Standard toolbar to see what your page will look like before it is sent to the printer. You can print directly from Print Preview.

If you are printing to a shared printer on a network, many other people might be sending print jobs at the same time you do. To avoid confusion, you will print the contents of both the Documentation sheet and the April Income sheet. You will use the Print command on the File menu since you need to print the entire workbook and not just the active worksheet (which is the default print setting). You will learn more about the Print Preview command in the next tutorial.

### To print the contents of the Lawn2 workbook:

**1.** Click **File** on the menu bar, and then click **Print** to open the Print dialog box. See Figure 1-29.

| Figure 1-29 | PRINT DIALOG BOX |
| --- | --- |

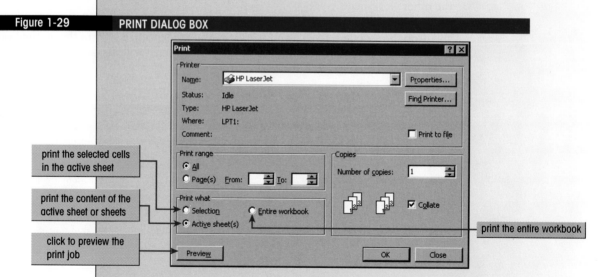

print the selected cells in the active sheet

print the content of the active sheet or sheets

click to preview the print job

print the entire workbook

**2.** Click the **Name** list box, and then select the printer to which you want to print.

Now you need to select what to print. To print the complete workbook, select the Entire workbook option button. To print the active worksheet, select the Active sheet(s) option button. To print the selected cells on the active sheet, click the Selection option button.

**3.** Click the **Entire workbook** option button.

**4.** Make sure "1" appears in the Number of copies list box, since you only need to print one copy of the workbook.

5. Click the **OK** button to send the workbook to the printer.

   **TROUBLE?** If the workbook does not print, see your instructor or technical resource person for help.

   You have completed your work on the Lawn2 workbook, so you can save your changes and exit Excel.

6. Click the **Save** button 🖫 on the Standard toolbar, and then click the **Close** button ⊠ on the title bar.

You give Mike the hard copy of the Lawn2 workbook. He will file the report for later reference. If he needs to add new information to the workbook or if he needs you to make further changes to the structure of the workbook, he will contact you.

## Session 1.2 QUICK CHECK

1. Indicate whether Excel treats the following cell entries as a value, text, or a formula:

   a. 11/09/2003          e. 201-19-1121
   b. Net Income          f. =D1-D9
   c. 321                 g. 44 Evans Avenue
   d. =C11*225

2. What formula would you enter to divide the value in cell E5 by the value in cell E6?

3. What formula would you enter to raise the value in cell E5 to the power of the value in cell E6?

4. When you insert a new row into a worksheet, the selected cells are moved
   _____.

5. When you insert a new column into a worksheet, the selected cells are moved
   _____.

6. To change the name of a worksheet, double-click the _____.

7. Which key do you press to clear the contents of the active cell?

8. How does clearing a cell differ from deleting a cell?

## REVIEW ASSIGNMENTS

Mike has another workbook in which he wants you to make some changes. This workbook contains the income and expense figures for May. Mike has already done some work on the file, but wants you to make some modifications and additions. To complete this task:

1. Start Excel and open the workbook **Income1** located in the Tutorial.01/Review folder on your Data Disk.

2. Save the workbook as **Income2** in the same folder.

3. Change the date in cell A3 to 5/1/2003.

4. Insert new cells in the range A12:C12, shifting the other cells down. In cell A12, enter the text "Rent". In cell B12, enter the value "4,100".

**Explore**
5. Edit the formula in cell C16 so that the formula includes the cost of rent in the liabilities total.

**Explore**
6. There is a mistake in the formula for the net income. Fix the formula so that it displays the difference between the assets and the liabilities in the month of May.

7. Move the income statement values in the range A5:C18 to the range C1:E14.

8. Resize the width of column C to 15 characters.

9. Insert a sheet named "Documentation" at the beginning of the workbook.

10. In the Documentation sheet, enter the following text:
   - Cell A1: Lawn Wizards
   - Cell A3: Date:
   - Cell B3: *Enter the current date*
   - Cell A4: Created By:
   - Cell B4: *Enter your name*
   - Cell A5: Purpose:
   - Cell B5: To record income and expenses for the month of May

11. Increase the width of column A in the Documentation worksheet to 20 characters.

12. Rename Sheet1 as **May Income**.

13. Delete Sheet2 and Sheet3.

14. Print the entire contents of the Income2 workbook.

15. Save and close the workbook, and then exit Excel.

## CASE PROBLEMS

*Case 1. Cash Flow Analysis at Madison Federal*  Lisa Wu is a financial consultant at Madison Federal. She is working on a financial plan for Tom and Carolyn Watkins. Lisa has a cash flow analysis for the couple, and she wants you to record this information for her. Here are the relevant financial figures:

Receipts
- Employment Income:      95,000
- Other Income:      5,000

Disbursements
- Insurance:      940
- Savings/Retirement:      8,400
- Living Expenses:      63,000
- Taxes:      16,300

Lisa wants you to calculate the total receipts and total disbursements and then to calculate the income surplus (receipts minus disbursements) in an Excel workbook that she has already started. To complete this task:

1. Open the **CFlow1** workbook located in the Tutorial.01/Cases folder on your Data Disk, and then save the workbook as **CFlow2** in the same folder.

2. Move the contents of the range A1:C12 to the range A3:C14.

3. Insert the text "Cash Flow Analysis" in cell A1.

4. Increase the width of column A to 130 pixels, the width of column B to 160 pixels, and the width of column C to 130 pixels.

5. Insert the financial numbers listed earlier into the appropriate cells in column C.

6. In cell C6, insert a formula to calculate the total receipts.

7. In cell C12, insert a formula to calculate the total disbursements.

8. Insert a formula to calculate the surplus in cell C14.

9. Rename Sheet1 as **Cash Flow**.

10. Insert a worksheet at the beginning of the workbook named "Documentation".

11. In the Documentation sheet, enter the following text:

   ■ Cell A1:  Cash Flow Report
   ■ Cell A3:  Date:
   ■ Cell B3:  *Enter the current date*
   ■ Cell A4:  Created By:
   ■ Cell B4:  *Enter your name*
   ■ Cell A5:  Purpose:
   ■ Cell B5:  Cash flow analysis for Tom and Carolyn Watkins

12. Increase the width of column A in the Documentation worksheet to 20 characters.

13. Delete Sheet2 and Sheet3.

14. Print the contents of the entire workbook.

**Explore** ▷ 15. What would the surplus be if the couple's taxes increased to 18,500? Enter this value into the Cash Flow worksheet, and then print just the Cash Flow worksheet.

16. Save and close the workbook, and then exit Excel.

*Case 2. Financial Report for EMS Industries*  Lee Evans is an agent at New Haven Financial Services. His job is to maintain financial information on stocks for client companies. He has the annual balance sheet for a company named EMS Industries in an Excel workbook and needs your help in finishing the workbook layout and contents. To complete this task:

1. Open the **Balance1** workbook located in the Tutorial.01/Cases folder on your Data Disk, and then save the workbook as **Balance2** in the same folder.

2. Select the cells A1:C2 and insert two new rows into the worksheet.

3. Insert the text "Annual Balance Sheet for EMS Industries" in cell A1.

4. Move the contents of the range A19:C33 to the range E3:G17.

5. Move the contents of the range B36:C38 to the range B19:C21.

6. Change the width of column B to 150 pixels, the width of column D to 20 pixels, and the width of column F to 150 pixels.

7. Insert a formula in cell C10 to calculate the total current assets, in cell C17 to calculate the total noncurrent assets, in cell G10 to calculate the total current liabilities, and in cell G17 to calculate the total noncurrent liabilities.

8. In cell C19, insert a formula to calculate the total of the current and noncurrent assets.

9. In cell C20, insert a formula to calculate the total of the current and noncurrent liabilities.

10. In cell C21, insert a formula to calculate the annual balance (the total assets minus the total liabilities).

11. Rename Sheet1 as **Annual Balance Sheet**.

12. Delete Sheet2 and Sheet3.

13. Insert a worksheet named "Documentation" at the front of the workbook.

14. Enter the following text into the Documentation sheet:
    - Cell A1: Annual Balance Report
    - Cell A3: Company:
    - Cell B3: EMS Industries
    - Cell A4: Date:
    - Cell B4: *Enter the current date*
    - Cell A5: Recorded By:
    - Cell B5: *Enter your name*
    - Cell A6: Summary:
    - Cell B6: Annual Balance Sheet

15. Increase the width of column A in the Documentation worksheet to 20 characters.

16. Print the entire contents of the workbook.

17. Save and close the workbook, and then exit Excel.

**Case 3. *Analyzing Sites for a New Factory for Kips Shoes*** Kips Shoes is planning to build a new factory. The company has narrowed the site down to four possible cities. Each city has been graded on a 1-to-10 scale for four categories: the size of the local market, the quality of the labor pool, the local tax base, and the local operating expenses. Each of these four factors is given a weight with the most important factor given the highest weight. After the sites are analyzed, the scores for each factor will be multiplied by their weights, and then a total weighted score will be calculated.

Gwen Sanchez has entered the weights and the scores for each city into an Excel workbook. She needs you to finish the workbook by inserting the formulas to calculate the weighted scores and the total overall score for each city. To complete this task:

1. Open the **Site1** workbook located in the Tutorial.01/Cases folder on your Data Disk, and then save the workbook as **Site2** in the same folder.

2. Switch to the Site Analysis sheet.

3. In cell B12, calculate the weighted Market Size score for Waukegan by inserting a formula that multiplies the value in cell B5 by the value in cell C5.

4. Insert formulas to calculate the weighted scores for the rest of the cells in the range B12:E15.

5. Insert formulas in the range B17:E17 that calculate the totals of the weighted scores for each of the four cities. Which city has the highest weighted score?

6. Switch to the Documentation sheet, and enter your name and the date in the appropriate location on the sheet.

7. Print the entire workbook.

*Explore*

8. Gwen reports that Brockton's score for market size should be 6 and not 5. Modify this entry in the table, and then print just the Site Analysis worksheet with the new total scores. Does this change your conclusions about which city is most preferable for the new factory?

9. Save and close the workbook, and then exit Excel.

*Case 4. Cash Counting Calculator*    Rob Stuben works at a local town beach in Narragansett where a fee is collected for parking. At the end of each day, the parking attendants turn in the cash they have collected with a statement of the daily total. Rob is responsible for receiving the daily cash from each attendant, checking the accuracy of the daily total, and taking the cash deposit to the bank.

Rob wants to set up a simple cash counter using Excel, so that he can insert the number of bills of each denomination into a worksheet so the total cash is automatically computed. By a simple cash counter method, he only has to count and enter the number of one-dollar bills, the number of fives, and so on. To complete this task:

1. Save a new workbook with the name **CashCounter** in the Tutorial.01/Cases folder on your Data Disk.

*Explore*

2. In the workbook, create a worksheet named **Counter** with the following properties:

   ■ All currency denominations (1, 5, 10, 20, 50, 100) should be listed in the first column of the worksheet.

   ■ In the second column, you will enter the number of bills of each denomination, but this column should be left blank initially.

   ■ In the third column, insert the formulas to calculate totals for each denomination, (that is, the number of bills multiplied by the denomination of each bill).

   ■ In a blank cell at the bottom of the third column, which contains the formulas for calculating the totals of each denomination, a formula that calculates the grand total of the cash received should be entered.

3. Create a Documentation sheet. The sheet should include the title of the workbook, the date the workbook was created, your name, and the purpose of the workbook. Make this worksheet the first worksheet in the workbook.

4. Adjust the widths of the columns, if necessary. Delete any blank worksheets from the workbook.

*Explore*

5. On Rob's first day using the worksheet, the cash reported by an attendant was $1,565. Rob counted the bills and separated them by denomination. Enter the following values into the worksheet:

   ■ 5 fifties

   ■ 23 twenties

   ■ 41 tens

   ■ 65 fives

   ■ 120 ones

6. Print the entire contents of your workbook.

**Explore**

7. On Rob's second day, the cash reported by an attendant was $1,395. Again, Rob counted the money and separated the bills by denomination. Clear the previous values, and then enter the new values for the distribution of the bills into the worksheet:

- 2 hundreds
- 4 fifties
- 17 twenties
- 34 tens
- 45 fives
- 90 ones

8. Print just the Counter worksheet.

9. Save and close the workbook, and then exit Excel.

## LAB ASSIGNMENTS

**Spreadsheets**

The New Perspectives Labs are designed to help you master some of the key computer concepts and skills presented in each chapter of the text. If you are using your school's lab computers, your instructor or technical support person should have installed the Labs software for you. If you want to use the Labs on your home computer, ask your instructor for the appropriate software. See the Read This Before You Begin page for more information on installing and starting the Lab.

Each Lab has two parts: Steps and Explore. Use Steps first to learn and review concepts. Read the information on each page and do the numbered steps. As you work through the Lab, you will be asked to answer Quick Check questions about what you have learned. At the end of the Lab, you will see a Summary Report of your answers to the Quick Checks. If your instructor wants you to turn in this Summary Report, click the Print button on the Summary Report screen.

When you have completed Steps, you can click the Explore button to complete the Lab Assignments. You can also use Explore to practice the skills you learned and to explore concepts on your own.

SPREADSHEETS  Spreadsheet software is used extensively in business, education, science, and humanities to simplify tasks that involve calculations. In this Lab you will learn how spreadsheet software works. You will use spreadsheet software to examine and modify worksheets, as well as to create your own worksheets.

1. Click the Steps button to learn how spreadsheet software works. As you proceed through the Steps, answer all of the Quick Check questions that appear. After you complete the Steps, you will see a Quick Check Summary Report. Follow the instructions on the screen to print this report.

2. Click the Explore button to begin this assignment. Click OK to display a new worksheet. Click File on the menu bar, and then click Open to display the Open dialog box. Click the file **Income.xls** and then press the Enter key to open the **Income and Expense Summary** workbook. Notice that the worksheet contains labels and values for income from consulting and training. It also contains labels and values for expenses

such as rent and salaries. The worksheet does not, however, contain formulas to calculate Total Income, Total Expenses, or Profit. Do the following:

a. Calculate the Total Income by entering the formula =SUM(C4:C5) in cell C6.
b. Calculate the Total Expenses by entering the formula =SUM(C9:C12) in C13.
c. Calculate Profit by entering the formula =C6-C13 in cell C15.
d. Manually check the results to make sure you entered the formulas correctly.
e. Print your completed worksheet showing your results.

3. You can use a spreadsheet to keep track of your grades in a class and to calculate your grade average. In Explore, click File on the menu bar, and then click Open to display the Open dialog box. Click the file **Grades.xls** to open the workbook. The worksheet contains the labels and formulas necessary to calculate your grade average based on four test scores. You receive a score of 88 out of 100 on the first test. On the second test, you score 42 out of 48. On the third test, you score 92 out of 100. You have not taken the fourth test yet. Enter the appropriate data in the **Grades.xls** worksheet to determine your grade average after taking three tests. Print out your worksheet.

4. Worksheets are handy for answering "what if" questions. Suppose you decide to open a lemonade stand. You're interested in how much profit you can make each day. What if you sell 20 cups of lemonade? What if you sell 100? What if the cost of lemons increases?

   In Explore, open the file **Lemons.xls** and use the worksheet to answer questions a through d. Then print the worksheet for question e:

   a. What is your profit if you sell 20 cups a day?
   b. What is your profit if you sell 100 cups a day?
   c. What is your profit if the price of lemons increases to $.07 and you sell 100 cups?
   d. What is your profit if you raise the price of a cup of lemonade to $.30? (Lemons still cost $.07 and assume you sell 100 cups.)
   e. Suppose your competitor boasts that she sold 50 cups of lemonade in one day and made exactly $12.00. On your worksheet adjust the cost of cups, water, lemons, and sugar, and the price per cup to show a profit of exactly $12.00 for 50 cups sold. Print this worksheet.

5. It is important to make sure the formulas in your worksheet are accurate. An easy way to test this is to enter 1's for all the values on your worksheet, then check the calculations manually. In Explore, open the file **Receipt.xls**, which contains a formula that calculates sales receipts. Enter "1" as the value for Item 1, Item 2, Item 3, and Sales Tax %. Now manually calculate what you would pay for three items that each cost $1.00 in a state where sales tax is 1% (.01). Do your manual calculations match those of the worksheet? If not, correct the formulas in the worksheet, and then print out a *formula report* of your revised worksheet.

6. In Explore, create your own worksheet showing your household budget for one month. Make up the numbers for the budget. Put a title at the top of the worksheet. Use formulas to calculate your total income and expenses for the month. Add another formula to calculate how much money you were able to save. Print a formula report of your worksheet. Also, print your worksheet showing realistic values for one month.

## INTERNET ASSIGNMENTS

**Student Union**

The purpose of the Internet Assignments is to challenge you to find information on the Internet that you can use to create effective spreadsheets. The actual assignments are updated and maintained on the Course Technology Web site. Log on to the Internet and use your Web browser to go to the Student Union on the New Perspectives Series site at **www.course.com/NewPerspectives/studentunion**. Click the Online Companions link, and then click the link for this text.

## QUICK CHECK ANSWERS

*Session 1.1*

1. cell
2. D2
3. Ctrl + Home
4. Click the Sheet2 tab.
5. Adjacent and nonadjacent. An adjacent range is a rectangular block of cells. A nonadjacent range consists of two or more separate adjacent ranges.
6. A5:F8
7. Select the cells you want to move, and then press and hold down the Alt key and drag the selection over the Sheet2 tab. When Sheet2 becomes the active sheet, continue to drag the selection to position it in its new location in the worksheet, and then release the left mouse button and the Alt key.

*Session 1.2*

1. a. value
   b. text
   c. value
   d. formula
   e. text
   f. formula
   g. text
2. =E5/E6
3. =E5^E6
4. down
5. to the right
6. sheet tab and then type the new name to replace the highlighted sheet tab name
7. Delete key
8. Clearing a cell deletes the cell's contents but does not affect the position of other cells in the workbook. Deleting a cell removes the cell from the worksheet, and other cells are shifted into the deleted cell's position.

## OBJECTIVES

In this tutorial you will:

- Work with the Insert Function button

- Learn about Excel's financial functions

- Copy and paste formulas and functions

- Work with absolute and relative references

- Learn to use Excel's Auto Fill features

- Create logical functions

- Work with Excel's date functions

# WORKING WITH FORMULAS AND FUNCTIONS

*Analyzing a Mortgage*

CASE

## Prime Realty

You work as an assistant at Prime Realty (PR) selling real estate. One of the agents at PR, Carol Malloy, has asked you to help her develop an Excel workbook that calculates mortgages. The workbook needs to include three values: the size of the loan, the number of payments, and the annual interest rate. Using this information in the workbook, you will be able to determine the monthly payment needed to pay off the loan and the total cost of the mortgage over the loan's history. Carol wants the workbook to display a table showing the monthly payments with information describing how much of the payment is for interest and how much is applied toward the principal. Carol also wants the workbook to be flexible enough so that if a client intends on making additional payments, beyond the required monthly payment, the workbook will show how the cost of the loan and subsequent payments are affected.

In this tutorial, you will use Excel's financial functions to create the workbook for the mortgage calculations.

## SESSION 2.1

In this session, you will learn about Excel's functions. You will insert functions and function arguments. You will copy and paste formulas and functions into your workbook. Finally, you will learn about absolute and relative references and how to insert them into your formulas.

# Working with Excel Functions

Carol has already started the loan workbook. She has not entered any values yet, but she has entered some text and a documentation sheet. Open her workbook now.

### To open Carol's workbook:

1. Start Excel and then open the **Loan1** workbook located in the Tutorial.02/Tutorial folder on your Data Disk.

2. On the Documentation sheet, enter your name in cell B3.

3. Click the **Mortgage** tab to make the sheet the active worksheet. See Figure 2-1.

| Figure 2-1 | THE LOAN WORKBOOK |

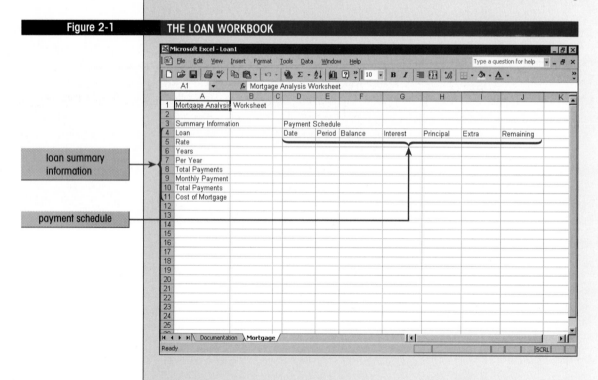

4. Save the workbook as **Loan2** in the Tutorial.02/Tutorial folder on your Data Disk.

The Mortgage worksheet is divided into two sections. The Summary Information section is the area in which you will enter the basic information about the loan, including the amount of the loan, the current interest rate, and the length of the mortgage. Figure 2-2 provides a description of the information that you will enter in the cells in that section.

| Figure 2-2 | CELLS IN THE SUMMARY INFORMATION SECTION |
|---|---|

| CELL | DESCRIPTION |
|---|---|
| B4 | Enter the amount of the loan |
| B5 | Enter the interest rate |
| B6 | Enter the length of the mortgage in years |
| B7 | Enter the number of periods (months) that the interest will be compounded each year |
| B8 | Calculate the total number of periods in the loan |
| B9 | Calculate the monthly payment |
| B10 | Calculate the total payments on the loan |
| B11 | Calculate the cost of the loan (total payments minus the amount of the loan) |

The other section of the worksheet contains the payment schedule; it indicates how much is paid toward the principal and how much is paid in interest each month. The schedule also indicates the balance remaining on the loan each month. Figure 2-3 describes the values to be placed in each column.

| Figure 2-3 | COLUMNS IN THE PAYMENT SCHEDULE |
|---|---|

| COLUMN | DESCRIPTION |
|---|---|
| Date | Date that loan payment is due |
| Period | Loan payment period |
| Balance | Balance of loan remaining to be paid |
| Interest | Interest due |
| Principal | Portion of the monthly payment used to reduce the principal |
| Extra | Extra payments beyond the scheduled monthly payment |
| Remaining | Balance of loan remaining after the monthly payment |

To make this worksheet operational, you need to use financial functions that are provided in Excel.

## Function Syntax

In the previous tutorial you used formulas to calculate values. For example, the formula =A1+A2+A3+A4 totals the values in the range A1:A4 and places the sum in the active cell. Although calculating sums this way for small ranges works fine, a formula that calculates the sum of 100 cells would be so large that it would become unmanageable. In Excel you can easily calculate the sum of a large number of cells by using a function. A **function** is a predefined, or built-in, formula for a commonly used calculation.

Each Excel function has a name and syntax. The **syntax** specifies the order in which you must enter the different parts of the function and the location in which you must insert commas, parentheses, and other punctuation. The general syntax for an Excel function is =FUNCTION(*argument1*, *argument2*, ...), where FUNCTION is the name of the Excel function, and *argument1*, *argument2*, and so on are **arguments**—the numbers, text, or cell references used by the function to calculate a value. Some arguments are **optional arguments** because they are not necessary for the function to return a value. If you omit an optional argument, Excel assumes a default value for it. By convention, optional arguments will appear in this text within square brackets along with the default value. For example, in the function =FUNCTION(*argument1*,[*argument2=value*]), the second argument is optional, and *value* is the default value assigned to *argument2* if a value is omitted from the argument list. A convention that you will follow in this text is to display function names in uppercase letters; however, when you enter formulas into your own Excel worksheets, you can use either uppercase or lowercase letters.

Excel supplies over 350 different functions organized into 10 categories:

- Database functions
- Date and Time functions
- Engineering functions
- Financial functions
- Information functions
- Logical functions
- Lookup functions
- Math functions
- Statistical functions
- Text and Data functions

You can learn about each function using Excel's online Help. Figure 2-4 describes some of the more important math and statistical functions that you may often use in your workbooks.

| Figure 2-4 | MATH AND STATISTICAL FUNCTIONS |
| --- | --- |
| **FUNCTION** | **DESCRIPTION** |
| AVERAGE(*values*) | Calculates the average value in a set of numbers, where *values* is either a cell reference or a collection of cell references separated by commas |
| COUNT(*values*) | Counts the number of cells containing numbers, where *values* is either a cell reference or a range of cell references separated by commas |
| MAX(*values*) | Calculates the largest value in a set of numbers, where *values* is either a cell reference or a range of cell references separated by commas |
| MIN(*values*) | Calculates the smallest value in a set of numbers, where *values* is either a cell reference or a range of cell references separated by commas |
| ROUND(*number, num_digits*) | Rounds a *number* to a specified number of digits, indicated by the *num_digits* arguments |
| SUM(*numbers*) | Calculates the sum of a collection of numbers, where *numbers* is either a cell or a range reference or a series of numbers separated by commas |

For example, the SUM function calculates the total for the values in a range of cells. The SUM function has only one argument, the cell reference containing the values to be totaled. To calculate the total of the cells in the range A1:A100, you would insert the expression =SUM(A1:A100) into the active cell.

Functions can also be combined with formulas. For example, the expression =MAX(A1:A100)/100 returns the maximum value in the range A1:A100 and then divides the value by 100. One function can also be nested inside the other. The expression =ROUND(AVERAGE(A1:A100),1) uses the AVERAGE function to calculate the average of the values in the range A1:A100 and then uses the ROUND function to round the average value off to the first decimal place.

By combining functions and formulas, you can create very sophisticated expressions to handle almost any situation.

## Financial Functions

In Carol's workbook, you will use one of Excel's financial functions to calculate information about the loan. Figure 2-5 describes a few of Excel's financial functions in more detail.

| Figure 2-5 | FINANCIAL FUNCTIONS |
|---|---|
| **FUNCTION** | **DESCRIPTION** |
| FV(*rate,nper,pmt,*[*pv*=0],[*type*=0]) | Calculates the future value of an investment based on periodic, constant payments, and a constant interest rate, where *rate* is the interest rate per period, *nper* is the number of periods, *pmt* is the payment per period, *pv* is the present value of the investment, and *type* indicates when payments are due (*type*=0 for payments at the end of each period, *type*=1 for payments at the beginning of each period) |
| IPMT(*rate,per,nper pv,*[*fv*=0],[*type*=0]) | Calculates the interest payment for a given period for an investment based on period cash payments and a constant interest rate, where *fv* is the future value of the investment |
| PMT(*rate,nper,pv,*[*fv*=0],[*type*=0] | Calculates the payment for a loan based on constant payments and a constant interest rate |
| PPMT(*rate,per,nper,pv,*[*fv*=0],[*type*=0]) | Calculates the payment on the principal for a given period for an investment based on period cash payments and a constant interest rate |
| PV(*rate,nper,pmt,*[*fv*=0],[*type*=0]) | Calculates the present value of an investment |

You need a function to calculate the monthly payment that will pay off a loan at a fixed interest rate. You can use Excel's PMT function to do just that. The syntax of the PMT function is PMT(*rate,nper,pv,*[*fv*=0],[*type*=0]) where *rate* is the interest rate per period of the loan, *nper* is the total number of periods, *pv* is the present value of the loan, *fv* is the future value, and *type* specifies whether the payment is made at the beginning of each period (*type*=1) or at the end of each period (*type*=0). Note that both the *fv* and *type* arguments are optional arguments. If you omit the *fv* argument, Excel assumes that the future value will be 0, in other words that the loan will be completely paid off. If you omit the *type* argument, Excel assumes a type value of 0 so that the loan is paid off at the end of each period.

For example, if Carol wanted to know the monthly payment for a $50,000 loan at 9% annual interest compounded monthly over 10 years, the arguments for the PMT function would be *PMT(0.09/12,10\*12,50000)*. Note that the yearly interest rate is divided by the number of periods (months) for the interest rate per period. Similarly, the number of periods (months) is multiplied by the number of years in order to arrive at the total number of periods.

The value returned by the PMT function is –633.38, indicating that a client would have to spend $633.38 per month to pay off the loan in 10 years. Excel uses a negative value to indicate that the value is an expense rather than income.

You can also use the PMT function for annuities other than loans. For example, if you want to determine how much money to save at a 6% annual interest rate compounded monthly so that you will have $5000 at the end of five years, you use the following PMT function: *=PMT(0.06/12,5\*12,0,5000)*. Note that the present value is 0 (since you are starting out with no money in the account) and the future value is 5000 (since that is the amount you want to have after 5 years). In this case, Excel will return a value of –71.66, indicating that you would have to invest $71.66 per month to achieve $5000 in your savings account after 5 years.

## Inserting a Function

Carol wants to calculate the monthly payment for a 20-year loan of $150,000 at 7.5% annual interest compounded monthly. First you need to enter this information into the workbook. You also need to enter a formula that will calculate the total number of monthly payments.

### *To add the loan information:*

1. Click cell **B4**, type **$150,000** and then press the **Enter** key. Even though you have added a dollar symbol in writing the loan amount, Excel still interprets cell B4 as a numeric value and not a text string.

2. In cell B5, type **7.5%** and then press the **Enter** key. Note that when you type a percentage into a worksheet cell, Excel interprets the percentage as a value. The actual value in cell B5 is 0.075; the value is just *formatted* to appear with the percent sign. You will learn more about how Excel formats numbers in the next tutorial.

3. In cell B6, type **20** and then press the **Enter** key.

4. In cell B7, type **12** since there are 12 payment periods in each year, and then press the **Enter** key.

   Note that in this text you can *enter* a cell reference in a formula or function by clicking the cell or by typing the cell reference.

5. In cell B8, enter the formula **=B6\*B7** for the total number of payments in the mortgage, and then press the **Enter** key. The value 240 appears in cell B8, and cell B9 is now the active cell.

Now you will use the PMT function to calculate the required monthly payment to pay off the loan under the terms of the mortgage. You could simply type the function and its arguments into the cell, but you will often find that you have forgotten which arguments are required by the function and the correct order in which the arguments need to be entered. To assist you, Excel provides the Insert Function button on the Formula bar. Clicking this button displays a dialog box from which you can choose the function you want to enter. Once you choose a function, another dialog box opens in which you specify values for all of the function's arguments.

### REFERENCE WINDOW                                                    RW

#### Inserting a Function
- Click the cell in which you will insert the function.
- Click the Insert Function button on the Formula bar.
- Select the type of function you want from the select a category list box, and then select the function category; or type information about the function in the Search for a function text box, and then click the Go button.
- Select the function in the Select a function list box.
- Click the OK button to view the arguments for the selected function.
- Enter values for each required argument in the Function Arguments dialog box.
- Click the OK button.

You will insert the PMT function in the Summary Information section of the Mortgage worksheet to determine the monthly payment required to pay off a mortgage. You will use the Insert Function button on the Formula bar to insert the PMT function.

## To insert the PMT function:

1. With cell B9 as the active cell, click the **Insert Function** button 𝑓𝑥 on the Formula bar. The Insert Function dialog box opens. See Figure 2-6.

| Figure 2-6 | INSERT FUNCTION DIALOG BOX |

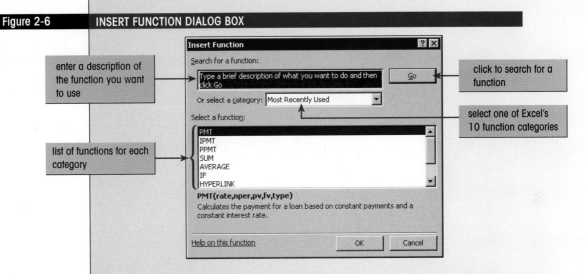

There are two ways to select a function using this dialog box. If you know something about the function but are not sure in which category the function belongs, enter a text description in the Search for a function text box and click the Go button. Excel will search for the functions that match your description. If you know the general category, select the category from the select a category list box; then Excel will list all of the functions in that category. Browse through the function list to find the function you need.

2. Type **calculate mortgage payments** in the Search for a function text box, and then click the **Go** button. Excel returns the PMT, IPMT, and NPER functions in the Select a function list box. Note that a description of the selected function and its arguments appears at the bottom of the dialog box. See Figure 2-7.

**Figure 2-7**    **SEARCHING FOR A FUNCTION**

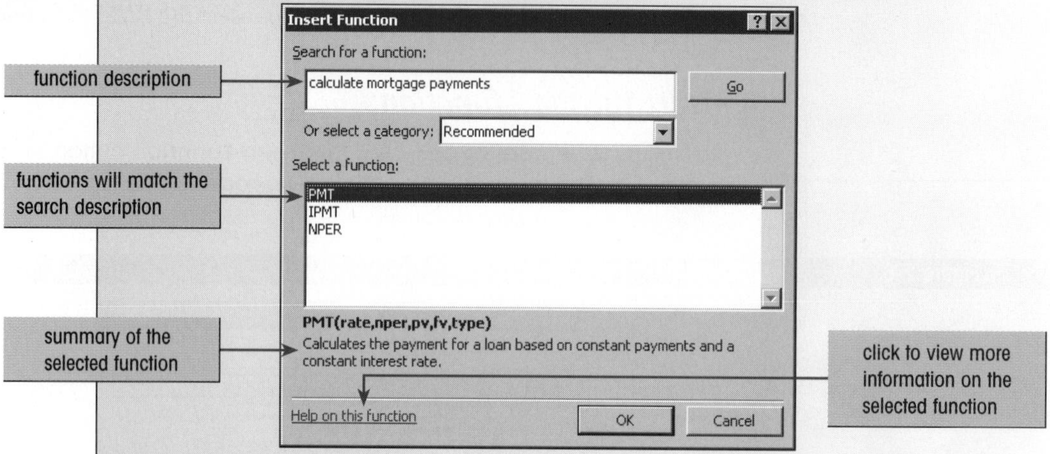

function description

functions will match the
search description

summary of the
selected function

click to view more
information on the
selected function

**Insert Function**

Search for a function:

calculate mortgage payments                    Go

Or select a category:  Recommended

Select a function:

PMT
IPMT
NPER

**PMT(rate,nper,pv,fv,type)**
Calculates the payment for a loan based on constant payments and a
constant interest rate.

Help on this function                    OK          Cancel

**3.** Verify that the PMT function is selected in the Select a function list box, and
then click the **OK** button.

Excel next displays the Function Arguments dialog box, which provides all of the arguments in
the selected function and the description of each argument. From this dialog box, you can select
the cells in the workbook that contain the values required for each argument. Note that the
expression =*PMT()* appears in both the Formula bar and cell B9. This display indicates that Excel
is starting to insert the PMT function for you. You have to use the Function Arguments dialog
box to complete the process.

You will start by entering the value for the Rate argument. Remember that rate refers to the
interest rate per period. In this case, that value is 7.5% divided by 12, or if you use the cells in the
worksheet, the value in cell B5 is divided by the value in cell B7. You can enter the cell references
either by typing them into the appropriate argument boxes or by pointing to a cell with the mouse
pointer, in which case Excel will automatically insert the cell reference into the appropriate box.

## To insert values into the PMT function:

**1.** With the blinking insertion point in the Rate argument box, click cell **B5**, type **/**,
and then click cell **B7**. The expression *B5/B7* appears in the box and the value
0.00625 appears to the right of the box.

> **TROUBLE?** If necessary, move the dialog box to view column B before clicking cell B5.

**2.** Press the **Tab** key to move to the Nper argument box.

**3.** Click cell **B8** for the 240 total payments needed for this loan, and then press the
**Tab** key.

The present value of the loan is $150,000, which is found in cell B4.

**4.** Click cell **B4** to enter the value of the loan in the Pv argument box. Figure 2-8
shows the completed Function Arguments dialog box.

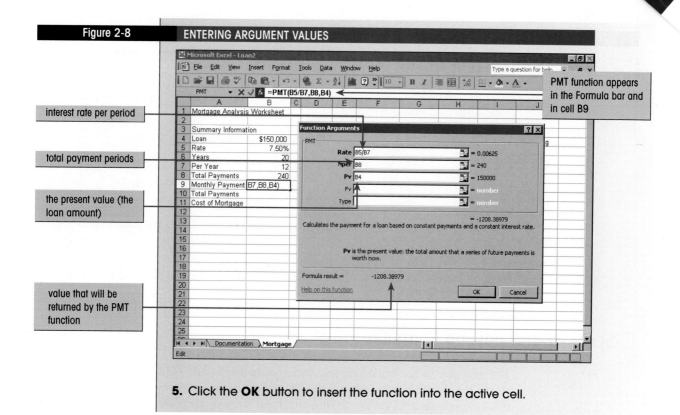

**Figure 2-8**  ENTERING ARGUMENT VALUES

interest rate per period

total payment periods

the present value (the loan amount)

value that will be returned by the PMT function

PMT function appears in the Formula bar and in cell B9

**5.** Click the **OK** button to insert the function into the active cell.

Excel displays the value ($1,208.39) with a red colored font in cell B9. This is a general format that Excel uses to display negative currency values. Carol would rather have the monthly payment appear as a positive value, so you will have to insert a negative sign in front of the PMT function to switch the monthly payment to a positive value. You will also complete the rest of the Summary Information section.

## To complete the Summary Information section:

**1.** Double-click cell **B9** to enter edit mode.

**2.** Click directly to the right of the = (equal sign), type **–** so that the expression changes to =-PMT(B5/B7,B8,B4), and then press the **Enter** key.

**3.** In cell B10, enter **=B9*B8** and then press the **Enter** key.

**4.** In cell B11, enter **=B10-B4** and then press the **Enter** key. Figure 2-9 shows the complete summary information for this loan.

| Figure 2-9 | MORTGAGE SUMMARY |

The required monthly payment for this loan will be $1,208.39. The total interest payments will be $140,013.55.

# Copying and Pasting Formulas

The next part of the worksheet that you need to work with is the payment schedule, which details the monthly payments on the mortgage. Before entering values into the payment schedule, you should consider the functions that you will use in the schedule. Each row of the payment schedule represents the condition of the loan for a single month of the mortgage.

The Date column (column D in the worksheet) will contain the date on which a payment is due. At this point you will not enter any date information (you will do that later in the tutorial). The Period column specifies the number of periods in the mortgage. The first month is period 1, the second month is period 2, and so forth. Since there are 240 payment periods, this payment schedule will extend from row 5 down to row 244 in the worksheet. The Balance column displays the balance left on the loan at the beginning of each period. The initial balance value is the amount of the loan, which is found in cell B4. After the initial period, the balance will be equal to the remaining balance from the previous period.

The Interest column is the amount of interest due on the balance, which is equal to: Balance * Interest rate per period. In this example, the interest rate per period is the annual interest rate (in cell B5) divided by the number of periods in a year (in cell B7).

Subtracting the interest due from the monthly payment (cell B9) tells you how much is paid toward reducing the principal. This value is placed in column H of the worksheet. Carol knows that sometimes clients will want to make extra payments each month in order to pay off the loan quicker (and thereby reduce the overall cost of the mortgage). The Extra column (column I in the worksheet) is used for recording these values. Finally, the remaining balance will be equal to the balance at the beginning of the month minus the payment toward the principal and any extra payments.

Now that you have reviewed what values and functions will go into each column of the payment schedule, you are ready to insert the first row of the schedule.

# To insert the first row of values in the payment schedule:

1. Click cell **E5**, type **1** and then press the **Tab** key.

   Now you will enter the initial balance, which is equal to the amount of the loan found in cell B4. Rather than typing in the value itself, you will enter a reference to the cell. If you change the amount of the loan, this change will be automatically reflected in the payment schedule.

2. In cell F5, enter **=B4** and then press the **Tab** key.

   Next you will enter the interest due in this period, which is equal to the balance multiplied by the interest rate per period (cell B5 divided by cell B7).

3. In cell G5, enter **=F5\*B5/B7** and then press the **Tab** key.

   **TROUBLE?** Note that if the values in cells F5 and G5 are displayed with a different number of decimal places, do not worry. You will learn more about formatting cells in Tutorial 3.

   The payment toward the principal is equal to the monthly payment (cell B9) minus the interest payment (cell G5).

4. In cell H5, enter **=B9-G5** and then press the **Tab** key.

   At this point there are no extra payments toward the mortgage so you will enter $0 in the Extra column. The balance remaining is equal to the present balance minus the payment towards the principal and any extra payments.

5. In cell I5, type **$0** and then press the **Tab** key.

6. In cell J5, enter **=F5-(H5+I5)** and then press the **Enter** key. Figure 2-10 shows the first period values in the payment schedule.

| Figure 2-10 | FIRST PERIOD VALUES IN THE PAYMENT SCHEDULE |

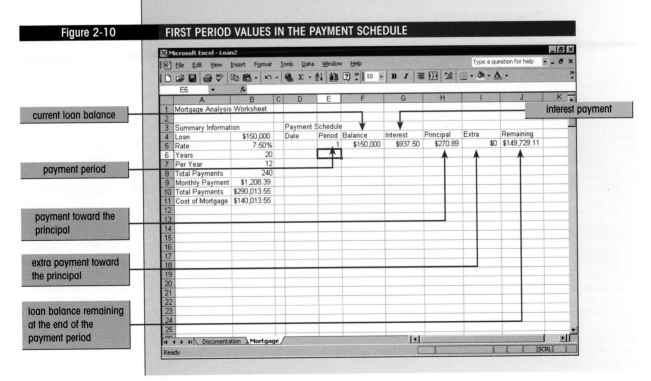

current loan balance

interest payment

payment period

payment toward the principal

extra payment toward the principal

loan balance remaining at the end of the payment period

You could have also calculated the monthly interest payment using Excel's IPMT function and the monthly payment toward the principal using the PPMT function. However, both of these functions assume that there will be no extra payments toward the principal. This assumption is something that Carol does not want to omit in her payment schedule.

The second row of the payment schedule is similar to the first. The only difference is that the balance (to be displayed in cell F6) will be carried over from the remaining balance (displayed in cell J5) in the previous row. At this point, you could retype the formulas that you used in the first row of the payment schedule. However, it is much easier and more efficient to copy and paste the formulas. When you **copy** the contents of a range, Excel places the formulas and values in those cells in a memory location called the **Clipboard**. The contents remain on the Clipboard until you **paste** them. You can paste the contents of the selected cells into another location on your worksheet, into a different worksheet or workbook, or even into another Windows application.

---

**REFERENCE WINDOW**                                                          **RW**

**Copying and Pasting a Cell or Range**
- Select the cell or range to be copied.
- Click the Copy button on the Standard toolbar.
- Select the cell or range into which you want to copy the selection.
- Click the Paste button on the Standard toolbar.
- If necessary, click the Paste Options button to apply a paste-related option to the pasted selection.
- Press the Esc key to deselect the selection.

---

Next you will copy and paste a range of values in the worksheet.

*To insert the second row of values in the payment schedule:*

1. Click cell **E6**, type **2** and then press the **Tab** key.

2. In cell F6, enter **=J5** (since the remaining balance needs to be carried over into the second payment period), and then press the **Enter** key.

   Now you will copy the formulas from the range G5:J5 to the range G6:J6.

3. Select the range **G5:J5** and then click the **Copy** button on the Standard toolbar.

   TROUBLE? If you do not see the Copy button on the Standard toolbar, click the Toolbar Options button on the Standard toolbar, and then click.

   Note that the range that you copied has a moving border surrounding it. This moving border is a visual reminder of what range values are currently in the paste buffer.

4. Click cell **G6** to make it the active cell, and then click the **Paste** button on the Standard toolbar. Note that you did not have to select a range of cells equal to the range you were copying because the cells adjacent to cell G6 were empty and could accommodate the pasted range.

The formulas from the G5:J5 range are pasted into the G6:J6 range. See Figure 2-11.

| Figure 2-11 | COPYING AND PASTING FORMULAS |

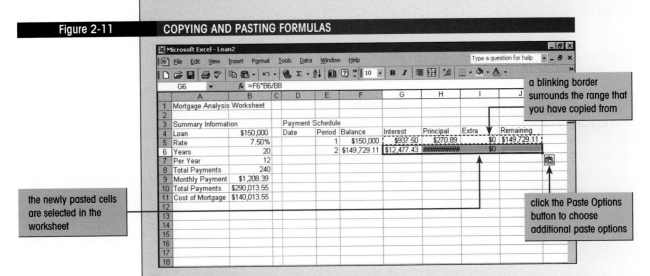

the newly pasted cells are selected in the worksheet

a blinking border surrounds the range that you have copied from

click the Paste Options button to choose additional paste options

Note that next to the pasted range is the Paste Options button. You can click this button to apply one of the available options for pasting cell values into the new range. By default, Excel pastes the values and formulas along with the format used to display those values and formulas. You will learn more about the Paste Options button in the next session.

**5.** Press the **Esc** key to remove the moving border.

Apparently something is wrong. Note that the interest payment in cell G6 has jumped to $12,477.43, and the principal payment in cell H6 and the remaining balance are represented with ########. Excel uses this string of symbols to represent a value that is so large that it cannot be displayed within the width of the cell. To view the value in the cell, you must either increase the width of the column or hover your mouse pointer over the cell.

## To view the value in cell H6:

**1.** Hover your mouse pointer over cell H6. After a brief interval, the value $277,536.12 appears in a ScreenTip.

**2.** Click cell **G6** to make it the active cell. The Formula bar displays the formula =F6*B6/B8.

The interest payment value jumped to $12,477.43 and the payment on the principal became $277,536.12. The absurdity of these values results from the way in which Excel copies formulas. When Excel copies formulas to a new location, Excel automatically adjusts the cell references in those formulas. For example, to calculate the remaining balance for the first payment period in cell J5, the formula is =F5-(H5+I5). For the second payment period, the remaining balance in cell J6 uses the formula =F6-(H6+I6). The cell references are shifted down one row.

This automatic update of the cell references works fine for this formula, but the updating does not work for the calculation of the interest payment. The interest payment should be the balance multiplied by the interest rate per period; therefore, for the first three rows of the payment schedule, the formulas should be =F5*B5/B7, =F6*B5/B7, and =F7*B5/B7.

However, when you copied the first formula to the second row, *all* of the cell references shifted down one row and the formula automatically became *=F6\*B6/B8*. You have a different formula; therefore, the result is a nonsensical value. Note that this is an issue only when copying a cell, not moving a cell. When you move a cell, Excel does *not* modify the cell references.

You need to be able to control how Excel adjusts cell references, so that Excel adjusts some of the cell references in the interest due formula, but not others. You can control this automatic adjusting of cell references through the use of relative and absolute references.

# Relative **and** Absolute References

A **relative reference** is a cell reference that shifts when you copy it to a new location on the worksheet. As you saw in the preceding set of steps, a relative reference changes in relation to the change of location. If you copy a formula to a cell three rows down and five columns to the right, the relative cell reference shifts three rows down and five columns to the right. For example, the relative reference B5 becomes G8.

An **absolute reference** is a cell reference that does not change when you copy the formula to a new location on the workbook. To create an absolute reference, you preface the column and row designations with a dollar sign ($). For example, the absolute reference for B5 would be $B$5. No matter where you copy the formula, this cell reference would stay the same. (Relative references do not include dollars signs.)

A **mixed reference** combines both relative and absolute cell references. A mixed reference for B5 would be either $B5 or B$5. In the case of $B5, the row reference would shift, but the column reference would not. In the case of B$5, only the column reference shifts.

You can switch between absolute, relative, and mixed references by selecting the cell reference in the formula (either using edit mode or the Formula bar) and then pressing the F4 key on your keyboard repeatedly.

The problem you have encountered with the payment schedule formulas is that you need a relative reference for the remaining balance but an absolute reference for the interest rate divided by the payment periods per year (since those values are always located in the same place in the worksheet). So instead of the formula *=F5\*B5/B7*, you need to use the formula *=F5\*$B$5/$B$7*.

Next you will revise the formulas in the payment schedule to use relative and absolute references, and then copy the revised formulas.

---

### *To use relative and absolute references in the payment schedule:*

1. Double-click cell **G5** to enter edit mode, use an arrow key to position the insertion point to the left of the column heading B if necessary, and then type **$**. Continue to use the arrow keys to position the insertion point in the formula before typing three more $ to change the formula to *=F5\*$B$5/$B$7*. Press the **Enter** key.

   You also have to change the formula in cell H5, so that the formula subtracts the interest payment from the required monthly payment to calculate the payment toward the principal. Instead of typing the dollar signs to change a relative reference to an absolute reference, you will use the F4 key.

2. Double-click cell **H5**, make sure the insertion point is positioned in the B9 cell reference, and then press the **F4** key to change the formula to *=$B$9–G5*. Press the **Enter** key.

   Now copy these new formulas into the second row of the payment schedule. Note that you do not have to delete the contents of the range into which you are copying the updated formulas.

**3.** Select the range **G5:H5**, and then click the **Copy** button  on the Standard toolbar.

**4.** Click cell **G6** and then click the **Paste** button on the Standard toolbar.

The new values are much more reasonable. The interest payment has decreased to $935.81, and the payment toward the principal has increased to $272.58. You will now add one more row to the payment schedule and copy the formulas.

## To add a third row to the payment schedule:

**1.** Click cell **E7**, type **3** and then press the **Tab** key.

**2.** Select the range **F6:J6**, and then click the **Copy** button on the Standard toolbar.

**3.** Click cell **F7** and then click the **Paste** button on the Standard toolbar.

Figure 2-12 shows the first three rows of the payment schedule.

| Figure 2-12 | PASTING THE THIRD ROW OF THE PAYMENT SCHEDULE |
| --- | --- |

Microsoft Excel - Loan2

File  Edit  View  Insert  Format  Tools  Data  Window  Help        Type a question for help

F7          =J6

|  | A | B | C | D | E | F | G | H | I | J | K |
|---|---|---|---|---|---|---|---|---|---|---|---|
| 1 | Mortgage Analysis Worksheet | | | | | | | | | | |
| 2 | | | | | | | | | | | |
| 3 | Summary Information | | | Payment Schedule | | | | | | | |
| 4 | Loan | $150,000 | | Date | Period | Balance | Interest | Principal | Extra | Remaining | |
| 5 | Rate | 7.50% | | | 1 | $150,000 | $937.50 | $270.89 | $0 | $149,729.11 | |
| 6 | Years | 20 | | | 2 | $149,729.11 | $935.81 | $272.58 | $0 | $149,456.53 | |
| 7 | Per Year | 12 | | | 3 | $149,456.53 | $934.10 | $274.29 | $0 | $149,182.24 | |
| 8 | Total Payments | 240 | | | | | | | | | |
| 9 | Monthly Payment | $1,208.39 | | | | | | | | | |
| 10 | Total Payments | $290,013.55 | | | | | | | | | |
| 11 | Cost of Mortgage | $140,013.55 | | | | | | | | | |
| 12 | | | | | | | | | | | |

**4.** Examine the formulas in cells G5, G6, and G7. Note that the relative reference to the balance remaining on the loan changes from F5 to F6 to F7 as you proceed down the schedule, but the interest rate per period keeps the same absolute reference, $B$5/$B$7.

As you would expect, the interest payment schedule decreases as the remaining balance decreases, and the monthly payment that goes to the principal steadily increases. Carol would like you to complete the rest of the payment schedule for all 240 payment periods. You will explore how to complete the rest of the payment schedule in a quick and efficient way in the next session.

## To close the Loan2 workbook:

**1.** Click **File** on the menu bar, and then click **Exit**.

**2.** When prompted to save your changes to Loan2.xls, click the **Yes** button.

## Session 2.1 QUICK CHECK

1. Which function would you enter to calculate the minimum value in the range B1:B50?

2. What function would you enter to calculate the ratio between the maximum value in the range B1:B50 and the minimum value?

3. A 5-year loan for $10,000 has been taken out at 7% interest compounded quarterly. What function would you enter to calculate the quarterly payment on the loan?

4. Which function would you use to determine the amount of interest due in the second quarter of the first year of the loan discussed in question 3?

5. In the formula *A8+$C$1*, *$C$1* is an example of a(n) _____ reference.

6. Cell A10 contains the formula *=A1+B1*. If the contents of this cell were copied to cell B11, what formula would be inserted into that cell?

7. Cell A10 contains the formula *=$A1+B$1*. If this cell were copied to cell B11, what formula would be inserted into that cell? What would the formula be if you moved cell A10 to B11?

---

## SESSION 2.2

In this session you will use Excel's Auto Fill feature to automatically fill in formulas, series, and dates. You will use Excel's logical functions to create functions that return different values based on different conditions. Finally, you will learn how Excel stores dates, and then you will work with dates using Excel's library of date and time functions.

## Filling in Formulas and Values

So far you have entered only three periods of the 240 total payment periods into the payment schedule. You used the copy and paste technique to enter the values for the second and third rows. You could continue to copy and paste the remaining rows of the payment schedule, but you can use a more efficient technique—the fill handle. The **fill handle** is a small black square located in the lower-right corner of a selected cell or range. When you drag the fill handle, Excel automatically fills in the formulas or formats used in the selected cells. This technique is also referred to as **Auto Fill**.

---

**REFERENCE WINDOW**                                                        **RW**

**Copying Formulas Using Auto Fill**

- Select the range that contains the formulas you want to copy.
- Click and drag the fill handle in the direction you want to copy the formulas.
- Release the mouse button.
- If necessary, click the Auto Fill Options button, and then select the Auto Fill option you want to apply to the selected range.

---

### Copying Formulas

Carol wants you to copy the formulas from the range F6:J7 into the larger range F7:J244. Copying the formulas into the larger range will, in effect, calculate the monthly payments for all 240 periods of the loan—all 20 years of the mortgage.

## To copy the formulas using the fill handle:

1. If you took a break after the previous session, make sure Excel is running and the Loan2 workbook is open.

2. Verify that the Mortgage sheet is the active worksheet.

3. Select the range **F6:J7**.

4. Position the pointer over the fill handle (the square box in the lower-right corner of cell J7) until the pointer changes to **+**.

5. Click and drag the fill handle down the worksheet to cell **J244**. As you drag the fill handle, an outline appears displaying the selected cells, and the worksheet automatically scrolls down.

6. Release the mouse button. By default, Excel copies the values and formulas found in the original range F6:J7 into the new range F7:J244. See Figure 2-13.

| Figure 2-13 | FILLING IN THE REST OF THE PAYMENT SCHEDULE VALUES |

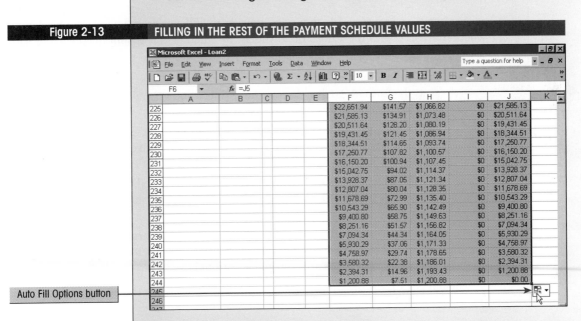

Auto Fill Options button

TROUBLE? It is very easy to "overshoot the mark" when dragging the fill handle down. If this happens, you can either click the Undo button 🔙 on the Standard toolbar and try again, or simply select the extras formulas you created and delete them.

Excel has copied the formulas from the first few rows of the payment schedule into the rest of the rows and has also automatically adjusted any relative references in the formulas. For example, the formula in cell G244 is =F244*$B$5/$B$7, which is the interest due on the last loan payment, an amount of $7.51. The last row in the payment schedule shows a remaining balance of $0.00 in cell J244. The loan is paid off.

Note that to the right of the filled values is the Auto Fill Options button. Clicking this button displays the available options that you can choose from to specify how Excel should perform the Auto Fill. Click this button now to view the options.

## To view the Auto Fill options:

**1.** Click the **Auto Fill Options** button 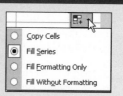 to the right of cell J244. Excel displays the Auto Fill Options menu, as shown in Figure 2-14.

---

| Figure 2-14 | AUTO FILL OPTIONS |
|---|---|

○ Copy Cells
◉ Fill Series
○ Fill Formatting Only
○ Fill Without Formatting

**2.** Click anywhere outside of the menu to hide it.

---

As shown in Figure 2-14, there are four Auto Fill options. These options determine whether Excel copies the values or formulas, or whether Excel simply copies the formats used to display those values and formulas. The four options and their descriptions are:

- **Copy Cells**: Copies the values and formulas into the selected range, as well as the formats used to display those values and formulas. Relative references are adjusted accordingly. This is the default option.

- **Fill Series**: Copies the values and formulas into the selected range, and completes any arithmetic or geometric series. Relative references are adjusted accordingly.

- **Fill Formatting Only**: Copies only the formats used to display the values or formulas in the cells. Values and formulas are not copied into the selected range.

- **Fill Without Formatting**: Copies the values and formulas into the selected range. The formats used to display those values and formulas are not copied. Relative references are adjusted accordingly.

You will learn more about formatting values and formulas in the next tutorial.

## Filling a Series

Missing from the payment schedule are the numbers in column E. There should be a sequence of numbers starting with the value 1 in cell E5 and ending with the value 240 in cell E244. Since these numbers are all different, you cannot simply copy and paste the values. You can, however, use the fill handle to complete a series of numbers, as long as you include the first few numbers of the series. If the numbers increase by a constant value in an arithmetic series, dragging the fill handle will continue that same increase over the length of the newly selected cells.

Use the fill handle to enter the numbers for the Period column in the payment schedule.

## To fill in the payment period values:

**1.** Press **Ctrl + Home** to return to the top of the worksheet.

**2.** Select the range **E5:E7**.

3. Click and drag the fill handle down to cell **E244**. Note that as you drag the fill handle a label appears indicating the current value in the series. When you reach cell E244, the label displays the value *240*.

4. Release the mouse button. Figure 2-15 shows the values in the payment schedule through the 240th payment.

| Figure 2-15 | FILLING IN THE PAYMENT PERIOD NUMBERS |

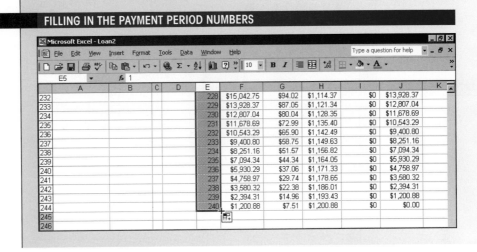

## Filling In Dates

You can also use the fill handle to fill in dates—the one part of the payment schedule you have not entered yet. As with filling in a series, if you specify the initial date or dates, Excel will automatically insert the rest of the dates. The series of dates that Excel fills in depends on the dates you start with. If you start with dates that are separated by a single day, Excel will fill in a series of days. If you start with dates separated by a single month, Excel will fill in a series of months and so forth. You can also specify how to fill in the date values using the Auto Fill Options button.

Next you will insert an initial date for the loan as August 1, 2003, and then specify that each payment period is due at the beginning of the next month.

### To insert the payment dates:

1. Type **8/1/2003** in cell D5, and then click the **Enter** button ✓ on the Formula bar. Note that clicking the Enter button on the Formula bar inserts the value in the cell and keeps it the active cell.

2. Drag the fill handle down to cell **D244**, and then release the mouse button. Note that as you drag the fill handle down, the date appears in the pop-up label; the date *3/27/2004* appears when you reach cell D244.

   **TROUBLE?** Don't worry if your computer is set up to display dates in a different format. The format doesn't affect the date value.

   By default, Excel created a series of consecutive days. You need to change the consecutive days to consecutive months.

3. Click the **Auto Fill Options** button 🖳 located to the lower-right corner of cell D244.

**4.** Click the **Fill Months** option button. Excel fills in consecutive months in the payment schedule. The last payment date is 7/1/2023. See Figure 2-16.

Figure 2-16 — ADDING DATES TO THE PAYMENT SCHEDULE

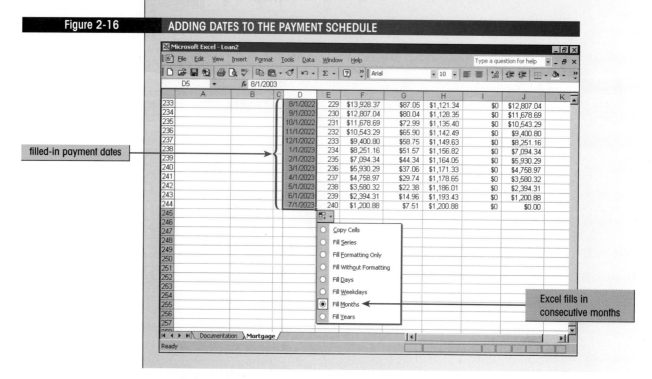

filled-in payment dates

Excel fills in consecutive months

Excel provides other techniques for automatically inserting series of numbers into your worksheets. You can even create your own customized fill series. You can use the online Help to learn how to use the other Auto Fill options. For now though, you have completed the payment schedule.

Carol wants to verify that the numbers you have inserted into the payment schedule are correct. She suggests that, as a check, you add up the interest payments in column G. The total should match the cost of the mortgage that you calculated in cell B11.

## To calculate the total interest payments:

**1.** Click cell **A13**, and type **Observed Payments**, and then press the **Enter** key.

**2.** In cell A14, type **Cost of Mortgage**, and then press the **Tab** key. The observed cost of the mortgage is the sum of interest payments in the range G5:G244.

**3.** In cell B14, type **=SUM(G5:G244)**, and then press the **Enter** key. As shown in Figure 2-17, the total cost of the interest payments in the payment schedule, $140,013.55, matches what was calculated in cell B11.

**Figure 2-17**  **TOTAL INTEREST PAYMENTS FROM THE PAYMENT SCHEDULE**

| | A | B | C | D | E | F | G | H | I | J | K |
|---|---|---|---|---|---|---|---|---|---|---|---|
| 1 | Mortgage Analysis Worksheet | | | | | | | | | | |
| 2 | | | | | | | | | | | |
| 3 | Summary Information | | | Payment Schedule | | | | | | | |
| 4 | Loan | $150,000 | | Date | Period | Balance | Interest | Principal | Extra | Remaining | |
| 5 | Rate | 7.50% | | 8/1/2003 | 1 | $150,000 | $937.50 | $270.89 | $0 | $149,729.11 | |
| 6 | Years | 20 | | 9/1/2003 | 2 | $149,729.11 | $935.81 | $272.58 | $0 | $149,456.53 | |
| 7 | Per Year | 12 | | 10/1/2003 | 3 | $149,456.53 | $934.10 | $274.29 | $0 | $149,182.24 | |
| 8 | Total Payments | 240 | | 11/1/2003 | 4 | $149,182.24 | $932.39 | $276.00 | $0 | $148,906.24 | |
| 9 | Monthly Payment | $1,208.39 | | 12/1/2003 | 5 | $148,906.24 | $930.66 | $277.73 | $0 | $148,628.51 | |
| 10 | Total Payments | $290,013.55 | | 1/1/2004 | 6 | $148,628.51 | $928.93 | $279.46 | $0 | $148,349.05 | |
| 11 | Cost of Mortgage | $140,013.55 | | 2/1/2004 | 7 | $148,349.05 | $927.18 | $281.21 | $0 | $148,067.84 | |
| 12 | | | | 3/1/2004 | 8 | $148,067.84 | $925.42 | $282.97 | $0 | $147,784.88 | |
| 13 | Observed Payments | | | 4/1/2004 | 9 | $147,784.88 | $923.66 | $284.73 | $0 | $147,500.14 | |
| 14 | Cost of Mortgage | $140,013.55 | | 5/1/2004 | 10 | $147,500.14 | $921.88 | $286.51 | $0 | $147,213.63 | |
| 15 | | | | 6/1/2004 | 11 | $147,213.63 | $920.09 | $288.30 | $0 | $146,925.33 | |
| 16 | | | | 7/1/2004 | 12 | $146,925.33 | $918.28 | $290.11 | $0 | $146,635.22 | |

# Using Excel's Logical Functions

So far you have assumed that there are no extra payments toward the principal. In fact, the PMT function assumes constant periodic deposits with no additional payments. If extra payments were made, they would reduce the cost of the mortgage and speed up the payment of the loan. Carol would like to see what the effect would be on the payment schedule and the cost of the mortgage if an extra payment were made.

## To add an extra payment to the schedule:

1. Click cell **I22**, which corresponds to the payment period for 1/1/2005.

   Now assume that a client makes an extra payment of $20,000 toward the principal on this date.

2. Type **$20,000** in cell I22, and then press the **Enter** key. The observed cost of the mortgage shown in cell B14 drops to $80,262.15.

3. Scroll down the worksheet until row **190** comes into view (corresponding to the date of 1/1/2019). See Figure 2-18.

**Figure 2-18**  **NEGATIVE INTEREST PAYMENTS**

after 12/1/2018, the remaining balance on the loan appears as a negative value

| | D | E | F | G | H | I | J |
|---|---|---|---|---|---|---|---|
| 187 | 10/1/2018 | 183 | $3,072.52 | $19.20 | $1,189.19 | $0 | $1,883.33 |
| 188 | 11/1/2018 | 184 | $1,883.33 | $11.77 | $1,196.62 | $0 | $686.71 |
| 189 | 12/1/2018 | 185 | $686.71 | $4.29 | $1,204.10 | $0 | ($517.39) |
| 190 | 1/1/2019 | 186 | ($517.39) | ($3.23) | $1,211.62 | $0 | ($1,729.01) |
| 191 | 2/1/2019 | 187 | ($1,729.01) | ($10.81) | $1,219.20 | $0 | ($2,948.21) |
| 192 | 3/1/2019 | 188 | ($2,948.21) | ($18.43) | $1,226.82 | $0 | ($4,175.02) |
| 193 | 4/1/2019 | 189 | ($4,175.02) | ($26.09) | $1,234.48 | $0 | ($5,409.51) |
| 194 | 5/1/2019 | 190 | ($5,409.51) | ($33.81) | $1,242.20 | $0 | ($6,651.70) |
| 195 | 6/1/2019 | 191 | ($6,651.70) | ($41.57) | $1,249.96 | $0 | ($7,901.67) |
| 196 | 7/1/2019 | 192 | ($7,901.67) | ($49.39) | $1,257.78 | $0 | ($9,159.44) |
| 197 | 8/1/2019 | 193 | ($9,159.44) | ($57.25) | $1,265.64 | $0 | ($10,425.08) |
| 198 | 9/1/2019 | 194 | ($10,425.08) | ($65.16) | $1,273.55 | $0 | ($11,698.63) |
| 199 | 10/1/2019 | 195 | ($11,698.63) | ($73.12) | $1,281.51 | $0 | ($12,980.13) |
| 200 | 11/1/2019 | 196 | ($12,980.13) | ($81.13) | $1,289.52 | $0 | ($14,269.65) |
| 201 | 12/1/2019 | 197 | ($14,269.65) | ($89.19) | $1,297.58 | $0 | ($15,567.22) |
| 202 | 1/1/2020 | 198 | ($15,567.22) | ($97.30) | $1,305.68 | $0 | ($16,872.91) |
| 203 | 2/1/2020 | 199 | ($16,872.91) | ($105.46) | $1,313.85 | $0 | ($18,186.75) |
| 204 | 3/1/2020 | 200 | ($18,186.75) | ($113.67) | $1,322.06 | $0 | ($19,508.81) |
| 205 | 4/1/2020 | 201 | ($19,508.81) | ($121.93) | $1,330.32 | $0 | ($20,839.13) |

Documentation / Mortgage

Something is wrong. With the extra payment, the loan is paid off early, at the end of the 185th payment period; but starting with 12/1/2018, the payment schedule no longer makes sense. It appears that the client is still making payments on a loan that is already paid off.

The effect of this error is that the remaining balance and the interest payments appear as negative values after the loan is paid off. But remember, in cell B14, you calculated the sum of the interest payments to determine the observed cost of the mortgage. With those negative interest payment values included, that total will be wrong.

To correct this problem, you need to revise the PMT function that determines the monthly payment directed toward the principal. Currently, this function subtracts the interest due from the monthly mortgage payment to arrive at the amount of the principal payment. You need to use a function that decides which of the two following situations is true:

- The remaining balance is greater than the payment toward the principal.
- The remaining balance is less than the payment toward the principal.

A function that determines whether a condition is true or false is called a **logical function**. Excel supports several logical functions, which are described in Figure 2-19.

| Figure 2-19 | EXCEL'S LOGICAL FUNCTIONS |
| --- | --- |
| **FUNCTION** | **DESCRIPTION** |
| AND(*logical1*,[*logical2*], …) | Returns the value TRUE if all arguments are true; returns FALSE if one or more arguments is false |
| FALSE() | Returns the value FALSE |
| IF(*logical_test*,*value_if_true*,*value_if_false*) | Returns *value_if_true* if the *logical_test* argument is true; returns the *value_if_false* if the *logical_test* argument is false |
| NOT(*logical*) | Returns the value TRUE if *logical* is false; returns the value FALSE if *logical* is true |
| OR(*logical1*,[*logical2*], …) | Returns the value TRUE if at least one argument is true; returns FALSE if all arguments are false |
| TRUE() | Returns the value TRUE |

In this loan workbook, you will be using an IF function. The syntax of the IF function is =IF(*logical_test*,*value_if_true*,*value_if_false*) where *logical_test* is an expression that is either true or false, *value_if_true* is an expression that Excel will run if the *logical_test* is true, and *value_if_false* is an expression that runs when the *logical_test* is false. The logical test is constructed using a comparison operator. A **comparison operator** checks whether two expressions are equal, whether one is greater than the other, and so forth. Figure 2-20 describes the six comparison operators supported by Excel.

| Figure 2-20 | COMPARISON OPERATORS | |
| --- | --- | --- |
| **OPERATOR** | **EXAMPLE** | **DESCRIPTION** |
| = | A1=B1 | Checks if the value in cell A1 equals the value in cell B1 |
| > | A1>B1 | Checks if the value in cell A1 is greater than B1 |
| < | A1<B1 | Checks if the value in cell A1 is less than B1 |
| >= | A1>=B1 | Checks if the value in cell A1 is greater than or equal to B1 |
| <= | A1<=B1 | Checks if the value in cell A1 is less than or equal to B1 |
| <> | A1<>B1 | Checks if the value in cell A1 is not equal to the value in cell B1 |

For example, the function =IF(A1=10,20,30) tests whether the value in cell A1 is equal to 10. If so, the function returns the value 20, otherwise the function returns the value 30. You can also use cell references in place of values.

The function =IF(A1=10,B1,B2) returns the value from cell B1 if A1 equals 10, otherwise the function returns the value stored in cell B2.

You can also make comparisons with text strings. When you do, the text strings must be enclosed in quotation marks. For example, the function =IF(A1="RETAIL",B1,B2) tests whether the text RETAIL has been entered into cell A1. If so, the function returns the value from cell B1, otherwise it returns the value from cell B2.

Because some functions are very complex, you might find it easier to enter a logical function, such as the IF function, using Excel's Insert Function option. You will use the Insert Function option to enter an IF function in the first row of the payment schedule.

## To enter the IF function in the first row of the payment schedule:

1. Click cell **H5** in the payment schedule, and then press the **Delete** key to clear the cell contents.

2. Click the **Insert Function** button 𝑓ₓ on the Formula bar.

3. Click the **Or select a category** list arrow, and then click **Logical** in the list of categories displayed.

4. Click **IF** in the Select a Function list box, and then click the **OK** button to open the Function Arguments dialog box.

   First, you need to enter the logical test. The test is whether the remaining balance in cell F5 is greater than the usual amount of payment toward the principal, which is equal to the monthly loan payment ($B$9) minus the interest payment (G5). The logical test is therefore F5>($B$9–G5).

5. In the Logical_test argument box, enter **F5>($B$9-G5)**, and then press the **Tab** key.

   If the logical test is true (in other words, if the remaining balance is greater than the principal payment), Excel should return the usual principal payment. In this case, that value is the expression $B$9–G5.

6. In the Value_if_true argument box, enter **$B$9-G5**, and then press the **Tab** key.

   If the logical test is false (which means that the balance remaining is *less* than the usual principal payment), the payment should be set equal to the remaining balance—which has the effect of paying off the loan. In this case, Excel should return the value in cell F5.

7. In the Value_if_false argument box, enter **F5**. Figure 2-21 shows the completed dialog box.

| Figure 2-21 | INSERTING THE IF FUNCTION |
|---|---|

tests whether the remaining balance is greater than the payment toward the principal

**Function Arguments** ? ✕

IF

Logical_test  `F5>($B$9-G5)`  = TRUE

Value_if_true  `$B$9-G5`  = 270.8897903

Value_if_false  `F5`  = 150000

= 270.8897903

Checks whether a condition is met, and returns one value if TRUE, and another value if FALSE.

if true, the principal payment is equal to the monthly loan payment minus the interest due

**Value_if_false** is the value that is returned if Logical_test is FALSE. If omitted, FALSE is returned.

if false, the payment is equal to the remaining balance

Formula result =        $270.89

Help on this function                    OK        Cancel

**8.** Click the **OK** button.

Now copy this new formula into the rest of the payment schedule.

## To fill in the rest of the payment schedule:

**1.** With cell H5 the active cell, click the fill handle and drag it down to cell **H244**.

**2.** Scroll up to row **190**. As shown in Figure 2-22, the payment schedule now accurately shows that once the remaining balance reaches $0, the interest payments and the payments toward the principal also become $0.

| Figure 2-22 | NEW PAYMENT VALUES |
|---|---|

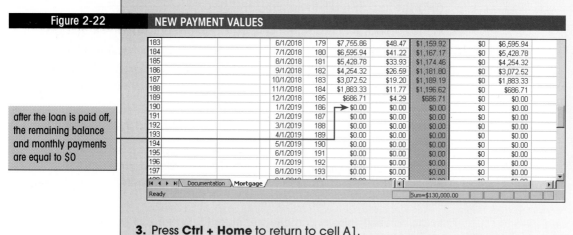

after the loan is paid off, the remaining balance and monthly payments are equal to $0

| | | | | | | | |
|---|---|---|---|---|---|---|---|
| 183 | | | 6/1/2018 | 179 | $7,755.86 | $48.47 | $1,159.92 | $0 | $6,595.94 |
| 184 | | | 7/1/2018 | 180 | $6,595.94 | $41.22 | $1,167.17 | $0 | $5,428.78 |
| 185 | | | 8/1/2018 | 181 | $5,428.78 | $33.93 | $1,174.46 | $0 | $4,254.32 |
| 186 | | | 9/1/2018 | 182 | $4,254.32 | $26.59 | $1,181.80 | $0 | $3,072.52 |
| 187 | | | 10/1/2018 | 183 | $3,072.52 | $19.20 | $1,189.19 | $0 | $1,883.33 |
| 188 | | | 11/1/2018 | 184 | $1,883.33 | $11.77 | $1,196.62 | $0 | $686.71 |
| 189 | | | 12/1/2018 | 185 | $686.71 | $4.29 | $686.71 | $0 | $0.00 |
| 190 | | | 1/1/2019 | 186 | $0.00 | $0.00 | $0.00 | $0 | $0.00 |
| 191 | | | 2/1/2019 | 187 | $0.00 | $0.00 | $0.00 | $0 | $0.00 |
| 192 | | | 3/1/2019 | 188 | $0.00 | $0.00 | $0.00 | $0 | $0.00 |
| 193 | | | 4/1/2019 | 189 | $0.00 | $0.00 | $0.00 | $0 | $0.00 |
| 194 | | | 5/1/2019 | 190 | $0.00 | $0.00 | $0.00 | $0 | $0.00 |
| 195 | | | 6/1/2019 | 191 | $0.00 | $0.00 | $0.00 | $0 | $0.00 |
| 196 | | | 7/1/2019 | 192 | $0.00 | $0.00 | $0.00 | $0 | $0.00 |
| 197 | | | 8/1/2019 | 193 | $0.00 | $0.00 | $0.00 | $0 | $0.00 |

Documentation \ Mortgage

Ready                                    Sum=$130,000.00

**3.** Press **Ctrl + Home** to return to cell A1.

Note that with the extra payment, the observed cost of the mortgage is $93,034.73. Thus, if a client were to make an extra payment of $20,000 on 1/1/2005, Carol could tell the client that there would be a savings of almost $47,000 over the history of the loan.

Making an extra payment or payments will greatly affect the number of payment periods. From the payment schedule, you can tell that the number of payment periods would be 185. The question is how can you include this information in the summary section at the top of the worksheet. To include the information, you will have to make the following change to the payment period values in column E of the payment schedule:

■ If the balance is greater than 0, the period number should be one higher than the previous period number.

■ If the balance is 0, set the period number to 0.

You'll make this change to the payment schedule now.

### To add an IF function that adjusts the period numbers in case of extra payments:

1. Click cell **E6** to make it the active cell, and then press the **Delete** key.

2. Click the **Insert Function** button 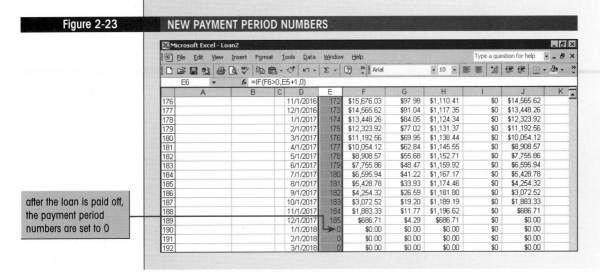 on the Formula toolbar.

3. Click **IF** in the Select a function list box, and then click the **OK** button.

   The logical test is whether the balance (in cell F6) is greater than $0 or not.

4. In the Logical_test argument box, enter **F6>0**, and then press the **Tab** key.

   If the logical test is true, the period number should be equal to the previous period number (E5) plus 1.

5. In the Value_if_true argument box, enter **E5+1**, and then press the **Tab** key.

   If the logical test is false, the balance is 0. Set the period number to 0.

6. In the Value_if_false argument box, type **0**, and then click the **OK** button.

7. Verify that E6 is still the active cell, and then click and drag the fill handle down to cell **E244**.

8. Scroll up the worksheet to row **190**. Note that once the loan is paid off, the period number is equal to 0. See Figure 2-23.

| Figure 2-23 | NEW PAYMENT PERIOD NUMBERS |

after the loan is paid off, the payment period numbers are set to 0

Microsoft Excel - Loan2

E6     fx =IF(F6>0,E5+1,0)

| | A | B | C | D | E | F | G | H | I | J | K |
|---|---|---|---|---|---|---|---|---|---|---|---|
| 176 | | | | 11/1/2016 | 172 | $15,676.03 | $97.98 | $1,110.41 | $0 | $14,565.62 | |
| 177 | | | | 12/1/2016 | 173 | $14,565.62 | $91.04 | $1,117.35 | $0 | $13,448.26 | |
| 178 | | | | 1/1/2017 | 174 | $13,448.26 | $84.05 | $1,124.34 | $0 | $12,323.92 | |
| 179 | | | | 2/1/2017 | 175 | $12,323.92 | $77.02 | $1,131.37 | $0 | $11,192.56 | |
| 180 | | | | 3/1/2017 | 176 | $11,192.56 | $69.95 | $1,138.44 | $0 | $10,054.12 | |
| 181 | | | | 4/1/2017 | 177 | $10,054.12 | $62.84 | $1,145.55 | $0 | $8,908.57 | |
| 182 | | | | 5/1/2017 | 178 | $8,908.57 | $55.68 | $1,152.71 | $0 | $7,755.86 | |
| 183 | | | | 6/1/2017 | 179 | $7,755.86 | $48.47 | $1,159.92 | $0 | $6,595.94 | |
| 184 | | | | 7/1/2017 | 180 | $6,595.94 | $41.22 | $1,167.17 | $0 | $5,428.78 | |
| 185 | | | | 8/1/2017 | 181 | $5,428.78 | $33.93 | $1,174.46 | $0 | $4,254.32 | |
| 186 | | | | 9/1/2017 | 182 | $4,254.32 | $26.59 | $1,181.80 | $0 | $3,072.52 | |
| 187 | | | | 10/1/2017 | 183 | $3,072.52 | $19.20 | $1,189.19 | $0 | $1,883.33 | |
| 188 | | | | 11/1/2017 | 184 | $1,883.33 | $11.77 | $1,196.62 | $0 | $686.71 | |
| 189 | | | | 12/1/2017 | 185 | $686.71 | $4.29 | $686.71 | $0 | $0.00 | |
| 190 | | | | 1/1/2018 | 0 | $0.00 | $0.00 | $0.00 | $0 | $0.00 | |
| 191 | | | | 2/1/2018 | 0 | $0.00 | $0.00 | $0.00 | $0 | $0.00 | |
| 192 | | | | 3/1/2018 | 0 | $0.00 | $0.00 | $0.00 | $0 | $0.00 | |

## Using the AutoSum Button

Since the period numbers are all equal to zero after the loan is paid off, the last period number in the payment schedule will also be the largest. You can, therefore, use the MAX function to calculate the maximum, or last, payment period in the schedule. You can enter the MAX function either by typing the function directly into the active cell or by using the

Insert Function button on the Formula bar. However, Excel also provides the AutoSum button on the Standard toolbar to give you quick access to the SUM, AVERAGE, COUNT, MIN, and MAX functions. The AutoSum button can be a real timesaver, so you will use it in this situation.

### To use the AutoSum button to calculate the maximum payment period:

1. Scroll to the top of the worksheet.

2. Click cell **A15**, type **Total Payments** and then press the **Tab** key.

3. Click the **list arrow** for the AutoSum button $\Sigma \cdot$ on the Standard toolbar to display a list of summary functions. See Figure 2-24.

| Figure 2-24 | USING THE AUTOSUM BUTTON |
| --- | --- |

AutoSum button

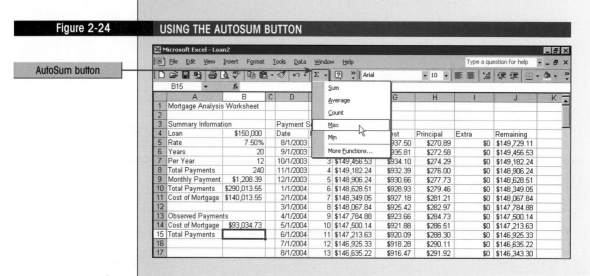

4. Click **Max** in the list, and then drag the pointer over the range **E5:E244** (the range containing the payment period numbers from the payment schedule).

5. Press the **Enter** key. The formula *=MAX(E5:E244)* is automatically entered into cell B15, and the value 185 appears in the cell.

Carol suggests you test the new payment schedule one more time. She asks what the effect would be if the extra payment on 1/1/2005 was increased from $20,000 to $25,000.

**To test the new payment figures:**

**1.** Click cell **I22**.

**2.** Type **$25,000** and then press the **Enter** key.

The cost of the mortgage decreases to $84,368.07 and the number of payments decreases to 174.

## Using Excel's Date Functions

Excel stores dates as integers, where the integer values represent the number of days since January 1, 1900. For example, the integer value for the date January 1, 2008 is 39448 because that date is 39,448 days after January 1, 1900. Most of the time you do not see these values because Excel automatically formats the integers to appear as dates, such as 1/1/2008. This method of storing the dates allows you to work with dates in the same way you work with numbers. For example, if you subtract one date from another, the answer will be the number of days separating the two dates.

In addition to creating simple formulas with date values, you can use Excel's date functions to create dates or to extract information about date values. To insert the current date into your workbook, you could use the TODAY function, for example. To determine which day of the week a particular date falls on, you could use the WEEKDAY function. Note that the date functions use your computer's system clock to return a value. Figure 2-25 describes some of Excel's more commonly used date functions.

| Figure 2-25 | EXCEL'S DATE FUNCTIONS |
| --- | --- |
| **FUNCTION** | **DESCRIPTION** |
| DATE(*year, month, day*) | Returns the integer for the date represented by the *year, month,* and *day* arguments |
| DAY(*date*) | Extracts the day of the month from the *date* value |
| MONTH(*date*) | Extracts the month number from the *date* value, where January=1, February=2, and so forth |
| NOW(), TODAY() | Returns the integer for the current date and time |
| WEEKDAY(*date*) | Calculates the day of the week using the *date* value, where Sunday=1, Monday=2, and so forth |
| YEAR(*date*) | Extracts the year number from the *date* value |

On the Documentation sheet, there is a cell for entering the current date. Rather than typing the date in manually, you will enter it using the TODAY function.

## To use the TODAY function:

**1.** Click the **Documentation** tab to make it the active worksheet, and then click cell **B4**.

**2.** Click the **Insert Function** button 🔎 on the Formula bar.

**3.** Select **Date & Time** from the function category list.

**4.** Scroll down the list, click **TODAY**, and then click the **OK** button twice. Note that the second dialog box indicated that there are no arguments for the TODAY function. The current date is entered into cell B4 (your date will most likely be different). See Figure 2-26.

| Figure 2-26 | INSERTING THE CURRENT DATE |

the TODAY function inserts the current date into the cell

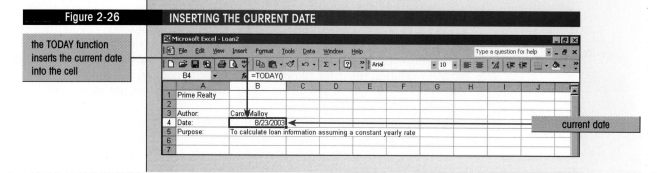

current date

The TODAY and NOW functions will always display the current date and time. Thus, if you reopen this workbook on a different date, the date in cell B4 will be updated to reflect that change. If you want a permanent date (that might reflect when the workbook was initially developed), you enter the date directly into the cell without using a function.

You have completed your work on the Loan workbook. Carol will examine the workbook and get back to you with more assignments. For now, you can close Excel and save your work.

## To save your work:

**1.** Click **File** on the menu bar, and then click **Exit**.

**2.** Click the **Yes** button when prompted to save your changes.

# Session 2.2 QUICK CHECK

1. Describe how you would create a series of odd numbers from 1 to 99 in column A of your worksheet.

2. Describe how you would create a series of yearly dates, ranging from 1/1/2003 to 1/1/2030, in column A of your worksheet.

3. What function would you enter to return the text string "Yes" if cell A1 is greater than cell B1 and "No" if cell A1 is not greater than cell B1?

4. Describe three ways of entering the SUM function into a worksheet cell.

5. Which function would you enter to extract the year value from the date entered into cell A1?

6. Which function would you enter to display the current date in the worksheet?

7. Which function would you enter to determine which day of the week a date entered into cell A1 falls on?

## REVIEW ASSIGNMENTS

Carol has another workbook for you to examine. Although the loan workbook was helpful, Carol realizes that most of the time she will be working with clients who can make only a specified monthly payment. She wants to have a workbook in which she enters a specific monthly payment and from that amount determine how large a mortgage her client can afford.

To determine this information, you will use the PV function: PV(*rate,nper,pmt*,[*fv*=0],[*type*=0]) where *rate* is the interest per period, *nper* is the number of payment periods, *pmt* is the monthly payment, *fv* is the future value of the loan (assumed to be 0), and *type* specifies when the loan will be paid (assumed to be 0 at the beginning of each payment period). For a loan, the *pmt* argument must be a negative number since it represents an expense and not income. The PV function then returns the present value of the loan or annuity. In Carol's workbook, the return would be the largest mortgage her clients can afford for a given monthly payment.

As with the previous workbook, Carol wants this new workbook to contain a payment schedule. The current annual interest rate is 7.5% compounded monthly. Carol wants the payment schedule to assume a 20-year mortgage with a monthly payment of $950. What is the largest mortgage her clients could get under those conditions, and how much would the interest payments total?

To complete this task:

1. Start Excel and open the **Mort1** workbook located in the Tutorial.02/Review folder on your Data Disk.

2. Save the workbook as **Mort2** in the same folder.

3. Enter your name and the current date in the Documentation sheet (use a function to automatically insert the date). Switch to the Mortgage worksheet.

4. Enter "$950" for the monthly payment in cell B4, "7.5%" as the interest rate in cell B5, "20" as the number of years, and "12" as the number of periods per year.

5. Enter a formula in cell B8 to calculate the total number of payments over the history of the loan.

**Explore**
6. In cell B10, use the PV function to calculate the largest mortgage a client could receive under those conditions. Also, assume that the payments are made at the beginning of each month. Remember that you need to make the monthly payment, which appears in cell B4, a negative, so the return is a positive number.

7. Complete the first row of the payment schedule, with the following formulas:

   ■ The initial value of the payment period should be equal to 1.
   ■ The initial balance should be equal to the amount of the mortgage.
   ■ The interest due should be equal to the balance multiplied by the interest rate per period.
   ■ Use the IF function to test whether the balance is greater than the monthly payment minus the interest due. If so, the principal payment should be equal to the monthly payment minus the interest due. If not, the principal payment should be equal to the balance.
   ■ Set the extra payment value to $0.
   ■ The remaining balance should be equal to the initial balance minus the principal payment and any extra payment.

8. Complete the second row of the payment schedule with the following formulas:

   ■ Carry the remaining balance from cell J3 into the current balance in cell F4.
   ■ If the current balance is equal to 0, set the period number to 0, otherwise set the period number equal to cell E3 plus 1.
   ■ Copy the formulas in the range G3:J3 to the range G4:J4.

9. Select the range E4:J4 and then drag the fill handle down to fill range E242:J242. What happens to the values in the Extra column when you release the mouse button?

**Explore**
10. Click the Auto Fill Options button next to the filled in values. Which option button is selected? Does this help you understand what happened in the previous step? Click the Copy Cells option button to fix the problem.

11. In cell D3, enter the initial date of the loan as "4/1/2003".

12. Payments are due at the beginning of each month. Fill in the rest of the payment dates in the range D3:D242 using the appropriate Auto Fill option.

13. In cell B11, enter the cost of the mortgage, which is equal to the sum of the interest payments in the payment schedule.

14. In cell B12, enter the number of observed payments, which is equal to the maximum payment period number in the payment schedule.

*Explore*

15. If a client pays an extra $100 for each period of the first five years of the loan, what is the cost of the mortgage and how many months will it take to pay off the loan? On what date will the loan be paid?

16. Print the entire Mort2 workbook.

17. Save and close the workbook, and then exit Excel.

## CASE PROBLEMS

*Case 1. Setting Up a College Fund*   Lynn and Peter Chao have recently celebrated the birth of their first daughter. The couple is acutely aware of how expensive a college education is. Although the couple does not have much money, they realize that if they start saving now, they can hopefully save a nice sum for their daughter's education. They have asked you for help in setting up a college fund for their daughter.

The couple has set a goal of saving $75,000 that they will use in 18 years for college. Current annual interest rates for such funds are 6.5% compounded monthly. Lynn and Peter want you to determine how much money they would have to set aside each month to reach their goal. They would also like you to create a schedule so they can see how fast their savings will grow over the next few years.

You can calculate how fast monthly contributions to a savings account will grow using the same financial functions used to determine how fast monthly payments can pay back a loan. In this case, the present value is equal to 0 (since the couple is starting out with no savings in the college fund) and the future value is $75,000 (the amount that the couple wants to have saved after 18 years.)

To complete this task:

1. Open the **School1** workbook located in the Tutorial.02/Cases folder on your Data Disk, and then save the workbook as **School2** in the same folder.

2. Enter your name and the current date in the Documentation sheet. Switch to the College Fund worksheet.

3. Enter the Chaos' saving goal in cell B3 and the assumed annual interest rate in cell B4. Enter the number of years they plan to save in cell B5 and the number of payments per year in cell B6.

4. Enter a formula to calculate the total number of payments in cell B7.

*Explore*

5. In cell B9, use the PMT function to calculate the monthly payment required for the Chaos to meet their savings goal. Express your answer as a positive value rather than a negative value.

6. Begin filling out the savings schedule. In the first row, enter the following information:

   ■ The initial date is 1/1/2003.
   ■ The payment period is 1.
   ■ The starting balance is equal to the first monthly payment.

*Explore*

   ■ Calculate the accrued interest using the IPMT function, assuming that payments are made at the end of each month. (*Hint*: Scroll the IPMT arguments list to display all the necessary arguments.)
   ■ Calculate the ending balance, which is equal to the starting balance plus the interest accrued in the current month.

7. Enter the second row of the table, using the following guidelines:

   ■ The date is one month later than the previous date.
   ■ The payment period is 2.
   ■ The starting balance is equal to the previous month's ending balance plus the monthly payment.
   ■ Use the IPMT function to calculate the interest for the second payment period.
   ■ The ending balance is once again equal to the starting balance plus the accrued interest.

8. Use the fill handle to fill in the remaining 214 months of the savings schedule. Choose the appropriate fill options to ensure that the values in the dates and the period and interest values fill in correctly.

9. Save your changes.

10. Print a copy of the College Fund worksheet, and then indicate on the printout how much the couple will have to save each month to reach their savings goal.

11. Save and close the workbook, and then exit Excel.

*Case 2. Payroll Information at Sonic Sounds*  Jeff Gwydion manages the payroll at Sonic Sounds. He has asked you for help in setting up a worksheet to store payroll values. The payroll contains three elements: the employee's salary, the 401(k) contribution, and the employee's health insurance cost. The company's 401(k) contribution is 3% of the employee's salary for employees who have worked for the company at least one year; otherwise the company's contribution is zero. Sonic Sounds also supports two health insurance plans: Premier and Standard. The cost of the Premier plan is $6,500, and the cost of the Standard plan is $5,500.

The workbook has already been set up for you. Your job is to enter the functions and formulas to calculate the 401(k) contributions and health insurance costs for each employee.

To complete this task:

1. Open the **Sonic1** workbook located in the Tutorial.02/Cases folder on your Data Disk, and save the workbook as **Sonic2** in the same folder.

2. Enter your name and the current date (calculated using a function) in the Documentation sheet. Switch to the Payroll worksheet.

3. In cell C13, determine the number of years the employee Abbot has been employed by subtracting the date Abbot was hired from the current date and then dividing the difference by 365.

4. Use the fill handle to compute the years employed for the rest of the employees.

**Explore**  5. Use an IF function to compute the 401(k) contribution for each employee (*Note*: Remember that an employee must have worked at Sonic for at least one year to be eligible for the 401(k) contribution.)

**Explore**  6. Use an IF function to calculate the health insurance cost for each employee at the company. (*Hint*: Test whether the employee's health plan listed in column E is equal to the value in cell B4. If so, the employee is using the Premier plan, and the health cost is equal to the value in cell C4. If not, the employee is using the Standard plan, and the health cost is equal to the value in cell C5.)

7. Calculate the total salaries, total 401(k) contributions, and total health insurance expenses for all of the employees at Sonic Sounds. Place the functions in the range B7:B9.

8. Print the contents of the **Sonic2** workbook.

9. Redo the analysis, assuming that the cost of the Premier plan has risen to $7,000 and the cost of the Standard plan has risen to $6,100. What is the total health insurance cost to the company's employees?

10. Print just the Payroll sheet.

11. Save and close the workbook, and then exit Excel.

*Case 3. Depreciation at Leland Hospital*  Leland Hospital in Leland, Ohio, has purchased a new x-ray machine for its operating room. Debra Sanchez in purchasing wants your assistance in calculating the yearly depreciation of the machine. **Depreciation** is the declining value of an asset over its lifetime. To calculate the depreciation, you need the initial cost of the asset, the number of years or periods that the asset will be used, and the final or salvage value of the asset. The new x-ray machine costs $450,000. The hospital expects that the x-ray machine will be used for 10 years and that at the end of the 10-year period the salvage value will be $50,000. Debra wants you to calculate the depreciation of the machine for each year in that 10-year period.

Accountants use several different methods to calculate depreciation. The difference between each method lies in how fast the asset declines in value. Figure 2-27 describes four Excel functions that you can use to calculate depreciation.

| Figure 2-27 | EXCEL'S DEPRECIATION FUNCTIONS | |
|---|---|---|
| **METHOD** | **FUNCTION** | **DESCRIPTION** |
| Straight-line | SLN(*cost, salvage, life*) | The straight-line method distributes the depreciation evenly over the life of the asset, so that the depreciation is the same in each period. The argument *cost* is the cost of the asset, *salvage* is the salvage value at the end of the life of the asset, and *life* is the number of periods that the asset is being depreciated. |
| Sum-of-years | SYD(*cost, salvage, life, per*) | The sum-of-years method concentrates the most depreciation in the earliest periods of the lifetime of the asset. The argument *per* is the period that you want to calculate the depreciation for. |
| Fixed-declining balance | DB(*cost, salvage, life, period,* [*month*=12]) | The fixed-declining balance method is an accelerated depreciation method in which the highest depreciation occurs in the earliest periods. The argument *month* is an optional argument that specifies the number of months in the first year (assumed to be 12). |
| Double-declining balance | DDB(*cost, salvage, life, period,* [*factor*=2]) | The double-declining balance method is an accelerated method in which the highest depreciation occurs in the earliest periods. The optional *factor* argument controls that rate at which the balance declines. |

Debra wants you to calculate the depreciation using all four methods so that she can see the impact on each method on the asset's value. She has already created the workbook containing the basic figures; she needs you to add the formulas.

To complete this task:

1. Open the **Leland1** workbook located in the Tutorial.02/Cases folder on your Data Disk and save the workbook as **Leland2** in the same folder.

2. Enter your name and the current date (calculated using a function) in the Documentation sheet. Switch to the Depreciation worksheet.

3. Enter the cost of the x-ray machine in cell B3, the lifetime of the machine in cell B4, and the salvage value in B5.

*Explore*    4. In the range B9:B18, enter the depreciation of the x-ray machine using the straight-line method.

5. In the range C9:C18, enter the yearly value of the machine after the depreciation is applied (*Hint*: After the first year, you must subtract the yearly depreciation from the previous year's value).

*Explore*    6. In the range F9:F18, enter the depreciation using the sum-of-years method.

7. In the range G9:G18, calculate the yearly value of the machine after the sum-of-years depreciation.

*Explore*    8. In the range B22:B31, calculate the fixed-declining depreciation for each year.

9. In the range C22:C31, calculate the value of the x-ray machine after applying the fixed-declining depreciation.

**Explore**

10. In the range F22:F31, calculate the double-declining depreciation for each year.

11. In the range G22:G31, calculate the yearly value of the x-ray machine after applying the double-declining depreciation.

12. Print the entire workbook.

13. Save and close the workbook, and then exit Excel.

**Case 4. Analyzing Faculty Salaries at Glenmore Junior College**   A complaint has been raised at Glenmore Junior College, a liberal arts college in upstate New York, that female faculty members are being paid less than their male counterparts. Professor Lawton, a member of the faculty senate, has asked you to compile basic statistics on faculty salaries, broken down by gender. The current salary figures are shown in Figure 2-28.

**Figure 2-28     FACULTY SALARIES**

| MALE FACULTY | MALE FACULTY | MALE FACULTY | FEMALE FACULTY | FEMALE FACULTY |
| --- | --- | --- | --- | --- |
| $40,000 | $55,000 | $75,000 | $25,000 | $60,000 |
| $45,000 | $55,000 | $75,000 | $30,000 | $60,000 |
| $45,000 | $60,000 | $75,000 | $35,000 | $60,000 |
| $45,000 | $60,000 | $75,000 | $40,000 | $60,000 |
| $45,000 | $60,000 | $80,000 | $42,000 | $62,000 |
| $45,000 | $62,000 | $85,000 | $45,000 | $62,000 |
| $45,000 | $62,000 | $95,000 | $47,000 | $65,000 |
| $50,000 | $65,000 | $115,000 | $50,000 | $65,000 |
| $50,000 | $65,000 | | $55,000 | $67,000 |
| $52,000 | $65,000 | | $55,000 | $70,000 |
| $55,000 | $70,000 | | $57,000 | $75,000 |

To complete this task:

1. Create a new workbook named **JrCol** and store it in the Tutorial.02/Cases folder on your Data Disk.

2. Insert a Documentation sheet into the workbook containing your name, the current date (calculated using a function), and the purpose of the workbook.

3. Rename Sheet1 as "Statistical Analysis" and delete any unused worksheets.

4. In the Statistical Analysis worksheet, enter the male and female faculty salaries in two separate columns labeled "Male Faculty" and "Female Faculty."

*Explore*

5. Use Excel's statistical functions to create a table of the following statistics for all faculty members, male faculty members, and female faculty members:

- the count
- the sum of the salaries
- the average salary
- the median salary
- the minimum salary
- the maximum salary
- the range of salary values (maximum minus minimum)
- the standard deviation of the salary values
- the standard error of the salary values (the standard deviation divided by the square root of the number of salaries)

6. Compare the average male salary to the average female salary. Is there evidence that the female faculty members are paid significantly less?

7. Average values can sometimes be skewed by high values. Compare the median male salary to the median female salary. Is the evidence supporting the complaint stronger or weaker using the median salary figures?

*Explore*

8. Select the cell range containing the statistics you calculated, and then print only that selected range.

9. Save and close the workbook, and then exit Excel.

## INTERNET ASSIGNMENTS

**Student Union**

The purpose of the Internet Assignments is to challenge you to find information on the Internet that you can use to create effective spreadsheets. The actual assignments are updated and maintained on the Course Technology Web site. Log on to the Internet and use your Web browser to go to the Student Union on the New Perspectives Series site at **www.course.com/NewPerspectives/studentunion**. Click the Online Companions link, and then click the link for this text.

## QUICK CHECK ANSWERS

*Session 2.1*

1. =MIN(B1:B50)
2. =MAX(B1:50)/MIN(B1:B50)
3. =PMT(0.07/4,20,10000)
4. =IPMT(0.07/4,2,20,10000)
5. absolute reference
6. =B2+C2
7. =$A2+C$1; if moved, the formula would stay the same, =$A1+B$1

## Session 2.2

1. Enter the values *1* and *3* in the first two rows of column A. Select the two cells and then drag the fill handle down to complete the rest of the series.

2. Enter *1/1/2003* in the first cell. Select the first cell and then drag the fill handle down 27 rows. Click the Auto Fill Options button, and then click the Fill Years option button.

3. =IF(A1>B1,"Yes","No")

4. Type the SUM function directly into the cell while in edit mode, using the Insert Function button on the Formula bar or using the AutoSum button on the Standard toolbar.

5. =YEAR(A1)

6. =TODAY()

7. =WEEKDAY(A1)

In this tutorial you will:

- Format data using different fonts, sizes, and font styles

- Align cell contents

- Add cell borders and backgrounds

- Merge cells and hide rows and columns

- Format the worksheet background and sheet tabs

- Find and replace formats within a worksheet

- Create and apply styles

- Apply an AutoFormat to a table

- Format a printout using Print Preview

- Create a header and footer for a printed worksheet

- Define a print area and add a page break to a printed worksheet

# DEVELOPING A PROFESSIONAL-LOOKING WORKSHEET

*Formatting a Sales Report*

CASE

## NewGeneration Monitors

NewGeneration Monitors is a computer equipment company that specializes in computer monitors. Joan Sanchez has been entering sales data on three of the company's monitors into an Excel workbook. She plans on including the sales data in a report to be presented later in the week. Joan has made no attempt to make this data presentable to her coworkers. She has simply entered the numbers. She needs you to transform her raw figures into a presentable report.

To create a professional-looking document, you will learn how to work with Excel's formatting tools to modify the appearance of the data in each cell, the cell itself, and the entire worksheet. You will also learn how to format printouts that Joan wants to generate based on her workbook. You will learn how to create headers and footers, and control which parts of the worksheet are printed on which pages.

# SESSION 3.1

In this session, you will format the contents of individual cells in your worksheet by modifying the font used in the cell or by changing the font size or style. You will also use color in your worksheet, modifying the background color of worksheet cells as well as the color of the text in a cell. You will also have an opportunity to examine various Excel commands that you can use to control text alignment and to wrap a line of text within a single cell. Finally, you will create borders around individual cells and cell ranges.

## Formatting Worksheet Data

The data for Joan's sales report has already been stored in an Excel workbook. Before going further, open the workbook and save it with a new filename.

### To open the Sales report workbook:

1. Start Excel, and open the **Sales1** workbook located in the Tutorial.03/Tutorial folder on your Data Disk.

2. On the Documentation worksheet, enter your name in cell B3, and enter the current date in cell B4.

3. Save the workbook as **Sales2** in the Tutorial.03/Tutorial folder on your Data Disk.

4. Click the **Sales** tab. Figure 3-1 shows the current appearance of the sales report, which is unformatted.

---

**Figure 3-1**        THE UNFORMATTED SALES WORKSHEET

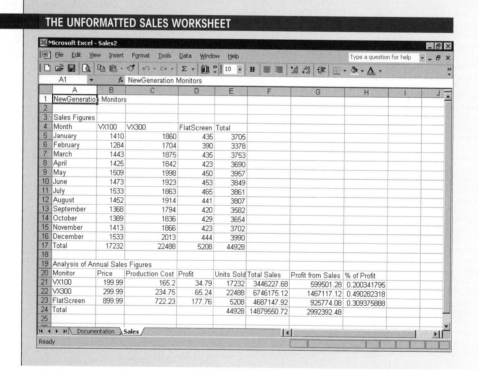

---

The Sales worksheet contains two tables. The first table displays the monthly sales for three of NewGeneration's monitors: the VX100, VX300, and the FlatScreen. The second table presents an analysis of these sales figures, showing the profit from the monitor sales and the percentage that each monitor contributes to the overall profit. In its current state, the worksheet is difficult to read and interpret. This is a problem that Joan wants you to solve by using Excel's formatting tools.

**Formatting** is the process of changing the appearance of your workbook. A properly formatted workbook can be easier to read, appear more professional, and help draw attention to important points you want to make. Formatting changes only the appearance of the data; formatting does not affect the data itself. For example, if a cell contains the value 0.124168, and you format the cell to display only up to the thousandths place (for example, 0.124), the cell still contains the precise value, even though you cannot see it displayed in the worksheet.

Up to now, Excel has been automatically formatting your cell entries using a formatting style called the General format. The **General format** aligns numbers with the right edge of the cell without dollar signs or commas, uses the minus sign for negative values, and truncates any trailing zeros to the right of the decimal point. For more control over your data's appearance, you can choose from a wide variety of other number formats. Formats can be applied using either the Formatting toolbar or the Format menu from Excel's menu bar. Formats can also be copied from one cell to another, giving you the ability to apply a common format to different cells in your worksheet.

## Using the Formatting Toolbar

The Formatting toolbar is the fastest way to format your worksheet. By clicking a single button on the Formatting toolbar you can increase or decrease the number of decimal places displayed in a selected range of cells, display a value as a currency or percentage, or change the color or size of the font used in a cell.

When Joan typed in the monthly sales figures for the three monitors, she neglected to include a comma to separate the thousands from the hundreds and so forth. Rather than retype these values, you can use the Comma Style button on the Formatting toolbar to format the values with a comma. You can use the Increase Decimal or Decrease Decimal button on the Formatting toolbar to change the number of decimal places displayed in a number.

*To apply the Comma format and adjust the number of decimal places displayed:*

1. Select the range **B5:E17** in the Sales worksheet.

2. Click the **Comma Style** button on the Formatting toolbar. Excel adds the comma separator to each of the values in the table and displays the values with two digits to the right of the decimal point.

   TROUBLE? If you do not see the Comma Style button on the Formatting toolbar, click the Toolbar Options button on the Formatting toolbar, and then click it.

   TROUBLE? If the Standard and Formatting toolbars appear on separate rows on your computer, then the Toolbar Options button might look slightly different from the Toolbar Options button used throughout this text. If you are unsure about the function of a toolbar button, hover the pointer over the button to display its name.

   Because all of the sales figures are whole numbers, you will remove the zeros.

3. Click the **Decrease Decimal** button on the Formatting toolbar twice to remove the zeros. See Figure 3-2.

**Figure 3-2** | **APPLYING THE COMMA STYLE TO THE SALES FIGURES**

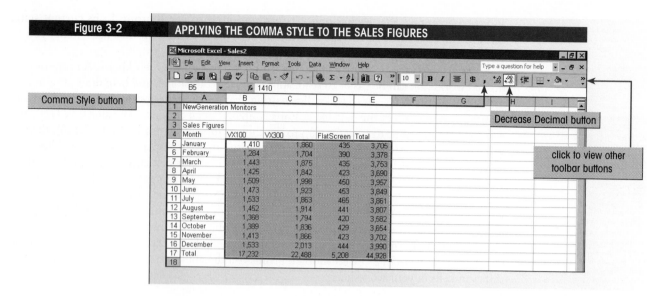

Joan's worksheet also displays the price and production cost of each monitor as well as last year's total sales and profit. She wants this information displayed using dollar signs, commas, and two decimal places. To format the values with these attributes, you can apply the Currency style.

## To apply the Currency format:

1. Select the nonadjacent range **B21:D23;F21:G24**.

   TROUBLE? To select a nonadjacent range, select the first range, press and hold the Ctrl key, and then select the next range.

2. Click the **Currency Style** button 📧 on the Formatting toolbar. Excel adds the dollar signs and commas to the currency values and displays each value (price) to two decimal places. See Figure 3-3.

**Figure 3-3**          APPLYING THE CURRENCY STYLE

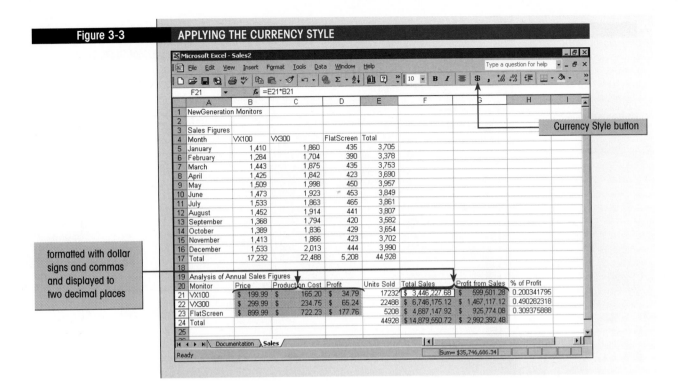

Finally, the range H21:H23 displays the percentage that each monitor contributes to the overall profit from sales. Joan wants these values displayed with a percent sign and to two decimal places. You will apply the Percent format; however, Excel, by default, does not display any decimal places with the Percent format. You need to increase the number of decimal places displayed.

### To apply the Percent format and increase the number of decimal places:

1. Select the range **H21:H23**.

2. Click the **Percent Style** button 🔲 on the Formatting toolbar.

3. Click the **Increase Decimal** button 🔲 on the Formatting toolbar twice to display the percentages to two decimal places. See Figure 3-4.

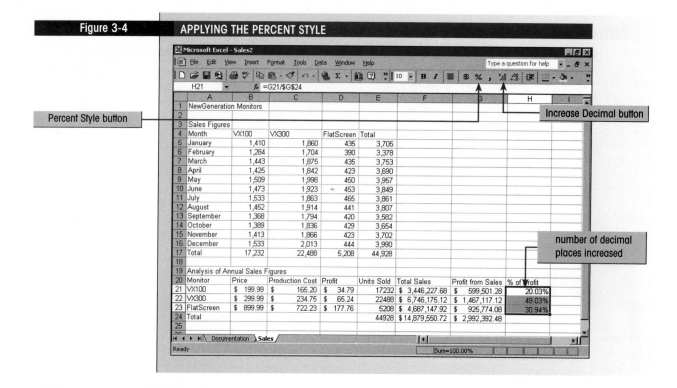

Figure 3-4  APPLYING THE PERCENT STYLE

By displaying the percent values using the Percent format, you can quickly see that one monitor, the VX300, accounts for almost half of the profit from monitor sales.

## Copying Formats

As you look over the sales figures, you see that one area of the worksheet still needs to be formatted. The Units Sold column in the range E21:E24 still does not display the comma separator you used in the sales figures table. To fix a formatting problem like this one, you can use one of the methods that Excel provides for copying a format from one location to another.

One of these methods is the Format Painter button located on the Standard toolbar. When you use the Format Painter option, you "paint" a format from one cell to another cell or to a range of cells. You can also use the fill handle and its Auto Fill options to copy a format from one cell to another. Another method for copying a format is using the Copy and Paste commands, which are available on both the Standard toolbar and the Edit menu. The Copy and Paste method requires you to click the Formatting Only option button that appears when you paste the selected cell, so that only the formatting of the pasted cell, not its content, is applied. Using the Format Painter button does all of this in fewer steps.

You will use the Format Painter button to copy the format used in the sales figures table and to paste that format into the range E21:E24.

### To copy the format using the Format Painter button:

1. Select cell **B5**, which contains the formatting that you want to copy. You do not have to copy the entire range, because the range is formatted in the same way.

2. Click the **Format Painter** button 🖌 on the Standard toolbar.

   As you move the pointer over the worksheet area, the pointer changes to 🔁🖌.

**TROUBLE?** If you do not see the Format Painter button, click the Toolbar Options button ⬚ on the Standard toolbar, and then click ⬚.

3. Select the range **E21:E23**. The format that you used in the sales figures table is applied to the cells in the range E21:E23.

You have not applied the format to cell E24 yet. Rather than using the Format Painter button again, you can drag the fill handle down over the cell. Recall that you can use the fill handle to copy formulas and values from one range into another. You can also use the fill handle to copy formats.

## To copy the format using the fill handle:

1. Click and drag the fill handle down to the range **E21:E24**.

   When you release the mouse button, the word "Price" appears. This occurs because the default action of the fill handle in this case is to fill the values in the range E21:E23 into cell E24. You'll override this default behavior by choosing a different option from the list of Auto Fill options.

2. Click the **Auto Fill Options** button ⬚ located at the lower-right corner of the selected range.

3. Click the **Fill Formatting Only** option button. Excel extends the format from the range E21:E23 into cell E24.

The Formatting toolbar is a fast and easy way to copy and apply cell formats, but there are other ways of formatting your data.

## Using the Format Cells Dialog Box

Joan stops by to view your progress. She agrees that formatting the values has made the worksheet easier to read, but she has a few suggestions. She does not like the way the currency values are displayed with the dollar signs ($) placed at the left edge of the cell, leaving a large blank space between the dollar sign and the numbers. She would like to have the dollar sign placed directly to the left of the dollar amounts, leaving no blank spaces.

The convenience of the Formatting toolbar's one-click access to many of the formatting tasks you will want to perform does have its limits. As you can see in the worksheet, when you use the Formatting toolbar, you cannot specify how the format is applied. To make the change that Joan suggests, you need to open the Format Cells dialog box, which gives you more control over the formatting.

## To open the Format Cells dialog box:

1. Select the nonadjacent range **B21:D23;F21:G24**.

2. Click **Format** on the menu bar, and then click **Cells**. The Format Cells dialog box opens. See Figure 3-5.

**Figure 3-5**    **FORMAT CELLS DIALOG BOX**

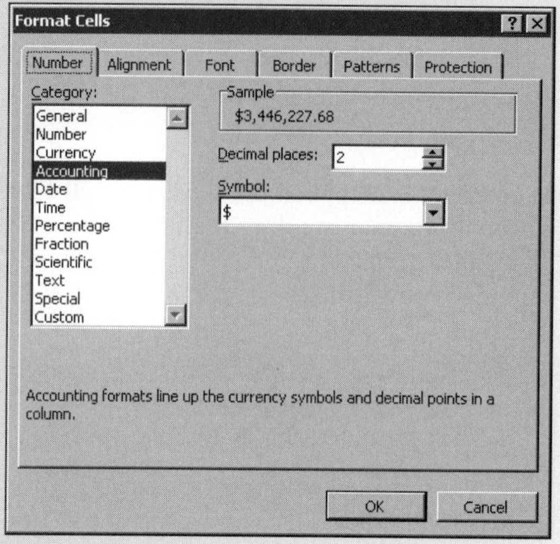

The Format Cells dialog box contains the following six tabs, each dedicated to a different set of format properties:

- **Number**—used to format the appearance of text and values within selected cells
- **Alignment**—used to control how text and values are aligned within a cell
- **Font**—used to choose the font type, size, and style
- **Border**—used to create borders around selected cells
- **Patterns**—used to create and apply background colors and patterns for selected cells
- **Protection**—used to lock or hide selected cells, preventing other users from modifying the cells' contents

So far, you have worked with number formats only. Excel supports several categories of number formats, ranging from Accounting and Currency formats to Scientific formats that might be used for recording engineering data. Figure 3-6 describes some of the number format categories.

**Figure 3-6**    **NUMBER FORMAT CATEGORIES**

| CATEGORY | DESCRIPTION |
| --- | --- |
| General | Default format; numbers are displayed without dollar signs, commas, or trailing decimal places |
| Number | Used for a general display of numbers |
| Currency, Accounting | Used for displaying monetary values; use Accounting formats to align decimal points within a column |
| Date, Time | Used for displaying date and time values |
| Percentage | Used for displaying decimal values as percentages |
| Fraction, Scientific | Used for displaying values as fractions or in scientific notation |
| Text | Used for displaying values as text strings |
| Special | Used for displaying zip codes, phone numbers, and social security numbers |

As shown in Figure 3-5, Excel applied an Accounting format, displaying the dollar sign and two decimal places, to the sales figures. The Accounting format differs from the Currency format; the Accounting format lines up the decimal points and the dollar signs for values within a column so that all the dollar signs appear at the left edge of the cell border. To align the dollar signs closer to the numbers, you can change the format to the Currency format.

### To apply the Currency format:

1. On the Number tab, click **Currency** in the Category list box.

   As shown in the Negative numbers list box, Excel displays negative currency values either with a minus sign (-) or with a combination of a red font and parentheses. Joan wants any negative currency values to be displayed with a minus sign.

2. Click the first entry in the Negative numbers list box.

3. Click the **OK** button. Excel changes the format of the currency values, removing the blank spaces between the dollar signs and the currency values, rather than having the dollar signs lined up within each column.

By using the Format Cells dialog box, you can control the formatting to ensure that text and values are displayed the way you want them to be.

## Working with Fonts and Colors

A **font** is the design applied to characters, letters, and punctuation marks. Each font is identified by a **font name** (or **typeface**). Some of the more commonly used fonts are Arial, Times Roman, and Courier. Each font can be displayed using one of the following styles: regular, italic, bold, or bold italic. Fonts can also be displayed with special effects, such as strikeout, underline, and color.

Fonts can also be rendered in different sizes. Sizes are measured using "points." By default, Excel displays characters using a 10-point Arial font in a regular style. To change the font used in a selected cell, you either click the appropriate buttons on the Formatting toolbar or select options in the Format Cells dialog box.

In the logo that the company uses on all its correspondence and advertising materials, the name "NewGeneration Monitors" appears in a large Times New Roman font. Joan wants you to modify the title in cell A1 to reflect this company-wide format.

### To change the font and font size of the title:

1. Click cell **A1** to make it the active cell.

2. Click the **list arrow** for the Font button Arial on the Formatting toolbar, scroll down the list of available fonts, and then click **Times New Roman**.

   **TROUBLE?** If you do not have the Times New Roman font installed on your computer, choose a different Times Roman font or choose MS Serif in the list.

3. Click the **list arrow** for the Font Size button 10 on the Formatting toolbar, and then click **18**. Figure 3-7 shows the revised format for the title in cell A1.

| Figure 3-7 | CHANGING THE FONT AND FONT SIZE |
|---|---|

Times New Roman font, 18 point

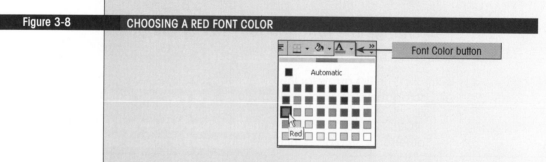

Joan wants the column titles of both tables displayed in bold font and the word "Total" in both tables displayed in italics. To make these modifications, you will again use the Formatting toolbar.

### To apply the bold and italic styles:

1. Select the nonadjacent range **A4:E4;A20:H20**.

2. Click the **Bold** button **B** on the Formatting toolbar. The titles in the two tables now appear in a boldface font.

3. Select cell **A17**, press and hold the **Ctrl** key, and then click cell **A24**.

4. Click the **Italic** button **I** on the Formatting toolbar. The word "Total" in cells A17 and A24 is now italicized.

Joan points out that NewGeneration's logo usually appears in a red font. Color is another one of Excel's formatting tools. Excel allows you to choose a text color from a palette of 40 different colors. If the color you want is not listed, you can modify Excel's color configuration to create a different color palette. Excel's default color settings will work for most situations, so in this case you will not modify Excel's color settings.

### To change the font color of the title to red:

1. Click cell **A1** to make it the active cell.

2. Click the **list arrow** for the Font Color button **A ·** on the Formatting toolbar. A color palette appears. See Figure 3-8.

| Figure 3-8 | CHOOSING A RED FONT COLOR |
|---|---|

Font Color button

3. In the color palette, click the **Red** square (third row, first column). Excel changes the color of the font in cell A1 to red. See Figure 3-9.

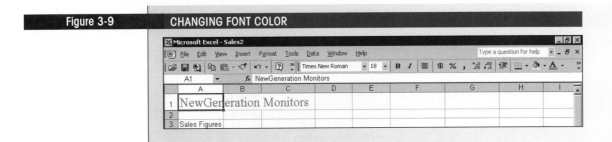

**Figure 3-9** | **CHANGING FONT COLOR**

# Aligning Cell Contents

When you enter numbers and formulas into a cell, Excel automatically aligns them with the cell's right edge and bottom border. Text entries are aligned with the left edge and bottom border. The default Excel alignment does not always create the most readable worksheets. As a general rule, you should center column titles, format columns of numbers so that the decimal places are lined up within a column, and align text with the left edge of the cell. You can change alignment using the alignment tools on the Formatting toolbar or the options on the Alignment tab in the Format Cells dialog box.

Joan wants the column titles centered above the values in each column.

## To center the column titles using the Formatting toolbar:

1. Select the nonadjacent range **B4:E4;B20:H20**.

2. Click the **Center** button on the Formatting toolbar. Excel centers the text in the selected cells in each column.

The Formatting toolbar also provides the Align Left button and the Align Right button so that you can left- and right-align cell contents. If you want to align the cell's contents vertically, you have to open the Format Cells dialog box and choose the vertical alignment options on the Alignment tab.

Another alignment option available in the Format Cells dialog box is the Merge and Center option, which centers the text in one cell across a range of cells. Joan wants the company logo to be centered at the top of the worksheet. In other words, she wants the contents of cell A1 to be centered across the range A1:H1.

## To center the text across the range A1:H1:

1. Select the range **A1:H1**.

2. Click **Format** on the menu bar, and then click **Cells**.

3. Click the **Alignment** tab.

4. Click the **Horizontal** list arrow in the Text alignment pane, and then click **Center Across Selection**. See Figure 3-10.

**Figure 3-10**    **ALIGNMENT TAB**

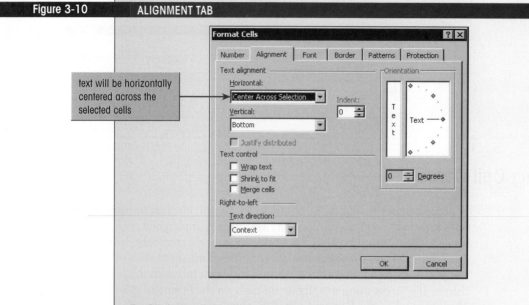

text will be horizontally centered across the selected cells

**5.** Click the **OK** button. See Figure 3-11.

**Figure 3-11**    **CENTERING TEXT WITHIN CELLS AND ACROSS COLUMNS**

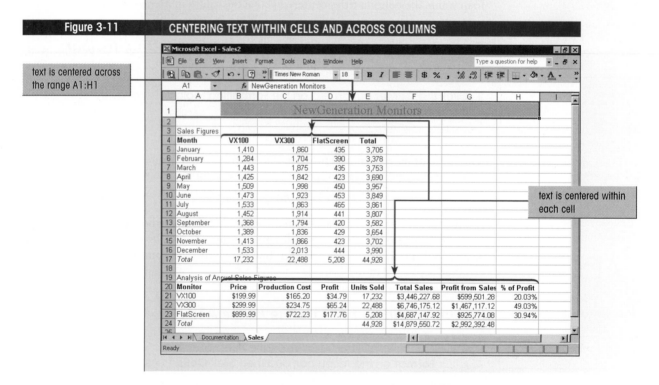

text is centered across the range A1:H1

text is centered within each cell

## Indenting and Wrapping Text

Sometimes you will want a cell's contents offset, or indented, a few spaces from the cell's edge. This is particularly true for text entries that are aligned with the left edge of the cell. Indenting is often used for cell entries that are considered "subsections" of your worksheet. In the sales figures table, Joan wants you to indent the names of the months in the range A5:A16 and the monitor titles in the range A21:A23.

## To indent the months and monitor titles:

1. Select the nonadjacent range **A5:A16;A21:A23**.

2. Click the **Increase Indent** button 📇 on the Formatting toolbar. Excel shifts the contents of the selected cells to the right.

   **TROUBLE?** You may have to click the Toolbar Options button 📳, and then choose the Add or Remove Buttons option before you can click the Increase Indent button. As you use more buttons on the Formatting toolbar, they are added to the toolbar. If your Standard and Formatting toolbars now appear on separate rows, that is okay. The rest of the figures in this book might not look exactly like your screen, but this will not affect your work.

Clicking the Increase Indent button increases the amount of indentation by roughly one character. To decrease or remove an indentation, click the Decrease Indent button or modify the indent value using the Format Cells dialog box.

If you enter text that is too wide for a cell, Excel either extends the text into the adjoining cells (if the cells are empty) or truncates the display of the text. You can also have Excel wrap the text within the cell so that the excess text is displayed on additional lines within the cell. To wrap text, you use the Format Cells dialog box.

Joan notes that some of the column titles in the second table are long. For example, the "Production Cost" label in cell C20 is much longer than the values below it. This formatting has caused some of the columns to be wider than they need to be. Joan suggests that you wrap the text within the column titles and then reduce the width of the columns.

## To wrap the title text within a cell and reduce the column widths:

1. Select the cell range **A20:H20**.

2. Click **Format** on the menu bar, and then click **Cells**.

3. Click the **Wrap text** check box in the Text control pane.

4. Click the **OK** button. The text in cells C20 and G20 now appears on two rows within the cells.

5. Reduce the width of column **C** to about **10** characters.

6. Reduce the width of column **G** to about **12** characters.

7. Reduce the width of column **H** to about **8** characters. See Figure 3-12.

| Figure 3-12 | WRAPPING TEXT WITHIN A CELL |
|---|---|

long column titles wrap to a new line and the widths of the columns are reduced

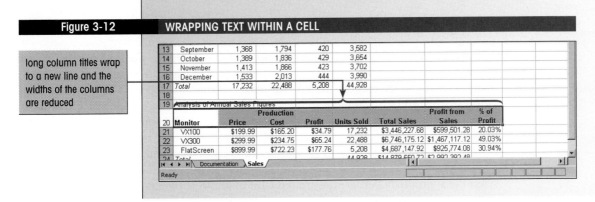

**TROUBLE?** Different monitors have different screen resolutions and column widths. If your screen does not match Figure 3-12, resize the columns accordingly.

## Other Formatting Options

Excel supports even more formatting options than have been discussed so far. For example, instead of wrapping the text, you can have Excel shrink it to fit the size of the cell. If you reduce the cell later on, Excel will automatically resize the text to match. You can also rotate the contents of the cell, displaying the cell entry at almost any angle (see Figure 3-13). Joan does not need to use either of these options in her workbook, but they might be useful later on another project.

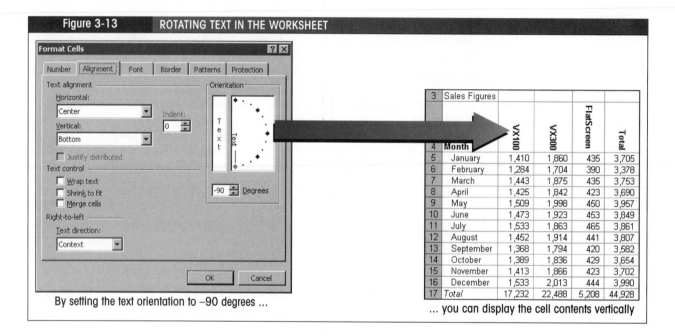

Figure 3-13    ROTATING TEXT IN THE WORKSHEET

By setting the text orientation to –90 degrees …

… you can display the cell contents vertically

# Working with Cell Borders and Backgrounds

Up to now, all the formatting you have done has been applied to the contents of a cell. Excel also provides a range of tools to format the cells themselves. Specifically, you can add borders to the cells and color the cell backgrounds.

## Adding a Cell Border

As you may have noticed from the printouts of other worksheets, the gridlines that appear in the worksheet window are not displayed on the printed page. In some cases, however, you might want to display borders around individual cells in a worksheet. This would be particularly true when you have different sections or tables in a worksheet, as in Joan's Sales worksheet.

You can add a border to a cell using either the Borders button on the Formatting toolbar or the options on the Border tab in the Format Cells dialog box. The Borders button allows you to create borders quickly, whereas the Format Cells dialog box lets you further refine your choices.

Joan wants you to place a border around each cell in the two tables in the worksheet. You'll select the appropriate border style from the list of available options on the Borders palette.

## *To create a grid of cell borders in the two tables:*

**1.** Select the nonadjacent range **A4:E17;A20:H24**.

**2.** Click the **list arrow** for the Borders button on the Formatting toolbar. See Figure 3-14.

**Figure 3-14**     BORDER OPTIONS

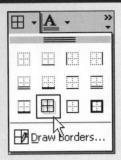

**3.** Click the **All Borders** option (third row, second column) in the gallery of border options. A thin border appears around each cell in the selected range.

**4.** Click cell **A1** to deselect the range.

You can also place a border around the entire range itself (and not the individual cells) by selecting a different border style. Try this by creating a thick border around the cell range.

## *To create a thick border around the selected range:*

**1.** Select the range **A4:E17;A20:H24** again.

**2.** Click the **list arrow** for the Borders button on the Formatting toolbar, and then click the **Thick Box Border** option (third row, fourth column) in the border gallery.

**3.** Click cell **A2**. Figure 3-15 shows the two tables with their borders.

| Figure 3-15 | BORDERS WITHIN AND AROUND THE TWO SALES TABLES |
| --- | --- |

If you want a more interactive way of drawing borders on your worksheet, you can use the Draw Border button, which is also one of the options on the Borders palette. To see how this option works, you will add a thick black line under the column titles in both of the tables.

## To draw borders using the Draw Border tool:

1. Click the **list arrow** for the Borders button ⬚▾ on the Formatting toolbar, and then click the **Draw Border** button ⊞ at the bottom of the border gallery.

   The pointer changes to ✎, and a floating Borders toolbar opens with four tools. The Draw Border button ✎▾ (currently selected) draws a border line on the worksheet; the Erase Border button ⬚ erases border lines; the Line Style button ⬚▾ specifies the style of the border line; and the Line Color button ✎ specifies the line color.

2. Click the **list arrow** for the Line Style button ⬚▾, and then click the **thick line** option (the eighth from the top) in the list.

3. Click and drag the pointer over the lower border of the range **A4:E4**.

4. Click and drag the pointer over the lower border of the range **A20:H20**.

5. Click the **Close** button ✕ on the floating Borders toolbar to close it.

Finally, you will add a double line above the Total row in each table. You will add the line using the options in the Format Cells dialog box.

## To create the double border lines:

1. Select the nonadjacent range **A16:E16;A23:H23**.

2. Click **Format** on the menu bar, and then click **Cells**.

3. Click the **Border** tab. The Border tab displays a diagram showing what borders, if any, are currently surrounding the selected cells.

   The bottom border is currently a single thin line. You want to change this to a double line.

4. Click the **double line** style in the Line Style list box located on the right side of the tab.

5. Click the **bottom border** in the border diagram. The bottom border changes to a double line. See Figure 3-16.

**Figure 3-16          BORDER TAB**

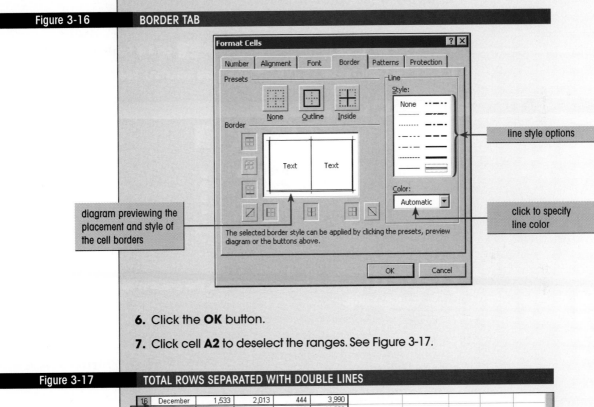

diagram previewing the placement and style of the cell borders

line style options

click to specify line color

6. Click the **OK** button.

7. Click cell **A2** to deselect the ranges. See Figure 3-17.

**Figure 3-17          TOTAL ROWS SEPARATED WITH DOUBLE LINES**

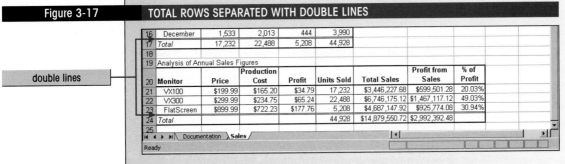

double lines

| | | | | Production | | | | Profit from | % of |
|---|---|---|---|---|---|---|---|---|---|
| 16 | December | 1,533 | 2,013 | 444 | 3,990 | | | | |
| 17 | Total | 17,232 | 22,488 | 5,208 | 44,928 | | | | |
| 18 | | | | | | | | | |
| 19 | Analysis of Annual Sales Figures | | | | | | | | |
| 20 | Monitor | Price | Production Cost | Profit | Units Sold | Total Sales | Profit from Sales | % of Profit | |
| 21 | VX100 | $199.99 | $165.20 | $34.79 | 17,232 | $3,446,227.68 | $599,501.28 | 20.03% | |
| 22 | VX300 | $299.99 | $234.75 | $65.24 | 22,488 | $6,746,175.12 | $1,467,117.12 | 49.03% | |
| 23 | FlatScreen | $899.99 | $722.23 | $177.76 | 5,208 | $4,687,147.92 | $925,774.08 | 30.94% | |
| 24 | Total | | | | 44,928 | $14,879,550.72 | $2,992,392.48 | | |
| 25 | | | | | | | | | |

You can also specify a color for the cell borders by using the Color list box located on the Border tab (see Figure 3-16). Joan does not need to change the border colors, but she would like you to change the background color for the column title cells.

## Setting the Background Color and Pattern

Patterns and color can be used to enliven a dull worksheet or provide visual emphasis to the sections of the worksheet that you want to stress. If you have a color printer or a color projection device, you might want to take advantage of Excel's color tools. By default, worksheet cells are not filled with any color (the white you see in your worksheet is not a fill color for the cells). To change the background color in a worksheet, you can use the Fill Color button on the Formatting toolbar, or you can use the Format Cells dialog box, which also provides patterns that you can apply to the background.

Joan wants to change the background color of the worksheet. When she makes her report later in the week, she will be using the company's color laser printer. So she would like you to explore using background color in the column titles for the two sales tables. She suggests that you try formatting the column titles with a light yellow background.

### To apply a fill color to the column titles:

1. Select the nonadjacent range **A4:E4;A20:H20**.

2. Click the **list arrow** for the Fill Color button 🎨 ▾ on the Formatting toolbar.

3. Click the **Light Yellow** square (fifth row, third column). See Figure 3-18.

| Figure 3-18 | SELECTING A FILL COLOR |

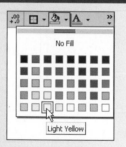

4. Click cell **A2** to deselect the column titles. The column titles now have light yellow backgrounds.

Joan would also like to investigate whether you can apply a pattern to the fill background. Excel supports 18 different fill patterns. To create and apply a fill pattern, you have to open the Format Cells dialog box.

### To apply a fill pattern to the column titles:

1. Select the nonadjacent range **A4:E4;A20:H20**.

2. Click **Format** on the menu bar, and then click **Cells**.

3. Click the **Patterns** tab.

4. Click the **Pattern** list arrow. Clicking the Pattern list arrow displays a gallery of patterns and a palette of colors applied to the selected pattern. The default pattern color is black. You will choose just a pattern now.

5. Click the **50% Gray** pattern (first row, third column) in the pattern gallery. See Figure 3-19.

**Figure 3-19**    SELECTING A FILL PATTERN

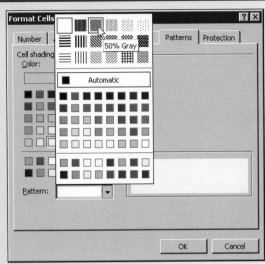

6. Click the **OK** button.

7. Click cell **A2** to deselect the ranges and to see the pattern.

The background pattern you have chosen overwhelms the text in these column titles. You can improve the appearance by changing the color of the pattern itself from black to a light orange.

## To change the pattern color:

1. Select the range **A4:E4;A20:H20** again.

2. Click **Format** on the menu bar, and then click **Cells**.

3. Click the **Pattern** list arrow. The default (or automatic) color of a selected pattern is black. You can choose a different color for the pattern using the color palette below the patterns.

4. Click the **Light Orange** square (third row, second column) in the color palette.

5. Click the **OK** button.

6. Click cell **A2** to deselect the ranges. Figure 3-20 shows the patterned background applied to the column titles. Note that the light orange pattern does not overwhelm the column titles.

**Figure 3-20**    **COLUMN TITLES WITH FORMATTED BACKGROUND**

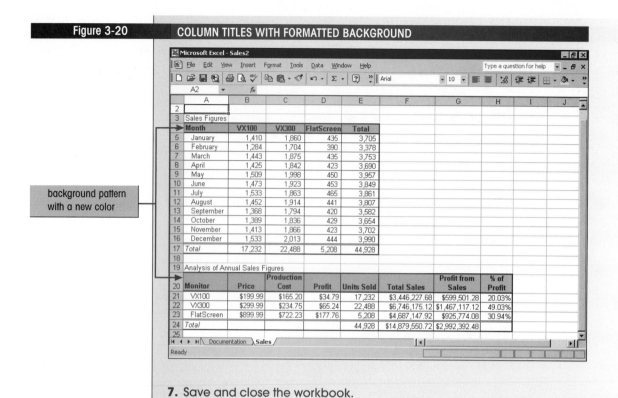

background pattern with a new color

**7.** Save and close the workbook.

Joan is pleased with the progress you have made. In the next session, you will explore other formatting features.

## Session 3.1 QUICK CHECK

1. Describe two ways of applying a Currency format to cells in your worksheet.

2. If the number 0.05765 has been entered into a cell, what will Excel display if you:
    **a.** format the number using the Percent format with one decimal place?
    **b.** format the number using the Currency format with two decimal places and a dollar sign?

3. Which two buttons can you use to copy a format from one cell range to another?

4. A long text string in one of your worksheet cells has been truncated. List three ways to correct this problem.

5. How do you center the contents of a single cell across a range of cells?

6. Describe three ways of creating a cell border.

7. How would you apply a background pattern to a selected cell range?

**SESSION 3.2**

In this session, you will format a worksheet by merging cells, hiding rows and columns, inserting a background image, and finding and replacing formats. You will also be introduced to styles. You will see how to create and apply styles, and you will learn how styles can be used to make formatting more efficient. You will also learn about Excel's gallery of AutoFormats. Finally, you will work with the Print Preview window to control the formatting applied to your printed worksheets.

## Formatting the Worksheet

In the previous session you formatted individual cells within the worksheet. Excel also provides tools for formatting the entire worksheet or the entire workbook. You will explore some of these tools as you continue to work on Joan's Sales report.

### Merging Cells into One Cell

Joan has reviewed the Sales worksheet and has a few suggestions. She would like you to format the titles for the two tables in her report so that they are centered in a bold font above the tables. You could do this by centering the cell title across a cell range, as you did for the title in the last session. Another way is to merge several cells into one cell and then center the contents of that single cell. Merging a range of cells into a single cell removes all of the cells from the worksheet, except the cell in the upper-left corner of the range. Any content in the other cells of the range is deleted. To merge a range of cells into a single cell, you can use the Merge option on the Alignment tab in the Format Cells dialog box or click the Merge and Center button on the Formatting toolbar.

### To merge and center the cell ranges containing the table titles:

1. If you took a break after the previous session, start Excel and open the Sales2 workbook.

2. In the Sales worksheet, select the range **A3:E3**.

3. Click the **Merge and Center** button ⊞ on the Formatting toolbar. The cells in the range A3:E3 are merged into one cell at the cell location, A3. The text in the merged cell is centered as well.

4. Click the **Bold** button B on the Formatting toolbar.

5. Select the range **A19:H19**, click ⊞, and then click B.

6. Click cell **A2** to deselect the range. Figure 3-21 shows the merged and centered table titles.

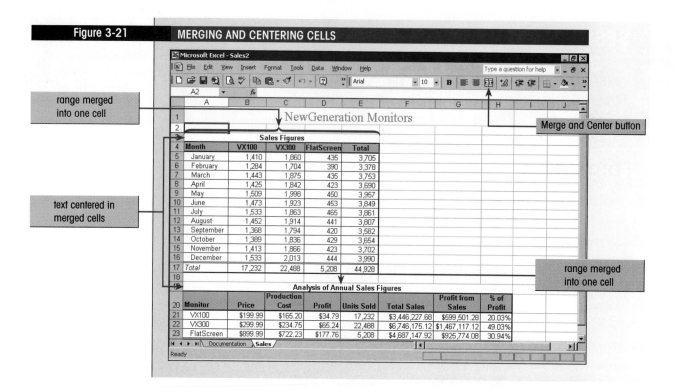

**Figure 3-21**     MERGING AND CENTERING CELLS

To split a merged cell back into individual cells, regardless of the method you used to merge the cells, you select the merged cell and then click the Merge and Center button again. You can also merge and unmerge cells using the Alignment tab in the Format Cells dialog box.

## Hiding Rows and Columns

Sometimes Joan does not need to view the monthly sales for the three monitors. She does not want to remove this information from the worksheet, but she would like the option of temporarily hiding that information. Excel provides this capability. Hiding a row or column does not affect the data stored there, nor does it affect any other cell that might have a formula referencing a cell in the hidden row or column. Hiding part of your worksheet is a good way of removing extraneous information, allowing you to concentrate on the more important data contained in your worksheet. To hide a row or column, first you must select the row(s) or column(s) you want to hide. You can then use the Row or Column option on the Format menu or right-click the selection to open its shortcut menu.

You will hide the monthly sales figures in the first table in the worksheet.

### To hide the monthly sales figures:

1. Select the headings for rows **5** through **16**.

2. Right-click the selection, and then click **Hide** on the shortcut menu. Excel hides rows 5 through 16. Note that the total sales figures in the range B17:E17 are not affected by hiding the monthly sales figures. See Figure 3-22.

**Figure 3-22**    **HIDING WORKSHEET ROWS**

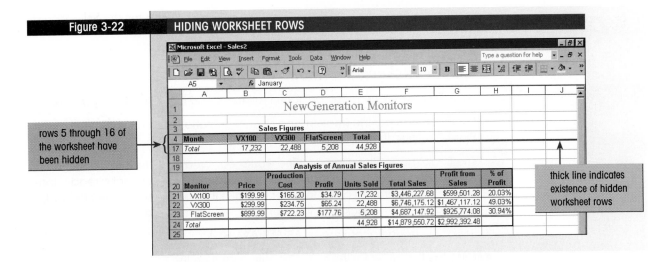

rows 5 through 16 of
the worksheet have
been hidden

thick line indicates
existence of hidden
worksheet rows

To unhide a hidden row or column, you must select the headings of the rows or columns that border the hidden area; then you can use the right-click method or the Row or Column command on the Format menu. You will let Joan know that it is easy to hide any row or column that she does not want to view. But for now you will redisplay the hidden sales figures.

### To unhide the monthly sales figures:

1. Select the row headings for rows **4** and **17**.

2. Right-click the selection, and then click **Unhide** on the shortcut menu. Excel redisplays rows 5 through 16.

3. Click cell **A2** to deselect the rows.

Hiding and unhiding a column follows the same process, except that you select the worksheet column headings rather than the row headings.

## Formatting the Sheet Background

In the previous session you learned how to create a background color for individual cells within the worksheet. Excel also allows you to use an image file as a background. The image from the file is tiled repeatedly until the images fill up the entire worksheet. Images can be used to give the background a textured appearance, like that of granite, wood, or fibered paper. The background image does not affect the format or content of any cell in the worksheet, and if you have already defined a background color for a cell, Excel displays the color on top, hiding that portion of the image.

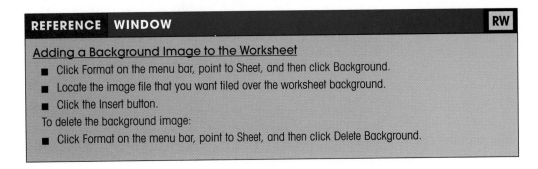

**REFERENCE WINDOW**    **RW**

Adding a Background Image to the Worksheet
- Click Format on the menu bar, point to Sheet, and then click Background.
- Locate the image file that you want tiled over the worksheet background.
- Click the Insert button.
To delete the background image:
- Click Format on the menu bar, point to Sheet, and then click Delete Background.

Joan wants you to experiment with using a background image for the Sales worksheet. She has an image file that she wants you to try.

### To add a background image to the worksheet:

1. Click **Format** on the menu bar, point to **Sheet**, and then click **Background**.

2. Locate and select the **Back** image file in the Tutorial.03/Tutorial folder on your Data Disk, and then click the **Insert** button.

   The Back image file is tiled over the worksheet, creating a textured background for the Sales sheet. Notice that the tiling is hidden in the cells that already contained a background color. In order to make the sales figures easier to read, you'll change the background color of those cells to white.

3. Select the nonadjacent range **A5:E17;A21:H24**.

4. Click the **list arrow** for the Fill Color button on the Formatting toolbar, and then click the **White** square (last row, last column) in the color palette.

5. Click cell **A2**. Figure 3-23 shows the Sales worksheet with the formatted background.

| Figure 3-23 | ADDING A BACKGROUND IMAGE |

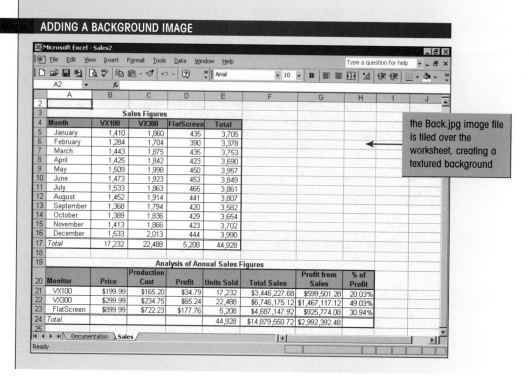

Note that you cannot apply a background image to all of the sheets in a workbook at the same time. If you want to apply the same background to several sheets, you must format each sheet separately.

## Formatting Sheet Tabs

In addition to the sheet background, you can also format the background color of worksheet tabs. This color is only visible when the worksheet is not the active sheet in the workbook; the background color for the active sheet is always white. You can use tab colors to better organize the various sheets in your workbook. For example, worksheets that contain sales information could be formatted with blue tabs, and sheets that describe the company's cash flow or budget could be formatted with green tabs.

If Joan's workbook contained many sheets, it would be easier to locate information if the sheet tabs were different colors. To explore how to color sheet tabs, you will change the tab color of the Sales worksheet to light orange.

### To change the tab color:

1. Right-click the **Sales** tab, and then click **Tab Color** on the shortcut menu.

2. Click the **Light Orange** square (third row, second column) in the color palette.

3. Click the **OK** button. A light orange horizontal stripe appears at the bottom of the tab, but because Sales is the active worksheet, the background color is still white.

4. Click the **Documentation** tab. Now that Documentation is the active sheet, you can see the light orange color of the Sales sheet tab.

5. Click the **Sales** tab to make it the active sheet again.

# Clearing and Replacing Formats

Sometimes you might want to change or remove some of the formatting from your workbooks. As you experiment with different formats, you will find a lot of use for the Undo button on the Standard toolbar as you remove formatting choices that did not work out as well as you expected. Another choice is to clear the formatting from the selected cells, returning the cells to their initial, unformatted appearance. To see how this option works, you will remove the formatting from the company name in cell A1 on the Sales worksheet.

### To clear the format from cell A1:

1. Click cell **A1** to select it.

2. Click **Edit** on the menu bar, point to **Clear**, and then click **Formats**. Excel removes the formatting that was applied to the cell text and removes the formatting that centered the text across the range A1:H1.

3. Click the **Undo** button 🔄 on the Standard toolbar to undo your action, restoring the formats you cleared.

Sometimes you will want to make a formatting change that applies to several different cells. If those cells are scattered throughout the workbook, you may find it time-consuming to search and replace the formats for each individual cell. If the cells share a common format that you want to change, you can use the Find and Replace command to locate the formats and modify them.

---

**REFERENCE WINDOW**                                          **RW**

Finding and Replacing a Format
- Click Edit on the menu bar, and then click Replace.
- Click the Options >> button, if necessary, to display the format choices.
- Click the top Format list arrow, and then click Format.
- Specify the format you want to find in the Find Format dialog box, and then click the OK button.
- Click the bottom Format list arrow, and then click Format.
- Enter a new format with which you want to replace the old format, and then click the OK button.
- Click the Replace All button to replace all occurrences of the old format; or click the Replace button to replace the currently selected cell containing the old format; or click the Find Next button to find the next occurrence of the old format before replacing it.
- Click the Close button.

---

For example, in the Sales worksheet, the table titles and column titles are displayed in a bold font. After seeing how the use of color has made the worksheet come alive, Joan wants you to change the titles to a boldface blue. Rather than selecting the cells that contain the table and column titles and formatting them, you can replace all occurrences of the boldface text with blue boldface text.

## To find and replace formats:

1. Click **Edit** on the menu bar, and then click **Replace**. The Find and Replace dialog box opens. You can use this dialog box to find and replace the contents of the cells. In this case, you will use it only for finding and replacing formats, leaving the contents of the cells unchanged.

2. Click the **Options >>** button to display additional find and replace options. See Figure 3-24.

   **TROUBLE?** If the button on your workbook appears as Options <<, the additional options are already displayed, and you do not need to click any buttons.

---

**Figure 3-24**          **FIND AND REPLACE DIALOG BOX**

previews the selected formatting

click to replace the next occurrence in the worksheet

click to replace all occurrences in the worksheet

click to specify the format to search for

click to specify the new format

click to find but not necessarily to replace

---

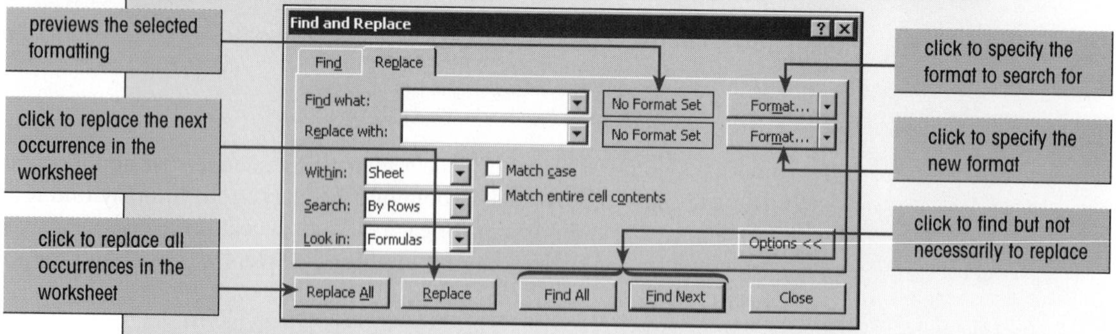

The dialog box expands to display options that allow you to find and replace cell formats. It also includes options to determine whether to search within the active sheet or the entire workbook. Currently no format options have been set.

3. Click the top **Format** list arrow, and then click **Format**.

   The Find Format dialog box opens. Here is where you specify the format you want to search for. In this case, you are searching for cells that contain boldface text.

4. Click the **Font** tab, and then click **Bold** in the Font style list box. See Figure 3-25.

---

**Figure 3-25**         **FIND FORMAT DIALOG BOX**

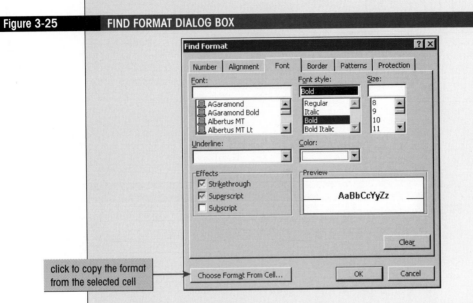

click to copy the format
from the selected cell

---

5. Click the **OK** button.

   Next, you have to specify the new format that you want to use to replace the boldface text. In this case, you need to specify a blue boldface text.

6. Click the bottom **Format** list arrow, and then click **Format**.

7. Click **Bold** in the Font style list box.

8. Click the **Color** list box, and then click the **Blue** square (second row, sixth column) in the color palette.

9. Click the **OK** button.

10. Click the **Replace All** button to replace all boldface text in the worksheet with boldface blue text. Excel indicates that it has completed its search and made 15 replacements.

11. Click the **OK** button, and then click the **Close** button. See Figure 3-26.

**Figure 3-26** SALES WORKSHEET WITH BOLDFACE BLUE TEXT

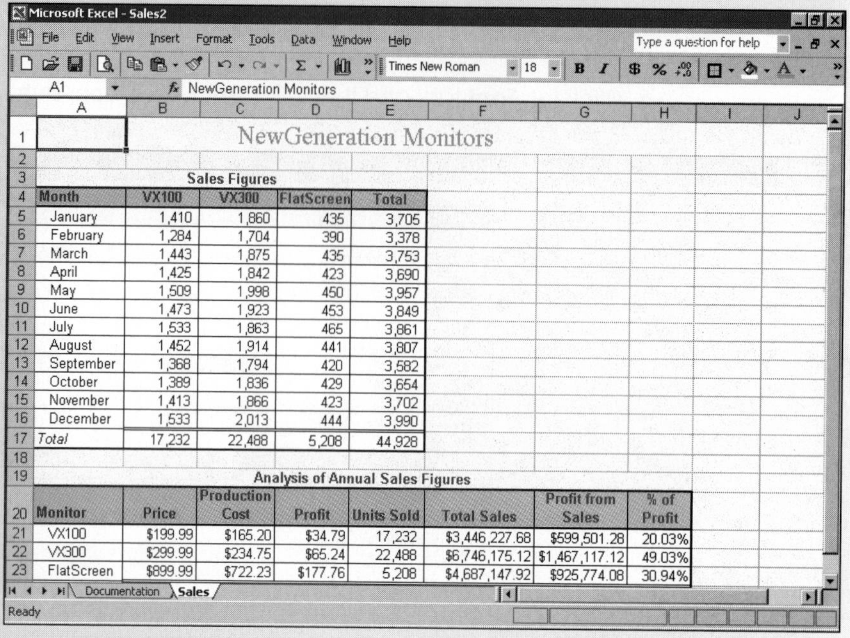

NewGeneration Monitors

Sales Figures

| Month | VX100 | VX300 | FlatScreen | Total |
|---|---|---|---|---|
| January | 1,410 | 1,860 | 435 | 3,705 |
| February | 1,284 | 1,704 | 390 | 3,378 |
| March | 1,443 | 1,875 | 435 | 3,753 |
| April | 1,425 | 1,842 | 423 | 3,690 |
| May | 1,509 | 1,998 | 450 | 3,957 |
| June | 1,473 | 1,923 | 453 | 3,849 |
| July | 1,533 | 1,863 | 465 | 3,861 |
| August | 1,452 | 1,914 | 441 | 3,807 |
| September | 1,368 | 1,794 | 420 | 3,582 |
| October | 1,389 | 1,836 | 429 | 3,654 |
| November | 1,413 | 1,866 | 423 | 3,702 |
| December | 1,533 | 2,013 | 444 | 3,990 |
| *Total* | 17,232 | 22,488 | 5,208 | 44,928 |

Analysis of Annual Sales Figures

| Monitor | Price | Production Cost | Profit | Units Sold | Total Sales | Profit from Sales | % of Profit |
|---|---|---|---|---|---|---|---|
| VX100 | $199.99 | $165.20 | $34.79 | 17,232 | $3,446,227.68 | $599,501.28 | 20.03% |
| VX300 | $299.99 | $234.75 | $65.24 | 22,488 | $6,746,175.12 | $1,467,117.12 | 49.03% |
| FlatScreen | $899.99 | $722.23 | $177.76 | 5,208 | $4,687,147.92 | $925,774.08 | 30.94% |

# Using Styles

If you have several cells that employ the same format, you can create a style for those cells. A **style** is a saved collection of formatting options—number formats; text alignment; font sizes and colors; borders; and background fills—that can be applied to cells in the worksheet. When you apply a style, Excel remembers which styles are associated with which cells in the workbook. If you want to change the appearance of a particular type of cell, you need only modify the specifications for the style, and the appearance of any cell associated with that style would be automatically changed to reflect the new style.

You can create a style in one of two ways: by selecting a cell from the worksheet and basing the style definition on the formatting choices already defined for that cell or by manually entering the style definitions into a dialog box. Once you create and name a style, you can apply it to cells in the workbook.

Excel has eight built-in styles named Comma, Comma [0], Currency, Currency [0], Followed Hyperlink, Hyperlink, Normal, and Percent. You have been using styles all of this time without knowing it. Most cells are formatted with the Normal style, but when you enter a percentage, Excel formats it using the Percent style. Similarly, currency values are automatically formatted using the Currency style, and so forth.

## Creating a Style

Joan wants you to further modify the appearance of the worksheet by changing the background color of the months in the first table and the monitor names in the second table to yellow. Rather than applying new formatting to the cells, you decide to create a new style called "Category" that you will apply to the category columns of the tables in your workbook. You will create the style using the format already applied to cell A5 of the worksheet as a basis.

## *To create a style using a formatted cell:*

1. Click cell **A5** to select it. The format applied to this cell becomes the basis of the new style that you want to create.

2. Click **Format** on the menu bar, and then click **Style**. The Style dialog box opens. All of the formatting options associated with the style of the active cell are listed. For example, the font is 10-point Arial.

   To create a new style for this cell, you simply type a different name into the list box.

3. Verify that Normal is highlighted in the Style name list box, and then type **Category**. See Figure 3-27.

| Figure 3-27 | STYLE DIALOG BOX |
|---|---|

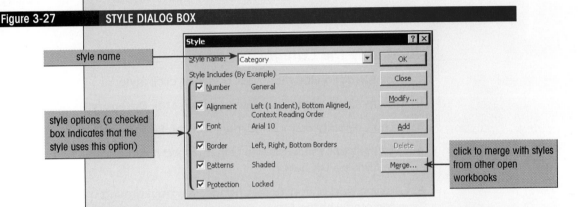

If you do not want all of these formatting options to be part of the Category style, you can deselect the options you no longer want included. You can also modify a current format option or add a new format option. You'll change the background color in the Category style to yellow.

4. Click the **Modify** button. The Format Cells dialog box opens.

5. Click the **Patterns** tab, and then click the **Yellow** square (fourth row, third column) in the color palette.

6. Click the **OK** button to close the Format Cells dialog box.

   If you click the OK button in the Style dialog box, the style definition changes and the updated style is applied to the active cell. If you click the Add button in the dialog box, the change is added, or saved, to the style definition but the updated style is not applied to the active cell.

7. Click the **OK** button. The background color of cell A5 changes to yellow.

Now you need to apply this style to other cells in the workbook.

## Applying a Style

To apply a style to cells in a worksheet, you first select the cells you want associated with the style and then open the Styles dialog box.

## To apply the Category style:

1. Select the nonadjacent range **A6:A16;A21:A23**.

2. Click **Format** on the menu bar, and then click **Style**.

3. Click the **Style name** list arrow, and then click **Category**.

4. Click the **OK** button, and then click cell **A2** to deselect the cells. A yellow background color is applied to all of the category cells in the two tables.

The yellow background appears a bit too strong. You decide to change it to a light yellow background. Since all the category cells are now associated with the Category style, you need only modify the definition of the Category style to make this change.

## To modify the Category style:

1. Click **Format** on the menu bar, and then click **Style**.

2. Click the **Style name** list arrow, and then click **Category**.

3. Click the **Modify** button, and then click the **Patterns** tab, if necessary.

4. Click the **Light Yellow** square (fifth row, third column) in the color palette, and then click the **OK** button.

5. Click the **Add** button. Excel changes the background color of all the cells associated with the Category style.

   TROUBLE? Do not click the OK button. Clicking the OK button will apply the Category style only to the active cell.

6. Click the **Close** button. See Figure 3-28.

Figure 3-28    CATEGORY STYLE IN THE SALES WORKSHEET

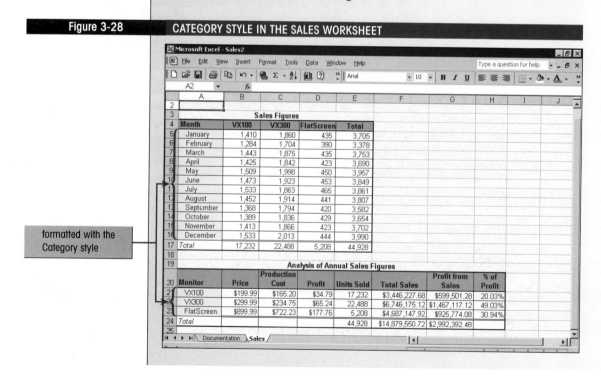

formatted with the Category style

You can also copy styles from one workbook to another. Copying styles allows you to create a collection of workbooks that share a common look and feel.

# Using AutoFormat

Excel's **AutoFormat** feature lets you choose an appearance for your worksheet cells from a gallery of 17 predefined formats. Rather than spending time testing different combinations of fonts, colors, and borders, you can apply a professionally designed format to your worksheet by choosing one from the AutoFormat Gallery. You have done a lot of work already formatting the data in the Sales workbook to give it a more professional and polished look, but you decide to see how the formatting you have done compares to one of Excel's AutoFormat designs.

Apply an AutoFormat to the Sales Figures table so that you can compare the professionally designed format to the format you have worked on.

## To apply an AutoFormat to the table:

1. Select the range **A3:E17**.

2. Click **Format** on the menu bar, and then click **AutoFormat**. The AutoFormat dialog box opens. See Figure 3-29.

| Figure 3-29 | AUTOFORMAT GALLERY |
|---|---|

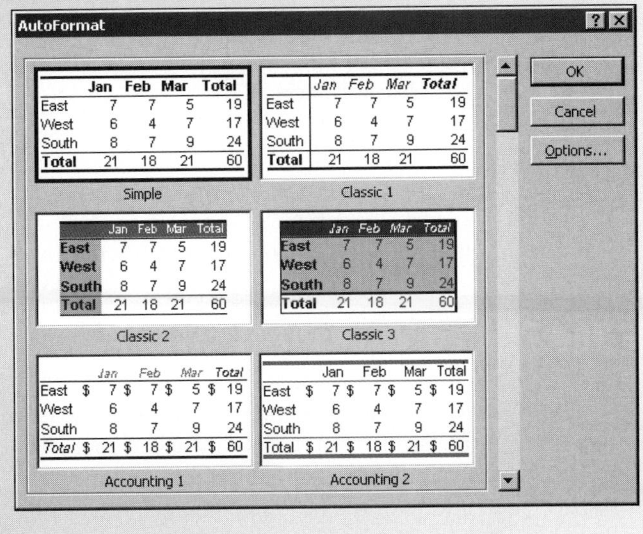

The dialog box displays a preview of how each format will appear when applied to cells in a worksheet.

3. Click **Classic 3** in the list of available designs, and then click the **OK** button.

4. Click cell **A2** to remove the highlighting from the first table. Figure 3-30 shows the appearance of the Classic 3 design in your workbook.

**Figure 3-30**    APPLYING AN AUTOFORMAT

table formatted with the
Classic 3 design

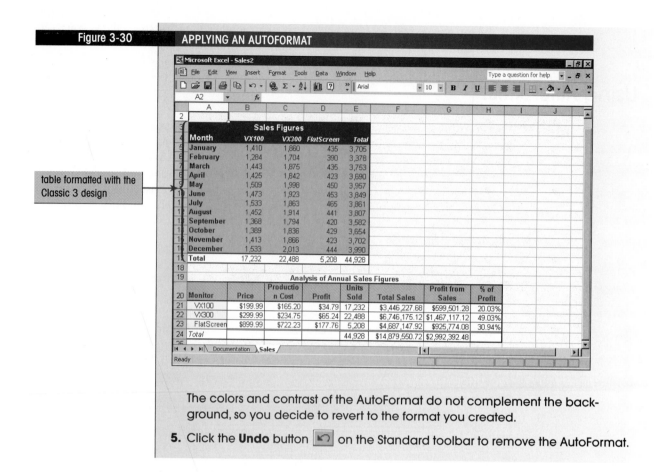

The colors and contrast of the AutoFormat do not complement the background, so you decide to revert to the format you created.

**5.** Click the **Undo** button on the Standard toolbar to remove the AutoFormat.

Although you will not use an AutoFormat in this case, you can see how an AutoFormat can be used as a starting point. You could start with Excel's professional design and then make modifications to the worksheet to fit your own needs.

# Formatting the Printed Worksheet

You have settled on an appearance for the Sales worksheet—at least the appearance that is displayed on your screen. But that is only half of your job. Joan also wants you to format the appearance of this worksheet when it is printed out. You have to decide how to arrange the report on the page, the size of the page margins, the orientation of the page, and whether the page will have any headers or footers. You can make many of these choices through Excel's Print Preview.

## Opening the Print Preview Window

As the name implies, the **Print Preview window** shows you how each page of your worksheet will look when it is printed. From the Print Preview window, you can make changes to the page layout before you print your worksheet.

### To preview the Sales worksheet printout:

**1.** Click the **Print Preview** button on the Standard toolbar. The Print Preview window opens, displaying the worksheet as it will appear on the printed page. See Figure 3-31.

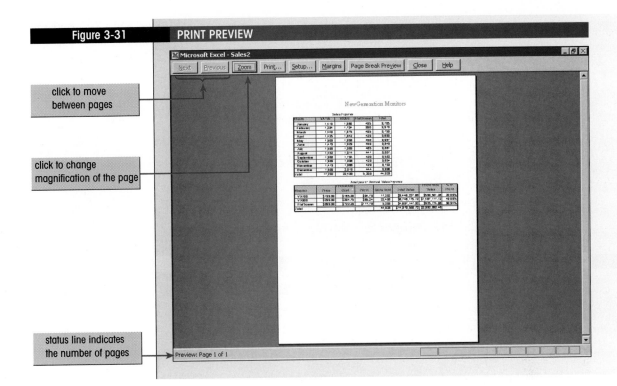

Figure 3-31   PRINT PREVIEW

click to move between pages

click to change magnification of the page

status line indicates the number of pages

Excel displays the full page in the Print Preview window. You might have difficulty reading the text because it is so small. Do not worry if the preview is not completely readable. One purpose of Print Preview is to see the overall layout of the worksheet. If you want a better view of the text, you can increase the magnification by either using the Zoom button on the Print Preview toolbar or by clicking the page with the 🔍 pointer. Clicking the Zoom button again, or clicking the page a second time with the pointer, reduces the magnification, bringing the whole page back into view.

### To enlarge the preview:

**1.** Click the **Zoom** button on the Print Preview toolbar.

**2.** Use the horizontal and vertical scroll bars to move around the worksheet.

**3.** Click anywhere within the page with the pointer to reduce the magnification.

You can also make changes to the layout of a worksheet page using the Setup and Margins buttons on the Print Preview toolbar.

## Defining the Page Setup

You can use the Page Setup dialog box to control how a worksheet is placed on a page. You can adjust the size of the **margins**, which are the spaces between the page content and the edges of the page. You can center the worksheet text between the top and bottom margins (horizontally) or between the right and left margins (vertically). You can change the **page orientation**, which determines if the page is wider than it is tall or taller than it is wide. You can also use the Page Setup dialog box to display text that will appear at the top (a header) or bottom (a footer) of each page of a worksheet. You can open the Page Setup dialog box using the File menu or using the Print Preview toolbar.

By default, Excel places a 1-inch margin above and below the report and a ¼-inch margin to the left and right. Excel also aligns column A in a worksheet at the left margin and row 1 at the top margin. Depending on how many columns and rows there are in the worksheet, you might want to increase or decrease the page margins or center the worksheet between the left and right margins or between the top and bottom margins.

You want to increase the margin size for the Sales worksheet to 1 inch all around. You also want the worksheet to be centered between the right and left margins.

## To change the margins and center the worksheet horizontally on the page:

1. Click the **Setup** button on the Print Preview toolbar.

2. Click the **Margins** tab. See Figure 3-32.

**Figure 3-32**   **MARGINS TAB**

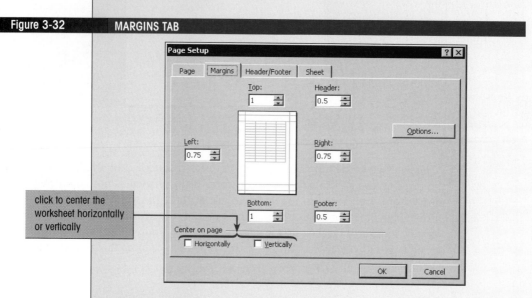

click to center the worksheet horizontally or vertically

The Margins tab provides a diagram showing the placement of the worksheet on the page. In addition to adjusting the sizes of the margins, you can also adjust the space allotted to the header and footer.

3. Click the **Left** up arrow to set the size of the left margin to **1** inch.

4. Click the **Right** up arrow to increase the size of the right margin to **1** inch.

5. Click the **Horizontally** check box, and then click the **OK** button.

The left and right margins change, but there is now less room for the worksheet. As indicated in the status line located in the lower-left corner of the Print Preview window, the worksheet now covers two pages instead of one; the last column in the Sales Analysis table has been moved to the second page. You can restore the margins to their default sizes, and the worksheet will once again fit on a single page. Another option is to change the orientation of the page from portrait to landscape. **Portrait orientation** (which is the default) displays the page taller than it is wide. **Landscape orientation** displays the page wider than it is tall.

You want to change the page orientation to landscape so the last column of the Sales Analysis table will fit on the same page as the rest of the columns in the table.

## To change the page orientation:

1. Click the **Setup** button, and then click the **Page** tab.

2. Click the **Landscape** option button. See Figure 3-33.

**Figure 3-33**    PAGE SETUP DIALOG BOX

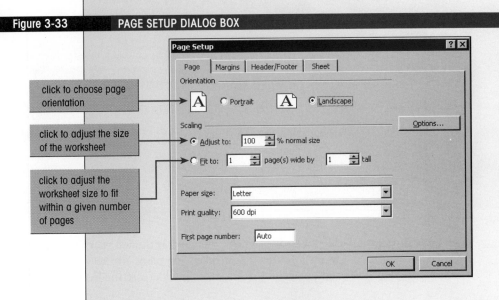

click to choose page orientation

click to adjust the size of the worksheet

click to adjust the worksheet size to fit within a given number of pages

3. Click the **OK** button. Excel changes the orientation to landscape. Note that the entire report now fits on a single page.

The Page tab in the Page Setup dialog box contains other useful formatting features. You can reduce or increase the size of the worksheet on the printed page. The default size is 100%. You can also have Excel automatically reduce the size of the report to fit within a specified number of pages.

## Working with Headers and Footers

Joan wants you to add a header and footer to the report. A **header** is text printed in the top margin of every worksheet page. A **footer** is text printed at the bottom of every page. Headers and footers can add important information to your printouts. For example, you can create a header that displays your name and the date the report was created. If the report covers multiple pages, you can use a footer to display the page number and the total number of pages. You use the Page Setup dialog box to add headers and footers to a worksheet.

Excel tries to anticipate headers and footers that you might want to include in your worksheet. Clicking the Header or Footer list arrow displays a list of possible headers or footers (the list is the same for both). For example, the "Page 1" entry inserts the page number of the worksheet prefaced by the word "Page" in the header; the "Page 1 of ?" displays the page number and the total number of pages. Other entries in the list include the name or the worksheet or workbook.

If you want to use a header or footer not available in the lists, you click the Custom Header or Custom Footer button and create your own header and footer. The Header dialog box and the Footer dialog box are similar. Each dialog box is divided into three sections, left, center, and right. If you want to enter information such as the filename or the day's date into the header or footer, you can either type the text or click one of the format buttons located above the three section boxes. Figure 3-34 describes the format buttons and the corresponding format codes.

**Figure 3-34**   **HEADER/FOOTER FORMATTING BUTTONS**

| BUTTON | NAME | FORMATTING CODE | ACTION |
|---|---|---|---|
| A | Font | None | Sets font, text style, and font size |
| # | Page number | &[Page] | Inserts page number |
|  | Total pages | &[Pages] | Inserts total number of pages |
|  | Date | &[Date] | Inserts current date |
|  | Time | &[Time] | Insert current time |
|  | Path | &[Path]&[File] | Inserts path and filename |
|  | Filename | &[File] | Insert filename |
|  | Sheet name | &[Tab] | Inserts name of active worksheet |
|  | Picture | &[Picture] | Inserts an image file |
|  | Format picture | None | Formats the picture inserted into the header/footer |

Joan wants a header that displays the filename at the left margin and today's date at the right margin. She wants a footer that displays the name of the workbook author, with the text aligned at the right margin of the footer. You'll create the header and footer now.

## To add a custom header to the workbook:

1. Click the **Setup** button on the Print Preview toolbar, and then click the **Header/Footer** tab.

2. Click the **Custom Header** button. The Header dialog box opens. See Figure 3-35.

**Figure 3-35**   **HEADER DIALOG BOX**

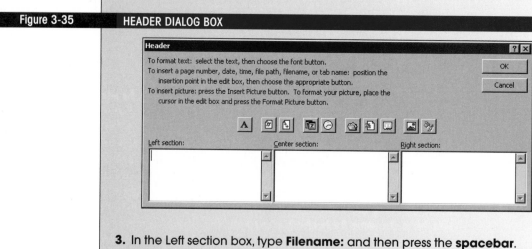

3. In the Left section box, type **Filename:** and then press the **spacebar**.

4. Click the **Filename** button  to insert the format code. The formatting code for the name of the file, &(File), appears after the text string that you entered in the Left section box.

5. Click the **Right section** box, and then click the **Date** button . Excel inserts the &(DATE) format code into the section box.

6. Click the **OK** button to close the Header dialog box.

7. Click the **Custom Footer** button. The Footer dialog box opens.

8. Click the **Right section** box, type **Prepared by:** and then type your name.

9. Click the **OK** button. The Page Setup dialog box displays the custom header and footer that you created.

10. Click the **OK** button. The Print Preview window displays the worksheet with the new header and footer.

11. Click the **Close** button on the Print Preview toolbar.

## Working with the Print Area and Page Breaks

When you displayed the worksheet in the Print Preview window, how did Excel know which parts of the active worksheet you were going to print? The default action is to print all parts of the active worksheet that contain text, formulas, or values, which will not always be what you want. If you want to print only a part of the worksheet , you can define a **print area** that contains the content you want to print. To define a print area, you must first select the cells you want to print, and then select the Print Area option on the File menu.

A print area can include an adjacent range or nonadjacent ranges. You can also hide rows or columns in the worksheet in order to print nonadjacent ranges. For her report, Joan might decide against printing the sales analysis information. To remove those cells from the printout, you need to define a print area that excludes the cells for the second table.

### To define the print area:

1. Select the range **A1:H17**.

2. Click **File** on the menu bar, point to **Print Area**, and then click **Set Print Area**.

3. Click cell **A2**. Excel places a dotted black line around the selected cells of the print area. This is a visual indicator of what parts of the worksheet will be printed.

4. Click the **Print Preview** button [image] on the Standard toolbar. The Print Preview window displays only the first table. The second table has been removed from the printout because it is not in the defined print area.

5. Click the **Close** button on the Print Preview toolbar.

Another approach that Joan might take is to place the two tables on separate pages. You can do this for her by creating a **page break**, which forces Excel to place a portion of a worksheet on a new page.

Before inserting a page break, you must first redefine the print area to include the second table.

### To redefine the print area, and then insert a page break:

1. Select the range **A1:H24**.

2. Click **File** on the menu bar, point to **Print Area**, and then click **Set Print Area**.

Before you insert the page break, you need to indicate where in the worksheet you want the break to occur. Because you want to print the second table on a separate page, you will set the page break at cell A18, which will force rows 18 through 24 to a new page.

3. Click cell **A18**, click **Insert** on the menu bar, and then click **Page Break**. Another blank dotted line appears—this time above cell A18, indicating there is a page break at this point in the print area. See Figure 3-36.

**Figure 3-36** ADDING A PAGE BREAK TO THE PRINT AREA

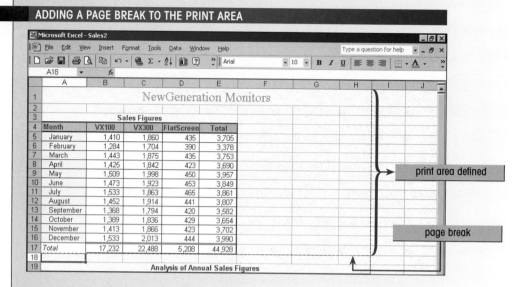

4. Click the **Print Preview** button on the Standard toolbar. Excel displays the first table on page 1 in the Print Preview window.

5. Click the **Next** button to display page 2.

6. Click the **Close** button on the Print Preview toolbar.

You show the print preview to Joan and she notices that the name of the company, "NewGeneration Monitors," appears on the first page, but not on the second. That is not surprising because the range that includes the company name is limited to the first page of the printout. However, Joan would like to have this information repeated on the second page.

You can repeat information, such as the company name, by specifying which cells in the print area should be repeated on each page. This is particularly useful in long tables which extend over many pages. In such cases, you can have the column titles repeated for each page in the printout.

To set rows or columns to repeat on each page, you have to open the Page Setup dialog box from the worksheet window.

## To repeat the first row on each page:

1. Click **File** on the menu bar, and then click **Page Setup**.

2. Click the **Sheet** tab. See Figure 3-37.

**Figure 3-37**     ADDING A PAGE BREAK TO THE PRINT AREA

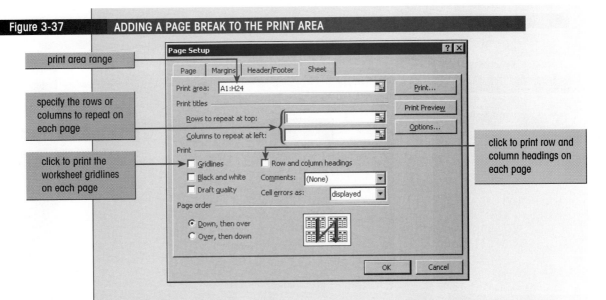

- print area range
- specify the rows or columns to repeat on each page
- click to print the worksheet gridlines on each page
- click to print row and column headings on each page

The Sheet tab displays options you can use to control how the worksheet is printed. As shown in Figure 3-37, the print area you have defined is already entered into the Print area box. Joan wants the company name to appear above the second table, so you need to have Excel repeat the first row on the second page.

3. Click the **Rows to repeat at top** box.

4. Click cell **A1**. A flashing border appears around the first row in the worksheet. This is a visual indicator that the contents of the first row will be repeated on all pages of the printout. In the Rows to repeat at top box, the format code *$1:$1* appears.

5. Click the **OK** button.

The Sheet tab also provides other options, such as the ability to print the worksheet's gridlines or row and column headings. You can also have Excel print the worksheet in black and white or draft quality. If there are multiple pages in the printout, you can indicate whether the pages should be ordered going down the worksheet first and then across, or across first and then down.

Next, you'll preview the worksheet to see how the pages look with the company name above each table, and then you'll print the worksheet.

### To preview and print the worksheet:

1. Click the **Print Preview** button on the Standard toolbar. The first page of the printout appears in the Print Preview window.

2. Click the **Next** button to display the second page of the printout. Note that the title "NewGeneration Monitors" appears on the page. See Figure 3-38.

| Figure 3-38 | SECOND PAGE OF THE SALES PRINTOUT |

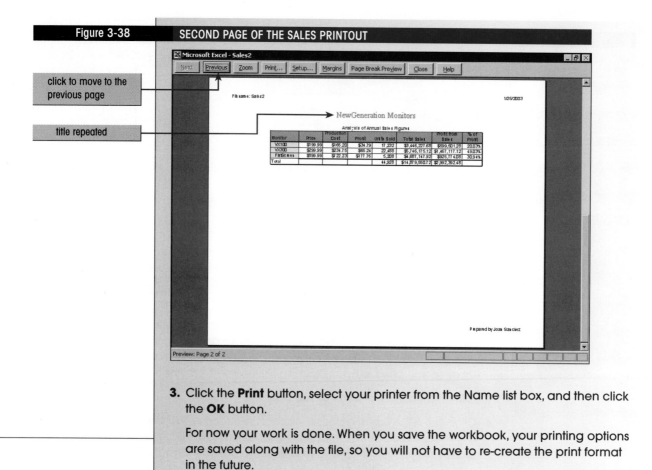

click to move to the previous page

title repeated

**3.** Click the **Print** button, select your printer from the Name list box, and then click the **OK** button.

For now your work is done. When you save the workbook, your printing options are saved along with the file, so you will not have to re-create the print format in the future.

**4.** Save and close the workbook, and then exit Excel.

You show the final version of the workbook and the printout to Joan. She is very happy with the way in which you have formatted her report. She will spend some time going over the printout and will get back to you with any further changes she wants you to make.

# Session 3.2 QUICK CHECK

1. Describe two ways of merging a range of cells into one.

2. How do you clear a format from a cell without affecting the underlying data?

3. How do you add a background image to the active worksheet?

4. To control the amount of space between the content on a page and its edges, you can adjust the page's _____.

5. By default, Excel prints what part of the active worksheet?

6. How do you define a print area? How do you remove a print area?

7. How do you insert a page break into your worksheet?

## REVIEW ASSIGNMENTS

Joan Sanchez has another report that she wants to format. The report displays regional sales for the three monitor brands you worked on earlier. As before, Joan wants to work on the overall appearance of the worksheet so the printout of the report is polished and professional looking.

To format the report:

1. Start Excel and open the **Region1** workbook located in the Tutorial.03/Review folder on your Data Disk.

2. Save the workbook as **Region2** in the same folder.

*Explore* 3. Enter your name and the current date in the Documentation sheet. Format the date to display the day of the week and the name of the month as well as the day and year. Switch to the Regional Sales worksheet.

4. Format the text in cell A1 with a 20-point, boldfaced, italicized, red Times New Roman font. Select the cell range A1:F1, and then center the text in cell A1 across the selection (do not merge the cells).

5. Select the range A3:E14, and then apply the List 2 format from the AutoFormat Gallery.

6. Change the format of all the values in the Sales by Region table to display a comma separator, but no decimal places.

7. Change the format of the units sold values in the second table to display a comma separator, but no decimal places.

8. Indent the region names in the range A5:A13 by one character.

9. Display the text in cell A16 in bold.

10. Change the format of the values in the Total Sales and Profit from Sales columns to display a dollar sign directly to the left of the values and no decimal places.

11. Change the format of the % of Profit column as percentages with two decimal places.

12. Allow the text in the range A17:F17 to wrap to a second line of text. Change the font of the text to bold.

*Explore* 13. Merge the cells in the range A18:A20, and then vertically align the text with the top of the cell. Apply this format to the cells in the following ranges: A21:A23, A24:A26, and A27:A29.

14. Change the background color of the cells in the range A17:F17;A18:A29 to Sea Green (third row, fourth column of the color palette). Change the font color to white.

15. Change the background color of the cells in the range B18:F29 to white. Change the background color of the cells in the range B20:F20;B23:F23;B26:F26;B29:F29 to Light Green (fifth row, fourth column of the color palette).

16. Surround the borders of all cells in the range A17:F29 with a black line.

*Explore* 17. Place a double red line on the bottom border of the cells in the range B20:F20;B23:F23;B26:F26.

18. Set the print area as the range A1:F29. Insert a page break above row 16. Repeat the first row of the worksheet on every page of any printouts you produce from this worksheet.

19. Set up the page to print in portrait orientation with 1-inch margins on all sides. Center the contents of the worksheet horizontally on the page.

20. Add a footer with the following text in the Left section box of the footer (with the date on a separate line): "Filename: *the name of the file*" and "Date: *current date*," and then the following text in the Right section box of the footer: "Prepared by: *your name*."

*Explore*      21. Add a header with the text "Regional Sales Report" displayed in the Center section using a 14-point Times New Roman font with a double underline. (*Hint*: Select the text in the Center section, and then use the Formatting toolbar to change the appearance of the text.)

22. Print the Regional Sales worksheet.

23. Save and close the workbook, and then exit Excel.

## CASE PROBLEMS

*Case 1. Jenson Sports Wear Quarterly Sales*  Carol Roberts is the national sales manager for Jenson Sports Wear, a company that sells sportswear to major department stores. She has been using an Excel worksheet to track the results of her staff's sales incentive program. She has asked you to format the worksheet so that it looks professional. She also wants a printout before she presents the worksheet at the next sales meeting.

Complete these steps to format and print the worksheet:

1. Open the **Running1** workbook located in the Tutorial.03/Cases folder on your Data Disk, and then save the file as **Running2** in the same folder.

2. Enter your name and the current date in the Documentation sheet. Switch to the Sales worksheet.

3. Complete the following calculations:
   a. Calculate the totals for each product.
   b. Calculate the quarterly subtotals for the Shoes and Shirts departments.
   c. Calculate the totals for each quarter and an overall total.

*Explore*      4. Format the data in the range A1:F14 so that it resembles the table shown in Figure 3-39.

**Figure 3-39**

| Jenson Sports Wear Quarterly Sales by Product | | | | | |
|---|---|---|---|---|---|
| **Shoes** | **Qtr1** | **Qtr2** | **Qtr3** | **Qtr4** | **Total** |
| Running | 2,250 | 2,550 | 2,650 | 2,800 | 10,250 |
| Tennis | 2,800 | 1,500 | 2,300 | 2,450 | 9,050 |
| Basketball | 1,250 | 1,400 | 1,550 | 1,550 | 5,750 |
| Subtotal | 6,300 | 5,450 | 6,500 | 6,800 | 25,050 |
| | | | | | |
| **Shirts** | **Qtr1** | **Qtr2** | **Qtr3** | **Qtr4** | **Total** |
| Tee | 1,000 | 1,150 | 1,250 | 1,150 | 4,550 |
| Polo | 2,100 | 2,200 | 2,300 | 2,400 | 9,000 |
| Sweat | 250 | 250 | 275 | 300 | 1,075 |
| Subtotal | 3,350 | 3,600 | 3,825 | 3,850 | 14,625 |
| **Grand Total** | **9,650** | **9,050** | **10,325** | **10,650** | **39,675** |

*Explore*      5. Create a style named "Subtotal" that is based on the font, border, and pattern formats found in the cell ranges A7:F7 and A13:F13.

6. Use the Page Setup dialog box to center the table both horizontally and vertically on the printed page and to change the page orientation to landscape.

7. Add the filename, your name, and the date on separate lines in the Right section box of the footer.

8. Print the sales report.

9. Save and close the workbook, and then exit Excel.

**Case 2. Wisconsin Department of Revenue**  Ted Crawford works for the Wisconsin Department of Revenue. Recently he compiled a list of the top 50 women-owned businesses in the state. He would like your help in formatting the report, in regard to both how it appears in the worksheet window and how it appears on the printed page.

Complete the following:

1. Open the **WBus1** workbook located in the Tutorial.03/Cases folder on your Data Disk, and then save the file as **WBus2** in the same folder.

2. Enter your name and the current date in the Documentation sheet. Switch to the Business Data worksheet.

3. Change the font in cell A1 to a boldface font that is 14 points in size. Merge and center the title across the range A1:F1.

4. Display the text in the range A2:F2 in bold, and then center the text in the range C2:F2. Place a double line on the bottom border of the range A2:F2.

5. Display the sales information in the Accounting format with no decimal places; enlarge the width of the column, if necessary.

6. Display the employees' data using a comma separator with no decimal places.

7. Change the background color of the cells in the range A3:F3 to light green. Change the background color of the cells in A4:F4 to white.

**Explore**  8. Select the range A3:F4 and use the Format Painter to apply the format to the cells in the range A5:F52. How is the format applied to the cells?

9. Change the page orientation of the worksheet to landscape. Set the bottom margin to 1.5 inches. Center the contents of the worksheet horizontally on the page.

10. Set the print area as the cell range A1:F52. Repeat the first two rows of the worksheet in any printouts.

11. Remove any header from the printed page. Display the following text on separate lines in the Right section box of the footer: "Compiled by *your name*," "*the current date*," "Page *the current page* of *total number of pages*."

**Explore**  12. Fit the worksheet on output that is 1 page wide by 2 pages tall.

13. Preview the worksheet, and then print it.

14. Save and close the workbook, and then exit Excel.

**Case 3. Sales Report at Davis Blades**  Andrew Malki is a financial officer at Davis Blades, a leading manufacturer of roller blades. He has recently finished entering data for the yearly sales report. Andrew has asked you to help him with the design of the main table in the report. A preview of the format you will apply is shown in Figure 3-40.

Figure 3-40

**Davis Blades Yearly Sales Report**
Units Sold

| | | Northeast | East | Southeast | Midwest | Southwest | West | All Regions |
|---|---|---|---|---|---|---|---|---|
| Black Hawk | Qtr 1 | 641 | 748 | 733 | 676 | 691 | 783 | 4,272 |
| | Qtr 2 | 708 | 826 | 811 | 748 | 763 | 866 | 4,722 |
| | Qtr 3 | 681 | 795 | 780 | 719 | 734 | 833 | 4,542 |
| | Qtr 4 | 668 | 779 | 764 | 705 | 720 | 816 | 4,452 |
| | Total | 2,698 | 3,148 | 3,088 | 2,848 | 2,908 | 3,298 | 17,988 |
| Blademaster | Qtr 1 | 513 | 598 | 587 | 541 | 552 | 627 | 3,418 |
| | Qtr 2 | 567 | 661 | 648 | 598 | 611 | 693 | 3,778 |
| | Qtr 3 | 545 | 636 | 624 | 575 | 587 | 666 | 3,633 |
| | Qtr 4 | 534 | 623 | 611 | 564 | 576 | 653 | 3,561 |
| | Total | 2,159 | 2,518 | 2,470 | 2,278 | 2,326 | 2,639 | 14,390 |
| The Professional | Qtr 1 | 342 | 399 | 391 | 361 | 368 | 418 | 2,279 |
| | Qtr 2 | 378 | 441 | 432 | 399 | 407 | 462 | 2,519 |
| | Qtr 3 | 363 | 424 | 416 | 383 | 391 | 444 | 2,421 |
| | Qtr 4 | 356 | 415 | 407 | 376 | 384 | 435 | 2,373 |
| | Total | 1,439 | 1,679 | 1,646 | 1,519 | 1,550 | 1,759 | 9,592 |
| All Models | Qtr 1 | 1,496 | 1,745 | 1,711 | 1,578 | 1,611 | 1,828 | 9,969 |
| | Qtr 2 | 1,653 | 1,928 | 1,891 | 1,745 | 1,781 | 2,021 | 11,019 |
| | Qtr 3 | 1,589 | 1,855 | 1,820 | 1,677 | 1,712 | 1,943 | 10,596 |
| | Qtr 4 | 1,558 | 1,817 | 1,782 | 1,645 | 1,680 | 1,904 | 10,386 |
| | Total | 6,296 | 7,345 | 7,204 | 6,645 | 6,784 | 7,696 | 41,970 |

Complete the following:

1. Open the **Blades1** workbook located in the Tutorial.03/Cases folder on your Data Disk, and then save the file as **Blades2** in the same folder.

2. Enter your name and the current date in the Documentation sheet. Switch to the Sales worksheet.

3. Change the font of the title in cell A1 to a 14–point, dark blue, boldface Arial font. Change the subtitle in cell A2 to a 12-point, dark blue, boldface Arial font.

*Explore* 4. Merge the cells in the range A4:A8, and align the contents of the cell with the upper-left corner of the cell. Repeat this for the following ranges: A9:A13, A14:A18, and A19:A23.

5. Change the background color of the cell range A4:I8 to light yellow. Change the background color of the range A9:I13 to light green. Change the background color of the range A14:I18 to light turquoise. Change the background color of the range A19:I23 to pale blue.

6. Reverse the color scheme for the subtotal values in the range B8:I8, so that instead of black on light yellow, the font color is light yellow on a black background. Reverse the subtotal values for the other products in the table.

7. Apply the gridlines as displayed in Figure 3-40 to the cells in the range A4:I23.

*Explore* 8. Rotate the column titles in the range C3:I3 by 45 degrees. Align the contents of each cell with the cell's bottom right border. Change the background color of these cells to white and add a border to each cell.

9. Set the print area as the range A1:K23.

10. Leave the page orientation as portrait, but center the worksheet horizontally on the page.

11. Remove any headers from the page. Create a custom footer with the the text "Filename: *name of the file*" left-aligned, and "Prepared by: *your name*" and "*the current date*" right-aligned, with your name and date on separate lines.

12. Print the worksheet.

13. Save and close the workbook, and then exit Excel.

*Case 4. Oritz Marine Services*  Vince DiOrio is an information systems major at a local college. He works three days a week at a nearby marina, Oritz Marine Services, to help pay for his tuition. Vince works in the business office, and his responsibilities range from making coffee to keeping the company's books.

Recently, Jim Oritz, the owner of the marina, asked Vince if he could help computerize the payroll for the employees. He explained that the employees work a different number of hours each week at different rates of pay. Jim does the payroll manually now and finds it time-consuming. Moreover, whenever he makes an error, he is annoyed at having to take the additional time to correct it. Jim is hoping that Vince can help him.

Vince immediately agrees to help. He tells Jim that he knows how to use Excel and that he can build a worksheet that will save him time and reduce errors. Jim and Vince meet to review the present payroll process and discuss the desired outcome of the payroll spreadsheet. Figure 3-41 displays the type of information that Jim records in the spreadsheet.

**Figure 3-41**

Oritz Marine Service Payroll
Week Ending

| Employee | Hours | Pay Rate | Gross Pay | Federal Withholding | State Withholding | Total Deductions | Net Pay |
|---|---|---|---|---|---|---|---|
| Bramble | 16 | 9.50 | | | | | |
| Juarez | 25 | 12.00 | | | | | |
| Smith | 30 | 13.50 | | | | | |
| DiOrio | 25 | 12.50 | | | | | |
| Smiken | 10 | 9.00 | | | | | |
| Cortez | 30 | 10.50 | | | | | |
| Fulton | 20 | 9.50 | | | | | |
| Total | | | | | | | |

Complete the following:

1. Create a new workbook named **Payroll** and save it in the Tutorial.03/Cases folder on your Data Disk.

2. Name two worksheets Documentation and Payroll.

3. On the Documentation sheet, include the name of the company, your name, the date, and a brief description of the purpose of the workbook.

4. On the Payroll worksheet, enter the payroll table shown in Figure 3-41.

5. Use the following formulas in the table to calculate total hours, gross pay, federal withholding, state withholding, total deductions, and net pay:
   a. Gross pay is hours times pay rate
   b. Federal withholding is 15% of gross pay
   c. State withholding is 4% of gross pay
   d. Total deductions are the sum of federal and state withholdings
   e. Net pay is the difference between gross pay and total deductions

*Explore*  6. Format the appearance of the payroll table using the techniques you learned in this tutorial. The appearance of the payroll table is up to you; however, do not use an AutoFormat to format the table.

*Explore*  7. Format the printed page, setting the print area and inserting an appropriate header and footer. Only a few employees are entered into the table at present. However, after Jim Oritz approves your layout, many additional employees will be added, which will cause the report to cover multiple pages. Format your printout so that the page title and column titles will appear on every page.

8. Remove the hours for the seven employees, and enter the following new values: 18 for Bramble, 25 for Juarez, 35 for Smith, 20 for DiOrio, 15 for Smiken, 35 for Cortez, and 22 for Fulton.

9. Print the worksheet.

10. Save and close the workbook, and then exit Excel.

## INTERNET ASSIGNMENTS

**Student Union**

The purpose of the Internet Assignments is to challenge you to find information on the Internet that you can use to create effective spreadsheets. The actual assignments are updated and maintained on the Course Technology Web site. Log on to the Internet and use your Web browser to go to the Student Union on the New Perspectives Series site at **www.course.com/NewPerspectives/studentunion**. Click the Online Companions link, and then click the link for this text.

## QUICK CHECK ANSWERS

*Session 3.1*

1. Click the Currency Style button on the Formatting toolbar; or click Cells on the Format menu, click the Number tab, and then select Currency from the Category list box.

2. Excel will display the following:
   a. 5.8%
   b. $0.06

3. the Format Painter button and the Copy button

4. Increase the width of the column; decrease the font size of the text; or select the Shrink to fit check box or the Wrap text check box on the Alignment tab in the Format cells dialog box.

5. Select the range, click Cells on the Format menu, click the Alignment tab, and then choose Center Across Selection from the Horizontal list box.

6. Use the Borders button on the Formatting toolbar; use the Draw Borders tool in the Border gallery; or click Cells on the Format menu, click the Border tab, and then choose the border options in the dialog box.

7. Click Cells on the Format menu, click the Patterns tab, and then click the Pattern list arrow to choose the pattern type and color.

*Session 3.2*

1. Select the cells and either click the Merge and Center button on the Formatting toolbar; or click Cells on the Format menu, click the Alignment tab, and then click the Merge cells check box.

2. Select the cell, point to Clear on the Edit menu, and then click Formats.

3. Point to Sheet on the Format menu, and then click Background. Locate and select an image file to use for the background.

4. margins

5. Excel prints all parts of the active worksheet that contain text, formulas, or values.

6. To define a print area, select a range in the worksheet, point to Print Area on the File menu, and then click Set Print Area. To remove a print area, point to Print Area on the File menu, and then click Clear Print Area.

7. Select the first cell below the intended place for the page break, and then click Page Break on the Insert menu.

*New Perspectives on*

# MICROSOFT®
# ACCESS 2002

# Read This Before You Begin

## To the Student

### Data Disks

To complete these tutorials, Review Assignments, and Case Problems, you need six Data Disks. Your instructor will either provide you with these Data Disks or ask you to make your own.

If you are making your own Data Disks, you will need **six** blank, formatted high-density disks. You will need to copy a set of files and/or folders from a file server, standalone computer, or the Web onto your disks. Your instructor will tell you which computer, drive letter, and folders contain the files you need. You could also download the files by going to www.course.com and following the instructions on the screen.

The information below shows you which folders go on each of your disks, so that you will have enough disk space to complete all the tutorials, Review Assignments, and Case Problems:

### Data Disk 1

Write this on the disk label:
Data Disk 1: Access 2002 Tutorial Files

Put these folders on the disk:
Tutorial

### Data Disk 2

Write this on the disk label:
Data Disk 2: Access 2002 Review Assignments

Put this folder on the disk:
Review

### Data Disk 3

Write this on the disk label:
Data Disk 3: Access 2002 Case Problem 1

Put this folder on the disk:
Cases

### Data Disk 4

Write this on the disk label:
Data Disk 4: Access 2002 Case Problem 2

Put this folder on the disk:
Cases

### Data Disk 5

Write this on the disk label:
Data Disk 5: Access 2002 Case Problem 3

Put this folder on the disk:
Cases

### Data Disk 6

Write this on the disk label:
Data Disk 6: Access 2002 Case Problem 4

Put this folder on the disk:
Cases

When you begin each tutorial, be sure you are using the correct Data Disk. Refer to the "File Finder" chart at the back of this text for more detailed information on which files are used in which tutorials, and make sure you carefully read the note above the chart. See the inside front or inside back cover of this book for more information on Data Disk files, or ask your instructor or technical support person for assistance.

### Course Labs

The Access tutorials feature an interactive Course Lab to help you understand database concepts. There are Lab Assignments at the end of Tutorial 1 that relate to this Lab.

To start a Lab, click the **Start** button on the Windows taskbar, point to **Programs**, point to **Course Labs**, point to **New Perspectives Course Labs**, and then click the name of the Lab you want to use.

### Using Your Own Computer

If you are going to work through this book using your own computer, you need:

- **Computer System** Microsoft Windows 98, NT, 2000 Professional, or higher must be installed on your computer. This book assumes a typical installation of Microsoft Access.

- **Data Disks** You will not be able to complete the tutorials or exercises in this book using your own computer until you have your Data Disks.

- **Course Labs** See your instructor or technical support person to obtain the Course Lab software for use on your own computer.

### Visit Our World Wide Web Site

Additional materials designed especially for you are available on the World Wide Web.

Go to www.course.com/NewPerspectives.

## To the Instructor

The Data Disk Files and Course Labs are available on the Instructor's Resource Kit for this title. Follow the instructions in the Help file on the CD-ROM to install the programs to your network or standalone computer. For information on creating Data Disks or the Course Labs, see the "To the Student" section above.

You are granted a license to copy the Data Files and Course Labs to any computer or computer network used by students who have purchased this book.

AC 1.03

## OBJECTIVES

In this tutorial you will:

- Define the terms field, record, table, relational database, primary key, and foreign key

- Open an existing database

- Identify the components of the Access and Database windows

- Open and navigate a table

- Learn how Access saves a database

- Open an existing query, and create, sort, and navigate a new query

- Create and navigate a form

- Create, preview, and navigate a report

- Learn how to manage a database by backing up, restoring, compacting, and converting a database

## LAB

databases

# INTRODUCTION
## TO MICROSOFT
## ACCESS 2002

*Viewing and Working with a Table Containing Employer Data*

CASE

## Northeast Seasonal Jobs International (NSJI)

During her high school and college years, Elsa Jensen spent her summers working as a lifeguard for some of the most popular beaches on Cape Cod, Massachusetts. Throughout those years, Elsa met many foreign students who had come to the United States to work for the summer, both at the beaches and at other seasonal businesses, such as restaurants and hotels. Elsa formed friendships with several students and kept in contact with them beyond college. Through discussions with her friends, Elsa realized that foreign students often have a difficult time finding appropriate seasonal work, relying mainly on "word-of-mouth" references to locate jobs. Elsa became convinced that there must be an easier way.

Several years ago, Elsa founded Northeast Seasonal Jobs, a small firm located in Boston that served as a job broker between foreign students seeking part-time, seasonal work and resort businesses located in New England. Recently Elsa expanded her business to include resorts in the eastern provinces of Canada, and consequently she changed her company's name to Northeast Seasonal Jobs International (NSJI). At first the company focused mainly on summer employment, but as the business continued to grow, Elsa increased the scope of operations to include all types of seasonal opportunities, including foliage tour companies in the fall and ski resorts in the winter.

Elsa depends on computers to help her manage all areas of NSJI's operations, including financial management, sales, and information management. Several months ago the company upgraded to Microsoft Windows and **Microsoft Access 2002** (or simply **Access**), a computer program used to enter, maintain, and retrieve related data in a format known as a database. Elsa and her staff use Access to maintain data such as information about employers, positions they have available for seasonal work, and foreign students seeking employment. Elsa recently created a database named Seasonal to track the company's employer customers and data about their available positions. She asks for your help in completing and maintaining this database.

**SESSION 1.1**

In this session, you will learn key database terms and concepts, open an existing database, identify components of the Access and Database windows, open and navigate a table, and learn how Access saves a database.

# Introduction to Database Concepts

databases

Before you begin working on Elsa's database and using Access, you need to understand a few key terms and concepts associated with databases.

## Organizing Data

Data is a valuable resource to any business. At NSJI, for example, important data includes employers' names and addresses, and available positions and wages. Organizing, storing, maintaining, retrieving, and sorting this type of data are critical activities that enable a business to find and use information effectively. Before storing data on a computer, however, you first must organize the data.

Your first step in organizing data is to identify the individual fields. A **field** is a single characteristic or attribute of a person, place, object, event, or idea. For example, some of the many fields that NSJI tracks are employer ID, employer name, employer address, employer phone number, position, wage, and start date.

Next, you group related fields together into tables. A **table** is a collection of fields that describe a person, place, object, event, or idea. Figure 1-1 shows an example of an Employer table consisting of four fields: EmployerID, EmployerName, EmployerAddress, and PhoneNumber.

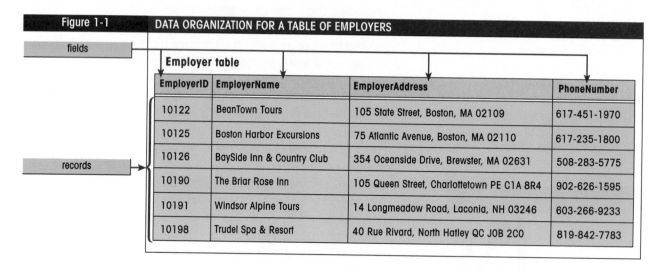

| Figure 1-1 | DATA ORGANIZATION FOR A TABLE OF EMPLOYERS |

**Employer table**

| EmployerID | EmployerName | EmployerAddress | PhoneNumber |
|---|---|---|---|
| 10122 | BeanTown Tours | 105 State Street, Boston, MA 02109 | 617-451-1970 |
| 10125 | Boston Harbor Excursions | 75 Atlantic Avenue, Boston, MA 02110 | 617-235-1800 |
| 10126 | BaySide Inn & Country Club | 354 Oceanside Drive, Brewster, MA 02631 | 508-283-5775 |
| 10190 | The Briar Rose Inn | 105 Queen Street, Charlottetown PE C1A 8R4 | 902-626-1595 |
| 10191 | Windsor Alpine Tours | 14 Longmeadow Road, Laconia, NH 03246 | 603-266-9233 |
| 10198 | Trudel Spa & Resort | 40 Rue Rivard, North Hatley QC J0B 2C0 | 819-842-7783 |

The specific value, or content, of a field is called the **field value**. In Figure 1-1, the first set of field values for EmployerID, EmployerName, EmployerAddress, and PhoneNumber are, respectively: 10122; BeanTown Tours; 105 State Street, Boston, MA 02109; and 617-451-1970. This set of field values is called a **record**. In the Employer table, the data for each employer is stored as a separate record. Figure 1-1 shows six records; each row of field values is a record.

## Databases and Relationships

A collection of related tables is called a **database**, or a **relational database**. NSJI's Seasonal database contains two related tables: the Employer and NAICS tables, which Elsa created. (The NAICS table contains North American Industry Classification System codes, which are used to classify businesses by the type of activity in which they are engaged.) In Tutorial 2, you will create a Position table to store information about the available positions at NSJI's employer clients.

Sometimes you might want information about employers and their available positions. To obtain this information, you must have a way to connect records in the Employer table to records in the Position table. You connect the records in the separate tables through a **common field** that appears in both tables.

In the sample database shown in Figure 1-2, each record in the Employer table has a field named EmployerID, which is also a field in the Position table. For example, BaySide Inn & Country Club is the third employer in the Employer table and has an EmployerID of 10126. This same EmployerID field value, 10126, appears in three records in the Position table. Therefore, BaySide Inn & Country Club is the employer with these three positions available.

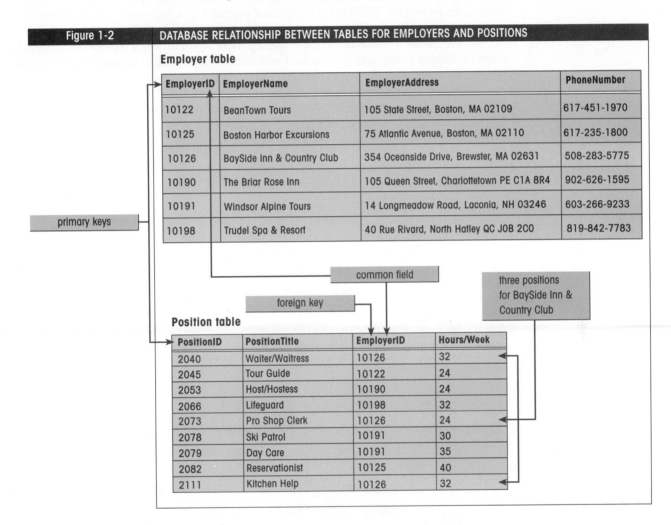

| Figure 1-2 | DATABASE RELATIONSHIP BETWEEN TABLES FOR EMPLOYERS AND POSITIONS |
|---|---|

**Employer table**

| EmployerID | EmployerName | EmployerAddress | PhoneNumber |
|---|---|---|---|
| 10122 | BeanTown Tours | 105 State Street, Boston, MA 02109 | 617-451-1970 |
| 10125 | Boston Harbor Excursions | 75 Atlantic Avenue, Boston, MA 02110 | 617-235-1800 |
| 10126 | BaySide Inn & Country Club | 354 Oceanside Drive, Brewster, MA 02631 | 508-283-5775 |
| 10190 | The Briar Rose Inn | 105 Queen Street, Charlottetown PE C1A 8R4 | 902-626-1595 |
| 10191 | Windsor Alpine Tours | 14 Longmeadow Road, Laconia, NH 03246 | 603-266-9233 |
| 10198 | Trudel Spa & Resort | 40 Rue Rivard, North Hatley QC J0B 2C0 | 819-842-7783 |

primary keys

common field

foreign key

three positions for BaySide Inn & Country Club

**Position table**

| PositionID | PositionTitle | EmployerID | Hours/Week |
|---|---|---|---|
| 2040 | Waiter/Waitress | 10126 | 32 |
| 2045 | Tour Guide | 10122 | 24 |
| 2053 | Host/Hostess | 10190 | 24 |
| 2066 | Lifeguard | 10198 | 32 |
| 2073 | Pro Shop Clerk | 10126 | 24 |
| 2078 | Ski Patrol | 10191 | 30 |
| 2079 | Day Care | 10191 | 35 |
| 2082 | Reservationist | 10125 | 40 |
| 2111 | Kitchen Help | 10126 | 32 |

Each EmployerID in the Employer table must be unique, so that you can distinguish one employer from another and identify the employer's specific positions available in the Position table. The EmployerID field is referred to as the primary key of the Employer table. A **primary key** is a field, or a collection of fields, whose values uniquely identify each record in a table. In the Position table, PositionID is the primary key.

When you include the primary key from one table as a field in a second table to form a relationship between the two tables, it is called a **foreign key** in the second table, as shown in Figure 1-2. For example, EmployerID is the primary key in the Employer table and a foreign key in the Position table. Although the primary key EmployerID has unique values in the Employer table, the same field as a foreign key in the Position table does not have unique values. The EmployerID value 10126, for example, appears three times in the Position table because the BaySide Inn & Country Club has three available positions. Each foreign key value, however, must match one of the field values for the primary key in the other table. In the example shown in Figure 1-2, each EmployerID value in the Position table must match an EmployerID value in the Employer table. The two tables are related, enabling users to connect the facts about employers with the facts about their employment positions.

## Relational Database Management Systems

To manage its databases, a company purchases a database management system. A **database management system (DBMS)** is a software program that lets you create databases and then manipulate data in them. Most of today's database management systems, including Access, are called relational database management systems. In a **relational database management system**, data is organized as a collection of tables. As stated earlier, a relationship between two tables in a relational DBMS is formed through a common field.

A relational DBMS controls the storage of databases on disk by carrying out data creation and manipulation requests. Specifically, a relational DBMS provides the following functions, which are illustrated in Figure 1-3:

- It allows you to create database structures containing fields, tables, and table relationships.

- It lets you easily add new records, change field values in existing records, and delete records.

- It contains a built-in query language, which lets you obtain immediate answers to the questions you ask about your data.

- It contains a built-in report generator, which lets you produce professional-looking, formatted reports from your data.

- It provides protection of databases through security, control, and recovery facilities.

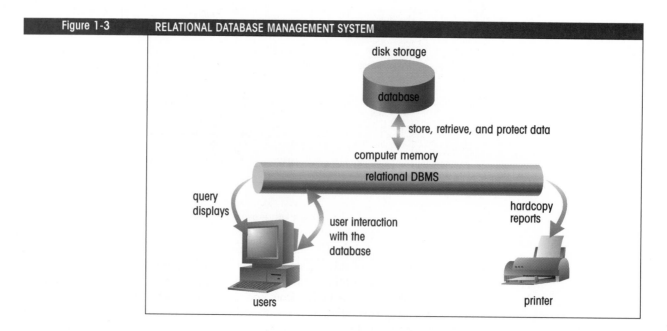

Figure 1-3    RELATIONAL DATABASE MANAGEMENT SYSTEM

A company such as NSJI benefits from a relational DBMS because it allows users working in different departments to share the same data. More than one user can enter data into a database, and more than one user can retrieve and analyze data that was entered by others. For example, NSJI will store only one copy of the Employer table, and all employees will be able to use it to meet their specific requests for employer information.

Finally, unlike other software programs, such as spreadsheets, a DBMS can handle massive amounts of data and can easily form relationships among multiple tables. Each Access database, for example, can be up to two gigabytes in size and can contain up to 32,768 objects (tables, queries, and so on).

# Opening **an Existing Database**

Now that you've learned some database terms and concepts, you're ready to start Access and open the Seasonal database.

## To start Access and open the Seasonal database:

1. Click the **Start** button on the taskbar, point to **Programs**, and then point to **Microsoft Access**. See Figure 1-4.

| Figure 1-4 | STARTING MICROSOFT ACCESS |
| --- | --- |

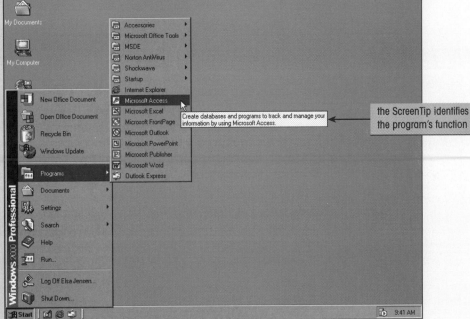

the ScreenTip identifies the program's function

**TROUBLE?** If your screen differs slightly from the figure, don't worry. Although the figures in this tutorial were created on a computer running Windows 2000 in its default settings, the different Windows operating systems share the same basic user interface, and Microsoft Access runs equally well using Windows 98, Windows NT, or Windows 2000.

**TROUBLE?** If you don't see the Microsoft Access option on the Programs menu, you might need to click the double arrow on the Programs menu to display more options. If you still cannot find the Microsoft Access option, ask your instructor or technical support person for help.

**2.** Click **Microsoft Access** to start Access. After a short pause, the Access copyright information appears in a message box and remains on the screen until the Access window opens. See Figure 1-5.

**Figure 1-5**    MICROSOFT ACCESS WINDOW

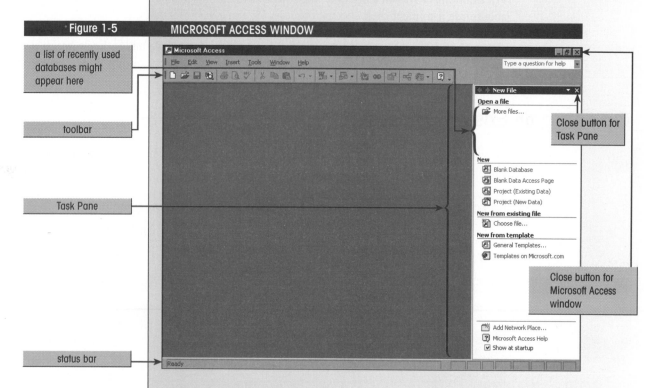

When you start Access, the Access window contains a Task Pane that allows you to create a new database or to open an existing database. You can click the "Blank Database" option in the "New" section of the Task Pane to create a new database on your own, or you can click the "General Templates" option in the "New from template" section of the Task Pane to let Access guide you through the steps for creating one of the standard databases provided by Microsoft. In this case, you need to open an existing database.

To open an existing database, you can select the name of a database in the list of recently opened databases (if the list appears), or you can click the "More files" option to open a database not listed. You need to open an existing database—the Seasonal database on your Data Disk.

**3.** Make sure you have created your copy of the Access Data Disk, and then place your Data Disk in the appropriate disk drive.

**TROUBLE?** If you don't have a Data Disk, you need to get one before you can proceed. Your instructor will either give you one or ask you to make your own. (See your instructor for more information.) In either case, be sure that you have made a backup copy of your Data Disk before you begin working, so that the original Data Files will be available on the copied disk in case you need to start over because of an error or problem.

**4.** In the "Open a file" section of the Task Pane, click the **More files** option. The Open dialog box is displayed. See Figure 1-6.

| Figure 1-6 | OPEN DIALOG BOX |

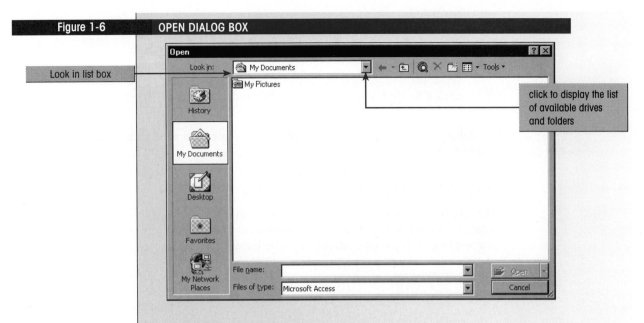

Look in list box

click to display the list of available drives and folders

**TROUBLE?** The list of folders and files on your screen might be different from the list in Figure 1-6.

5. Click the **Look in** list arrow, and then click the drive that contains your Data Disk.

6. Click **Tutorial** in the list box (if necessary), and then click the **Open** button to display a list of the files in the Tutorial folder.

7. Click **Seasonal** in the list box, and then click the **Open** button. The Seasonal database opens in the Access window. See Figure 1-7.

| Figure 1-7 | ACCESS AND DATABASE WINDOWS |

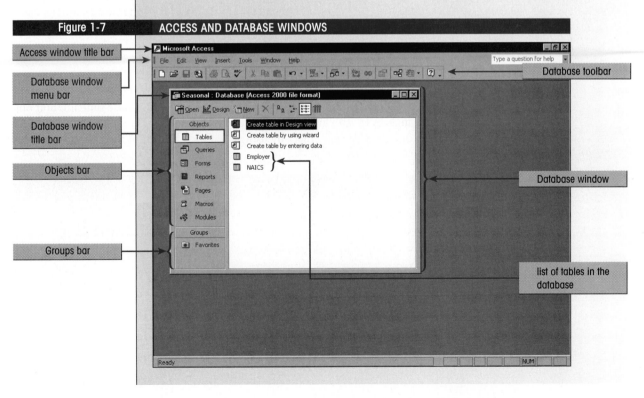

Access window title bar

Database window menu bar

Database window title bar

Objects bar

Groups bar

Database toolbar

Database window

list of tables in the database

> **TROUBLE?** The filename on your screen might be Seasonal.mdb instead of Seasonal, depending on your computer's default settings. The extension ".mdb" identifies the file as a Microsoft Access database.
>
> **TROUBLE?** If Tables is not selected in the Objects bar of the Database window, click it to display the list of tables in the database.

Before you can begin working with the database, you need to become familiar with the components of the Access and Database windows.

## The Access and Database Windows

The **Access window** is the program window that appears when you start the program. The **Database window** appears when you open a database; this window is the main control center for working with an open Access database. Except for the Access window title bar, all screen components now on your screen are associated with the Database window (see Figure 1-7). Most of these screen components—including the title bars, window sizing buttons, menu bar, toolbar, and status bar—are the same as the components in other Windows programs.

Notice that the Database window title bar includes the notation "(Access 2000 file format)." By default, databases that you create in Access 2002 use the Access 2000 database file format. This feature ensures that you can use and share databases originally created in Access 2002 without converting them to Access 2000, and vice versa. (You'll learn more about database file formats and converting databases later in this tutorial.)

The Database window provides a variety of options for viewing and manipulating database objects. Each item in the **Objects bar** controls one of the major object groups—such as tables, queries, forms, and reports—in an Access database. The **Groups bar** allows you to organize different types of database objects into groups, with shortcuts to those objects, so that you can work with them more easily. The Database window also provides buttons for quickly creating, opening, and managing objects, as well as shortcut options for some of these tasks.

Elsa has already created the Employer and NAICS tables in the Seasonal database. She asks you to open the Employer table and view its contents.

## Opening an Access Table

As noted earlier, tables contain all the data in a database. Tables are the fundamental objects for your work in Access. To view, add, change, or delete data in a table, you first open the table. You can open any Access object by using the Open button in the Database window.

---

**REFERENCE WINDOW**                                                        **RW**

<u>Opening an Access Object</u>
- In the Objects bar of the Database window, click the type of object you want to open.
- If necessary, scroll the object list box until the object name appears, and then click the object name.
- Click the Open button in the Database window.

You need to open the Employer table, which is one of two tables in the Seasonal database.

### To open the Employer table:

1. In the Database window, click **Employer** to select it.

2. Click the **Open** button in the Database window. The Employer table opens in Datasheet view on top of the Database and Access windows. See Figure 1-8.

| Figure 1-8 | EMPLOYER TABLE DISPLAYED IN DATASHEET VIEW |
|---|---|

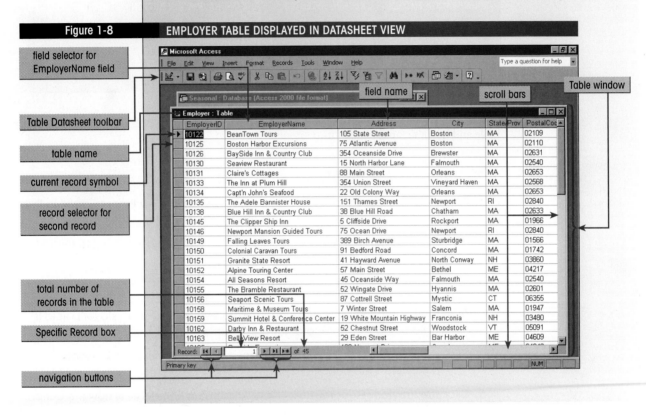

**Datasheet view** shows a table's contents as a **datasheet** in rows and columns, similar to a table or spreadsheet. Each row is a separate record in the table, and each column contains the field values for one field in the table. Each column is headed by a field name inside a field selector, and each row has a record selector to its left. Clicking a **field selector** or a **record selector** selects that entire column or row (respectively), which you then can manipulate. A field selector is also called a **column selector**, and a record selector is also called a **row selector**.

## Navigating an Access Datasheet

When you first open a datasheet, Access selects the first field value in the first record. Notice that this field value is highlighted and that a darkened triangle symbol, called the current record symbol, appears in the record selector to the left of the first record. The **current record symbol** identifies the currently selected record. Clicking a record selector or field value in another row moves the current record symbol to that row. You can also move the pointer over the data on the screen and click one of the field values to position the insertion point.

The Employer table currently has 13 fields and 45 records. To view fields or records not currently visible in the datasheet, you can use the horizontal and vertical scroll bars shown in Figure 1-8 to navigate through the data. The **navigation buttons**, also shown in Figure 1-8, provide another way to move vertically through the records. Figure 1-9 shows which record becomes the current record when you click each navigation button. The **Specific Record box**, which appears between the two sets of navigation buttons, displays the current record number. The total number of records in the table appears to the right of the navigation buttons.

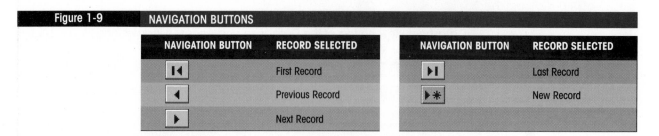

| Figure 1-9 | NAVIGATION BUTTONS | | | |

| NAVIGATION BUTTON | RECORD SELECTED | NAVIGATION BUTTON | RECORD SELECTED |
| --- | --- | --- | --- |
| ⏮ | First Record | ⏭ | Last Record |
| ◀ | Previous Record | ▶※ | New Record |
| ▶ | Next Record | | |

Elsa suggests that you use the various navigation techniques to move through the Employer table and become familiar with its contents.

### To navigate the Employer datasheet:

1. Click the right scroll arrow in the horizontal scroll bar a few times to scroll to the right and view the remaining fields in the Employer table.

2. Drag the scroll box in the horizontal scroll bar all the way to the left to return to the previous display of the datasheet.

3. Click the **Next Record** navigation button ▶ . The second record is now the current record, as indicated by the current record symbol in the second record selector. Also, notice that the second record's value for the EmployerID field is highlighted, and "2" (for record number 2) appears in the Specific Record box.

4. Click the **Last Record** navigation button ⏭ . The last record in the table, record 45, is now the current record.

5. Click the **Previous Record** navigation button ◀ . Record 44 is now the current record.

6. Click the **First Record** navigation button ⏮ . The first record is now the current record.

## Saving a Database

Notice the Save button 🖫 on the Table Datasheet toolbar. Unlike the Save buttons in other Windows programs, this Save button does not save the active document (database) to your disk. Instead, you use the Save button to save the design of an Access object, such as a table, or to save datasheet format changes. Access does not have a button or option you can use to save the active database.

Access saves changes to the active database to your disk automatically, when a record is changed or added and when you close the database. If your database is stored on a disk in drive A, you should never remove the disk while the database file is open. If you remove the disk, Access will encounter problems when it tries to save the database, which might damage the database.

Now that you've viewed the Employer table, you can exit Access.

### To exit Access:

1. Click the **Close** button ☒ on the Access window title bar. The Employer table and the Seasonal database close, Access closes, and you return to the Windows desktop.

Now that you've become familiar with Access and the Seasonal database, in the next session, you'll be ready to work with the data stored in the database.

## Session 1.1 QUICK CHECK

1. A(n) _____ is a single characteristic of a person, place, object, event, or idea.

2. You connect the records in two separate tables through a(n) _____ that appears in both tables.

3. The _____, whose values uniquely identify each record in a table, is called a(n) _____ when it is placed in a second table to form a relationship between the two tables.

4. In a table, the rows are also called _____, and the columns are also called _____.

5. The _____ identifies the selected record in an Access table.

6. Describe two methods for navigating through a table.

---

## SESSION 1.2

In this session, you will open an existing query and create and navigate a new query; create and navigate a form; and create, preview, and navigate a report. You will also learn how to manage databases by backing up and restoring, compacting and repairing, and converting databases.

---

## Working with Queries

A **query** is a question you ask about the data stored in a database. In response to a query, Access displays the specific records and fields that answer your question. When you create a query, you tell Access which fields you need and what criteria Access should use to select the records. Then Access displays only the information you want, so you don't have to navigate through the entire database for the information.

Before creating a new query, you will open a query that Elsa created recently so that she could view information in the Employer table in a different way.

### Opening an Existing Query

Queries that you create and save appear in the Queries list of the Database window. To see the results of a query, you simply open, or run, the query. Elsa created and saved a query named "Contacts" in the Seasonal database. This query shows all the fields from the Employer table, but in a different order. Elsa suggests that you open this query to see its results.

## *To open the Contacts query:*

1. Insert your Data Disk into the appropriate disk drive.

2. Start Access, and then click the **More files** option in the Task Pane to display the Open dialog box.

3. Click the **Look in** list arrow, click the drive that contains your Data Disk, click **Tutorial** in the list box, and then click the **Open** button to display the list of files in the Tutorial folder.

4. Click **Seasonal** in the list box, and then click the **Open** button.

5. Click **Queries** in the Objects bar of the Database window to display the Queries list. The Queries list box contains one object—the Contacts query. See Figure 1-10.

| Figure 1-10 | LIST OF QUERIES IN THE SEASONAL DATABASE |
|---|---|

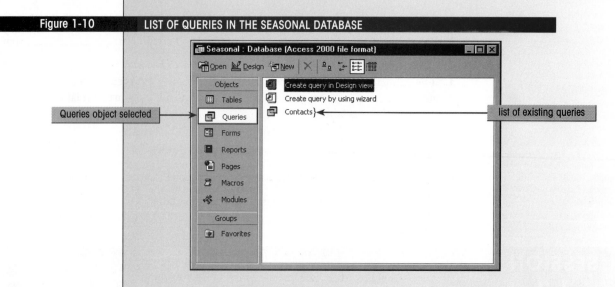

Queries object selected

list of existing queries

Now you will run the Contacts query by opening it.

6. Click **Contacts** to select it, and then click the **Open** button in the Database window. Access displays the results of the query in Datasheet view. See Figure 1-11.

| Figure 1-11 | RESULT OF RUNNING THE CONTACTS QUERY |
|---|---|

fields appear in a different order

Notice that the query displays the fields from the Employer table, but in a different order. For example, the first and last names of each contact, as well as the contact's phone number, appear next to the employer name. This arrangement lets Elsa view pertinent contact information without having to scroll through the table. Rearranging the display of table data is one task you can perform with queries, so that table information appears in a different order to suit how you want to work with the information.

**7.** Click the **Close** button ☒ on the Query window title bar to close the Contacts query.

Even though a query can display table information in a different way, the information still exists in the table as it was originally entered. If you opened the Employer table, it would still show the fields in their original order.

Zack Ward, the director of marketing at NSJI, wants a list of all employers so that his staff can call them to check on their satisfaction with NSJI's services and recruits. He doesn't want the list to include all the fields in the Employer table (such as PostalCode and NAICSCode). To produce this list for Zack, you need to create a query using the Employer table.

## Creating, Sorting, and Navigating a Query

You can design your own queries or use an Access **Query Wizard**, which guides you through the steps to create a query. The Simple Query Wizard allows you to select records and fields quickly, and it is an appropriate choice for producing the employer list Zack wants. You can choose this Wizard either by clicking the New button, which opens a dialog box from which you can choose among several different Wizards to create your query, or by double-clicking the "Create query by using wizard" option, which automatically starts the Simple Query Wizard.

### *To start the Simple Query Wizard:*

**1.** Double-click **Create query by using wizard**. The first Simple Query Wizard dialog box opens. See Figure 1-12.

| Figure 1-12 | FIRST SIMPLE QUERY WIZARD DIALOG BOX |

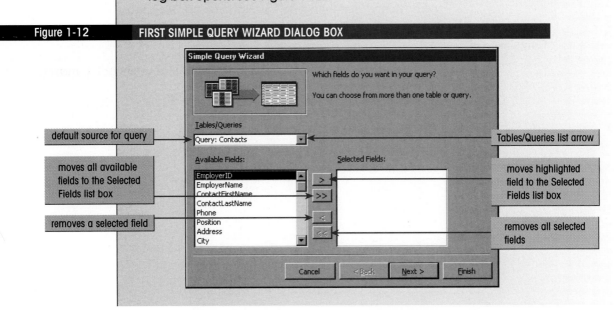

Because Contacts is the only query object currently in the Seasonal database, it is listed in the Tables/Queries box by default. You need to base the query you're creating on the Employer table.

**2.** Click the **Tables/Queries** list arrow, and then click **Table: Employer** to select the Employer table as the source for the new query. The Available Fields list box now lists the fields in the Employer table.

You need to select fields from the Available Fields list to include them in the query. To select fields one at a time, click a field and then click the ▢ > button. The selected field moves from the Available Fields list box on the left to the Selected Fields list box on the right. To select all the fields, click the ▢ >> button. If you change your mind or make a mistake, you can remove a field by clicking it in the Selected Fields list box and then clicking the ▢ < button. To remove all selected fields, click the ▢ << button.

Each Wizard dialog box contains buttons on the bottom that allow you to move to the previous dialog box (Back button), move to the next dialog box (Next button), or cancel the creation process (Cancel button) and return to the Database window. You can also finish creating the object (Finish button) and accept the Wizard's defaults for the remaining options.

Zack wants his list to include data from only the following fields: EmployerName, City, State/Prov, ContactFirstName, ContactLastName, and Phone. You need to select these fields to include them in the query.

## To create the query using the Simple Query Wizard:

**1.** Click **EmployerName** in the Available Fields list box, and then click the ▢ > button. The EmployerName field moves to the Selected Fields list box.

**2.** Repeat Step 1 for the fields **City**, **State/Prov**, **ContactFirstName**, **ContactLastName**, and **Phone**, and then click the **Next** button. The second, and final, Simple Query Wizard dialog box opens and asks you to choose a name for your query. This name will appear in the Queries list in the Database window. You'll change the suggested name (Employer Query) to "Employer List."

**3.** Click at the end of the highlighted name, use the Backspace key to delete the word "Query," and then type **List**. Now you can view the query results.

**4.** Click the **Finish** button to complete the query. Access displays the query results in Datasheet view.

**5.** Click the **Maximize** button ▢ on the Query window title bar to maximize the window. See Figure 1-13.

**Figure 1-13**                    **QUERY RESULTS**

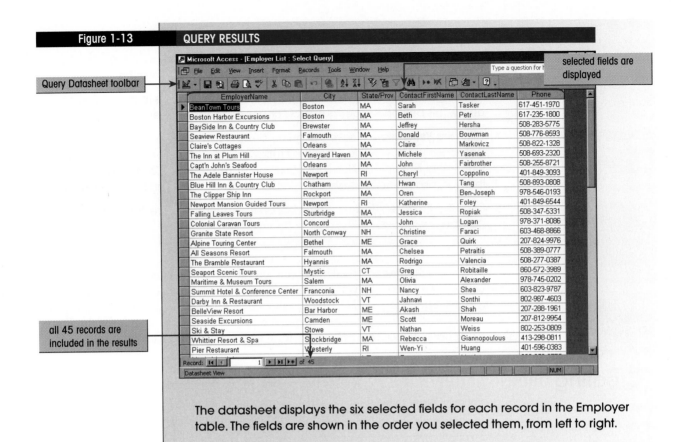

Query Datasheet toolbar

selected fields are displayed

all 45 records are included in the results

The datasheet displays the six selected fields for each record in the Employer table. The fields are shown in the order you selected them, from left to right.

The records are currently listed in order by the primary key field (EmployerID from the Employer table). This is true even though the EmployerID field is not included in the display of the query results. Zack prefers the records listed in order by state or province, so that his staff members can focus on all records for the employers in a particular state or province. To display the records in the order Zack wants, you need to sort the query results by the State/Prov field.

## To sort the query results:

1. Click to position the insertion point anywhere in the State/Prov column. This establishes the State/Prov column as the current field.

2. Click the **Sort Ascending** button 🔼 on the Query Datasheet toolbar. Now the records are sorted in ascending alphabetical order by the values in the State/Prov field. All the records for Connecticut (CT) are listed first, followed by the records for Massachusetts (MA), Maine (ME), and so on.

   Notice that the navigation buttons are located at the bottom of the window. You navigate through a query datasheet in the same way that you navigate through a table datasheet.

3. Click the **Last Record** navigation button ▶️. The last record in the query datasheet, for the Darby Inn & Restaurant, is now the current record.

4. Click the **Previous Record** navigation button ◀. Record 44 in the query datasheet is now the current record.

5. Click the **First Record** navigation button ⏮. The first record is now the current record.

6. Click the **Close Window** button ✕ on the menu bar to close the query.

    A dialog box opens and asks if you want to save changes to the design of the query. This box opens because you changed the sort order of the query results.

7. Click the **Yes** button to save the query design changes and return to the Database window. Notice that the Employer List query now appears in the Queries list box. In addition, because you maximized the Query window, now the Database window is also maximized. You need to restore the window.

8. Click the **Restore Window** button 🗗 on the menu bar to restore the Database window.

The query results are not stored in the database; however, the query design is stored as part of the database with the name you specified. You can re-create the query results at any time by running the query again. You'll learn more about creating and running queries in Tutorial 3.

After Zack views the query results, Elsa then asks you to create a form for the Employer table so that her staff members can use the form to enter and work with data in the table easily.

# Creating and Navigating a Form

A **form** is an object you use to maintain, view, and print records in a database. Although you can perform these same functions with tables and queries, forms can present data in many customized and useful ways.

In Access, you can design your own forms or use a Form Wizard to create your forms automatically. A **Form Wizard** is an Access tool that asks you a series of questions, and then creates a form based on your answers. The quickest way to create a form is to use an **AutoForm Wizard**, which places all the fields from a selected table (or query) on a form automatically, without asking you any questions, and then displays the form on the screen.

Elsa wants a form for the Employer table that will show all the fields for one record at a time, with fields listed one below another in a column. This type of form will make it easier for her staff to focus on all the data for a particular employer. You'll use the AutoForm: Columnar Wizard to create the form.

### To create the form using an AutoForm Wizard:

1. Click **Forms** in the Objects bar of the Database window to display the Forms list. The Forms list box does not contain any forms yet.

2. Click the **New** button in the Database window to open the New Form dialog box. See Figure 1-14.

| Figure 1-14 | NEW FORM DIALOG BOX |

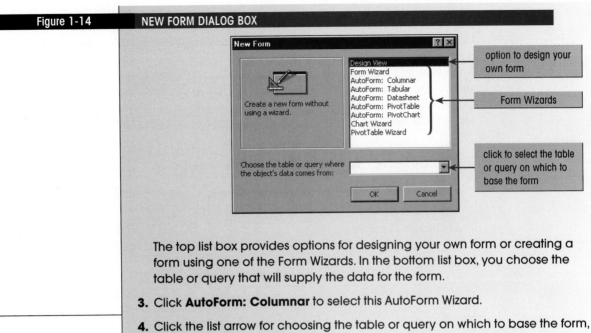

The top list box provides options for designing your own form or creating a form using one of the Form Wizards. In the bottom list box, you choose the table or query that will supply the data for the form.

3. Click **AutoForm: Columnar** to select this AutoForm Wizard.

4. Click the list arrow for choosing the table or query on which to base the form, and then click **Employer**.

5. Click the **OK** button. The AutoForm Wizard creates the form and displays it in Form view. See Figure 1-15.

| Figure 1-15 | FORM CREATED BY THE AUTOFORM: COLUMNAR WIZARD |

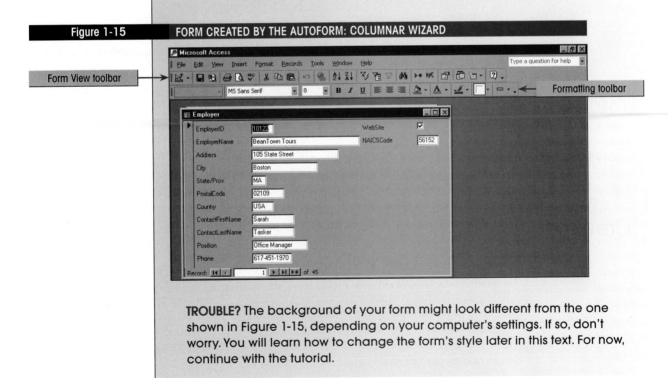

**TROUBLE?** The background of your form might look different from the one shown in Figure 1-15, depending on your computer's settings. If so, don't worry. You will learn how to change the form's style later in this text. For now, continue with the tutorial.

The form displays one record at a time in the Employer table. Access displays the field values for the first record in the table and selects the first field value (EmployerID). Each field name appears on a separate line (spread over two columns) and on the same line as its field value, which appears in a box. The widths of the boxes are different to accommodate the different sizes of the displayed field values; for example, compare the small box for the State/Prov field value with the larger box for the EmployerName field value. The AutoForm: Columnar Wizard automatically placed the field names and values on the form and supplied the background style.

To view and maintain data using a form, you must know how to move from field to field and from record to record. Notice that the Form window contains navigation buttons, similar to those available in Datasheet view, which you can use to display different records in the form. You'll use these now to navigate through the form; then you'll save and close the form.

---

### To navigate, save, and close the form:

1. Click the **Next Record** navigation button ▶. The form now displays the values for the second record in the Employer table.

2. Click the **Last Record** navigation button ▶❙ to move to the last record in the table. The form displays the information for record 45, Lighthouse Tours.

3. Click the **Previous Record** navigation button ◀ to move to record 44.

4. Click the **First Record** navigation button ❙◀ to return to the first record in the Employer table.

   Next, you'll save the form with the name "Employer Data" in the Seasonal database. Then the form will be available for later use. You'll learn more about creating and customizing forms in Tutorial 4.

5. Click the **Save** button 🖫 on the Form View toolbar. The Save As dialog box opens.

6. In the Form Name text box, click at the end of the highlighted word "Employer," press the **spacebar**, type **Data**, and then press the **Enter** key. Access saves the form as Employer Data in the Seasonal database and closes the dialog box.

7. Click the **Close** button ✕ on the Form window title bar to close the form and return to the Database window. Note that the Employer Data form is now listed in the Forms list box.

---

After attending a staff meeting, Zack returns with another request. He wants the same employer list you produced earlier when you created the Employer List query, but he'd like the information presented in a more readable format. You'll help Zack by creating a report.

## Creating, Previewing, and Navigating a Report

A **report** is a formatted printout (or screen display) of the contents of one or more tables in a database. Although you can print data appearing in tables, queries, and forms, reports provide you with the greatest flexibility for formatting printed output. As with forms, you can design your own reports or use a Report Wizard to create reports automatically.

Zack wants a report showing the same information contained in the Employer List query that you created earlier. However, he wants the data for each employer to be grouped together, with one employer record below another, as shown in the report sketch in Figure 1-16.

**Figure 1-16**     **SKETCH OF ZACK'S REPORT**

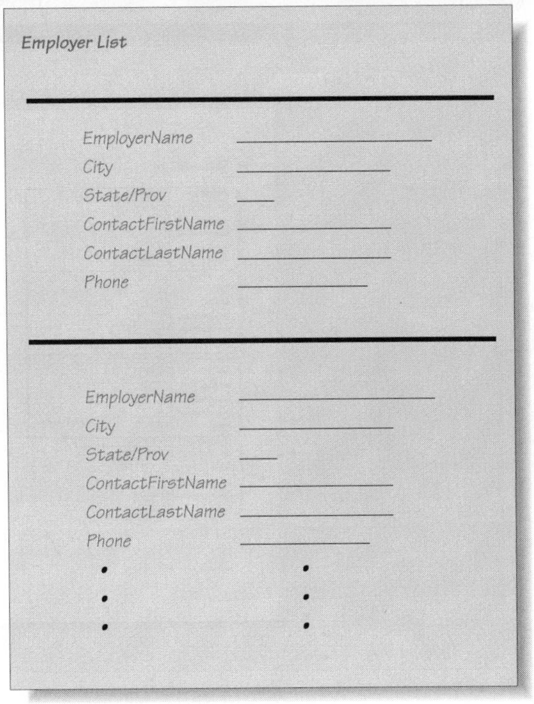

To produce the report for Zack, you'll use the AutoReport: Columnar Wizard, which is similar to the AutoForm: Columnar Wizard you used earlier when creating the Employer Data form.

## To create the report using the AutoReport: Columnar Wizard:

1. Click **Reports** in the Objects bar of the Database window, and then click the **New** button in the Database window to open the New Report dialog box, which is similar to the New Form dialog box you saw earlier.

2. Click **AutoReport: Columnar** to select this Wizard for creating the report.

   Because Zack wants the same data as in the Employer List query, you need to choose that query as the basis for the report.

3. Click the list arrow for choosing the table or query on which to base the report, and then click **Employer List**.

4. Click the **OK** button. The AutoReport Wizard creates the report and displays it in Print Preview, which shows exactly how the report will look when printed.

   To view the report better, you'll maximize the window and change the Zoom setting so that you can see the entire page.

5. Click the **Maximize** button 🔲 on the Report window title bar, click the **Zoom** list arrow (to the right of the value 100%) on the Print Preview toolbar, and then click **Fit**. The entire first page of the report is displayed in the window. See Figure 1-17.

| Figure 1-17 | FIRST PAGE OF THE REPORT IN PRINT PREVIEW |

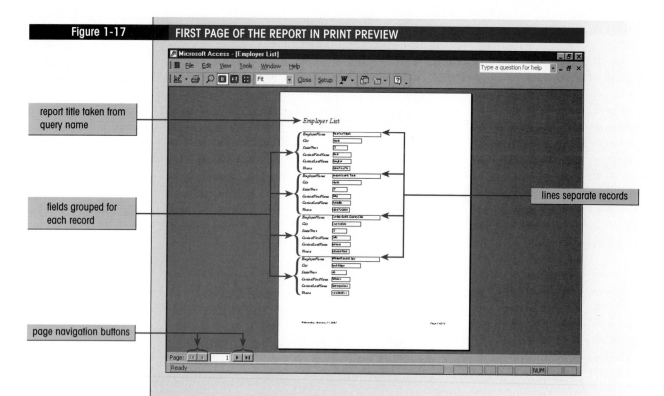

report title taken from query name

fields grouped for each record

page navigation buttons

lines separate records

**TROUBLE?** The fonts used in your report might look different from the ones shown in Figure 1-17, depending on your computer's settings. If so, don't worry. You will learn how to change the report's style later in this text.

Each field from the Employer List query appears on its own line, with the corresponding field value to the right and in a box. Horizontal lines separate one record from the next, visually grouping all the fields for each record. The name of the query—Employer List—appears as the report's title.

Notice that the Print Preview window provides page navigation buttons at the bottom of the window, similar to the navigation buttons you've used to move through records in a table, query, and form. You use these buttons to move through the pages of a report.

6. Click the **Next Page** navigation button ▶. The second page of the report is displayed in Print Preview.

7. Click the **Last Page** navigation button ▶| to move to the last page of the report. Note that this page contains the fields for only one record. Also note that the box in the middle of the navigation buttons displays the number "12"; there are 12 pages in this report.

**TROUBLE?** Depending on the printer you are using, your report might have more or fewer pages. If so, don't worry. Different printers format reports in different ways, sometimes affecting the total number of pages.

8. Click the **First Page** navigation button |◀ to return to the first page of the report.

At this point, you could close the report without saving it because you can easily re-create it at any time. In general, it's best to save an object—report, form, or query—only if you anticipate using the object frequently or if it is time-consuming to create, because these objects use considerable storage space on your disk. However, Zack wants to show the report to his staff members, so he asks you to save it.

---

### To close and save the report:

1. Click the **Close Window** button ☒ on the menu bar. *Do not* click the Close button on the Print Preview toolbar.

   **TROUBLE?** If you clicked the Close button on the Print Preview toolbar, you switched to Design view. Simply click the Close Window button ☒ on the menu bar, and then continue with the steps.

   A dialog box opens and asks if you want to save the changes to the report design.

2. Click the **Yes** button. The Save As dialog box opens.

3. Click to the right of the highlighted text in the Report Name text box, press the **spacebar** once, type **Report**, and then click the **OK** button. Access saves the report as "Employer List Report" and returns to the Database window.

---

You'll learn more about creating and customizing reports in Tutorial 4.

# Managing a Database

One of the main tasks involved in working with database software is managing your databases and the data they contain. By managing your databases, you can ensure that they operate in the most efficient way, that the data they contain is secure, and that you can work with the data effectively. Some of the activities involved in database management include backing up and restoring a database, compacting and repairing a database, and converting a database for use in other versions of Access.

## Backing Up and Restoring a Database

You make a backup copy of a database file to protect your database against loss or damage. You can make the backup copy using one of several methods: Windows Explorer, My Computer, Microsoft Backup, or other backup software. If you back up your database file to a floppy disk, and the file size exceeds the size of the disk, you cannot use Windows Explorer or My Computer; you must use Microsoft Backup or some other backup software so that you can copy the file over more than one disk.

To restore a backup database file, choose the same method you used to make the backup copy. For example, if you used the Microsoft Backup tool (which is one of the System Tools available from the Programs menu and Accessories submenu in Windows 2000), you must choose the Restore option for this tool to copy the database file to your database folder. If the existing database file and the backup copy have the same name, restoring the backup copy might replace the existing file. If you want to save the existing file, rename it before you restore it.

## Compacting and Repairing a Database

Whenever you open an Access database and work in it, the size of the database increases. Likewise, when you delete records and when you delete or replace database objects—such as queries, forms, and reports—the space that had been occupied on the disk by the deleted or replaced records or objects does not become available for other records or objects. To make the space available, you must compact the database. **Compacting** a database rearranges the data and objects in a database to decrease its file size. Unlike making a copy of a database file, which you do to protect your database against loss or damage, you compact a database to make it smaller, thereby making more space available on your disk and speeding up the process of opening and closing the database. Figure 1-18 illustrates the compacting process; the orange colored elements in the figure represent database records and objects.

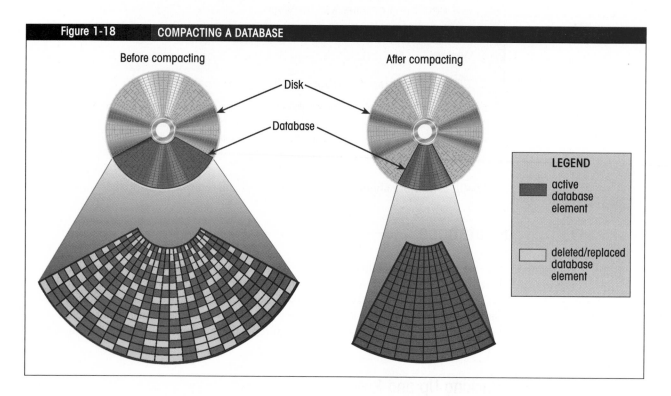

**Figure 1-18    COMPACTING A DATABASE**

Before compacting

After compacting

Disk

Database

LEGEND

active database element

deleted/replaced database element

When you compact a database, Access repairs the database at the same time. In many cases, Access detects that a database is damaged when you try to open it and gives you the option to compact and repair it at that time. If you think your database might be damaged because it is behaving unpredictably, you can use the "Compact and Repair Database" option to fix it. With your database file open, point to the Database Utilities option on the Tools menu, and then choose the Compact and Repair Database option.

## Compacting a Database Automatically

Access also allows you to set an option for your database file so that every time you close the database, it will be compacted automatically.

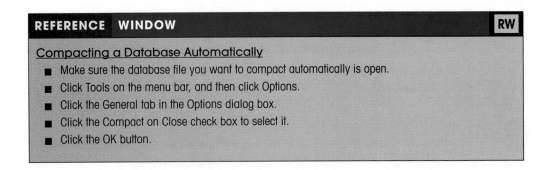

**Compacting a Database Automatically**
- Make sure the database file you want to compact automatically is open.
- Click Tools on the menu bar, and then click Options.
- Click the General tab in the Options dialog box.
- Click the Compact on Close check box to select it.
- Click the OK button.

You'll set the compact option now for the Seasonal database. Then, every time you subsequently close the Seasonal database, Access will compact the database file for you. After setting this option, you'll exit Access.

### To set the option for compacting the Seasonal database:

1. Make sure the Seasonal Database window is open on your screen.

2. Click **Tools** on the menu bar, and then click **Options**. The Options dialog box opens.

3. Click the **General** tab in the dialog box, and then click the **Compact on Close** check box to select it. See Figure 1-19.

Figure 1-19   GENERAL TAB OF THE OPTIONS DIALOG BOX

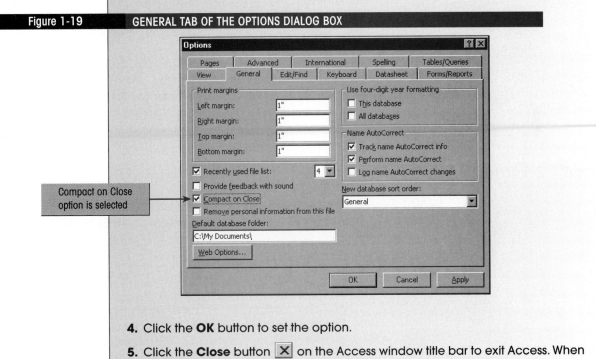

Compact on Close option is selected

4. Click the **OK** button to set the option.

5. Click the **Close** button X on the Access window title bar to exit Access. When you exit, Access closes the Seasonal database file and compacts it automatically.

## Converting an Access 2000 Database

Another important database management task is converting a database so that you can work with it in a different version of Access. As noted earlier in this tutorial, the default file format for databases you create in Access 2002 is Access 2000. This enables you to work with the database in either the Access 2000 or 2002 versions of the software, without having to convert it. This compatibility makes it easy for multiple users working with different versions of the software to share the same database and work more efficiently.

Sometimes, however, you might need to convert an Access 2000 database to another version. For example, if you needed to share an Access 2000 database with a colleague who worked on a laptop computer with Access 97 installed on it, you could convert the Access 2000 database to the Access 97 format. Likewise, you might want to convert an Access 2000 database to the Access 2002 file format if the database becomes very large in size. Access 2002 is enhanced so that large databases run faster in the Access 2002 file format, making it more efficient for you to work with the information contained in them.

To convert a database, follow these steps:

1. Make sure the database you want to convert is closed and the Access window is open.

2. Click Tools on the menu bar, point to Database Utilities, point to Convert Database, and then choose the format you want to convert to—To Access 97 File Format, To Access 2000 File Format, or To Access 2002 File Format.

3. In the Database to Convert From dialog box, select the name of the database you want to convert, and then click the Convert button.

4. In the Convert Database Into dialog box, enter a new name for the converted database in the File name text box, and then click the Save button.

After converting a database, you can use it in the version of Access to which you converted the file. Note, however, that when you convert to a previous file format, such as converting from the Access 2000 file format to the Access 97 file format, you might lose some of the advanced features of the newer version and you might need to make some adjustments to the converted database.

With the Employer and NAICS tables in place, Elsa can continue to build the Seasonal database and use it to store, manipulate, and retrieve important data for NSJI. In the following tutorials, you'll help Elsa complete and maintain the database, and you'll use it to meet the specific information needs of other NSJI employees.

# Session 1.2 QUICK CHECK

1. A(n) _____ is a question you ask about the data stored in a database.

2. Unless you specify otherwise, the records resulting from a query are listed in order by the _____.

3. The quickest way to create a form is to use a(n) _____.

4. Describe the form created by the AutoForm: Columnar Wizard.

5. After creating a report, the AutoReport Wizard displays the report in _____.

6. _____ a database rearranges the data and objects in a database to decrease its file size.

## REVIEW ASSIGNMENTS

In the Review Assignments, you'll work with the **Seasons** database, which is similar to the database you worked with in the tutorial. Complete the following:

1. Make sure your Data Disk is in the disk drive.

2. Start Access and open the **Seasons** database, which is located in the Review folder on your Data Disk.

*Explore* ➤ 3. Open the Microsoft Access Help window, and then display the Contents tab. Double-click the topic "Microsoft Access Help" (if necessary), and then double-click the topic "Queries," and then click "About types of queries." Read the displayed information, and then click "Select queries." Read the displayed information. In the Contents tab, double-click the topic "Forms," and then click the topic "About forms." Read the displayed information. In the Contents tab, scroll down and double-click the topic "Reports and Report Snapshots," and then click the topic "About reports." Read the displayed information. When finished reading all the topics, close the Microsoft Access Help window. Use Notepad, Word, or some other text editor to write a brief summary of what you learned.

*Explore* ➤ 4. Use the "Ask a Question" box to ask the following question: "How do I rename an object?" Click the topic "Rename a database object" and read the displayed information. Close the Microsoft Access Help window. Then, in the **Seasons** database, rename the **Table1** table as **Employers**.

5. Open the **Employers** table.

*Explore* ➤ 6. Open the Microsoft Access Help window, and then display the Index tab. Type the keyword "print" in the Type keywords text box, and then click the Search button. Click the topic "Set page setup options for printing" and then click "For a table, query, form, or report." Read the displayed information. Close the Microsoft Access Help window. Set the option for printing in landscape orientation, and then print the first page only of the **Employers** table datasheet. Close the **Employers** table.

*Explore* ➤ 7. Use the Simple Query Wizard to create a query that includes the City, EmployerName, ContactFirstName, ContactLastName, and Phone fields (in that order) from the **Employers** table. Name the query **Employer Phone List**. Sort the query results in ascending order by City. Set the option for printing in landscape orientation, and then print the second page only of the query results. Close and save the query.

8. Use the AutoForm: Columnar Wizard to create a form for the **Employers** table.

*Explore* ➤ 9. Use context-sensitive Help to find out how to move to a particular record and display it in the form. Click the What's This? command from the Help menu, and then use the Help pointer to click the number 1 in the Specific Record box at the bottom of the form. Read the displayed information. Click to close the Help box, and then use the Specific Record box to move to record 42 (for Whitney's Resort & Spa) in the **Employers** table.

*Explore* ➤ 10. Print the form for the current record (42). (*Hint:* Click the Selected Record(s) option in the Print dialog box to print the current record.)

11. Save the form as **Employer Info**, and then close the form.

*Explore* ➤ 12. Use the AutoReport: Tabular Wizard to create a report based on the **Employers** table. Print the first page of the report, and then close and save the report as **Employers**.

13. Set the option for compacting the **Seasons** database on close.

*Explore* ▶ 14. Convert the **Seasons** database to Access 2002 file format, saving the converted file as **Seasons2002** in the Review folder. Then convert the **Seasons** database to Access 97 file format, saving the converted file as **Seasons97** in the Review folder. Using Windows Explorer or My Computer, view the contents of your Review folder, and note the file sizes of the three versions of the **Seasons** database. Describe the results.

15. Exit Access.

## CASE PROBLEMS

*Case 1. Lim's Video Photography*  Several years ago, Youngho Lim left his position at a commercial photographer's studio and started his own business, Lim's Video Photography, located in San Francisco, California. Youngho quickly established a reputation as one of the area's best videographers, specializing in digital video photography. Youngho offers customers the option of storing edited videos on CD or DVD. His video shoots include weddings and other special events, as well as recording personal and commercial inventories for insurance purposes.

As his business continues to grow, Youngho relies on Access to keep track of information about clients, contracts, and so on. Youngho recently created an Access database named **Videos** to store data about his clients. You'll help Youngho complete and maintain the **Videos** database. Complete the following:

1. Make sure your Data Disk is in the disk drive.

2. Start Access and open the **Videos** database, which is located in the Cases folder on your Data Disk.

3. Open the **Client** table, print the table datasheet, and then close the table.

4. Use the Simple Query Wizard to create a query that includes the ClientName, Phone, and City fields (in that order) from the **Client** table. Name the query **Client List**. Print the query results, and then close the query.

*Explore* ▶ 5. Use the AutoForm: Tabular Wizard to create a form for the **Contract** table. Print the form, save it as **Contract Info**, and then close it.

*Explore* ▶ 6. Use the AutoReport: Columnar Wizard to create a report based on the **Contract** table. Maximize the Report window and change the Zoom setting to Fit. Use the Two Pages button on the Print Preview toolbar to view the first two pages of the report in Print Preview. Print the first page of the report, and then close and save it as **Contracts**.

7. Set the option for compacting the **Videos** database on close.

*Explore* ▶ 8. Convert the **Videos** database to Access 2002 file format, saving the converted file as **Videos2002** in the Cases folder. Then convert the **Videos** database to Access 97 file format, saving the converted file as **Videos97** in the Cases folder. Using Windows Explorer or My Computer, view the contents of your Cases folder, and note the file sizes of the three versions of the **Videos** database. Describe the results.

9. Exit Access.

*Case 2. DineAtHome.course.com*  After working as both a concierge in a local hotel and a manager of several restaurants, Claire Picard founded DineAtHome.course.com in Naples, Florida. Her idea for this e-commerce company was a simple one: to provide people with an easy-to-use, online service that would allow them to order meals from one or more area restaurants and have the meals delivered to their homes. DineAtHome acts as a sort of broker between restaurants and customers. The participating restaurants offer everything from simple fare to gourmet feasts. Claire's staff performs a variety of services, from simply picking up and delivering the meals to providing linens and table service for more formal occasions.

Claire created the **Meals** database in Access to maintain information about participating restaurants and their menu offerings. She needs your help in working with this database. Complete the following:

1. Make sure your Data Disk is in the disk drive.

2. Start Access and open the **Meals** database, which is located in the Cases folder on your Data Disk.

*Explore*   3. Open the **Restaurant** table, print the table datasheet in landscape orientation, and then close the table.

4. Use the Simple Query Wizard to create a query that includes the RestaurantName, OwnerFirstName, OwnerLastName, and City fields (in that order) from the **Restaurant** table. Name the query **Owner List**.

*Explore*   5. Sort the query results in descending order by the City field. (*Hint*: Use a toolbar button.)

*Explore*   6. Use the "Ask a Question" box to ask the following question: "How do I select multiple records?" Click the topic "Select fields and records," and then click the topic "Select fields and records in a datasheet." Read the displayed information, and then close the Help window. Select the four records with "Marco Island" as the value in the City field, and then print just the selected records. (*Hint:* Use the Selected Record(s) option in the Print dialog box to print them.) Close the query, and save your changes to the design.

*Explore*   7. Use the AutoForm: Columnar Wizard to create a form for the **Restaurant** table. Use context-sensitive Help to find out how to move to a particular record and display it in the form. Click the What's This? command from the Help menu, and then use the Help pointer to click the number 1 in the Specific Record box at the bottom of the form. Read the displayed information. Click to close the Help box, use the Specific Record box to move to record 11 (for The Gazebo), and then print the form for the current record only. (*Hint:* Use the Selected Record(s) option in the Print dialog box to print the current record.) Save the form as **Restaurant Info**, and then close the form.

8. Use the AutoReport: Columnar Wizard to create a report based on the **Restaurant** table. Maximize the Report window and change the Zoom setting to Fit.

*Explore*   9. Use the View menu to view all eight pages of the report at the same time in Print Preview.

10. Print just the first page of the report, and then close and save the report as **Restaurants**.

11. Set the option for compacting the **Meals** database on close.

*Explore*   12. Convert the **Meals** database to Access 2002 file format, saving the converted file as **Meals2002** in the Cases folder. Then convert the **Meals** database to Access 97 file format, saving the converted file as **Meals97** in the Cases folder. Using Windows Explorer or My Computer, view the contents of your Cases folder, and note the file sizes of the three versions of the **Meals** database. Describe the results.

13. Exit Access.

*Case 3. Redwood Zoo*   The Redwood Zoo is a small zoo located in the picturesque city of Gig Harbor, Washington, on the shores of Puget Sound. The zoo is ideally situated, with the natural beauty of the site providing the perfect backdrop for the zoo's varied exhibits. Although there are larger zoos in the greater Seattle area, the Redwood Zoo is considered to have some of the best exhibits of marine animals. The newly constructed polar bear habitat is a particular favorite among patrons.

Michael Rosenfeld is the director of fundraising activities for the Redwood Zoo. The zoo relies heavily on donations to fund both ongoing exhibits and temporary displays, especially those involving exotic animals. Michael created an Access database named **Redwood** to keep track of information about donors, their pledges, and the status of funds. You'll help Michael maintain the **Redwood** database. Complete the following:

1. Make sure your Data Disk is in the disk drive.

2. Start Access and open the **Redwood** database, which is located in the Cases folder on your Data Disk.

3. Open the **Donor** table, print the table datasheet, and then close the table.

*Explore*   4. Use the Simple Query Wizard to create a query that includes all the fields in the **Donor** table *except* the MI field. (*Hint*: Use the >> and < buttons to select the necessary fields.) Name the query **Donors**.

*Explore*   5. Sort the query results in descending order by the Class field. (*Hint*: Use a toolbar button.) Print the query results, and then close and save the query.

*Explore*   6. Use the AutoForm: Columnar Wizard to create a form for the **Fund** table. Use context-sensitive Help to find out how to move to a particular record and display it in the form. Click the What's This? command from the Help menu, and then use the Help pointer to click the number 1 in the Specific Record box at the bottom of the form. Read the displayed information. Click to close the Help box, use the Specific Record box to move to record 7 (Polar Bear Park), and then print the form for the current record only. (*Hint:* Use the Selected Record(s) option in the Print dialog box to print the current record.) Save the form as **Fund Info**, and then close it.

7. Use the AutoReport: Columnar Wizard to create a report based on the **Donor** table. Maximize the Report window and change the Zoom setting to Fit.

*Explore*   8. Use the View menu to view all seven pages of the report at the same time in Print Preview.

9. Print just the first page of the report, and then close and save the report as **Donors**.

10. Set the option for compacting the **Redwood** database on close.

*Explore*   11. Convert the **Redwood** database to Access 2002 file format, saving the converted file as **Redwood2002** in the Cases folder. Then convert the **Redwood** database to Access 97 file format, saving the converted file as **Redwood97** in the Cases folder. Using Windows Explorer or My Computer, view the contents of your Cases folder, and note the file sizes of the three versions of the **Redwood** database. Describe the results.

12. Exit Access.

**Case 4. Mountain River Adventures**   Several years ago, Connor and Siobhan Dempsey moved to Boulder, Colorado, drawn by their love of the mountains and their interest in outdoor activities of all kinds. This interest led them to form the Mountain River Adventures center. The center began as a whitewater rafting tour provider, but quickly grew to encompass other activities, such as canoeing, hiking, camping, fishing, and rock climbing.

From the beginning, Connor and Siobhan have used computers to help them manage all aspects of their business. They recently installed Access and created a database named **Trips** to store information about clients, equipment, and the types of guided tours they provide. You'll work with the **Trips** database to manage this information. Complete the following:

1. Make sure your Data Disk is in the disk drive.

2. Start Access and open the **Trips** database, which is located in the Cases folder on your Data Disk.

3. Open the **Client** table.

*Explore* 4. Print the **Client** table datasheet in landscape orientation, and then close the table.

5. Use the Simple Query Wizard to create a query that includes the ClientName, City, State/Prov, and Phone fields (in that order) from the **Client** table. Name the query **Client Info**.

*Explore* 6. Sort the query results in descending order by State/Prov. (*Hint:* Use a toolbar button.)

7. Print the query results, and then close and save the query.

*Explore* 8. Use the AutoForm: Columnar Wizard to create a form for the **Client** table. Use context-sensitive Help to find out how to move to a particular record and display it in the form. Click the What's This? command from the Help menu, and then use the Help pointer to click the number 1 in the Specific Record box at the bottom of the form. Read the displayed information. Click to close the Help box, use the Specific Record box to move to record 18, and then print the form for the current record only. (*Hint:* Use the Selected Record(s) option in the Print dialog box to print the current record.) Save the form as **Client Info**, and then close it.

*Explore* 9. Use the AutoReport: Tabular Wizard to create a report based on the **Client** table. Maximize the Report window and change the Zoom setting to Fit. Use the Two Pages button on the Print Preview toolbar to view both pages of the report in Print Preview. Print the first page of the report in landscape orientation, and then close and save the report as **Clients**.

10. Set the option for compacting the **Trips** database on close.

*Explore* 11. Convert the **Trips** database to Access 2002 file format, saving the converted file as **Trips2002** in the Cases folder. Then convert the **Trips** database to Access 97 file format, saving the converted file as **Trips97** in the Cases folder. Using Windows Explorer or My Computer, view the contents of your Cases folder, and note the file sizes of the three versions of the **Trips** database. Describe the results.

12. Exit Access.

## LAB ASSIGNMENTS

These Lab Assignments are designed to accompany the interactive Course Lab called Databases. To start the Databases Lab, click the Start button on the Windows taskbar, point to Programs, point to Course Labs, point to New Perspectives Course Labs, and then click Databases. If you do not see Course Labs on your Programs menu, see your instructor or technical support person.

*Databases* This Databases Lab demonstrates the essential concepts of file and database management systems. You will use the Lab to search, sort, and report the data contained in a file of classic books.

1. Click the Steps button to review basic database terminology and to learn how to manipulate the classic books database. As you proceed through the Steps, answer all of the Quick Check questions that appear. After you complete the Steps, you will see a Quick Check summary report. Follow the instructions on the screen to print this report.

2. Click the Explore button. Make sure you can apply basic database terminology to describe the classic books database by answering the following questions:
   a. How many records does the file contain?
   b. How many fields does each record contain?

    c. What are the contents of the Catalog # field for the book written by Margaret Mitchell?

    d. What are the contents of the Title field for the record with Thoreau in the Author field?

    e. Which field has been used to sort the records?

3. In Explore, manipulate the database as necessary to answer the following questions:

    a. When the books are sorted by title, what is the first record in the file?

    b. Use the Search button to search for all the books in the West location. How many do you find?

    c. Use the Search button to search for all the books in the Main location that are checked in. What do you find?

4. Use the Report button to print out a report that groups the books by Status and sorts them by Title. On your report, circle the four field names. Draw a box around the summary statistics showing which books are currently checked in and which books are currently checked out.

## INTERNET ASSIGNMENTS

**Student Union**

The purpose of the Internet Assignments is to challenge you to find information on the Internet that you can use to create effective documents. The actual assignments are updated and maintained on the Course Technology Web site. Log on to the Internet and use your Web browser to go to the Student Union on the New Perspectives Series site at **www.course.com/NewPerspectives/studentunion**. Click the Online Companions link, and then click the link for this text.

## QUICK CHECK ANSWERS

*Session 1.1*

1. field

2. common field

3. primary key; foreign key

4. records; fields

5. current record symbol

6. Use the horizontal and vertical scroll bars to view fields or records not currently visible in the datasheet; use the navigation buttons to move vertically through the records.

*Session 1.2*

1. query

2. primary key

3. AutoForm Wizard

4. The form displays each field name to the left of its field value, which appears in a box; the widths of the boxes represent the size of the fields.

5. Print Preview

6. Compacting

## OBJECTIVES

In this tutorial you will:

- Learn the guidelines for designing databases and setting field properties

- Create a new database

- Create and save a table

- Define fields and specify a table's primary key

- Add records to a table

- Modify the structure of a table

- Delete, move, and add fields

- Change field properties

- Copy records and import tables from another Access database

- Delete and change records

# CREATING
## AND MAINTAINING
## A DATABASE

*Creating the Northeast Database, and Creating, Modifying, and Updating the Position Table*

CASE

### Northeast Seasonal Jobs International (NSJI)

The Seasonal database contains two tables—the Employer table and the NAICS table. These tables store data about NSJI's employer customers and the NAICS codes for pertinent job positions, respectively. Elsa Jensen also wants to track information about each position that is available at each employer's place of business. This information includes the position title and wage. Elsa asks you to create a third table, named Position, in which to store the position data.

Because this is your first time creating a new table, Elsa suggests that you first create a new database, named "Northeast," and then create the new Position table in this database. This will keep the Seasonal database intact. Once the Position table is completed, you then can import the Employer and NAICS tables from the Seasonal database into your new Northeast database.

Some of the position data Elsa needs is already stored in another NSJI database. After creating the Position table and adding some records to it, you'll copy the records from the other database into the Position table. Then you'll maintain the Position table by modifying it and updating it to meet Elsa's specific data requirements.

## SESSION 2.1

In this session, you will learn the guidelines for designing databases and setting field properties. You'll also learn how to create a new database, create a table, define the fields for a table, select the primary key for a table, and save the table structure.

## Guidelines for Designing Databases

A database management system can be a useful tool, but only if you first carefully design the database so that it meets the needs of its users. In database design, you determine the fields, tables, and relationships needed to satisfy the data and processing requirements. When you design a database, you should follow these guidelines:

- **Identify all the fields needed to produce the required information.** For example, Elsa needs information about employers, NAICS codes, and positions. Figure 2-1 shows the fields that satisfy these information requirements.

| Figure 2-1 | ELSA'S DATA REQUIREMENTS |
| --- | --- |

| | |
| --- | --- |
| EmployerID | ContactFirstName |
| PositionID | ContactLastName |
| PositionTitle | Position |
| EmployerName | Wage |
| Address | Hours/Week |
| City | NAICSCode |
| State/Prov | NAICSDesc |
| PostalCode | StartDate |
| Country | EndDate |
| Phone | ReferredBy |
| Openings | WebSite |

- **Group related fields into tables.** For example, Elsa grouped the fields relating to employers into the Employer table and the fields related to NAICS codes into the NAICS table. The other fields are grouped logically into the Position table, which you will create, as shown in Figure 2-2.

| Figure 2-2 | ELSA'S FIELDS GROUPED INTO TABLES |
| --- | --- |

| Employer table | NAICS table | Position table |
| --- | --- | --- |
| EmployerID | NAICSCode | PositionID |
| EmployerName | NAICSDesc | PositionTitle |
| Address | | Wage |
| City | | Hours/Week |
| State/Prov | | Openings |
| PostalCode | | ReferredBy |
| Country | | StartDate |
| ContactFirstName | | EndDate |
| ContactLastName | | |
| Position | | |
| Phone | | |
| WebSite | | |

■ **Determine each table's primary key.** Recall that a primary key uniquely identifies each record in a table. Although a primary key is not mandatory in Access, it's usually a good idea to include one in each table. Without a primary key, selecting the exact record that you want can be a problem. For some tables, one of the fields, such as a Social Security or credit card number, naturally serves the function of a primary key. For other tables, two or more fields might be needed to function as the primary key. In these cases, the primary key is referred to as a **composite key**. For example, a school grade table would use a combination of student number and course code to serve as the primary key. For a third category of tables, no single field or combination of fields can uniquely identify a record in a table. In these cases, you need to add a field whose sole purpose is to serve as the table's primary key.

For Elsa's tables, EmployerID is the primary key for the Employer table, NAICSCode is the primary key for the NAICS table, and PositionID will be the primary key for the Position table.

■ **Include a common field in related tables.** You use the common field to connect one table logically with another table. For example, Elsa's Employer and Position tables will include the EmployerID field as a common field. Recall that when you include the primary key from one table as a field in a second table to form a relationship, the field is called a foreign key in the second table; therefore, the EmployerID field will be a foreign key in the Position table. With this common field, Elsa can find all positions available at a particular employer; she can use the EmployerID value for an employer and search the Position table for all records with that EmployerID value. Likewise, she can determine which employer has a particular position available by searching the Employer table to find the one record with the same EmployerID value as the corresponding value in the Position table.

■ **Avoid data redundancy.** Data redundancy occurs when you store the same data in more than one place. With the exception of common fields to connect tables, you should avoid redundancy because it wastes storage space and can cause inconsistencies, if, for instance, you type a field value one way in one table and a different way in the same table or in a second table. Figure 2-3, which contains portions of potential data to be stored in the Employer and Position tables, shows an example of incorrect database design that has data redundancy in the Position table; the EmployerName field is redundant, and one value was entered incorrectly, in three different ways.

| Figure 2-3 | INCORRECT DATABASE DESIGN WITH DATA REDUNDANCY |
|---|---|

**Employer table**

| EmployerID | EmployerName | Address | Phone |
|---|---|---|---|
| 10122 | BeanTown Tours | 105 State Street, Boston, MA 02109 | 617-451-1970 |
| 10125 | Boston Harbor Excursions | 75 Atlantic Avenue, Boston, MA 02110 | 617-235-1800 |
| 10126 | BaySide Inn & Country Club | 354 Oceanside Drive, Brewster, MA 02631 | 508-283-5775 |
| 10190 | The Briar Rose Inn | 105 Queen Street, Charlottetown PE C1A 8R4 | 902-626-1595 |
| 10191 | Windsor Alpine Tours | 14 Longmeadow Road, Laconia, NH 03246 | 603-266-9233 |
| 10198 | Trudel Spa & Resort | 40 Rue Rivard, North Hatley QC J0B 2C0 | 819-842-7783 |

data redundancy

**Position table**

| PositionID | EmployerID | EmployerName | PositionTitle | Hours/Week |
|---|---|---|---|---|
| 2040 | 10126 | DaySide Inn & Country Club | Waiter/Waitress | 32 |
| 2045 | 10122 | BeanTown Tours | Tour Guide | 24 |
| 2053 | 10190 | The Briar Rose Inn | Host/Hostess | 24 |
| 2066 | 10198 | Trudel Spa & Resort | Lifeguard | 32 |
| 2073 | 10126 | Baside Inn & Country Club | Pro Shop Clerk | 24 |
| 2078 | 10191 | Windsor Alpine Tours | Ski Patrol | 30 |
| 2079 | 10191 | Windsor Alpine Tours | Day Care | 35 |
| 2082 | 10125 | Boston Harbor Excursions | Reservationist | 40 |
| 2111 | 10126 | BaySide Inn Club | Kitchen Help | 32 |

inconsistent data

■ **Determine the properties of each field.** You need to identify the **properties**, or characteristics, of each field so that the DBMS knows how to store, display, and process the field values. These properties include the field's name, maximum number of characters or digits, description, valid values, and other field characteristics. You will learn more about field properties later in this tutorial.

The Position table you need to create will contain the fields shown in Figure 2-2, plus the EmployerID field as a foreign key. Before you create the new Northeast database and the Position table, you first need to learn some guidelines for setting field properties.

# Guidelines for Setting Field Properties

As just noted, the last step of database design is to determine which values to assign to the properties, such as the name and data type, of each field. When you select or enter a value for a property, you **set** the property. Access has rules for naming fields, choosing data types, and setting other properties for fields.

## Naming Fields and Objects

You must name each field, table, and other object in an Access database. Access then stores these items in the database, using the names you supply. It's best to choose a field or object name that describes the purpose or contents of the field or object, so that later you can easily remember what the name represents. For example, the three tables in the Northeast database will be named Employer, NAICS, and Position, because these names suggest their contents.

The following rules apply to naming fields and objects:

- A name can be up to 64 characters long.
- A name can contain letters, numbers, spaces, and special characters, except for a period (.), exclamation mark (!), accent grave (`), and square brackets ([ ]).
- A name cannot start with a space.
- A table or query name must be unique within a database. A field name must be unique within a table, but it can be used again in another table.

In addition, experienced users of databases follow these conventions for naming fields and objects:

- Capitalize the first letter of each word in the name.
- Avoid extremely long names because they are difficult to remember and reference.
- Use standard abbreviations, such as Num for Number, Amt for Amount, and Qty for Quantity.
- Do not use spaces in field names because these names will appear in column headings on datasheets and on labels in forms and reports. By not using spaces, you'll be able to show more fields in these objects at one time.

## Assigning Field Data Types

You must assign a data type for each field. The **data type** determines what field values you can enter for the field and what other properties the field will have. For example, the Position table will include a StartDate field, which will store date values, so you will assign the date/time data type to this field. Then Access will allow you to enter and manipulate only dates or times as values in the StartDate field.

Figure 2-4 lists the 10 data types available in Access, describes the field values allowed for each data type, explains when you should use each data type, and indicates the field size of each data type.

| Figure 2-4 | DATA TYPES FOR FIELDS | |
|---|---|---|
| **DATA TYPE** | **DESCRIPTION** | **FIELD SIZE** |
| Text | Allows field values containing letters, digits, spaces, and special characters. Use for names, addresses, descriptions, and fields containing digits that are not used in calculations. | 0 to 255 characters; 50 characters default |
| Memo | Allows field values containing letters, digits, spaces, and special characters. Use for long comments and explanations. | 1 to 65,535 characters; exact size is determined by entry |
| Number | Allows positive and negative numbers as field values. Numbers can contain digits, a decimal point, commas, a plus sign, and a minus sign. Use for fields that you will use in calculations, except calculations involving money. | 1 to 15 digits |
| Date/Time | Allows field values containing valid dates and times from January 1, 100 to December 31, 9999. Dates can be entered in mm/dd/yy (month, day, year) format, several other date formats, or a variety of time formats, such as 10:35 PM. You can perform calculations on dates and times, and you can sort them. For example, you can determine the number of days between two dates. | 8 bytes |
| Currency | Allows field values similar to those for the number data type. Unlike calculations with number data type decimal values, calculations performed using the currency data type are not subject to round-off error. | Accurate to 15 digits on the left side of the decimal separator and to 4 digits on the right side |

| Figure 2-4 | DATA TYPES FOR FIELDS, CONTINUED | |
|---|---|---|
| DATA TYPE | DESCRIPTION | FIELD SIZE |
| AutoNumber | Consists of integers with values controlled by Access. Access automatically inserts a value in the field as each new record is created. You can specify sequential numbering or random numbering, which guarantees a unique field value, so that such a field can serve as a table's primary key. | 9 digits |
| Yes/No | Limits field values to yes and no, on and off, or true and false. Use for fields that indicate the presence or absence of a condition, such as whether an order has been filled or whether an employee is eligible for the company dental plan. | 1 character |
| OLE Object | Allows field values that are created in other programs as objects, such as photographs, video images, graphics, drawings, sound recordings, voice-mail messages, spreadsheets, and word-processing documents. These objects can be linked or embedded. | 1 gigabyte maximum; exact size depends on object size |
| Hyperlink | Consists of text used as a hyperlink address. A hyperlink address can have up to three parts: the text that appears in a field or control; the path to a file or page; and a location within the file or page. Hyperlinks help you to connect your application easily to the Internet or an intranet. | Up to 64,000 characters total for the three parts of a hyperlink data type |
| Lookup Wizard | Creates a field that lets you look up a value in another table or in a predefined list of values. | Same size as the primary key field used to perform the lookup |

## Setting Field Sizes

The **Field Size** property defines a field value's maximum storage size for text, number, and AutoNumber fields only. The other data types have no Field Size property because their storage size is either a fixed, predetermined amount or is determined automatically by the field value itself, as shown in Figure 2-4. A text field has a default field size of 50 characters; you can also set its field size by entering a number from 0 to 255. For example, the PositionTitle and ReferredBy fields in the Position table will be text fields with a size of 30 each.

When you use the number data type to define a field, you should set the field's Field Size property based on the largest value that you expect to store in that field. Access processes smaller data sizes faster using less memory, so you can optimize your database's performance and its storage space by selecting the correct field size for each field. For example, it would be wasteful to use the Long Integer setting when defining a field that will store only whole numbers ranging from 0 to 255, because the Long Integer setting will use four bytes of storage space. A better choice would be the Byte setting, which uses one byte of storage space to store the same values. Field Size property settings for number fields are as follows:

- **Byte:** Stores whole numbers (numbers with no fractions) from 0 to 255 in one byte
- **Integer:** Stores whole numbers from –32,768 to 32,767 in two bytes
- **Long Integer** (default): Stores whole numbers from –2,147,483,648 to 2,147,483,647 in four bytes
- **Single:** Stores positive and negative numbers to precisely seven decimal places and uses four bytes
- **Double:** Stores positive and negative numbers to precisely 15 decimal places and uses eight bytes
- **Replication ID:** Establishes a unique identifier for replication of tables, records, and other objects and uses 16 bytes
- **Decimal:** Stores positive and negative numbers to precisely 28 decimal places and uses 12 bytes

Elsa documented the design for the new Position table by listing each field's name, data type, size (if applicable), and description, as shown in Figure 2-5. Note that Elsa assigned the text data type to the PositionID, PositionTitle, EmployerID, and ReferredBy fields; the currency data type to the Wage field; the number data type to the Hours/Week and Openings fields; and the date/time data type to the StartDate and EndDate fields.

| Figure 2-5 | DESIGN FOR THE POSITION TABLE | | | |
|---|---|---|---|---|
| Field Name | Data Type | Field Size | Description | |
| PositionID | Text | 4 | Primary key | |
| PositionTitle | Text | 30 | | |
| EmployerID | Text | 5 | Foreign key | |
| Wage | Currency | | Rate per hour | |
| Hours/Week | Number | Integer | Work hours per week | |
| Openings | Number | Integer | Number of openings | |
| ReferredBy | Text | 30 | | |
| StartDate | Date/Time | | Month and day | |
| EndDate | Date/Time | | Month and day | |

With Elsa's design in place, you're ready to create the new Northeast database and the Position table.

## Creating a New Database

Access provides two ways for you to create a new database: using a Database Wizard or creating a blank database. When you use a Wizard, the Wizard guides you through the database creation process and provides the necessary tables, forms, and reports for the type of database you choose—all in one operation. Using a Database Wizard is an easy way to start creating a database, but only if your data requirements closely match one of the supplied templates. When you choose to create a blank database, you need to add all the tables, forms, reports, and other objects after you create the database file. Creating a blank database provides the most flexibility, allowing you to define objects in the way that you want, but it does require that you define each object separately. Whichever method you choose, you can always modify or add to your database after you create it.

The following steps outline the process for creating a new database using a Database Wizard:

1. If necessary, click the New button on the Database toolbar to display the Task Pane.

2. In the "New from template" section of the Task Pane, click General Templates. The Templates dialog box opens.

3. Click the Databases tab, and then choose the Database Wizard that most closely matches the type of database you want to create. Click the OK button.

4. In the File New Database dialog box, choose the location in which to save the new database, specify its name, and then click the Create button.

5. Complete each of the Wizard dialog boxes, clicking the Next button to move through them after making your selections.

6. Click the Finish button when you have completed all the Wizard dialog boxes.

None of the Database Wizards matches the requirements of the new Northeast database, so you'll use the Blank Database option to create it.

### To create the Northeast database:

1. Place your Data Disk in the appropriate disk drive, and then start Access.

2. In the New section of the Task Pane, click **Blank Database**. The File New Database dialog box opens. This dialog box is similar to the Open dialog box.

3. Click the **Save in** list arrow, and then click the drive that contains your Data Disk.

4. Click **Tutorial** in the list box, and then click the **Open** button.

5. In the File name text box, double-click the text **db1** to select it, and then type **Northeast**.

   TROUBLE? Your File name text box might contain an entry other than "db1." Just select whatever text is in this text box, and continue with the steps.

6. Click the **Create** button. Access creates the Northeast database in the Tutorial folder on your Data Disk, and then displays the Database window for the new database with the Tables object selected.

Now you can create the Position table in the Northeast database.

## Creating a Table

Creating a table consists of naming the fields and defining the properties for the fields, specifying a primary key (and a foreign key, if applicable) for the table, and then saving the table structure. You will use Elsa's design (Figure 2-5) as a guide for creating the Position table in the Northeast database.

### To begin creating the Position table:

1. Click the **New** button in the Database window. The New Table dialog box opens. See Figure 2-6.

| Figure 2-6 | NEW TABLE DIALOG BOX |
| --- | --- |

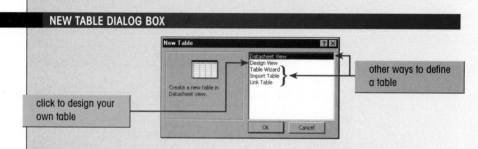

click to design your own table

other ways to define a table

TROUBLE? If the Task Pane opens and displays "New File" at the top, you clicked the New button on the Database toolbar instead of the New button in the Database window. Click the Close button to close the Task Pane, and then repeat Step 1.

In Access, you can create a table from entered data (Datasheet View), define your own table (Design View), use a Wizard to automate the table creation process (Table Wizard), or use a Wizard to import or link data from another database or other data source (Import Table or Link Table). For the Position table, you will define your own table.

2. Click **Design View** in the list box, and then click the **OK** button. The Table window opens in Design view. (Note that you can also double-click the "Create table in Design view" option in the Database window to open the Table window in Design view.) See Figure 2-7.

| Figure 2-7 | TABLE WINDOW IN DESIGN VIEW |
| --- | --- |

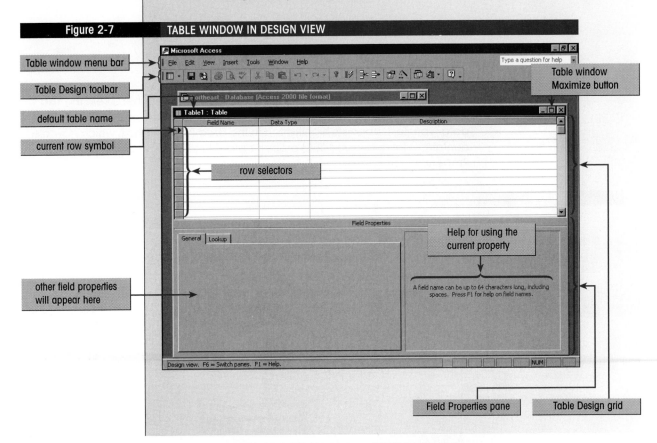

Table window menu bar
Table Design toolbar
default table name
current row symbol
row selectors
other field properties will appear here
Table window Maximize button
Help for using the current property
A field name can be up to 64 characters long, including spaces. Press F1 for help on field names.
Field Properties pane
Table Design grid

You use Design view to define or modify a table structure or the properties of the fields in a table. If you create a table without using a Wizard, you enter the fields and their properties for your table directly in the Table window in Design view.

## Defining Fields

Initially, the default table name, Table1, appears on the Table window title bar, the current row symbol is positioned in the first row selector of the Table Design grid, and the insertion point is located in the first row's Field Name box. The purpose or characteristics of the current property (Field Name, in this case) appear in the right side of the Field Properties pane. You can display more complete information about the current property by pressing the F1 key.

You enter values for the Field Name, Data Type, and Description field properties in the Table Design grid. You select values for all other field properties, most of which are optional, in the Field Properties pane. These other properties will appear when you move to the first row's Data Type text box.

---

### REFERENCE WINDOW    RW

#### Defining a Field in a Table

- In the Database window, select the table, and then click the Design button to open the Table window in Design view.
- Type the field name.
- Select the data type.
- Type or select other field properties, as appropriate.

---

The first field you need to define is PositionID.

## To define the PositionID field:

1. Type **PositionID** in the first row's Field Name text box, and then press the **Tab** key (or press the **Enter** key) to advance to the Data Type text box. The default data type, Text, appears highlighted in the Data Type text box, which now also contains a list arrow, and field properties for a text field appear in the Field Properties pane. See Figure 2-8.

| Figure 2-8 | TABLE WINDOW AFTER ENTERING THE FIRST FIELD NAME |
|---|---|

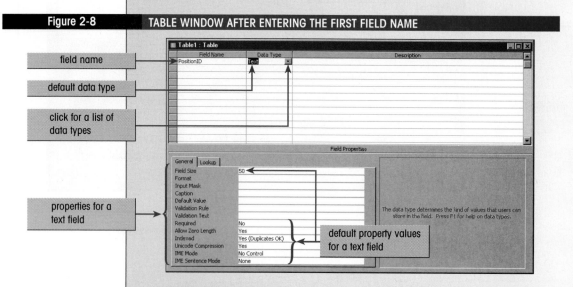

Notice that the right side of the Field Properties pane now provides an explanation for the current property, Data Type.

**TROUBLE?** If you make a typing error, you can correct it by clicking the mouse to position the insertion point, and then using either the Backspace key to delete characters to the left of the insertion point or the Delete key to delete characters to the right of the insertion point. Then type the correct text.

Because the PositionID numbers will not be used in calculations, you will assign the text data type (as opposed to the number data type) to the PositionID field.

2. Press the **Tab** key to accept Text as the data type and to advance to the Description text box.

Next you'll enter the Description property value as "Primary key." You can use the Description property to enter an optional description for a field to explain its purpose or usage. A field's Description property can be up to 255 characters long, and its value appears on the status bar when you view the table datasheet.

3. Type **Primary key** in the Description text box.

Notice the Field Size property for the text field. The default setting of "50" is displayed. You need to change this number to "4" because all PositionID values at NSJI contain only 4 digits. (Refer to the Access Help system for a complete description of all the properties available for the different data types.)

4. Double-click the number **50** in the Field Size property box to select it, and then type **4**. The definition of the first field is completed. See Figure 2-9.

| Figure 2-9 | PositionID FIELD DEFINED |
| --- | --- |

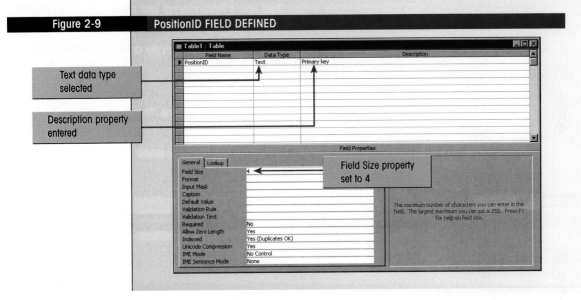

Text data type selected

Description property entered

Field Size property set to 4

Elsa's Position table design shows PositionTitle as the second field. You will define PositionTitle as a text field with a Field Size of 30, which is a sufficient length for any title values that will be entered.

## To define the PositionTitle field:

1. Place the insertion point in the second row's Field Name text box, type **PositionTitle** in the text box, and then press the **Tab** key to advance to the Data Type text box.

2. Press the **Tab** key to accept Text as the field's data type.

According to Elsa's design (Figure 2-5), you do not need to enter a description for this field. If you've assigned a descriptive field name and the field does not fulfill a special function (such as primary key), you usually do not enter a value for the optional Description property. PositionTitle is a field that does not require a value for its Description property.

Next, you'll change the Field Size property to 30. Note that when defining the fields in a table, you can move between the Table Design grid and the Field Properties pane of the Table window by pressing the F6 key.

3. Press the **F6** key to move to the Field Properties pane. The current entry for the Field Size property, 50, is highlighted.

4. Type **30** to set the Field Size property. You have completed the definition of the second field.

The third field in the Position table is the EmployerID field. Recall that this field will serve as the foreign key in the Position table, allowing you to relate data from the Position table to data in the Employer table. The field must be defined in the same way in both tables—that is, a text field with a field size of 5.

## To define the EmployerID field:

1. Place the insertion point in the third row's Field Name text box, type **EmployerID** in the text box, and then press the **Tab** key to advance to the Data Type text box.

2. Press the **Tab** key to accept Text as the field's data type and to advance to the Description text box.

3. Type **Foreign key** in the Description text box.

4. Press the **F6** key to move to the Field Properties pane. The current entry for the Field Size property, 50, is highlighted.

5. Type **5** to set the Field Size property. You have completed the definition of the third field. See Figure 2-10.

| Figure 2-10 | TABLE WINDOW AFTER DEFINING THE FIRST THREE FIELDS |

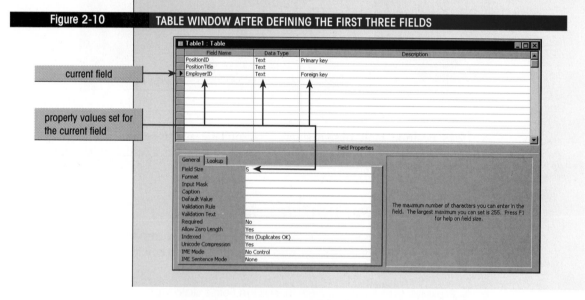

The fourth field is the Wage field, which will display values in the currency format.

## To define the Wage field:

1. Place the insertion point in the fourth row's Field Name text box, type **Wage** in the text box, and then press the **Tab** key to advance to the Data Type text box.

2. Click the **Data Type** list arrow, click **Currency** in the list box, and then press the **Tab** key to advance to the Description text box.

3. Type **Rate per hour** in the Description text box.

   Elsa wants the Wage field values to be displayed with two decimal places, and she does not want any value to be displayed by default for new records. So, you need to set the Decimal Places and Default Value properties accordingly.

4. Click the **Decimal Places** text box to position the insertion point there. A list arrow appears on the right side of the Decimal Places text box.

   When you position the insertion point or select text in many Access text boxes, Access displays a list arrow, which you can click to display a list box with options. You can display the list arrow and the list box simultaneously if you click the text box near its right side.

5. Click the **Decimal Places** list arrow, and then click **2** in the list box to specify two decimal places for the Wage field values.

   Next, notice the Default Value property, which specifies the value that will be automatically entered into the field when you add a new record. Currently this property has a setting of 0. Elsa wants the Wage field to be empty (that is, to contain *no* default value) when a new record is added. Therefore, you need to change the Default Value property to the setting "Null." Setting the Default Value property to "Null" tells Access to display no value in the Wage field, by default.

6. Select **0** in the Default Value text box either by dragging the pointer or double-clicking the mouse, and then type **Null**.

The next two fields in the Position table—Hours/Week and Openings—are number fields with a field size of Integer. Also, for each of these fields, Elsa wants the values displayed with no decimal places, and she does not want a default value displayed for the fields when new records are added. You'll define these two fields next.

## To define the Hours/Week and Openings fields:

1. Position the insertion point in the fifth row's Field Name text box, type **Hours/Week** in the text box, and then press the **Tab** key to advance to the Data Type text box.

2. Click the **Data Type** list arrow, click **Number** in the list box, and then press the **Tab** key to advance to the Description text box.

3. Type **Work hours per week** in the Description text box.

4. Click the right side of the **Field Size** text box, and then click **Integer** to choose this setting. Recall that the Integer field size stores whole numbers in two bytes.

5. Click the right side of the **Decimal Places** text box, and then click **0** to specify no decimal places.

6. Select the value **0** in the Default Value text box, and then type **Null**.

7. Repeat Steps 1 through 6 to define the **Openings** field as the sixth field in the Position table. For the Description, enter the text **Number of openings**.

According to Elsa's design (Figure 2-5), the final three fields to be defined in the Position table are ReferredBy, a text field, and StartDate and EndDate, both date/time fields. You'll define these three fields next.

## To define the ReferredBy, StartDate, and EndDate fields:

1. Position the insertion point in the seventh row's Field Name text box, type **ReferredBy** in the text box, press the **Tab** key to advance to the Data Type text box, and then press the **Tab** key again to accept the default Text data type.

2. Change the default Field Size of 50 to **30** for the ReferredBy field.

3. Position the insertion point in the eighth row's Field Name text box, type **StartDate**, and then press the **Tab** key to advance to the Data Type text box.

4. Click the **Data Type** list arrow, click **Date/Time** to select this type, press the **Tab** key, and then type **Month and day** in the Description text box.

   Elsa wants the values in the StartDate field to be displayed in a format showing only the month and day, as in the following example: 03/11. You use the Format property to control the display of a field value.

5. In the Field Properties pane, click the right side of the **Format** text box to display the list of predefined formats. As noted in the right side of the Field Properties pane, you can either choose a predefined format or enter a custom format.

   **TROUBLE?** If you see a list arrow instead of a list of predefined formats, click the list arrow to display the list.

   None of the predefined formats matches the layout Elsa wants for the StartDate values. Therefore, you need to create a custom date format. Figure 2-11 shows some of the symbols available for custom date and time formats. (A complete description of all the custom formats is available in Help.)

**Figure 2-11**   SYMBOLS FOR SOME CUSTOM DATE FORMATS

| SYMBOL | DESCRIPTION |
|---|---|
| / | date separator |
| d | day of the month in one or two numeric digits, as needed (1 to 31) |
| dd | day of the month in two numeric digits (01 to 31) |
| ddd | first three letters of the weekday (Sun to Sat) |
| dddd | full name of the weekday (Sunday to Saturday) |
| w | day of the week (1 to 7) |
| ww | week of the year (1 to 53) |
| m | month of the year in one or two numeric digits, as needed (1 to 12) |
| mm | month of the year in two numeric digits (01 to 12) |
| mmm | first three letters of the month (Jan to Dec) |
| mmmm | full name of the month (January to December) |
| yy | last two digits of the year (01 to 99) |
| yyyy | full year (0100 to 9999) |

Elsa wants the dates to be displayed with a two-digit month (mm) and a two-digit day (dd). You'll enter this custom format now.

6. Click the **Format** list arrow to close the list of predefined formats, and then type **mm/dd** in the Format text box. See Figure 2-12.

Figure 2-12 **SPECIFYING THE CUSTOM DATE FORMAT**

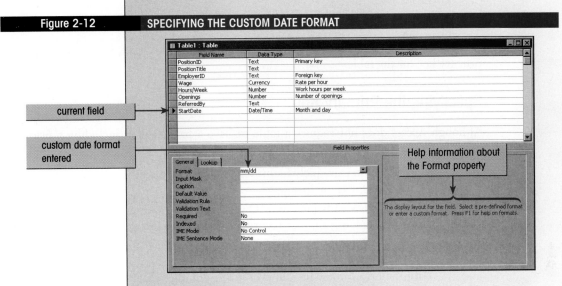

current field

custom date format entered

Next, you'll define the ninth and final field, EndDate. This field will have the same definition and properties as the StartDate field.

7. Place the insertion point in the ninth row's Field Name text box, type **EndDate**, and then press the **Tab** key to advance to the Data Type text box.

You can select a value from the Data Type list box as you did for the StartDate field. Alternately, you can type the property value in the text box or type just the first character of the property value.

8. Type **d**. The value in the ninth row's Data Type text box changes to "date/Time," with the letters "ate/Time" highlighted. See Figure 2-13.

Figure 2-13 **SELECTING A VALUE FOR THE DATA TYPE PROPERTY**

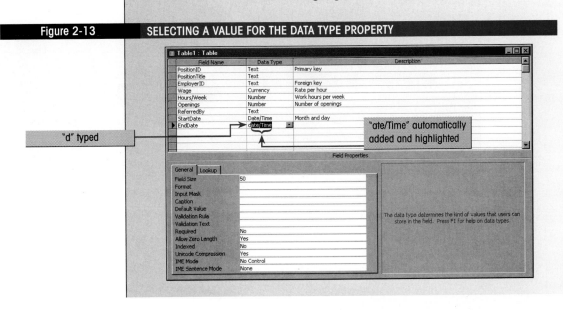

"d" typed

> **9.** Press the **Tab** key to advance to the Description text box, and then type **Month and day**. Note that Access changes the value for the Data Type property to Date/Time.
>
> **10.** In the Format text box, type **mm/dd** to specify the custom date format for the EndDate field.

You've finished defining the fields for the Position table. Next, you need to specify the primary key for the table.

## Specifying the Primary Key

Although Access does not require a table to have a primary key, including a primary key offers several advantages:

- A primary key uniquely identifies each record in a table.

- Access does not allow duplicate values in the primary key field. If a record already exists with a PositionID value of 1320, for example, Access prevents you from adding another record with this same value in the PositionID field. Preventing duplicate values ensures the uniqueness of the primary key field.

- When a primary key has been specified, Access forces you to enter a value for the primary key field in every record in the table. This is known as **entity integrity**. If you do not enter a value for a field, you have actually given the field what is known as a **null value**. You cannot give a null value to the primary key field because entity integrity prevents Access from accepting and processing that record.

- Access stores records on disk in the same order as you enter them but displays them in order by the field values of the primary key. If you enter records in no specific order, you are ensured that you will later be able to work with them in a more meaningful, primary key sequence.

- Access responds faster to your requests for specific records based on the primary key.

---

**REFERENCE WINDOW**                                                    **RW**

**Specifying a Primary Key for a Table**
- In the Table window in Design view, click the row selector for the field you've chosen to be the primary key.
- If the primary key will consist of two or more fields, press and hold down the Ctrl key, and then click the row selector for each additional primary key field.
- Click the Primary Key button on the Table Design toolbar.

---

According to Elsa's design, you need to specify PositionID as the primary key for the Position table.

## To specify PositionID as the primary key:

1. Position the pointer on the row selector for the PositionID field until the pointer changes to a ➡ shape. See Figure 2-14.

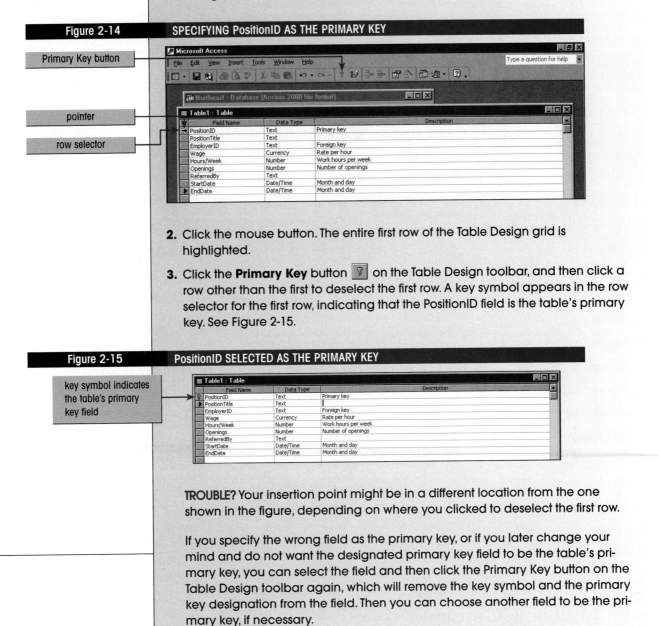

| Figure 2-14 | SPECIFYING PositionID AS THE PRIMARY KEY |

Primary Key button

pointer

row selector

2. Click the mouse button. The entire first row of the Table Design grid is highlighted.

3. Click the **Primary Key** button 🔑 on the Table Design toolbar, and then click a row other than the first to deselect the first row. A key symbol appears in the row selector for the first row, indicating that the PositionID field is the table's primary key. See Figure 2-15.

| Figure 2-15 | PositionID SELECTED AS THE PRIMARY KEY |

key symbol indicates the table's primary key field

**TROUBLE?** Your insertion point might be in a different location from the one shown in the figure, depending on where you clicked to deselect the first row.

If you specify the wrong field as the primary key, or if you later change your mind and do not want the designated primary key field to be the table's primary key, you can select the field and then click the Primary Key button on the Table Design toolbar again, which will remove the key symbol and the primary key designation from the field. Then you can choose another field to be the primary key, if necessary.

You've defined the fields for the Position table and specified its primary key, so you can now save the table structure.

## Saving the Table Structure

The last step in creating a table is to name the table and save the table's structure on disk. Once the table is saved, you can use it to enter data in the table.

> **REFERENCE    WINDOW**                                    **RW**
>
> Saving a Table Structure
> - Click the Save button on the Table Design toolbar.
> - Type the name of the table in the Table Name text box of the Save As dialog box.
> - Click the OK button (or press the Enter key).

According to Elsa's plan, you need to save the table you've defined as "Position."

### To name and save the Position table:

1. Click the **Save** button 🖫 on the Table Design toolbar. The Save As dialog box opens.

2. Type **Position** in the Table Name text box, and then press the **Enter** key. Access saves the table with the name Position in the Northeast database on your Data Disk. Notice that Position now appears instead of Table1 in the Table window title bar.

Recall that in Tutorial 1 you set the Compact on Close option for the Seasonal database so that it would be compacted automatically each time you closed it. Now you'll set this option for your new Northeast database, so that it will be compacted automatically.

### To set the option for compacting the Northeast database automatically:

1. Click **Tools** on the menu bar, and then click **Options**. The Options dialog box opens.

2. Click the **General** tab in the dialog box, and then click the **Compact on Close** check box to select it.

3. Click the **OK** button to set the option.

The Position table is now complete. In Session 2.2, you'll continue to work with the Position table by entering records in it, modifying its structure, and maintaining data in the table. You will also import two tables, Employer and NAICS, from the Seasonal database into the Northeast database.

## Session 2.1 QUICK CHECK

1. What guidelines should you follow when designing a database?

2. What is the purpose of the Data Type property for a field?

3. For which three types of fields can you assign a field size?

4. In Design view, which key do you press to move between the Table Design grid and the Field Properties pane?

5. You use the _____ property to control the display of a field value.

6. A(n) _____ value, which results when you do not enter a value for a field, is not permitted for a primary key.

---

**SESSION 2.2**

In this session, you will add records to a table; modify the structure of an existing table by deleting, moving, and adding fields and changing field properties; copy records from another Access database; import tables from another Access database; and update an existing database by deleting and changing records.

---

# Adding Records to a Table

You can add records to an Access table in several ways. A table datasheet provides a simple way for you to add records. As you learned in Tutorial 1, a datasheet shows a table's contents in rows and columns. Each row is a separate record in the table, and each column contains the field values for one field in the table. If you are currently working in Design view, you first must change from Design view to Datasheet view in order to view the table's datasheet.

Elsa asks you to add the two records shown in Figure 2-16 to the Position table. These two records contain data for positions that have recently become available at two employers.

| Figure 2-16 | RECORDS TO BE ADDED TO THE POSITION TABLE |
|---|---|

| PositionID | PositionTitle | EmployerID | Wage | Hours/Week | Openings | ReferredBy | StartDate | EndDate |
|---|---|---|---|---|---|---|---|---|
| 2021 | Waiter/Waitress | 10155 | 9.50 | 30 | 1 | Sue Brown | 6/30 | 9/15 |
| 2017 | Tour Guide | 10149 | 15.00 | 20 | 1 | Ed Curran | 9/21 | 11/1 |

---

### To add the records in the Position table datasheet:

1. If you took a break after the previous session, make sure that Access is running and that the Position table of the Northeast database is open in Design view. To open the table in Design view from the Database window, right-click the **Position** table, and then click **Design View** on the shortcut menu.

   Access displays the fields you defined for the Position table in Design view. Now you need to switch to Datasheet view so that you can enter the two records for Elsa.

2. Click the **View** button for Datasheet view 🖽 on the Table Design toolbar. The Table window opens in Datasheet view. See Figure 2-17.

**Figure 2-17**    TABLE WINDOW IN DATASHEET VIEW

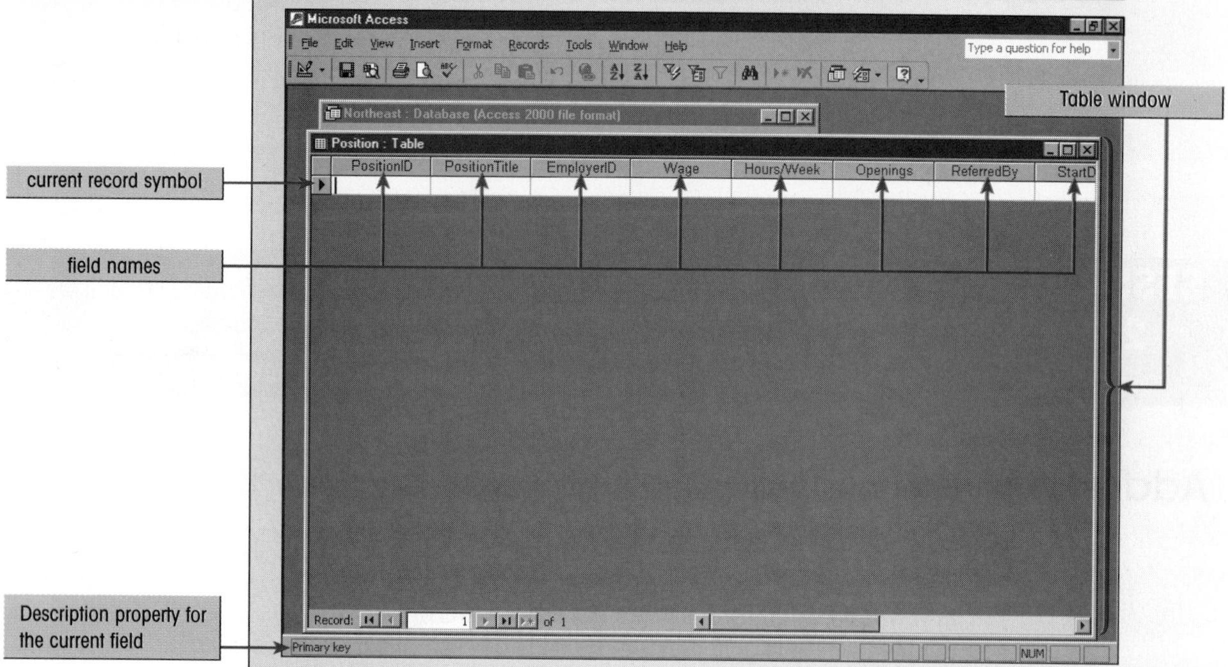

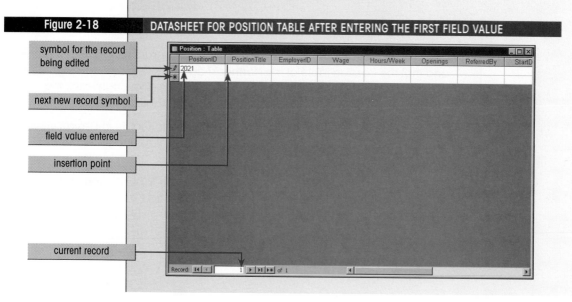

current record symbol

field names

Table window

Description property for
the current field

The table's nine field names appear at the top of the datasheet. Some of the
field names might not be visible. The current record symbol in the first row's
record selector identifies the currently selected record, which contains no data
until you enter the first record. The insertion point is located in the first row's
PositionID field, whose Description property appears on the status bar.

3. Type **2021**, which is the first record's PositionID field value, and then press the
**Tab** key. Each time you press the Tab key, the insertion point moves to the right
to the next field in the record. See Figure 2-18.

**Figure 2-18**    DATASHEET FOR POSITION TABLE AFTER ENTERING THE FIRST FIELD VALUE

symbol for the record
being edited

next new record symbol

field value entered

insertion point

current record

**TROUBLE?** If you make a mistake when typing a value, use the Backspace key to delete characters to the left of the insertion point or the Delete key to delete characters to the right of the insertion point. Then type the correct value. If you want to correct a value by replacing it entirely, double-click the value to select it, and then type the correct value.

The pencil symbol in the first row's record selector indicates that the record is being edited. The star symbol in the second row's record selector identifies the second row as the next one available for a new record. Notice that all the fields are initially empty; this occurs because you set the Default Value property for the fields (as appropriate) to Null.

4. Type **Waiter/Waitress** in the PositionTitle field, and then press the **Tab** key. The insertion point moves to the EmployerID field.

5. Type **10155** and then press the **Tab** key. The insertion point moves to the right side of the Wage field.

Recall that the PositionID, PositionTitle, and EmployerID fields are all text fields and that the Wage field is a currency field. Field values for text fields are left-aligned in their boxes, and field values for number, date/time, and currency fields are right-aligned in their boxes.

6. Type **9.5** and then press the **Tab** key. Access displays the field value with a dollar sign and two decimal places ($9.50), as specified by the currency format. You do not need to type the dollar sign, commas, or decimal point (for whole dollar amounts) because Access adds these symbols automatically for you.

7. In the Hours/Week field, type **30**, press the **Tab** key, type **1** in the Openings field, and then press the **Tab** key.

8. Type **Sue Brown** in the ReferredBy field, and then press the **Tab** key. Depending on your monitor's resolution and size, the display of the datasheet might shift so that the next field, StartDate, is completely visible.

9. Type **6/30** in the StartDate field, and then press the **Tab** key. Access displays the value as 06/30, as specified by the custom date format (mm/dd) you set for this field. The insertion point moves to the final field in the table, EndDate.

10. Type **9/15** in the EndDate field, and then press the **Tab** key. Access displays the value as 09/15, shifts the display of the datasheet back to the left, stores the first completed record in the Position table, removes the pencil symbol from the first row's record selector, advances the insertion point to the second row's PositionID text box, and places the current record symbol in the second row's record selector.

Now you can enter the values for the second record.

11. Refer to Figure 2-16, and repeat Steps 3 through 10 to add the second record to the table. Access saves the record in the Position table, and moves the insertion point to the beginning of the third row. See Figure 2-19.

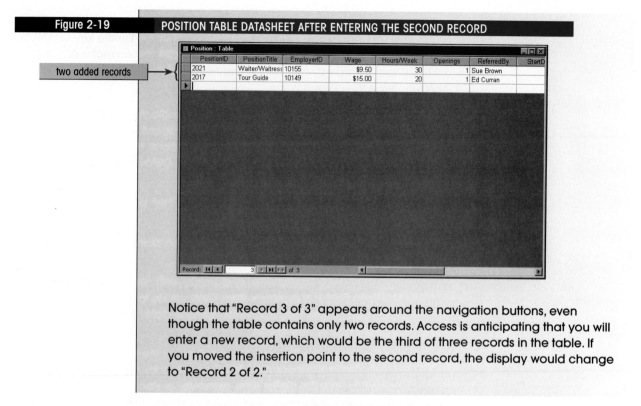

Figure 2-19    POSITION TABLE DATASHEET AFTER ENTERING THE SECOND RECORD

two added records

Notice that "Record 3 of 3" appears around the navigation buttons, even though the table contains only two records. Access is anticipating that you will enter a new record, which would be the third of three records in the table. If you moved the insertion point to the second record, the display would change to "Record 2 of 2."

Notice that the two records are currently listed in the order in which you entered them. However, once you close the table or change to another view, and then redisplay the table datasheet, the records will be listed in primary key order by the values in the PositionID field.

## Modifying the Structure of an Access Table

Even a well-designed table might need to be modified. For example, the government at all levels and competitors place demands on a company to track more data and to modify the data it already tracks. Access allows you to modify a table's structure in Design view: you can add and delete fields, change the order of fields, and change the properties of the fields.

After holding a meeting with her staff members and reviewing the structure of the Position table and the format of the field values in the datasheet, Elsa has several changes she wants you to make to the table. First, she has decided that it's not necessary to keep track of the name of the person who originally requested a particular position, so she wants you to delete the ReferredBy field. Also, she thinks that the Wage field should remain a currency field, but she wants the dollar signs removed from the displayed field values in the datasheet. She also wants the Openings field moved to the end of the table. Finally, she wants you to add a new yes/no field, named Experience, to the table to indicate whether the available position requires that potential recruits have prior experience in that type of work. The Experience field will be inserted between the Hours/Week and StartDate fields. Figure 2-20 shows Elsa's modified design for the Position table.

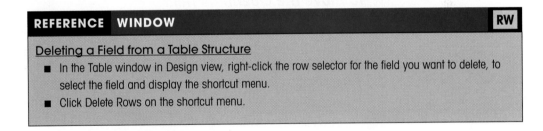

**Figure 2-20  MODIFIED DESIGN FOR THE POSITION TABLE**

| Field Name | Data Type | Field Size | Description |
|---|---|---|---|
| PositionID | Text | 4 | Primary key |
| PositionTitle | Text | 30 | |
| EmployerID | Text | 5 | Foreign key |
| Wage | Currency | | Rate per hour |
| Hours/Week | Number | Integer | Work hours per week |
| Experience | Yes/No | | Experience required |
| StartDate | Date/Time | | Month and day |
| EndDate | Date/Time | | Month and day |
| Openings | Number | Integer | Number of openings |

You'll begin modifying the table by deleting the ReferredBy field.

## Deleting a Field

After you've defined a table structure and added records to the table, you can delete a field from the table structure. When you delete a field, you also delete all the values for the field from the table. Therefore, you should make sure that you need to delete a field and that you delete the correct field.

**REFERENCE WINDOW**                                                     **RW**

**Deleting a Field from a Table Structure**
- In the Table window in Design view, right-click the row selector for the field you want to delete, to select the field and display the shortcut menu.
- Click Delete Rows on the shortcut menu.

You need to delete the ReferredBy field from the Position table structure.

**To delete the ReferredBy field:**

1. Click the **View** button for Design view on the Table Datasheet toolbar. The Table window for the Position table opens in Design view.

2. Position the pointer on the row selector for the ReferredBy field until the pointer changes to a ➡ shape.

3. Right-click to select the entire row for the ReferredBy field and display the shortcut menu, and then click **Delete Rows**.

   A dialog box opens asking you to confirm the deletion.

4. Click the **Yes** button to close the dialog box and to delete the field and its values from the table. See Figure 2-21.

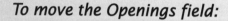

| Figure 2-21 | TABLE STRUCTURE AFTER DELETING ReferredBy FIELD |
|---|---|

**field was deleted from here**

| Field Name | Data Type | Description |
|---|---|---|
| PositionID | Text | Primary key |
| PositionTitle | Text | |
| EmployerID | Text | Foreign key |
| Wage | Currency | Rate per hour |
| Hours/Week | Number | Work hours per week |
| Openings | Number | Number of openings |
| StartDate | Date/Time | Month and day |
| EndDate | Date/Time | Month and day |

You have deleted the ReferredBy field in the Table window, but the change doesn't take place in the table on disk until you save the table structure. Because you have other modifications to make to the table, you'll wait until you finish them all before saving the modified table structure to disk.

## Moving a Field

To move a field, you use the mouse to drag it to a new location in the Table window in Design view. Your next modification to the Position table structure is to move the Openings field to the end of the table, as Elsa requested.

### To move the Openings field:

1. Click the **row selector** for the Openings field to select the entire row.

2. Place the pointer in the row selector for the Openings field, click the ↳ pointer, and then drag the ↳ pointer to the row selector below the EndDate row selector. See Figure 2-22.

| Figure 2-22 | MOVING A FIELD IN THE TABLE STRUCTURE |
|---|---|

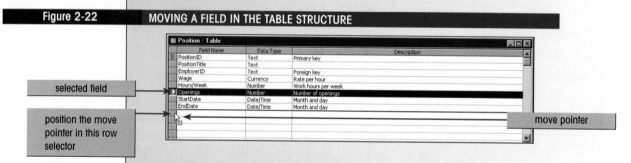

**selected field**

**position the move pointer in this row selector**

**move pointer**

3. Release the mouse button. Access moves the Openings field below the EndDate field in the table structure.

**TROUBLE?** If the Openings field did not move, repeat Steps 1 through 3, making sure you firmly hold down the mouse button during the drag operation.

## Adding a Field

Next, you need to add the Experience field to the table structure between the Hours/Week and StartDate fields. To add a new field between existing fields, you must insert a row. You begin by selecting the field that will be below the new field you want to insert.

## To add the Experience field to the Position table:

1. Right-click the **row selector** for the StartDate field to select this field and display the shortcut menu, and then click **Insert Rows**. Access adds a new, blank row between the Hours/Week and StartDate fields. See Figure 2-23.

**Figure 2-23**          AFTER INSERTING A ROW IN THE TABLE STRUCTURE

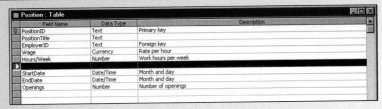

You'll define the Experience field in the new row of the Position table. Access will add this new field to the Position table structure between the Hours/Week and StartDate fields.

2. Click the **Field Name** text box for the new row, type **Experience**, and then press the **Tab** key.

The Experience field will be a yes/no field that will specify whether prior work experience is required for the position.

3. Type **y**. Access completes the data type as "yes/No."

4. Press the **Tab** key to select the yes/no data type and to move to the Description text box.

Notice that Access changes the value in the Data Type text box from "yes/No" to "Yes/No."

5. Type **Experience required** in the Description text box.

Elsa wants the Experience field to have a Default Value property value of "No," so you need to set this property.

6. In the Field Properties pane, click the **Default Value** text box, type **no**, and then click somewhere outside of the Default Value text box to deselect the value. Notice that Access changes the Default Value property value from "no" to "No." See Figure 2-24.

| Figure 2-24 | EXPERIENCE FIELD ADDED TO THE POSITION TABLE |

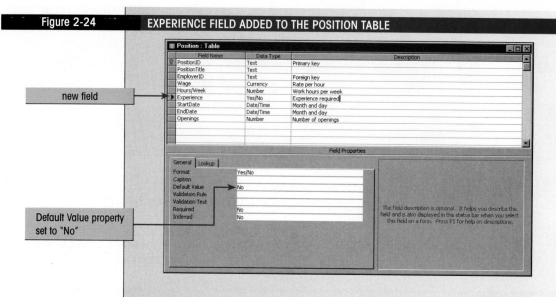

new field

Default Value property
set to "No"

**TROUBLE?** Your insertion point might be in a different location from the one shown in the figure, depending on where you clicked to deselect the value.

You've completed adding the Experience field to the Position table in Design view. As with the other changes you've made in Design view, however, the Experience field is not added to the Position table in the Northeast database until you save the changes to the table structure.

## Changing Field Properties

Elsa's last modification to the table structure is to remove the dollar signs from the Wage field values displayed in the datasheet—repeated dollar signs are unnecessary and they clutter the datasheet. As you learned earlier when defining the StartDate and EndDate fields, you use the Format property to control the display of a field value.

### To change the Format property of the Wage field:

1. Click the **Description** text box for the Wage field. The Wage field is now the current field.

2. Click the right side of the **Format** text box to display the Format list box. See Figure 2-25.

| Figure 2-25 | FORMAT LIST BOX FOR THE WAGE FIELD |
|---|---|

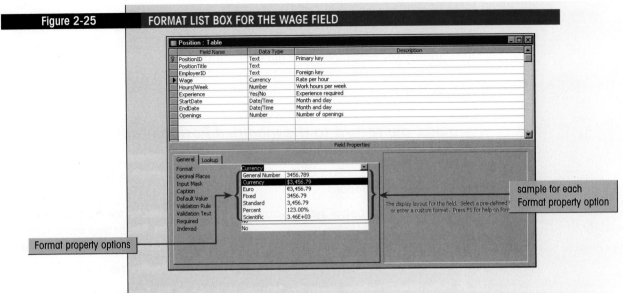

Format property options

sample for each Format property option

To the right of each Format property option is a field value whose appearance represents a sample of the option. The Standard option specifies the format Elsa wants for the Wage field.

**3.** Click **Standard** in the Format list box to accept this option for the Format property.

Elsa wants you to add a third record to the Position table datasheet. Before you can add the record, you must save the modified table structure, and then switch to the Position table datasheet.

### To save the modified table structure, and then switch to the datasheet:

**1.** Click the **Save** button 🖫 on the Table Design toolbar. The modified table structure for the Position table is stored in the Northeast database. Note that if you forget to save the modified structure and try to close the table or switch to another view, Access will prompt you to save the table before you can continue.

**2.** Click the **View** button for Datasheet view 🖽 on the Table Design toolbar. The Position table datasheet opens. See Figure 2-26.

| Figure 2-26 | DATASHEET FOR THE MODIFIED POSITION TABLE |
|---|---|

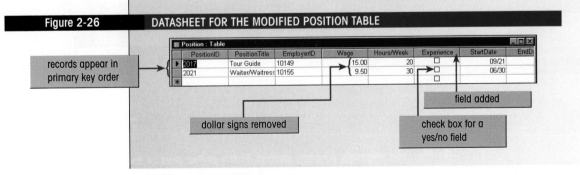

records appear in primary key order

dollar signs removed

field added

check box for a yes/no field

Notice that the ReferredBy field no longer appears in the datasheet, the Openings field is now the rightmost column (you might need to scroll the datasheet to see it), the Wage field values do not contain dollar signs, and the Experience field appears between the Hours/Week and StartDate fields. The Experience column contains check boxes to represent the yes/no field values. Empty check boxes signify "No," which is the default value you assigned to the Experience field. A check mark in the check box indicates a "Yes" value. Also notice that the records appear in ascending order based on the value in the PositionID field, the Position table's primary key, even though you did not enter the records in this order.

Elsa asks you to add a third record to the table. This record is for a position that requires prior work experience.

### To add the record to the modified Position table:

1. Click the **New Record** button ▶* on the Table Datasheet toolbar. The insertion point moves to the PositionID field for the third row, which is the next row available for a new record.

2. Type **2020**. The pencil symbol appears in the row selector for the third row, and the star appears in the row selector for the fourth row. Recall that these symbols represent a record being edited and the next available record, respectively.

3. Press the **Tab** key. The insertion point moves to the PositionTitle field.

4. Type **Host/Hostess**, press the **Tab** key to move to the EmployerID field, type **10163**, and then press the **Tab** key. The Wage field is now the current field.

5. Type **18.5** and then press the **Tab** key. Access displays the value as "18.50" (with no dollar sign).

6. Type **32** in the Hours/Week field, and then press the **Tab** key. The Experience field is now the current field.

   Recall that the default value for this field is "No," which means the check box is initially empty. For yes/no fields with check boxes, you press the Tab key to leave the check box unchecked; you press the spacebar or click the check box to add or remove a check mark in the check box. Because this position requires experience, you need to insert a check mark in the check box.

7. Press the **spacebar**. A check mark appears in the check box.

8. Press the **Tab** key, type **6/15** in the StartDate field, press the **Tab** key, and then type **10/1** in the EndDate field.

9. Press the **Tab** key, type **1** in the Openings field, and then press the **Tab** key. Access saves the record in the Position table and moves the insertion point to the beginning of the fourth row. See Figure 2-27.

| Figure 2-27 | POSITION TABLE DATASHEET WITH THIRD RECORD ADDED |

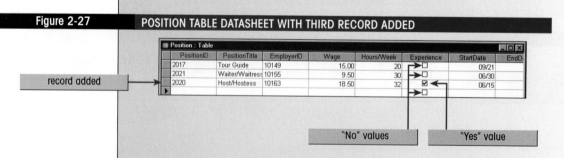

As you add records, Access places them at the end of the datasheet. If you switch to Design view and then return to the datasheet, or if you close the table and then open the datasheet, Access will display the records in primary key sequence.

For many of the fields, the columns are wider than necessary for the field values. You can resize the datasheet columns so that they are only as wide as needed to display the longest value in the column, including the field name. Resizing datasheet columns to their best fit improves the display of the datasheet and allows you to view more fields at the same time.

## To resize the Position datasheet columns to their best fit:

1. Place the pointer on the line between the PositionID and PositionTitle field names until the pointer changes to a ➕ shape.

2. Double-click the pointer. The PositionID column is resized so that it is only as wide as the longest value in the column (the field name, in this case).

3. Double-click the ➕ pointer on the line to the right of each remaining field name to resize all the columns in the datasheet to their best fit. See Figure 2-28.

| Figure 2-28 | DATASHEET AFTER RESIZING ALL COLUMNS TO THEIR BEST FIT |

| PositionID | PositionTitle | EmployerID | Wage | Hours/Week | Experience | StartDate | EndDate | Openings |
|---|---|---|---|---|---|---|---|---|
| 2017 | Tour Guide | 10149 | 15.00 | 20 | ☐ | 09/21 | 11/01 | 1 |
| 2020 | Host/Hostess | 10163 | 18.50 | 32 | ☑ | 06/15 | 10/01 | 1 |
| 2021 | Waiter/Waitress | 10155 | 9.50 | 30 | ☐ | 06/30 | 09/15 | 1 |

Notice that all nine fields in the Position table are now visible in the datasheet.

You have modified the Position table structure and added one record. Next you need to obtain the rest of the records for this table from another database, and then import the two tables from the Seasonal database (Employer and NAICS) into your Northeast database.

# Obtaining Data from Another Access Database

Sometimes the data you need for your database might already exist in another Access database. You can save time in obtaining this data by copying and pasting records from one database table into another or by importing an entire table from one database into another.

## Copying Records from Another Access Database

You can copy and paste records from a table in the same database or in a different database only if the tables have the same structure—that is, the tables contain the same fields in the same order. Elsa's NEJobs database in the Tutorial folder on your Data Disk has a table named Available Positions that has the same table structure as the Position table. The records in the Available Positions table are the records Elsa wants you to copy into the Position table.

Other programs, such as Microsoft Word and Microsoft Excel, allow you to have two or more documents open at a time. However, you can have only one Access database open at a time. Therefore, you need to close the Northeast database, open the Available Positions table in the NEJobs database, select and copy the table records, close the NEJobs database, reopen the Position table in the Northeast database, and then paste the copied records. (*Note*: If you have a database open and then open a second database, Access will automatically close the first database for you.)

## To copy the records from the Available Positions table:

1. Click the **Close** button ☒ on the Table window title bar to close the Position table. A message box opens asking if you want to save the changes to the layout of the Position table. This box appears because you resized the datasheet columns to their best fit.

2. Click the **Yes** button in the message box.

3. Click ☒ on the Database window title bar to close the Northeast database.

4. Click the **Open** button 🖝 on the Database toolbar to display the Open dialog box.

5. If necessary, display the list of files on your Data Disk, and then open the **Tutorial** folder.

6. Open the database file named **NEJobs**. The Database window opens. Notice that the NEJobs database contains only one table, the Available Positions table. This table contains the records you need to copy.

7. Click **Available Positions** in the Tables list box (if necessary), and then click the **Open** button in the Database window. The datasheet for the Available Positions table opens. See Figure 2-29. Note that this table contains a total of 62 records.

| Figure 2-29 | DATASHEET FOR THE NEJobs DATABASE'S AVAILABLE POSITIONS TABLE |

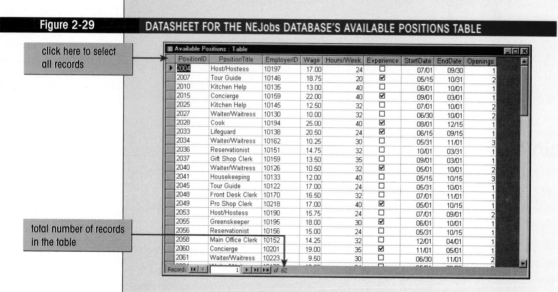

click here to select all records

total number of records in the table

Elsa wants you to copy all the records in the Available Positions table. You can select all records by clicking the row selector for the field name row.

8. Click the **row selector** for the field name row (see Figure 2-29). All the records in the table are now highlighted, which means that Access has selected all of them.

9. Click the **Copy** button 🗈 on the Table Datasheet toolbar. All the records are copied to the Windows Clipboard.

**TROUBLE?** If a Clipboard panel opens in the Task Pane, click its Close button to close it, and then continue with Step 10.

10. Click ☒ on the Table window title bar. A dialog box opens asking if you want to save the data you copied to the Windows Clipboard.

**11.** Click the **Yes** button in the dialog box. The dialog box closes, and then the table closes.

**12.** Click [X] on the Database window title bar to close the NEJobs database.

To finish copying and pasting the records, you must open the Position table and paste the copied records into the table.

## To paste the copied records into the Position table:

**1.** Click **File** on the menu bar, and then click **Northeast** in the list of recently opened databases. The Database window opens, showing the tables for the Northeast database.

**2.** In the Tables list box, click **Position** (if necessary), and then click the **Open** button in the Database window. The datasheet for the Position table opens.

You must paste the records at the end of the table.

**3.** Click the **row selector** for row four, which is the next row available for a new record.

**4.** Click the **Paste** button [📋] on the Table Datasheet toolbar. A dialog box opens asking if you are sure you want to paste the records (62 in all).

**5.** Click the **Yes** button. All the records are pasted from the Windows Clipboard, and the pasted records remain highlighted. See Figure 2-30. Notice that the table now contains a total of 65 records—the three original records plus the 62 copied records.

| Figure 2-30 | TABLE AFTER COPYING AND PASTING RECORDS |
| --- | --- |

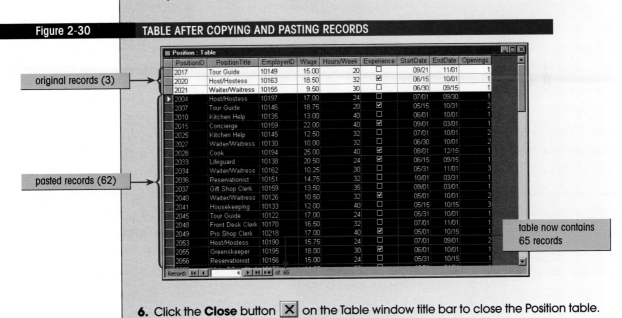

original records (3)

pasted records (62)

table now contains 65 records

**6.** Click the **Close** button [X] on the Table window title bar to close the Position table.

## Importing a Table from Another Access Database

When you import a table from one Access database to another, you place a copy of the table—including its structure, field definitions, and field values—in the database into which you import it. There are two ways to import a table from another Access database into your current database: using the Get External Data option on the File menu, or using the Import Table Wizard, which is available in the New Table dialog box. You'll use both methods to import the two tables from the Seasonal database into your Northeast database.

### To import the Employer and NAICS tables:

1. Make sure the Northeast Database window is open on your screen.

2. Click **File** on the menu bar, position the pointer on the double-arrow at the bottom of the File menu to display the full menu (if necessary), point to **Get External Data**, and then click **Import**. The Import dialog box opens. This dialog box is similar to the Open dialog box.

3. Display the list of files in your Tutorial folder, click **Seasonal**, and then click the **Import** button. The Import Objects dialog box opens. See Figure 2-31.

| Figure 2-31 | IMPORT OBJECTS DIALOG BOX |

table objects in the Seasonal database

The Tables tab of the dialog box lists both tables in the Seasonal database—Employer and NAICS. Note that you can import other objects as well (queries, forms, reports, and so on).

4. Click **Employer** in the list of tables, and then click the **OK** button. The Import Objects dialog box closes, and the Employer table is now listed in the Northeast Database window.

Now you'll use the Import Table Wizard to import the NAICS table. (Note that you could also use the Select All button in the Import Objects dialog box to import all the objects listed on the current tab at the same time.)

5. Click the **New** button in the Database window, click **Import Table** in the New Table dialog box, and then click the **OK** button. The Import dialog box opens.

6. If necessary, display the list of files in your Tutorial folder, click **Seasonal**, and then click the **Import** button. The Import Objects dialog box opens, again displaying the tables in the Seasonal database.

7. Click **NAICS** in the list of tables, and then click the **OK** button to import the NAICS table into the Northeast database.

Now that you have all the records in the Position table and all three tables in the Northeast database, Elsa examines the records to make sure they are correct. She finds one record in the Position table that she wants you to delete and another record that needs changes to its field values.

# Updating a Database

**Updating**, or **maintaining**, a database is the process of adding, changing, and deleting records in database tables to keep them current and accurate. You've already added records to the Position table. Now Elsa wants you to delete and change records.

## Deleting Records

To delete a record, you need to select the record in Datasheet view, and then delete it using the Delete Record button on the Table Datasheet toolbar or the Delete Record option on the shortcut menu.

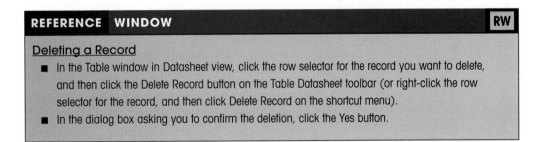

**REFERENCE WINDOW**                                                    **RW**

### Deleting a Record
- In the Table window in Datasheet view, click the row selector for the record you want to delete, and then click the Delete Record button on the Table Datasheet toolbar (or right-click the row selector for the record, and then click Delete Record on the shortcut menu).
- In the dialog box asking you to confirm the deletion, click the Yes button.

Elsa asks you to delete the record whose PositionID is 2015 because this record was entered in error; the position for this record does not exist. The fourth record in the table has a PositionID value of 2015. This record is the one you need to delete.

### To delete the record:

**1.** Open the Position table in Datasheet view.

**2.** Right-click the **row selector** for row four. Access selects the fourth record and displays the shortcut menu. See Figure 2-32.

**Figure 2-32**         **DELETING A RECORD**

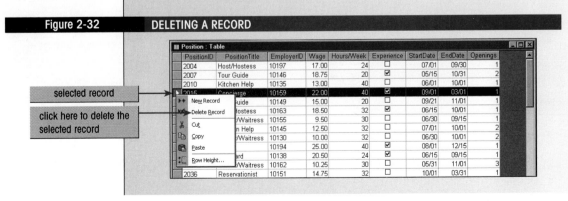

**3.** Click **Delete Record** on the shortcut menu. Access deletes the record and opens a dialog box asking you to confirm the deletion. Because the deletion of a record is permanent and cannot be undone, Access prompts you to make sure that you want to delete the record.

**TROUBLE?** If you selected the wrong record for deletion, click the No button. Access ends the deletion process and continues to display the selected record. Repeat Steps 2 and 3 to delete the correct record.

**4.** Click the **Yes** button to confirm the deletion and close the dialog box.

Elsa's final update to the Position table involves changes to field values in one of the records.

## Changing Records

To change the field values in a record, you first must make the record the current record. Then you position the insertion point in the field value to make minor changes or select the field value to replace it entirely. In Tutorial 1, you used the mouse with the scroll bars and the navigation buttons to navigate through the records in a datasheet. You can also use keystroke combinations and the F2 key to navigate a datasheet and to select field values.

The **F2 key** is a toggle that you use to switch between navigation mode and editing mode:

- In **navigation mode**, Access selects an entire field value. If you type while you are in navigation mode, your typed entry replaces the highlighted field value.

- In **editing mode**, you can insert or delete characters in a field value based on the location of the insertion point.

Figure 2-33 shows some of the navigation mode and editing mode keystroke techniques.

| Figure 2-33 | NAVIGATION MODE AND EDITING MODE KEYSTROKE TECHNIQUES | |
|---|---|---|
| **PRESS** | **TO MOVE THE SELECTION IN NAVIGATION MODE** | **TO MOVE THE INSERTION POINT IN EDITING MODE** |
| ← | Left one field value at a time | Left one character at a time |
| → | Right one field value at a time | Right one character at a time |
| Home | Left to the first field value in the record | To the left of the first character in the field value |
| End | Right to the last field value in the record | To the right of the last character in the field value |
| ↑ or ↓ | Up or down one record at a time | Up or down one record at a time and switch to navigation mode |
| Tab or Enter | Right one field value at a time | Right one field value at a time and switch to navigation mode |
| Ctrl + Home | To the first field value in the first record | To the left of the first character in the field value |
| Ctrl + End | To the last field value in the last record | To the right of the last character in the field value |

The record Elsa wants you to change has a PositionID field value of 2125. Some of the values were entered incorrectly for this record, and you need to enter the correct values.

## To modify the record:

1. Make sure the PositionID field value for the fourth record is still highlighted, indicating that the table is in navigation mode.

2. Press **Ctrl + End**. Access displays records from the end of the table and selects the last field value in the last record. This field value is for the Openings field.

3. Press the **Home** key. The first field value in the last record is now selected. This field value is for the PositionID field.

4. Press the ↑ key. The PositionID field value for the previous record (PositionID 2125) is selected. This record is the one you need to change.

   Elsa wants you to change these field values in the record: PositionID to 2124, EmployerID to 10163, Wage to 14.50, Experience to "Yes" (checked), and EndDate to 10/15.

5. Type **2124**, press the **Tab** key twice, type **10163**, press the **Tab** key, type **14.5**, press the **Tab** key twice, press the **spacebar** to insert a check mark in the Experience check box, press the **Tab** key twice, and then type **10/15**. The changes to the record are complete. See Figure 2-34.

| Figure 2-34 | TABLE AFTER CHANGING FIELD VALUES IN A RECORD |
|---|---|

field values changed

| | | | | | | | | |
|---|---|---|---|---|---|---|---|---|
| 2115 | Gift Shop Clerk | 10154 | 13.00 | 25 | ☐ | 05/01 | 09/30 | 1 |
| 2117 | Housekeeping | 10220 | 13.50 | 30 | ☐ | 06/30 | 09/30 | 3 |
| 2118 | Greenskeeper | 10218 | 17.00 | 32 | ☐ | 05/01 | 11/01 | 1 |
| 2120 | Lifeguard | 10154 | 19.00 | 32 | ☑ | 06/15 | 09/30 | 2 |
| 2122 | Kitchen Help | 10151 | 13.00 | 35 | ☐ | 09/01 | 03/31 | 3 |
| 2123 | Main Office Clerk | 10170 | 14.50 | 32 | ☐ | 07/01 | 11/15 | 1 |
| 2124 | Kitchen Help | 10163 | 14.50 | 40 | ☑ | 06/01 | 10/15 | 2 |
| 2127 | Waiter/Waitress | 10185 | 10.50 | 40 | ☐ | 12/01 | 05/01 | 1 |

Record: 14 ◄ | 63 ► ►I ►* of 64

You've completed all of Elsa's updates to the Position table. Now you can exit Access.

6. Click the **Close** button ⊠ on the Access window title bar to close the Position table and the Northeast database, and to exit Access.

Elsa and her staff members approve of the revised table structure for the Position table. They are confident that the table will allow them to easily track position data for NSJI's employer customers.

# Session 2.2 QUICK CHECK

1. What does a pencil symbol in a datasheet's row selector represent? A star symbol?

2. What is the effect of deleting a field from a table structure?

3. How do you insert a field between existing fields in a table structure?

4. A field with the _____ data type can appear in the table datasheet as a check box.

5. Describe the two ways in which you can display the Import dialog box, so that you can import a table from one Access database to another.

6. In Datasheet view, what is the difference between navigation mode and editing mode?

## REVIEW ASSIGNMENTS

Elsa needs a database to track data about the students recruited by NSJI and about the recruiters who find jobs for the students. She asks you to create the database by completing the following:

1. Make sure your Data Disk is in the appropriate disk drive, and then start Access.

2. Create a new, blank database named **Recruits** and save it in the Review folder on your Data Disk.

*Explore*

3. Use the Table Wizard to create a new table named **Recruiter** in the **Recruits** database, as follows:

   a. Base the new table on the Employees sample table, which is one of the sample tables in the Business category.

   b. Add the following fields to your table (in the order shown): SocialSecurityNumber, Salary, FirstName, MiddleName, and LastName.

   c. Click SocialSecurityNumber in the "Fields in my new table" list, and then use the Rename Field button to change the name of this field to SSN. Click the Next button.

   d. Name the new table **Recruiter**, and choose the option for setting the primary key yourself. Click the Next button.

   e. Specify SSN as the primary key field and accept the default data type. Click the Next button.

   f. In the final Table Wizard dialog box, click the Finish button to display the table in Datasheet view. (*Note:* The field names appear with spaces between words; this is how the Table Wizard is set up to format these field names when they appear in Datasheet view.)

4. Add the recruiter records shown in Figure 2-35 to the **Recruiter** table. (*Note:* You do not have to type the dashes in the SSN field values or commas in the Salary field values; the Table Wizard formatted these fields so that these symbols are entered automatically for you.)

**Figure 2-35**

| SSN | Salary | First Name | Middle Name | Last Name |
|-----|--------|-----------|-------------|-----------|
| 892-77-1201 | 40,000 | Kate | Teresa | Foster |
| 901-63-1554 | 38,500 | Paul | Michael | Kirnicki |
| 893-91-0178 | 40,000 | Ryan | James | DuBrava |

5. Make the following changes to the structure of the **Recruiter** table:

   a. Move the Salary field so that it appears after the LastName field.

   b. Add a new field between the LastName and Salary fields, using the following properties:

   | | |
   |---|---|
   | Field Name: | BonusQuota |
   | Data Type: | Number |
   | Description: | Number of recruited students needed to receive bonus |
   | Field Size: | Byte |
   | Decimal Places: | 0 |

   c. Change the format of the Salary field so that commas are displayed, dollar signs are not displayed, and no decimal places are displayed in the field values.

   d. Save the revised table structure.

6. Use the **Recruiter** datasheet to update the database as follows:

   a. Enter these BonusQuota values for the three records: 60 for Kate Foster; 60 for Ryan DuBrava; and 50 for Paul Kirnicki.

   b. Add a record to the **Recruiter** datasheet with the following field values:

   | | |
   |---|---|
   | SSN: | 899-40-2937 |
   | First Name: | Sonia |
   | Middle Name: | Lee |
   | Last Name: | Xu |
   | BonusQuota: | 50 |
   | Salary: | 39,250 |

7. Close the **Recruiter** table, and then set the option for compacting the **Recruits** database on close.
8. Elsa created a database with her name as the database name. The **Recruiter Employees** table in that database has the same format as the **Recruiter** table you created. Copy all the records from the **Recruiter Employees** table in the **Elsa** database (located in the Review folder on your Data Disk) to the end of the **Recruiter** table in the **Recruits** database.

*Explore*
9. Because you added a number of records to the database, its size has increased. Compact the database manually using the Compact and Repair Database option.
10. Delete the MiddleName field from the **Recruiter** table structure, and then save the table structure.
11. Resize all columns in the datasheet for the **Recruiter** table to their best fit.
12. Print the **Recruiter** table datasheet, and then save and close the table.
13. Create a table named **Student** using the Import Table Wizard. The table you need to import is named **Student**, which is one of the tables in the **Elsa** database located in the Review folder on your Data Disk.
14. Make the following modifications to the structure of the **Student** table in the **Recruits** database:
    a. Enter the following Description property values:
       StudentID:           Primary key
       SSN:                 Foreign key value of the recruiter for this student
    b. Change the Field Size property for both the FirstName field and the LastName field to 15.
    c. Move the BirthDate field so that it appears between the Nation and Gender fields.
    d. Change the format of the BirthDate field so that it displays only two digits for the year instead of four.
    e. Save the table structure changes. (Answer "Yes" to any warning messages about property changes and lost data.)
15. Switch to Datasheet view, and then resize all columns in the datasheet to fit the data.
16. Delete the record with the StudentID DRI9901 from the **Student** table.
17. Save, print, and then close the **Student** datasheet.
18. Close the **Recruits** database, and then exit Access.

## CASE PROBLEMS

*Case 1. Lim's Video Photography*  Youngho Lim uses the **Videos** database to maintain information about the clients, contracts, and events for his video photography business. Youngho asks you to help him maintain the database by completing the following:
1. Make sure your Data Disk is in the appropriate disk drive.
2. Start Access and open the **Videos** database located in the Cases folder on your Data Disk.

*Explore*
3. Use Design view to create a table using the table design shown in Figure 2-36.

**Figure 2-36**

| Field Name | Data Type | Description | Field Size | Other Properties |
|---|---|---|---|---|
| Shoot# | Number | Primary key | Long Integer | Decimal Places: 0<br>Default Value: Null |
| ShootType | Text | | 2 | |
| ShootTime | Date/Time | | | Format: Medium Time |
| Duration | Number | # of hours | Single | Default Value: Null |
| Contact | Text | Person who booked shoot | 30 | |
| Location | Text | | 30 | |
| ShootDate | Date/Time | | | Format: mm/dd/yyyy |
| Contract# | Number | Foreign key | Integer | Decimal Places: 0<br>Default Value: Null |

4. Specify Shoot# as the primary key, and then save the table as **Shoot**.

5. Add the records shown in Figure 2-37 to the **Shoot** table.

| Figure 2-37 |
|---|

| Shoot# | ShootType | ShootTime | Duration | Contact | Location | ShootDate | Contract# |
|---|---|---|---|---|---|---|---|
| 927032 | AP | 4:00 PM | 3.5 | Ellen Quirk | Elm Lodge | 9/27/2003 | 2412 |
| 103031 | HP | 9:00 AM | 3.5 | Tom Bradbury | Client's home | 10/30/2003 | 2611 |

6. Youngho created a database named **Events** that contains a table with shoot data named **Shoot Events**. The **Shoot** table you created has the same format as the **Shoot Events** table. Copy all the records from the **Shoot Events** table in the **Events** database (located in the Cases folder on your Data Disk) to the end of the **Shoot** table in the **Videos** database.

7. Modify the structure of the **Shoot** table by completing the following:

    a. Delete the Contact field.

    b. Move the ShootDate field so that it appears between the ShootType and ShootTime fields.

8. Switch to Datasheet view and resize all columns in the datasheet for the **Shoot** table to their best fit.

9. Use the **Shoot** datasheet to update the database as follows:

    a. For Shoot# 421032, change the ShootTime value to 7:00 PM, and change the Location value to Le Bistro.

    b. Add a record to the **Shoot** datasheet with the following field values:

    Shoot#:        913032
    ShootType:    SE
    ShootDate:    9/13/2003
    ShootTime:    1:00 PM
    Duration:      2.5
    Location:      High School football field
    Contract#:    2501

10. Switch to Design view, and then switch back to Datasheet view so that the records appear in primary key sequence by Shoot#. Resize any datasheet columns to their best fit, as necessary.

11. Print the **Shoot** table datasheet, and then save and close the table.

**Explore** ▶ 12. Create a table named **ShootDesc**, based on the data shown in Figure 2-38 and according to the following steps:

| Figure 2-38 |
|---|

| ShootType | ShootDesc |
|---|---|
| AP | Anniversary Party |
| BM | Bar/Bat Mitzvah |
| BP | Birthday Party |
| CP | Insurance Commercial Property |
| DR | Dance Recital |
| GR | Graduation |
| HP | Insurance Home Property |
| LS | Legal Services |
| RC | Religious Ceremony |
| SE | Sports Event |
| WE | Wedding |

    a. Select the Datasheet View option in the New Table dialog box.

    b. Enter the 11 records shown in Figure 2-38. (Do *not* enter the field names at this point.)

    c. Switch to Design view, supply the table name, and then answer "No" if asked if you want to create a primary key.

   d. Type the following field names and set the following properties for the two text fields:

ShootType

| | |
|---|---|
| Description: | Primary key |
| Field Size: | 2 |

ShootDesc

| | |
|---|---|
| Description: | Description of shoot |
| Field Size: | 30 |

   e. Specify the primary key, save the table structure changes, and then switch back to Datasheet view. If you receive any warning messages, answer "Yes" to continue.

   f. Resize both datasheet columns to their best fit; then save, print, and close the datasheet.

13. Close the **Videos** database, and then exit Access.

*Case 2. DineAtHome.course.com*  Claire Picard uses the **Meals** database to track information about local restaurants and orders placed at the restaurants by the customers of her e-commerce business. You'll help her maintain this database by completing the following:

1. Make sure your Data Disk is in the appropriate disk drive.

2. Start Access and open the **Meals** database located in the Cases folder on your Data Disk.

3. Use Design view to create a table using the table design shown in Figure 2-39.

**Figure 2-39**

| Field Name | Data Type | Description | Field Size | Other Properties |
|---|---|---|---|---|
| Order# | Number | Primary key | Long Integer | Decimal Places: 0<br>Default Value: Null |
| Restaurant# | Number | Foreign key | Long Integer | Decimal Places: 0 |
| OrderAmt | Currency | Total amount of order | | Format: Fixed |

4. Specify Order# as the primary key, and then save the table as **Order**.

5. Add the records shown in Figure 2-40 to the **Order** table.

**Figure 2-40**

| Order# | Restaurant# | OrderAmt |
|---|---|---|
| 3117 | 131 | 155.35 |
| 3123 | 115 | 45.42 |
| 3020 | 120 | 85.50 |

**Explore**

6. Modify the structure of the **Order** table by adding a new field between the Restaurant# and OrderAmt fields, with the following properties:

| | |
|---|---|
| Field Name: | OrderDate |
| Data Type: | Date/Time |
| Format: | Long Date |

7. Use the revised **Order** datasheet to update the database as follows:

   a. Enter the following OrderDate values for the three records: 1/15/03 for Order# 3020, 4/2/03 for Order# 3117, and 5/1/03 for Order# 3123.

   b. Add a new record to the **Order** datasheet with the following field values:

| | |
|---|---|
| Order#: | 3045 |
| Restaurant#: | 108 |
| OrderDate: | 3/16/03 |
| OrderAmt: | 50.25 |

8. Claire created a database named **Customer** that contains a table with order data named **Order Records**. The **Order** table you created has the same format as the **Order Records** table. Copy all the records from the **Order Records** table in the **Customer** database (located in the Cases folder on your Data Disk) to the end of the **Order** table in the **Meals** database.

9. Resize all columns in the datasheet for the **Order** table to their best fit.

10. For Order# 3039, change the OrderAmt value to 87.30.

11. Delete the record for Order# 3068.

12. Print the **Order** table datasheet, and then save and close the table.

13. Close the **Meals** database, and then exit Access.

*Case 3. Redwood Zoo*  Michael Rosenfeld continues to track information about donors, their pledges, and the status of funds to benefit the Redwood Zoo. Help him maintain the **Redwood** database by completing the following:

1. Make sure your Data Disk is in the appropriate disk drive.

2. Start Access and open the **Redwood** database located in the Cases folder on your Data Disk.

3. Create a table named **Pledge** using the Import Table Wizard. The table you need to import is named **Pledge Records**, which is located in the **Pledge** database in the Cases folder on your Data Disk.

*Explore* ▷ 4. After importing the **Pledge Records** table, use the shortcut menu to rename the table to **Pledge** in the Database window.

*Explore* ▷ 5. Modify the structure of the **Pledge** table by completing the following:

    a. Enter the following Description property values:

| | |
|---|---|
| Pledge#: | Primary key |
| DonorID: | Foreign key |
| FundCode: | Foreign key |

    b. Change the format of the PledgeDate field to mm/dd/yyyy.

    c. Change the Data Type of the TotalPledged field to Currency with the Standard format.

    d. Specify a Default Value of B for the PaymentMethod field.

    e. Specify a Default Value of F for the PaymentSchedule field.

    f. Save the modified table structure.

6. Switch to Datasheet view, and then resize all columns in the datasheet to their best fit.

7. Use the **Pledge** datasheet to update the database as follows:

    a. Add a new record to the **Pledge** table with the following field values:

| | |
|---|---|
| Pledge#: | 2695 |
| DonorID: | 59045 |
| FundCode: | P15 |
| PledgeDate: | 7/11/2003 |
| TotalPledged: | 1000 |
| PaymentMethod: | B |
| PaymentSchedule: | M |

    b. Change the TotalPledged value for Pledge# 2499 to 150.

    c. Change the FundCode value for Pledge# 2332 to B03.

8. Print the **Pledge** table datasheet, and then save and close the table.

9. Close the **Redwood** database, and then exit Access.

*Case 4. Mountain River Adventures*  Connor and Siobhan Dempsey use the **Trips** database to track the data about the guided tours they provide. You'll help them maintain this database by completing the following:

1. Make sure your Data Disk is in the appropriate disk drive.

2. Start Access and open the **Trips** database located in the Cases folder on your Data Disk.

*Explore* ▷ 3. Use the Import Spreadsheet Wizard to create a new table named **Rafting Trip**. The data you need to import is contained in the **Rafting** workbook, which is a Microsoft Excel file located in the Cases folder on your Data Disk.

    a. Select the Import Table option in the New Table dialog box.

    b. Change the entry in the Files of type list box to display the list of Excel workbook files in the Cases folder.

c. Select the **Rafting** file and then click the Import button.

d. In the Import Spreadsheet Wizard dialog boxes, choose the Sheet1 worksheet; choose the option for using column headings as field names; select the option for choosing your own primary key; specify Trip# as the primary key; and enter the table name (**Rafting Trip**). Otherwise, accept the Wizard's choices for all other options for the imported data.

4. Open the **Rafting Trip** table and resize all datasheet columns to their best fit.

5. Modify the structure of the **Rafting Trip** table by completing the following:

   a. For the Trip# field, enter a Description property of "Primary key", change the Field Size to Long Integer, and set the Decimal Places property to 0.

   b. For the River field, change the Field Size to 45.

   c. For the TripDistance field, enter a Description property of "Distance in miles", change the Field Size to Integer, and set the Decimal Places property to 0.

   d. For the TripDays field, enter a Description property of "Number of days for the trip", and change the Field Size to Single.

   e. For the Fee/Person field, change the Data Type to Currency and set the Format property to Fixed.

   f. Save the table structure. If you receive any warning messages about lost data or integrity rules, click the Yes button.

6. Use the **Rafting Trip** datasheet to update the database as follows:

   a. For Trip# 3142, change the TripDistance value to 20.

   b. Add a new record to the **Rafting Trip** table with the following field values:

   | | |
   |---|---|
   | Trip#: | 3675 |
   | River: | Colorado River (Grand Canyon) |
   | TripDistance: | 110 |
   | TripDays: | 2.5 |
   | Fee/Person: | 215 |

   c. Delete the record for Trip# 3423.

7. Print the **Rafting Trip** table datasheet, and then close the table.

8. Use Design view to create a new table named **Booking** using the table design shown in Figure 2-41.

**Figure 2-41**

| Field Name | Data Type | Description | Field Size | Other Properties |
|---|---|---|---|---|
| Booking# | Number | Primary key | Long Integer | Decimal Places: 0<br>Default Value: Null |
| Client# | Number | Foreign key | Integer | Decimal Places: 0 |
| TripDate | Date/Time | | | Format: Short Date |
| Trip# | Number | Foreign key | Long Integer | Decimal Places: 0 |
| People | Number | Number of people in the group | Byte | Decimal Places: 0 |

9. Specify Booking# as the primary key, and then save the table as **Booking**.

10. Add the records shown in Figure 2-42 to the **Booking** table.

**Figure 2-42**

| Booking# | Client# | TripDate | Trip# | People |
|---|---|---|---|---|
| 410 | 330 | 6/5/03 | 3529 | 4 |
| 403 | 315 | 7/1/03 | 3107 | 7 |
| 411 | 311 | 7/5/03 | 3222 | 5 |

11. Connor created a database named **Groups** that contains a table with booking data named **Group Info**. The **Booking** table you created has the same format as the **Group Info** table. Copy all the records from the **Group Info** table in the **Groups** database (located in the Cases folder on your Data Disk) to the end of the **Booking** table in the **Trips** database.

12. Resize all columns in the **Booking** datasheet to their best fit.

13. Print the **Booking** datasheet, and then save and close the table.

14. Close the **Trips** database, and then exit Access.

## INTERNET ASSIGNMENTS

**Student Union**

The purpose of the Internet Assignments is to challenge you to find information on the Internet that you can use to create effective documents. The actual assignments are updated and maintained on the Course Technology Web site. Log on to the Internet and use your Web browser to go to the Student Union on the New Perspectives Series site at **www.course.com/NewPerspectives/studentunion**. Click the Online Companions link, and then click the link for this text.

## QUICK CHECK ANSWERS

*Session 2.1*

1. Identify all the fields needed to produce the required information, group related fields into tables, determine each table's primary key, include a common field in related tables, avoid data redundancy, and determine the properties of each field.

2. The Data Type property determines what field values you can enter for the field and what other properties the field will have.

3. text, number, and AutoNumber fields

4. F6

5. Format

6. null

*Session 2.2*

1. the record being edited; the next row available for a new record

2. The field and all its values are removed from the table.

3. In Design view, right-click the row selector for the row above which you want to insert the field, click Insert Rows on the shortcut menu, and then define the new field.

4. yes/no

5. Make sure the database into which you want to import a table is open, click the File menu, point to Get External Data, and then click Import; or, click the New button in the Database window, click Import Table in the New Table dialog box, and then click the OK button.

6. In navigation mode, the entire field value is selected, and anything you type replaces the field value; in editing mode, you can insert or delete characters in a field value based on the location of the insertion point.

## OBJECTIVES

In this tutorial you will:

- Learn how to use the Query window in Design view

- Create, run, and save queries

- Update data using a query

- Define a relationship between two tables

- Sort data in a query

- Filter data in a query

- Specify an exact match condition in a query

- Change a datasheet's appearance

- Use a comparison operator to match a range of values

- Use the And and Or logical operators

- Use multiple undo and redo

- Perform calculations in a query using calculated fields, aggregate functions, and record group calculations

# QUERYING A DATABASE

*Retrieving Information About Employers and Their Positions*

CASE

## Northeast Seasonal Jobs International (NSJI)

At a recent company meeting, Elsa Jensen and other NSJI employees discussed the importance of regularly monitoring the business activity of the company's employer clients. For example, Zack Ward and his marketing staff track employer activity to develop new strategies for promoting NSJI's services. Matt Griffin, the manager of recruitment, needs to track information about available positions, so that he can find student recruits to fill those positions. In addition, Elsa is interested in analyzing other aspects of the business, such as the wage amounts paid for different positions at different employers. All of these informational needs can be satisfied by queries that retrieve information from the Northeast database.

# SESSION 3.1

In this session, you will use the Query window in Design view to create, run, and save queries; update data using a query; define a one-to-many relationship between two tables; sort data with a toolbar button and in Design view; and filter data in a query datasheet.

## Introduction to Queries

As you learned in Tutorial 1, a query is a question you ask about data stored in a database. For example, Zack might create a query to find records in the Employer table for only those employers located in a specific state or province. When you create a query, you tell Access which fields you need and what criteria Access should use to select the records.

Access provides powerful query capabilities that allow you to:

- display selected fields and records from a table
- sort records
- perform calculations
- generate data for forms, reports, and other queries
- update data in the tables in a database
- find and display data from two or more tables

Most questions about data are generalized queries in which you specify the fields and records you want Access to select. These common requests for information, such as "Which employers are located in Quebec?" or "How many waiter/waitress positions are available?" are called **select queries**. The answer to a select query is returned in the form of a datasheet. The result of a query is also referred to as a **recordset**, because the query produces a set of records that answers your question.

More specialized, technical queries, such as finding duplicate records in a table, are best formulated using a Query Wizard. A Query Wizard prompts you for information by asking a series of questions and then creates the appropriate query based on your answers. In Tutorial 1, you used the Simple Query Wizard to display only some of the fields in the Employer table; Access provides other Query Wizards for more complex queries. For common, informational queries, it is easier for you to design your own query than to use a Query Wizard.

Zack wants you to create a query to display the employer ID, employer name, city, contact first name, contact last name, and Web site information for each record in the Employer table. He needs this information for a market analysis his staff is completing on NSJI's employer clients. You'll open the Query window to create the query for Zack.

## Query Window

You use the Query window in Design view to create a query. In Design view, you specify the data you want to view by constructing a query by example. When you use **query by example** (**QBE**), you give Access an example of the information you are requesting. Access then retrieves the information that precisely matches your example.

For Zack's query, you need to display data from the Employer table. You'll begin by starting Access, opening the Northeast database, and displaying the Query window in Design view.

## To start Access, open the Northeast database, and open the Query window in Design view:

1. Place your Data Disk in the appropriate disk drive.

2. Start Access and open the **Northeast** database located in the Tutorial folder on your Data Disk. The Northeast database is displayed in the Database window.

3. Click **Queries** in the Objects bar of the Database window, and then click the **New** button. The New Query dialog box opens. See Figure 3-1.

 Figure 3-1            NEW QUERY DIALOG BOX

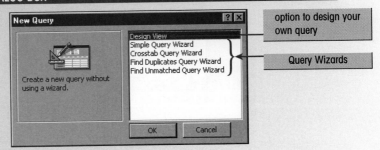

You'll design your own query instead of using a Query Wizard.

4. If necessary, click **Design View** in the list box.

5. Click the **OK** button. Access opens the Show Table dialog box on top of the Query window. (Note that you could also have double-clicked the "Create query in Design view" option in the Database window.) Notice that the title bar of the Query window shows that you are creating a select query.

   The query you are creating will retrieve data from the Employer table, so you need to add this table to the Select Query window.

6. Click **Employer** in the Tables list box (if necessary), click the **Add** button, and then click the **Close** button. Access places the Employer table's field list in the Select Query window and closes the Show Table dialog box.

   To display more of the fields you'll be using for creating queries, you'll maximize the Select Query window.

7. Click the **Maximize** button ▫ on the Select Query window title bar. See Figure 3-2.

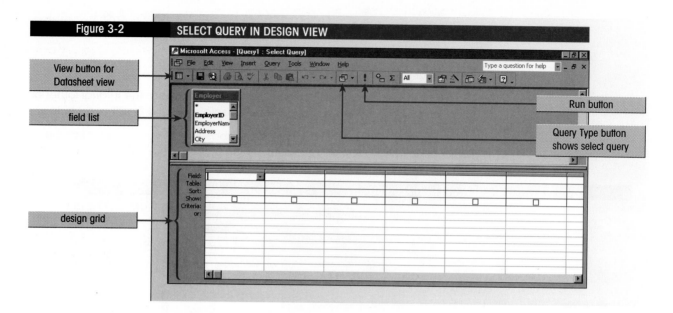

Figure 3-2

SELECT QUERY IN DESIGN VIEW

View button for
Datasheet view

field list

design grid

Run button

Query Type button
shows select query

In Design view, the Select Query window contains the standard title bar, the menu bar, the status bar, and the Query Design toolbar. On the toolbar, the Query Type button shows a select query; the icon on this button changes according to the type of query you are creating. The title bar on the Select Query window displays the query type (Select Query) and the default query name (Query1). You'll change the default query name to a more meaningful one later when you save the query.

The Select Query window in Design view contains a field list and the design grid. The **field list** contains the fields for the table you are querying. The table name appears at the top of the list box, and the fields are listed in the order in which they appear in the table. You can scroll the field list to see more fields; or, you can expand the field list to display all the fields and the complete field names by resizing the field list box.

In the **design grid**, you include the fields and record selection criteria for the information you want to see. Each column in the design grid contains specifications about a field you will use in the query. You can choose a single field for your query by dragging its name from the field list to the design grid in the lower portion of the window. Alternatively, you can double-click a field name to place it in the next available design grid column.

When you are constructing a query, you can see the query results at any time by clicking the View button or the Run button on the Query Design toolbar. In response, Access displays the datasheet, which contains the set of fields and records that results from answering, or **running**, the query. The order of the fields in the datasheet is the same as the order of the fields in the design grid. Although the datasheet looks just like a table datasheet and appears in Datasheet view, a query datasheet is temporary, and its contents are based on the criteria you establish in the design grid. In contrast, a table datasheet shows the permanent data in a table. However, you can update data while viewing a query datasheet, just as you can when working in a table datasheet or form.

If the query you are creating includes every field from the specified table, you can use one of the following three methods to transfer all the fields from the field list to the design grid:

■ Click and drag each field individually from the field list to the design grid. Use this method if you want the fields in your query to appear in an order that is different from the order in the field list.

■ Double-click the asterisk in the field list. Access places the table name followed by a period and an asterisk (as in "Employer.*") in the design grid, which signifies that the order of the fields will be the same in the query as it is in the field list. Use this method if you don't need to sort the query or specify conditions for the records you want to select. The advantage of using this method is that you do not need to change the query if you add or delete fields from the underlying table structure. Such changes are reflected automatically in the query.

■ Double-click the field list title bar to highlight all the fields, and then click and drag one of the highlighted fields to the design grid. Access places each field in a separate column and arranges the fields in the order in which they appear in the field list. Use this method when you need to sort your query or include record selection criteria.

Now you'll create and run Zack's query to display selected fields from the Employer table.

# Creating and Running a Query

The default table datasheet displays all the fields in the table, in the same order as they appear in the table. In contrast, a query datasheet can display selected fields from a table, and the order of the fields can be different from that of the table.

Zack wants the Employer table's EmployerID, EmployerName, City, ContactFirstName, ContactLastName, and WebSite fields to appear in the query results. You'll add each of these fields to the design grid.

*To select the fields for the query, and then run the query:*

1. Drag **EmployerID** from the Employer field list to the design grid's first column Field text box, and then release the mouse button. See Figure 3-3.

| Figure 3-3 | FIELD ADDED TO THE DESIGN GRID |
| --- | --- |

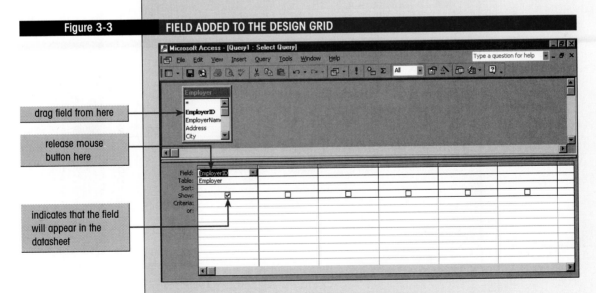

drag field from here

release mouse button here

indicates that the field will appear in the datasheet

In the design grid's first column, the field name EmployerID appears in the Field text box, the table name Employer appears in the Table text box, and the check mark in the Show check box indicates that the field will be displayed in the datasheet when you run the query. Sometimes you might not want to display a field and its values in the query results. For example, if you are creating a query to show all employers located in Massachusetts, and you assign the name "Employers in Massachusetts" to the query, you do not need to include the State/Prov field value for each record in the query results—every State/Prov field value would be "MA" for Massachusetts. Even if you choose not to include a field in the display of the query results, you can still use the field as part of the query to select specific records or to specify a particular sequence for the records in the datasheet.

2. Double-click **EmployerName** in the Employer field list. Access adds this field to the second column of the design grid.

3. Scrolling the Employer field list as necessary, repeat Step 2 for the **City**, **ContactFirstName**, **ContactLastName**, and **WebSite** fields to add these fields to the design grid in that order.

   **TROUBLE?** If you double-click the wrong field and accidentally add it to the design grid, you can remove the field from the grid. Select the field's column by clicking the pointer ↓ on the bar above the Field text box for the field you want to delete, and then press the Delete key (or click Edit on the menu bar, and then click Delete Columns).

   Having selected the fields for Zack's query, you now can run the query.

4. Click the **Run** button ! on the Query Design toolbar. Access runs the query and displays the results in Datasheet view. See Figure 3-4.

| Figure 3-4 | DATASHEET DISPLAYED AFTER RUNNING THE QUERY |

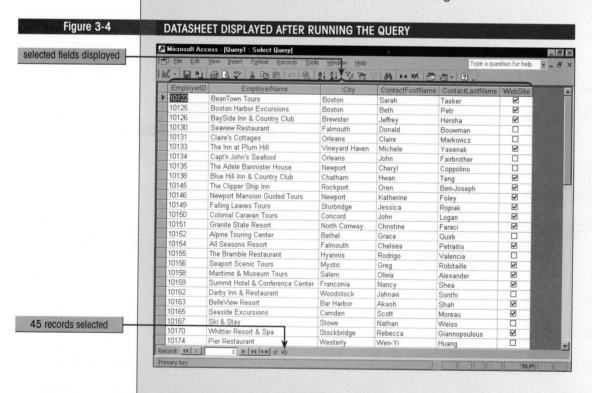

selected fields displayed

45 records selected

The six fields you added to the design grid appear in the datasheet, and the records are displayed in primary key sequence by EmployerID. Access selected a total of 45 records for display in the datasheet.

Zack asks you to save the query as "Employer Analysis" so that he can easily retrieve the same data again.

5. Click the **Save** button 🖫 on the Query Datasheet toolbar. The Save As dialog box opens.

6. Type **Employer Analysis** in the Query Name text box, and then press the **Enter** key. Access saves the query with the specified name in the Northeast database on your Data Disk and displays the name in the title bar.

When viewing the results of the query, Zack noticed a couple of changes that need to be made to the data in the Employer table. The Adele Bannister House recently developed a Web site, so the WebSite field for this record needs to be updated. In addition, the contact information has changed for the Alpine Touring Center.

## Updating Data Using a Query

Although a query datasheet is temporary and its contents are based on the criteria in the query design grid, you can update the data in a table using a query datasheet. In this case, Zack has changes he wants you to make to records in the Employer table. Instead of making the changes in the table datasheet, you can make them in the Employer Analysis query datasheet. The underlying Employer table will be updated with the changes you make.

### To update data using the Employer Analysis query datasheet:

1. For the record with EmployerID 10135 (The Adele Bannister House), click the check box in the WebSite field to place a check mark in it.

2. For the record with EmployerID 10152 (Alpine Touring Center), change the ContactFirstName field value to **Mary** and change the ContactLastName field value to **Grant**.

3. Click the **Close Window** button ☒ on the menu bar to close the query. Note that the Employer Analysis query appears in the list of queries.

4. Click the **Restore Window** button 🗗 on the menu bar to return the Database window to its original size.

   Now you will check the Employer table to verify that the changes you made in the query datasheet were also made to the Employer table records.

5. Click **Tables** in the Objects bar of the Database window, click **Employer** in the list of tables, and then click the **Open** button. The Employer table datasheet opens.

6. For the record with EmployerID 10135, scroll the datasheet to the right to verify that the WebSite field contains a check mark. For the record with EmployerID 10152, scroll to the right to see the new contact information (Mary Grant).

7. Click the **Close** button ☒ on the Employer table window to close it.

Matt also wants to view specific information in the Northeast database. However, he needs to see data from both the Employer table and the Position table at the same time. To view data from two tables at the same time, you need to define a relationship between the tables.

# Defining Table Relationships

One of the most powerful features of a relational database management system is its ability to define relationships between tables. You use a common field to relate one table to another. The process of relating tables is often called performing a **join**. When you join tables that have a common field, you can extract data from them as if they were one larger table. For example, you can join the Employer and Position tables by using the EmployerID field in both tables as the common field. Then you can use a query, a form, or a report to extract selected data from each table, even though the data is contained in two separate tables, as shown in Figure 3-5. In the Positions query shown in Figure 3-5, the PositionID, PositionTitle, and Wage columns are fields from the Position table, and the EmployerName and State/Prov columns are fields from the Employer table. The joining of records is based on the common field of EmployerID. The Employer and Position tables have a type of relationship called a one-to-many relationship.

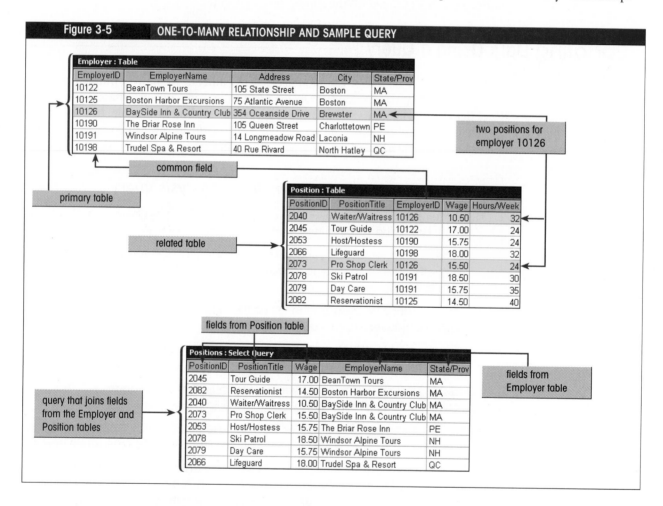

**Figure 3-5**    ONE-TO-MANY RELATIONSHIP AND SAMPLE QUERY

## One-to-Many Relationships

A **one-to-many relationship** exists between two tables when one record in the first table matches zero, one, or many records in the second table, and when one record in the second table matches exactly one record in the first table. For example, as shown in Figure 3-5, employers 10126 and 10191 each have two available positions, and employers 10122, 10125, 10190, and 10198 each have one available position. Every position has a single matching employer.

Access refers to the two tables that form a relationship as the primary table and the related table. The **primary table** is the "one" table in a one-to-many relationship; in Figure 3-5, the Employer table is the primary table because there is only one employer for each available position. The **related table** is the "many" table; in Figure 3-5, the Position table is the related table because there can be many positions offered by each employer.

Because related data is stored in two tables, inconsistencies between the tables can occur. Consider the following scenarios:

- Matt adds a position record to the Position table for a new employer, Glen Cove Inn, using EmployerID 10132. Matt did not first add the new employer's information to the Employer table, so this position does not have a matching record in the Employer table. The data is inconsistent, and the position record is considered to be an **orphaned** record.

- Matt changes the EmployerID in the Employer table for BaySide Inn & Country Club from 10126 to 10128. Two orphaned records for employer 10126 now exist in the Position table, and the database is inconsistent.

- Matt deletes the record for Boston Harbor Excursions, employer 10125, in the Employer table because this employer is no longer an NSJI client. The database is again inconsistent; one record for employer 10125 in the Position table has no matching record in the Employer table.

You can avoid these problems by specifying referential integrity between tables when you define their relationships.

## Referential Integrity

**Referential integrity** is a set of rules that Access enforces to maintain consistency between related tables when you update data in a database. Specifically, the referential integrity rules are as follows:

- When you add a record to a related table, a matching record must already exist in the primary table, thereby preventing the possibility of orphaned records.

- If you attempt to change the value of the primary key in the primary table, Access prevents this change if matching records exist in a related table. However, if you choose the **cascade updates** option, Access permits the change in value to the primary key and changes the appropriate foreign key values in the related table, thereby eliminating the possibility of inconsistent data.

- When you delete a record in the primary table, Access prevents the deletion if matching records exist in a related table. However, if you choose the **cascade deletes** option, Access deletes the record in the primary table and also deletes all records in related tables that have matching foreign key values.

Now you'll define a one-to-many relationship between the Employer and Position tables so that you can use fields from both tables to create a query that will retrieve the information Matt needs. You will also define a one-to-many relationship between the NAICS (primary) table and the Employer (related) table.

## Defining a Relationship Between Two Tables

When two tables have a common field, you can define a relationship between them in the Relationships window. The **Relationships window** illustrates the relationships among a database's tables. In this window, you can view or change existing relationships, define new relationships between tables, and rearrange the layout of the tables in the window.

You need to open the Relationships window and define the relationship between the Employer and Position tables. You'll define a one-to-many relationship between the two tables, with Employer as the primary table and Position as the related table, and with EmployerID as the common field (the primary key in the Employer table and a foreign key in the Position table). You'll also define a one-to-many relationship between the NAICS and Employer tables, with NAICS as the primary table and Employer as the related table, and with NAICSCode as the common field (the primary key in the NAICS table and a foreign key in the Employer table).

## To define the one-to-many relationship between the Employer and Position tables:

**1.** Click the **Relationships** button 🔲 on the Database toolbar. The Show Table dialog box opens on top of the Relationships window. See Figure 3-6.

| Figure 3-6 | SHOW TABLE DIALOG BOX |

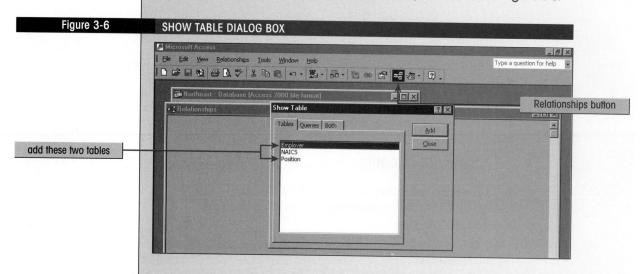

You must add each table participating in a relationship to the Relationships window.

**2.** Click **Employer** (if necessary), and then click the **Add** button. The Employer field list is added to the Relationships window.

**3.** Click **Position**, and then click the **Add** button. The Position field list is added to the Relationships window.

**4.** Click the **Close** button in the Show Table dialog box to close it and reveal the entire Relationships window.

To form the relationship between the two tables, you drag the common field of EmployerID from the primary table to the related table. Then Access opens the Edit Relationships dialog box, in which you select the relationship options for the two tables.

**5.** Click **EmployerID** in the Employer field list, and drag it to **EmployerID** in the Position field list. When you release the mouse button, the Edit Relationships dialog box opens. See Figure 3-7.

| Figure 3-7 | EDIT RELATIONSHIPS DIALOG BOX |
|---|---|

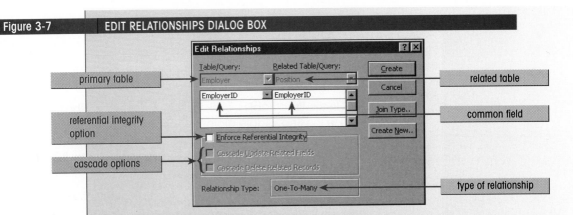

primary table

referential integrity option

cascade options

related table

common field

type of relationship

The primary table, related table, and common field appear at the top of the dialog box. The type of relationship, One-To-Many, appears at the bottom of the dialog box. When you click the Enforce Referential Integrity check box, the two cascade options become available. If you select the Cascade Update Related Fields option, Access will change the appropriate foreign key values in the related table when you change a primary key value in the primary table. If you select the Cascade Delete Related Records option, when you delete a record in the primary table, Access will delete all records in the related table that have a matching foreign key value.

6. Click the **Enforce Referential Integrity** check box, click the **Cascade Update Related Fields** check box, and then click the **Cascade Delete Related Records** check box. **Note:** You should select this option with caution because you might inadvertently delete records you do not want deleted.

7. Click the **Create** button to define the one-to-many relationship between the two tables and to close the dialog box. The completed relationship appears in the Relationships window. See Figure 3-8.

| Figure 3-8 | DEFINED RELATIONSHIP IN THE RELATIONSHIPS WINDOW |
|---|---|

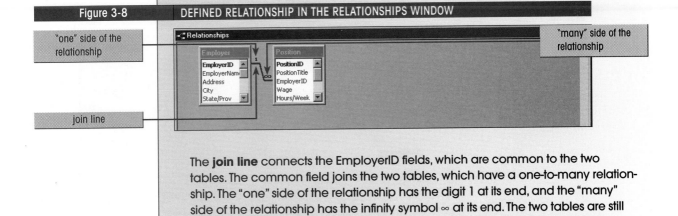

"one" side of the relationship

"many" side of the relationship

join line

The **join line** connects the EmployerID fields, which are common to the two tables. The common field joins the two tables, which have a one-to-many relationship. The "one" side of the relationship has the digit 1 at its end, and the "many" side of the relationship has the infinity symbol ∞ at its end. The two tables are still separate tables, but you can use the data in them as if they were one table.

Now you need to define the one-to-many relationship between the NAICS and Employer tables. In this relationship, NAICS is the primary ("one") table because there is only one code for each employer. Employer is the related ("many") table because there are multiple employers with the same NAICS code.

## To define the one-to-many relationship between the NAICS and Employer tables:

1. Click the **Show Table** button on the Relationship toolbar. The Show Table dialog box opens on top of the Relationships window.

2. Click **NAICS** in the list of tables, click the **Add** button, and then click the **Close** button to close the Show Table dialog box. The NAICS field list appears in the Relationships window to the right of the Position field list. To make it easier to define the relationship, you'll move the NAICS field list below the Employer and Position field lists.

3. Click the NAICS field list title bar and drag the list until it is below the Position table (see Figure 3-9), and then release the mouse button.

4. Scroll the Employer field list until the NAICSCode field is visible. Because the NAICS table is the primary table in this relationship, you need to drag the NAICSCode field from the NAICS field list to the Employer field list. Notice that the NAICSCode field in the NAICS table appears in a bold font; this indicates that the field is the table's primary key. On the other hand, the NAICSCode field in the Employer table is not bold, which is a reminder that this field is the foreign key in this table.

5. Click and drag the **NAICSCode** field in the NAICS field list to the **NAICSCode** field in the Employer field list. When you release the mouse button, the Edit Relationships dialog box opens.

6. Click the **Enforce Referential Integrity** check box, click the **Cascade Update Related Fields** check box, and then click the **Cascade Delete Related Records** check box. You now have selected all the necessary relationship options.

7. Click the **Create** button to define the one-to-many relationship between the two tables and close the dialog box. The completed relationship appears in the Relationships window. See Figure 3-9.

| Figure 3-9 | BOTH RELATIONSHIPS DEFINED |

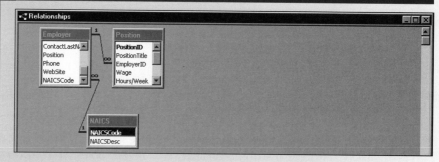

With both relationships defined, you have connected the data among the three tables in the Northeast database.

8. Click the **Save** button on the Relationship toolbar to save the layout in the Relationships window.

9. Click the **Close** button on the Relationships window title bar. The Relationships window closes, and you return to the Database window.

# Creating a Multi-table Query

Now that you have joined the Employer and Position tables, you can create a query to produce the information Matt wants. To help him determine his recruiting needs, Matt wants a query that displays the EmployerName, City, and State/Prov fields from the Employer table and the Openings, PositionTitle, StartDate, and EndDate fields from the Position table.

## To create, run, and save the query using the Employer and Position tables:

1. Click **Queries** in the Objects bar of the Database window, and then double-click **Create query in Design view**. The Show Table dialog box opens on top of the Query window in Design view.

   You need to add the Employer and Position tables to the Query window.

2. Click **Employer** in the Tables list box (if necessary), click the **Add** button, click **Position**, click the **Add** button, and then click the **Close** button. The Employer and Position field lists appear in the Query window, and the Show Table dialog box closes. Note that the one-to-many relationship that exists between the two tables is shown in the Query window. Also, notice that the join line is thick at both ends; this signifies that you selected the option to enforce referential integrity. If you had not selected this option, the join line would be thin at both ends and neither the "1" nor the infinity symbol would appear, even though there is a one-to-many relationship between the two tables.

   You need to place the EmployerName, City, and State/Prov fields from the Employer field list into the design grid, and then place the Openings, PositionTitle, StartDate, and EndDate fields from the Position field list into the design grid.

3. Double-click **EmployerName** in the Employer field list to place EmployerName in the design grid's first column Field text box.

4. Repeat Step 3 to add the **City** and **State/Prov** fields from the Employer table, so that these fields are placed in the second and third columns of the design grid.

5. Repeat Step 3 to add the **Openings**, **PositionTitle**, **StartDate**, and **EndDate** fields (in that order) from the Position table, so that these fields are placed in the fourth through seventh columns of the design grid.

   The query specifications are completed, so you now can run the query.

6. Click the **Run** button on the Query Design toolbar. Access runs the query and displays the results in the datasheet.

7. Click the **Maximize** button on the Query window title bar. See Figure 3-10.

Figure 3-10    DATASHEET FOR THE QUERY BASED ON THE EMPLOYER AND POSITION TABLES

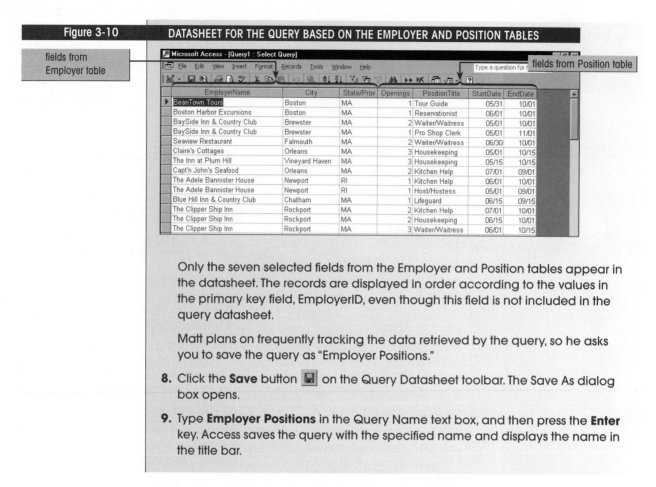

fields from Employer table

fields from Position table

Only the seven selected fields from the Employer and Position tables appear in the datasheet. The records are displayed in order according to the values in the primary key field, EmployerID, even though this field is not included in the query datasheet.

Matt plans on frequently tracking the data retrieved by the query, so he asks you to save the query as "Employer Positions."

8. Click the **Save** button 🖫 on the Query Datasheet toolbar. The Save As dialog box opens.

9. Type **Employer Positions** in the Query Name text box, and then press the **Enter** key. Access saves the query with the specified name and displays the name in the title bar.

Matt decides he wants the records displayed in alphabetical order by employer name. Because the query displays data in order by the field value of EmployerID, which is the primary key for the Employer table, you need to sort the records by EmployerName to display the data in the order Matt wants.

## Sorting Data in a Query

**Sorting** is the process of rearranging records in a specified order or sequence. Sometimes you might need to sort data before displaying or printing it to meet a specific request. For example, Matt might want to review position information arranged by the StartDate field because he needs to know which positions are available earliest in the year. On the other hand, Elsa might want to view position information arranged by the Openings field for each employer, because she monitors employer activity for NSJI.

When you sort data in a query, you do not change the sequence of the records in the underlying tables. Only the records in the query datasheet are rearranged according to your specifications.

To sort records, you must select the **sort key**, which is the field used to determine the order of records in the datasheet. In this case, Matt wants the data sorted by the employer name, so you need to specify the EmployerName field as the sort key. Sort keys can be text, number, date/time, currency, AutoNumber, yes/no, or Lookup Wizard fields, but not memo, OLE object, or hyperlink fields. You sort records in either ascending (increasing) or descending (decreasing) order. Figure 3-11 shows the results of each type of sort for different data types.

| Figure 3-11 | SORTING RESULTS FOR DIFFERENT DATA TYPES | |
|---|---|---|
| **DATA TYPE** | **ASCENDING SORT RESULTS** | **DESCENDING SORT RESULTS** |
| Text | A to Z | Z to A |
| Number | lowest to highest numeric value | highest to lowest numeric value |
| Date/Time | oldest to most recent date | most recent to oldest date |
| Currency | lowest to highest numeric value | highest to lowest numeric value |
| AutoNumber | lowest to highest numeric value | highest to lowest numeric value |
| Yes/No | yes (check mark in check box) then no values | no then yes values |

Access provides several methods for sorting data in a table or query datasheet and in a form. One method, clicking a toolbar sort button, lets you sort the displayed records quickly.

## Using a Toolbar Button to Sort Data

The **Sort Ascending** and **Sort Descending** buttons on the toolbar allow you to sort records immediately, based on the values in the selected field. First you select the column on which you want to base the sort, and then you click the appropriate sort button on the toolbar to rearrange the records in either ascending or descending order. Unless you save the datasheet or form after you've sorted the records, the rearrangement of records is temporary.

Recall that in Tutorial 1 you used the Sort Ascending button to sort query results by the State/Prov field. You'll use this same button to sort the Employer Positions query results by the EmployerName field.

### To sort the records using a toolbar sort button:

1. Click any visible EmployerName field value to establish the field as the current field (if necessary).

2. Click the **Sort Ascending** button 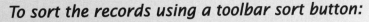 on the Query Datasheet toolbar. The records are rearranged in ascending order by employer name. See Figure 3-12.

| Figure 3-12 | SORTING RECORDS ON A SINGLE FIELD IN A DATASHEET |
|---|---|

Sort Ascending button

Sort Descending button

records sorted in ascending order by EmployerName

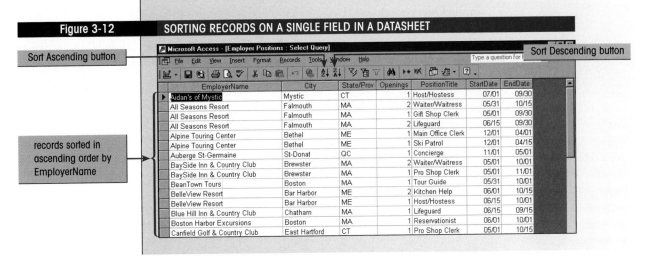

After viewing the query results, Matt decides that he'd prefer to see the records arranged by the value in the PositionTitle field, so that he can identify the types of positions he needs to fill. He also wants to display the records in descending order according to the value of the Openings field, so that he can easily see how many openings there are for each position. To do this you need to sort using two fields.

## Sorting Multiple Fields in Design View

Sort keys can be unique or nonunique. A sort key is **unique** if the value of the sort key field for each record is different. The EmployerID field in the Employer table is an example of a unique sort key because each employer record has a different value in this field. A sort key is **nonunique** if more than one record can have the same value for the sort key field. For example, the PositionTitle field in the Position table is a nonunique sort key because more than one record can have the same PositionTitle value.

When the sort key is nonunique, records with the same sort key value are grouped together, but they are not in a specific order within the group. To arrange these grouped records in a specific order, you can specify a **secondary sort key**, which is a second sort key field. The first sort key field is called the **primary sort key**. Note that the primary sort key is *not* the same as a table's primary key field. A table has at most one primary key, which must be unique, whereas any field in a table can serve as a primary sort key.

Access lets you select up to 10 different sort keys. When you use the toolbar sort buttons, the sort key fields must be in adjacent columns in the datasheet. You highlight the adjacent columns, and Access sorts first by the first column and then by each other highlighted column in order from left to right.

Matt wants the records sorted first by the PositionTitle field and then by the Openings field. The two fields are adjacent, but not in the correct left-to-right order, so you cannot use the toolbar buttons to sort them. You could move the Openings field to the right of the PositionTitle field in the query datasheet. However, you can specify only one type of sort—either ascending or descending—for selected columns in the query datasheet. This is not what Matt wants; he wants the PositionTitle field values to be sorted in ascending alphabetical order and the Openings field values to be sorted in descending order.

In this case, you need to specify the sort keys for the query in Design view. Any time you want to sort on multiple fields that are nonadjacent or in the wrong order, but do not want to rearrange the columns in the query datasheet to accomplish the sort, you must specify the sort keys in Design view.

In the Query window in Design view, Access first uses the sort key that is leftmost in the design grid. Therefore, you must arrange the fields you want to sort from left to right in the design grid, with the primary sort key being the leftmost sort key field. In Design view, multiple sort fields do not have to be adjacent to each other, as they do in Datasheet view; however, they must be in the correct left-to-right order.

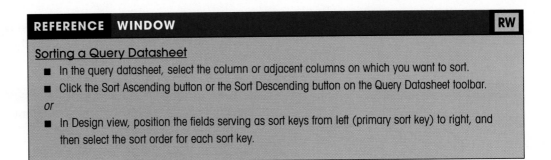

**REFERENCE   WINDOW**                                                          **RW**

Sorting a Query Datasheet
- In the query datasheet, select the column or adjacent columns on which you want to sort.
- Click the Sort Ascending button or the Sort Descending button on the Query Datasheet toolbar.

*or*
- In Design view, position the fields serving as sort keys from left (primary sort key) to right, and then select the sort order for each sort key.

To achieve the results Matt wants, you need to switch to Design view, move the Openings field to the right of the EndDate field, and then specify the sort order for the two fields.

### To select the two sort keys in Design view:

1. Click the **View** button for Design view [icon] on the Query Datasheet toolbar to open the query in Design view.

   First, you'll move the Openings field to the right of the EndDate field. Remember, in Design view, the sort fields do not have to be adjacent, and non-sort key fields can appear between sort key fields. So, you will move the Openings field to the end of the query design, following the EndDate field.

2. If necessary, click the right arrow in the design grid's horizontal scroll bar a few times to scroll to the right so that both the Openings and EndDate fields are completely visible.

3. Position the pointer in the Openings field selector until the pointer changes to a ↓ shape, and then click to select the field. See Figure 3-13.

| Figure 3-13 | SELECTED OPENINGS FIELD |

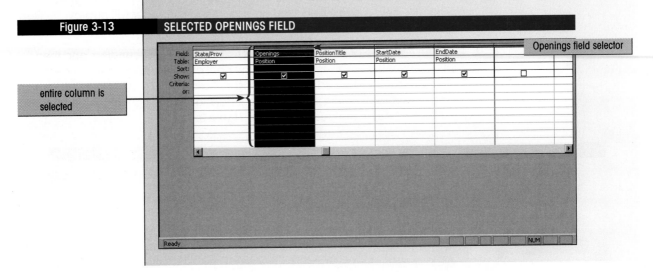

Openings field selector

entire column is selected

4. Position the pointer in the Openings field selector, and then click and drag the pointer to the right until the vertical line on the right of the EndDate field is highlighted. See Figure 3-14.

**Figure 3-14          DRAGGING THE FIELD IN THE DESIGN GRID**

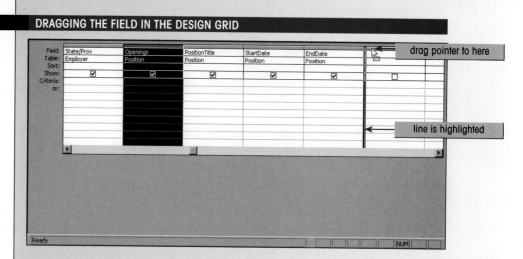

5. Release the mouse button. The Openings field moves to the right of the EndDate field.

   The fields are now in the correct order for the sort. Next, you need to specify an ascending sort order for the PositionTitle field and a descending sort order for the Openings field.

6. Click the right side of the **PositionTitle Sort** text box to display the list arrow and the sort options, and then click **Ascending**. You've selected an ascending sort order for the PositionTitle field, which will be the primary sort key. The PositionTitle field is a text field, and an ascending sort order will display the field values in alphabetical order.

7. Click the right side of the **Openings Sort** text box, click **Descending**, and then click in one of the empty text boxes to the right of the Openings field to deselect the setting. You've selected a descending sort order for the Openings field, which will be the secondary sort key, because it appears to the right of the primary sort key (PositionTitle) in the design grid. See Figure 3-15.

**Figure 3-15          SELECTING TWO SORT KEYS IN DESIGN VIEW**

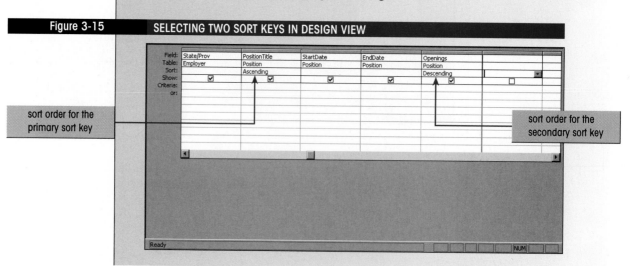

You have finished your query changes, so now you can run the query and then save the modified query with the same query name.

8. Click the **Run** button ! on the Query Design toolbar. Access runs the query and displays the query datasheet. The records appear in ascending order, based on the values of the PositionTitle field. Within groups of records with the same PositionTitle field value, the records appear in descending order by the values of the Openings field. See Figure 3-16.

| Figure 3-16 | DATASHEET SORTED ON TWO FIELDS |

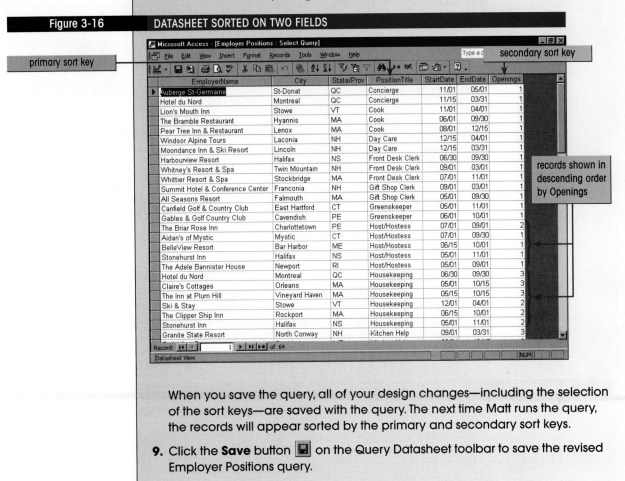

When you save the query, all of your design changes—including the selection of the sort keys—are saved with the query. The next time Matt runs the query, the records will appear sorted by the primary and secondary sort keys.

9. Click the **Save** button on the Query Datasheet toolbar to save the revised Employer Positions query.

Matt wants to concentrate on the positions in the datasheet with a start date sometime in May, to see how many recruits he will need to fill these positions. Selecting only the records with a StartDate field value in May is a temporary change that Matt wants in the datasheet, so you do not need to switch to Design view and change the query. Instead, you can apply a filter.

# Filtering Data

A **filter** is a set of restrictions you place on the records in an open datasheet or form to *temporarily* isolate a subset of the records. A filter lets you view different subsets of displayed records so that you can focus on only the data you need. Unless you save a query or form with a filter applied, an applied filter is not available the next time you run the query or open the form.

The simplest technique for filtering records is Filter By Selection. **Filter By Selection** lets you select all or part of a field value in a datasheet or form, and then display only those records that contain the selected value in the field. Another technique for filtering records is to use **Filter By Form**, which changes your datasheet to display empty fields. Then you can select a value from the list arrow that appears when you click any blank field to apply a filter that selects only those records containing that value.

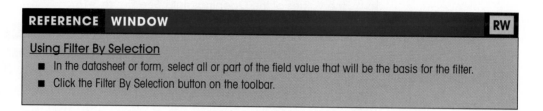

**REFERENCE WINDOW**        **RW**

Using Filter By Selection
- In the datasheet or form, select all or part of the field value that will be the basis for the filter.
- Click the Filter By Selection button on the toolbar.

For Matt's request, you need to select just the beginning digits "05" in the StartDate field, to view all the records with a May start date, and then use Filter By Selection to display only those query records with this same partial value.

## To display the records using Filter By Selection:

1. In the query datasheet, locate the first occurrence of a May date in the StartDate field, and then select **05** in that field value.

2. Click the **Filter By Selection** button 💥 on the Query Datasheet toolbar. Access displays the filtered results. Only the 17 query records that have a StartDate field value with the beginning digits "05" appear in the datasheet. The status bar's display (FLTR), the area next to the navigation buttons, and the selected Remove Filter button on the toolbar all indicate that the records have been filtered. See Figure 3-17.

| Figure 3-17 | USING FILTER BY SELECTION |
| --- | --- |

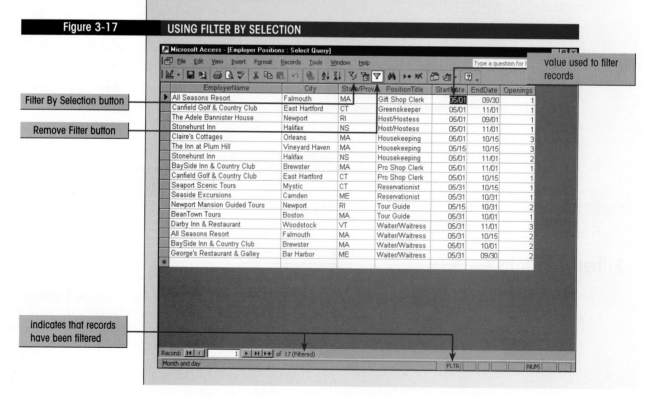

TROUBLE? If you are unable to select only the digits "05" in the StartDate field because the entire field value (including a four-digit year) is displayed when you click in the field, your Windows date settings might be affecting the display of the field values. In this case, you can either read through the remaining steps on this page without completing them, or ask your instructor for assistance.

Next, Matt wants to view only those records with a StartDate value of 05/01, because he needs to fill those positions before the other May positions. So, you need to filter by the complete field value of 05/01.

3. Click in any StartDate field value of **05/01**, and then click ▼. The filtered display now shows only the 9 records with a value of 05/01 in the StartDate field.

Now you can redisplay all the query records by clicking the Remove Filter button; this button works as a toggle to switch between the filtered and nonfiltered displays.

4. Click the **Remove Filter** button ▼ on the Query Datasheet toolbar. Access redisplays all the records in the query datasheet.

5. Click the **Save** button 🖫 on the Query Datasheet toolbar, and then click the **Close Window** button ✕ on the menu bar to save and close the query and return to the Database window.

6. Click the **Restore Window** button 🗗 on the menu bar to return the Database window to its original size.

The queries you've created will help NSJI employees retrieve just the information they want to view. In the next session, you'll continue to create queries to meet their information needs.

# Session 3.1 QUICK CHECK

1. What is a select query?

2. Describe the field list and the design grid in the Query window in Design view.

3. How are a table datasheet and a query datasheet similar? How are they different?

4. The _____ is the "one" table in a one-to-many relationship, and the _____ is the "many" table in the relationship.

5. _____ is a set of rules that Access enforces to maintain consistency between related tables when you update data in a database.

6. For a date/time field, how do the records appear when sorted in ascending order?

7. When must you define multiple sort keys in Design view instead of in the query datasheet?

8. A(n) _____ is a set of restrictions you place on the records in an open datasheet or form to isolate a subset of records temporarily.

## SESSION 3.2

In this session, you will specify an exact match condition in a query, change a datasheet's appearance, use a comparison operator to match a range of values, use the And and Or logical operators to define multiple selection criteria for queries, use multiple undo and redo, and perform calculations in queries.

# Defining Record Selection Criteria for Queries

Matt wants to display employer and position information for all positions with a start date of 07/01, so that he can plan his recruitment efforts accordingly. For this request, you could create a query to select the correct fields and all records in the Employer and Position tables, select a StartDate field value of 07/01 in the query datasheet, and then click the Filter By Selection button to filter the query results to display only those positions starting on July 1. However, a faster way of displaying the data Matt needs is to create a query that displays the selected fields and only those records in the Employer and Position tables that satisfy a condition.

Just as you can display selected fields from a database in a query datasheet, you can display selected records. To tell Access which records you want to select, you must specify a condition as part of the query. A **condition** is a criterion, or rule, that determines which records are selected. To define a condition for a field, you place the condition in the field's Criteria text box in the design grid.

A condition usually consists of an operator, often a comparison operator, and a value. A **comparison operator** asks Access to compare the value in a database field to the condition value and to select all the records for which the relationship is true. For example, the condition >15.00 for the Wage field selects all records in the Position table having Wage field values greater than 15.00. Figure 3-18 shows the Access comparison operators.

**Figure 3-18** | **ACCESS COMPARISON OPERATORS**

| OPERATOR | MEANING | EXAMPLE |
|---|---|---|
| = | equal to (optional; default operator) | ="Hall" |
| < | less than | <#1/1/99# |
| <= | less than or equal to | <=100 |
| > | greater than | >"C400" |
| >= | greater than or equal to | >=18.75 |
| <> | not equal to | <>"Hall" |
| Between ... And... | between two values (inclusive) | Between 50 And 325 |
| In () | in a list of values | In ("Hall", "Seeger") |
| Like | matches a pattern that includes wildcards | Like "706*" |

## Specifying an Exact Match

For Matt's request, you need to create a query that will display only those records in the Position table with the value 07/01 in the StartDate field. This type of condition is called an **exact match** because the value in the specified field must match the condition exactly in order for the record to be included in the query results. You'll use the Simple Query Wizard to create the query, and then you'll specify the exact match condition.

## To create the query using the Simple Query Wizard:

1. If you took a break after the previous session, make sure that Access is running, the Northeast database is open, and the Queries object is selected in the Database window.

2. Double-click **Create query by using wizard**. Access opens the first Simple Query Wizard dialog box, in which you select the tables (or queries) and fields for the query.

3. Click the **Tables/Queries** list arrow, and then click **Table: Position**. The fields in the Position table appear in the Available Fields list box. Except for the PositionID and EmployerID fields, you will include all fields from the Position table in the query.

4. Click the >> button. All the fields from the Available Fields list box move to the Selected Fields list box.

5. Scroll up and click **PositionID** in the Selected Fields list box, click the < button to move the PositionID field back to the Available Fields list box, click **EmployerID** in the Selected Fields list box, and then click the < button to move the EmployerID field back to the Available Fields list box.

   Matt also wants certain information from the Employer table included in the query results. Because he wants the fields from the Employer table to appear in the query datasheet to the right of the fields from the Position table fields, you need to click the last field in the Selected Fields list box so that the new Employer fields will be inserted below it in the list.

6. Click **Openings** in the Selected Fields list box.

7. Click the **Tables/Queries** list arrow, and then click **Table: Employer**. The fields in the Employer table now appear in the Available Fields list box. Notice that the fields you selected from the Position table remain in the Selected Fields list box.

8. Click **EmployerName** in the Available Fields list box, and then click the > button to move EmployerName to the Selected Fields list box, below the Openings field.

9. Repeat Step 8 to move the **State/Prov**, **ContactFirstName**, **ContactLastName**, and **Phone** fields into the Selected Fields list box. (Note that you can also double-click a field to move it from the Available Fields list box to the Selected Fields list box.)

10. Click the **Next** button to open the second Simple Query Wizard dialog box, in which you choose whether the query will display records from the selected tables or a summary of those records. Summary options show calculations such as average, minimum, maximum, and so on. Matt wants to view the details for the records, not a summary.

11. Make sure the **Detail (shows every field of every record)** option button is selected, and then click the **Next** button to open the last Simple Query Wizard dialog box, in which you choose a name for the query and complete the Wizard. You need to enter a condition for the query, so you'll want to modify the query's design.

12. Type **July 1 Positions**, click the **Modify the query design** option button, and then click the **Finish** button. Access saves the query as July 1 Positions and opens the query in Design view. See Figure 3-19.

Figure 3-19   QUERY IN DESIGN VIEW

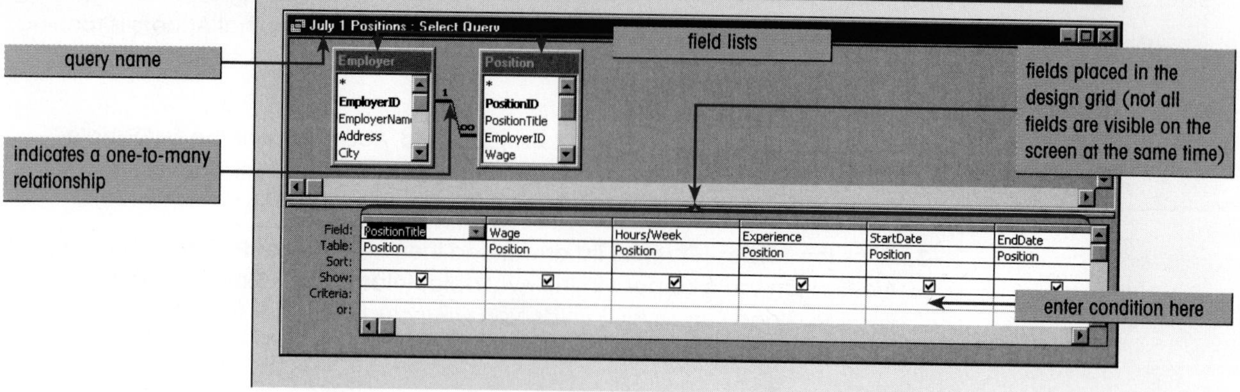

query name

indicates a one-to-many relationship

field lists

fields placed in the design grid (not all fields are visible on the screen at the same time)

enter condition here

The field lists for the Employer and Position tables appear in the top portion of the window, and the join line indicating a one-to-many relationship connects the two tables. The selected fields appear in the design grid. Not all of the fields are visible in the grid; to see the other selected fields, you need to scroll to the right using the horizontal scroll bar.

To display the information Matt wants, you need to enter the condition for the StartDate field in its Criteria text box. Matt wants to display only those records with a start date of 07/01.

### To enter the exact match condition, and then run the query:

1. Click the **StartDate Criteria** text box, type **7/01**, and then press the **Enter** key. The condition changes to #7/01/2003#.

   TROUBLE? If your date is displayed with a two-digit year, or if it shows a different year, don't worry. You can customize Windows to display different date formats.

   Access automatically placed number signs (#) before and after the condition. You must place date and time values inside number signs when using these values as selection criteria. If you omit the number signs, however, Access will include them automatically.

2. Click the **Run** button on the Query Design toolbar. Access runs the query and displays the selected field values for only those records with a StartDate field value of 07/01. A total of 9 records are selected and displayed in the datasheet. See Figure 3-20.

   TROUBLE? If your query does not produce the results shown in Figure 3-20, you probably need to specify the year "01" as part of the StartDate criteria. To do so, return to the query in Design view, enter the criteria "7/01/01" for the StartDate, and then repeat Step 2.

| Figure 3-20 | DATASHEET DISPLAYING SELECTED FIELDS AND RECORDS |
|---|---|

**July 1 Positions : Select Query**

| PositionTitle | Wage | Hours/Week | Experience | StartDate | EndDate | Openings | EmployerName |
|---|---|---|---|---|---|---|---|
| Host/Hostess | 17.00 | 24 | ☐ | 07/01 | 09/30 | 1 | Aidan's of Mystic |
| Kitchen Help | 12.50 | 32 | ☐ | 07/01 | 10/01 | 2 | The Clipper Ship Inn |
| Front Desk Clerk | 16.50 | 32 | ☐ | 07/01 | 11/01 | 1 | Whittier Resort & Spa |
| Host/Hostess | 15.75 | 24 | ☐ | 07/01 | 09/01 | 2 | The Briar Rose Inn |
| Kitchen Help | 12.00 | 40 | ☐ | 07/01 | 09/01 | 2 | Capt'n John's Seafood |
| Tour Guide | 16.00 | 24 | ☑ | 07/01 | 09/30 | 1 | Harbor Whale Watch Tours |
| Pro Shop Clerk | 16.00 | 30 | ☑ | 07/01 | 10/31 | 1 | Gables & Golf Country Club |
| Kitchen Help | 13.00 | 32 | ☐ | 07/01 | 10/31 | 1 | The Berkshire House |
| Main Office Clerk | 14.50 | 32 | ☐ | 07/01 | 11/15 | 1 | Whittier Resort & Spa |

only records with a StartDate value of 07/01 are selected

9 records selected

Record: |◄| ◄| 1 |►| |►| |►*| of 9

Matt would like to see more fields and records on the screen at one time. He asks you to maximize the datasheet, change the datasheet's font size, and resize all the columns to their best fit.

## Changing a Datasheet's Appearance

You can change the characteristics of a datasheet, including the font type and size of text in the datasheet, to improve its appearance or readability. As you learned in Tutorial 2, you can also resize the datasheet columns to view more columns on the screen at the same time.

You'll maximize the datasheet, change the font size from the default 10 points to 8, and then resize the datasheet columns.

### To change the font size and resize columns in the datasheet:

1. Click the **Maximize** button 🗖 on the Query window title bar.

2. Click **Format** on the menu bar, and then click **Font** to open the Font dialog box.

3. Scroll the Size list box, click **8**, and then click the **OK** button. The font size for the entire datasheet changes to 8.

   Next you need to resize the columns to their best fit, so that each column is just wide enough to fit the longest value in the column. Instead of resizing each column individually, as you did in Tutorial 2, you'll select all the columns and resize them at the same time.

4. Position the pointer in the PositionTitle field selector. When the pointer changes to a ▼ shape, click to select the entire column.

5. Click the right arrow on the horizontal scroll bar until the Phone field is fully visible, and then position the pointer in the Phone field selector until the pointer changes to a ▼ shape.

6. Press and hold the **Shift** key, and then click the mouse button. All the columns are selected. Now you can resize all of them at once.

7. Position the pointer at the right edge of the Phone field selector until the pointer changes to a ↔ shape. See Figure 3-21.

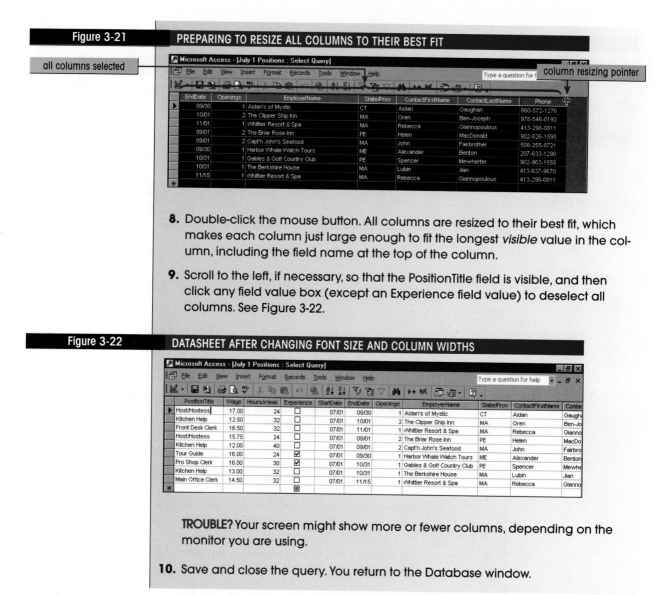

Figure 3-21    PREPARING TO RESIZE ALL COLUMNS TO THEIR BEST FIT

all columns selected

column resizing pointer

8. Double-click the mouse button. All columns are resized to their best fit, which makes each column just large enough to fit the longest *visible* value in the column, including the field name at the top of the column.

9. Scroll to the left, if necessary, so that the PositionTitle field is visible, and then click any field value box (except an Experience field value) to deselect all columns. See Figure 3-22.

Figure 3-22    DATASHEET AFTER CHANGING FONT SIZE AND COLUMN WIDTHS

**TROUBLE?** Your screen might show more or fewer columns, depending on the monitor you are using.

10. Save and close the query. You return to the Database window.

After viewing the query results, Matt decides that he would like to see the same fields, but only for those records whose Wage field value is equal to or greater than 17.00. He needs this information when he recruits students who will require a higher wage per hour for the available positions. To create the query needed to produce these results, you need to use a comparison operator to match a range of values—in this case, any Wage value greater than or equal to 17.00.

## Using a Comparison Operator to Match a Range of Values

Once you create and save a query, you can click the Open button to run it again, or you can click the Design button to change its design. Because the design of the query you need to create next is similar to the July 1 Positions query, you will change its design, run the query to test it, and then save the query with a new name, which keeps the July 1 Positions query intact.

## To change the July 1 Positions query design to create a new query:

1. Click the **July 1 Positions** query in the Database window (if necessary), and then click the **Design** button to open the July 1 Positions query in Design view.

2. Click the **Wage Criteria** text box, type **>=17**, and then press the **Tab** key three times. See Figure 3-23.

| Figure 3-23 | CHANGING A QUERY'S DESIGN TO CREATE A NEW QUERY |
|---|---|

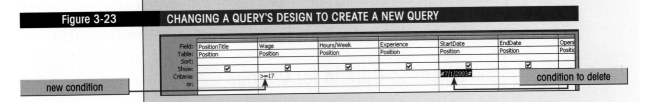

new condition

| Field: | PositionTitle | Wage | Hours/Week | Experience | StartDate | EndDate | Openi |
|---|---|---|---|---|---|---|---|
| Table: | Position | Position | Position | Position | Position | Position | Positi |
| Sort: | | | | | | | |
| Show: | ☑ | ☑ | ☑ | ☑ | | ☑ | |
| Criteria: | | >=17 | | | #7/1/2003# | | |
| or: | | | | | | | |

condition to delete

Matt's new condition specifies that a record will be selected only if its Wage field value is 17.00 or higher. Before you run the query, you need to delete the condition for the StartDate field.

3. With the StartDate field condition highlighted, press the **Delete** key. Now there is no condition for the StartDate field.

4. Click the **Run** button [!] on the Query Design toolbar. Access runs the query and displays the selected fields for only those records with a Wage field value greater than or equal to 17.00. A total of 19 records are selected. See Figure 3-24.

| Figure 3-24 | RUNNING THE MODIFIED QUERY |
|---|---|

only records with a Wage value greater than or equal to 17.00 are selected

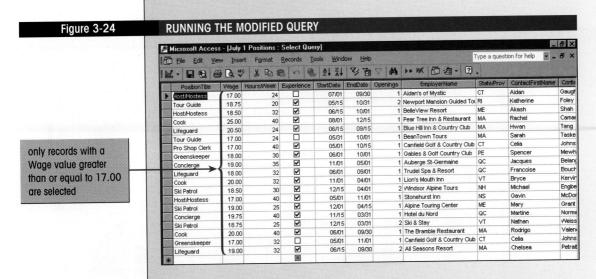

So that Matt can display this information again, as necessary, you'll save the query as High Wage Amounts.

5. Click **File** on the menu bar, click the double-arrow at the bottom of the menu to display the full menu (if necessary), and then click **Save As** to open the Save As dialog box.

6. In the text box for the new query name, type **High Wage Amounts**. Notice that the As text box specifies that you are saving the data as a query.

**7.** Click the **OK** button to save the query using the new name. The new query name appears in the title bar.

**8.** Close the Query window and return to the Database window.

Elsa asks Matt for a list of the positions with a start date of 07/01 for only the employers in Prince Edward Island. She wants to increase NSJI's business activity throughout eastern Canada (Prince Edward Island in particular), especially in the latter half of the year. To produce this data, you need to create a query containing two conditions—one for the position's start date and another to specify only the employers in Prince Edward Island (PE).

# Defining **Multiple Selection Criteria for Queries**

Multiple conditions require you to use **logical operators** to combine two or more conditions. When you want a record selected only if two or more conditions are met, you need to use the **And logical operator**. In this case, Elsa wants to see only those records with a StartDate field value of 07/01 *and* a State/Prov field value of PE. If you place conditions in separate fields in the *same* Criteria row of the design grid, all conditions in that row must be met in order for a record to be included in the query results. However, if you place conditions in *different* Criteria rows, a record will be selected if at least one of the conditions is met. If none of the conditions is met, Access does not select the record. When you place conditions in different Criteria rows, you are using the **Or logical operator**. Figure 3-25 illustrates the difference between the And and Or logical operators.

| Figure 3-25 | LOGICAL OPERATORS And AND Or FOR MULTIPLE SELECTION CRITERIA |
|---|---|

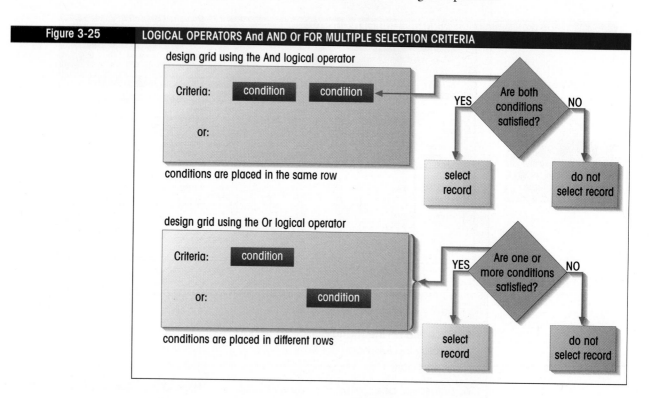

## The And Logical Operator

To create Elsa's query, you need to modify the existing July 1 Positions query to show only the records for employers located in Prince Edward Island and offering positions starting on 07/01. For the modified query, you must add a second condition in the same Criteria row. The existing condition for the StartDate field finds records for positions that start on July 1; the new condition "PE" in the State/Prov field will find records for employers in Prince Edward Island. Because the conditions appear in the same Criteria row, the query will select records only if both conditions are met.

After modifying the query, you'll save it and then rename it as "PE July 1 Positions," overwriting the July 1 Positions query, which Matt no longer needs.

### To modify the July 1 Positions query and use the And logical operator:

1. With the Queries object selected in the Database window, click **July 1 Positions** (if necessary), and then click the **Design** button to open the query in Design view.

2. Scroll the design grid to the right, click the **State/Prov Criteria** text box, type **PE**, and then press the ↓ key. See Figure 3-26.

| Figure 3-26 | QUERY TO FIND POSITIONS IN PE THAT START ON 07/01 |
| --- | --- |

And logical operator; conditions entered in the same row

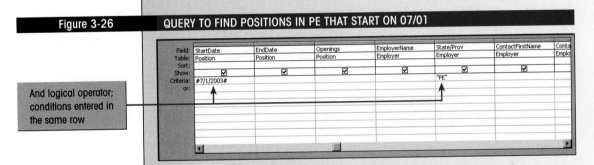

Notice that Access added quotation marks around the entry "PE"; you can type the quotation marks when you enter the condition, but if you forget to do so, Access will add them for you automatically.

The condition for the StartDate field is already entered, so you can run the query.

3. Run the query. Access displays in the datasheet only those records that meet both conditions: a StartDate field value of 07/01 and a State/Prov field value of PE. Two records are selected. See Figure 3-27.

| Figure 3-27 | RESULTS OF QUERY USING THE AND LOGICAL OPERATOR |
| --- | --- |

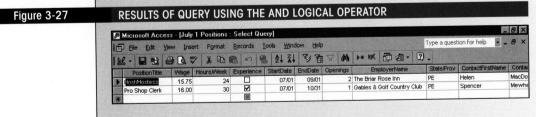

Now you can save the changes to the query and rename it.

4. Save and close the query. You return to the Database window.

5. Right-click **July 1 Positions** in the Queries list box, and then click **Rename** on the shortcut menu.

6. Click to position the insertion point to the left of the word "July," type **PE**, press the **spacebar**, and then press the **Enter** key. The query name is now PE July 1 Positions.

## Using Multiple Undo and Redo

In previous versions of Access, you could not undo certain actions. Now Access allows you to undo and redo multiple actions when you are working in Design view for tables, queries, forms, reports, and so on. For example, when working in the Query window in Design view, if you specify multiple selection criteria for a query, you can use the multiple undo feature to remove the criteria—even after you run and save the query.

To see how this feature works, you will reopen the PE July 1 Positions query in Design view, delete the two criteria, and then reinsert them using multiple undo.

### To modify the PE July 1 Positions query and use the multiple undo feature:

1. Open the **PE July 1 Positions** query in Design view.

2. Select the StartDate Criteria value, **#7/1/2003#**, and then press the **Delete** key. The StartDate Criteria text box is now empty.

3. Press the **Tab** key four times to move to and select **"PE"**, the State/Prov Criteria value, and then press the **Delete** key.

4. Run the query. Notice that the results display all records for the fields specified in the query design grid.

5. Switch back to Design view.

   Now you will use multiple undo to reverse the edits you made and reinsert the two conditions.

6. Click the **list arrow** for the Undo button on the Query Design toolbar. A menu appears listing the actions you can undo. See Figure 3-28.

Figure 3-28    USING MULTIPLE UNDO

Undo list arrow

list of actions you can undo

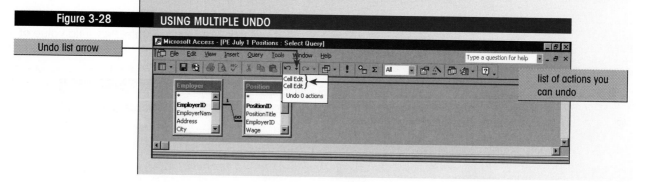

Two items, both named "Cell Edit," are listed in the Undo list box. These items represent the two changes you made to the query design—first deleting the StartDate condition and then deleting the State/Prov condition. If you select an action that is below other items in the list, you will undo all the actions above the one you select, in addition to the one you select. Currently no actions are selected, so the list box indicates "Undo 0 actions."

7. Position the pointer over the second occurrence of **Cell Edit** in the list. Notice that both undo actions are highlighted, and the list box indicates that you can undo two actions.

8. Click the second occurrence of **Cell Edit**. Both actions are "undone," and the two conditions are redisplayed in the query design grid. The multiple undo feature makes it easy for you to test different criteria for a query and, when necessary, to undo your actions based on the query results.

   Notice that the Redo button and list arrow are now available. You can redo the actions you've just undone.

9. Click the **list arrow** for the Redo button 🔄 on the Query Design toolbar. The Redo list box indicates that you can redo the two cell edits.

10. Click the **list arrow** for the Redo button 🔄 again to close the Redo list box without selecting any option.

11. Close the query. Click the **No** button in the message box that opens, asking if you want to save your changes. You return to the Database window.

Matt has another request for information. He knows that it can be difficult to find student recruits for positions that offer fewer than 30 hours of work per week or that require prior work experience. So that his staff can focus on such positions, Matt wants to see a list of those positions that provide less than 30 hours of work or that require experience. To create this query, you need to use the Or logical operator.

## The Or Logical Operator

For Matt's request, you need a query that selects a record when either one of two conditions is satisfied or when both conditions are satisfied. That is, a record is selected if the Hours/Week field value is less than 30 *or* if the Experience field value is "Yes" (checked). You will enter the condition for the Hours/Week field in one Criteria row and the condition for the Experience field in another Criteria row, thereby using the Or logical operator.

To display the information Matt wants to view, you'll create a new query containing the EmployerName and City fields from the Employer table and the PositionTitle, Hours/Week, and Experience fields from the Position table. Then you'll specify the conditions using the Or logical operator.

## *To create the query and use the Or logical operator:*

1. In the Database window, double-click **Create query in Design view**. The Show Table dialog box opens on top of the Query window in Design view.

2. Click **Employer** in the Tables list box (if necessary), click the **Add** button, click **Position**, click the **Add** button, and then click the **Close** button. The Employer and Position field lists appear in the Query window and the Show Table dialog box closes.

3. Double-click **EmployerName** in the Employer field list to add the EmployerName field to the design grid's first column Field text box.

4. Repeat Step 3 to add the **City** field from the Employer table, and then add the **PositionTitle**, **Hours/Week**, and **Experience** fields from the Position table.

   Now you need to specify the first condition, <30, in the Hours/Week field.

5. Click the **Hours/Week Criteria** text box, type **<30** and then press the **Tab** key.

   Because you want records selected if either of the conditions for the Hours/Week or Experience fields is satisfied, you must enter the condition for the Experience field in the "or" row of the design grid.

6. Press the ↓ key, and then type **Yes** in the "or" text box for Experience. See Figure 3-29.

| Figure 3-29 | QUERY WINDOW WITH THE OR LOGICAL OPERATOR |
|---|---|

Or logical operator; conditions entered in different rows

| Field: | EmployerName | City | PositionTitle | Hours/Week | Experience | |
|---|---|---|---|---|---|---|
| Table: | Employer | Employer | Position | Position | Position | |
| Sort: | | | | | | |
| Show: | ☑ | ☑ | ☑ | ☑ | ☑ | ☐ |
| Criteria: | | | | <30 | | |
| or: | | | | | Yes | |

7. Run the query. Access displays only those records that meet either condition: an Hours/Week field value less than 30 or an Experience field value of "Yes" (checked). A total of 35 records are selected.

   Matt wants the list displayed in alphabetical order by EmployerName. The first record's EmployerName field is highlighted, indicating the current field.

8. Click the **Sort Ascending** button [⇅] on the Query Datasheet toolbar.

9. Resize all datasheet columns to their best fit. Scroll through the entire datasheet to make sure that all values are completely displayed. Deselect all columns when you are finished resizing them, and then return to the top of the datasheet. See Figure 3-30.

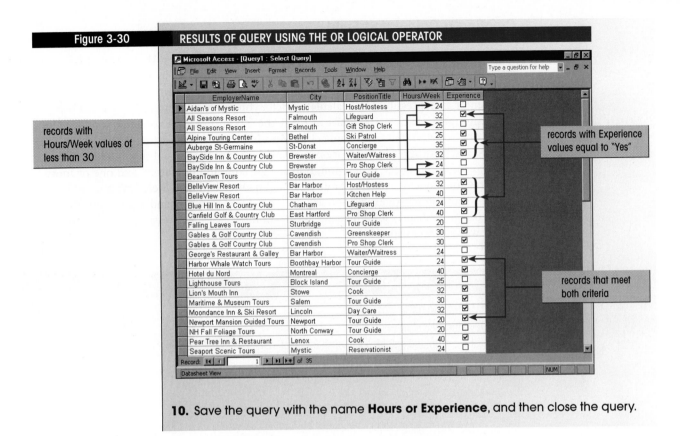

Figure 3-30 | RESULTS OF QUERY USING THE OR LOGICAL OPERATOR

records with Hours/Week values of less than 30

records with Experience values equal to "Yes"

records that meet both criteria

10. Save the query with the name **Hours or Experience**, and then close the query.

Next, Elsa wants to use the Northeast database to perform calculations. She is considering offering a 2% bonus per week to the student recruits in higher paid positions, based on employer recommendation, and she wants to know exactly what these bonuses would be.

# Performing Calculations

In addition to using queries to retrieve, sort, and filter data in a database, you can use a query to perform calculations. To perform a calculation, you define an **expression** containing a combination of database fields, constants, and operators. For numeric expressions, the data types of the database fields must be number, currency, or date/time; the constants are numbers such as .02 (for the 2% bonus); and the operators can be arithmetic operators (+ – * /) or other specialized operators. In complex expressions, you can enclose calculations in parentheses to indicate which one should be performed first. In expressions without parentheses, Access calculates in the following order of precedence: multiplication and division before addition and subtraction. When operators have equal precedence, Access calculates them in order from left to right.

To perform a calculation in a query, you add a calculated field to the query. A **calculated field** is a field that displays the results of an expression. A calculated field appears in a query datasheet or in a form or report; however, it does not exist in a database. When you run a query that contains a calculated field, Access evaluates the expression defined by the calculated field and displays the resulting value in the datasheet, form, or report.

## Creating a Calculated Field

To produce the information Elsa wants, you need to open the High Wage Amounts query and create a calculated field that will multiply each Wage field value by each Hours/Week value, and then multiply that amount by .02 to determine the 2% weekly bonus Elsa is considering.

To enter an expression for a calculated field, you can type it directly in a Field text box in the design grid. Alternately, you can open the Zoom box or Expression Builder and use either one to enter the expression. The **Zoom box** is a large text box for entering text, expressions, or other values. **Expression Builder** is an Access tool that contains an expression box for entering the expression, buttons for common operators, and one or more lists of expression elements, such as table and field names. Unlike a Field text box, which is too small to show an entire expression at one time, the Zoom box and Expression Builder are large enough to display lengthy expressions. In most cases, Expression Builder provides the easiest way to enter expressions.

---

**REFERENCE WINDOW**         **RW**

### Using Expression Builder

- Open the query in Design view.
- In the design grid, position the insertion point in the Field text box of the field for which you want to create an expression.
- Click the Build button on the Query Design toolbar.
- Use the expression elements and common operators to build the expression, or type the expression directly.
- Click the OK button.

---

You'll begin by copying, pasting, and renaming the High Wage Amounts query, keeping the original query intact. You'll name the new query "High Wages with Bonus." Then you'll modify this query in Design view to show only the information Elsa wants to view.

---

### To copy the High Wage Amounts query and paste the copy with a new name:

1. Right-click the **High Wage Amounts** query in the list of queries, and then click **Copy** on the shortcut menu.

2. Right-click an empty area of the Database window, and then click **Paste** on the shortcut menu. The Paste As dialog box opens.

3. Type **High Wages with Bonus** in the Query Name text box, and then press the **Enter** key. The new query appears in the query list, along with the original High Wage Amounts query.

---

Now you're ready to modify the High Wages with Bonus query to create the calculated field for Elsa.

## To modify the High Wages with Bonus query:

1. Open the **High Wages with Bonus** query in Design view.

   Elsa wants to see only the EmployerName, PositionTitle, and Wage fields in the query results. First, you'll delete the unnecessary fields, and then you'll move the EmployerName field so that it appears first in the query results.

2. Scroll the design grid to the right until the Hours/Week and EmployerName fields are visible at the same time.

3. Position the pointer on the Hours/Week field until the pointer changes to a ↓ shape, click and hold down the mouse button, drag the mouse to the right to highlight the Hours/Week, Experience, StartDate, EndDate, and Openings fields, and then release the mouse button.

4. Press the **Delete** key to delete the five selected fields.

5. Repeat Steps 3 and 4 to delete the State/Prov, ContactFirstName, ContactLastName, and Phone fields from the query design grid.

   Next you'll move the EmployerName field to the left of the PositionTitle field so that the Wage values will appear next to the calculated field values in the query results.

6. Scroll the design grid back to the left (if necessary), select the **EmployerName** field, and then use the pointer ⬚ to drag the field to the left of the PositionTitle field. See Figure 3-31.

| Figure 3-31 | MODIFIED QUERY BEFORE ADDING THE CALCULATED FIELD |

EmployerName field positioned to the left of PositionTitle field

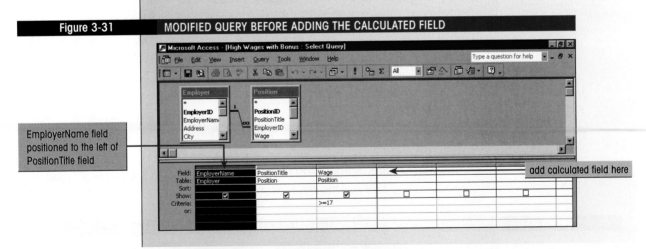

add calculated field here

Now you're ready to use Expression Builder to enter the calculated field in the High Wages with Bonus query.

## To add the calculated field to the High Wages with Bonus query:

1. Position the insertion point in the Field text box to the right of the Wage field, and then click the **Build** button ⬚ on the Query Design toolbar. The Expression Builder dialog box opens. See Figure 3-32.

| Figure 3-32 | INITIAL EXPRESSION BUILDER DIALOG BOX |
|---|---|

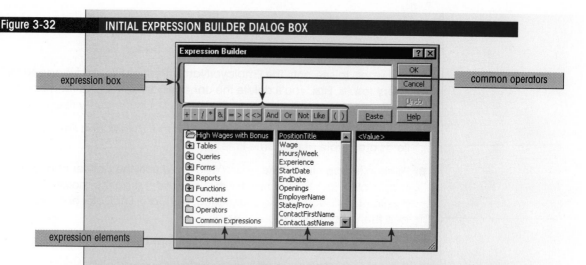

You use the common operators and expression elements to help you build an expression. Note that the High Wages with Bonus query is already selected in the list box on the lower left; the fields included in the original version of the query are listed in the center box.

The expression for the calculated field will multiply the Wage field values by the Hours/Week field values, and then multiply that amount by the numeric constant .02 (which represents a 2% bonus). To include a field in the expression, you select the field and then click the Paste button. To include a numeric constant, you simply type the constant in the expression.

2. Click **Wage** in the field list, and then click the **Paste** button. [Wage] appears in the expression box.

   To include the multiplication operator in the expression, you click the asterisk (**\***) button.

3. Click the **\*** button in the row of common operators, click **Hours/Week** in the field list, and then click the **Paste** button. The expression multiplies the Wage values by the Hours/Week values.

4. Click the **\*** button in the row of common operators, and then type **.02**. You have finished entering the expression. See Figure 3-33.

| Figure 3-33 | COMPLETED EXPRESSION FOR THE CALCULATED FIELD |
|---|---|

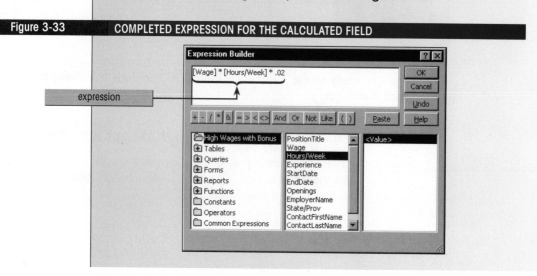

Note that you also could have typed the expression directly into the expression box, instead of clicking the field names and the operator.

5. Click the **OK** button. Access closes the Expression Builder dialog box and adds the expression to the design grid in the Field text box for the calculated field.

Next, you need to specify a name for the calculated field as it will appear in the query results.

6. Press the **Home** key to position the insertion point to the left of the expression.

You'll enter the name WeeklyBonus, which is descriptive of the field's contents; then you'll run the query.

7. Type **WeeklyBonus**:. *Make sure you include the colon following the field name. The colon is needed to separate the field name from its expression.*

8. Run the query. Access displays the query datasheet, which contains the three specified fields and the calculated field with the name "WeeklyBonus." Resize all datasheet columns to their best fit. See Figure 3-34.

| Figure 3-34 | DATASHEET DISPLAYING THE CALCULATED FIELD |

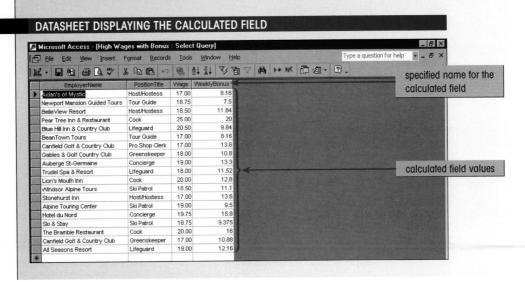

Notice the WeeklyBonus value for Ski & Stay; the value appears with three decimal places (9.375). Currency values should have only two decimal places, so you need to format the WeeklyBonus calculated field so that all values appear in the Fixed format with two decimal places.

## To format the calculated field:

1. Switch to Design view.

2. Right-click the **WeeklyBonus** calculated field in the design grid to open the shortcut menu, and then click **Properties**. The property sheet for the selected field opens. The property sheet for a field provides options for changing the display of field values in the datasheet.

3. Click the right side of the **Format** text box to display the list of formats, and then click **Fixed**.

**4.** Click the right side of the **Decimal Places** text box, and then click **2**.

**5.** Click in the **Description** text box to deselect the Decimal Places setting. See Figure 3-35.

| Figure 3-35 | PROPERTY SHEET SETTINGS TO FORMAT THE CALCULATED FIELD |
|---|---|

Now that you have formatted the calculated field, you can run the query.

**6.** Close the Field Properties window, and then save and run the query. The value for Ski & Stay now correctly appears as 9.38.

**7.** Close the query.

Elsa prepares a report on a regular basis that includes a summary of information about the wages paid to student recruits. She lists the minimum hourly wage paid, the average wage amount, and the maximum hourly wage paid. She asks you to create a query to determine these statistics from data in the Position table.

## Using Aggregate Functions

You can calculate statistical information, such as totals and averages, on the records selected by a query. To do this, you use the Access aggregate functions. **Aggregate functions** perform arithmetic operations on selected records in a database. Figure 3-36 lists the most frequently used aggregate functions. Aggregate functions operate on the records that meet a query's selection criteria. You specify an aggregate function for a specific field, and the appropriate operation applies to that field's values for the selected records.

| Figure 3-36 | FREQUENTLY USED AGGREGATE FUNCTIONS | |
|---|---|---|

| AGGREGATE FUNCTION | DETERMINES | DATA TYPES SUPPORTED |
|---|---|---|
| Avg | Average of the field values for the selected records | AutoNumber, Currency, Date/Time, Number |
| Count | Number of records selected | AutoNumber, Currency, Date/Time, Memo, Number, OLE Object, Text, Yes/No |
| Max | Highest field value for the selected records | AutoNumber, Currency, Date/Time, Number, Text |
| Min | Lowest field value for the selected records | AutoNumber, Currency, Date/Time, Number, Text |
| Sum | Total of the field values for the selected records | AutoNumber, Currency, Date/Time, Number |

To display the minimum, average, and maximum of all the wage amounts in the Position table, you will use the Min, Avg, and Max aggregate functions for the Wage field.

## To calculate the minimum, average, and maximum of all wage amounts:

1. Double-click **Create query in Design view**, click **Position**, click the **Add** button, and then click the **Close** button. The Position field list is added to the Query window and the Show Table dialog box closes.

   To perform the three calculations on the Wage field, you need to add the field to the design grid three times.

2. Double-click **Wage** in the Position field list three times to add three copies of the field to the design grid.

   You need to select an aggregate function for each Wage field. When you click the Totals button on the Query Design toolbar, a row labeled "Total" is added to the design grid. The Total row provides a list of the aggregate functions that you can select.

3. Click the **Totals** button $\Sigma$ on the Query Design toolbar. A new row labeled "Total" appears between the Table and Sort rows in the design grid. See Figure 3-37.

| Figure 3-37 | TOTAL ROW INSERTED IN THE DESIGN GRID |
|---|---|

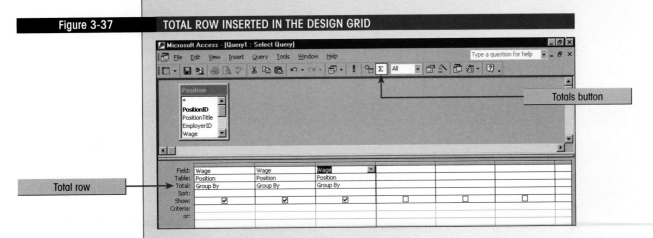

In the Total row, you specify the aggregate function you want to use for a field.

4. Click the right side of the first column's **Total** text box, and then click **Min**. This field will calculate the minimum amount of all the Wage field values.

   When you run the query, Access automatically will assign a datasheet column name of "MinOfWage" for this field. You can change the datasheet column name to a more descriptive or readable name by entering the name you want in the Field text box. However, you must also keep the field name Wage in the Field text box, because it identifies the field whose values will be calculated. The Field text box will contain the datasheet column name you specify followed by the field name (Wage) with a colon separating the two names.

5. Position the insertion point to the left of Wage in the first column's Field text box, and then type **MinimumWage**:. Be sure that you type the colon.

6. Click the right side of the second column's **Total** text box, and then click **Avg**. This field will calculate the average of all the Wage field values.

7. Position the insertion point to the left of Wage in the second column's Field text box, and then type **AverageWage**:.

8. Click the right side of the third column's **Total** text box, and then click **Max**. This field will calculate the maximum amount of all the Wage field values.

9. Position the insertion point to the left of Wage in the third column's Field text box, and then type **MaximumWage**:.

   The query design is completed, so you can run the query.

10. Run the query. Access displays one record containing the three aggregate function values. The single row of summary statistics represents calculations based on the 64 records selected by the query.

    You need to resize the three columns to their best fit to see the column names.

11. Resize all columns to their best fit, and then position the insertion point in the field value in the first column. See Figure 3-38.

| Figure 3-38 | RESULTS OF THE QUERY USING AGGREGATE FUNCTIONS |
|---|---|

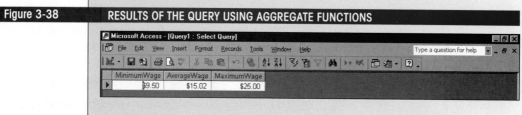

12. Save the query as **Wage Statistics**, and then close the query.

Elsa also wants her report to include the same wage statistics (minimum, average, and maximum) for each type of position. She asks you to display the wage statistics for each different PositionTitle value in the Position table.

## Using Record Group Calculations

In addition to calculating statistical information on all or selected records in selected tables, you can calculate statistics for groups of records. For example, you can determine the number of employers in each state or province, or the average wage amount by position.

To create a query for Elsa's latest request, you can modify the current query by adding the PositionTitle field and assigning the Group By operator to it. The **Group By operator** divides the selected records into groups based on the values in the specified field. Those records with the same value for the field are grouped together, and the datasheet displays one record for each group. Aggregate functions, which appear in the other columns of the design grid, provide statistical information for each group.

You need to modify the current query to add the Group By operator for the PositionTitle field. This will display the statistical information grouped by position for the 64 selected records in the query. As you did earlier, you will copy the Wage Statistics query and paste it with a new name, keeping the original query intact, to create the new query.

### To copy and paste the query, and then add the PositionTitle field with the Group By operator:

1. Right-click the **Wage Statistics** query in the list of queries, and then click **Copy** on the shortcut menu.

2. Right-click an empty area of the Database window, and then click **Paste** on the shortcut menu.

3. Type **Wage Statistics by Position** in the Query Name text box, and then press the **Enter** key.

   Now you're ready to modify the query design.

4. Open the **Wage Statistics by Position** query in Design view.

5. Double-click **PositionTitle** in the Position field list to add the field to the design grid. Group By, which is the default option in the Total row, appears for the PositionTitle field.

   You've completed the query changes, so you can run the query.

6. Run the query. Access displays 16 records—one for each PositionTitle group. Each record contains the three aggregate function values and the PositionTitle field value for the group. Again, the summary statistics represent calculations based on the 64 records selected by the query. See Figure 3-39.

| Figure 3-39 | AGGREGATE FUNCTIONS GROUPED BY PositionTitle |
|---|---|

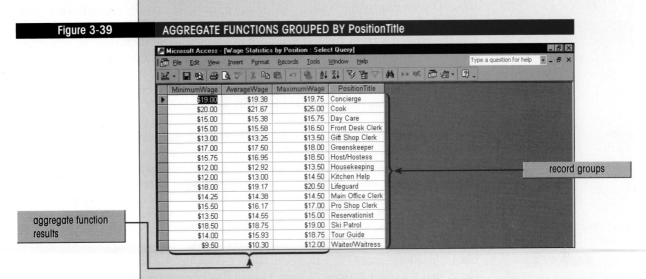

7. Save and close the query, and then click the **Close** button ☒ on the Access window title bar to close the Northeast database and to exit Access.

   TROUBLE? If a dialog box opens and asks if you want to empty the Clipboard, click the Yes button.

The queries you've created and saved will help Elsa, Zack, Matt, and other employees to monitor and analyze the business activity of NSJI's employer customers. Now any NSJI staff member can run the queries at any time, modify them as needed, or use them as the basis for designing new queries to meet additional information requirements.

# Session 3.2 QUICK CHECK

1. A(n) _____ is a criterion, or rule, that determines which records are selected for a query datasheet.

2. In the design grid, where do you place the conditions for two different fields when you use the And logical operator? The Or logical operator?

3. To perform a calculation in a query, you define a(n) _____ containing a combination of database fields, constants, and operators.
4. How does a calculated field differ from a table field?
5. What is an aggregate function?
6. The _____ operator divides selected records into groups based on the values in a field.

## REVIEW ASSIGNMENTS

Elsa needs information from the **Recruits** database, and she asks you to query the database by completing the following:

1. Make sure your Data Disk is in the appropriate disk drive, start Access, and then open the **Recruits** database located in the Review folder on your Data Disk.

2. Create a select query based on the **Student** table. Display the StudentID, FirstName, and LastName fields in the query results; sort in ascending order based on the LastName field values; and select only those records whose Nation value equals Ireland. (*Hint*: Do not display the Nation field values in the query results.) Save the query as **Students from Ireland**, run the query, and then print the query datasheet.

3. Use the **Students from Ireland** datasheet to update the **Student** table by changing the FirstName field value for StudentID OMA9956 to Richard. Print the query datasheet, and then close the query.

4. Define a one-to-many relationship between the primary **Recruiter** table and the related **Student** table. Select the referential integrity option and both cascade options for the relationship.

5. Use Design view to create a select query based on the **Recruiter** and **Student** tables. Select the fields FirstName (from the **Student** table), LastName (from the **Student** table), City, Nation, BonusQuota, Salary, and SSN (from the **Student** table), in that order. Sort in ascending order based on the Nation field values. Select only those records whose SSN equals "977071798." (*Hint*: Do not type the dashes for the SSN criterion, and do not display the SSN field values in the query results.) Save the query as **Wolfe Recruits**, and then run the query. Resize all columns in the datasheet to fit the data. Print the datasheet, and then save the query.

*Explore* 6. Use Help to learn about Filter By Form. In the Ask a Question box, type, "How do I create a filter?" and then click the topic "Create a filter." Read the portions of the topic pertaining to Filter By Selection and Filter By Form, and then close the Microsoft Access Help window.

*Explore* 7. Use the Filter By Form button on the Query Datasheet toolbar to filter the records in the **Wolfe Recruits** datasheet that have a Nation field value of "Spain," and then apply the filter. Print the query datasheet.

*Explore* 8. Remove the filter to display all records, and then save and close the query.

*Explore* 9. Use Design view to create a query based on the **Recruiter** table that shows all recruiters with a BonusQuota field value between 40 and 50, and whose Salary field value is greater than 35000. (*Hint*: Refer to Figure 3-18 to determine the correct comparison operator to use.) Display all fields except SSN from the **Recruiter** table. Save the query as **Bonus Info**, and then run the query.

*Explore* 10. Switch to Design view for the **Bonus Info** query. Create a calculated field named RaiseAmt that displays the net amount of a 3% raise to the Salary values. Display the results in descending order by RaiseAmt. Save the query as **Salaries with Raises**, run the query, resize all columns in the datasheet to fit the data, print the query datasheet, and then save and close the query.

11. In the Database window, copy the **Students from Ireland** query, and then paste it with the new name **Students from Holland Plus Younger Students**. Open the new query in Design view. Modify the query to display only those records with a Nation field value of Holland or with a BirthDate field value greater than 1/1/84. Also, modify the query to include the Nation field values in the query results. Save and run the query. Resize all columns in the datasheet to fit the data, print the query datasheet, and then save and close the query.

12. Create a new query based on the **Recruiter** table. Use the Min, Max, and Avg aggregate functions to find the lowest, highest, and average values in the Salary field. Name the three aggregate fields LowestSalary, HighestSalary, and AverageSalary, respectively. Save the query as **Salary Statistics**, and then run the query. Resize all columns in the datasheet to fit the data, print the query datasheet, and then save and close the query.

13. Open the **Salary Statistics** query in Design view. Modify the query so that the records are grouped by the BonusQuota field. Save the query as **Salary Statistics by BonusQuota**, run the query, print the query datasheet, and then close the query.

14. Close the **Recruits** database, and then exit Access.

## CASE PROBLEMS

*Case 1. Lim's Video Photography*   Youngho Lim wants to view specific information about his clients and video shoot events. He asks you to query the **Videos** database by completing the following:

1. Make sure your Data Disk is in the appropriate disk drive, start Access, and then open the **Videos** database located in the Cases folder on your Data Disk.

> **Explore**

2. Define the necessary one-to-many relationships between the database tables, as follows: between the primary **Client** table and the related **Contract** table, between the primary **Contract** table and the related **Shoot** table, and between the primary **ShootDesc** table and the related **Shoot** table. (*Hint*: Add all four tables to the Relationships window, and then define the three relationships.) Select the referential integrity option and both cascade options for each relationship.

3. Create a select query based on the **Client** and **Contract** tables. Display the ClientName, City, ContractDate, and ContractAmt fields, in that order. Sort in ascending order based on the ClientName field values. Run the query, save the query as **Client Contracts**, and then print the datasheet.

4. Use Filter By Selection to display only those records with a City field value of Oakland in the **Client Contracts** datasheet. Print the datasheet and then remove the filter. Save and close the query.

5. Open the **Client Contracts** query in Design view. Modify the query to display only those records with a ContractAmt value greater than or equal to 600. Run the query, save the query as **Contract Amounts**, and then print the datasheet.

6. Switch to Design view for the **Contract Amounts** query. Modify the query to display only those records with a ContractAmt value greater than or equal to 600 and with a City value of San Francisco. Also modify the query so that the City field values are not displayed in the query results. Run the query, save it as **SF Contract Amounts**, print the datasheet, and then close the query.

7. Close the **Videos** database, and then exit Access.

*Case 2. DineAtHome.course.com*   Claire Picard is completing an analysis of the orders placed at restaurants that use her company's services. To help her find the information she needs, you'll query the **Meals** database by completing the following:

1. Make sure your Data Disk is in the appropriate disk drive, start Access, and then open the **Meals** database located in the Cases folder on your Data Disk.

2. Define a one-to-many relationship between the primary **Restaurant** table and the related **Order** table. Select the referential integrity option and both cascade options for the relationship.

3. Use Design view to create a select query based on the **Restaurant** and **Order** tables. Display the fields RestaurantName, City, OrderAmt, and OrderDate, in that order. Sort in descending order based on the OrderAmt field values. Select only those records whose OrderAmt is greater than 150. Save the query as **Large Orders**, and then run the query.

4. Use the **Large Orders** datasheet to update the **Order** table by changing the OrderAmt value for the first record in the datasheet to 240.25. Print the datasheet, and then close the query.

5. Use Design view to create a select query based on the **Restaurant** and **Order** tables. For all orders placed on 03/21/2003, display the Order#, OrderAmt, OrderDate, and RestaurantName fields. Save the query as **March 21 Orders**, and then run the query. Switch to Design view, modify the query so that the OrderDate values do not appear in the query results, and then save the modified query. Run the query, print the query results, and then close the query.

6. Use Design view to create a select query based on the **Restaurant** table. For all restaurants that have a Website and are located in Naples, display the RestaurantName, OwnerFirstName, OwnerLastName, and Phone fields. Save the query as **Naples Restaurants with Websites**, run the query, print the query results, and then close the query.

7. Use Design view to create a select query based on the **Restaurant** and **Order** tables. For all orders placed on 03/14/2003 or 03/15/2003, display the fields OrderDate, OrderAmt, RestaurantName, and Restaurant# (from the **Restaurant** table). Display the results in ascending order by OrderDate and then in descending order by OrderAmt. Save the query as **Selected Dates**, run the query, print the query datasheet, and then close the query.

**Explore** ▶ 8. Use the **Order** table to display the highest, lowest, total, average, and count of the OrderAmt field for all orders. Then do the following:

   a. Specify column names of HighestOrder, LowestOrder, TotalOrders, AverageOrder, and #Orders. Use the property sheet for each column (except #Orders) to format the results as Fixed with two decimal places. Save the query as **Order Statistics**, and then run the query. Resize all datasheet columns to their best fit, save the query, and then print the query results.

   b. Change the query to display the same statistics grouped by RestaurantName. (*Hint*: Use the Show Table button on the Query Design toolbar to add the **Restaurant** table to the query.) Save the query as **Order Statistics by Restaurant**. Run the query, print the query results, and then close the query.

9. Close the **Meals** database, and then exit Access.

*Case 3. Redwood Zoo*   Michael Rosenfeld wants to find specific information about the donors and their pledge amounts for the Redwood Zoo. You'll help them find the information in the **Redwood** database by completing the following:

1. Make sure your Data Disk is in the appropriate disk drive, start Access, and then open the **Redwood** database located in the Cases folder on your Data Disk.

**Explore** ▶ 2. Define the necessary one-to-many relationships between the database tables, as follows: between the primary **Donor** table and the related **Pledge** table, and between the primary **Fund** table and the related **Pledge** table. (*Hint*: Add all three tables to the Relationships window, and then define the two relationships.) Select the referential integrity option and both cascade options for each relationship.

3. Use Design view to create a select query that, for all pledges with a TotalPledged field value of greater than 200, displays the DonorID (from the **Donor** table), FirstName, LastName, Pledge#, TotalPledged, and FundName fields. Sort the query in ascending order by TotalPledged. Save the query as **Large Pledges**, and then run the query.

4. Use the **Large Pledges** datasheet to update the **Pledge** table by changing the TotalPledged field value for Pledge# 2976 to 750. Print the query datasheet, and then close the query.

5. Use Design view to create a select query that, for all donors who pledged less than $150 or who donated to the Whale Watchers fund, displays the Pledge#, PledgeDate, TotalPledged, FirstName, and LastName fields. Save the revised query as **Pledged or Whale Watchers**, run the query, and then print the query datasheet. Change the query to select all donors who pledged less than $150 and who donated to the Whale Watchers fund. Save the revised query as **Pledged and Whale Watchers**, and then run the query. Close the query.

**Explore** ▶ 6. Use Design view to create a select query that displays the DonorID (from the **Donor** table), TotalPledged, PaymentMethod, PledgeDate, and FundName fields. Save the query as **Pledges after Costs**. Create a calculated field named Overhead that displays the results of multiplying the TotalPledged field values by 15% (to account for overhead costs). Save the query, and then create a second calculated field named NetPledge that displays the results of subtracting the Overhead field values from the TotalPledged field values.

Format the calculated fields as Fixed. Display the results in ascending order by TotalPledged. Save the modified query, and then run the query. Resize all datasheet columns to their best fit, print the query results, and then save and close the query.

**Explore** ▷ 7. Use the **Pledge** table to display the sum, average, and count of the TotalPledged field for all pledges. Then do the following:

a. Specify column names of TotalPledge, AveragePledge, and #Pledges.

b. Change properties so that the values in the TotalPledge and AveragePledge columns display two decimal places and the Fixed format.

c. Save the query as **Pledge Statistics**, run the query, resize all datasheet columns to their best fit, and then print the query datasheet. Save the query.

d. Change the query to display the sum, average, and count of the TotalPledged field for all pledges by FundName. (*Hint*: Use the Show Table button on the Query Design toolbar to add the **Fund** table to the query.) Save the query as **Pledge Statistics by Fund**, run the query, print the query datasheet, and then close the query.

8. Close the **Redwood** database, and then exit Access.

*Case 4. Mountain River Adventures* Connor and Siobhan Dempsey want to analyze data about their clients and the rafting trips they take. Help them query the **Trips** database by completing the following:

1. Make sure your Data Disk is in the appropriate disk drive, start Access, and then open the **Trips** database located in the Cases folder on your Data Disk.

**Explore** ▷ 2. Define the necessary one-to-many relationships between the database tables, as follows: between the primary **Client** table and the related **Booking** table, and between the primary **Rafting Trip** table and the related **Booking** table. (*Hint*: Add all three tables to the Relationships window, and then define the two relationships.) Select the referential integrity option and both cascade options for each relationship.

3. For all clients, display the ClientName, City, State/Prov, Booking#, and TripDate fields. Save the query as **Client Trip Dates**, and then run the query. Resize all datasheet columns to their best fit. In Datasheet view, sort the query results in ascending order by the TripDate field. Print the query datasheet, and then save and close the query.

4. For all clients from Colorado (CO), display the ClientName, City, State/Prov, Trip#, People, and TripDate fields. Sort the query in ascending order by City. Save the query as **Colorado Clients**, and then run the query. Modify the query to remove the display of the State/Prov field values from the query results. Save the modified query, run the query, print the query datasheet, and then close the query.

**Explore** ▷ 5. For all clients who are not from Colorado or who are taking a rafting trip in the month of July 2003, display the ClientName, City, State/Prov, Booking#, TripDate, and Trip# fields. (*Hint*: Refer to Figure 3-18 to determine the correct comparison operators to use.) Sort the query in descending order by TripDate. Save the query as **Out of State or July**, run the query, and then print the query datasheet. Change the query to select all clients who are not from Colorado and who are taking a rafting trip in the month of July 2003. Sort the query in ascending order by State/Prov. Save the query as **Out of State and July**, run the query, print the query datasheet, and then close the query.

6. For all bookings, display the Booking#, TripDate, Trip# (from the **Booking** table), River, People, and Fee/Person fields. Save the query as **Trip Cost**. Then create a calculated field named TripCost that displays the results of multiplying the People field values by the Fee/Person field values. Display the results in descending order by TripCost. Run the query, resize all datasheet columns to their best fit, print the query datasheet, and then save and close the query.

**Explore** ▷ 7. Use the **Rafting Trip** table to determine the minimum, average, and maximum Fee/Person for all trips. Use the Ask a Question box to ask the question, "What is a caption?" and then locate and click the topic "Change a field name in a query." Read the displayed information, and then click and read the subtopic "Change a field's caption."

Close the Help window. Set the Caption property of the three fields to Lowest Fee, Average Fee, and Highest Fee, respectively. Also set the properties so that the results of the three fields are displayed as Fixed with two decimal places. Save the query as **Fee Statistics**, run the query, resize all datasheet columns to their best fit, print the query datasheet, and then save the query again. Revise the query to show the fee statistics grouped by People. (*Hint*: Use the Show Table button on the Query Design toolbar to display the Show Table dialog box.) Save the revised query as **Fee Statistics by People**, run the query, print the query datasheet, and then close the query.

*Explore*

8. Use the Ask a Question box to ask the following question: "How do I create a Top Values query?" Click the topic "Show only the high or low values in a query." Read the displayed information, and then close the Help window. Open the **Trip Cost** query in Design view, and then modify the query to display only the top five values for the TripCost field. Save the query as **Top Trip Cost**, run the query, print the query datasheet, and then close the query.

9. Close the **Trips** database, and then exit Access.

## INTERNET ASSIGNMENTS

**Student Union**

The purpose of the Internet Assignments is to challenge you to find information on the Internet that you can use to create effective documents. The actual assignments are updated and maintained on the Course Technology Web site. Log on to the Internet and use your Web browser to go to the Student Union on the New Perspectives Series site at **www.course.com/NewPerspectives/studentunion**. Click the Online Companions link, and then click the link for this text.

# QUICK CHECK ANSWERS

## Session 3.1

1. a general query in which you specify the fields and records you want Access to select
2. The field list contains the table name at the top of the list box and the table's fields listed in the order in which they appear in the table; the design grid displays columns that contain specifications about a field you will use in the query.
3. A table datasheet and a query datasheet look the same, appearing in Datasheet view, and can be used to update data in a database. A table datasheet shows the permanent data in a table, whereas a query datasheet is temporary and its contents are based on the criteria you establish in the design grid.
4. primary table; related table
5. Referential integrity
6. oldest to most recent date
7. when you want to perform different types of sorts (both ascending and descending, for example) on multiple fields, and when you want to sort on multiple fields that are nonadjacent or in the wrong order, but you do not want to rearrange the columns in the query datasheet to accomplish the sort
8. filter

## Session 3.2

1. condition
2. in the same Criteria row; in different Criteria rows
3. expression
4. A calculated field appears in a query datasheet, form, or report but does not exist in a database, as does a table field.
5. a function that performs an arithmetic operation on selected records in a database
6. Group By

*New Perspectives on*

# MICROSOFT®

# POWERPOINT®

# 2002

## TUTORIAL 1   PPT 1.03

*Creating a PowerPoint Presentation*

Presentation on Information about Global Humanitarian

# Read This Before You Begin

## To the Student

### Data Disks

To complete this tutorial, Review Assignments, and Case Problems, you need one Data Disk. Your instructor will either provide you with the Data Disk or ask you to make your own.

If you are making your own Data Disk, you will need **one** blank, formatted high-density disk. You will need to copy a set of files and/or folders from a file server, standalone computer, or the Web onto your disk. Your instructor will tell you which computer, drive letter, and folders contain the files you need. You could also download the files by going to www.course.com and following the instructions on the screen.

The information below shows you which folders go on your disk, so that you will have enough disk space to complete the tutorial, Review Assignments, and Case Problems:

### Data Disk 1

Write this on the disk label:
Data Disk 1: PowerPoint 2002 Tutorial 1
Put these folders on the disk:
Tutorial.01

When you begin the tutorial, be sure you are using the correct Data Disk. Refer to the "File Finder" chart at the back of this text for more detailed information on which files are used in which tutorials. See the inside front or inside back cover of this book for more information on Data Disk files, or ask your instructor or technical support person for assistance.

### Using Your Own Computer

If you are going to work through this book using your own computer, you need:

■ **Computer System** Microsoft Windows 98, NT, 2000 Professional, or higher must be installed on your computer. This book assumes a full installation of Microsoft PowerPoint.

■ **Data Disk** You will not be able to complete the tutorials or exercises in this book using your own computer until you have your Data Disk.

### Visit Our World Wide Web Site

Additional materials designed especially for you are available on the World Wide Web.
Go to www.course.com/NewPerspectives.

## To the Instructor

The Data Disk Files are available on the Instructor's Resource Kit for this title. Follow the instructions in the Help file on the CD-ROM to install the programs to your network or standalone computer. For information on creating Data Disks, see the "To the Student" section above.

You are granted a license to copy the Data Files to any computer or computer network used by students who have purchased this book.

# CREATING A POWERPOINT PRESENTATION

*Presentation on Information about Global Humanitarian*

## OBJECTIVES

In this tutorial you will:

- Identify components of the PowerPoint window
- Open and view an existing PowerPoint presentation
- Create a folder for saving presentations
- Create a presentation using the AutoContent Wizard
- Add, move, and delete slides
- Promote and demote text in the Outline tab
- Create speaker notes for slides
- Check the spelling and style in a presentation
- Preview and print slides
- Print outlines, handouts, and speaker notes

## Global Humanitarian, Austin Office

In 1985, a group of Austin, Texas, business leaders established a not-for-profit organization called Global Humanitarian. Its goal was to alleviate abject poverty through public awareness and personal involvement in sustainable self-help initiatives in Third World villages. Today, Global Humanitarian is a large umbrella organization and clearinghouse for national and international humanitarian organizations. Its five major functions are to help provide the following:

- **Entrepreneurial support** in less-developed countries, which includes providing low-interest loans and assistance for home and family businesses, and mentoring in basic business practices
- **Service expeditions** to less-developed countries, where participants help: build homes and schools; dig wells and build culinary water systems; build, and train people to use, healthy, fuel-efficient stoves; provide medical, dental, and ophthalmologic services; teach personal hygiene, basic living skills, and literacy; and teach gardening skills and water purification
- **Inventory surplus exchange**, including the collection, exchange, and distribution of clothing, furniture, and other goods
- **Funding** to obtain personal and corporate contributions for humanitarian purposes, and to help write grant proposals to agencies and foundations
- **Student Internships** in less-developed countries to perform service-learning activities, learn about other peoples and cultures, study foreign languages, develop leadership, and obtain practical experience for future employment

The president of Global Humanitarian is Norma Flores, who sits on the Board of Directors and carries out its policies and procedures. The managing director of the Austin office is Miriam Schwartz, and the managing director in Latin America is Pablo Fuentes, who lives and works in Lima, Peru.

Miriam decides to prepare presentations to potential donors, expedition participants, and student interns. She asks you to develop a PowerPoint presentation that provides general information about Global Humanitarian.

## SESSION 1.1

In this session, you'll identify the parts of the PowerPoint window; open and view an existing presentation; create a new presentation using the AutoContent Wizard; and insert and modify text in both the Slide Pane and the Outline tab.

# What Is PowerPoint?

**PowerPoint** is a powerful presentation graphics program that provides everything you need to produce an effective presentation in the form of black-and-white or color over-heads, 35-mm photographic slides, or on-screen slides. You may have already seen your instructors use PowerPoint presentations to enhance their classroom lectures.

Using PowerPoint, you can prepare each component of a presentation: individual slides, speaker notes, an outline, and audience handouts. The presentation you'll create for Miriam will include slides, notes, and handouts. Before you begin creating this presentation, how-ever, you'll first preview an existing presentation recently prepared under Norma's and Miriam's direction. You'll learn about some PowerPoint capabilities that can help make your presentations more interesting and effective.

### To start PowerPoint:

1. Make sure Windows 98/2000 is running on your computer, and that the Windows desktop appears on your screen.

    **TROUBLE?** If you're running Windows NT Workstation on your computer or net-work, don't worry. Although the figures in this book were created while running Windows 2000, Windows NT and Windows 98 or 2000 share the same interface, and PowerPoint 2002 runs well under any of these operating systems.

2. Click the **Start** button on the taskbar to display the Start menu, and then point to **Programs** to display the Programs menu.

3. Point to **Microsoft PowerPoint** on the Programs menu. See Figure 1-1.

| Figure 1-1 | STARTING MICROSOFT POWERPOINT |
| --- | --- |

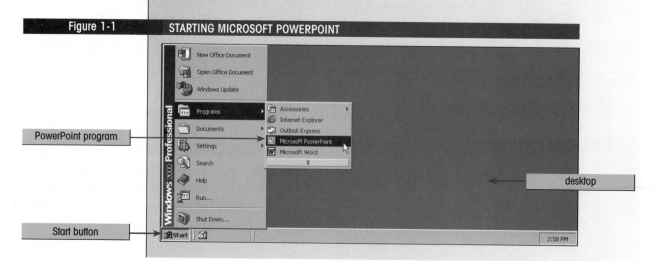

**TROUBLE?** If you don't see Microsoft PowerPoint on the Programs menu, ask your instructor or technical support person for help.

4. Click **Microsoft PowerPoint**. After a short pause, PowerPoint opens. If necessary, click the **Maximize** button ☐ so that the PowerPoint window fills the entire screen. See Figure 1-2.

| Figure 1-2 | BLANK POWERPOINT WINDOW |
| --- | --- |

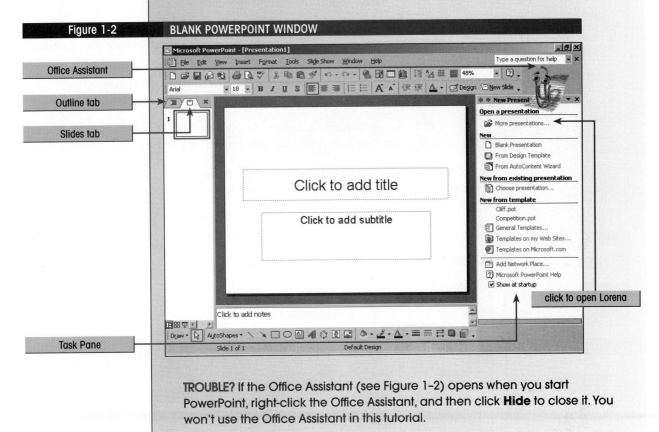

**TROUBLE?** If the Office Assistant (see Figure 1-2) opens when you start PowerPoint, right-click the Office Assistant, and then click **Hide** to close it. You won't use the Office Assistant in this tutorial.

Now that you've started PowerPoint, you're ready to open Miriam's existing presentation.

## Opening **an Existing PowerPoint Presentation**

Before you prepare the presentation on Global Humanitarian, Miriam suggests that you view the previously prepared presentation as an example of PowerPoint features. She gives you a disk with a PowerPoint file so you can open and view it. You'll do that now.

### *To open an existing presentation:*

1. Place your Data Disk in the appropriate drive.

**TROUBLE?** If you don't have a Data Disk, you need to get one before you can proceed. Your instructor or technical support person will either give you one or ask you to make your own by following the instructions on the "Read This Before You Begin" page preceding this tutorial. See your instructor or technical support person for more information.

**2.** Make sure the New Presentation Task Pane appears on the right side of the PowerPoint window. If no Task Pane appears, click **View** on the menu bar, and then click **Task Pane**. If the Task Pane appears but isn't labeled "New Presentation", click the **Task Pane** list arrow (located at the top of the pane), and then click **New Presentation**.

**3.** Under Open a presentation, click **More Presentations**. The Open dialog box appears on the screen.

**4.** Click the **Look in** list arrow to display the list of disk drives on your computer, and then click the drive that contains your Data Disk.

**5.** Double-click the **Tutorial.01** folder, double-click the **Tutorial** folder, click **Lorena**, and then click the **Open** button to display Miriam's presentation.

TROUBLE? If you see filename extensions on your screen (such as ".ppt" appended to "Lorena" in the filename), don't be concerned; they won't affect your work.

**6.** If necessary, click the **Maximize** button 🔲 so the presentation window fills the screen, and then, if necessary, click the **Normal View** button 🔲 near the lower-left corner of the screen. See Figure 1-3.

| Figure 1-3 | POWERPOINT WINDOW WITH PRESENTATION |

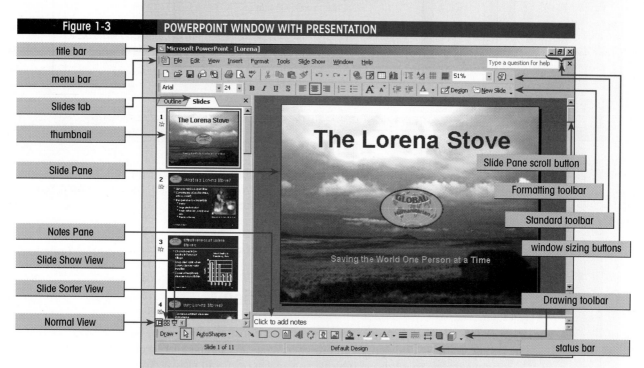

TROUBLE? If your screen doesn't show the Drawing toolbar (located near the bottom of the screen, with the word "Draw" on the left edge), click View on the menu bar, point to Toolbars, and then click Drawing.

TROUBLE? If your screen shows both the Standard toolbar and the Formatting toolbar on the same line, drag the double vertical bar immediately to the left of the Font box so that the Formatting toolbar is positioned below the Standard toolbar, as shown in Figure 1-3.

TROUBLE? If your screen still displays the Task Pane, close it by clicking the Close button in the upper-right corner of the pane.

Now that you've opened Miriam's presentation, you're ready to view some PowerPoint features. You'll begin by reviewing the PowerPoint window.

# Understanding the PowerPoint Window

The PowerPoint window contains features common to all Windows programs, as well as features specific to PowerPoint, such as the options available on the toolbars.

## Common Windows Elements

You'll recognize that several elements of the PowerPoint window are common to other Windows programs. For example, as shown in Figure 1-3, the PowerPoint window has a title bar with window sizing buttons, menu bar with sizing buttons, Standard toolbar, and Formatting toolbar. These elements function the same way in PowerPoint as they do in other Windows programs. However, the PowerPoint window also includes items that are specific to PowerPoint, such as some of the toolbar buttons and the panes.

## The Toolbars

Like many Windows programs, PowerPoint supplies several toolbars, as shown in Figure 1-3. Although many of the toolbar buttons accomplish the same tasks in PowerPoint as they do in other Windows programs, you'll also notice some differences. For example, the Drawing toolbar contains specific buttons for adding shapes, lines, and other graphic objects to the slides in your PowerPoint presentation.

Further, just above the Drawing toolbar on the left side of the screen is the View toolbar, which contains three buttons that allow you to change the way you view a slide presentation. You're currently in Normal View. Clicking the Slide Sorter View button 🔠 changes the view to miniature images (thumbnails) of all the slides at once and lets you reorder the slides or set special features for your slide show. To present your slide show, you click the Slide Show button 🖵.

## The PowerPoint Tabs

Along the left edge of the PowerPoint window, you can see two tabs, the Outline tab and the Slides tab. The **Outline tab** shows an outline of your presentation, including the titles and text of each slide. The **Slides tab** shows a column of numbered slide thumbnails so you can see a visual representation of several slides at once. You can also use the Slides tab to jump quickly to another slide by clicking the desired slide.

## The PowerPoint Panes

In Normal View, the PowerPoint window contains not only the two tabs, but also up to three panes: the Slide Pane, the Notes Pane, and the Task Pane (not shown in Figure 1-3, but shown in Figure 1-2). The **Slide Pane** shows the current slide as it will look during your slide show. You can use either the Slide Pane or the Outline tab to add or edit text, but you must use the Slide Pane to add or edit graphics and to change a slide's design and animations. The **Notes Pane** contains any notes (also called speaker notes) that you might prepare on each slide. For example, the Notes Pane might contain points to cover or phrases to say during the presentation.

Now that you're familiar with the PowerPoint window, you're ready to view Miriam's presentation.

## Viewing **a Presentation in Slide Show View**

You want to see how Miriam's presentation will appear when she shows it in Slide Show View at Global Humanitarian's executive meeting. You'll then have a better understanding of how Miriam used PowerPoint features to make her presentation informative and interesting.

### *To view the presentation in Slide Show View:*

1. Make sure Slide 1, "The Lorena Stove," appears in the Slide Pane. (If you prefer to start the slide show on a different slide, you can click the desired slide in the Slides tab or use the Slide Pane scroll bar to move to the desired slide, and then start the slide show.)

   TROUBLE? If a different slide is in the Slide Pane, drag the scroll button in the vertical scroll bar (located on the right side of the Slide Pane) to the top of the scroll bar, or click the Slide 1 thumbnail in the Slides tab.

2. Click the **Slide Show** button 🖳 on the View toolbar (just below the Slides tab). The slide show begins by filling the entire viewing area of the screen with Slide 1 of Miriam's presentation. See Figure 1-4.

| Figure 1-4 | SLIDE 1 IN SLIDE SHOW VIEW |
| --- | --- |

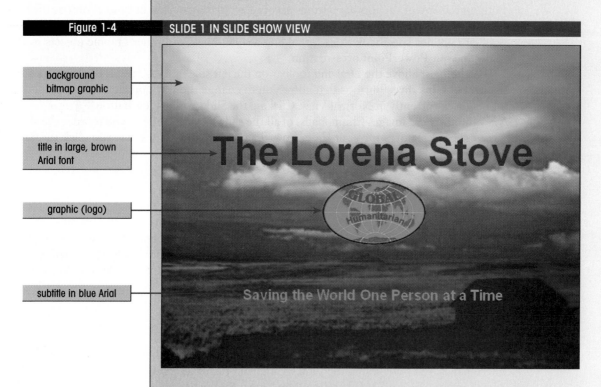

background
bitmap graphic

title in large, brown
Arial font

graphic (logo)

subtitle in blue Arial

As you view this first slide, you can already see some of the types of objects that PowerPoint allows you to place on a slide: text in different fonts, font sizes, and font colors (to differentiate between the slide title and subtitle); graphics (the Global Humanitarian logo, to clearly identify the company); background picture (the scene of the high-altitude plains in Peru, an example of a bitmap image); and custom animation (the motion of the slide title and the gradual appearance of the logo and institution motto, "Saving the World One Person at a Time"). A **bitmap image** is a grid (or "map") of colored dots (picture elements or **pixels**) that form a picture.

3. Press the **spacebar**. The slide show goes from Slide 1 to Slide 2. See Figure 1-5. You can also press the → key or click the left mouse button to advance to the next slide.

**Figure 1-5**   **SLIDE 2 IN SLIDE SHOW VIEW**

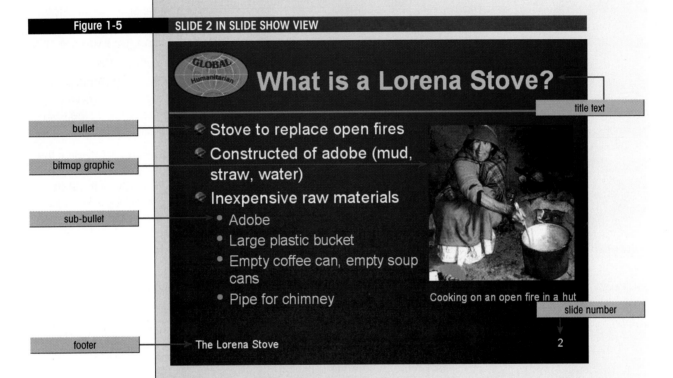

Additionally, PowerPoint provides a method for jumping from one slide to any other slide in the presentation during the slide show: right-click anywhere on the screen, point to Go, and then click Slide Navigator. The **Slide Navigator** is a dialog box that displays a list of all the slides by title. Simply click a title, and then click the Go To button to go to that slide. You also can right-click the screen during a slide show, and then click other options to view other slide features.

Notice that during the transition from Slide 1 to Slide 2, the presentation displayed Slide 2 by scrolling down from the top of the screen and covering up Slide 1. (This is an example of a **slide transition**, the manner in which a new slide appears on the screen during a slide show.) PowerPoint slide transitions can be entertaining and will reinforce the information on the slide, but they should be used sparingly.

**TROUBLE?** If you missed some of the action during the transition from Slide 1 to Slide 2, or if you want to see it again, press the ← key to redisplay Slide 1, and then press the spacebar to go to Slide 2 again.

Notice in Figure 1-5 that Slide 2 displays: (1) a colored background with a gradient fill, (2) Global Humanitarian's logo, (3) a title in a large yellow font, (4) a bulleted list (with green textured bullets and white text, or solid cyan bullets with light yellow text), (5) a footer, (6) the slide number (in the lower-right corner of the slide), and (7) a bitmap image (photograph) of a villager using an open fire. A **gradient fill** is a type of shading in which one color blends into another, making the slide more eye-catching; for example, in Figure 1-5, the blue-green at the top blends into black at the bottom. A **bulleted list** is a list of paragraphs with a special character (dot, circle, box, star, or other character) to the left of each paragraph. A **bulleted item** is one paragraph in a bulleted list. Bullets can appear at different outline levels. A **first-level** bullet is a main paragraph in a bulleted list; a **second-level** bullet is a sub-bullet beneath (and indented from) a first-level bullet. Using bulleted lists reminds both the speaker and the audience of the main points of the presentation. A **footer** is a word or phrase that appears at the bottom of each slide in the presentation (for example, "The Lorena Stove" in the lower-left corner of Figure 1-5).

In addition to bulleted lists, PowerPoint also supports numbered lists. A **numbered list** is a list of paragraphs that are numbered consecutively within a main text box (also called the body text). To number a list automatically, select the text box, and then click the Numbering button 📋 on the Formatting toolbar.

4. Read the information on Slide 2, and then press the **spacebar** (or left-click the mouse) to proceed to Slide 3. During the transition from Slide 2 to Slide 3, you again see the slide scroll down onto the screen from the top. Once the slide appears on the screen, you see a chart fade onto the screen. PowerPoint supports features for creating and customizing not only this type of chart, but also graphs, diagrams, tables, and organization charts. What you don't see on the screen is the bulleted list because this slide is designed for **progressive disclosure**, which is the appearance of the bulleted list one item at a time.

5. Press the **spacebar** to reveal the first bulleted item on Slide 3. Notice that the item flies onto the screen from the bottom. Press the **spacebar** twice to reveal the subsequent bulleted items. As one item appears, the previous item dims. See Figure 1-6. Dimming the previous bulleted items helps focus the audience's attention on the current bulleted item. Press the **spacebar** again to dim the final item in the bulleted list.

| Figure 1-6 | SLIDE 3 WITH PROGRESSIVE DISCLOSURE OF BULLETED ITEMS |

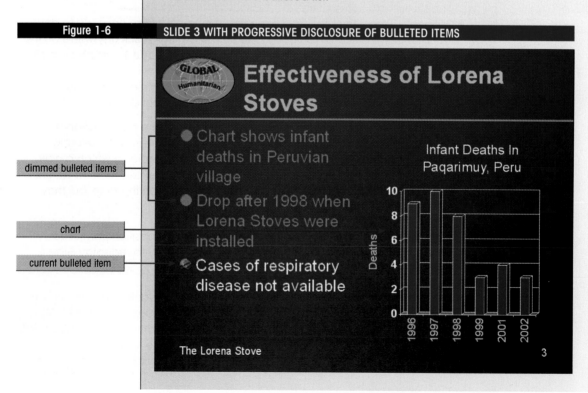

dimmed bulleted items

chart

current bulleted item

6. Read Slide 3, press the **spacebar** three times to display Slide 4 and the two groups of bulleted items, and then read the slide and view the bitmap image of the Peruvian boy. Press the **spacebar** twice, once to dim the final bulleted items, and once to go to Slide 5. Here you'll see an example of custom animation supported by PowerPoint. **Custom animation** is a user-defined special visual (or sound) effect applied to text or graphics. For example, in Slide 1 you saw custom animation in the motion of the title and the gradual appearance of Global Humanitarian's logo and motto. Here you'll see custom animation that helps explain the parts and function of the Lorena adobe stove.

7. Press the **spacebar** to cause the label "Fuel chamber" and its accompanying arrow to fade onto the screen. This and subsequent items appear one at a time while the speaker explains that aspect of the stove; the custom animation draws the audience's attention to the particular item on the screen.

8. Press the **spacebar** three more times, pausing between each to allow the label and arrow to fade onto the screen, and then press the **spacebar** one more time to hear the sound of wind (or a breeze) as the graphic labeled "smoke" appears on the Lorena stove. The smoke object is an example of a user-drawn graphic. Press the **spacebar** to animate the smoke graphic and repeat the sound effect. This custom animation shows how smoke goes through the stove and up the chimney rather than into the villager's hut. See Figure 1-7.

| Figure 1-7 | SLIDE 5 AFTER ADDING TEXT |

animated user-drawn object

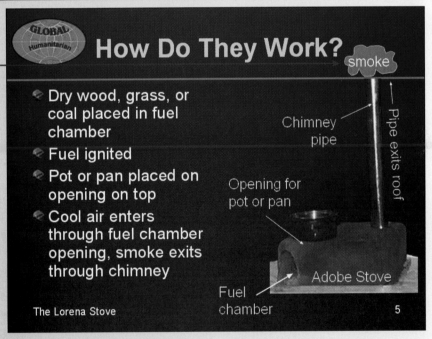

9. Go to Slide 6 where you can see a simple diagram drawn using PowerPoint drawing tools—which include shapes like circles, ovals, squares, rectangles, arrows, boxes, stars, and banners.

10. Continue to look through all the slides, pausing at each one to read the bulleted items and view the graphics. Once you reach Slide 11 at the end of the slide show and press the **spacebar** once more, PowerPoint displays a black, nearly blank screen. This signals that the slide show is over, as indicated by the line of text on the screen. Press the **spacebar** or click the mouse button to return to Normal View.

As you can see from this slide show, PowerPoint has many powerful features. You'll learn how to use many of these features in your own presentations as you work through these tutorials. Now that you've finished viewing Miriam's presentation, you're ready to close it.

---

### To close the presentation and exit PowerPoint:

1. Click the **Close Window** button ☒ on the right side of the menu bar, immediately to the right of the Help text box. The presentation window closes but leaves the PowerPoint window on the screen.

   **TROUBLE?** If you clicked the PowerPoint Close button in the extreme upper-right corner of the screen, the entire PowerPoint window closed. If this happened, just omit the next step.

2. Click the **Close** button ☒ in the upper-right corner of the screen to exit PowerPoint. You should now see your computer desktop on your screen (unless other programs are running).

---

You're now ready to create Miriam's presentation on general information about Global Humanitarian. Before you begin, however, you should plan the presentation.

## Planning a Presentation

Planning a presentation before you create it improves the quality of your presentation, makes your presentation more effective and enjoyable, and, in the long run, saves you time and effort. As you plan your presentation, you should answer several questions: What is my purpose or objective for this presentation? What type of presentation is needed? Who is the audience? What information does that audience need? What is the physical location of my presentation? What is the best format for presenting the information contained in this presentation, given the location of the presentation?

In planning your presentation, you identify the following elements:

- **Purpose of the presentation**: To provide general information about Global Humanitarian
- **Type of presentation**: Selling an idea (becoming involved with Global Humanitarian)
- **Audience for the presentation**: Potential donors, potential participants in humanitarian expeditions, and potential student interns
- **Audience needs**: To understand Global Humanitarian's mission
- **Location of the presentation**: Small conference rooms to large classrooms
- **Format**: Oral presentation; electronic slide show of 10 to 12 slides

You have carefully planned your presentation. Now you'll use the PowerPoint AutoContent Wizard to create your presentation.

## Using the AutoContent Wizard

PowerPoint helps you quickly create effective presentations by using a Wizard, which asks you a series of questions about your tasks, and then helps you perform them. The AutoContent Wizard lets you choose a presentation category, such as "Recommending a Strategy," "Brainstorming Session," or "Selling Your Ideas." After you select the type of presentation you want, the AutoContent Wizard creates a general outline for you to follow and formats the slides using a built-in design template. A **design template** is a file that contains the colors and format of the background and the type style of the titles, accents, and other text. Once you start creating a presentation with a given design template, you can change to any other PowerPoint design template or create a custom design template. In this tutorial, you'll use the AutoContent Wizard to sell your idea, the donation of time or money for humanitarian projects. Because "Selling Your Ideas" is predefined, you'll use the AutoContent Wizard, which will automatically create a title slide and standard outline that you then can edit to fit Miriam's needs.

### To create the presentation with the AutoContent Wizard:

1. Start PowerPoint, and then click **From AutoContent Wizard** on the New Presentation Task Pane on the right side of the PowerPoint window. The first of several AutoContent Wizard dialog boxes opens. See Figure 1-8.

Figure 1-8          OPENING DIALOG BOX OF AUTOCONTENT WIZARD

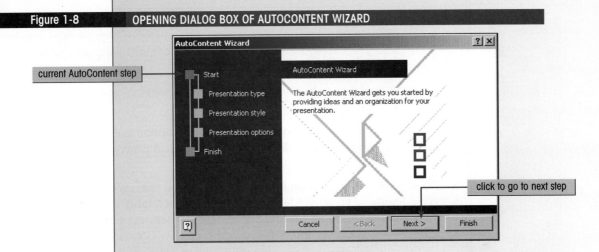

TROUBLE? If the New Presentation Task Pane doesn't appear on your screen, click View on the menu bar, and then click Task Pane. If the Task Pane isn't New Presentation, click the Other Task Panes list arrow at the top of the Task Pane, click New from Existing Presentation, and then click From AutoContent Wizard.

2. Read the information in the AutoContent Wizard dialog box, and then click the **Next** button to display the next dialog box of the AutoContent Wizard. This dialog box allows you to select the type of presentation.

3. Click the **Carnegie Coach** button (which provides AutoContent presentations based upon Dale Carnegie Training principles), and then, if necessary, click **Selling Your Ideas**. See Figure 1-9.

**Figure 1-9**   SELECTING TYPE OF PRESENTATION IN AUTOCONTENT WIZARD

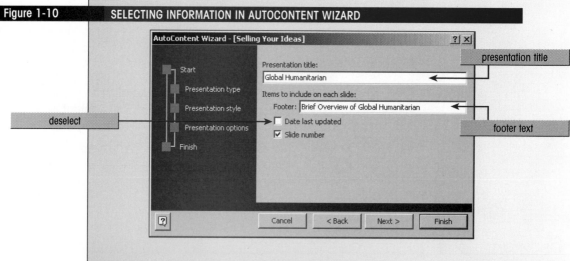

The **Carnegie Coach** is a special feature of PowerPoint in which the AutoContent Wizard can help you create different types of presentations (listed in the dialog box in Figure 1-9) using principles of the Dale Carnegie Training system.

4. Click the **Next** button to display the dialog box with the question, "What type of output will you use?"

5. If necessary, click the **On-screen presentation** option button to select it, and then click the **Next** button. In this dialog box, you'll specify the title and footer (if any) of the presentation.

6. Click ⌶ in the **Presentation title** text box and type **Global Humanitarian**, click ⌶ in the **Footer** text box and type **Brief Overview of Global Humanitarian**, and then click the **Date last updated** check box to deselect it. Leave the Slide Number box checked. The dialog box should now look like Figure 1-10.

**Figure 1-10**   SELECTING INFORMATION IN AUTOCONTENT WIZARD

7. Click the **Next** button. The final AutoContent Wizard dialog box opens, letting you know that you completed the AutoContent Wizard.

8. Click the **Finish** button. PowerPoint now displays the AutoContent outline in the Outline tab and the title slide (Slide 1) in the Slide Pane. See Figure 1-11. The

AutoContent Wizard automatically displays the presenter's name (actually the name of the computer's owner) below the title in Slide 1. The name that appears on your screen will be different from the one in Figure 1-11.

| Figure 1-11 | OUTLINE AND SLIDE AFTER COMPLETING AUTOCONTENT WIZARD |
| --- | --- |

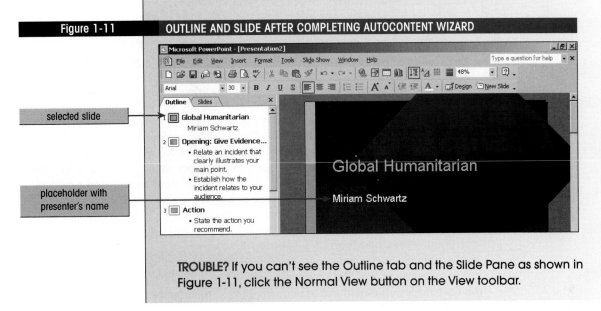

**TROUBLE?** If you can't see the Outline tab and the Slide Pane as shown in Figure 1-11, click the Normal View button on the View toolbar.

Now that you've used the AutoContent Wizard, you're ready to edit its default outline to fit Miriam's specific presentation needs.

## Editing **AutoContent Slides**

The AutoContent Wizard automatically creates the title slide, as well as other slides, with suggested text located in placeholders. A **placeholder** is a region of a slide, or a location in an outline, reserved for inserting text or graphics. To edit the AutoContent outline to fit Miriam's needs, you must select the placeholders one at a time, and then replace them with other text.

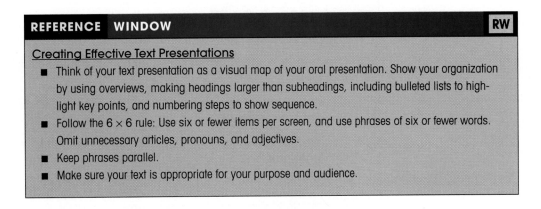

**REFERENCE WINDOW**                                                                 **RW**

Creating Effective Text Presentations
- Think of your text presentation as a visual map of your oral presentation. Show your organization by using overviews, making headings larger than subheadings, including bulleted lists to highlight key points, and numbering steps to show sequence.
- Follow the 6 × 6 rule: Use six or fewer items per screen, and use phrases of six or fewer words. Omit unnecessary articles, pronouns, and adjectives.
- Keep phrases parallel.
- Make sure your text is appropriate for your purpose and audience.

You'll now begin to edit and replace the text to fit Miriam's presentation. The first text you'll change is the presenter's name placeholder.

## *To edit and replace text in a slide:*

1. In the Slide Pane, drag $\text{I}$ across the text of the presenter's name (currently the computer owner's name) to select it. When the text is selected, it appears as black text on a violet background.

2. Type your first and last name (so your instructor can identify you as the author of this presentation), and then click anywhere else on the slide. As soon as you start to type, the placeholder disappears, and the typed text appears in its place. The figures in this book will leave the name as Miriam Schwartz.

   TROUBLE? If PowerPoint marks your name with a red wavy underline, this indicates that the word is not found in the PowerPoint dictionary. In most cases, this means the word might be misspelled. If that were the case here, you would right-click the red wavy underlined word to display a list of suggested spellings, and then click the correct word, or simply edit the misspelled word. In this case, however, you want to tell PowerPoint to ignore what it thinks is a misspelling.

3. If your name was marked as a misspelling, right-click the word to display the shortcut menu, and then click **Ignore All**.

You have made substantial progress in creating Miriam's presentation. Now you'll create a folder for your presentation files, and save this presentation. Then, you'll exit PowerPoint.

## Creating a Folder for Saving Presentations

As a general rule, you should save your PowerPoint work often, about every 15 minutes (or as often as your instructor recommends), so you won't lose your work in case of a power outage, a power surge, or some other computer or software glitch.

## *To create a folder and save a presentation for the first time:*

1. If necessary, place your Data Disk into the appropriate drive.

2. Click the **Save** button 🖫 on the Standard toolbar. The Save As dialog box opens.

3. Click the **Save in** list arrow, and then click the drive that contains your Data Disk.

4. Double-click the **Tutorial.01** folder, and then double-click **Tutorial** to open that folder.

5. Click the **Create New Folder** button 🗂 on the Save As dialog box toolbar. The New Folder dialog box opens.

6. Type **My Files** (see Figure 1-12), and click the **OK** button, edit the default filename (probably Global Humanitarian) in the File name text box so that it becomes **Global Humanitarian Overview**, and then click the **Save** button. PowerPoint saves the presentation to the disk using the filename Global Humanitarian Overview. That name now appears in the title bar of the PowerPoint window. Now that you have saved your work, you're ready to exit PowerPoint.

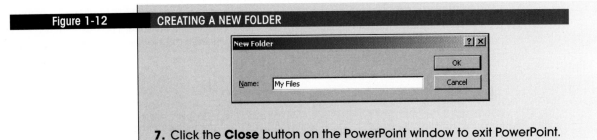

Figure 1-12 | CREATING A NEW FOLDER

**7.** Click the **Close** button on the PowerPoint window to exit PowerPoint.

In addition to the Save command, PowerPoint also has a Save As command, which allows you to save the current presentation to a new file. For example, if you make modifications to an existing presentation but you want to keep the old version and save the new version to the disk, you would use the Save As command to save the modified presentation with a new filename.

In the next session, you'll continue to edit the text of Miriam's presentation, as well as create notes.

## Session 1.1 QUICK CHECK

1. In one to three sentences, describe the purpose of PowerPoint and the components of a presentation that you can create with this program.

2. Name and describe the PowerPoint tabs and panes visible within Normal View.

3. Define or describe the following:
   a. gradient fill
   b. footer
   c. slide transition
   d. custom animation
   e. placeholder
   f. bulleted list

4. Why should you plan a presentation before you create it? What are some of the presentation elements that should be considered?

5. Describe the purpose of the AutoContent Wizard.

6. What is the 6 × 6 rule?

7. What does a red wavy underline indicate?

8. Why is it important to save your work frequently?

---

## SESSION 1.2

In this session, you'll learn how to move from one slide to the next, modify bulleted lists, add new slides with a specified layout, delete slides, change the order of slides, promote and demote outline text, create notes, use the Style Checker, and preview and print a presentation.

---

## Modifying a Presentation

Miriam reviewed your presentation and she has several suggestions for improvement. First, she wants you to replace text in the placeholders with information about Global Humanitarian. Most of the slides in the presentation contain two placeholder text boxes.

The slide **title text** is a text box at the top of the slide that gives the title of the information on that slide; the slide **main text** (also called **body text**) is a large text box in which you type a bulleted or numbered list. In this presentation, you'll modify or create title text and main text in all but the title slide (Slide 1).

## Editing Slides

You'll now edit Slides 2 through 5 by replacing the placeholder text and by adding new text.

### To edit the text in the slides:

1. If you took a break after the previous session, start PowerPoint, and then open the presentation **Global Humanitarian Overview** located in the My Files folder of the Tutorial.01\Tutorial folder. Notice that this filename appears in the New Presentation Task Pane, so you can click the filename to open the presentation.

2. With Slide 1 in the Slide Pane, click the **Next Slide** button ⏬.

3. Select the title text ("Opening: Give Evidence...") so that the title text box becomes active (as indicated by the hatched lines around the box and the resize handles at each corner and on each side of the text box) and the text becomes highlighted. See Figure 1-13. Now you're ready to type the desired title.

| Figure 1-13 | SELECTING TITLE TEXT |
|---|---|

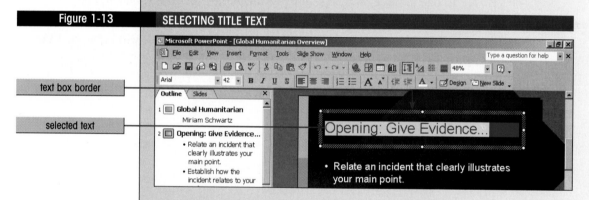

text box border

selected text

4. Type **Are You Rich?** and click in a blank space just outside the edge of the slide to deselect the text box. The hatched lines and resize handles disappear. This title is meant to give evidence of the ability and need to help villagers in less-developed countries. Now you're ready to replace the placeholder text in the bulleted list on this slide.

   TROUBLE? If you click somewhere on the slide that selects another item, such as the main text, click another place, preferably just outside the edge of the slide, to deselect all items.

5. Within the main text box, select the text of the first bulleted item, **Relate an incident that clearly illustrates your main point**, and then type **If you live in a non dirt floor home, top 50%**. Don't include a period at the end of the phrase. Notice how this bulleted item is an incomplete sentence, short for "If you live in a home with a non dirt floor, you're in the top 50% of wealthiest people on earth." Keep in mind that the bulleted lists are not meant to be the complete presentation; instead they remind the speaker of key points and to emphasize the key points to the audience. In all your presentations, you should follow the 6 × 6 rule as much as possible: keep each bulleted item as close to six words as possible, and if possible, have six or fewer bulleted items.

6. Select the text of the second bulleted item, then and type **Home has window and more than one room, top 20%** (without a period). With the insertion point at the end of the second bulleted item, you're ready to create additional bulleted items.

7. Press the **Enter** key. PowerPoint creates a new bullet and leaves the insertion point to the right of the indent after the bullet, waiting for you to type the text.

8. Type **If you can read and have more than one pair of shoes, top 5%**, press the **Enter** key, and then type the last two bulleted items, as shown in Figure 1-14. Notice that as you add more text to a bulleted list, PowerPoint automatically adjusts the font size to fit in the main text placeholder.

   **TROUBLE?** If the font size doesn't automatically adjust so that the text fits within the main text placeholder, click the AutoFit icon ⊞ and then click AutoFit Text to Placeholder.

| Figure 1-14 | SLIDE 2 AFTER ADDING TEXT |
| --- | --- |

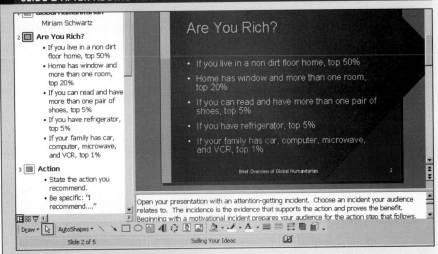

9. Click in a blank area of the slide to deselect the bulleted list text box. The completed Slide 2 should look like Figure 1-14.

You're now ready to go to other slides and edit text.

## To edit the other slides:

1. Click the **Next Slide** button ⬇ to go to Slide 3.

2. Select the title placeholder ("Action") and type **How You Can Help** (with no punctuation).

3. Select all the text in the main text placeholder, and type **Become a member of Global Humanitarian**, press the **Enter** key, and then type **Contribute to humanitarian projects**. Now you'll add some sub-bullets (second-level bulleted items) beneath the current (first-level) bulleted item.

4. Press the **Enter** key to insert a new bullet, and then press the **Tab** key to indent. The bullet changes to a second-level bullet (a dash in this case).

5. Type **Health**, press the **Enter** key (the bullet stays second level), type **Education**, press the **Enter** key, type **Water and Environment**, press the **Enter** key, type **Income Generation and Agriculture**, press the **Enter** key, and type **Leaderships and Cultural Enhancement**. Now you want the next bullet to return to the first level.

6. Press the **Enter** key to create a new second-level bullet, and then click the **Decrease Indent** button 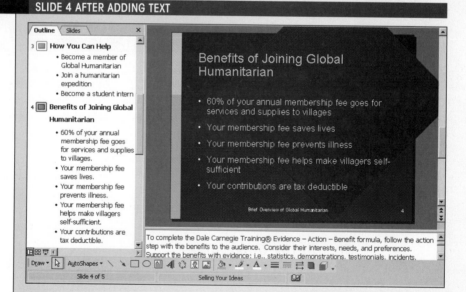 on the Formatting toolbar to convert the item to a first-level bullet. You can also press the Shift + Tab key combination. Type the remaining two bulleted items: **Join a humanitarian expedition** and **Become a student intern**. The slide exceeds the 6 × 6 rule in the number of bulleted items, but you'll fix that later.

You have completed editing and adding text to Slide 3. Now you'll edit the other slides and save your work.

## To edit the slides and save the presentation:

1. Go to Slide 4 and edit the title text to read **Benefits of Joining Global Humanitarian**.

2. Select all the text, not just the text of the first bulleted item, in the main text placeholder, and then add the bulleted items, as shown in Figure 1-15.

**Figure 1-15**    SLIDE 4 AFTER ADDING TEXT

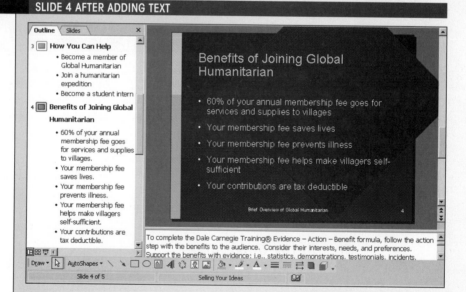

3. Go to Slide 5 (currently the last slide in the presentation), and then modify the title and text boxes so that the slide looks like Figure 1-16.

**Figure 1-16**   **COMPLETED SLIDE 5**

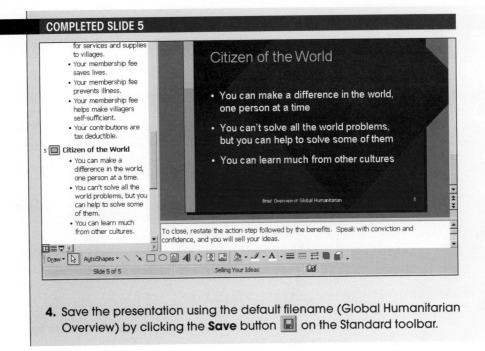

4. Save the presentation using the default filename (Global Humanitarian Overview) by clicking the **Save** button 🖫 on the Standard toolbar.

You have completed the first draft of the Global Humanitarian presentation. Now you'll add a slide to provide additional information about Global Humanitarian.

## Adding a New Slide and Choosing a Layout

Miriam wants you to add a new slide at the end of the presentation explaining how individuals and families can join Global Humanitarian. When you add a new slide, PowerPoint formats the slide using a **slide layout**, which is an arrangement of placeholders. PowerPoint supports four **text layouts**: Title Slide (placeholders for a title and a subtitle, usually used as the first slide in a presentation); Title Only (a title placeholder but not main text placeholder); Text (the default slide layout, with a title and a main text placeholder); and 2 Column Text (same as Text, but with two columns). PowerPoint also supports several **content layouts**—slide layouts that contain from zero to four charts, diagrams, images, tables, or movie clips. In addition, PowerPoint supports combination layouts, called **text and content layouts**, and several other types of layouts. When you add a new Slide 6, you'll use the Text layout.

### To insert a new slide:

1. Because you want to add a slide after Slide 5, make sure Slide 5 is still in the Slide Pane. In general, when you add a new slide, it will appear immediately after the current one.

2. Click the **New Slide** button 🗐 on the Formatting toolbar. The new slide appears in the Slide Pane. See Figure 1-17. The Slide Layout Task Pane appears, with the Text layout as the default for the new slide. You'll accept the default layout for this slide. If you wanted a different layout, you would click the desired layout in the Slide Layout Task Pane.

Figure 1-17 NEW SLIDE

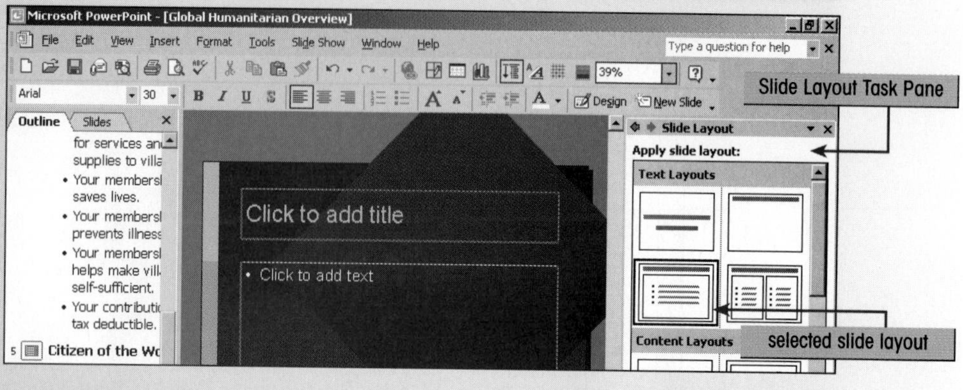

**TROUBLE?** If the Slide Layout Task Pane doesn't automatically appear in the PowerPoint window, make sure the Task Pane is in view by clicking View on the menu bar and clicking Task Pane. Then if necessary, click the Task Pane list arrow, and click Slide Layout.

3. Click anywhere in the title placeholder, and then type the title **Global Humanitarian Membership**.

4. Click in the main text placeholder. The insertion point appears just to the right of the first bullet.

5. Type **$75 per year individual membership**, press the **Enter** key to start a new bulleted item, type **$150 per year family membership**, press the **Enter** key, type **Visit our Web site at www.globalhumanitiarian.org** (which PowerPoint will automatically mark as a link by changing its color and underlining it), press the Enter key, and then type **Call 523-555-SERV**.

You have inserted a new slide at the end of the presentation and added text to the slide. Next you'll create a new slide by promoting text in the Outline tab.

## Promoting, Demoting, and Moving Outline Text

To **promote** an item means to increase the outline level of that item—for example, to change a bulleted item into a slide title or to change a sub-bullet (a second-level bullet) into a first-level bullet. To **demote** an item means to decrease the outline level—for example, to change a slide title into a bulleted item within another slide or to change a bulleted item into a sub-bulleted item. You'll begin by promoting a bulleted item to a slide title, thus creating a new slide.

### To create a new slide by promoting outline text:

1. Go to Slide 3 by dragging the Slide Pane scroll bar up until the ScreenTip displays "Slide: 3 of 6" and the title "How You Can Help." Notice that the text of that slide appears in the Outline tab. You can modify text of a slide not only in the Slide Pane, but also in the Outline tab. Currently, the Outline tab is so narrow that you can't see much of the text. One way to increase its size is to close the Task Pane.

**2.** Click the **Close** button ☒ at the top of the Task Pane.

   **TROUBLE?** If you accidentally click the Close button of the PowerPoint window or Presentation window, PowerPoint will ask you if you want to save the changes to your presentation. Click the Cancel button so that the presentation doesn't close, and then click the correct Close button so that the Task Pane closes.

**3.** In the Outline tab, move the pointer to the bullet to the left of "Contribute to humanitarian projects" so that the pointer becomes ✛, and then click the bullet. The text for that bullet and all its sub-bullets becomes selected. You have to do this in the Outline tab rather than the Slide Pane so that you can decrease indent (promote) the text to a new slide. Now you'll promote that text so that it becomes title text and first-level bullets.

**4.** Click the **Decrease Indent** button 🔤 on the Formatting toolbar. PowerPoint promotes the text to a slide title, and automatically creates a new Slide 4. See Figure 1-18. As you can see, the new slide appears with the title text "Contribute to humanitarian projects." Now you'll edit this text, and then move some of the bulleted items to another slide.

| Figure 1-18 | PROMOTING A BULLETED ITEM TO BECOME A NEW SLIDE |
| --- | --- |

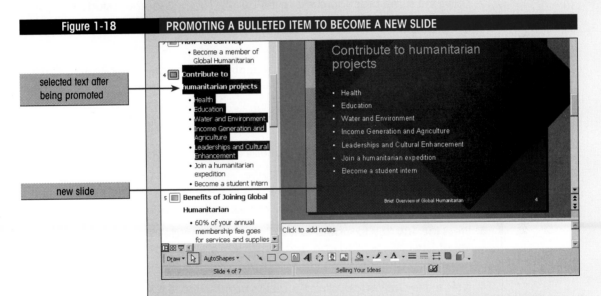

selected text after being promoted

new slide

**5.** Edit the title of the new Slide 4 to **Types of Humanitarian Projects in Third-World Villages**. You can make these changes either in the Slide Pane or Outline tab.

**6.** In the Outline tab, click ✛ on the bullet to the left of "Join a humanitarian expedition." While holding down the left mouse button, drag the bullet and its text up until the horizontal line position marker is just under the bulleted item "Become a member of Global Humanitarian" in Slide 3, as shown in Figure 1-19, and then release the mouse button.

| Figure 1-19 | MOVING TEXT IN THE OUTLINE TAB |
| --- | --- |

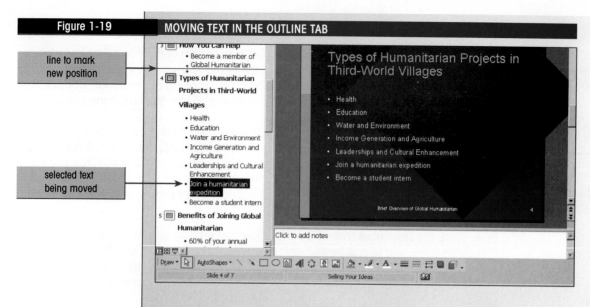

line to mark
new position

selected text
being moved

**7.** Using the same procedure, move the bulleted item "Become a student intern" from the end of Slide 4 to the end of Slide 3 in the Outline tab.

As you review your slides, you notice that in Slide 5, the phrase "Your membership fee" is unnecessarily repeated three times. You decide to fix the problem by demoting some of the text.

## To demote text:

**1.** Go to Slide 5 in the Outline tab, "Benefits of Joining Global Humanitarian."

**2.** Click immediately to the right of "Your membership fee" in the second bulleted item, and then press the **Enter** key. Notice that "saves lives" becomes a new bulleted item, but you want that item to appear indented at a lower outline level.

**3.** Press the **Tab** key to indent "saves lives," and then delete any spaces to the left of "saves lives." You can also click the Increase Indent button on the Formatting toolbar.

**4.** Now, in the Outline tab, click on the bullet to the left of "Your membership fee prevents illness," press and hold down the **Shift** key, and then click the bullet to the left of "Your membership fee helps make villagers self-sufficient." This selects both bulleted items at the same time.

**5.** Click the **Increase Indent** button on the Formatting toolbar to demote the two bulleted items.

**6.** Delete the phrase "Your membership fee" and the space after it from the two items that you just demoted. Your slide now looks like Figure 1-20.

| Figure 1-20 | SLIDE 5 AFTER DEMOTING TEXT TO SUB-BULLETS |
|---|---|

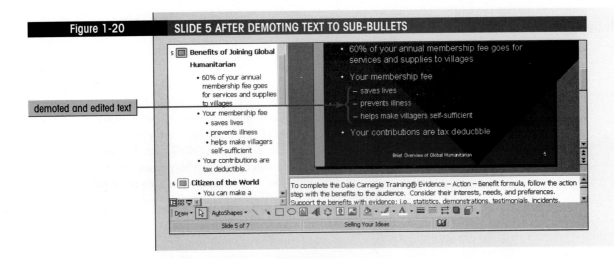

demoted and edited text

Miriam looks at your presentation and suggests that you move the current Slide 4 ahead of Slide 3. You could make this change by clicking ⊹ on the slide icon ▣ and dragging it up above the slide icon for Slide 3. Instead, you'll move the slide in Slide Sorter View.

## Moving Slides in Slide Sorter View

In Slide Sorter View, PowerPoint displays all the slides as thumbnails, so that 12 or more slides can appear on the screen at once. This view not only provides you with a good overview of your presentation, but also allows you to easily change the order of the slides and modify the slides in other ways.

### *To move the slide:*

1. Click the **Slide Sorter View** button 🔲 on the View toolbar. You now see your presentation in Slide Sorter view. Move the pointer ▷ over Slide 4. As you can see, a frame appears around the slide.

2. Click **Slide 4**. Notice that the frame around the slide becomes thicker, indicating that the slide is selected.

3. Press and hold down the left mouse button, drag the slide to the left so that the vertical line position marker appears on the other side of Slide 3, as shown in Figure 1-21, and then release the mouse button. The old Slides 3 and 4 switch places.

| Figure 1-21 | MOVING A SLIDE IN SLIDE SORTER VIEW |
|---|---|

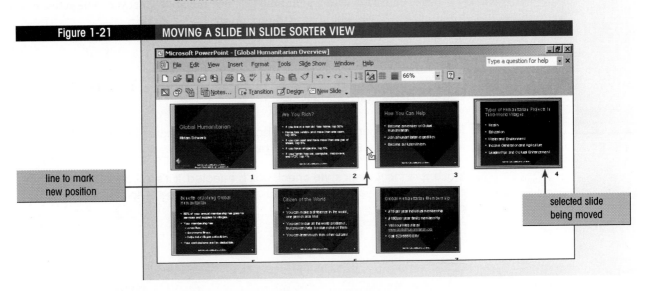

line to mark
new position

selected slide
being moved

Miriam is pleased with your presentation, but suggests that you delete one of the slides.

## Deleting Slides

When creating a presentation, you'll often delete slides. The AutoContent Wizard may create slides that you don't think are necessary, or you may create slides that you no longer want. For this presentation, Miriam asks you to delete Slide 6, titled "Citizen of the World." You can delete slides in the Outline tab by clicking the slide icon and pressing the Delete key, in Slide Sorter View by selecting the slide and pressing the Delete key, or in Normal View by using the menus. Keep in mind that once you delete a slide, you can recover it by immediately clicking the Undo button, but once you've done several other operations, you may not be able to recover the deleted slide. Now you'll use the menu method to delete a slide.

### To delete Slide 6:

1. In Slide Sorter View, click **Slide 6**, and then click the **Normal View** button ⊞. This step causes Slide 6 to appear in the Slide Pane in Normal View. Now you're ready to delete the slide.

2. Click **Edit** on the menu bar, and then, if necessary, point to the double-arrow (at the bottom of the menu) to display the hidden menu items. PowerPoint, like other Office programs, initially displays the commands that are used most frequently on that computer. When you leave the menu open for a few seconds, or click the double-arrow, PowerPoint anticipates that you are looking for an item not currently displayed, and it expands the list of possible options. For the rest of these tutorials, click the double-arrow if you don't see the option you're looking for.

3. Click **Delete Slide**. The entire slide is deleted from the presentation. The slide that was Slide 7 becomes Slide 6 and appears in the Slide Pane.

This completes the presentation slides. Your next task is to use the Style Checker to check consistency and style within your presentation.

## Using the Style Checker

The **Style Checker** automatically checks your presentation for consistency and style, and marks problems on a slide with a light bulb 💡. For the Style Checker to be active in your PowerPoint program, you might have to turn on the Style Checker.

### To turn on the Style Checker:

1. Click **Tools** on the menu bar, click **Options** to open the Options dialog box, and click the **Spelling and Style** tab.

   TROUBLE? If you get the message about the Style Checker using the Office Assistant, click the Enable Assistant button.

2. Make sure the **Check style** check box is selected. If it's not checked, click the check box. Now you'll check to make sure the desired Style Checker options are selected.

**3.** Click the **Style Options** button on the Options dialog box, make sure each item is checked or unchecked, as shown in Figure 1-22, and then click the **OK** button.

| Figure 1-22 | STYLE OPTIONS DIALOG BOX |
|---|---|

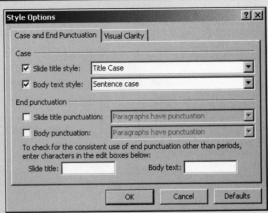

**4.** Click the **OK** button on the Options dialog box.

You don't have to show the Office Assistant for the style checking to work, but the Office Assistant will automatically appear on the screen when you click 💡 to view the style error. From now on, PowerPoint will check the style in your presentation as you display each slide in the Slide Pane. Now you'll go through your presentation and check for style problems. As you display a slide, PowerPoint will mark any potential style errors with 💡.

## To fix the problems marked by the Style Checker:

**1.** Go to Slide 1. As you can see, no style error occurs on this slide.

**2.** Go to Slide 2, where you will find no style error marked, and then to Slide 3, where 💡 appears next to the title. Often you won't know the style problem, but you can determine it by clicking the light bulb.

TROUBLE? If, in this or subsequent steps, the light bulb doesn't appear by the main text, go to the next or the previous slide, and then return to the current slide as a way of telling the Office Assistant to recheck the slide.

**3.** Click 💡. The Office Assistant appears and displays the problem. See Figure 1-23. The Style Checker can automatically fix the problem if you clicks the blue bullet of the first option in the Office Assistant dialog box.

Figure 1-23     **USING THE STYLE CHECKER**

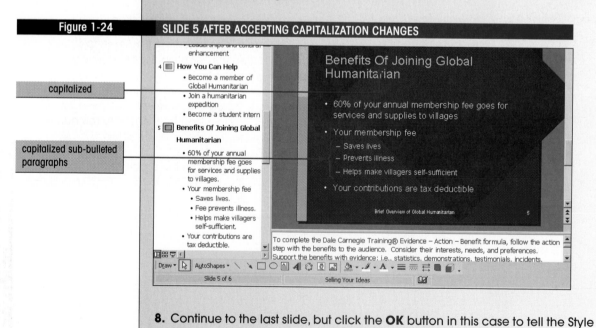

click to accept suggested changes

message from Style Checker

4. Click the **Change the text to title case** option button. The words "Of" and "In" are capitalized. Now the light bulb appears by the main text (the bulleted list).

5. Click 💡 to see the error in the bulleted list, and then click **Change the text to sentence case**. All the words (except the first word in each bulleted item) in the last three bulleted items are converted to lowercase; that is, all the bulleted items are converted to sentence case.

6. Go to Slide 4. Here the Style Checker detects that the first bulleted item is in mixed case (Global Humanitarian is capitalized), but you don't want to make any changes here. Click 💡 to read the error, but don't click any of the bulleted options. Instead, just click the **OK** button. When you click OK without selecting any of the other options, PowerPoint ignores the style for that slide.

7. Go to Slide 5 and use the same method to correct the capitalization problems in the title. Notice that in the main body of this slide, the sub-bullets need to be capitalized. See Figure 1-24.

Figure 1-24     **SLIDE 5 AFTER ACCEPTING CAPITALIZATION CHANGES**

capitalized

capitalized sub-bulleted paragraphs

8. Continue to the last slide, but click the **OK** button in this case to tell the Style Checker to ignore the suggested style error because you don't want to change the capitalization on this slide.

As you create your own presentations, watch for the problems marked by the Style Checker. Of course, in some cases, you might want a certain capitalization that the Style Checker detects as an error. In these cases, just ignore the light bulb, or click it, and then click the OK button. The light bulb never appears on the screen during a slide show or when you print a presentation.

# Creating **Speaker Notes**

When you show the presentation to Miriam, she is satisfied. Now you're ready to prepare the other parts of Miriam's presentation: the notes (also called speaker notes) and audience handouts (a printout of the slides). **Notes** are printed pages that contain a picture of and notes about each slide. They help the speaker remember what to say while a particular slide appears during the presentation.

You'll create notes, or modify existing notes, for only two of the slides in the presentation.

## To create notes:

1. Go to Slide 1. As you can see, notes already appear in the Notes Pane, just below the Slide Pane. First you'll delete them.

2. Click anywhere in the Notes Pane, press **Ctrl + A** to select all the text in the Notes Pane, and then press the **Delete** key. The current notes, which gave hints on how to sell your ideas to your audience, disappear from the pane. Now you're ready to type your own notes. Miriam wants to remember to acknowledge special guests or Global Humanitarian executives at any meeting where she might use this presentation.

3. Type **Acknowledge special guests and Global Humanitarian executives.** See Figure 1-25.

| Figure 1-25 | NOTES ON SLIDE 1 |
| --- | --- |

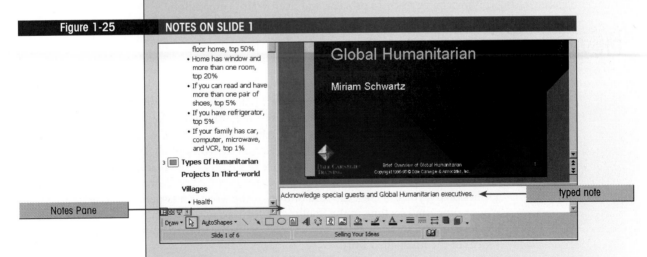

4. Go to Slide 2, delete all the current text from the Notes Pane, and then type **Everyone in this room is in the top 99th percentile of wealthy people who have ever lived on earth**.

5. Go to Slide 3, click in the Notes Pane, and then type **Give an example of each of these project types**. These are all the notes that Miriam wants.

**6.** Go through the rest of the slides in the presentation and delete any comments currently found in the Notes Pane.

**7.** Make sure your Data Disk is still in the disk drive, go back to Slide 1, and then save the presentation using the default filename. An updated copy of your presentation is now on your Data Disk.

Before Miriam gives her presentation, she'll print the Notes Panes of the presentation so she'll have the notes available during her presentations. Miriam also might want the Notes Panes to include headers and footers. Similar to a footer, a **header** is a word or phrase that appears at the top of each page. You'll practice inserting a footer (through the AutoContent Wizard) in an exercise at the end of the tutorial.

You can now view the completed presentation to make sure that it is accurate, informative, and visually pleasing.

### To view the slide show:

**1.** Click the **Slide Show View** button 🖵.

**2.** Proceed through the slide show as you did earlier, clicking the left mouse button or pressing the spacebar to advance from one slide to the next.

**3.** When you reach the end of your slide show, press the **spacebar** to move to the blank screen, and then press the **spacebar** again to return to Normal View.

If you see a problem on one of your slides, press the Esc key to abort the slide show. The slide on the screen at the time you press the Esc key will appear in the Slide Pane. After you fix any problems, save the completed presentation again.

Now you're ready to preview and print your presentation.

## Previewing **and Printing the Presentation**

Before you print or present a slide show, you should always do a final spell check of all the slides and speaker notes by clicking the Spelling button to start the PowerPoint Spell Checker feature. If PowerPoint finds a word that's not in its dictionary, the word is marked in the Slide Pane, and the Spelling dialog box appears. If the word is actually spelled correctly, but not found in the PowerPoint dictionary, you can click the Ignore button to tell the Spell Checker to ignore that occurrence of the word, or click Ignore All to tell the Spell Checker to ignore all occurrences of the word. If you want PowerPoint to add the word to its dictionary, you can click the Add button. If the word is misspelled, PowerPoint often displays a suggested spelling in the Spelling dialog box; in that case, you would click the correct suggestion, and then click Change or Change All to correct that occurrence or all occurrences of the misspelled word.

Before printing on your black-and-white printer, you should preview the presentation to make sure the text is legible in grayscale (shades of black and white).

### To preview the presentation in grayscale:

**1.** Make sure Slide 1 appears in the Slide Pane, click the **Color/Grayscale** button 🖼 on the Standard toolbar, and then click **Grayscale**. See Figure 1-26.

| Figure 1-26 | SLIDE 1 IN GRAYSCALE |
|---|---|

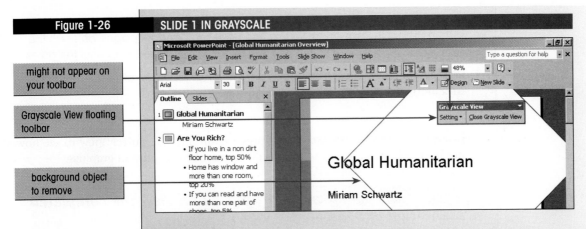

might not appear on your toolbar

Grayscale View floating toolbar

background object to remove

2. Look at the text on each slide to make sure it is legible. Depending on your Windows printer driver, the background graphics (a square tipped on a corner, in this case) might make some of the text hard to read, so you might want to omit the graphics from the slides.

3. Click **Format** on the menu bar, click **Background** to display the Background dialog box, click the **Omit background graphics from master** check box, and then click the **Apply to All** button. The slide appears as before, but without the background graphics.

4. Click **File** on the menu bar, and then click **Print** to open the Print dialog box. PowerPoint provides several printing options. For example, you can print the slides in color using a color printer; print in grayscale using a black-and-white printer; print handouts with 2, 3, 4, 6, or 9 slides per page; or print the Notes Pages (printed notes below a picture of the corresponding slide). You can also format and then print the presentation onto overhead transparency film (available in most office supply stores).

5. Click the **Print what** list arrow, click **Handouts**, then in the Handouts section, click the **Slides per page** list arrow, and then click **4**. Make sure the Frame slides check box is selected, and the Color/grayscale text box is set to Grayscale. See Figure 1-27.

| Figure 1-27 | PRINT DIALOG BOX |
|---|---|

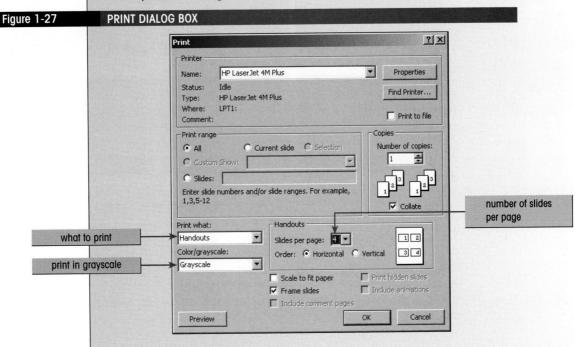

number of slides per page

what to print

print in grayscale

**6.** Make sure all the other options are set as in Figure 1-27, and then click the **OK** button to print the handouts. You should have two handout pages, one with the first four slides, and another with the last two. Now you're ready to print the notes.

**7.** Display the Print dialog box, click the **Print what** list arrow, click **Notes Pages**, and then click the **OK** button to print the notes.

Your last task is to view the completed presentation in Slide Sorter View to see how all the slides look together. First, however, you'll restore the background graphics.

### To restore the background graphics and view the completed presentation in Slide Sorter View:

**1.** Click the **Color/Grayscale** button 🔲 on the Standard toolbar, and then click **Color** to return to color view.

**2.** Click **Format** on the menu bar, click **Background**, click the **Omit background graphics from master** check box to deselect it, and then click the **Apply to All** button. The background graphics are restored to the slides.

**3.** Click the **Slide Sorter View** button 🔳 on the View toolbar.

**4.** To see the slides better, click the **Zoom** list arrow on the Standard toolbar, and change the Zoom to **100%**. Compare your handouts with the six slides shown in Figure 1-28.

| Figure 1-28 | COMPLETED PRESENTATION IN SLIDE SORTER VIEW |

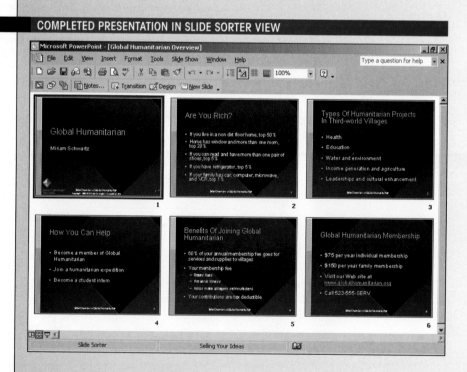

**TROUBLE?** If the thumbnail views of the slides are too big for all to be seen at once, set the Zoom to a lower value.

Now that you have created, edited, saved, and printed Miriam's presentation, you can exit PowerPoint.

### To exit PowerPoint:

1. Click ☒ in the upper-right corner of the PowerPoint window. Because you have made changes since the last time you saved the presentation, PowerPoint displays a dialog box with the message "Do you want to save the changes you made to Global Humanitarian Overview.ppt?"

2. Click the **No** button to exit PowerPoint without saving the current version of the presentation, because you already saved the final version.

You have created a presentation using the AutoContent Wizard, edited it according to Miriam's wishes, and created and printed notes and handouts. Miriam thanks you for your help; she believes that your work will enable her to make an effective presentation.

## Session 1.2 QUICK CHECK

1. Explain how to do the following in the Outline tab:
   a. move text up
   b. delete a slide
   c. promote text
   d. edit text

2. What does it mean to promote a bulleted item in the Outline tab? To demote a bulleted item?

3. Explain a benefit of using the Outline tab rather than the Slide Pane, and a benefit of using the Slide Pane rather than the Outline tab.

4. Explain how to add a slide to a presentation.

5. What is the Style Checker? What is an example of a consistency or style problem that it might mark?

6. What are speaker notes? How do you create them?

7. Why is it beneficial to preview a presentation before printing it?

## REVIEW ASSIGNMENTS

Miriam Schwartz, the managing director of the Austin, Texas, headquarters of Global Humanitarian, asks you to prepare a PowerPoint presentation explaining the Village Outreach Program to potential donors and volunteers. She gives you a disk with a rough draft of a PowerPoint presentation that provides most of the information about the Village Outreach Program. Your job is to edit the presentation. Complete the following:

1. Start PowerPoint and make sure your Data Disk is in the disk drive.

*Explore*
2. Open the presentation **VillagOP** in the Review folder of the Tutorial.01 folder, and then save the file using the new filename **Village Outreach Program** in the same Review folder. (*Hint*: To save a file with a different filename, click File on the menu bar, and then click Save As.)

3. In Slide 1, change the subtitle placeholder ("Global Humanitarian") to your name.

4. In Slide 2, use the Outline tab to demote the bulleted items "Health," "Education," "Clean water and environment," and "Leadership" and make them sub-bulleted items. (*Hint*: Select all four items at once by clicking the bullet of the first item, pressing and holding down the Shift key, and clicking the bullet of the last item.)

5. Below the sub-bulleted item "Clean water and environment," insert another sub-bulleted item "Agriculture and Income Generation."

6. In Slide 3, delete all occurrences of the word "the" to approach the 6 × 6 rule by reducing the number of words in each bulleted item.

7. Use the Outline tab to move the last bulleted item ("Assist villagers in organizing health committees") so it becomes the second bulleted item in the main text.

8. In Slide 4, right-click the misspelled word (marked with the wavy red underline), and then click the correctly spelled word.

9. In the Outline tab of Slide 5, promote the bulleted item "Agriculture and Income Generation" so it becomes the title of a new slide (Slide 6).

10. Return to Slide 5 and promote the last three sub-bulleted items so they become bullets on the same level as "Help villagers construct."

**Explore** ▷ 11. Still in Slide 5, tell PowerPoint Spell Checker to ignore all occurrences of the word "catchment," which is not found in PowerPoint's dictionary. (*Hint*: Right-click the word.)

12. In the new Slide 6, edit the typographical error "load," which should be "loan." (This exercise is to remind you of the importance of proofreading your presentation. Don't leave it to the PowerPoint Spell Checker to find all your errors.)

13. Edit the final bulleted item so that each phrase after "Encourage weekly meetings to discuss" is a sub-bulleted item with no punctuation. You should end up with five sub-bulleted items.

14. Go to Slide 7, and then add a new Slide 8.

15. In Slide 8, type the title "Household Interventions."

16. Type the following as bulleted items in Slide 8: "Wells," "Pumps," "Greenhouses," "Lorena Stoves," "First aid supplies," and "Bookkeeping supplies."

17. In Slide 2, add the following speaker note: "Relate personal experiences for each of these items."

18. In Slide 3, add the following speaker note: "Remind audience that we need volunteer physicians, dentists, optometrists, nurses, and social workers."

**Explore** ▷ 19. Make sure the Style Checker is turned on, and then set the Style Options for Visual Clarity so that the maximum number of bullets should not exceed six, the number of lines per title should not exceed two, and number of lines per bulleted item should not exceed two. (*Hint*: Use the Legibility section of the Visual Clarity tab on the Style Options dialog box.)

20. Go through each slide of the presentation to see if the Style Checker marks any potential problems. When you see the light bulb, click it, and assess whether you want to accept or reject the suggested change. For example, in Slide 2, make sure you keep "Village Outreach Programs" capitalized.

**Explore** ▷ 21. If any of the bulleted text (for example, the text in Slide 7) doesn't fit on the slide, but drops below the main text box, set the text box to AutoFit. (*Hint*: Select the text box, click the AutoFit icon ⊞, which appears near the lower-left corner of the text box, and select the desired option.)

**Explore** ▷ 22. Add to the presentation the design template called "Cliff," which has a green gradient-filled background. (*Hint*: Open the Task Pane, if necessary, and change the Task Pane to Slide Design—Design Templates using the drop-down menu. Then move the pointer over a design template thumbnail so the design template name appears. Click the thumbnail of the desired template.) If you can't find the "Cliff" design template, choose a different design template.

23. Spell check the presentation by clicking the Spelling button.

24. View the presentation in Slide Show View.

25. Save the presentation using its default filename.

*Explore* ▷ 26. View the presentation again in Slide Show View, except this time start with Slide 4 and go only to Slide 6. (*Hint*: The slide show starts with the slide in the Slide Pane. To terminate a slide show, press the Esc key.)

27. Preview the presentation in grayscale.

28. Print the presentation in grayscale as handouts with four slides per page.

29. Close the file, and then exit PowerPoint.

## CASE PROBLEMS

**Case 1. e-Commerce Consultants**   Two years ago, Whitney Harris of Rockford, Illinois, founded a consulting business that helps local businesses with their e-commerce needs, including Web page design, order fulfillment, and security. Whitney asks you to prepare a presentation to businesses to sell the services of e-Commerce Consultants. Do the following:

1. Create a new onscreen PowerPoint presentation and start the AutoContent Wizard.

2. In the Sales/Marketing category, select Selling a Product or Service.

3. Type the presentation title as "e-Commerce: Your Strategy for the Future," and type the footer as "e-Commerce Consultants."

4. Omit the Date last updated from the presentation, but include the slide number.

5. In Slide 1, change the subtitle placeholder, if necessary, to your name.

6. In Slide 2 ("Objective"), include the following bulleted items (here and in the other slides, delete the current items in the main text placeholder): "How to manage change," "How to overcome barriers to e-commerce," "How to change managerial styles," "How to set up your Web site," "How to manage orders," and "What we offer to your business."

7. In Slide 3 ("Customer Requirements"), keep the radial diagram that automatically appears here, and then include the following bulleted items: "Company management issues," "Web site design and set-up," "Order taking and fulfillment," "Security," and "Other?"

*Explore* ▷ 8. Go to Slide 4, open the Slide Layout Task Pane, and change the slide layout to Text. (*Hint*: Click the slide layout thumbnail that contains only a title and a bulleted list.)

9. Delete the three pyramid diagrams by clicking each one and pressing the Delete key.

10. In Slide 4, change the title to "Meeting Your Needs," and then include the following bulleted items: "We supply labor or help you find employees," "We provide know-how, graphic design, software, programming, security systems," "We can help promote your product, secure startup funding, arrange for credit card accounts," and "We can answer all your questions."

11. Delete Slides 5 and 6.

12. In the new Slide 5 ("Key Benefits"), include the following bulleted items: "You focus on your products, your services, your bottom line," and "We help you sell your product on the Internet."

13. In Slide 6, ("Next Steps"), include the following bulleted items: "Make a list of the things that you want us to do," "Draw up an agreement," "Set a timeline for implementation," "Establish your order-fulfillment operation," and "Launch your Web site and e-commerce system."

14. Save the presentation to the Cases folder in the Tutorial.01 folder using the filename **e-Commerce Consultants**.

15. In Slide 1, delete the space between "e-Commerce:" and "Your," and then press Enter to move the phrase "Your Strategy for the Future" to the second line of the title.

*Explore* ▷ 16. Center the text in the title text box. (*Hint*: Use the Answer Wizard of the Help system and ask the question, "How do I center a paragraph?")

17. In Slide 2, move "manage change" down to a new bulleted item, indent (demote) that item so it is a sub-bullet under "How to," delete "How to" from the next four bulleted items, and then make them sub-bullets under "How to."

18. In Slide 4, edit the second bulleted item to be "We provide," and then make sub-bulleted items of "know how," "graphic design," "software," "programming," and "security systems."

19. Similarly in Slide 4, do the same type of editing for the next bulleted item, making "We can help" the main bullet and the other phrases the sub-bullets.

**Explore** 20. Still in Slide 4, move the third bullet "We can help" (along with all its sub-bullets) up to become the second bullet. (*Hint*: In the Outline tab or Slide Pane, when you select a bulleted item, PowerPoint automatically selects all its sub-bullets.)

21. Move the last bulleted item "We can answer all your questions" up to become the first bulleted item.

22. Promote the bulleted item "We provide" (and all its sub-bullets) to become a new separate slide, and then add the word "What" at the beginning of the slide title.

23. In Slide 6 ("Key Benefits"), edit the first bulleted item to be "You focus on your," and then make sub-bulleted items of "products," "services," and "bottom line."

24. In Slide 7 ("Next Steps"), delete excess words like "a," "an," "the," and "that" to achieve the 6 × 6 rule as closely as possible.

**Explore** 25. Make sure the Style Checker is turned on, and then set the Style Options for Visual Clarity so that the maximum number of bullets should not exceed six, the number of lines per title should not exceed two, and the number of lines per bulleted item should not exceed two. (*Hint*: Use the Legibility section of the Visual Clarity tab on the Style Options dialog box.)

26. Go through each slide of the presentation to see if the Style Checker marks any potential problems. When you see the light bulb, click it, and assess whether you want to accept or reject the suggested change. You'll want to accept most of the suggested changes, but make sure you leave words like "Web" and "Internet" capitalized.

27. Spell check the presentation by clicking the Spelling button.

28. View the presentation in Slide Show View.

30. Save the current version of the presentation using its default filename, preview the presentation in grayscale, and then print the presentation in grayscale as handouts with four slides per page.

31. Close the file, and then exit PowerPoint.

*Case 2. Northeast Seafoods*    Paul Neibaur is president of Northeast Seafoods, a seafood distribution company with headquarters in Halifax, Nova Scotia. He buys fish and other seafood from suppliers and sells to restaurant and grocery store chains. Although his company has been in business and profitable for 27 years, Paul wants to sell the company and retire. He wants you to help him create a PowerPoint presentation to prospective buyers. Do the following:

1. Open the file **Seafoods** in the Cases folder in the Tutorial.01 folder of your Data Disk, and save it back to the same folder using the filename **Northeast Seafoods**.

2. In Slide 1, replace the subtitle placeholder ("Paul Neibaur") with your name.

3. In Slide 2, add the speaker's note "Mention that the regular customers are all large grocery store and restaurant chains."

**Explore** 4. Run the Spell Checker. Tell it to ignore all occurrences of the word "preapproved" which are not found in the PowerPoint dictionary. (*Hint*: Click the Ignore All button on the Spelling dialog box.) Do the same for other correctly spelled words, if any, not found in the PowerPoint dictionary. Correct all the misspelled words.

**Explore** 5. Move the third bulleted item ("19% to 28% profit . . .") from Slide 2 to become the last bulleted item in Slide 4. (*Hint*: You can use the Outline tab to drag the bullet, or you can use the cut-and-paste method.)

6. In Slide 3, edit the third bulleted item so that "freezers," "saws," "packagers," and "other equipment" are sub-bulleted items below the main bullet.

7. Do the same for the items after the colon in the fifth main bulleted item, and then delete the colon.

8. Move the last bulleted item ("Contracts with . . .") to become the second bulleted item.

9. Promote the bulleted item "Experienced employees" and its sub-bullets so that they become a new separate slide.

*Explore* ▶ 10. Use the Slides tab to move Slide 4 ("Experienced Employees") to become Slide 3. (*Hint*: Drag and drop the slide.)

11. In Slide 5, find the typographical error (if you haven't already) and correct it. This demonstrates the importance of proofreading your presentation carefully, because PowerPoint doesn't pick up this type of error.

12. Make sure the Style Checker is turned on, and then go through all the slides correcting problems of case (capitalization). Be sure not to let the Style Checker change the case for "Small Business Administration;" otherwise, accept the Style Checker's suggested case changes.

*Explore* ▶ 13. Add to the presentation the design template called "Ocean," which has a blue gradient-filled background with lighter colors near the upper-left corner. (*Hint*: Open the Task Pane, if necessary, and change the Task Pane to Slide Design—Design Templates. Then move the pointer over a design template thumbnail so the design template name appears. Click the thumbnail of the desired template.) If you can't find the "Ocean" design template, choose a different design template.

14. View the presentation in Slide Show View.

15. Save the presentation using its default filename.

16. Preview the presentation in grayscale.

17. Print the presentation in grayscale as handouts with four slides per page.

18. Close the file and then exit PowerPoint.

**Case 3. *Magnolia Gardens Eye Center*** Dr. Carol Wang, the head ophthalmologist at the Magnolia Gardens Eye Center in Charleston, South Carolina, performs over 20 surgeries per week using laser in situ keratomileusis, also called laser-assisted in situ keratomileusis (LASIK), to correct vision problems of myopia (nearsightedness), hyperopia (farsightedness), and astigmatism. She asks you to help prepare a PowerPoint presentation to those interested in learning more about LASIK. Do the following:

1. Open the file **LASIK** in the Cases folder in the Tutorial.01 folder of your Data Disk, and save it back to the same folder using the filename **Magnolia LASIK**.

2. In Slide 1, replace the subtitle placeholder ("Magnolia Gardens Eye Center") with your name.

3. In Slide 2, move the third bulleted item up to become the first bulleted item.

4. Add a fourth bulleted item with the text "Improves how patients see without corrective lenses."

5. Edit the third bulleted item so that "myopia," "hyperopia," and "astigmatism" are sub-bulleted items below the main bullet.

*Explore* ▶ 6. In Slide 3, change the bulleted list to a numbered list.

*Explore* ▶ 7. Have PowerPoint automatically split Slide 3 into two slides. (*Hint*: With the main text box selected, click the AutoFit Options icon 🟰 and select the appropriate option.)

*Explore* ▶ 8. On the new Slide 4, change the numbering so it starts at 5 rather than 1, to continue from the previous slide. (*Hint*: Select the numbered text box, click Format on the menu bar, click Bullets and Numbering, click the Numbered tab, and change the Start at value.)

9. At the end of the title in Slide 4, add a space and "(cont.)," the abbreviation for continued.

10. In Slide 5, demote the two bullets under "With low to moderate myopia," so they become sub-bullets.

11. In Slide 6, demote the final two bullets to become sub-bullets.

12. In Slide 7, move the sixth bulleted item ("Greater the correction, longer the time to heal") to become the second item.

13. In Slide 8, edit the bulleted item ("Analysis of . . .") so that "eye pressure," "shape of cornea," and "thickness of cornea" are sub-bullets below "Analysis of."

14. Add a Slide 9. Select the Title Only layout in the Text Layout section of the Slide Layout Task Pane.

*Explore*   15. In Slide 9, add the title "Magnolia Gardens Eye Center," and then create a new text box near the center of the slide, with the address and phone number ("8184 Magnolia Drive" on the first line, "Charleston, SC 29406" on the second line, and "(843) 555-EYES" on the third line). (*Hint*: Click the Text Box button on the Drawing toolbar, and then click on the slide at the desired location.)

*Explore*   16. Change the font size of the new text box on Slide 9 so that it's 32 points. If you're not sure how to do it, use the Help system to get help on changing the font size. If necessary, drag the edge of the text box so the box is positioned near the center of the slide.

*Explore*   17. Make sure the Style Checker is turned on, and then set the Style Options for Visual Clarity so that the maximum number of bullets should not exceed six, the number of lines per title should not exceed two, and the number of lines per bulleted item should not exceed two. Also turn on body punctuation, so that the Style Checker checks for punctuation at the end of paragraphs in the main text, but make sure title punctuation is turned off. (*Hint*: Use the Legibility section of the Visual Clarity tab and the Body punctuation section of the Case and End Punctuation tab on the Style Options dialog box.)

18. Go through all the slides, correcting problems of case (capitalization) and punctuation. Be sure not to let the Style Checker change the case for proper nouns; otherwise, accept the Style Checker's suggested case changes. Let the Style Checker correct end punctuation for complete sentences, but you shouldn't allow (or you should remove) punctuation for words or phrases that don't form complete sentences.

*Explore*   19. Add to the presentation the design template called "Watermark," which has a white background with violet circles. (*Hint*: Open the Task Pane, if necessary, and change the Task Pane to Slide Design – Design Templates. Then move the pointer over a design template thumbnail so the design template name appears. Click the thumbnail of the desired template. The Watermark template is the last one in the Task Pane.) If you can't find the "Watermark" design template, choose a different design template.

20. View the presentation in Slide Show View.

21. Save the presentation using its default filename.

22. Preview the presentation in grayscale.

23. Print the presentation in grayscale as handouts with four slides per page.

24. Close the files and then exit PowerPoint.

*Case 4. Textbook Review*   Your English teacher asks you to prepare a book review for presentation to the class. The teacher asks you to review any textbook for any class, current or past. To help you give your class presentation, you want to use PowerPoint slides. Your task is to prepare a presentation of at least six PowerPoint slides. Do the following:

1. Use the AutoContent Wizard to begin developing slides based on "Generic" from the General category of presentation types.

2. Make the presentation "Review of" followed by your textbook title, and make the footer "Review of" followed by the textbook subject. For example, the title might be "Review of *Earth's Dynamic Systems*" and the footer "Review of Geology Textbook."

3. In the footer, include both the date and the slide number.

4. Edit Slide 1 so that the textbook title is italicized. If you don't know how to italicize existing text, use PowerPoint's Help.

5. Also in Slide 1, if necessary, change the subtitle to your name.

6. In Slide 2 ("Introduction"), include the following type of information in the bulleted list: title, authors, publisher, publication year, number of pages, and college course using the book.

7. In Slide 3 ("Topics of Discussion"), include the categories used in reviewing the book; for example, "Level of writing," "Clarity of explanations," "Completeness of explanations," "Figures and tables," "End-of-chapter materials," and "End-of-book supplementary material."

8. Delete Slides 4 through 9. (*Hint*: The easiest way to delete many slides at once is to select the slides in Slide Sorter View.)

9. Create at least one slide for each of the topics you listed on Slide 3, and then include bulleted lists explaining that topic.

10. Create a slide titled "Summary and Recommendation" as the last slide in your presentation, giving your overall impression of the book and your recommendation for whether or not it should be continued.

**Explore** 11. Make sure the Style Checker is turned on, and then set the Style Options for Visual Clarity so that the maximum number of bullets should not exceed six, the number of lines per title should not exceed two, and the number of lines per bulleted item should not exceed two. Also turn on body punctuation, so that the Style Checker checks for punctuation at the end of paragraphs in the main text, but make sure title punctuation is turned off. (*Hint*: Use the Legibility section of the Visual Clarity tab and the End punctuation section of the Case and End Punctuation tab on the Style Options dialog box.)

12. Go through all the slides, correcting problems of case (capitalization), punctuation, number of bulleted items per slide, and the number of lines per bulleted item. Be sure not to let the Style Checker change the case for proper nouns. Let the Style Checker correct end punctuation for complete sentences, but you shouldn't allow (or you should remove) punctuation for words or phrases that don't form complete sentences.

**Explore** 13. Add to the presentation an appropriate design template. For example, if you're reviewing a geology textbook, you might apply the "Globe" design style. (*Hint*: Open the Task Pane, if necessary, and change the Task Pane to Slide Design – Design Templates.)

14. Check the spelling of your presentation.

15. View the presentation in Slide Show View. If you see any typographical errors or other problems, stop the slide show, correct the problems, and then continue the slide show.

16. If necessary, change the order of the bulleted items on slides, or change the order of slides.

17. If you find slides with more than six bulleted items, split the slide in two.

18. If you find slides that aren't necessary, delete them.

19. Save the presentation in the Cases folder of the Tutorial.01 folder, using the filename **Textbook Review**.

20. Preview the presentation in grayscale.

21. Print the presentation in grayscale as handouts with four slides per page.

22. Close the file, and then exit PowerPoint.

## INTERNET ASSIGNMENTS

**Student Union**

The purpose of the Internet Assignments is to challenge you to find information on the Internet that you can use to create effective documents. The actual assignments are updated and maintained on the Course Technology Web site. Log on to the Internet and use your Web browser to go to the Student Union on the New Perspectives Series site at **www.course.com/NewPerspectives/studentunion**. Click the Online Companions link, and then click the link for this text.

# QUICK | CHECK ANSWERS

*Session 1.1*

1. PowerPoint provides everything you need to produce a presentation that consists of black-and-white or color overheads, 35-mm slides, or on-screen slides. The presentation's components can consist of individual slides, speaker notes, an outline, and audience handouts.

2. The Outline tab shows an outline of your presentation, including titles and text of each slide. The Slides tab displays thumbnails of each slide in your presentation. The Slide Pane shows the slide as it will look during your slide show. The Notes Pane contains any notes that you might prepare on each slide. The Task Pane displays lists or sets of tasks that you can apply to your slide.

3. a. gradient fill: a type of shading in which one color blends into another
   b. footer: a word or phrase that appears at the bottom of each slide in the presentation
   c. slide transition: the special effect of how a slide appears on the monitor screen
   d. custom animation: user-defined motion or appearance of items on the slide
   e. placeholder: a region of a slide, or a location in an outline, reserved for inserting text or graphics
   f. bulleted list: a list of paragraphs with a special character (dot, circle, box, star, or other character) to the left of each paragraph

4. Planning improves the quality of your presentation, makes your presentation more effective and enjoyable, and saves you time and effort. You should answer several questions: What is my purpose or objective? What type of presentation is needed? What is the physical location of my presentation? What is the best format for presenting the information?

5. The AutoContent Wizard lets you choose a presentation category and then creates a general outline of the presentation.

6. Use six or fewer items per screen, and use phrases of six or fewer words

7. a word that is not located in the PowerPoint dictionary, usually a misspelled word.

8. so that you won't lose all your work if, for example, a power failure suddenly shuts down your computer

*Session 1.2*

1. a. Click a slide or bullet icon, and drag the selected item up.
   b. Select the slide to be deleted, click Edit on the menu bar, and then click Delete Slide. Or, select the slide to be deleted and press the Delete key.
   c. Unindent or move it from a lower to a higher outline level.
   d. Drag the I-beam pointer to select the text, and then delete or retype it.

2. Promote means to decrease the level (for example, from level 2 to level 1) of an outline item; demote means to increase the level (for example, from level 1 to level 2) of an outline item.

3. In the Outline tab you can see the text of several slides at once, which makes it easier to work with text. In the Slide Pane, you can see the design and layout of the slide.

4. Click the New Slide button on the Standard toolbar, then select the desired layout from the New Slide dialog box. You can also promote (unindent) a bulleted item using the Outline tab.

5. The Style Checker automatically checks your presentation for consistency and style. For example, it will check for consistency in punctuation.

6. Speaker notes are printed pages that contain a picture of and notes about each slide. Create them by typing text into the Notes Pane.

7. By previewing your presentation, you make sure that the slides are satisfactory, and that the presentation is legible in grayscale if you use a monochrome printer.

*New Perspectives on*

# MICROSOFT®
# OUTLOOK® 2002

## TUTORIAL 1   OUT 1.03

*Communicating with Outlook 2002*

Sending and Receiving E-mail Messages for The Express Lane

# Read This Before You Begin

## To the Student

### Data Disks

To complete this tutorial, Review Assignments, and Case Problems, you need one Data Disk. Your instructor will either provide you with the Data Disk or ask you to make your own.

If you are making your own Data Disk, you will need one blank, formatted high-density disk. You will need to copy a set of files and/or folders from a file server, standalone computer, or the Web onto your disk. Your instructor will tell you which computer, drive letter, and folders contain the files you need. You could also download the files by going to www.course.com and following the instructions on the screen.

The information below shows you which folders go on your disk, so that you will have enough disk space to complete the tutorial, Review Assignments, and Case Problems:

### Data Disk

Write this on the disk label.
Data Disk 1: Outlook Tutorial 1

Put this folder on the disk:
Tutorial 0.1

When you begin each tutorial, be sure you are using the correct Data Disk. Refer to the "File Finder" chart at the back of this text for more detailed information on which files are used in which tutorials. See the inside front or inside back cover of this book for more information on Data Disk files, or ask your instructor or technical support person for assistance.

### Using Your Own Computer

If you are going to work through this book using your own computer, you need:

- **Computer System** Microsoft Windows 98, NT, 2000 Professional, or higher must be installed on your computer. This book assumes a typical installation of Microsoft Office XP (including Outlook, Word, Excel, PowerPoint, and Access). You may need to install some features on first use, including the Import/Export feature and the Mail Merge feature.

- **Data Disks** You will not be able to complete the tutorials or exercises in this book using your own computer until you have your Data Disk.

### Visit Our World Wide Web Site

Additional materials designed especially for you are available on the World Wide Web.
Go to www.course.com/NewPerspectives.

## To the Instructor

The Data Disk Files are available on the Instructor's Resource Kit for this title. Follow the instructions in the Help file on the CD-ROM to install the programs to your network or standalone computer. For information on creating Data Disks, see the "To the Student" section above.

You are granted a license to copy the Data Files to any computer or computer network used by students who have purchased this book.

OBJECTIVES

In this tutorial you will:

- Start and exit Outlook

- Explore the Outlook window

- Navigate between Outlook components

- Create, send, read, and respond to e-mail messages

- Create and edit contact information

- Attach files to e-mail messages

- File, sort, save, and archive messages

# COMMUNICATING WITH OUTLOOK 2002

*Sending and Receiving E-mail Messages for The Express Lane*

CASE

## The Express Lane

The Express Lane is a complete and affordable online grocery store in the San Francisco Bay Area, specializing in natural and organic foods. When Alan Gregory and Lora Shaw began The Express Lane in 1998, fewer than 200,000 U.S. households were using online services to purchase food and other household goods and services; by 2007, this number is expected to reach 15 to 20 million. These households span a wide demographic range and will spend approximately $85 billion a year on foods and other goods purchased online (Andersen Consulting, January 20, 1998). Customers span all income and educational levels, ages, and locations.

Unlike traditional groceries, The Express Lane does not have a storefront where customers come to shop. Instead it stores both packaged goods and fresh produce in its warehouse. Customers place orders using fax, e-mail, or the company's Web site. The Express Lane staff then selects and packs the requested items, bills the customer's credit card for the cost of the groceries plus a $5 service fee, and delivers the groceries to the customer's front door within 4 to 6 hours. To coordinate these activities, The Express Lane relies on **Microsoft Outlook**, an information management program. You can use Outlook to perform a wide range of communication and organizational tasks, such as sending, receiving, and filing e-mail; organizing contact information; scheduling appointments, events, and meetings; creating a to-do list and delegating tasks; and writing notes.

To help manage their company's growth, Alan and Lora hire you to assist them with the variety of tasks they perform using Outlook. In this tutorial, you'll explore the Outlook window and its components. You'll use e-mail to send information about increasing an order to a supplier. You'll also set up contact information for suppliers and The Express Lane staff. Then you'll receive, read, and respond to e-mail messages. Finally you'll organize messages by filing, filtering, sorting, and archiving them.

# SESSION 1.1

In this session, you'll learn about the Outlook components, start Outlook, view its window elements, and navigate between components. Then you'll create and send an e-mail message. Finally you'll create and organize a contact list.

## Exploring Outlook

There are six main components in Outlook, described in Figure 1-1. As you work with these components, you create items such as e-mail messages, appointments, contacts, tasks, journal entries, and notes. An **item** is the basic element that holds information in Outlook, similar to a file in other programs. Items are organized into **folders**. Unlike folders in other Office programs, however, which you can view and open in Windows Explorer, Outlook folders are available only from within Outlook.

| Figure 1-1 | OUTLOOK COMPONENTS |
|---|---|
| **COMPONENT** | **DESCRIPTION** |
| Mail | A messaging/communication tool for receiving, sending, storing, and managing e-mail; the Inbox folder stores messages you have received; the Outbox folder stores messages you have written but not sent; the Sent Items folder stores copies of messages you have sent; you also can create other folders to save and organize e-mail you've received and written |
| Calendar | A scheduling tool for planning appointments, events, and meetings |
| Contacts | An address book for compiling postal addresses, phone numbers, e-mail and Web addresses, and other personal and business information about people and businesses with whom you communicate |
| Notes | A notepad for jotting down ideas and thoughts that you can group, sort, and categorize |
| Tasks | A to-do list for organizing and tracking items you need to complete or delegate |
| Journal | A diary for recording your activities, such as talking on the phone, sending an e-mail message, or working on a document |

### Starting Outlook

You can start Outlook in any of several ways. You can click the Launch Microsoft Outlook button on the Quick Launch toolbar in the taskbar, double-click the Microsoft Outlook icon on your desktop, or use the Start menu.

### To start Outlook:

1. Make sure that Windows is running on your computer and that the Windows desktop appears on your screen.

2. Click the **Start** button on the taskbar to display the Start menu, and then point to **Programs** to display the Programs menu.

3. Point to (but don't click) **Microsoft Outlook** on the Programs menu.

   **TROUBLE?** If you don't see Microsoft Outlook on the Programs menu, point to Microsoft Office, and then point to Microsoft Outlook. If you still can't find Microsoft Outlook, click the Launch Microsoft Outlook button on the Quick Launch toolbar or double-click the Microsoft Outlook icon on your desktop and skip Step 4. If none of the above is available, ask your instructor or technical support person for help.

4. Click **Microsoft Outlook**. After a short pause, the Outlook program window, displaying Outlook Today, appears.

   **TROUBLE?** If a dialog box opens, indicating that you need to set up an e-mail account, click the Cancel button and contine with Step 5.

   **TROUBLE?** If a dialog box opens, asking whether you want to import e-mail messages and addresses from Outlook Express or another e-mail program, click the No button.

   **TROUBLE?** If a dialog box opens, asking whether you want to make Outlook the default manager for Mail, News, and Contacts, click the No button.

5. If necessary, click the **Maximize** button ▣. Figure 1-2 shows the maximized Outlook window.

| Figure 1-2 | OUTLOOK TODAY |
| --- | --- |

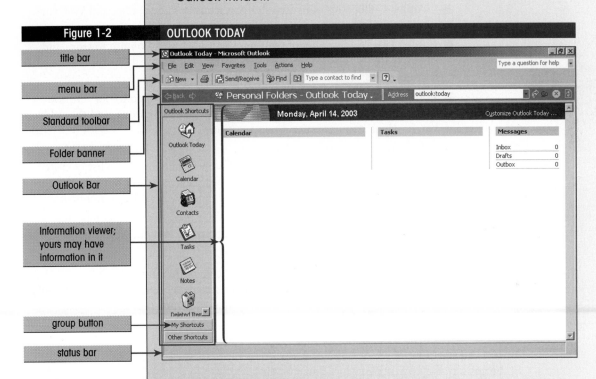

- title bar
- menu bar
- Standard toolbar
- Folder banner
- Outlook Bar
- Information viewer; yours may have information in it
- group button
- status bar

   **TROUBLE?** If your screen does not look exactly like the one in Figure 1-2, just continue. You'll learn how to hide and display Outlook elements next.

   **TROUBLE?** If a dialog box opens, asking whether you want to AutoArchive your old items now, click the No button.

   **TROUBLE?** Don't worry if your screen differs slightly from Figure 1-2. Although the figures in this book were created while running Windows 2000 in its default settings, all Windows operating systems share the same basic user interface. Microsoft Outlook should run equally well using Windows 98, Windows NT, or Windows Me.

The Outlook window contains some elements that might be familiar to you from other programs, such as Word or Excel. Other elements are specific to Outlook. The Outlook window includes the following:

- **Menu bar:** A collection of menus that you click to access commands. You use menu **commands** to tell Outlook what tasks you want it to perform. Menu commands vary, depending on the displayed Outlook folder.

- **Standard toolbar:** A collection of buttons that are shortcuts to frequently used commands. The toolbar buttons vary, depending on the displayed Outlook folder. Additional toolbars are available in different folders.

- **Outlook Bar:** Groups of shortcut icons that you can click to open frequently used Outlook folders or files and folders on your system or network. You can add shortcut icons to the Outlook Bar as needed.

- **Groups:** Collections of related shortcut icons to folders, files, and Web sites. Click a group button to display its contents.

- **Folder List:** A hierarchy of the Outlook folders that you use to store and organize items. The Folder List is not shown in Figure 1-2; you'll work with it later in this tutorial.

- **Folder banner:** A bar that displays the name of the open folder (Outlook Today in Figure 1-2), Back and Forward navigation buttons, and the Address bar, in which you can enter a new location.

- **Information viewer:** The display of items stored in the selected folder; may be divided into panes. For example, the upper pane displays a list of stored items, such as e-mail messages in the Inbox, and the lower pane displays a preview of the item selected in the upper pane, such as the contents of the selected e-mail message.

- **Status bar:** A banner of helpful details about the current view, such as the number of items stored in that folder.

No matter which component you use, these elements of the Outlook window work in the same way. You can display or hide any of these elements, depending on your needs and preferences. You'll customize the Outlook window to match Figure 1-2.

## To customize the Outlook window:

1. Click **View** on the menu bar. The View menu opens, displaying the list of commands you can click to change the "view" in Outlook—you click the commands to display or hide the various elements. (You may need to pause a moment or click the double arrow at the bottom of the menu to display the full menu.)

    Commands that are preceded by a check mark or whose icon appears pressed in indicate that those elements are currently displayed in the Outlook window. Clicking those commands hides the corresponding Outlook element. Likewise, commands that are not preceded by a check mark or whose icon doesn't appear pressed in indicate that those elements are not currently displayed; clicking the command displays the corresponding element.

2. Click **Outlook Bar**. The menu closes and the Outlook Bar disappears from the window.

    **TROUBLE?** If the Outlook Bar was not already displayed, then it appears rather than disappears. Skip to Step 4.

> You want to display the Outlook Bar, Preview pane, status bar, and Folder List.
>
> 3. Click **View** on the menu bar, and then click **Outlook Bar**. The Outlook Bar reappears.
>
> 4. If necessary, use the View menu to display the **Status Bar** and the **Folder List**. Your screen should now look similar to Figure 1-2 with the addition of the Folder List.

As you can see, the Folder List duplicates the information in the Outlook Bar. Both enable you to move between Outlook folders. Your Folder List may have different items than the Outlook Bar if either one is customized.

## Navigating Between Outlook Components

You can click any icon in the Outlook Bar to display that folder's contents in the Information viewer. The Outlook Bar contains three groups (collections of related shortcut icons): the Outlook Shortcuts group, which contains shortcut buttons for most of the installed Outlook components—Outlook Today, Calendar, Contacts, Tasks, Notes, Deleted Items, and Inbox; the My Shortcuts group, which contains shortcut buttons to access the Drafts and Journal folders and the Outlook Update Web page; and the Other Shortcuts group, which contains buttons for My Computer and the My Documents and Favorites folders. You click a group button to display its contents in the Outlook Bar. You can add shortcuts to any group, and you can also add more groups.

> ### To navigate with the Outlook Bar:
>
> 1. Click the **Outlook Shortcuts** group button on the Outlook Bar to display its buttons in the Outlook Bar. If that button was already selected, your view will not change.
>
> 2. Click **Calendar** on the Outlook Bar to switch to the Calendar, and then click the **Day** button on the Standard toolbar. The daily planner, current and next month calendar, and the TaskPad appear in the Information viewer.
>
> 3. Click the **My Shortcuts** group button on the Outlook Bar to display its shortcuts.
>
> 4. Click **Journal** on the Outlook Bar to switch to the Journal. The Journal displays a timeline. If the Journal is turned on, you will see icons representing your e-mail messages, files, phone calls, tasks, and other items organized by date.
>
>    TROUBLE? If a dialog box opens, asking whether you want to turn on the Journal, click the No button.
>
> 5. Click the **Outlook Shortcuts** group button on the Outlook Bar again, and then click **Contacts**. The list of contacts is displayed; yours is probably empty, but you will still see letter buttons along the right side that you use to scroll the contacts list.

A second way to navigate between folders is with the Folder List. You can click any folder icon in the Folder List to display the folder's contents in the Information viewer.

> ### To navigate with the Folder List:
>
> 1. Click the **Calendar** icon in the Folder List. The Calendar reappears.
>
> 2. Click the **Inbox** icon in the Folder List. The Inbox appears. See Figure 1-3.

Figure 1-3    INBOX

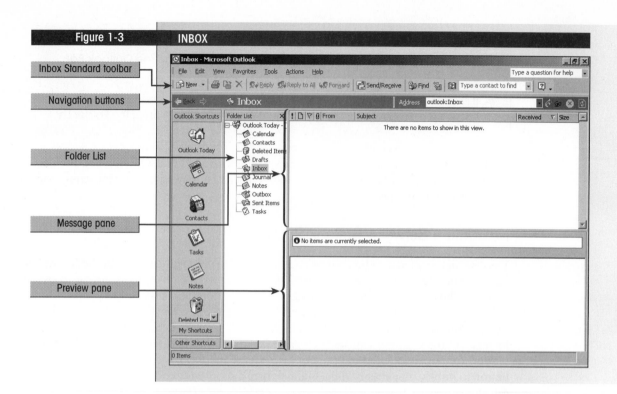

Inbox Standard toolbar

Navigation buttons

Folder List

Message pane

Preview pane

After you've switched between a few folders, you can use the Back and Forward buttons to return to them in reverse order. You'll try these buttons and then hide the Outlook Bar, leaving more room for the Information viewer.

### To navigate with the Folder List:

1. Click the **Back** button ⟵ Back on the Folder banner. The Calendar appears.

2. Click the **Forward** button ➡ on the Folder banner. The Inbox appears.

3. Click **View** on the menu bar, and then click **Outlook Bar**. The Outlook Bar disappears, and the Information viewer expands to fill the extra space.

The Information viewer currently displays the contents of the Inbox folder, where you receive, create, and send e-mail messages.

## Creating and Sending E-mail Messages

**E-mail**, the electronic transfer of messages between computers, is a simple and inexpensive way to communicate with friends around the corner, family across the country, and colleagues in the same building or around the world. The messages you send are delivered immediately and stored until recipients can read those messages at their convenience. The Express Lane staff uses e-mail to correspond with its customers, suppliers, and each other because it is fast, convenient, and inexpensive. In addition, it saves the company the cost of paper, ink or toner, and other supplies.

Before you can send and receive e-mail messages with Outlook, you must have access to an e-mail server or Internet service provider (ISP), an e-mail address, and a password. An **e-mail address** is a series of characters that you use to send and receive e-mail messages. It consists of a user ID and a host name separated by the @ symbol. A **user ID** (or user name or account name) is a unique name that identifies you to your mail server. The **host name** consists of the name of your ISP's computer on the Internet plus its domain or level. For example, in the e-mail address "alan@theexpresslane.com," "alan" is the user ID and "theexpresslane.com" is the host name. Although many people might use the same host, each user ID is unique, enabling the host to distinguish one user from another. A **password** is a private code that you enter to access your account. (In this tutorial, you'll use your own e-mail address to send all messages.)

If you haven't already set up an Outlook mail account, you'll need to do so now by completing the following steps.

## To set up an Outlook mail account:

1. Click **Tools** on the menu bar, and then click **E-mail Accounts**. The E-mail Accounts dialog box opens. You choose whether you want to create a new account or modify an existing one.

2. Click the **Add a new e-mail account** option button, and then click the **Next** button. The second dialog box has various server types. See Figure 1-4.

| Figure 1-4 | SECOND E-MAIL ACCOUNTS DIALOG BOX |
| --- | --- |

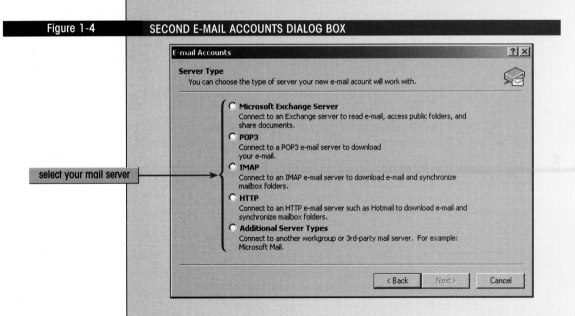

select your mail server

3. Select the type of server you will use to access your e-mail, and then click the **Next** button. The third dialog box varies, depending on the type of server you selected. See Figure 1-5.

**Figure 1-5**      THIRD E-MAIL ACCOUNTS DIALOG BOX

options vary depending on server type selected in previous dialog box

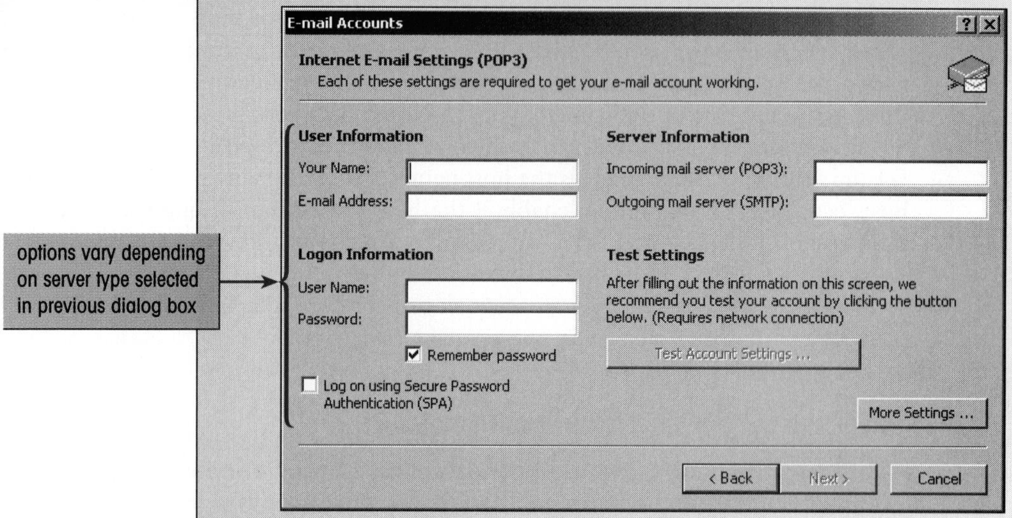

4. Enter the requested information in the E-mail Accounts dialog box, and then click the **Next** button.

   **TROUBLE?** If you are unsure of what information to enter, ask your instructor or technical support person.

5. Click the **Finish** button to set up your account based on the information you entered.

Once your account is set up, you can send and receive e-mail messages.

## Choosing a Message Format

Outlook can send and receive messages in three formats: HTML, Rich Text, and Plain Text. Although you specify one of these formats as the default for your messages, you can always switch formats for an individual message. **HTML** provides the most formatting features and options (text formatting, numbering, bullets, alignment, horizontal lines, backgrounds, HTML styles, and Web pages). **Rich Text** provides some formatting options (text formatting, bullets, and alignment), but some recipients will not be able to see the formatting if you send messages over the Internet. **Plain Text** messages include no formatting, and the recipient specifies which font is used for the message. When you reply to a message, Outlook uses the same format in which the message was created, unless you specify otherwise. For example, if you reply to a message sent to you in Plain Text, Outlook sends the response in Plain Text.

You'll set the message format to HTML so you can customize your messages.

### To choose a default message format:

1. Click **Tools** on the menu bar, and then click **Options**.

2. Click the **Mail Format** tab in the Options dialog box.

3. If it's not already selected, select **HTML** in the Compose in this message format list box.

**4.** If it is not already checked, click the **Use Microsoft Word to edit e-mail messages** check box. See Figure 1-6.

| Figure 1-6 | MAIL FORMAT TAB IN OPTIONS DIALOG BOX |

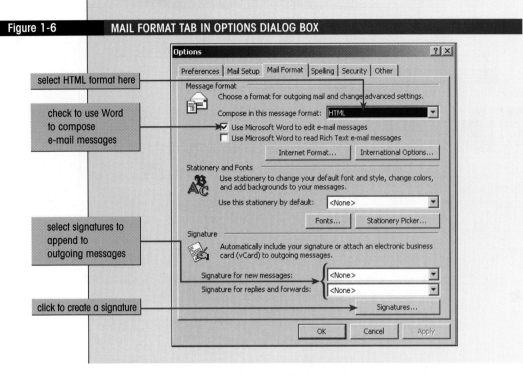

Each time you create a message, Outlook will use the HTML format, unless you select a different format for that message. Because you selected HTML as your message format, you can customize your messages with a formatted signature. You'll do that before closing the Options dialog box.

## Adding a Signature

A **signature** is text that is automatically added to every e-mail message you send. A signature can contain any text you want. For example, you might create a signature with your name, job title, company name, and phone number. The Express Lane might create a signature containing a paragraph that describes how to order groceries. You also can create more than one signature and then use the Signature button on the Standard toolbar to select which one you want to include in a particular message. Although you can attach a signature to a message in any format, the HTML and Rich Text formats enable you to apply font and paragraph formatting. For now, you'll create a simple signature with your name and the company name.

### To create a signature:

**1.** Click the **Signatures** button, and then click the **New** button in the Create Signature dialog box.

**2.** Type your name in the Enter a name for your new signature text box, click the **Start with a blank signature** option button if necessary, and then click the **Next** button. The Edit Signature dialog box opens.

**3.** In the Signature text box, type your name, press the **Enter** key, and then type **The Express Lane**. See Figure 1-7.

**Figure 1-7**    **EDIT SIGNATURE DIALOG BOX**

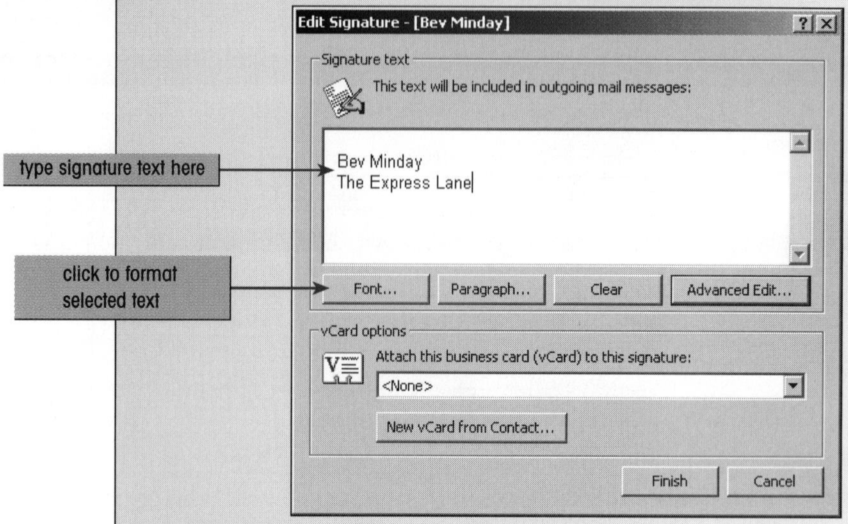

type signature text here →

click to format
selected text →

4. Select **The Express Lane**, click the **Font** button, change the font to **10-point, Bold Italic, Arial**, and then click the **OK** button.

5. Click the **Finish** button, preview your signature in the Create Signature dialog box, and then click the **OK** button to return to the Options dialog box.

You'll add your signature to new messages you create, but not to messages you respond to.

6. Click the **Signature for new messages** list arrow, and then click your name.

7. If necessary, select **<None>** in the Signature for replies and forwards list box.

8. Click the **OK** button.

Whenever you create a new e-mail, your signature will appear at the end of the message.

## Using Stationery

With Outlook, you can select a special look for your messages, much as you would select special letterhead paper for your business correspondence. **Stationery templates** are HTML files that include complementary fonts, background colors, and images for your outgoing e-mail messages. They also increase the size of your message. To use one of the stationery templates that comes with Outlook, including announcements, invitations, greetings, and other designs, you click Actions on the menu bar, point to New Mail Message Using, and then click the More Stationery command to open a dialog box with stationery options. Previously selected stationeries will appear below the More Stationery command. You also can create your own stationery. Stationery uses HTML message format, so recipients whose e-mail programs don't read HTML e-mail won't see the stationery, but they will still be able to read the text.

## Creating an E-mail Message

An e-mail message looks similar to a memo, with header lines for Date, To, From, Cc, and Subject, followed by the body of the message. Outlook fills in the Date line with the date on which you send the message and the From line with your name or e-mail address; these lines are not visible in the Message window. You complete the other lines. The To line lists the e-mail addresses of one or more recipients. The Cc line lists the e-mail addresses of anyone who will receive a courtesy copy of the message. An optional Bcc line lists the e-mail addresses of anyone who will receive a blind courtesy copy of the message; the Bcc recipients are not visible to each other or to the To and Cc recipients. The Subject line provides a quick overview of the message topic, similar to a headline. The main part of the e-mail is the message body.

E-mail, like other types of communication, is governed by its own customs of behavior, called **netiquette** (short for Internet etiquette), which helps prevent miscommunication. As you write and send e-mail messages, keep in mind the following guidelines:

- **Think before you send.** Your words can have a lasting impact. Be sure your messages convey the thoughts you intend and want others to attribute to you. Your name and e-mail address are attached to every message that you send, and your message can be forwarded swiftly to others.

- **Be concise.** The recipient should be able to read and understand your message quickly.

- **Use standard capitalization.** Excessive use of uppercase is considered shouting, and exclusive use of lowercase is incorrect and is difficult to read.

- **Check spelling and grammar.** Create and maintain a professional image by using standard spelling and grammar. What you say is just as important as how you say it.

- **Avoid sarcasm.** Without vocal intonations and body language, a recipient may read your words with emotions or feelings you didn't intend. You can use punctuation marks to create smileys such as :-) to convey the intent of your words. To learn additional smileys, use your favorite search engine and search on the keywords "smiley dictionary" for good Web sites.

- **Don't send confidential information.** E-mail is not private; once you send a message, you lose control over where it may go and who might read it. Also, employers and schools usually can access their employees' and students' e-mail messages.

The adage "Act in haste; repent in leisure" is particularly apt for writing e-mail.

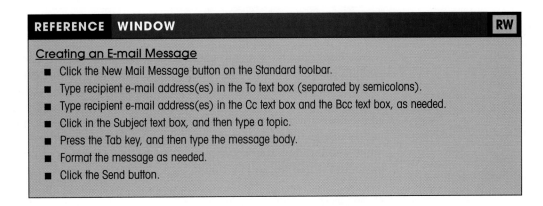

You'll create an e-mail message. Although you would usually send messages to other people, you will send messages to yourself in this tutorial so you can practice sending and receiving messages.

## To create an e-mail message:

1. Click the **New Mail Message** button on the Standard toolbar. A new Message window opens in Word. If necessary, maximize the window. Your signature appears in the message body; you'll type your message above the signature.

2. Type your e-mail address in the To text box. You could send the e-mail to multiple recipients by typing a semicolon between each address.

3. Press the **Tab** key twice to move to the Subject text box. You skipped the Cc text box because you aren't sending a courtesy copy of this e-mail to anyone.

   **TROUBLE?** If the insertion point is not in the Subject text box, then the Bcc text box is displayed. Press the Tab key again to move to the Subject text box, and then continue with Step 4.

4. Type **Peach Order** in the Subject text box, and then press the **Tab** key to move to the message body, just above the signature.

5. Type **Your peaches are a big hit with The Express Lane customers. Please double our order for the next three weeks.**, press the **Enter** key twice, and then type **Thank you,** (including the comma). See Figure 1-8.

| Figure 1-8 | COMPLETED E-MAIL MESSAGE IN WORD |
| --- | --- |

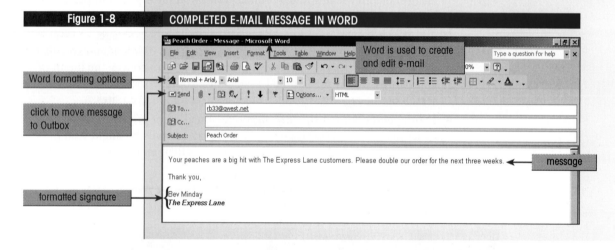

Word formatting options

click to move message to Outbox

formatted signature

message

You don't need to type your name because you included it as part of the signature. Before sending your message, however, you want to add some text formatting. You set up Outlook to use Word as your e-mail editor, which means that you are actually using Word to create the message rather than Outlook; notice the title bar in Figure 1-8. This gives you access to all the formatting features available in Word. For example, you can set bold, underline, and italics; change the font, font size, and font color; align and indent text; create a bulleted or numbered list; and even apply paragraph styles. People whose e-mail programs can't read formatted e-mail will still be able to read your messages in plain text.

## To format text in an e-mail message:

1. Select the text **a big hit** in the message body. You'll make this text bold and orange.

2. Click the **Bold** button **B** on the Formatting toolbar.

> **TROUBLE?** If you don't see the Bold button, click the Toolbar Options list arrow, and then click the Bold button.
>
> 3. Click the **Font Color** button list arrow [A▾] on the Formatting toolbar, and then click the **Orange** tile in the palette that opens.
>
> **TROUBLE?** If you don't see the Font Color button, click the Toolbar Options list arrow, and then click the Font Color button.

You could add more formatting, but a little goes a long way. Try to be judicious in your use of text formatting. Use it to enhance your message rather than overwhelm it.

## Sending E-mail

There are a variety of ways you can set up Outlook for sending messages. Your messages can be sent immediately (assuming your computer is connected to your e-mail server), or you can set it up so messages remain in the Outbox until you click the Send/Receive button. You also can set up a schedule, where Outlook automatically sends and receives messages at regular intervals that you specify (such as every 5 minutes or every few hours).

If you are **working offline** (not connected to your e-mail server) or if you have a dial-up connection, any messages you write remain in the Outbox until you choose to send them. In this case, it is usually a more efficient practice to create all of your messages before you send them. You select how messages are sent in the Options dialog box. You'll set these options now.

> ### To change your message delivery options:
>
> 1. Click the **Inbox - Microsoft Outlook** button on the taskbar to return to the Inbox.
> 2. Click **Tools** on the menu bar, and then click **Options**.
> 3. Click the **Mail Setup** tab.
> 4. In the Send/Receive section, click the **Send immediately when connected** check box to remove the check mark, if necessary. Now Outlook will move your completed messages into the Outbox until you choose to send them rather than immediately sending them to your e-mail server.
> 5. Click the **OK** button.

When you click the Send button in the Message window, the message will move to the Outbox. You then must click the Send/Receive button on the Standard toolbar to check for and deliver new messages.

> ### To send a message to the Outbox:
>
> 1. Click the **Peach Order - Message - Microsoft Word** button on the taskbar to return to your message.
> 2. Click the **Send** button [Send] on the Standard toolbar. The message moves to the Outbox.

The Outbox changes to boldface and is followed by (1), which indicates that there is one outgoing message. You can send and receive e-mail from the Inbox or the Outbox; you'll switch to the Outbox to deliver this message.

### To switch to the Outbox and send the message:

**1.** Click **Outbox** in the Folder List. The message appears in the Information viewer. See Figure 1-9.

Figure 1-9          MESSAGE IN OUTBOX

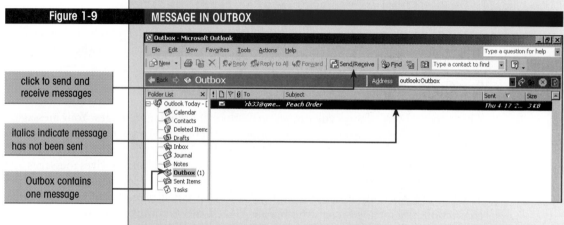

click to send and receive messages

italics indicate message has not been sent

Outbox contains one message

**2.** Click the **Send/Receive** button [Send/Receive] on the Standard toolbar to send the message. You may see the Outlook Send/Receive Progress dialog box until the message is sent. After the message is sent, the Outbox is empty and the boldface and (1) have disappeared.

**TROUBLE?** If Outlook requests a password, you might need to enter your password before you can send and receive your messages. Type your password, and then click the OK button.

A copy of the message is stored in the Sent Items folder, which provides a record of all the messages you sent. The time your e-mail takes to arrive at its destination will vary, depending on the size of the message, the speed of your Internet connection, and the number of other users on the Internet.

While sending your outgoing messages, Outlook may check your mail server for messages you have received since you last checked. If you have messages, they will be delivered to your Inbox.

## Organizing Contact Information

The **Contacts** folder is an address book where you store information about the people and businesses with whom you communicate. Each person or organization is called a **contact**. You can store business-related information about each contact, including job title, phone and fax numbers, postal and Web addresses, and e-mail addresses, as well as more personal information, such as birthdays, anniversaries, and spouse and children's names.

Each piece of information you enter about a contact is called a **field**. For example, a complete contact name, such as Mr. Salvador F. Aiello, Jr., is comprised of a Title field, First field, Middle field, Last field, and Suffix field. The field's name or label identifies what information is stored in that field. You can use fields to sort, group, or look up contacts by any part of the name.

## Creating Contacts

The Express Lane stores information about its suppliers and customers in the Contacts folder. Alan has asked you to create new contacts for several suppliers. You can start a new contact from any folder by clicking the New button list arrow on the Standard toolbar and then clicking New Contact. Instead, you'll switch to the Contacts folder.

---

### To create a contact:

1. Switch to the **Contacts** folder. The New button changes to reflect the most likely item you'll want to create from this folder.

2. Click the **New Contact** button [New] on the Standard toolbar. A new Contact window opens, displaying text boxes in which to enter the contact information.

3. Maximize the Contact window, if necessary.

---

Contact information is entered on two tabs. The General tab stores the most pertinent information about a contact, including the contact's name, job title and company, phone numbers, and addresses. The Details tab contains less frequently needed information, such as the names of the contact's manager, assistant, and spouse, as well as the contact's birthday, anniversary, and nickname.

---

**REFERENCE WINDOW** **RW**

Creating a Contact

■ Click the New button list arrow, and then click Contact to open a blank Contact window.
■ Enter the contact's name, job title, company, mailing address, phone numbers, e-mail addresses, and Web site (click the down arrow to select other address, number, or e-mail options).
■ Click the Details tab and enter other business or personal data as needed.
■ Click the Save and New button on the Standard toolbar to create another contact (or click the Save and Close button if this is the last contact).
■ If the Duplicate Contact Detected dialog box opens, select whether to add contact anyway or merge with existing contact, and then click the OK button.

---

You'll enter the first contact's name and company.

---

### To enter a contact's name and company:

1. Type **Mr. Salvador F. Aiello, Jr.** in the Full Name text box, and then press the **Enter** key. The insertion point moves to the next text box, and the contact name appears, last name first, in the File as text box. By default, Outlook organizes your contacts by their last names.

2. Click the **Full Name** button to open the Check Full Name dialog box. Although you entered the contact name in one text box, Outlook stores each part of the name as a separate field. See Figure 1-10.

| Figure 1-10 | CHECK FULL NAME DIALOG BOX |
|---|---|

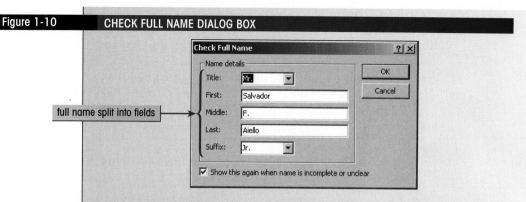

full name split into fields

3. Click the **Cancel** button to close the dialog box without making any changes. If Outlook cannot tell how to distinguish part of a name, the Check Full Name dialog box will open so that you can correct the fields.

4. Click in the **Job title** text box, and then type **President**.

5. Press the **Tab** key to move to the Company text box, and then type **Green Grocer Produce**.

Next you enter the contact's phone numbers. You can enter as many as 19 numbers per contact. No matter how you enter the numbers—with or without spaces, hyphens, or parentheses—Outlook formats them consistently, such as (415) 555-3928.

## To enter a contact's phone numbers, mailing address, and e-mail address:

1. Click in the **Business** text box. The button that appears provides access to a Check Phone Number dialog box, which is similar in function and appearance to the Check Full Name dialog box.

   TROUBLE? If the Location Information dialog box opens, enter the appropriate information about your location, and then click the OK button.

2. Type **415 555 9753**, and then press the **Tab** key. Outlook formats the phone number with parentheses around the area code and a hyphen after the prefix, even though you didn't type them.

   Next to each phone number text box is a list arrow that you can click to display other phone fields. Although you can display only four phone fields at a time, you can enter information in all the fields, using one text box or all four text boxes.

3. Click the **down arrow** button ▼ next to Home, click **Assistant** to change the field label, and then enter **415-555-9752** for the phone number of Salvador's assistant.

   You'll switch to the Details tab to enter the name of Salvador's assistant, and then return to the General tab to enter his fax number, postal address, and e-mail address.

4. Click the **Details** tab, and then type **Cynthia Lopez** in the Assistant's name text box.

5. Click the **General** tab, and then enter **415-555-6441** as the Business Fax.

6. Click in the **Address** text box, type **12 Haymarket Blvd.**, press the **Enter** key, and then type **San Francisco, CA 94102**. You could verify that Outlook recorded the address in the correct fields by clicking the Address button, but you don't need to do so for a simple address.

The This is the mailing address check box is checked. Outlook assumes that the first address you enter for a contact is the mailing address. You could enter additional addresses and specify any one of them as the mailing address.

7. Click in the **E-mail** text box, type your own e-mail address, and then press the **Tab** key. The Display as text box shows how the e-mail address will appear in the To text box of e-mail messages. See Figure 1-11.

| Figure 1-11 | COMPLETED CONTACT WINDOW |
| --- | --- |

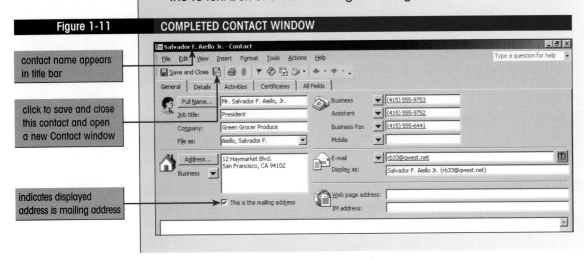

contact name appears in title bar

click to save and close this contact and open a new Contact window

indicates displayed address is mailing address

In most cases, each contact would have a unique e-mail address to which you would send e-mail messages. So far, you have completed the contact information for Salvador. You can close his Contact window and open a new Contact window in the same step.

## To create additional contacts:

1. Click the **Save and New** button [icon] on the Standard toolbar to save Salvador's contact information and open a new Contact window.

2. Enter the following information: **Julia Shang**, **Manager**, **Foods Naturally**, business phone **415-555-1224**, business fax **415-555-4331**, **19 Hillcrest Way**, **Novato, CA 94132**. Use your own e-mail address.

3. Click [icon]. Outlook detects that another contact already has the same e-mail address as Julia Shang and opens the Duplicate Contact Detected dialog box. Click the **Add this as a new contact anyway** option button, and then click the **OK** button.

4. Enter the following contact information: **Kelley Ming**, **Ming Nuts Company**, business phone **415-555-9797**, **2932 Post Street, San Francisco, CA 94110**. Use your own e-mail address.

5. Click [icon], add Kelley Ming as a new contact anyway, and then enter the following contact information: **Alan Gregory**, **The Express Lane**, and your e-mail address.

> **6.** Click the **Save and Close** button 🖫 Save and Close on the Standard toolbar and add Alan Gregory as a new contact anyway to save his contact information and return to the Contacts Information viewer.

There are a variety of ways to look at the information in the Contacts folder. **Views** specify how information in a folder is organized and which details are visible. Address Cards view displays names and addresses in blocks. Detailed Address Cards view displays additional information in this same format. Phone List view displays details about your contacts, such as name, job title, telephone numbers, in columns. Each Outlook folder has a set of standard views from which you can choose. You'll change the Contacts folder view to Detailed Address Cards.

### To change the Contacts view:

**1.** Click **View** on the menu bar, and then point to **Current View**. The submenu lists all the available standard views for the Contacts folder.

**2.** Click **Detailed Address Cards**. Detailed Address Cards view displays more contact information in the Information viewer than the Address Cards view. See Figure 1-12.

| Figure 1-12 | CONTACTS IN DETAILED ADDRESS CARDS VIEW |

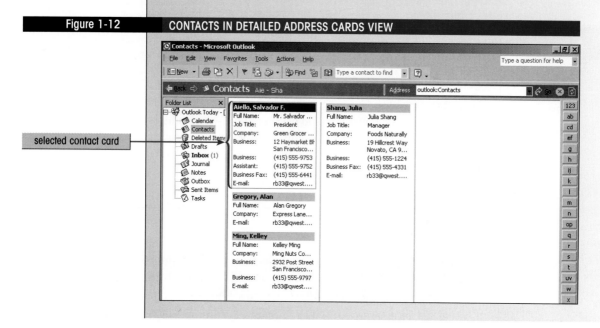

selected contact card

In the Detailed Address Cards view, Outlook organizes your contacts in alphabetical order by last name, as specified in the File as text box. When you have many contacts, you find a certain contact quickly by clicking the letter button along the right side of the Information viewer that corresponds to the first letter of a contact's last name. Then use the scroll bar at the bottom of the window to display that contact.

## Editing Contacts

Many aspects of a contact's information may change over time. A person or company may move to a new street address or be assigned a new area code. A person may change jobs periodically. You may discover that you entered information incorrectly. Rather than deleting the card and starting over, you can update the existing contact card as needed. Simply double-click the contact to open its Contact window, and edit the information as needed. You also can make the change directly in the Contacts Information viewer from the Address Cards or Detailed Address Cards view.

Alan tells you that the ZIP code for Foods Naturally is actually 94947. You'll make this correction directly in the Information viewer.

### To edit a contact:

1. Click the letter **S** along the right side of the Information viewer to select Julia Shang's contact card.

   **TROUBLE?** If your contacts list has additional contacts, the first contact beginning with "s" will be selected. Scroll until you can see Julia Shang's contact card.

2. Click the address portion of the contact card to place the insertion point.

3. Use the arrow keys to move the insertion point between the 4 and 1 in the ZIP code.

4. Type **947**, and then press the **Delete** key three times to erase the incorrect digits.

5. Click anywhere outside Julia Shang's contact card. Outlook saves the changes.

No matter how many changes you need to make to a contact's information, the contact card remains neat and organized.

## Session 1.1 QUICK CHECK

1. Describe the purposes of the Inbox and the Outbox.

2. Define e-mail and list two benefits of using it.

3. What is a signature?

4. List five types of contact information that you can store in Outlook.

## SESSION 1.2

In this session, you'll receive, read, reply to, forward, and print e-mail messages. Then you'll add and read attachments to e-mail messages. Finally you'll organize messages by filing, archiving, sorting, and filtering them.

## Receiving E-mail

You check for new e-mail messages by clicking the Send/Receive button on the Standard toolbar. Outlook connects to your e-mail server, if necessary, sends any messages in the Outbox, and receives any incoming messages that have arrived since you last checked. New messages are delivered into the Inbox.

You'll switch to the Inbox and download the message you sent yourself earlier.

## To receive e-mail:

**1.** If you took a break after the previous session, make sure Outlook is running.

**2.** Switch to the **Inbox**.

**3.** Click the **Send/Receive** button [Send/Receive] on the Standard toolbar. If necessary, connect to the Internet.

**4.** Watch for the new message to appear in the Inbox. The number of new messages you receive appears within parentheses. See Figure 1-13. Your Inbox might contain additional e-mail messages.

| Figure 1-13 | RECEIVED MESSAGE IN INBOX |

unread message icon

indicates one unread message in the inbox

Preview pane header information

formatted message in Preview pane

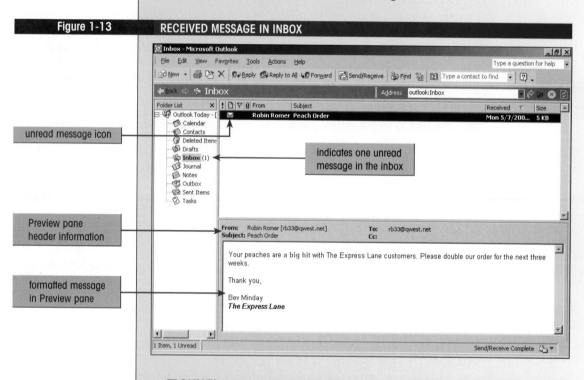

**TROUBLE?** If no messages appear, your e-mail server might not have received the message yet. Wait a few minutes, and then repeat Steps 3 and 4.

Once a message arrives, you can open and read it.

## Opening and Reading Messages

The Inbox Information viewer is divided into two panes. The upper pane displays a list of all e-mail messages that you have received, along with columns of information about the message. These columns include the sender's name, the message subject, and the date and time that the message was received, as well as icons that indicate the message's status (such as the message's importance level and whether the message has been read). You can change any column width by dragging the border of any column header.

The lower pane, called the Preview pane, displays the contents of the selected message. At the top of the Preview pane is the **message header**, which indicates the sender, all recipients (except Bcc recipients), and the subject. You can resize the panes by dragging the border above the message header up or down.

## To open and read a message:

1. In the message list, click the **Peach Order** message to display its contents in the Preview pane. In a moment, the mail icon changes from unread ✉ to read ✉, and the message no longer appears in boldface.

   **TROUBLE?** If the message header does not appear, right-click the top of the Preview pane and then click Header Information in the shortcut menu.

2. Double-click the **Peach Order** message in the message list. The message opens in an Outlook Message window.

3. Read the message. Because Outlook can view HTML messages, the formatting you added to the message earlier is visible.

   **TROUBLE?** If you don't see the HTML formatting, your mail server may not accept messages formatted in HTML. Just continue with the tutorial.

4. Click the **Close** button ✕ on the title bar.

After you read a message, you have several options—you can leave the message in the Inbox and deal with it later, reply to the message, forward the message to others, print it, file it, or delete it.

# Replying to and Forwarding Mail

Many messages you receive require some sort of response—for example, confirmation you received the information, the answer to a question, or sending the message to another person. The quickest way to respond to messages is to use the Reply, Reply to All, and Forward features. The **Reply** feature responds to the sender, and the **Reply to All** feature responds to the sender and all recipients (including any Bcc recipients); Outlook inserts the e-mail addresses into the appropriate text boxes. The **Forward** feature sends a copy of the message to one or more recipients you specify; you enter the e-mail addresses in the To or Cc text box. With both the Reply and Forward features, the original message is included for reference, separated from your new message by the text "Original Message" and the original message header information. By default, any new text you type is added at the top of the message body, above the original message. This makes it simpler for recipients to read your message because they don't have to scroll through the original message text to find the new text.

You'll reply to the Peach Order message. In reality, you would respond to someone other than yourself.

## To reply to a message:

1. Make sure that the **Peach Order** message is selected in the Inbox, and then click the **Reply** button on the Standard toolbar. A Message window opens in Word with the receiver's name or e-mail address in the To text box (in this case, your name or address) and RE: (short for Regarding) inserted at the beginning of the Subject line.

2. If necessary, click in the message area, and then type **You will receive double shipments of peaches for the next three weeks. Thank you for your order.**, press the **Enter** key twice, and then type your name (remember that your signature is not added for replies). Your reply message appears in blue type because you selected HTML format.

**TROUBLE?** Depending on how your computer is configured, you might not see the HTML formatting.

**3.** Click the **Send** button ⊟Send to move the message to the Outbox.

Next you'll forward the message to Julia Shang, the manager at Foods Naturally. Because Julia's contact information is in the Contacts folder, you can address the message to her quickly.

## To forward a message:

**1.** Make sure that the **Peach Order** message is selected in the Inbox, and then click the **Forward** button 🔁Forward on the Standard toolbar. This time, the insertion point is in the empty To text box and FW: (for Forward) precedes the Subject line.

**2.** Type **Julia Shang** in the To text box, and then press the **Tab** key. A wavy red line appears below the name, indicating that multiple contact information is available for that contact.

**3.** Right-click **Julia Shang**, and then click the option with the e-mail address. When Outlook recognizes the contact name as an item in the Contacts folder with a valid e-mail address, it underlines it.

**4.** Click at the top of the message body, and then type **Please update The Express Lane account.**

**5.** Click the **Send** button ⊟Send on the Standard toolbar to move the message to the Outbox.

**6.** Click the **Send/Receive** button 🗐Send/Receive if necessary.

Alan asks you to print the message for future reference.

## Printing Messages

Although e-mail eliminates the need for paper messages, sometimes you'll want a printed copy of a message to file or distribute, or to read when you're not at your computer. You can use the Print button on the Standard toolbar to print a selected message with the default settings, or you can use the Print command on the File menu to open the Print dialog box, where you can verify and change settings before you print. All default print styles include the print date, user name, and page number in the footer. You'll use the Print dialog box to verify the settings and then print the Peach Order message.

## To verify settings and print a message:

**1.** If necessary, select the **Peach Order** message in the Inbox.

**2.** Click **File** on the menu bar, and then click **Print**. The Print dialog box opens, as shown in Figure 1-14.

| Figure 1-14 | PRINT DIALOG BOX |

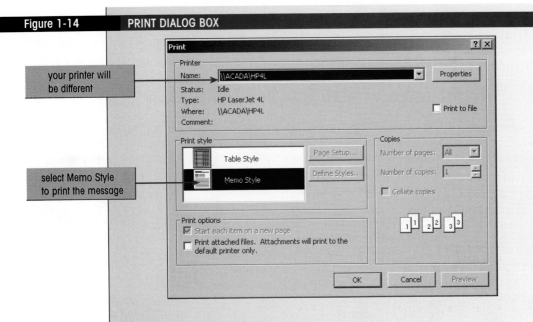

your printer will
be different

select Memo Style
to print the message

**3.** Make sure that the correct printer appears in the Name list box.

**TROUBLE?** If you're not sure which printer to use, ask your instructor or technical support person for assistance.

**4.** If necessary, click **Memo Style** in the Print style section to select it.

Memo style prints the contents of the selected item—in this case, the e-mail message. Table Style prints the view of the selected folder—in this case, the Inbox folder. Other folders have different print style options.

**5.** Click the **OK** button. The message prints.

In your work at The Express Lane, you'll often want to send information that is stored in a variety of files on your computer. Some of this information could be typed into an e-mail message, but many kinds of files (such as photos and spreadsheets) can't be inserted into e-mail messages. Instead, you can send files as attachments.

# Working **with Attachments**

An **attachment** is a file that you send with an e-mail message. Attachments can be any type of file, including documents (such as a Word document, Excel workbook, or PowerPoint slide presentation), images, sounds, and programs. For example, you might send an attachment containing The Express Lane's latest sales figures to Alan for his review. Recipients can then save and open the file; the recipient must have the original program or a program that can read that file type. For example, if Alan receives a Lotus 1-2-3 spreadsheet, he can open and save it with Excel.

## To attach a file to an e-mail:

**1.** Click the **New Mail Message** button [New] on the Inbox Standard toolbar.

**2.** Type **Alan Gregory** in the To text box.

3. Type **Latest Sales** in the Subject text box.

4. In the message body area, type **The attached Excel workbook contains the latest sales figures. It looks like we're on track. Let me know if you have any comments.**, and then press the **Enter** key.

5. Insert your Data Disk in the appropriate disk drive.

   **TROUBLE?** If you don't have a Data Disk, you need to get one before you can proceed. Your instructor or technical support person will either give you one or ask you to make your own by following the instructions on the "Read This Before You Begin" page preceding this tutorial. See your instructor or technical support person for more information.

6. Click the **Insert File** button 🔗 on the Standard toolbar. The Insert File dialog box opens and functions like the Open dialog box.

7. Change the Look in list box to the **Tutorial** folder within the **Tutorial.01** folder on your Data Disk.

8. Double-click the **Sales** document. The file is attached to your e-mail message, and the Insert File dialog box closes. See Figure 1-15. The message is ready to send.

| Figure 1-15 | MESSAGE WITH ATTACHED FILE |

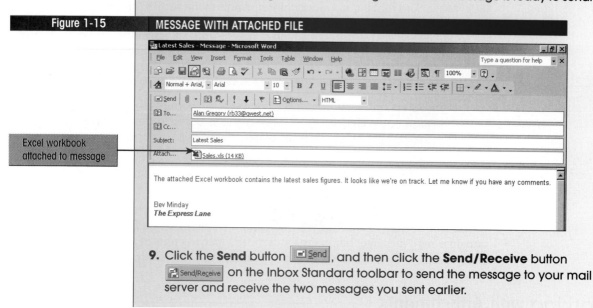

Excel workbook
attached to message

9. Click the **Send** button 🔲 Send, and then click the **Send/Receive** button 📧 Send/Receive on the Inbox Standard toolbar to send the message to your mail server and receive the two messages you sent earlier.

A message with an attachment may take a bit longer to send because it's larger than an e-mail message without an attachment. Messages with attached files display a paper clip icon in the message list. If the appropriate program is installed on your computer, you can open the attached file from the message itself. You also can save the attachment to your computer and then open, edit, and move it like any other file on your computer.

You can reply to or forward any message with an attachment, but the attachment is included only in the forwarded message because you will rarely, if ever, want to return the same file to the sender.

After you receive the message with the attachment, you'll save the attachment and then view it from within the message.

### To save and view the message attachment:

1. Click the **Send/Receive** button [Send/Receive] on the Standard toolbar to receive the message. Again, it might take a bit longer than usual to download the message with the attachment.

2. Click the **Latest Sales** message in the message list to view the message in the Preview pane. The attachment icon appears below the Subject, similar to when you created the message.

3. Right-click the **Sales** icon, and then click **Save As** on the shortcut menu. The Save Attachment dialog box opens, where you can select the location to save the attachment.

4. Change the Save in list box to the **Tutorial** folder within the **Tutorial.01** folder on your Data Disk.

5. Change the filename to **Second Quarter Sales**, and then click the **Save** button to save the attached file to your Data Disk. You can work with this file just as you would any other file on disk.

   You also can open the attached file from the Preview pane or the Message window.

6. Double-click the **Sales** icon. The Opening Mail Attachment dialog box opens.

7. Click the **Open it** option button, and then click the **OK** button. The attached file opens in its associated program—in this case, Excel. You can read, edit, format, and save the file just as you would any other Excel workbook.

   **TROUBLE?** If the file opens in a spreadsheet program other than Excel, your computer might be configured to associate the file extension .xls with spreadsheet programs other than Excel. Just continue with Step 8.

8. Review the sales figures, and then click the **Close** button [X] on the Excel title bar to close the workbook and exit Excel.

   **TROUBLE?** If a dialog box opens asking whether you want to save changes, click the No button.

# Managing **Messages**

As you can readily see, messages can collect quickly in your Inbox. Even if you respond to each message as it arrives, all of the original messages will still remain in your Inbox. Some messages you'll want to delete. Others you'll want to file and store, just as you would file and store paper memos in a file cabinet. The Folder List acts like an electronic file cabinet. You should create a logical folder structure in which to store your messages. For example, an employee of The Express Lane might create subfolders named Customers and Suppliers within the Inbox folder.

## Creating a Folder

You can create folders at the same level as the default folders, such as Inbox, Outbox, and Sent Messages, or you can create subfolders within these main folders. For now, you'll create one subfolder in the Inbox folder, named Suppliers. Once you create a subfolder, an Expand button or a Collapse button precedes the icon for the main folder, depending on whether the subfolders are displayed or hidden.

## To create a folder in the Inbox folder:

1. Right-click **Inbox** in the Folder List, and then click **New Folder**. The Create New Folder dialog box opens.

2. Select **Mail and Post Items** in the Folder contains list box. You can also create subfolders to store contacts, notes, tasks, and so on.

3. Type **Suppliers** in the Name text box.

4. Click the **Inbox** icon in the Select where to place the folder list box if it's not already selected. See Figure 1-16.

| Figure 1-16 | CREATE NEW FOLDER DIALOG BOX |
| --- | --- |

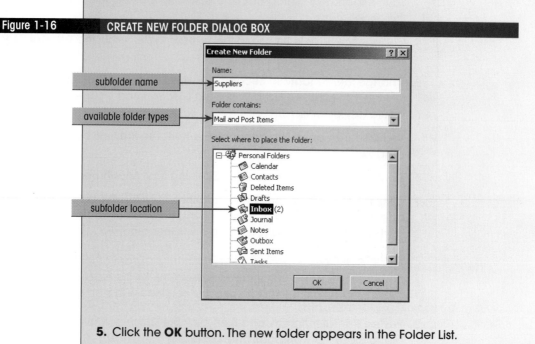

5. Click the **OK** button. The new folder appears in the Folder List.

Now you can file any messages related to The Express Lane in the new folder.

## Filing Messages

As soon as you've dealt with a message in the Inbox, you should move it out of the Inbox; otherwise it will become cluttered, and you won't know which messages you've dealt with and which you haven't. To file a message, you can drag selected messages from one folder to another or use the Move to Folder button on the Standard toolbar.

## To file messages:

1. If necessary, click the **Expand** button ⊞ next to the Inbox folder in the Folder List to display the Suppliers subfolder.

2. Select the **Peach Order** message in the Information viewer. It is the first message that you will move.

3. Drag the **Peach Order** message to the **Suppliers** subfolder in the Folder List, but do not release the mouse button. See Figure 1-17.

| Figure 1-17 | FILING A MESSAGE |
| --- | --- |

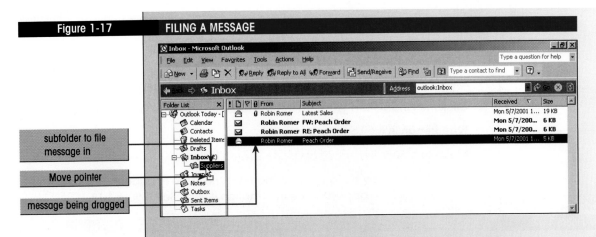

subfolder to file message in

Move pointer

message being dragged

**4.** Release the mouse button to move the message from the Inbox into the subfolder.

You want to move all messages related to The Express Lane into the subfolder. You could continue to move each message individually, but it's faster to move all of them at once.

### To file multiple messages:

**1.** Click the **Latest Sales** message, the first message you want to file.

**2.** Press and hold the **Ctrl** key and click the remaining two Peach Order messages ("RE: Peach Order" and "FW: Peach Order"). Use the Ctrl key to select nonadjacent messages. Press the Shift key to select a range of adjacent messages.

**3.** Release the **Ctrl** key. The three messages should be selected.

**4.** Drag all three selected messages from the Inbox into the **Suppliers** subfolder.

## Finding Messages

As your folder structure becomes more complex and you have more stored messages, it might become difficult to locate a specific message you filed. Rather than searching through multiple folders, you can have Outlook find the desired message. The Find command searches the From or Subject text boxes in a single folder for text that you specify. For searches of more than one criterion or multiple folders and subfolders, you must use the Advanced Find feature.

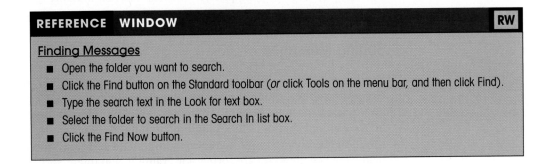

**REFERENCE WINDOW** **RW**

Finding Messages
- Open the folder you want to search.
- Click the Find button on the Standard toolbar (or click Tools on the menu bar, and then click Find).
- Type the search text in the Look for text box.
- Select the folder to search in the Search In list box.
- Click the Find Now button.

You'll use the Find feature to look for messages related to peaches in the Suppliers folder.

### To find all messages related to peach:

1. Click the **Suppliers** subfolder in the Folder List to display its contents.

2. Click the **Find** button 🔍 Find on the Standard toolbar. The Find pane opens.

3. Type **Peach** in the Look for text box.

4. Make sure **Suppliers** appears in the Search In list box.

5. Click the **Find Now** button. After a moment, the three messages that contain the word "peach" appear in the Information viewer. See Figure 1-18.

| Figure 1-18 | FIND RESULTS |

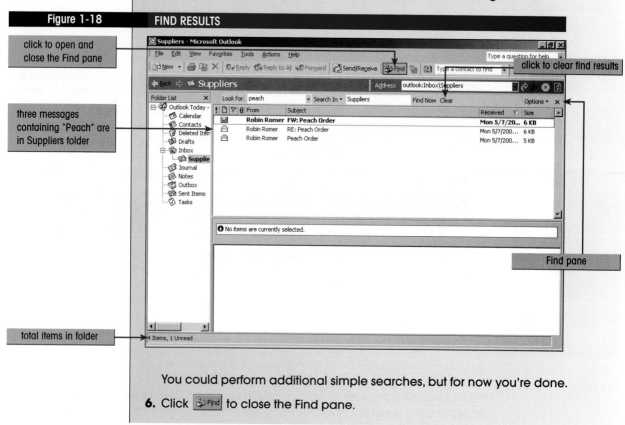

click to open and close the Find pane

three messages containing "Peach" are in Suppliers folder

click to clear find results

Find pane

total items in folder

You could perform additional simple searches, but for now you're done.

6. Click 🔍 Find to close the Find pane.

Once you close the Find pane, all messages in that folder reappear. Another way to manage files is to sort them.

## Sorting Messages

**Sorting** is a way to arrange items in a specific order—either ascending or descending. **Ascending order** arranges messages alphabetically from A to Z, chronologically from earliest to latest, or numerically from lowest to highest. **Descending order** arranges messages in reverse alphabetical, chronological, or numerical order. By default, all messages are sorted in descending order by their Received date and time. You can, however, change the field by which messages are sorted; for example, you might sort e-mail messages alphabetically by sender. Alternatively, you can sort messages by multiple fields; for example, you might sort e-mail messages alphabetically by sender and then by subject. The simplest way to change the sort order is to click a column heading in the Information viewer.

You'll sort your messages first by subject, and then by date received within each subject.

## To sort messages by subject and then date:

1. Click the **Subject** column heading. The sort order changes to ascending by subject, as indicated by the up arrow icon in the Subject column heading.

   **TROUBLE?** If the arrow icon points down, then the sort order is descending. Click the Subject column heading again to sort messages in ascending order by subject.

   Next you'll sort the messages within each subject in descending order by the received date.

2. Press and hold the **Shift** key while you click the **Received** column heading until the arrow icon points down, and then release the **Shift** key. See Figure 1-19. (If you clicked the Received column without pressing the Shift key, the messages would be sorted by only the date received, not by the subject first and then by the date received.)

| Figure 1-19 | SORTED MESSAGES |
| --- | --- |

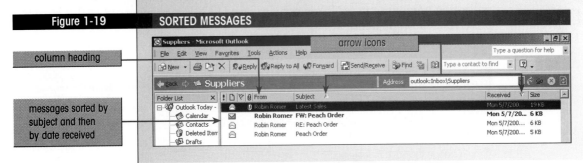

column heading

messages sorted by subject and then by date received

You can sort messages in any view except Message Timeline view. You'll switch between views now.

## To switch views:

1. Click **View** on the menu bar, and then point to **Current View** to display the list of default views.

2. Click **By Conversation Topic**. The messages are rearranged according to the information in the Subject box. Each subject, or conversation topic, becomes a different group. The Expand button indicates that a group contains the number of messages indicated after the conversation topic.

3. Click the **Expand** button [+] next to Peach Order. The messages in that group are displayed, and a Collapse button precedes the conversation topic. The other views arrange the e-mail messages in different ways.

4. Click the **Received** column heading to sort the messages within each group in ascending order by date.

   **TROUBLE?** If your messages are sorted in descending order, click the Received column heading again to sort in ascending order.

**5.** Switch to **Messages** view, and then sort the messages in descending order by the Received column.

You could further customize a view by removing some of the existing column headings and adding others.

## Storing Messages

After a time, you may not need immediate access to the messages you have compiled in the Outlook folders. You can store messages in other file formats or by archiving them.

### Saving Messages

You can use the Save As command to save messages and other Outlook items in other file formats so that you can save them on your hard drive or floppy disks, as you save your other files, and then delete them from Outlook. You can open such messages with other programs. For example, you can save an e-mail message as a Text Only (.txt) file that most word processing programs can read. You can also save HTML messages as HTML (.htm) files to preserve their original formatting.

---

**REFERENCE WINDOW**                                                    **RW**

**Saving Messages in Another File Format**
- Select the message or messages you want to save in another format.
- Click File on the menu bar, and then click Save As.
- Change the Save in location.
- Enter a new filename as needed.
- Click the Save as type list arrow, and the select the file format you want.
- Click the Save button.

---

You'll save the original Peach Order message as a Text Only file.

*To save a message in another format:*

**1.** Click the **Peach Order** message to select it.

**2.** Click **File** on the menu bar, and then click **Save As**. The Save As dialog box opens, with the subject listed in the File name text box.

**3.** Change the Save in location to the **Tutorial** folder within the **Tutorial.01** folder on your Data Disk.

**4.** Click the **Save as type** list arrow to display the file formats from which you can select. See Figure 1-20.

   **TROUBLE?** If your message did not retain the HTML formatting, then the format options available are Text Only, Outlook Template, and Message Format. Continue with Step 5.

| Figure 1-20 | SAVE AS DIALOG BOX |

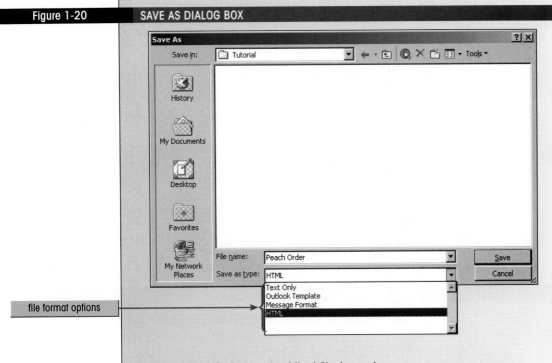

file format options

5. Click **Text Only** to select that file format.

6. Click the **Save** button. The message is saved to your Data Disk as a text file.

You or others can now open the file in Word or any other program that can read text files.

### To view the saved message in Word:

1. Start Word, and then click the **Open** button 📂 on the Standard toolbar. The Open dialog box opens.

2. Change the Look in location to the **Tutorial** folder within the **Tutorial.01** folder on your Data Disk.

3. Click the **Files of type** list arrow, click **Text Files**, and then double-click **Peach Order**. The Peach Order file opens.

4. Read the message, and then close the document and exit Word.

The process is the same for saving and viewing files in HTML.

## Archiving Mail Messages

Eventually, even the messages in your subfolders can become too numerous to manage easily. More often than not, you don't need immediate access to the older messages. Rather than reviewing your filed messages and moving older ones to a storage file, you can archive them. The **Archive** feature lets you manually transfer messages or other items stored in a folder (such as an attachment in the e-mail folder) to a personal folder file when the items have reached the age you specify. A **personal folder file** is a special storage file with a .pst extension that contains folders, messages, forms, and files; it can be viewed only in Outlook. Outlook calculates the age of an e-mail message from the date the message was sent or received, whichever is later.

When you create an archive, your existing folder structure from Outlook is recreated in the archive file and all the messages are moved from Outlook into the archive file. If you want to archive only a subfolder, the entire folder structure is still recreated in the archive file; however, only the messages from the selected subfolder are moved into the archive file. For example, if you archive the Suppliers folder, the archive file will include both the Inbox and the Suppliers subfolder, but only the messages in the Suppliers subfolder will be moved. Any messages in the Inbox remain in the Outlook Inbox. All folders remain in place within Outlook after archiving—even empty ones.

You can manually archive a folder at any time, such as when you finish a project or event. You specify which folders to archive, the age of items to archive, and the name and location of the archive file.

## To manually archive a folder:

1. Click **File** on the menu bar, and then click **Archive**. The Archive dialog box opens. See Figure 1-21.

| Figure 1-21 | ARCHIVE DIALOG BOX |
| --- | --- |

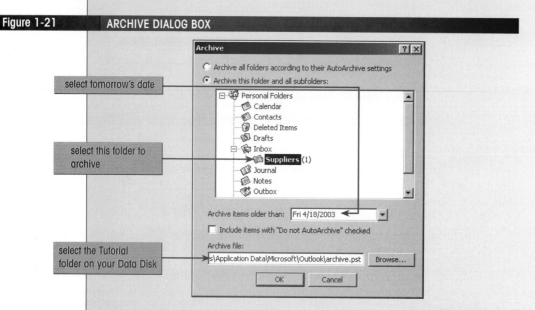

2. If necessary, click the **Archive this folder and all subfolders** option button.

3. If necessary, click the **Expand** button ⊞ next to Inbox to display the subfolders, and then click the **Suppliers** folder.

4. Type **tomorrow** in the Archive items older than text box, and then press the **Tab** key. Outlook will move any files dated with today's date or earlier to the archive file.

5. Click the **Browse** button. The Open Personal Folders dialog box opens.

6. Change the Save in location to the **Tutorial** folder within the **Tutorial.01** folder on your Data Disk, type **Suppliers Archive** as the filename, and then click the **OK** button.

7. Click the **OK** button in the Archive dialog box.

**8.** Click the **Yes** button to confirm that you want to archive all the items in the folder. All of the messages in the Suppliers folder are moved into the archive file you specified. The empty Suppliers folder remains in the folder structure.

**9.** Right-click the **Archived Folder** in the Folder list, and then click **Close "Archived Folders."**

Archived folders let you keep the contents of your folders manageable and current while providing the security of knowing older information is available if you need access to the information. You can access items in your archive files several ways: you can open the file using the Open command on the File menu and then drag the items you need to a current folder; you can add the archive file to your profile; or you can restore all the items in the archive file by using the Import and Export command on the File menu.

## Deleting Items and Exiting Outlook

When you finish using Outlook, you should **exit** (or close) the program. Unlike other programs, you don't need to save or close any other files. Before you exit, however, you'll delete each of the items you created in this tutorial. Deleted items are moved into the Deleted Items folder. This folder acts like the Recycle Bin in Windows. Items you delete stay in this folder until you empty it.

### To delete items:

**1.** Click the **Suppliers** folder in the Folder List.

**2.** Click the **Delete** button ⊠ on the Standard toolbar, and then click the **Yes** button to confirm that the folder and all of its messages should be moved to the Deleted Items folder.

**3.** Switch to the **Sent Items** folder, click the first message you sent in this tutorial, press and hold the **Ctrl** key as you click each additional message you sent in this tutorial, release the **Ctrl** key, and then click ⊠. The messages move to the Deleted Items folder.

**4.** Switch to the **Contacts** folder, and delete the contacts you created.

**5.** Right-click the **Deleted Items** folder in the Folder List, click **Empty "Deleted Items" folder**, and then click the **Yes** button to confirm the deletion. The folder empties.

Next you'll remove the signature you created.

### To delete a signature and exit Outlook:

**1.** Click **Tools** on the menu bar, click **Options**, and then click the **Mail Format** tab in the Options dialog box.

**2.** Click the **Signatures** button, click the name of your signature in the Signature list box, and then click the **Remove** button.

**3.** Click the **Yes** button to confirm that you want to permanently remove this signature, click the **OK** button, and then click the **OK** button. You're ready to exit Outlook.

**4.** Click the **Close** button ⊠ on the title bar to exit Outlook.

Alan thanks you for your help. The Express Lane can now fill all of its customers' orders for peaches until the end of the season. A happy customer means a profitable business.

## Session 1.2 QUICK CHECK

1. Explain the difference between the Reply button and the Reply to All button.

2. True or False: You can save a file attached to a message, but you cannot open the attachment from Outlook.

3. How do you move an e-mail message from the Inbox to a subfolder?

4. What does it mean to archive a folder?

## REVIEW ASSIGNMENTS

Lora Shaw asks you to help her with customer communication for The Express Lane. Complete the following:

1. Start Outlook and, if necessary, set up an account. Make sure that the Outlook screen and settings match those in the tutorial.

2. Create a signature that uses your name and the title "Customer Service Representative".

3. Create a new e-mail message addressed to your e-mail address with the subject "Welcome New Customer" and the message "Welcome to The Express Lane. We're sure you'll find our grocery delivery service more convenient and cheaper than your local grocery store—not to mention more healthful, because all our foods are certified organic. If you have any questions or comments, feel free to e-mail us."

4. Format the text of your e-mail in 12-point Times New Roman.

5. Send the e-mail to the Outbox and then to your mail server.

6. Create a contact card for Alan Gregory at The Express Lane with a fictional business mailing address and business phone number; use your own e-mail address.

*Explore*

7. Create a contact card for Lora based on Alan's contact card. Select Alan's contact card in the Contacts folder. Click Actions on the menu bar, and then click New Contact from Same Company. A Contact window opens with the company name, address, and phone number already entered. Type "Lora Shaw" in the Full Name text box. Type your own e-mail address in the E-mail text box.

8. Create contact cards for the following customers at their home addresses, using your e-mail address: (*Hint:* Click the down arrow button in the address section, and then click Home.)

   ■ Elliot Zander, 384 Leavenworth Street, San Francisco, CA 94103, 415-555-1232

   ■ Mai Ching, 1938 Grant Avenue, San Francisco, CA 94110, 415-555-0907

   ■ Lester Newhoun, 2938 Golden Gate Avenue, San Francisco, CA 94124, 415-555-6497

9. Edit Mai Ching's contact card to change the address to "1938 Presidio Street".

*Explore*

10. You can create an e-mail message already addressed to a specific contact. From the Contacts folder, click the contact card for Lora Shaw, and then click the New Message to Contact button. (Notice that her address is entered automatically in the To text box.) Type "Tea health benefits?" as the subject. Type "I've heard that drinking tea has health benefits. Do you have any information about this?" as the message body.

11. Send the e-mail to the Outbox and then to your mail server.

12. Download your new messages. If the Tea health benefits? message hasn't arrived, wait a few minutes and try again. Open, read, and then close the Tea health benefits? message.

13. Reply to the Tea health benefits? message with the text "In addition to being the world's second favorite drink to water, there is growing evidence of a link between tea and disease prevention, particularly cancer and heart disease. Check out our large selection of black, oolong, and green teas. The attached file has some information about teas. I hope this information is helpful."

14. Attach the **Tea** document located in the **Review** folder within the **Tutorial.01** folder on your Data Disk to the file.

*Explore*

15. Because Lora plans to update the tea information sheet next week, she asks you to recall the message if the customer hasn't read it within one week. Click the Options button on the toolbar, click the Expires after check box to insert a check mark, enter the date of one week from today, and then click the Close button. This option makes the message unavailable after the date you specified.

16. Send the message to the Outbox.

17. Forward the Tea health benefits? message to Alan Gregory with the message "Let's meet next week to talk about adding this information to our Web site."

18. Send the message to the Outbox and then to your mail server.

19. Create a Mail and Post subfolder named "Customers" located within the Inbox.

20. Download your messages, and then file the Welcome New Customer message and the Tea health benefits? messages in the Customers subfolder.

21. Sort the messages in the Customers folder in descending order by subject and then in descending order by date of receipt.

22. Find the messages in the Customers folder that contain the word "customer."

*Explore*

23. Save the messages that were found in HTML format to the **Review** folder in the **Tutorial.01** folder on your Data Disk (if your server does not support HTML, then save the messages in Text Only format). Close the Find pane.

24. Save the attachment in the RE: Tea health benefits? message as **Tea Health Benefits** to the **Review** folder within the **Tutorial.01** folder on your Data Disk.

*Explore*

25. Print the RE: Tea health benefits? message and its attachment. (*Hint:* In the Print dialog box, select the Print attached files with item(s) check box.)

*Explore*

26. Archive all the messages in the Customers folder to the **Review** folder within the **Tutorial.01** folder on your Data Disk, using the filename **Customer Archive**. Close the archive.

27. Delete each Outlook item you created, including the signature, subfolder, messages in the Sent Items folder, and contacts; empty the Deleted Items folder; and exit Outlook.

## CASE PROBLEMS

*Case 1. Answers Anytime*  Answers Anytime is a unique tutoring service where students can e-mail specific questions and problem areas to subject experts and receive quick answers. The subject experts reply to students within two hours, either by e-mail message or e-mail message with an attachment. Complete the following:

1. Start Outlook and, if necessary, set up an account.

2. Create a new e-mail message to your e-mail address with the subject "History questions" and the message "Please send information about the following: What was the Bill of Rights? When did women receive the right to vote? How does Rachel Carson fit into the environmental movement?" Press the Enter key after each question to place it on its own line, and then format the questions as a numbered list. Type your name at the end of the message. Send the message.

3. Create a contact card for Benji Tanago, Environmental History Expert, Answers Anytime, Pallas Road, Cincinnati, OH 45230, 513-555-6582, and your e-mail address.

4. Download your message.

*Explore*  5. Reply to the message using the following text formatted as a numbered list:
   1. See the attached document for information about the Bill of Rights.
   2. On August 26, 1920, Tennessee delivered the last needed vote and the Nineteenth Amendment was added to the Constitution. It stated that "the right of citizens of the United States to vote shall not be denied by the United States or by any State on account of sex."
   3. I've forwarded this question to Benji Tanago, our resident expert on the environmental movement.

6. Attach the **Amendments** document located in the **Cases** folder within the **Tutorial.01** folder on your Data Disk to the e-mail. Send the message to the Outbox.

*Explore*  7. Rather than retype Benji's information, you can send the contact card you just created. Switch to the Contacts folder, click Benji's contact card to select it, click Actions on the menu bar, and then click Forward as vCard. A Message window opens with the contact card included as an attachment. Enter your e-mail address in the To text box, and then send the message to the Outbox.

8. Forward the student's original message to Benji. Add the text "Hi Benji. Question 3 is yours. Thanks." Send the message to the Outbox.

9. Send all the messages in the Outbox.

10. Create a Mail and Post subfolder named "Answers" located in the Inbox.

11. Download your messages.

12. Find all messages in the Inbox related to the subject "History questions."

13. Save the messages you found as HTML files in the **Cases** folder within the **Tutorial.01** folder on your Data Disk.

14. File the found messages in the Answers folder, and then close the Find pane.

15. File the message with the vCard in the Answers folder.

16. Archive the Answers subfolder as **Answers Archive** in the **Cases** folder within the **Tutorial.01** folder on your Data Disk. Close the archive.

17. Delete the Answers folder, messages in the Sent Items folder, and the contact; empty the Deleted Items folder; and then exit Outlook.

***Case 2. Party Planners*** Jace Moran, owner of Party Planners, plans events ranging from company picnics to children's birthday parties to weddings. Right now, she is working on a graduation party. The graduate hosting the party has given Jace the e-mail addresses for the entire guest list so that Jace can send the invitations using Outlook. Complete the following:

1. Start Outlook, set up an account if necessary, and then switch to the Inbox.

*Explore*
2. Create a new e-mail message to your e-mail address with an appropriate subject using an Excel worksheet as the message body. Click Actions on the menu bar, point to New Mail Message Using, point to Microsoft Office, and then click Microsoft Excel Worksheet. In column A, enter a list of foods for the party. In column B, enter the probable cost for the food. Total the cost column. Send the e-mail to the Outbox and then to your mail server. Close Excel without saving the worksheet.

3. Create contact cards for at least five guests. Include their names, addresses, phone numbers, and e-mail addresses. Enter your own e-mail address for each contact.

4. Edit each contact to include one item of personal information, such as a birthday or spouse's name.

*Explore*
5. Use stationery to create the party invitation. From the Inbox, click Actions on the menu bar, point to New Mail Message Using, and then click More Stationery. Click Citrus Punch in the Stationery box, and then click the OK button (if you do not have the Citrus Punch stationery, select another appropriate stationery).

6. Address the invitation to each of the contacts you created. Remember to type a semi-colon between the names in the To text box. Type an appropriate subject.

*Explore*
7. Enter the Day, Time, and Place. Format the stationery, using Word's formatting features; try changing the font and color of existing text.

8. Send the message to the Outbox and then to your mail server.

9. Open, read, print, and close the food cost e-mail.

10. Switch to the Contacts folder, and then change the view to Detailed Address Cards.

*Explore*
11. Print the contact cards you created. If other contact cards exist in addition to the ones you created, press and hold the Ctrl key as you click the contact name for each card you created. Open the Print dialog box. Use Card Style as the Print style and, if you selected contact cards, click the Only selected items option button in the Print range. Click the OK button.

*Explore*
12. Create a Contacts subfolder named "Guests" located in the Contacts folder and move the contact cards you created into it.

*Explore*
13. Export your contact list. Click File on the menu bar, and then click Import and Export. Click Export to a file, and then click the Next button. Click Microsoft Access, and then click the Next button. If necessary, click the Expand button next to Contacts to display the Guests subfolder, select the subfolder, and then click the Next button. Use the Browse button to save the file as **Guest List** to the **Cases** folder within the **Tutorial.01** folder on your Data Disk. Click the Next button, and then click the Finish button. The contact list is exported as an Access database to your Data Disk.

14. Download your messages. Print one message, and save the party invitation message as an HTML file to the **Cases** folder within the **Tutorial.01** folder on your Data Disk.

15. Archive the messages in the Inbox as **Party Archive** in the **Cases** folder within the **Tutorial.01** folder on your Data Disk.

**Explore** ▶ 16. Expand the Archive folder files, and then copy the Guests subfolder to the archive. Click the Guests subfolder, press and hold the Ctrl key as you drag the folder to the archive file, and then release the Ctrl key. Close the archive file.

17. Delete the Guests subfolder, the messages in the Sent Items folder, and the contacts you created in Outlook; empty the Deleted Items folder; and then exit Outlook.

# QUICK | CHECK ANSWERS

*Session 1.1*

1. The Inbox stores e-mail messages you have received. The Outbox stores e-mail messages you have written but not yet sent.

2. E-mail is the electronic transfer of messages between computers on the Internet. It's inexpensive for communicating with others who are nearby or far away. You can send and read messages at your convenience.

3. text that is automatically added to every e-mail message you send, such as your name, job title, and company name

4. a contact's name, job title, company name and address, phone and fax numbers, as well as personal information such as birthdays, anniversaries, and children's names

*Session 1.2*

1. Reply responds to only the sender of the e-mail message; Reply to All responds to the sender and any other recipients of the e-mail message.

2. False

3. Drag the message from the message list to the subfolder in the Folder List.

4. moves items you selected from Outlook into a personal folder file

## I

**I-beam pointer, WIN 2000 2.05**
**icons, WIN 2000 1.05**
  display, WIN 2000 2.18–20
  file and folder, WIN 2000 2.19
  Places Bar, WIN 2000 2.08–09
  program, WIN 2000 2.19
**indenting**
  hanging indent, WD 2.25
  paragraph, WD 2.25-2.26
  right indent, WD 2.25
**Index tab, Help window,**
  **WIN 2000 1.26,**
  **WIN 2000 1.27–28**
**information viewer, Outlook,**
  **OUT 1.06**
**inserting characters in text,**
  **WIN 2000 2.07**
**insertion point, WIN 2000 2.04**
  moving, WIN 2000 2.05–06
  pointer compared, WIN 2000 2.5–6
**insertion point, moving in**
  **document, WD 2.07-2.08**
**integration, Office, OFF 7-9**
**Internet, WIN 2000 1.03,**
  **WIN 2000 2.01**
**Internet service provider (ISP),**
  **OUT 1.09**
**ISP.** *See* **Internet service provider**
**italicizing text.** *See also* **text**
  procedure, WD 2.33-2.34
**item, OUT 1.04**

## J

**join, tables, AC 3.08**

## K

**key**
  composite key, AC 2.03
  foreign key, AC 1.05
  primary key, AC 1.05, AC 2.03
    specifying, AC 2.16-2.17
  sort key, AC 3.14
**keyboard shortcut, Office, OFF 13**
**keyboard shortcuts, WIN 2000 1.21**

## L

**label.** *See also* **text**
  entering into worksheet,
    EX 1.20-1.21
**Large Icons view, WIN 2000 2.18,**
  **WIN 2000 2.19**
  switching to, WIN 2000 2.20

**layout.** *See also* **design**
  choosing, PPT 1.21-1.22
  content layout, PPT 1.21
  slide layout, PPT 1.21
  text and content layout, PPT 1.21
  text layout, PPT 1.21
**letter, preparing in Word,**
  **WD 1.14-1.16**
**line spacing**
  changing, WD 2.23-2.24
  1.5 line spacing, WD 2.23
    double spacing, WD 2.23
**list**
  bulleted list, PPT 1.10,
    WD 2.28-2.30
  numbered list, PPT 1.10, WD 2.29
**list arrows, WIN 2000 1.24**
**list boxes, WIN 2000 1.23–24**
**List view, WIN 2000 2.18,**
  **WIN 2000 2.19**
**location, considerations about,**
  **PPT 1.12, logical functions**
  in general, EX 2.21-2.25
    comparison operator, EX 2.22
**logical operator, AC 3.28**
  AND logical operator, AC 3.28,
    AC 3.29-3.30
  OR logical operator, AC 3.28,
    AC 3.31-3.33

## M

**margins**
  changing, WD 2.21-2.22
  paragraph indentation,
    WD 2.25-2.26
**Maximize button, WIN 2000 1.18,**
  **WIN 2000 1.19**
**maximizing windows,**
  **WIN 2000 1.18, WIN 2000 1.19**
**menu**
  Office, OFF 13-16
  personalized, OFF 13-14
**menu(s), WIN 2000 1.07.** *See also*
  **specific menus**
  conventions, WIN 2000 1.21–22
  hidden options, WIN 2000 1.10–11
  keyboard shortcuts, WIN 2000 1.21
  program. *See* program menus
  selecting options,
    WIN 2000 1.08–09
  shortcut. *See* shortcut menus
**menu bar, WIN 2000 1.16,**
  **WIN 2000 1.17**
**menu bar, Outlook, OUT 1.06**
**menu command, OFF 13**

**Microsoft Access 2002.** *See* **Access**
**Microsoft Excel 2002.** *See* **Excel**
**Microsoft Office XP.** *See* **Office**
**Microsoft Outlook 2002.** *See*
  **Outlook**
**Microsoft PowerPoint 2002.** *See*
  **PowerPoint**
**Microsoft Windows 2000**
  **Professional, WIN 2000 1.03**
**Microsoft Word 2002.** *See* **Word**
**Minimize button, WIN 2000 1.18,**
  **WIN 2000 1.19**
**minimizing windows,**
  **WIN 2000 1.17, WIN 2000 1.18,**
  **WIN 2000 1.19**
**mistakes.** *See also* **error correction**
  undoing, EX 1.32-1.33
**mistakes, correcting in text,**
  **WIN 2000 2.04**
**mouse, WIN 2000 1.05–06.** *See*
  *also* **pointing devices**
  types, WIN 2000 1.06
**mouse pads, WIN 2000 1.06**
**moving.** *See also* **navigating**
  files, WIN 2000 2.24,
    WIN 2000 2.25,
    WIN 2000 2.26–27
  insertion point, WIN 2000 2.05–06
  pointers, WIN 2000 1.06
  windows, WIN 2000 1.20
**multiple programs, running at**
  **same time.** *See* **multitasking**
**multitasking, WIN 2000 1.12–15**
  accessing desktop, WIN 2000 1.14
  closing inactive programs,
    WIN 2000 1.14–15
  switching between programs,
    WIN 2000 1.13
**My Computer window,**
  **WIN 2000 2.02,**
  **WIN 2000 2.16-21**
  changing icon display,
    WIN 2000 2.18–20
  controlling toolbar display,
    WIN 2000 2.17–18
  displaying files, WIN 2000 2.16–17
  restoring default settings,
    WIN 2000 2.21

## N

**names**
  drives, WIN 2000 2.16
  files. *See* filenames
**navigating**
  hierarchy of folders,
    WIN 2000 2.22–24

# TASK REFERENCE

| TASK | PAGE # | RECOMMENDED METHOD |
|------|--------|-------------------|
| Absolute reference, change to relative | EX 2.14 | Edit the formula, deleting the $ before the column and row references; or press F4 to switch between absolute, relative, and mixed references |
| Access, exit | AC 1.13 | Click ⊠ on the program window |
| Access, start | AC 1.07 | Click Start, point to Programs, click Microsoft Access |
| Action, redo | WD 2.11 | Click ⟳ or list arrow |
| Action, undo | WD 2.11 | Click ⟲ or list arrow |
| Actions, redo several | EX 1.33 | Click the list arrow for ⟳▾, select the action(s) to redo |
| Actions, undo several | EX 1.32 | Click the list arrow for ⟲▾, select the action(s) to undo |
| Aggregate functions, use in a query | AC 3.38 | Display the query in Design view, click Σ |
| Attachment, view in Outlook | OUT 1.27 | Double-click the attachment icon in the Preview pane or Message window, click the Open it option button, click OK |
| AutoContent Wizard, run | PPT 1.13 | Click File, click New, click From AutoContent Wizard on New Presentation Task Pane, follow instructions |
| AutoCorrect, use | WD 1.25 | Click ⚡▾, click correct spelling |
| Auto Fill, copy formulas | EX 2.16 | See Reference Window: Copying Formulas Using Auto Fill |
| Auto Fill, create series | EX 2.18 | Select the range, drag the fill handle down, release mouse button, click ⊞, click the option button to complete series |
| AutoFormat, apply | EX 3.31 | Select the range, click Format, click AutoFormat, select an AutoFormat design, click OK |
| AutoSum, apply | EX 2.25 | Click the cell in which you want the final value to appear, click the list arrow for Σ▾, select the AutoSum function to apply |
| Background color, apply | EX 3.18 | Select the range, click the list arrow for ⬛▾, select a color square in the color palette |
| Background pattern, apply | EX 3.18 | Open the Format Cells dialog box, click the Patterns tab, click the Pattern list arrow, click a pattern in the pattern gallery, click OK |
| Boldface, add to text | WD 2.32 | Select text, click **B** |
| Border, create | EX 3.15 | Click the list arrow for ⬛▾, select a border in the border gallery |
| Border, draw | EX 3.16 | Click the list arrow for ⬛▾, click ✎, draw the border using the Pencil tool |
| Bullets, add to paragraphs | WD 2.28 | Select paragraphs, click ☰ |
| Calculated field, add to a query | AC 3.34 | See Reference Window: Using Expression Builder |
| Cell, clear contents of | EX 1.27 | Click Edit, click Clear; or press Delete |
| Cell, edit | EX 1.31 | See Reference Window: Editing a Cell |
| Cells, delete from worksheet | EX 1.27 | Select the cell or range, click Edit, click Delete, select a delete option, click OK; or select the cell or range, click-right the selection, click Delete, select a delete option, click OK |
| Cells, insert into worksheet | EX 1.26 | See Reference Window: Inserting New Cells into a Worksheet |
| Cells, merge | EX 3.21 | Select the adjacent cells, open the Format Cells dialog box, click the Alignment tab, select the Merge check box, click OK |
| Cells, merge and center | EX 3.21 | Select the adjacent cells, click ⬛▾ |

| TASK | PAGE # | RECOMMENDED METHOD |
|---|---|---|
| Character, insert | WIN 2000 2.07 | Click where you want to insert the text, type the character |
| Clipboard Task Pane, open | WD 2.15 | Click Edit, click Office Clipboard |
| Clipboard Task Pane, use to cut, copy, and paste | WD 2.16 | See Reference Window: Cutting or Copying and Pasting Text |
| Column, change width | EX 1.30 | See Reference Window: Changing Column Width |
| Column, delete from worksheet | EX 1.27 | Select the column, click Edit, click Delete; or select the column, click-right the selection, click Delete |
| Column, hide | EX 3.22 | Select the headings for the columns you want to hide, right-click the selection, click Hide |
| Column, insert into worksheet | EX 1.30 | See Reference Window: Inserting Cells into a Worksheet |
| Column, resize width in a datasheet | AC 2.29 | Double-click ◄╫► on the right border of the column heading |
| Column, select | EX 1.19 | Click the column heading of the column you want to select. To select more than one column, hold down the Ctrl key and click each individual column heading. To select a range of columns, click the first column heading in the range, hold down the Shift key and click the last column in the range. |
| Column, unhide | EX 3.23 | Select the column headings left and right of the hidden columns, right-click the selection, click Unhide |
| Columns, repeat in printout | EX 3.38 | Open the Page Setup dialog box, click the Sheet tab, click the Column to repeat at left box, click the column that contain the information you want repeated, click OK |
| Comment, add or edit | WD 2.35 | Click comment, click 🔼 |
| Comment, display | WD 2.35 | Point to comment |
| Comment, insert | WD 2.35 | Click Insert, click Comment |
| Data Disk, create | WIN 2000 2.15 | Click 🏁Start , point to Programs, point to NP on Microsoft Windows 2000 – Level I, click Disk 1, click OK |
| Database, compact and repair | AC 1.24 | Click Tools, point to Database Utilities, click Compact and Repair Database |
| Database, compact on close | AC 1.25 | See Reference Window: Compacting a Database Automatically |
| Database, convert to another Access version | AC 1.26 | Close the database to convert, click Tools, point to Database Utilities, point to Convert Database, click the format to convert to |
| Database, create a blank | AC 2.07 | Click 🗋 on the Database toolbar, click Blank Database in the Task Pane, type the database name, select the drive and folder, click Create |
| Database, create using a Wizard | AC 2.07 | Click 🗋 on the Database toolbar, click General Templates in the Task Pane, click the Databases tab, select a template, click OK, type the database name, select the drive and folder, click Create, follow the instructions in the Wizard |
| Database, open | AC 1.07 | Click 📂 |
| Datasheet view, switch to | AC 2.19 | Click 📰 |
| Date, insert current | EX 2.28 | Insert the TODAY() or NOW() function |
| Date, insert with AutoComplete | WD 1.28 | Start typing date, press Enter |
| Dates, fill in with Auto Fill | EX 2.19 | Select the cell containing the initial date, drag and drop the fill handle to fill in the rest of the dates. Click the Auto Fill options button 🔽 and choose whether to fill in days, weekdays, months, or years. |

| TASK | PAGE # | RECOMMENDED METHOD |
|---|---|---|
| Desktop, access | WIN 2000 1.14 | Click ⬚ on the Quick Launch toolbar |
| Design view, switch to | AC 2.23 | Click ⬚ |
| Disk, format | WIN 2000 2.03 | Right-click the 3½ Floppy icon in My Computer, click Format on the shortcut menu, specify the capacity and file system of the disk, click Start. |
| Document, close | WD 1.33 | Click ⬚ |
| Document, open | WD 2.03 | Click ⬚, select drive and folder, click filename, click open |
| Document, open new | WD 1.15 | Click ⬚ |
| Document, preview | WD 1.36 | Click ⬚ |
| Document, print | WD 1.30 | Click ⬚ |
| Document, save with new name | WD 2.04 | Click File, click Save As, select drive and folder, enter new filename, click Save |
| Document, save with same name | WD 1.18 | Click ⬚ |
| Envelope, create | WD 1.33 | Click Tools, point to Letters and Mailings, click Envelopes and Labels, click Envelopes tab, type delivery and return addresses, click Print |
| Excel, exit | EX 1.19 | Click File and then click Exit. |
| Excel, start | EX 1.05 | Click Start, point to Programs, click Microsoft Excel |
| Field, add to a database table | AC 2.25 | See Reference Window: Adding a Field Between Two Existing Fields |
| Field, define in a database table | AC 2.10 | See Reference Window: Defining a Field in a Table |
| Field, delete from a database table | AC 2.23 | See Reference Window: Deleting a Field from a Table Structure |
| Field, move to a new location in a database table | AC 2.24 | Display the table in Design view, click the field's row selector, drag the field with the pointer |
| File, close | OFF 1.19 | Click ⬚ |
| File, copy | WIN 2000 2.24 | See Reference Window: Moving and Copying a File |
| File, delete | WIN 2000 2.26 | See Reference Window: Deleting a File |
| File, move | WIN 2000 2.24 | See Reference Window: Moving and Copying a File |
| File, open | OFF 1.20 | See Reference Window: Opening an Existing or New File |
| File, open from My Computer | WIN 2000 2.11 | Open My Computer, open the window containing the file, click the file, press Enter |
| File, open from within a program | WIN 2000 2.12 | Start the program, click File, click Open, select the file in theOpen dialog box, click Open |
| File, print | WIN 2000 2.13 | Click ⬚ |
| File, print | OFF 1.21 | See Reference Window: Printing a File |
| File, rename | WIN 2000 2.25 | See Reference Window: Renaming a File |
| File, save | WIN 2000 2.07 | Click ⬚ |
| File, save | OFF 1.17 | See Reference Window: Saving a File |

# TASK REFERENCE

| TASK | PAGE # | RECOMMENDED METHOD |
| --- | --- | --- |
| Files, view as large icons | WIN 2000 2.18 | Click View, click Large Icons |
| Files, view as small icons | WIN 2000 2.18 | Click View, click Small Icons |
| Files, view details | WIN 2000 2.18 | Click View, click Details |
| Files, view in list | WIN 2000 2.18 | Click View, click List |
| Files, view thumbnails | WIN 2000 2.18 | Click View, click Thumbnails |
| Filter By Selection, activate | AC 3.20 | See Reference Window: Using Filter By Selection |
| Find and replace text | WD 2.18 | See Reference Window: Finding and Replacing Text |
| Floppy disk, copy | WIN 2000 2.28 | See Reference Window: Copying a Disk |
| Folder, create | WIN 2000 2.22 | See Reference Window: Creating a Folder |
| Folder, create | PPT 1.16 | Click File, click Save As, click [icon], type folder name, click OK |
| Folder, create in Outlook | OUT 1.27 | Right-click the icon in the Folder List, click New Folder, type the folder name, select the folder type, select the folder location, click OK |
| Folder hierarchy, move back in the | WIN 2000 2.23 | Click the Back button [icon] |
| Folder hierarchy, move forward in the | WIN 2000 2.23 | Click the Forward button [icon] |
| Folder hierarchy, move up the | WIN 2000 2.23 | Click the Up button [icon] |
| Folder options, restore default settings | WIN 2000 2.21 | Click Tools, click Folder Options, click the General tab, click the Restore Defaults button; click the View tab, click the Restore Defaults button, click OK |
| Font, change color | EX 3.10 | Click the list arrow for [A icon], select a color from the color palette |
| Font, change size | EX 3.09 | Click the list arrow for [10 icon], click a size |
| Font, change style | EX 3.10 | Select the text, click [B], click [I], or click [U] |
| Font, change typeface | EX 3.09 | Click the list arrow for [Arial] button, click a font |
| Font, select | WD 1.10 | Click Format, click Font, click font name |
| Font and font size, change | WD 2.30 | See Reference Window: Changing the Font and Font Size |
| Font size, select | WD 1.11 | Click Format, click Font, click font size |
| Format, apply currency style, percent style, or comma style | EX 3.03 | Click [$], click [%], or click [,] or open the Format Cells dialog box, click the Number tab, select a style, specify style-related options, click OK |
| Format, clear | EX 3.25 | Click Edit, point to Clear, click Formats |
| Format, copy | WD 2.27 | Select text with desired format, double-click [icon], select paragraphs to format, click [icon] |
| Format, copy using fill handle | EX 3.07 | Select the cell or range that contains the formatting you want to copy, drag the fill handle down, click [icon], click the Fill Formatting Only option button |
| Format, copy using Format Painter | EX 3.06 | Select the cell or range that contains the formatting you want to copy, click [icon], drag the pointer over the cell or range to apply the formatting |
| Format, decrease decimal places | EX 3.03 | Click [icon] |

# TASK REFERENCE

| TASK | PAGE # | RECOMMENDED METHOD |
|------|--------|-------------------|
| Format, find and replace | EX 3.26 | See Reference Window: Finding and Replacing a Format |
| Format, increase decimal places | EX 3.05 | Click [icon] |
| Format Cells dialog box, open | EX 3.07 | Click Format, click Cells |
| Formula, copy | EX 2.12 | See Reference Window: Copying and Pasting a Cell or Range |
| Formula, copy with Auto Fill | EX 2.16 | See Reference Window: Copying Formulas Using Auto Fill |
| Formula, enter using keyboard | EX 1.23 | See Reference Window: Entering a Formula |
| Formula, enter using mouse | EX 1.23 | See Reference Window: Entering a Formula |
| Function, insert | EX 2.06 | See Reference Window: Inserting a Function |
| Grayscale, preview presentation in | PPT 1.30 | Click [icon] |
| Handouts, print | PPT 1.31 | Click File, click Print, click Print what list arrow, click Handouts, click Slides per page list arrow, click number, click OK |
| Header/footer, create | EX 3.35 | Open the Page Setup dialog box, click the Header/Footer tab, click list arrow for the Header button or the Footer button, select an available header or footer, click OK |
| Header/footer, create custom | EX 3.36 | Open Page Setup dialog box, click the Header/Footer tab, click the Custom Header or Customer Footer button, complete the header/footer related boxes, click OK |
| Help, display topic from Contents tab | WIN 2000 1.26 | In Help, click the Contents tab, click [icon] until you see the topic you want, click [?] to display topic |
| Help, display topic from Index tab | WIN 2000 1.27 | In Help, click the Index tab, scroll to locate topic, click topic, click Display |
| Help, get from Ask a Question box | OFF 1.23 | See Reference Window: Getting Help from the Ask a Question Box |
| Help, return to previous Help topic | WIN 2000 1.28 | Click [icon] |
| Help, start | WIN 2000 1.25 | See Reference Window: Starting Windows 2000 Help |
| Insertion point, move | WIN 2000 2.05 | Click the location in the document to which you want to move |
| Italics, add to text | WD 2.33 | Select text, click [I] |
| Item in Outlook, delete | OUT 1.35 | Click the item, click [X], click the Yes button |
| Items in Outlook, select multiple | OUT 1.35 | Click the first item, press and hold the Ctrl key, click additional items, release the Ctrl key |
| Line spacing, change | WD 2.23 | Select text to change, press Ctrl+1 for single spacing, Ctrl+5 for 1.5 line spacing, or Ctrl+2 for double spacing |
| List box, scroll | WIN 2000 1.23 | Click [icon] to scroll down the list box |
| Margins, change | WD 2.21 | Click File, click Page Setup, click Margins tab, enter margin values, click OK |
| Menu option, select | WIN 2000 1.08, WIN 2000 1.21 | Click the menu option, or, if it is a submenu, point to it |
| Messages, archive manually | OUT 1.33 | Click File, click Archive, click Archive this folder and all subfolders option button, click folder to archive, type date in Archive items older than text box, click the Browse button, select the save in location, click OK, click OK, click the Yes button |

| TASK | PAGE # | RECOMMENDED METHOD |
|---|---|---|
| Messages, file | OUT 1.28 | Select the message or messages in the Information viewer, drag to appropriate folder or subfolder |
| Messages, find | OUT 1.29 | See Reference Window: Finding Messages |
| Messages, save | OUT 1.32 | See Reference Window: Saving Messages in Another File Format |
| Messages, sort | OUT 1.30 | Click the column heading |
| Messages, sort by two or more columns | OUT 1.31 | Click the column heading, hold down the Shift key, click additional column headings, release the Shift key |
| My Computer, open | WIN 2000 2.16 | Click My Computer on the desktop, press Enter |
| Nonprinting characters, show | WD 1.12 | Click Show/Hide ¶ |
| Normal view, change to | WD 1.08 | Click ☰ |
| Notes, create | PPT 1.29 | Click in Notes Pane, type text |
| Notes, print | PPT 1.32 | Click File, click Print, click Print what list arrow, click Notes Pages, click OK |
| Numbering, add to paragraphs | WD 2.29 | Select paragraphs, click ⊞ |
| Object, open | AC 1.10 | Click the object's type in the Objects bar, click the object's name, click Open |
| Object, save | AC 1.20 | Click 💾, type the object name, click OK |
| Office files, open | OFF 1.09 | See Reference Window: Starting Office Programs and Files |
| Office programs, start | OFF 1.09 | See Reference Window: Starting Office Programs and Files |
| Outline text, demote | PPT 1.24 | Click Outline tab (if necessary), click paragraph, click ⊞ |
| Outline text, promote | PPT 1.23 | Click Outline tab (if necessary), click paragraph, click ⊞ |
| Outlook, exit | OUT 1.35 | Click ✕ on the Outlook title bar |
| Page, change orientation | EX 3.35 | Open the Page Setup dialog box, click the Page tab, click either the Landscape or the Portrait option button |
| Page, set margins | EX 3.34 | Open the Page Setup dialog box, click the Margins tab, specify the width of the margins, click OK |
| Page break, insert | EX 3.37 | Click the cell below where you want the page break to appear, click Insert, click Page Break. |
| Page Setup dialog box, open | EX 3.33 | Click File, click Page Setup; or click the Setup button on the Print Preview toolbar |
| Paragraph, decrease indent | WD 2.26 | Click ⊞ |
| Paragraph, indent | WD 2.26 | Click ⊞ |
| Paste options, select | WD 2.14 | Click ⊞ |
| Personalized menus and toolbars, turn on or off | OFF 1.15 | Click Tools, click Customize, click the Options tab, check or uncheck options, click Close |
| PowerPoint, exit | PPT 1.12 | Click ✕ of PowerPoint window |
| PowerPoint, start | PPT 1.04 | Click Start button, point to Programs, click Microsoft PowerPoint |
| Presentation, close | PPT 1.12 | Click ✕ on presentation window |
| Presentation, open | PPT 1.05 | Click 📂, select disk and folder, click filename, click Open |
| Primary key, specify | AC 2.16 | See Reference Window: Specifying a Primary Key for a Table |
| Print area, define | EX 3.37 | Select the range, click File, point to Print Area, click Set Print Area |
| Print Preview, open | EX 3.32 | Click 🔍 |

# TASK REFERENCE

| TASK | PAGE # | RECOMMENDED METHOD |
|---|---|---|
| Program, close | WIN 2000 1.11 | Click [X] |
| Program, close inactive | WIN 2000 1.14 | Right-click program button, click Close |
| Program, exit | OFF 1.25 | Click [X] |
| Program, start | WIN 2000 1.10 | See Reference Window: Starting a Program |
| Program, switch to another | WIN 2000 1.13 | See Reference Window: Switching Between Programs |
| Programs, switch between | OFF 1.12 | Click the program button on the taskbar |
| Property sheet, open | AC 3.37 | Right-click the object or control, click Properties |
| Query, define | AC 3.03 | Click Queries in the Objects bar, click New, click Design View, click OK |
| Query, run | AC 3.06 | Click [!] |
| Query results, sort | AC 3.17 | See Reference Window: Sorting a Query Datasheet |
| Range, copy | EX 1.18 | Select the cell or range, hold down the Ctrl key and drag the selection to the new location, release the mouse button and Ctrl |
| Range, move | EX 1.18 | Select the cell or range, drag the selection to the new location, release the mouse button |
| Range, select adjacent | EX 1.16 | See Reference Window: Selecting Adjacent or Nonadjacent Ranges of Cells |
| Range, select non-adjacent | EX 1.16 | See Reference Window: Selecting Adjacent or Nonadjacent Ranges of Cells |
| Record, add a new one | AC 2.28 | Click [▶*] |
| Record, delete | AC 2.33 | See Reference Window: Deleting a Record |
| Record, move to a specific one | AC 1.11 | Type the record number in the Specific Record box, press Enter |
| Record, move to first | AC 1.12 | Click [I◀] |
| Record, move to last | AC 1.12 | Click [▶I] |
| Record, move to next | AC 1.12 | Click [▶] |
| Record, move to previous | AC 1.12 | Click [◀] |
| Records, redisplay all after filter | AC 3.21 | Click [▽] |
| Redo command, use to redo multiple operations in a database object | AC 3.31 | Click the list arrow for [↻], click the action(s) to redo |
| Relationship, define between database tables | AC 3.10 | Click [▱] |
| Relative reference, change to absolute | EX 2.14 | Type $ before the column and row references; or press F4 to insert $ |
| Reviewing pane, open or close | WD 2.35 | Click [▣] on Reviewing toolbar |
| Row, change height | EX 1.30 | Move the pointer over the row heading border until the pointer changes to ╪, click and drag the border to increase or decrease the height of the row |
| Row, delete from worksheet | EX 1.27 | Select the row, click Edit, click Delete; or select the row, click-right the selection, click Delete |
| Row, hide | EX 3.22 | Select the headings for the rows you want to hide, right-click the selection, click Hide |

# TASK REFERENCE

| TASK | PAGE # | RECOMMENDED METHOD |
|---|---|---|
| Row, insert into worksheet | EX 1.30 | See Reference Window: Inserting Cells into a Worksheet |
| Row, unhide | EX 3.23 | Select the rows headings above and below the hidden rows, right-click the selection, click Unhide |
| Row, select | EX 1.19 | Click the heading of the row you want to select. To select more than one row, hold down the Ctrl key and click each individual row heading. To select a range of rows, click the first row heading in the range, hold down the Shift key and click the last row in the range |
| Rows, repeat in printout | EX 3.38 | Open the Page Setup dialog box, click the Sheet tab, click the Row to repeat at top box, click the row that contains the information |
| Ruler, display | WD 1.10 | Click View, click Ruler |
| ScreenTips, view | WIN 2000 1.07 | Position the pointer over the item |
| Sheet tabs, format | EX 3.25 | Right-click the sheet tab, click Tab Color, select a color from the color palette |
| Slide, add new | PPT 1.21 | Click ⬚ |
| Slide, delete | PPT 1.26 | In Slide Pane, click Edit, click Delete Slide. In Outline Tab, click ⬚, press Delete. In Slide Tab, click slide, click Delete |
| Slide, go to next | PPT 1.18 | Click ⬚ |
| Slide Show, view | PPT 1.08 | Click ⬚ |
| Slide Sorter View, switch to | PPT 1.25 | Click ⬚ |
| Smart Tag, remove | WD 1.29 | Click ⬚, click Remove this Smart Tag |
| Sort, specify ascending in datasheet | AC 3.15 | Click ⬚ |
| Sort, specify descending in datasheet | AC 3.15 | Click ⬚ |
| Speaker Notes, create | PPT 1.29 | Click in Notes Pane, type text |
| Spelling, correct individual word | WD 1.25 | Right-click misspelled word (as indicated by a wavy red line), click correctly spelled word |
| Spelling and grammar, check | WD 2.05 | See Reference Window: Checking a Document for Spelling and Grammatical Errors |
| Spelling and grammar, check document | WD 2.05 | Click ⬚, click correction, click change; click Ignore once to skip an item |
| Start menu, open | WIN 2000 1.07 | Click ⬚ Start |
| Style, apply | EX 3.29 | Select the range, click Format, click Style, select a style, click OK |
| Style, create | EX 3.29 | Select the cell that contains the formatting you want to use as the basis of the new style, click Format, click Style, type a name for the style, click Modify, specify format options using the Format Cells dialog box, click OK, click OK |
| Style, modify | EX 3.30 | Select the range, click Format, click Style, click Modify, change style attributes, click OK |
| Style Checker, fix style problem | PPT 1.27 | Click ⬚, click option to fix style problem |
| Style Checker, set options | PPT 1.27 | Click Tools, click Options, click Spelling and Style tab, click Style Options, set options, click OK, then click OK in the Options dialog box |

| TASK | PAGE # | RECOMMENDED METHOD |
|------|--------|--------------------|
| Style Checker, turn on | PPT 1.26 | Click Tools, click Options, click Spelling and Style tab, click Check style check box, click OK |
| Table, create in a database | AC 2.08 | Click Tables in the Objects bar, click New, click Design View, click OK |
| Table, import from another Access database | AC 2.32 | Click File, point to Get External Data, click Import, select the folder, click Import, select the table, click OK |
| Table, open in a database | AC 1.10 | Click Tables in the Objects bar, click the table name, click Open |
| Table structure, save in a database | AC 2.18 | See Reference Window: Saving a Table Structure |
| Task Pane, close | WD 1.08 | Click ⊠ |
| Text, align | WD 2.24 | Select text, click ▤, ▤, ▤, or ▤ |
| Text, align within a cell | EX 3.11 | Click ▤, click ▤, click ▤, click ▤, or click ▤; or open Format Cells dialog box, click the Alignment tab, select a text alignment, click OK |
| Text, bold | WD 2.32 | Select text, click **B** |
| Text box, move | — | Click text box, drag edge (not resize handle) of text box |
| Text, change indent | EX 3.11 | Click ▤, or ▤ |
| Text, copy and paste | WD 2.16 | Select text, click 📋, move to target location, click 📋 |
| Text, delete | WD 2.10 | Press Backspace to delete character to left of insertion point; press Delete to delete character to the right; press Ctrl+Backspace to delete to beginning of word; press Ctrl+Delete to delete to end of word |
| Text, enter into cell | EX 1.20 | Click the cell, type text entry, press Enter |
| Text, italicize | WD 2.33 | Select text, click *I* |
| Text, move by cut and paste | WD 2.15 | Select text, click ✂, move to target location, click 📋 |
| Text, move by drag and drop | WD 2.13 | Select text, drag pointer to target location, release mouse button |
| Text, replace | WD 2.18 | See Reference Window: Finding and Replacing Text |
| Text, select | WIN 2000 2.06 | Drag the pointer over the text |
| Text, select a block of | WD 2.09 | Click at beginning of block, press and hold Shift and click at end of block |
| Text, select entire document | WD 2.09 | Press Ctrl and click in selection bar |
| Text, select multiple adjacent lines | WD 2.09 | Click and drag in selection bar |
| Text, select multiple nonadjacent lines | WD 2.09 | Select text, press and hold Ctrl, and select next text |
| Text, select multiple paragraphs | WD 2.09 | Double-click and drag in selection bar |
| Text, select paragraph | WD 2.09 | Double-click in selection bar next to paragraph |
| Text, select sentence | WD 2.09 | Press Ctrl and click in sentence |
| Text, underline | WD 2.33 | Select text, click U |
| Text, wrap in cell | EX 3.13 | Open the Format Cells dialog box, click the Alignment tab, select the Text wrap check box, click OK |
| Toolbar, display | WD 1.09 | Right-click any visible toolbar, click toolbar name |
| Toolbar button, select | WIN 2000 1.22 | Click the toolbar button |

| TASK | PAGE # | RECOMMENDED METHOD |
|---|---|---|
| Toolbars, control display | WIN 2000 2.17 | Click View, point to Toolbars, select the toolbar options you want |
| Underline, add to text | WD 2.33 | Select text, click [U] |
| Undo command, use to undo multiple operations in a database object | AC 3.30 | Click the list arrow for [↶], click the action(s) to undo |
| Window, close | WIN 2000 1.18 | Click [X] |
| Window, maximize | WIN 2000 1.18 | Click [□] |
| Window, minimize | WIN 2000 1.18 | Click [_] |
| Window, move | WIN 2000 1.20 | Drag the title bar |
| Window, resize | WIN 2000 1.20 | Drag [⁄⁄] |
| Window, restore | WIN 2000 1.18 | Click [🗗] |
| Windows 2000, shut down | WIN 2000 1.15 | Click [Start], click Shut Down click the list arrow, click Shut Down, click OK |
| Windows 2000, start | WIN 2000 1.04 | Turn on the computer |
| Word, exit | WD 1.33 | Click [X] |
| Word, start | WD 1.05 | Click [Start], point to Programs, click Microsoft Word |
| Workbook, open | EX 1.12 | Click [📂]; (or click File and click Open or click the Workbook link in the Task Pane), locate the drive and folder that contains the workbook, click the file- name, click Open (or double-click the workbook file name in the Task Pane) |
| Workbook, print | EX 1.36 | Click [🖨]; or click File, click Print, select printer and print-related options, click OK |
| Workbook, save for first time | EX 1.14 | Click [💾] (or click File, click Save or Save As), locate the folder and drive in which to store the file, type a filename, click Save |
| Workbook, save in a different format | EX 1.14 | See Reference Window: Saving a Workbook in a Different Format |
| Workbook, save to update | EX 1.14 | Click [💾] [Insert Button B-0]; or click File, click Save |
| Workbook, save with new name | EX 1.14 | Click File, click Save As, locate the folder and drive in which to store the file, type a filename, click Save |
| Worksheet, add background image | EX 3.23 | See Reference Window: Adding a Background Image to the Worksheet |
| Worksheet, copy | EX 1.35 | See Reference Window: Moving or Copying a Worksheet |
| Worksheet, delete | EX 1.33 | Click the sheet tab, click Edit, click Delete Sheet; or right-click the sheet tab, click Delete |
| Worksheet, insert | EX 1.34 | Click Insert, click Worksheet; or right-click a sheet tab, click Insert, click Worksheet icon, click Insert |
| Worksheet, move | EX 1.35 | See Reference Window: Moving or Copying a Worksheet |
| Worksheet, rename | EX 1.35 | Double-click the sheet tab that you want to rename, type a new name, press Enter |
| Worksheets, move between | EX 1.11 | Click the sheet tab for the worksheet you want to view; or click one of the tab scrolling buttons, click the sheet tab |
| Zoom setting, change | WD 1.11 | Click Zoom list arrow, click zoom percentage |

## Windows 2000 File Finder

| Location in Tutorial | Name and Location of Data File | Student Saves File As... | Student Creates New File |
|---|---|---|---|
| **Tutorial 2**<br>Session 2.1 | | | Practice Text.doc |
| Session 2.2<br>*Note:* Students copy the contents of Disk 1 onto Disk 2 in this session. | Agenda.doc<br>Budget2001.xls<br>Budget2001.xls<br>Budget2002.xls<br>Exterior.bmp<br>Interior.bmp<br>Logo.bmp<br>Members.wdb<br>Minutes.wps<br>Newlogo.bmp<br>Opus27.mid<br>Parkcost.wks<br>Proposal.doc<br>Resume.doc<br>Sales.wks<br>Sample Text.doc<br>Tools.wks<br>Travel.wps<br><br>Practice Text.doc<br>*(Saved from Session 2.1)* | | |
| Review Assigments & Projects | *Note:* Students continue to use the Data Disks they used in the Tutorial. For certain Assignments, they will need a 3rd blank disk. | Woods Resume.doc<br>*(Saved from Resume.doc)* | Letter.doc<br>Song.doc<br>Poem.doc |

## Introducing Microsoft Office XP File Finder

| Location in Tutorial | Name and Location of Data File | Student Saves File As | Student Creates New File |
|---|---|---|---|
| Page OFF 17 | | | Tutorial.01\Tutorial\<br>Stockholder Meeting<br>Agenda.doc |
| Review Assignments | Tutorial.01\Review\Finances.xls | Tutorial.01\Review\Delmar Finances.xls | |
| Review Assignments | Tutorial.01\Review\Letter.doc | Tutorial.01\Review\Delmar Letter.doc | |

## Word 2002 File Finder

| Location in Tutorial | Name and Location of Data File | Student Saves File As... | Student Creates New File |
|---|---|---|---|
| **Tutorial 1** | | | |
| Session 1.2 | | | Tutorial.01\Tutorial\Web Time Contract Letter |
| Review Assignments | | | Tutorial.01\Review\Conference Call Memo |
| | | | Tutorial.01\Review\Web Time Envelope |
| Case Problem 1 | | | Tutorial.01\Cases\Water Park Information Letter |
| Case Problem 2 | | | Tutorial.01\Cases\Confirmation Letter |
| Case Problem 3 | | | Tutorial.01\Cases\Liza Morgan Letter |
| Case Problem 4 | | | Tutorial.01\Cases\Meeting Memo |
| **Tutorial 2** | | | |
| Session 2.1 | Tutorial.02\Tutorial\FAQ | Tutorial.02\Tutorial\Tree FAQ | |
| Review Assignments | Tutorial.02\Review\Statmnt | Tutorial.02\Review\Monthly Statement | Tutorial.02\Review\LMG Contact Information |
| Case Problem 1 | Tutorial.02\Cases\Form | Tutorial.02\Cases\Authorization Form | |
| Case Problem 2 | Tutorial.02\Cases\CCW | Tutorial.02\Cases\CCW Brochure | |
| Case Problem 3 | Tutorial.02\Cases\UpTime | Tutorial.02\Cases\UpTime Training Summary | |
| Case Problem 4 | Tutorial.02\Cases\Ridge | Tutorial.02\Cases\Ridge Top Guide | |

## Excel 2002 File Finder

| Location in Tutorial | Name and Location of Data Files | Student Saves File As... | Student Creates New File |
|---|---|---|---|
| **Tutorial 1** | | | |
| Session 1.1 | Tutorial.01\Tutorial\Lawn1.xls | Lawn2.xls | |
| Session 1.2 | | | |
| Review Assignments | Tutorial.01\Review\Income1.xls | Income2.xls | |
| Case Problem 1 | Tutorial.01\Cases\CFlow1.xls | CFlow2.xls | |
| Case Problem 2 | Tutorial.01\Cases\Balance1.xls | Balance2.xls | |
| Case Problem 3 | Tutorial.01\Cases\Site1.xls | Site2.xls | |
| Case Problem 4 | | | CashCounter.xls |
| **Tutorial 2** | | | |
| Session 2.1 | Tutorial.02\Tutorial\Loan1.xls | Loan2.xls | |
| Session 2.2 | | | |
| Review Assignments | Tutorial.02\Review\Mort1.xls | Mort2.xls | |
| Case Problem 1 | Tutorial.02\Cases\School1.xls | School2.xls | |
| Case Problem 2 | Tutorial.02\Cases\Sonic1.xls | Sonic2.xls | |
| Case Problem 3 | Tutorial.02\Cases\Leland1.xls | Leland2.xls | |
| Case Problem 4 | | | JrCol.xls |
| **Tutorial 3** | | | |
| Session 3.1 | Tutorial.03\Tutorial\Sales1.xls | Sales2.xls | |
| Session 3.2 | | | |

## Excel 2002 File Finder

| Location in Tutorial | Name and Location of Data Files | Student Saves File As... | Student Creates New File |
|---|---|---|---|
| **Tutorial 3** *(Continued)* | | | |
| Review Assignments | Tutorial.03\Review\Region1.xls | Region2.xls | |
| Case Problem 1 | Tutorial.03\Cases\Running1.xls | Running2.xls | |
| Case Problem 2 | Tutorial.03\Cases\WBus1.xls | WBus2.xls | |
| Case Problem 3 | Tutorial.03\Cases\Blades1.xls | Blades2.xls | |
| Case Problem 4 | | | Payroll.xls |

## Access 2002 File Finder

**Note:** *The Data Files supplied with this book and listed in the chart below are starting files for Tutorial 1. You will begin your work on each subsequent tutorial with the files that you created in the previous tutorial. For example, after completing Tutorial 1, you begin Tutorial 2 with your ending files from Tutorial 1. The Review Assignments and Case Problems also build on the starting Data Files in this way. You must complete each tutorial, Review Assignment, and Case Problem in order and finish them completely before continuing to the next tutorial, or your Data Files will not be correct for the next tutorial.*

| Location in Tutorial | Name and Location of Data File | Student Creates New File |
|---|---|---|
| **Tutorial 1** | | |
| Session 1.1 | Disk1\Tutorial\Seasonal.mdb | |
| Session 1.2 | Disk1\Tutorial\Seasonal.mdb *(continued from Session 1.1)* | |
| Review Assignments | Disk2\Review\Seasons.mdb | Disk2\Review\Seasons2002.mdb<br>Disk2\Review\Seasons97.mdb |
| Case Problem 1 | Disk3\Cases\Videos.mdb | Disk3\Cases\Videos2002.mdb<br>Disk3\Cases\Videos97.mdb |
| Case Problem 2 | Disk4\Cases\Meals.mdb | Disk4\Cases\Meals2002.mdb<br>Disk4\Cases\Meals97.mdb |
| Case Problem 3 | Disk5\Cases\Redwood.mdb | Disk5\Cases\Redwood.mdb<br>Disk5\Cases\Redwood.mdb |
| Case Problem 4 | Disk6\Cases\Trips.mdb | Disk6\Cases\Trips2002.mdb<br>Disk6\Cases\Trips97.mdb |
| **Tutorial 2** | | |
| Session 2.1 | | Disk1\Tutorial\Northeast.mdb |
| Session 2.2 | Disk1\Tutorial\Northeast.mdb *(continued from Session 2.1)*<br>Disk1\Tutorial\NEJobs.mdb<br>Disk1\Tutorial\Seasonal.mdb *(continued from Tutorial 1)* | |
| Review Assignments | Disk2\Review\Elsa.mdb | Disk2\Review\Recruits.mdb |
| Case Problem 1 | Disk3\Cases\Videos.mdb *(continued from Tutorial 1)*<br>Disk3\Cases\Events.mdb | |
| Case Problem 2 | Disk4\Cases\Meals.mdb *(continued from Tutorial 1)*<br>Disk4\Cases\Customer.mdb | |
| Case Problem 3 | Disk5\Cases\Redwood.mdb *(continued from Tutorial 1)*<br>Disk5\Cases\Pledge.mdb | |
| Case Problem 4 | Disk6\Cases\Trips.mdb *(continued from Tutorial 1)*<br>Disk6\Cases\Rafting.xls<br>Disk6\Cases\Groups.mdb | |
| **Tutorial 3** | | |
| Session 3.1 | Disk1\Tutorial\Northeast.mdb *(continued from Session 2.2)* | |
| Session 3.2 | Disk1\Tutorial\Northeast.mdb *(continued from Session 3.1)* | |
| Review Assignments | Disk2\Review\Recruits.mdb *(continued from Tutorial 2)* | |
| Case Problem 1 | Disk3\Cases\Videos.mdb *(continued from Tutorial 2)* | |
| Case Problem 2 | Disk4\Cases\Meals.mdb *(continued from Tutorial 2)* | |
| Case Problem 3 | Disk5\Cases\Redwood.mdb *(continued from Tutorial 2)* | |
| Case Problem 4 | Disk6\Cases\Trips.mdb *(continued from Tutorial 2)* | |

## PowerPoint 2002 File Finder

| Location in Tutorial | Name and Location of Data File | Student Saves File As... | Student Creates New File |
|---|---|---|---|
| **Tutorial 1** | | | |
| Session 1.1 | Tutorial.01\Tutorial\Lorena.ppt | | Tutorial.01\My Files\Global Humanitarian Overview.ppt |
| Session 1.2 | Tutorial.01\My Files\Global Humanitarian Overview.ppt | Tutorial.01\My Files\Global Humanitarian Overview.ppt | |
| Review Assignments | Tutorial.01\Review\Village OP.ppt | Tutorial.01\Review\Village Outreach Program.ppt | |
| Case Problem 1 | | | Tutorial.01\Cases\e-Commerce Consultants.ppt |
| Case Problem 2 | Tutorial.01\Cases\Seafoods.ppt | Tutorial.01\Cases\Northeast Seafoods.ppt | |
| Case Problem 3 | Tutorial.01\Cases\LASIK.ppt | Tutorial.01\Cases\Magnolia LASIK.ppt | |
| Case Problem 4 | | | Tutorial.01\Cases\Textbook Review.ppt |

## Outlook 2002 File Finder

| Location in Tutorial | Name and Location of Data File | Student Saves File As | Student Creates New File |
|---|---|---|---|
| **Tutorial 1** Session 1.2 | Tutorial.01\Tutorial\Sales.xls | Tutorial.01\Tutorial\Second Quarter Sales.xls | |
| Session 1.2 | | | Tutorial.01\Tutorial\Peach Order.txt |
| Session 1.2 | | | Tutorial.01\Tutorial\Suppliers Archive.pst |
| Review Assignments | Tutorial.01\Review\Tea.doc | | Tutorial.01\Review\Welcome New Customer.htm (or .txt) |
| | | | Tutorial.01\Review\Tea Health Benefits.htm (or .txt) |
| | | | Tutorial.01\Review\RE Tea Health Benefits.htm (or .txt) |
| | | | Tutorial.01\Review\FW Tea Health Benefits.htm (or .txt) |
| | | | Tutorial.01\Review\Customer Archive.pst |
| Case Problem 1 | Tutorial.01\Cases\Amendments.doc | | Tutorial.01\Cases\History questions |
| | | | Tutorial.01\Cases\RE History questions |
| | | | Tutorial.01\Cases\FW History questions |
| | | | Tutorial.01\Cases\Answers Archive.pst |
| Case Problem 2 | | | Tutorial.01\Cases\Guest List.mdb |
| | | | Tutorial.01\Cases\Party Invitation.htm (or .txt) |
| | | | Tutorial.01\Cases\Party Archive.pst |